Structural analysis in the social sciences 2

Social structures: a network approach

Structural analysis is characterized by a focus on social structure. Structural analysts reject approaches to social analysis that treat individuals as independent units and are skeptical of analyses that see social behavior as determined by norms injected into the psyches of people and organizations. By using the powerful techniques of network analysis, they directly study the concrete relations that exist among persons, organizations, interest groups, and nation-states. Their work forms part of a worldwide scientific shift away from the tradition of analyzing things in terms of the intrinsic characteristics of their individual parts, and toward structural analytic interpretation of phenomena in the light of their linkages with other members of systems.

This collection of original articles demonstrates the case for structural analysis. It contains a variety of studies addressing key sociological questions such as: How do social networks create supportive communities that enable people to cope with the stresses of modern times? How do people's relationships affect their social mobility? How do the social structures of relationships undergird the seemingly independent behavior of businesses and nations? And how are apparently spontaneous revolutionary changes based on underlying relationships between people and interest groups? Throughout, the authors use innovative network theories and methods as ways of moving beyond individualistic analysis to confront directly the structural basis of social life.

Structural analysis in the social sciences

Series Editor: Mark Granovetter

The series *Structural analysis in the social sciences* will present approaches that explain social behaviour and institutions by reference to relations among such concrete social entities as persons and organizations. This contrasts with at least four other popular strategies: (1) reductionist attempts to explain by a focus on individuals alone; (2) explanations stressing the causal primacy of abstract concepts such as ideas, values, mental harmonies and cognitive maps (what is now called 'structuralism' on the Continent should be sharply distinguished from structural analysis in the present sense, though Claude Lévi-Strauss's early work on kinship is much closer to it); (3) technological and material determinism; (4) explanations that take 'variables' to be the main concepts of analysis, as for the 'structural equation' models that dominated much 1970s sociology, where the 'structure' is that connecting variables rather than concrete social entities.

The methodological core of structural analysis is the 'social network' approach but the series will also draw on a large body of work in areas such as political economy, conflict, human ecology, social psychology, organizational analysis, social mobility, sociology of science and biosociology, among others, that is not framed explicitly in network terms, but stresses the importance of relations rather than the atomization of reductionism or the determinism of ideas, technology or material conditions. The series will consist of edited and single-authored volumes; each will broadly synthesize one area of study and demonstrate the value of a structural perspective. Though this perspective has become extremely popular and influential in all the social sciences, it does not have a coherent identity, and no series yet brings together such work under a single rubric. It is my hope that the *Structural analysis* series will, by doing so, bring the achievements of structurally oriented scholars to a wider public, and thereby encourage others to approach their theory and research in this very fruitful way.

Mark Granovetter

Social structures:
a network approach

Edited by

Barry Wellman
University of Toronto

S. D. Berkowitz
University of Vermont

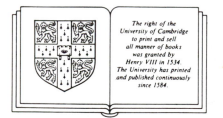

The right of the
University of Cambridge
to print and sell
all manner of books
was granted by
Henry VIII in 1534.
The University has printed
and published continuously
since 1584.

Cambridge University Press

Cambridge

New York   New Rochelle   Melbourne   Sydney

Published by the Press Syndicate of the University of Cambridge
The Pitt Building, Trumpington Street, Cambridge CB2 1RP
32 East 57th Street, New York, NY 10022, USA
10 Stamford Road, Oakleigh, Melbourne 3166, Australia

© Cambridge University Press 1988

First published 1988

Printed in the United States of America

Library of Congress Cataloging-in-Publication Data
Social structures: a network approach/edited by Barry Wellman,
S. D. Berkowitz.
p.   cm. – (Structural analysis in the social sciences; 2)
Includes index.
1. Social structure.   2. Social networks.   I. Wellman, Barry.
II. Berkowitz, Stephen D.   III. Series.
HM73.S6276   1988   87–17765
305 – dc 19

British Library Cataloguing in Publication Data
Social structures: a network approach.
– (Structural analysis in the social sciences; 2)
1. Social structure
I. Wellman, Barry   II. Berkowitz, S. D.
III. Series
305   HM131

ISBN 0 521 24441 2 hard covers
ISBN 0 521 28687 5 paperback

Contents

v

Part IV *Social change* 327

Part V *Social mobility* 401

Figures and tables

Figures

vii

Tables

Acknowledgments

We gratefully thank: *Social Forces* for permission to reprint as Chapter 4 Ronald Breiger's "The Duality of Persons and Groups" (*Social Forces*, Vol. 53, no. 2, pp. 181–90, 1974); and Holmes & Meier, for permission to reprint Charles Tilly's "Misreading, Then Rereading, Nineteenth Century Social Change," which appears here in slightly revised form as Chapter 12. [This work originally appeared in *French Cities in the Nineteenth Century*, edited by John Merriman (New York: Holmes & Meier, 1979).] Parts of Chapter 2 first appeared in Barry Wellman's "Network Analysis: Some Basic Principles" (*Sociological Theory 1983*) and in R. J. Richardson and Barry Wellman's "Structural Analysis" (*Canadian Review of Sociology and Anthropology*, vol. 22, no. 5, pp. 772–93, 1985).

We thank all the authors for their patience with our delays in editing this book.

The Structural Analysis Programme, Department of Sociology, University of Toronto supported the initial preparation of most of the manuscripts and also facilitated the visit of many contributors to Toronto. Partial support for Wellman's subsequent work came from the Centre for Urban and Community Studies, University of Toronto; the Social Science Research Council of Canada; and the National Welfare Grants division of Health and Welfare Canada. The final manuscript version was produced through the support and facilities of the University of Vermont's Academic Computing Center.

Sharon Bolt, Margot Bowlby, Susan Haggis, Lisa Handler, Kelley O'Malley, Ann Pahud, Beatrix Robinow, Cyndi Rottenberg, Alicia VanDerMeer, and Lori Witham deserve our thanks for their careful work in preparing this manuscript. Alicia VanDerMeer drew the complicated figures in Chapter 15. At Cambridge University Press, J. A. Barnes, Walter Lippincott, Susan Allen-Mills, Rhona Johnson, Edith Feinstein, and Vicky Macintyre provided patient guidance. Throughout this enterprise, our wives, Terry Berkowitz and Bev Wellman, gave us invaluable support and advice.

1

Introduction: Studying social structures

Barry Wellman and S. D. Berkowitz

Concerns and questions

When a new research group forms around a set of core ideas – a *paradigm* – its early adherents almost always seem like strange ducks. After all, academia is a conservative place. New views are seldom accepted easily, and novel ways of reexamining old findings are often greeted with skepticism. "Why isn't this new crowd," their colleagues often say, "content to look at the world in ways we've found so compelling in the past?"

In some respects, this attitude is healthy. As with other forms of concrete social activity, science is subject to fads or enthusiasms that turn out to be silly or unproductive in the end. But this inherent conservatism and skepticism also means that incomplete or outmoded sets of ideas often hang around long after the problems and circumstances that brought them about have changed. Hence, new scientific paradigms do not simply "surface": They *emerge* against the background of older frameworks or perspectives. They are not "new," but simply ascendant. Ironically, when a new approach to interpreting the world is finally recognized as such, someone almost always points out that its central ideas "have been around for a long time."

This is what has been happening to *structural analysis*. Although structural analysis has deep roots in older theoretical traditions, North American social scientists only began to recognize it as a distinct perspective less than two decades ago. Even though the foundation work had been done by 1965, its implications for the larger study of social structure were not yet clear. Other theory groups, in fact, could legitimately claim that they were studying regular patterns in the organization of social systems and that the tools they used were appropriate to the task. Few thought of themselves as "structural analysts." No well-defined core of animating concepts existed. Empirical work, often shored up by a few fragmentary theoretical assumptions, predominated.

By the mid-1970s, however, structural analysis had caught on to the point where meetings of self-defined practitioners could be held, a professional group – the International Network for Network Analysis – could be formed, and a journal (*Social Networks*) could be founded. In effect, the sinews that hold a scientific community together were in place. By the late 1970s exchanges among self-defined practitioners had led to the coalescence of a core set of concepts that made it possible to define overlapping concerns. Symptomatically, much of the work now being done in structural analysis addresses *open problems*: commonly recognized theoretical and methodological issues that must be tackled in order to advance the state of the art. This work can proceed only when at least the broad outlines of a paradigm have been defined.

Despite this evidence of the institutionalization of structural analysis as a paradigm, and despite the considerable amount of attention that it has attracted during the last few years, we still keep bumping into three persistent questions. First, "What's so special about structural analysis? Don't all sociologists care about social structure?" Second, "Isn't 'structural analysis' just another name for 'network analysis'? Aren't you really just peddling a new bag of methodological tricks?" Finally, "Isn't structural analysis something that nonsociologists do? After all, a number of the social science disciplines have some concept of structure?" Although the answers to these questions are clear to those involved in the development of structural analysis, we suspect that this might not be true for other social scientists.

The purpose of this book is to provide tentative answers to these questions. Our discussion could have taken several directions, but because we wanted to avoid the kind of niggling and unproductive definition mongering that often accompanies the birth of a new paradigm, we decided to present the structural analytic case through practical demonstrations. Hence, every chapter addresses an important, if not classic, sociological problem and demonstrates the utility of the structural analytic approach in dealing with it.

What's so special about structural analysis? Don't all sociologists care about social structure?

Sociologists are taught to believe, axiomatically, that enduring patterns in the relationships among the elementary parts of social systems constrain individual behavior. This view is what separates sociology from fields such as psychology or economics, which ultimately rest on individualistic assumptions.

Sociological practice tends to be quite different. Rather than working *from* social structure, sociologists often work *toward* it. One important reason for this approach is that contemporary sociological studies rely heavily on statistical analyses. Statistics and probability theory are seductive in their apparent ability to tease out the separate and conjoint effects of multiple variables. Aggregative analyses, however, assume that, for all practical purposes, individual units – be they persons, groups, organizations, or societies – can be treated as independent. This assumption has always been somewhat problematic given the kinds of phenomena in which sociologists have been interested. Nevertheless, until quite recently most quantitatively oriented social scientists thought that they could adequately represent the phenomena they were studying by juxtaposing them with various distributions of independent events. As a result, they began aggregating and cross-clarifying individual units in order to tease out their similarities and differences. Yet, sociologists following this strategy can, at best, only *infer* the presence of social structure when they discover aggregates of individuals thinking and behaving in similar ways.

Just because sociologists use statistical models, of course, does not mean that they are trapped into providing individualistic explanations. But the tendency of many analysts – both quantitative and qualitative in their approaches – to base their explanatory schema on the putative norms and values of idealized social actors has led many in this individualistic direction. Their analyses treat persons as automata, moving like compass needles, in response to internalized norms. Their explanations hinge on discovering that persons with similar attributes (e.g., gender, urban residence) behave similarly in response to shared norms. Such analyses, which are based upon an inferred vocabulary of motives, can detect social structure only indirectly.

By contrast, structural analysts believe that the main business of social scientists is to study social structure and its consequences. Rather than working toward an indirect understanding of "social structure" in the abstract, they study "social structures" directly and concretely. They analyze the ordered arrangements of relations that are contingent upon exchange among members of social systems. They map these structures, describe their patterns (often using a set of tools derived from mathematical graph theory), and seek to uncover the effects of these patterns on the behavior of the individual members of these structures – whether people, groups, or organizations. Reversing the traditional logic of inquiry in sociology, structural analysts argue that social categories (e.g., classes, races) and bounded groups are best discovered and analyzed by examining relations between social actors. Rather than beginning with an a priori classification of the observable world into a discrete set of categories, they begin with a set of relations, from which they derive maps and typologies of social structures. Thus they draw inferences from wholes to parts, from structures and relations to categories, and from behaviors to attitudes.

Isn't "structural analysis" just another name for "network analysis"?

Structural analysis is both less and more than network analysis. Some observers have mistakenly reduced network analysis to a mystifying jargon or an arcane bag of methodological tricks. They have confused the regalia of the network fraternity – with its talk of "zero-filled matrices" and "network density" or "blockmodeling" – with the essence of a network analytic approach. Nor has all the confusion been confined to the variable-happy: At the other end of the hard–soft continuum, some clinicians have invoked "the social network" as an incantation in praise of informal help supplied to individuals by kinfolk, friends, and neighbors.

We suggest that network analysis is neither a method nor a metaphor, but a fundamental intellectual tool for the study of social structures. In our view, an important key to understanding structural analysis is recognizing that social structures can be represented as *networks* – as sets of *nodes* (or social system members) and sets of *ties* depicting their interconnections.

This is a marvelously liberating idea. It immediately directs analysts to look at linked social relations and frees them from thinking of social systems as collections of individuals, two-person dyads, bounded groups, or simple categories. Usually, structural analysts have associated "nodes" with individual people, but they can, just as easily represent groups, corporations, households, nation-states, or other collectivities in this way. "Ties" are used to represent flows of resources, symmetrical friendships, transfers, or structured relationships between nodes.

Many of the authors in this book have used network tools to examine structures ranging in scale from small sets of friends, through tribes and villages, to large organizations, nation-states, and world systems. Their network tools are first that – instruments brought in to explicate patterns of relationships – and not ends in themselves. In some chapters, the word "network" appears fleetingly or not at all, and overtly network-based methods are not used. Yet, even in these instances, the structural analytic approach is evident in the ways in which the authors pose questions, gather information, and interpret evidence about the allocation of resources within social systems.

Isn't structural analysis something that nonsociologists do?

Many colleagues call our approach "network analysis" to distinguish it from the various forms of "structuralism" or relational analysis that float around the humanities or social and natural sciences. Indeed, in one sense, we agree with their usage: In the 1970s and 1980s it has often seemed that half the members of the avant-garde have been calling themselves "structural analysts." Hofstadter (1980), for instance, spent hundreds of pages telling millions of readers that Gödel, Escher, and Bach were related by their common relationalism.

This proliferation of "structuralism" across disciplinary boundaries is more than trendiness: It is the result of a broadly based scholarly movement away from the Aristotleian-Linnean tradition of analyzing things in terms of the intrinsic characteristics of their individual parts. It is, in other words, explicitly antireductionist. In the first influential shift toward this mode of analysis, in quantum physics, the very properties of parts are defined by the interactions between them (Schrödinger, 1951; Pagels, 1985). At the opposite end of the physical scale, this approach has spread to cosmology, in which the universe is now defined relationally (Gregory and Thompson, 1982). In biology, "constrained relationalism" argues that "the properties of organisms are consequences of the particular interactions that occur between bits and pieces of matter" (Lewontin, 1983; 36; see also Weyl, 1922; Boorman and Levitt, 1980; Prigogine, 1980; Mayr, 1982; Rose, 1982; Smith, 1982; Gould, 1983). In the same vein, philosophers of language have argued that mutual understanding of any utterance is possible "only by having implicit theory about how to understand a network of your possible utterances" (Hacking, 1984: 54; see also Hacking, 1975; Parret, 1976).

There are many "structuralisms" in the social sciences. All are concerned with interpreting processes in terms of patterned interrelationships rather than on the basis of individual essences. Consequently, they look at their subject matter in similar ways, pose similar questions, and construct similar analytic procedures to answer these questions. Perhaps the best known such approach is "structural anthropology," which systematically defines and studies sets of cultural symbols in terms of their patterned interrelationships (Lévi-Strauss, 1969). Structuralist ideas have cropped up in other social sciences in a variety of contexts: "general systems theory" (von Bertalanffy, 1968), "game theory" (Luce and Tucker, 1959), "structural linguistics" (Jakobson and Halle, 1971), "cybernetics" (Simon, 1952, 1957), "input–output economics" (Leontief, 1985), and "urban systems" geography (Simmons, 1983). Within sociology itself, a "structuralist" approach somewhat different from the one taken in this book analyzes social systems primarily in terms of the distributions of the characteristics of their component units – for example, differentiation, inequality, unequal resources – and secondarily derives linkage properties from these distributions (Mayhew and Levinger, 1976; Blau, 1977; Mayhew, 1980).

Although the structural analysis presented in this book fits comfortably into this extended structuralist family, it is not simply an extension of other forms of structuralism. It is distinguished from them by its focus on *concrete* social relations among specific social actors. Indeed, its emphasis on exchange puts it closer to input–output economics and quantum physics than to Lévi-Straussian structuralism. Symbols, meanings, and values – the primary concern of most European and some North American structuralists – are a derivative and often residual concern within the type of structural analysis presented in this book.

The intellectual context

The authors whose work appears in this book have come to structural analysis with a variety of substantive and methodological questions. Their interests range from Kalahari hunter-gatherers and Sardic villages to Toronto elites, upwardly mobile Americans, and multinational corporations. Thus the chapters here cover a wide range of topics, from abstract, mathematical models of social structure and processes to classic sociological issues, such as the organization of precapitalist and capitalist forms of social structure, the circumstances under which markets can form, and the conditions leading to stability or change in social systems.

Underlying this diverse content is a shared perspective much of which has bubbled up out of the intellectual ferment of the University of Toronto's Structural Analysis Programme. Scholars associated with SAP have been especially interested in linking structural analysis with political economy. Living in the shadow of the United States and in a trading nation with substantial regional inequality in wealth and power, great diversity in ethnic groups, and highly entrenched interests, Canadians habitually use neo-colonial relations of power and dependency to analyze local events. From this perspective, the world seems to operate through complex networks of unequal resource flows.[1]

Although many of the contributors are American, and not Canadian, almost all have been members of the Structural Analysis Programme or frequent visitors to SAP. They have come to share a common perspective. They focus on relationships among members of social systems, and not on the psychically driven behavior of individuals. Their analyses emphasize socio-logistic explanations of behavior and deemphasize psychologistic, normative ones. They tend to look at systems, not individuals; structural constraints, not internalized drives. Unlike some network analysts, they do not assume that the world is rife with voluntarily chosen, symmetrical relations. Instead, they are primarily concerned with how relationships structure resource allocation under conditions of scarcity and how these often asymmetrical relationships concatenate into complex, hierarchical and quasi-hierarchical networks of power and dependency.

In analyzing interpersonal relations, the authors are interested in understanding how network members use unevenly distributed resources for survival. Many of the contributors analyze complex links between large units: corporations, ethnic groups, worldwide structures of economic interest, and flows of persons through social systems. In analyzing large-scale phenomena, they aim for greater understanding of integration and cleavage in social structures.[2] Some seek to specify the conditions under which divisions of labor can integrate social systems, and others study complex networks that constitute the basis for conflict, cleavage, and coalition within structures.

The plan of the book

Thinking structurally

Our principal objective in putting this book together is to demonstrate the case for structural analysis, but not to overstate it. Indeed, as the author of one of the first textbooks on the subject (Berkowitz) and founding head of its professional society (Wellman), the editors are painfully aware of the long-standing gap between theoretical promise and empirical performance in structural analysis. Thus, even the orienting chapters in Part I, "Thinking structurally," contain many specific examples showing how classic problems in social inquiry can be rethought – and new insights developed – once the phenomena involved are seen as the systematic result of structural forces.

Barry Wellman's chapter traces the development of structural analysis and shows how its main tenets have been applied to a variety of substantive research problems. He demonstrates how network analysis, sociometry, and political economy are coalescing into a common structural analytic approach. In his review, Wellman distills common theoretical principles in structural analysis from hundreds of studies.

Nancy Howell looks at one of the most clearly defined examples of the reciprocal effects of social structure and individual behavior: the interaction between kinship roles and demography. In kinship, the units of analysis must be relational: There can be no "mothers" without "children," "husbands" without "wives." Howell uses the !Kung hunter-gatherers of the Kalahari desert to analyze the intersection of kinship structure with demographic changes. To do this, she must trace patterns over long periods of time. Yet reliable data about the !Kung do not go back very far. Howell deals with this problem by working with microsimulations that replicate population changes and point toward important social structural patterns and dynamics.

Ronald Breiger's chapter demonstrates important ways in which networks integrate or generate cleavages in social systems. He finds elegant ways of studying Simmel's classic insight that, in essence, intergroup networks simultaneously connect persons and institutions. Two persons may be connected through an interpersonal tie. But a single person may also connect two groups when he or she is a member of both. Such joint memberships form group-to-group ties that indirectly connect all persons in each separate group.

Bonnie Erickson is interested in understanding how the patterning of social structures affects the attitudes of their members. She first provides a guide to useful ways of detecting robust patterns in often obscuring surface noise. Then she discusses the implications that location in various positions of social networks hold for attitude formation. Thus her chapter points the way toward a structuralist social psychology.

Communities

Network models were first used to study interpersonal communities, the subject of the second part of this book. Recent work on communities has been largely descriptive – questioning in many cases whether communities exist in contemporary societies, given the buffeting of capitalism, industrialization, and urbanization. The success of network analysis in discovering communities under these circumstances has shifted the focus away from simply document-ing the continued existence of communities to demonstrating how large-scale structural patterns affect the ways in which specific community structures contribute to social production and reproduction. The authors in this section examine three widely divergent settings: a Canadian metropolis, a rapidly industrializing city in India, and a village in Sardinia. Although kinship and friendship provide the basis for interpersonal relations in all three examples, the community networks differ in the way they act as conduits for resources.

In the first chapter in Part II, *Barry Wellman, Peter Carrington*, and *Alan Hall* describe "personal community" networks formed by informal links between individuals and households. Although most Torontonians report a densely knit core of kin or friends, their ties with individuals, dyads, and small clusters are more fragmented. Their networks contribute much more to their domestic life than to their (paid) work life. They seldom receive a wide range of aid from any one network member, but, instead, utilize a variety of ties to obtain the emotional support, goods and services, companionship, information, and financial aid they need to deal with their everyday hassles and emergency crises.

In contrast, *Leslie Howard* reports that the personal communities of adult men in Ranchi, India, are greatly affected by the places in which these men obtain paid work. The authority structure of the workplace conditions interpersonal ties both on and off the job. Whereas many sociologists would expect nonfactory workers to be more involved than factory workers in rich, complex, communal bonds, Howard finds no such simple tradi-tional–modern distinction. Because personalistic, patron–client relations inhibit equal-status ties among nonfactory workers, the factory workers are better able to build broadly based communities.

Michal Bodemann extends the structural analysis of communities by showing that the ways in which patron–client relations articulate with larger political economic networks affects the structure and content of interpersonal networks within an isolated Sardinian village. He demonstrates that asymmetric patron–client relations are a mechanism for maintaining relations of production and, thus, class rule. He shows how the local operation of village networks are rooted in larger regional, national, and transnational economic and political relations. In response to the vast changes in Sardinia during the twentieth century, from a precapitalist to a national capitalist and then transnational economy, corresponding changes have taken place in the ties inside and outside villages.

Markets

Since the early 1970s, many structural analysts have been preoccupied with documenting the linkages among corporations, government bodies, and other institutions. As in their studies of communities, structural analysts have used network tools to establish and interpret patterns of ties between them. In this fashion, they have been able to address a variety of questions: Are enterprises truly "free," or do ties structure flows of resources through them? How are markets formed? And how do they structure relations among regions within a global economy?

In the first chapter in the "Markets" part, *Harrison White* explores the conditions under which buyers and sellers come together. White departs from the individualistic interpretation of economists and treats markets as a particular kind of social structure. He argues that markets exercise a distinctive form of social control through revealing actors to one another. Furthermore, markets are not created automatically, but develop through an elaborate process of mutual orientation in which actors come to recognize an "accustomed structure of deference and differentiated behavior" that allows them to interpret one another's actions.

But who are the effective collective actors within these markets? Given the footloose multinational conglomerates operating on a worldwide scale, firms have become less useful as units for measuring economic structure. *S. D. Berkowitz's* chapter explains how we can describe enterprises and producers' markets within complex industrial economies with the aid of network tools, which can be used to identify units and markets. This approach, Berkowitz argues, produces more powerful results than the ones based on the individualistic "structure–conduct–performance" paradigm that has dominated work in this area of research.

Harriet Friedmann moves from problems of market formation to the wider structural context within which market interactions take place. Since the 1960s, she observes, sociologists working within the "world-systems" paradigm have recognized the complexity of the world economic order and have sought to develop an analytic framework that takes part–whole relationships into account. Yet they, too, have had problems in determining the appropriate units of analysis: Although world-systems analysis have avoided the "modernization" theorists' mistake of treating nations as independent entities, they have sorted nations into "core" and "periphery" regions on a priori grounds. Friedmann argues the utility of using network tools to identify often asymmetric relations in world political economic structures. From her detailed study of the international wheat trade, she demonstrates how her approach may be used to interpret the location of nations within systems of exchange.

Social change

The problems in specifying units of analysis are also a central concern in Part IV, "Social change." Structural analysts have had a long-standing debate in this regard with modernization theorists who contend that changes in individuals' norms and values provide the motive force behind social change. "Relative deprivation" theorists, for instance, contend that members of radical political groups tend to be rootless individuals made anomic by social dislocations. In rebuttal, structural analysts have pointed out that such individualistic normative explanations ignore the ways in which social networks structure resource flows. They argue that political behavior arises out of contentions for resources between interest groups and not from social–psychic dislocations. They want to know how intergroup coalitions and cleavages mobilize and channel political activity. Thus structural studies associate social change with fundamental alterations in patterns of relationships between individuals, groups, and organizations. The underlying assumption of their analyses is that norms and values are byproducts of structural changes, not their source.

Charles Tilly has been in the forefront of the critique of traditional modernization theory, and his chapter here continues the argument. He maintains that modernization theories have failed to interpret successfully the consequences of important nineteenth-century European social change. Conventional, normatively driven analyses – treating each town and nation individually – find only chaos wherever industrialization, mobility, and complex structural transformations have affected the agrarian, immobile, homogeneous world, which they took as their contrast conception. Tilly contends that nineteenth-century changes in work, mobility, and population distributions are prime examples of structural analyses of economic relations that provide more satisfying interpretations than conventional ones.

Robert Brym's chapter analyzes how differences in structural location among Jewish intellectuals yielded divergences in their revolutionary roles and ideological positions in early twentieth century Russia. Traditional sociological explanations of the disproportionate role played by Jews in these movements have centered around their "rootlessness" or lack of integration into Russian society. In contrast, Brym maintains that the "rootedness" of Jewish intellectuals – the form of their ties to one another and to the larger social structure – provides a better explanation of both their disproportionate role in the revolutionary movements and the ideological connections of their participation. He documents this interpretation through detailed analyses of the careers of Jewish revolutionaries and the changing bases of Russian Jewish community life.

Douglas R. White and *H. Gilman McCann* analyze a different type of revolutionary change, the eighteenth century "chemical revolution." They use a new analytic technique, "material entailment analysis," to trace changing patterns of affiliation among scientists during this time. The technique enables them to reconstruct the underlying structural dynamics that led to the successful supplanting of the phlogiston model of combustion by one based on oxygen reactions.

Social mobility

The fifth part, "Social mobility," deals with the movement of individuals through relatively stable social systems. Mobility, at first sight, is an inherently individualistic subject. After all, individuals are the ones who "move." If social factors enter into conventional studies of mobility at all, it is because persons with similar attributes possess similar resources and motivations and hence move through social systems in similar ways. "Human capital" theory (Becker, 1975) and the classic Wisconsin studies of intergenerational mobility (Sewell, Haller, and Portes, 1969) are based on this model. Although such models often deal with large aggregates, their underlying assumptions are derived from the experiences of persons moving through the system as apparently isolated individuals.

However, ever since Harrison White (1970) demonstrated the utility of analyzing "vacancy chains" – by studying how openings in one locale in a social system create movement and subsequent mobility elsewhere – researchers have come to recognize that social mobility is governed by deeply rooted structural processes. Thus, in the first chapter of Part V, *Lorne Tepperman* argues that traditional political sociology has tended to favor "voluntaristic" explanations of elite behavior, dynastic persistence, social stratification, and social mobility. Using nineteenth-century Toronto as a case study, he argues that the survival of upper classes is a part of the larger problem of how groups are able to maintain social position over time. Groups, not individuals, he contends, are the appropriate units for analyzing this problem in that individual opportunities depend largely on the opportunities available to the groups to which individuals belong. Tepperman demonstrates how structural constraints – changes in class structure, demographic inundation, circulating succession, and family support – have affected the ability of Toronto elite families to help their children maintain elite status.

The other two chapters in this part deal with job mobility. *John Delany* looks at the processes through which mobility ultimately occurs – the locating and securing of employment. He is mainly interested in how individuals garner information about job opportunities through social networks and how, given this information, they are able to make job moves. Rather than using "real" data gathered through a survey, Delany relies on simulation techniques to test hypotheses about the effects of information transfers via social networks.

As *Joel Levine* and *John Spadaro* point out in their chapter, although job moves may appear to be individualistic, the players are inherently constrained by the occupational structure. Rather than forcing intergenerational occupational moves to fit into categories predetermined by the investigator, Levine and Spadaro argue that the intergenerational structure itself can only be determined empirically by tracing the shifts in jobs between the generations. Thus the model uses individual movements to trace the broad outlines of the structure of intergenerational change. The authors use this larger image of the structure of change to refine definitions of the categories into which individuals were initially placed. The result is a far better delineation of the parameters that govern social mobility than those obtained using traditional methods. By varying their parameters, Levine and Spadaro are able to predict the effects of structural shifts on patterns of intergenerational mobility over time.

S. D. Berkowitz's afterword is both retrospective and prospective. He sums up the developments in structural analysis, especially as they are represented in this book. He points out the value of holistic studies that deal simultaneously with individual and structural data, come to grips with questions of units of analysis and levels of interaction, and utilize truly structural methods to address sociological issues. Berkowitz sees the future of structural analysis in its ability to represent social structures and to model systemic processes in their own terms.

NOTES

1. Wellman's chapter further develops this point; see also, Richardson and Wellman, 1985.
2. Such studies are often quite Marxian in their focus on exploitative structures, even though they may not, in all cases, see relations of production as the dominant explanatory variable of social structure and social relations.

LITERATURE CITED

Becker, Gary. *Human Capital*. New York: Columbia University Press, 1975.

Bertalanffy, Ludwig von. *General System Theory*. New York: Braziller, 1968.

Blau, Peter. *Inequality and Heterogeneity*. New York: Free Press, 1977.

Boorman, Scott and Paul Levitt. *The Genetics of Altruism*. New York: Academic Press, 1980.

Gould, Stephen Jay "Utopia (Limited)." *New York Review of Books*, 3 March 1983:23-5.

Gregory, Stephen, and Laird Thompson. "Superclusters and Voids in the Distribution of Galaxies." *Scientific American* 246 (1982): 06-14.

Hacking, Ian. *Why Does Language Matter in Philosophy?* Cambridge: Cambridge University Press, 1975.

"On the Frontier." *New York Review of Books*, 20 December 1984: 54-8.

Hofstadter, Douglas. *Gödel, Escher, Bach*. Harmondsworth, England: Penguin, 1980.

Jakobson, Roman, and Morris Halle. *Fundamentals of Language*. The Hague: Mouton, 1971.

Lévi-Strauss, Claude. *Structural Anthropology*. Translated by Claire Jacobson and Brook Schoepf. Garden City, N.Y.: Doubleday, 1969.

Leontief, Wassily. *Input-Output Economics*, 2nd ed. New York: Oxford University Press, 1985.

Lewontin, R. C. "The Corpse in the Elevator." *New York Review of Books*, 20 January 1983:34-7.

Luce, R. D., and A. W. Tucker (eds.). *Contributions to the Theory of Games, IV*. Princeton, N.J.: Princeton University Press, 1959.

Mayhew, Bruce. "Structuralism versus Individualism. I. Shadowboxing in the Dark." *Social Forces* 59 (1980): 335-75.

Mayhew, Bruce, and Roger Levinger. "Size and Density of Interaction in Human Aggregates." *American Journal of Sociology* 82 (1976): 86-110.

Mayr, Ernst. *The Growth of Biological Thought*. Cambridge, Mass.: Harvard University Press, 1982.

Pagels, Heinz. *Perfect Symmetry*. New York: Simon & Schuster, 1985.

Parret, Herman. "Structuralism: A Methodology or an Ideology?" *Algemeen Netherlands Tidjschrift voor Wijsbegeerte* 68 (1976): 99-110.

Prigogine, Ilya. *From Being to Becoming*. San Francisco: W. H. Freeman, 1980.

Richardson, R. J., and Barry Wellman. "Structural Analysis," *Canadian Review of Sociology and Anthropology* 22 (1985): 771-93.

Rose, Steven (ed.). *Against Biological Determinism*. London: Allison & Busby, 1982.

Schrödinger, Erwin. *Science and Humanism*. Cambridge: Cambridge University Press, 1951.

Sewell, William, Archibald Haller, and Alejandro Portes. "The Educational and Early Occupational Attainment Process." *American Sociological Review* 34 (1969): 82-92.

Simmons, James. "The Canadian Urban System as a Political System. I and II." Research Papers 141 and 142, Centre for Urban and Community Studies, University of Toronto, 1983.

Simon, Herbert. "A Formal Theory of Interaction in Social Groups." *American Sociological Review* 17 (1952): 202–12.

(ed.). *Models of Man*. New York: Wiley, 1957.

Smith, John Maynard. "Storming the Fortress." *New York Review of Books*, 13 May 1982: 41–42.

Weyl, Hermann. *Space, Time, Matter*. New York: Dover, 1922.

White, Harrison. *Chains of Opportunity*. Cambridge, Mass.: Harvard University Press, 1970.

Part I
Thinking structurally

Although the concept of *social structure* has long played a critical role in distinguishing sociology from other social sciences, sociologists have only recently been able to develop systematic methods for analyzing concrete social structures. Instead of looking at the world in terms of *structures*, mainstream sociologists have tended to think in terms of *categories* of social actors who share similar characteristics: "women," "the elderly," "blue-collar workers," "emerging nations," and so on. These categories are close enough to those used by people in their ordinary discourse so that the process of working with them is familiar and reassuring to researchers. Indeed, much sociological research in this genre consists of nothing more elaborate than checking to see whether or not actors with one kind of characteristic are more likely than others to have another: "Do blondes have more fun?"

This kind of approach has its uses, but it has misled many sociologists into studying the *attributes* of aggregated sets of *individuals* rather than the structural nature of social systems. Analytically, it has encouraged them to produce increasingly sophisticated statistical techniques for interpreting what are, ultimately, distributions of independent events. No blonde in the previous example, for instance, has any inherent structural connection to any other blonde – whether or not he or she is having more fun.

A better way of looking at things, structural analysts contend, is to view *relations* as the basic units of social structure and groupings of similarly situated actors as the result. At present, such structural thinking is rare because it often requires the development of new intellectual habits. Yet, this structuralist way of interpreting phenomena also accords with our ordinary experience in another way. For instance, when we attend a social gathering, we often become aware of the marital, friendship, or occupational ties between the persons in attendance and use this information to navigate in that environment. When we meet people for the first time, we often ask them where they work, live, or went to school. The answers they provide enable us to place them into categories whose members occupy *similar positions* in social systems: "engineers at IBM who attended MIT," "artists from Soho who used to hang out at the Village Vanguard," "truck drivers from Cabbagetown who now work for General Electric." We generally assume that persons occupying structurally equivalent locations will share experiences and, hence, attitudes. But we normally do not stop there. We also

15

explore their particular interconnections: "Do you work for Joe Chambers?" we ask. "Did you know Henry Wong at MIT?" People are usually concerned with how others deal with these questions because their answers help to locate actors in occupational, educational, and friendship networks: If we can locate people in such networks, we can then make some useful estimates as to who and what they know, the resources to which they have access, the social constraints on their behavior, and how they are likely to think and act.

Structural analysts do the same thing, but on a larger scale and in a more systematic fashion: They seek to describe networks of relations as fully as possible, tease out the prominent patterns in such networks, trace the flow of resources through them, and discover what effects they have on individuals who are or are not connected into them in specific ways. They use the resulting information to study the fit between structure and behavior at each of several analytic levels within the structures.

Thinking structurally, then, requires that we pay attention primarily to the implications of patterns of relationships among units within social structures. It is in this sense that all the chapters in this part – and, indeed, in this book – are about how to "think structurally." In the lead chapter, *Barry Wellman* reviews several hundred studies to elaborate on some basic principles that distinguish structural from nonstructural analysis. He starts by asserting the underlying unity of three distinct structural analytic traditions: the (mostly British) development of social network concepts to analyze ethnographic data about villagers and urbanites; the (mostly American) development of quantitative network analysis to look at links between persons and organizations; the (mostly Canadian and American) application of structural analytic principles to analyze "political economic" links among nations, regions, and interest groups.

The underlying similarity in these approaches often is not perceived by their adherents because of differences in technique, subject matter, and rhetoric. Yet Wellman argues that these three traditions have common themes which distinguish structural analysis from mainstream social science. They all maintain that the study of patterns of social relationships yields more powerful sociological explanations than the study of personal attributes. They all reject the notion that norms and dyadic interactions are the building blocks of social systems, but instead, see systems of ties as the basis of social structure. Indeed, their analyses often treat large-scale social systems as "networks of networks," so that a network at a lower level of analysis is treated as a node in larger-scale networks.

Wellman's account emphasizes the usefulness of structural analysis for studying power, stratification, and interest groups. The other chapters in this section stress different dimensions of social systems. Just as traditional sociologists use a variety of techniques to simplify and explain complex social patterns – typologies, means, regressions, case studies – structural analysts have created some new ways of identifying, understanding, and summarizing important features of social structure. Although many structural analysts work by simplifying complex structures, Nancy Howell proposes the opposite solution in her chapter: start with social structures that are inherently simple enough to comprehend in their own right and then derive their implications from the study of more complex structures. She says, "My own inclination when faced with puzzles that are too difficult to solve directly is to ask easier questions. . . . Examining the demography of a remote hunter–gatherer people [the !Kung of the Kalahari desert] . . . is far simpler, both theoretically and substantively, than understanding networks of friends, relations, workers, and strangers in industrialized societies."

Howell describes how empirically based "microsimulations" of births, deaths, marriages, and divorce "can be used to find out if a kin system that operates according to given rules and probability schedules is viable." Keeping straight both levels and units of analysis turns out to be critical here. Her analysis depends on recognizing the key role played by sibling groups in orchestrating relations between individuals, their parents, and the larger kin system. Since kinship is the central organizing mechanism in hunter–gatherer populations, Howell is able to use her microsimulations of the demography of the !Kung to illustrate how, in a "simple" case, larger dimensions of social structure are formed, maintained, and transformed over time.

In his chapter, *Ronald Breiger* addresses one of the most powerful "dualities" in social structure: Just as persons can link groups, groups can link persons. A person links two groups by being a member of both, for example, when acting as the director of two corporations. At the same time, groups link persons who are members of them; for example, directors share the experience of being on several corporate boards with one another. The emphasis in the first instance is on the structure of interorganizational relationships; in the second, it is on the notion of social milieu or background.

At first blush, this notion of duality may appear to be trivial, but many researchers have not understood its implications. Their confusion has been most apparent in studies of the upper echelons of complex societies when analysts have mistaken links between elite *persons* for links between powerful *organizations* and interest *groups* (e.g., Clement, 1975). Although such confusion can lead researchers to discover transitory captains of industry and government, it does little to explicate the underlying economic structure of a nation-state.

Breiger bases his discussion on Simmel's (1922) insight that intergroup networks connect persons and groups. People in modern industrial societies typically belong to a wide variety of groups, and the membership of each of these groups typically varies. Hence the links that people make between groups – and the links that groups make between people – integrate and cleave social systems. By comparing networks of groups tied by individuals and individuals tied by groups, Breiger contends, we can begin to understand how changes in social structures shape individual and group activities.

Bonnie H. Erickson takes this notion about the relationship between social structure and individual actions or perceptions one step further by considering how individuals' attitudes are "made, maintained or modified primarily through interpersonal processes." She contends that the key to understanding attitude formation is to recognize that attitudes are by-products of interpersonal processes that depend both on aspects of interpersonal relations and on how these fit into larger social structures. Most studies, she finds, explain attitudes in terms of individual attributes. According to many social psychologists, for example, individuals form attitudes by comparing themselves to "similar" and "dissimilar" others. Yet "the chance that someone will compare and come to agree with a person . . . depends on the nature of their relationship as well as similarity in their attributes per se."

The social psychological perspective, she maintains, fails to account adequately for the social processes that lead to the creation and maintenance of comparison groups, and hence the social basis for comparisons. Many structural analysts, by contrast, have overlooked the fact that social ties have different consequences, depending on the particular contexts in which they occur. In Erickson's view, only methods that allow us to embed small-scale processes of attitude formation in a larger context can encompass both aspects of the problem simultaneously. She describes three tools widely used to study network structure – clique models, blockmodels, and spatial models – and draws out their implications for the study of attitude formation.

LITERATURE CITED

Clement, Wallace. *The Canadian Corporate Elite*. Toronto: McClelland and Stewart, 1975.

Simmel, Georg. "The Web of Group Affiliations." Translated by Reinhard Bendix. In Georg Simmel, *Conflict and the Web of Group Affiliations*. Glencoe, Ill.: Free Press [1922], 1955.

2

Structural analysis: from method and metaphor to theory and substance

Barry Wellman

(Mis)conceptions

Structural (or network) analysis has mystified many social scientists. Some have rejected it as mere methodology, which lacks due regard for substantive issues. Some have fled from its unusual terms and techniques, not having played with blocks and graphs since grammar school. Some have dismissed one portion for the whole, saying, for example, that their study of class structure has little need for the focus on friendship ties emphasized in network analysis. And some have scorned it as nothing new, claiming that they also study "social structure." Others have bolted on variables such as network "density" as they would a turbocharger in order to boost explained variance. Still others, attracted by the capability of studying nonhierarchical, nongroup structures, have expanded structural analysis into a network ideology that advocates egalitarian, open communities. Some have even used "network" as a verb and "networking" as a noun to advocate the deliberate creation and use of social networks for such desired ends as getting jobs or integrating communities.

These misconceptions have arisen because too many analysts and

This chapter was prepared with the significant assistance of members of the Structural Analysis Programme, University of Toronto. S. D. Berkowitz, Robert Brym, June Corman, Bonnie Erickson, Harriet Friedmann, Leslie Howard, Nancy Howell, R. J. Richardson, Lorne Tepperman, and Jack Wayne contributed ideas and commented on drafts. I have benefited as well from discussion with H. Russell Bernard, Jerome Bruner, Ronald Burt, Douglas Caulkins, Ivan Chase, Patrick Doreian, Linton Freeman, Beatrice de Gelder, Hans J. Hummell, Judith Kjellburg, Edward Laumann, J. Clyde Mitchell, Robert Mokken, Carolyn Mullins, Leslie Salzinger, Emanuel Schegloff, Neil Smelser, Albert Somit, Charles Tilly, Beverly Wellman and Harrison White.

Support for this work has been provided by the Social Sciences and Humanities Research Council of Canada; the National Welfare Grants Directorate of Health and Welfare Canada; the Center for Studies of Metropolitan Problems (U.S. National Institute of Mental Health); the Netherlands Institute for Advanced Studies; the Institute for Urban and Regional Development, University of California; and the Structural Analysis Programme and Centre for Urban and Community Studies, University of Toronto. Although I have benefited greatly from all this assistance and discussion, I take sole responsibility for the result.

practitioners have (mis)used "structural analysis" as a mixed bag of terms and techniques. Some have hardened it into a method, whereas others have softened it into a metaphor. Many have limited the power of the approach by treating all units as if they had the same resources, all ties as if they were symmetrical, and the contents of all ties as if they were equivalent.

Yet, structural analysis does not derive its power from the partial application of this concept or that measure. It is a comprehensive paradigmatic way of taking social structure seriously by studying directly how patterns of ties allocate resources in a social system. Thus, its strength lies in its integrated application of theoretical concepts, ways of collecting and analyzing data, and a growing, cumulating body of substantive findings.

Until recently, structural analysis has had neither a basic programmatic statement nor a standard text. Instead, it has tended to accumulate partial principles and conclusions from empirical studies and oral lore. There have been three distinct research traditions, and most adherents of each tradition have not assimilated the work of the other two. Hence, rather than adopt one standard model, structural analysts have used a number of different models with shared family resemblances. Now, much work is coalescing, and researchers are forming groups, starting their own journals, and publishing widely in mainstream books and journals.[1]

In the course of time, structural analysis has emerged as a distinctive form of social inquiry having five paradigmatic characteristics that provide its underlying intellectual unity:

1. Behavior is interpreted in terms of structural constraints on activity, rather than in terms of inner forces within units (e.g., "socialization to norms") that impel behavior in a voluntaristic, sometimes teleological, push toward a desired goal.
2. Analyses focus on the relations between units, instead of trying to sort units into categories defined by the inner attributes (or essences) of these units.
3. A central consideration is how the patterned relationships among multiple alters jointly affect network members' behavior. Hence, it is not assumed that network members engage only in multiple duets with separate alters.
4. Structure is treated as a network of networks that may or may not be partitioned into discrete groups. It is not assumed a priori that tightly bounded groups are, intrinsically, the building blocks of the structure.
5. Analytic methods deal directly with the patterned, relational nature of social structure in order to supplement – and sometimes supplant – mainstream statistical methods that demand independent units of analysis.

My objective in this chapter is to describe this structural analytic paradigm: its development, distinguishing characteristics, and analytic principles. Not all structural analysts will agree with my description. Indeed, some would not even call themselves "structural analysts." Nevertheless, I believe that I am able to show a fundamental unity underlying the many studies that I discuss.

Research traditions

The (mostly British) anthropological development of the social network concept

The concern of structural analysts with the direct study of networks of concrete social relations connects strongly back to post–World War II developments in British social anthropology.[2] Then as now, anthropologists paid a good deal of attention to cultural systems of normative rights and duties that prescribe proper behavior within such bounded groups as tribes, villages, and work units. Although British "structural-functionalists" had used network metaphors as partial, allusive descriptions of social structure (e.g., Radcliffe-Brown, 1940; see also Sundt, 1857; Bohannan, 1954), their research had focused on how cultures prescribe proper behavior within bounded groups (Boissevain, 1979). Not only were such cultural systems simpler to describe than the great variety of actual behavior, but the structural-functionalists believed that in focusing on culture they were reducing behavioral noise and thus getting at the essence of social systems.

Whatever the merits of such normative analyses when applied to bounded groups, they have difficulty in dealing with social systems in which ties cut across "the framework of bounded institutionalized groups or categories" in complex ways (Barnes, 1969: 72). To study these crosscutting ties, several anthropologists in the 1950s shifted attention away from cultural systems toward structural systems of concrete ties and networks (e.g., Nadel, 1957; Barnes, 1971) and began developing social network concepts more systematically and self-consciously. These analysts defined a network as a set of ties linking social system members across social categories and bounded groups.

Some anthropologists especially felt the need for network analytic tools after World War II when they began studying large streams of migrants leaving culturally homogeneous villages and tribes for polyglot cities and industrial areas. They feared that these migrants, in leaving behind the normative guidance of their homelands, would become isolated and disorganized in "mass societies." Administrators worried that these new urbanites would be prone to sink into apathetic despair or to strike out in unstructured, mindless mobs (these views are summarized in Kornhauser,

1968). Yet investigators soon discovered that not only were the migrants forming strong, supportive ties within their new urban milieux, they were retaining strong ties to their ancestral rural homelands. Rather than wilting under the impact of urbanization, industrialization, capitalism, and technological change, the migrants were enmeshed in complex and supportive social networks, cutting across tribal, residential, and workplace boundaries.[3]

This research focused on the migrants' actual ties rather than on the ties that normative prescriptions suggested that they *ought* to have. Such work soon came together with similar anthropological work on concrete social relations in western social systems. In 1954, Barnes had self-consciously used the concept of "the social network" to analyze the ties that cut across kinship groups and social classes in a Norwegian fishing village. Not only did the network concept help him to describe more accurately the social structure of the village, but it was more useful than normative concepts in explaining such key social processes as access to jobs and political activity. Soon afterward, Bott's (1957, 1971) work brought the network concept to the wider attention of social scientists. She developed the first distinct measure of network structure – "knit" (now called "density") – to show that densely knit, English extended families were more apt to contain married couples who did most things independently rather than jointly.

These anthropological network analysts shared with their structural-functional kindred a resolute British empiricism. They differed from them in emphasizing concrete social relations and not cultural prescriptions. They insisted on starting with these relations and then discerning the social structure inherent in the underlying patterns of behavioral exchanges.

At first, the anthropological network analysts saw the network concept as just one (albeit, important) addition to the social scientist's battery of intellectual tools, which provided a way to incorporate crosscutting relationships into analyses hitherto confined to bounded groups. They began to develop basic quantitative measures of properties such as density to describe the form of social networks. As their work progressed, these anthropologists gradually expanded the scope of their claims for the usefulness of "social network analysis" (as the approach came to be called).

The (mostly American) increase in quantitative analysis and substantive scope

Whereas the British anthropologists moved from questions of substance to the study of network form, much American structural analysis started with questions of network form: Do patterns of relations in networks, for example, affect the ways in which social systems operate? With the post–World War II translation of Georg Simmel's work into English (e.g., 1950,

1955, 1971), many American sociologists became acquainted with his early twentieth-century argument that the forms of social relations greatly determine their contents. They drew from his work an interest in how the size of social systems and the ways in which relationships are interconnected constrain individual behavior and dyadic exchange. To some, such a *structural* emphasis was a welcome challenge to the more psychologistic, needs-driven analyses advocated by the dominant American sociological brand of structural-functionalism (e.g., Parsons, 1951, 1960).

As knowledge of the British anthropologists' work diffused across the Atlantic, it intersected with, reinforced, and modified American sociological interest in structural analysis. The scope of inquiries expanded, as British empiricism fit well with the American penchant for quantitative measurement and statistical analysis.

American interest in structural form stimulated efforts to map interpersonal relations and to develop fine-grained methods for describing their patterns. "Sociometrists" started using network diagrams to represent interpersonal relations in small groups (e.g., Coleman, 1961; for a precursor, see Moreno, 1934). Subsequently, epidemiologists and information scientists began conceiving of the diffusion of disease, information, and sundry other things as a social network phenomenon (Coleman, Katz, and Manzel, 1966; Rapoport, 1979; Rogers and Kincaid, 1981).

Structural analysts then began using the vocabulary of rudimentary "graph theory" – the field of mathematics devoted to studying the arrangement of points and lines – to describe linkages among the members of social systems and to manipulate these representations in order to probe the underlying "deep structures" connecting and cleaving social systems (Harary, Norman, and Cartwright, 1965; Frank, 1981). Yet point-and-line diagrams are cluttered when used to study networks with more than about a dozen members; McCann and White's (Chapter 14) graphic depiction of the citation network of oxygen chemists in the 1780s is at about the outer limits of legibility (see Figure 2.1, which is based on Figure 14.6). Consequently analysts have come to use matrices to study social networks (Figure 2.2). The use of matrices has made it possible to study many more members of social systems and many more types of ties, and it has fit well with the use of computers to reveal such underlying structural features as cliques, central members, and indirect linkages.

The research group around Harrison White at Harvard in the 1960s and 1970s played an especially important role in these efforts. White wrote key programmatic papers (e.g., 1965, 1966) claiming all of sociologistic sociology for structural analysis. He also performed a variety of exemplary analyses (e.g., 1970a) and trained more than a score of graduate students in his lectures (unfortunately, unpublished) and seminars. In the words of one influential paper, "The presently existing, largely categorical descriptions of social

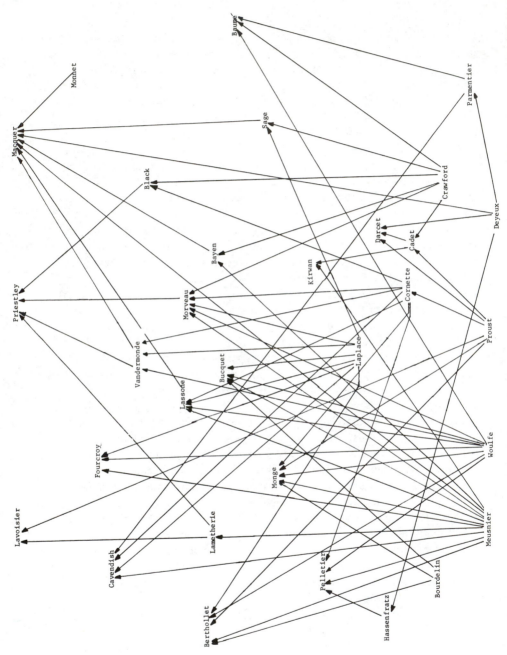

Figure 2.1. Entailment structure of network of chemists, 1781–88. $\phi \geqslant .3$; 2 exceptions; signal-to-noise ratio, 1:1.

FROM		1	2	3	4	5	6	7	8	9	10	11	12	13	14	15	16	17	18	19	20	21	22	23	24	25	26	27	28	29	30	31
Baume	1																															
Bayen	2																			X												
Berthollet	3																															
Black	4																											X				
Bourdelin	5			X		X															X											
Bucquet	6																															
Cadet	7											X			X																	
Cavendish	8																															
Cornette	9			X					X											X			X		X		X					X
Crawford	10	X	X		X			X																X						X		
Darcet	11																															
Deyeux	12											X			X					X				X								
Fourcroy	13																															
Hassenfratz	14																								X							
Kirwan	15																															
Lametherie	16																		X						X							
Laplace	17			X				X		X					X					X					X						X	X
Lassone	18																				X											
Lavoisier	19																															
Macquer	20																															
Meusneir	21		X	X			X		X				X			X	X		X		X		X		X		X					
Monge	22																			X												
Monnet	23																			X												
Morveau	24																								X							
Parmentier	25	X						X																								
Pelletier	26																															
Priestley	27																															
Proust	28			X						X		X		X						X			X									
Sage	29																				X											
Vandermonde	30																				X						X					
Woulfe	31	X	X		X								X							X			X		X							X

Figure 2.2. Matrix representation of Figure 2.1. Presence of tie represented by *X*; absence of tie represented by blank. [Note: Computer storage would be binary (1/0) or as a vector (e.g., Black–03:27).]

structure have no solid theoretical grounding; furthermore, network concepts may provide the only way to construct a theory of social structure" (White, Boorman, and Breiger, 1976: 732).

American structural analysts have had two distinct sensibilities. An influential minority are *formalists* (e.g., Lorrain and White, 1971; Fararo, 1973; also see many of the papers in Holland and Leinhardt, 1979). Concentrating on the form of network patterns rather than their content, they have shared a Simmelian sensibility that similar patterns of ties may have similar behavioral consequences, no matter what the substantive context. Pushed to its extreme, their argument has been that the pattern of relationships is substantially the same as the content.

The second sensibility, more widely represented in this book, has been a broad *structuralism*, using a variety of network analytic concepts and techniques to address the substantive questions that have preoccupied most sociologists. Structural analysts with this sensibility have approached these questions from two routes. Many view networks much as astronomers view the universe: as outside observers studying relationships linking all members of a population. The resulting *whole network* studies describe the comprehensive structure of role relationships in a social system. Through manipulating matrices, analysts can find patterns of connectivity and cleavage within social systems, "structurally equivalent" role relationships among system members, changes in network structures over time, and the ways in which system members are directly and indirectly connected.

A basic strength of the whole network approach is that it permits simultaneous views of the social system as a whole and of the parts that make up the system. Analysts are therefore able to trace lateral and vertical flows of information, identify sources and targets, and detect structural constraints operating on flows of resources. Whole network analysts either study the system for its own sake asking, for example, if it is socially integrated or if there is a ruling class or they analyze how the structure of a system affects the behavior and attitude of its members. They ask, for example, if sparsely knit networks lead to sensed social isolation or if persons with ties to two network clusters behave differently from those whose ties are wholly bound up within one cluster (e.g., Kapferer, 1972; Bernard and Killworth, 1973).

Some of the most interesting whole network studies have used memberships on boards of directors to describe relationships between large corporations. Here the nodes of the networks are the large corporations themselves, and the membership of a corporate executive on another corporation's board is used as a trace of a tie between the two corporations.[4] Such work has powerful implications even in its descriptive form: It graphically portrays the overall connectivity of dominant corporations and the presence of interest-group alliances among them. Moreover, the work has predictive power: For example, sectors of the Canadian economy in which the corporations are heavily interconnected tend to have high rates of profit (Carrington, 1981).

Whole network studies are not always methodologically feasible or analytically appropriate. Those who use them find that they must define the boundaries of a population, compile a list of all the members of this population, collect a list of all the direct ties (of the sort the analyst is interested in) between the members of this population, and employ a variety of statistical and mathematical techniques to tease out some underlying structural properties of the social systems. Yet, with the current limitations of computer hardware and software, analysts have been able to study only a few types of relationships in populations no larger than several hundred. Moreover, it is not feasible to obtain complete lists of population members

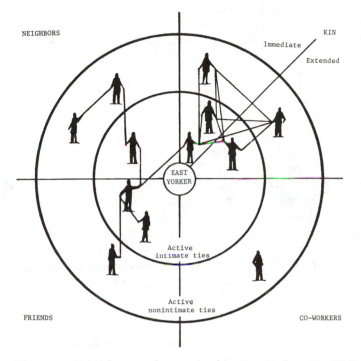

Figure 2.3. Typical personal network of an East Yorker. (See Wellman, Carrington, and Hall, Chapter 6.)

and their ties in many large, naturally occurring settings. Indeed, attempts to impose improper boundaries may often lead to analytic confusion, as was common before 1970 when urban sociologists ignored nonneighborhood friendships and wrongly declared urbanites to be isolated and lonely (see the review in Wellman and Leighton, 1979).

Because of such limitations, many structural analysts have concentrated on studying smaller *egocentric (or personal) networks* – defined from the standpoint of focal individuals. There are positive reasons as well for studying egocentric networks. Rather than showing the universe as it is perceived by an outside observer, they provide Ptolemaic views of networks as they may be perceived by the individuals at their centers.

Figure 2.3, for example, shows the significant interpersonal ties of a typical North American. She is directly tied with each network member (by definition), and she perceives many network members as being linked with each other. (For the sake of clarity, Figure 2.3 omits the direct ties between focal-person and network members.) She is aware of a densely knit core cluster of kin – three of whom she sees as her intimates – and more sparsely knit relations among half a dozen friends and neighbors. In her eyes, only her one work mate stands apart, the work mate's isolation reflecting both the focal person's separation of employed and social life, and her use of interpersonal ties to deal with domestic concerns and not problems of earning a living (see Wellman, 1985; Wellman, Carrington, and Hall, Chapter 6, for more details).

Egocentric network studies have often meshed well with traditional American survey techniques. Researchers have typically interviewed a (often large) sample of respondents, inquiring about the composition, relational patterns, and contents of "their" networks.

As in the many studies of urban "personal communities," such analyses have demonstrated the continued abundance and vitality of primary relations in social systems transformed by capitalism, urbanization, industrialization, bureaucratization, and technology. These egocentric network studies have documented the pervasiveness and importance of connectivity, thereby rebutting mass society contentions that recent large-scale social transformations have produced isolation and alienation. Numerous scholars have described how networks link individuals through strong and weak ties, situate them in larger social systems, and affect the flows of resources to and from them.

Questions of resource access are closely associated with questions of network form. How does one obtain material goods, emotional support, or information from other network members? A number of studies have demonstrated the effects of different network patterns of access to such diverse resources as jobs, scientific information, abortionists, and emotional support. Investigators have paid a great deal of attention to "social support," and many studies have suggested that the characteristics of their networks may significantly affect focal individuals' health, longevity, and well-being.[5]

In recent years, analysts of both whole and egocentric networks have been concerned with the effects of network properties on the integration of large-scale social systems, a sociological preoccupation since Émile Durkheim. In particular, they have studied:

- the conditions under which triads of ties concatenate to form larger networks (Davis and Leinhardt, 1972; Davis, 1979; Holland and Leinhardt, 1977)
- the addition of new members to networks through ramifying ties (Rapoport, 1979)
- the likelihood of network ties between members of large-scale social systems (Milgram, 1967: White, 1970b; Bernard and Killworth, 1978; Pool and Kochen, 1978)
- the impact of interpersonal network characteristics on the integration of large-scale social systems (Granovetter, 1973, 1982; Laumann, 1973; Brieger, Chapter 4).

Such studies are an important part of the contemporary movement away from treating network properties as just another interesting set of variables. Social network concepts, Simmelian sensibilities, quantitative techniques, and political economic awareness (see the next section) have expanded into a broadly comprehensive structural analytic approach. Having greatly increased the scope and claims of their work, many structural analysts now argue that all social behavior is best analyzed by looking first at the ways in which networks allocate flows of scarce resources to system members.

Structural explanations of political processes

At about the same time that many structural analysts were developing ethnographic and quantitative approaches to studying social networks, others were analyzing political processes as the result of ties of exchange and dependency between interest groups and nation-states. Researchers within this tradition have seldom used structural analytic tools or techniques. Few see themselves as structural analysts. Yet, some have personal and scholarly links with structural analysts and, like them, want to know how patterns of ties in social systems allocate resources unevenly.

One set of scholars in this tradition has been concerned with the ways in which networks and coalitions structure contentions for power *within* states. Their work began as a critique of psychologistic "relative deprivation" studies that sought to explain political behavior in terms of the personal attributes and internalized norms of individuals. Such analyses (e.g., Davies, 1962) usually portrayed politicized groups as collections of rootless individuals made anomic by the dislocations induced by large-scale change. Hence, these analyses have an intellectual tie with the "mass society" argument confronted by British anthropological network analysts and with the "loss-of-community" argument rejected by urban network researchers.

In contrast, structural analysts have developed "resource mobilization" analyses to explain political behavior. They showed such behavior to be due to structured vying for resources by interest groups – and not to reflect the aberrant cravings of a mob. Their work emphasized how patterns of links between interest groups structure coalitions, cleavages, and competitive relations and how direct and indirect ties differentially link individuals and groups to resources (Blok, 1974; Gold, 1975; Pickvance, 1975; Oberschall, 1978; Roberts, 1978; Tilly, 1978, 1979, 1981, Chapter 12; Bodemann, Chapter 8; Brym, Chapter 13). In documenting the existence and importance of connectivity within and between groups, their work has tied in neatly with recent historical research into the demography and structure of families and communities (Anderson, 1971; Laslett, 1971; Tilly and Scott, 1978, Foster, 1974; Katz, 1975; Maynes, 1981).

A second set of scholars has used structural analytic concepts, but not usually network methods, to study dependency links in systems of nation-states and among other macrostructural interest groups. Their work began in reaction to the prevailing scholarly view of the 1950s and 1960s, which attributed the underdevelopment of Third World states primarily to a state's *internally* "backward" social structure, norms, and values (e.g., McClelland, 1961; Hagen, 1962; Pye, 1962; Moore, 1979). These structural analysts have gone on to demonstrate that asymmetric relations of trade and power *between* states, regions, and interest groups have affected the course of Third World development much more than internal backwardness.

This "political economic" approach has adherents throughout the world, especially in Canada, which has been extensively involved in inter-national, interregional and intergroup dependency networks (Richardson and Wellman, 1985). A number of research groups with varying interests have contributed to this work: For example, "dependency" and "world-systems" analysts have studied how international terms of trade affect the internal structures of dependent countries (Frank, 1969; Wallerstein, 1974; Friedmann and Wayne, 1977; Friedmann, 1978, 1980, 1982, Chapter 11; Skocpol, 1979; Wayne, 1980; Delacroix and Ragin, 1981).

This work has led other structural analysts to consider more fully how power over access to resources affects relationships and to examine linkages between large-scale units as well as between persons. The reciprocal effect has been weaker. Whether through ignorance or distaste for quantitative reasoning, few "political economists" have used structural analytic tools to examine relationships between states and interest groups (see Berkowitz, Chapter 10; Friedmann, Chapter 11; Tilly, Chapter 12; White, Chapter 9). Yet the structural analytic approach shows particular promise for Marxian-informed studies of how power-dependency networks are associated with modes of production, consistent with Marx's injunction that class relation-ships be analyzed in structural rather than categorical terms (Godelier, 1978; *Insurgent Sociologist*, 1979).

The structural alternative

Structural analysis is more than a set of topics or a bag of methodological tricks with a new mystifying vocabulary. It is a distinctive way of tackling sociological questions that provides a means to the end of taking social structure seriously. In this section I present five general principles that together substantially guide structural analytic work in a wide variety of substantive areas.

Structured social relationships are a more powerful source of sociological explanation than personal attributes of system members

Many mainstream sociological studies treat social structure and process as the sum of individual actors' personal attributes. These attributes, whether derived genetically (e.g., age, gender) or socially (e.g., socioeconomic status, political attitudes), are treated as entities that individuals possess *as individuals*. Each is treated as an independent unit of analysis and lumped into social categories with others possessing similar attribute profiles. The method of analysis – be it cross-tabulation, correlation, or more complex multivariate techniques – proceeds by sorting individuals possessing similar combinations of attributes into similar analytic cells, for example, old women of high socioeconomic status who vote Republican.

Such taxonomic analyses group individuals into similar-attribute categories without regard for the structure of relationships in which such individuals are embedded – both internally within groups and externally between groups. For example, "there has been a tendency to examine the capitalist class and the petit bourgeoisie as distinct phenomena rather than as class analysis should demand, in relation to one another" (Clement, 1983: viii). Such analyses inevitably conclude that social behavior is the result of the fact that individuals possess common attributes rather than that they are involved in structured social relationships. Hence, although most mainstream sociologists profess to be studying social structure through attributional analyses, their inherent "methodological individualism" leads them to neglect social structure and the relations among individuals (Coleman, 1958:28). Their so-called structural techniques examine relationships between variables – not social system members. Such analyses, interrelating the personal attributes of discrete individuals, lead to a variety of problems.

1. Attribute analyses treat each social system member as an astructural independent unit. Since analyses of this kind must assume random linkages, they cannot take into account members' patterned connections (Berkowitz, Chapter 18). "But of course individuals do not act randomly with respect to one another. They form attachments to certain persons, they group together in cliques, they establish institutions" (Coleman, 1964: 88). Hence, aggregating each member's characteristics independently obscures or destroys structural information in the same way that centrifuging genes destroys structure while providing information about composition.

2. Such analyses concentrate on the attributes that discrete individuals possess. For example, they treat an inherently structural phenomenon, "social class," as a personal attribute, "socioeconomic status." Yet "it is as useful to tell me that 'power' is localized in the X club of New York as it is to

tell me that my soul resides in my pineal gland; the premise is false ... social vitalism" (Levine and Roy, 1979: 360–1).

3. Many analyses compare distributions and correlations of aggregated categories of attributes. They focus on the causes and correlates of internal variation within a social category, for example, relating socioeconomic status to voting behavior. At best, such analyses use categorical memberships as proxy measures of structured relationships (Friedmann, 1979; Breiger, 1981).

4. When analysts consider a category to be truly relevant rather than a proxy, they expect members of that category to behave in similar ways. However, coordinating ties among category members may be responsible for the similar behavior. How these ties come to exist and function is still open to question. Thus, the artisans of the Vendée did not all rise up spontaneously as the aggregated indignation of thousands of individuals. Rather, ties between local communities and occupational groups structured political activity (Tilly, 1967).

5. If analysts treat only categories and groups as relevant organizational units, this affects the ways in which they analyze ties that cut across category and group boundaries. They must treat such ties as marginal, when in fact the category or group may be truly irrelevant to the functioning of ties (Berkowitz, Chapter 18). For example, terming migrants "marginal" may well ignore their concrete urban relationships, while unduly positing attachments back to ancestral villages.

6. Aggregating individuals' attributes encourages analysts to interpret social behavior as a normatively guided phenomenon. The aggregation process has destroyed information about structural linkages but retained information about internalized norms. Analysts seize upon these norms to explain social behavior (Erickson, Chapter 5).

7. Normative interpretations lead analysts to look for behavior that is prescribed or common among category members. They either do not recognize other kinds of behavior or label it as deviant. Yet it may be deviant only because analysts persist in misidentifying it with a categorical reference group.[6]

These observations lead structural analysts to wonder if "the stuff of social action is, in fact, waiting to be discovered in the network of interstices that exist outside the normative constructs and the attribute breakdowns of our everyday categories." To find out, analysts "must aggregate (social) regularities in a fashion consistent with their inherent nature as networks" – that is, they must group individuals by equivalent structural location rather than equivalent categorical memberships (White, Boorman, and Breiger, 1976: 734).

People belong to networks as well as to categories. Structural analysts believe that categorical memberships reflect underlying structural relationships, that is, patterned differences in the kinds of resources with which they are linked. They do not treat social class, for example, as a set of statuses occupied by members of a population, but as a summary label for economic relations of power and dependency (Wright, 1977, 1980).

> This shift in perspective markedly affects analysis: Once we assume that the unit of analysis is ... a "world system" and not the "state" or the "nation" or the "people" ... we shift from a concern with the attributive characteristics of states to concern with relational characteristics of states. We shift from seeing classes (and status-groups) as groups within a state to seeing them as groups within a world-economy. (Wallerstein, 1976: xi)

Norms emerge from location in structured systems of social relationships

Although many mainstream sociologists do use the structural location of persons to explain their acquisition of norms and values, they still treat persons as individuals acting in response to their internalized norms. They find purportedly sociological regularities when persons who have similar personal attributes behave similarly in response to shared norms. Such explanations, concerned as they are with aggregated sets of individual motives for action, are ultimately psychological and not sociological in character, as they neglect the ways in which variations in structured access to scarce resources determine opportunities and constraints for behavior. These explanations – with their strong echoes of Durkheim's views (e.g., 1893) – implicitly treat social integration as the normal state. They define the relationship of persons to social systems "in terms of shared consciousness, commitments, normative orientations, values, systems of explanation" (Howard, 1974: 5).

In contrast, structural analysts first seek explanations in the regularities of how people and collectivities actually behave rather than in the regularities of their beliefs about how they *ought* to behave. They interpret behavior in terms of structural constraints on activity instead of assuming that inner forces (i.e., internalized norms) impel actors in voluntaristic, sometimes teleological, behavior toward desired goals. Thus, they treat norms as effects of structural location, not causes (see Erickson, Chapter 5).

Structural analysts contend that accounting for individual motives is a job better left to psychologists. They suggest that sociologists should explain behavior by analyzing the social distribution of possibilities: the unequal availability of resources – such as information, wealth, and influence – and the structures through which people may gain access to them. They study the processes through which resources are garnered or mobilized – such as exchange, dependency, competition, and coalition – and the social systems that develop out of these processes (White, Chapter 9).

If norms are to be treated as effects, then how can analysts explain why people behave the way they do? Structural analysts deal with normative motivation in four ways:

1. Some analysts exclude questions of human motivation and concentrate on describing and explaining social systems only in systemic terms (e.g., Boorman and Levitt, 1980; Levine and Spadaro, Chapter 17). One study, for example, modeled systems of social mobility in the American Episcopal church (White, 1970a; Stewman and Konda, 1983). It found the Episcopal ministers' motives for changing positions to be irrelevant to their regular movements through linked "vacancy chains." Another set of studies has mapped a variety of relations among major Canadian corporations, showing links to the state, continuity in intercorporate control over time, and associations between densely knit corporate relations in business sectors and high rates of profit (e.g., Berkowitz, 1980, Chapter 10; Carrington, 1981; Niosi, 1981; Corman, 1983).

2. Many analysts concentrate on analyzing the structural determinants of human freedom and behavior. They do not deny the existence and force of norms, but assume that norms operate only within the constraints and opportunities social structures provide for human behavior. As White argues:

> My personal *values* are voluntaristic individualism. I wish for myself, and others, as much freedom as possible, i.e., as much dignity as possible. This value becomes a mockery without facing the constraints of social structure. Much better a twig of genuine freedom wrung from a tree of constraint than an artificial tinsel forest of freedom....
>
> Most sociology and social science, especially in the U.S., takes the *view* of voluntaristic individualism: basic reality is in individuals' values and choices, social structure being derived therefrom, being merely epiphenomenal.... The fruit of much sociology theory is this deception: social structure must be the sum of individual values so you can define it *a priori* out of your head. Or in recent versions, you can find it by pooling responses of populations of questionnaires.   (White, 1968)

3. Some analysts have placed structural and normative explanations head to head, arguing that structural constraints and opportunities explain social behavior more fully that normative motivation: "Most studies find little or no correlation between an individual's attitudes or normative beliefs and his behavior" (Cancian, 1975: 112; see also Deutscher, 1973). In one experiment, many persons obeyed orders to shock strangers and kin "lethally":

> [Many were] against what they did to the learner, and many protested even while they obeyed. But between thoughts, words, and the critical step of disobeying a malevolent authority, lies

another ingredient, the capacity for transforming beliefs and values into action. Some subjects were totally convinced of the wrongness of what they were doing but could not bring themselves to make an open break with authority. Some derived satisfaction from their thoughts and felt that – within themselves, at least – they had been on the side of the angels. What they failed to realize is that subjective feelings are largely irrelevant to the moral issue at hand so long as they are transformed into action. (Milgram, 1974: 10)

There is a clear contrast between normative and structural studies of "modernization." Normative studies, on the one hand, argue that rural Third World inhabitants go through an attitudinal change of "becoming modern" *before* they participate in urban industrial social systems (Inkeles and Smith, 1974). Structural studies, on the other hand, argue that rural villagers do not migrate to an industrial city *because* of newly adopted modern norms and values, but because previously migrated kin, friends, and neighbors have promised to help them find homes and jobs. Migration is rarely a once-and-for-all, uprooting and isolating experience. Rather, migrants travel and communicate back and forth between their new residences and ancestral homelands (Jacobson, 1973; Mitchell, 1973a; Roberts, 1973; Howard, 1974; Mayer and Mayer, 1974).

4. Some structural analysts explain the uneven distribution of norms in a population as a systemic phenomenon. They argue that people acquire norms, as they do other pieces of information, through network ties. Thus Erickson and Nosanchuk (1984) have shown that the allocation of esteem and disesteem in the Ottawa bridge world has everything to do with the players' behavior in bridge circles and little to do with their location in outside social structures (e.g., work, gender, age). On a much larger scale, argues White (1981, Chapter 9), perceptions of corporations are strongly affected by the kinds of structural niches they occupy in competitive markets. Thus, not only is normatively guided behavior structurally constrained, but the inculcation of these norms, itself, is differentially reproduced through network structures (see Cohen, 1969; Schildkraut, 1974; Brym, Chapter 13).

Social structures determine the operation of dyadic relationships

Many sociologists use another form of reductionist aggregation: They treat dyadic (two-person) interaction as the basic relational unit of analysis (e.g., Homans, 1961; Backman, 1981). They look at factors affecting the initiation, continuation, and loss of ties; the types of resources each dyad member exchanges with the other; and the extent to which such resources are reciprocally exchanged. They disregard structural form, making an implicit bet that they can adequately analyze ties in structural isolation, without reference to the nature of other ties in the network or how they fit together. Thus, many studies of "social support" see interpersonal help as emerging from multiple duets with separate others (Hall and Wellman, 1985).

Structural analysts point out, however, that social structural features greatly determine the milieux in which dyadic ties operate. For starters, the social structures create relatively homogeneous "foci" within which most individuals choose their dyadic partners: kinship groups, cafes, workplaces, neighborhoods, and the like (Feld, 1981). As a result, "institutionally complete" ethnic groups – supplying a broad range of services to members – tend to retain comparatively high proportions of their members' informal contacts (Breton, 1964).

Once a relationship begins, its structural location continues to affect it strongly. The pattern of ties in a social system significantly affects the flow of resources through specific ties, so that densely knit kinship groups pull apart spouses (Bott, 1957), and densely knit corporate relations bring high profit levels (Carrington, 1981). Many personal community ties persist because the participants are embedded in social structures – kinship, work groups, friendship circles, neighboring networks – that constrain them to continue, and not because either dyad member enjoys being with the other. Indeed, the amount of reciprocity is more evenly balanced in the overall networks than it is among the specific ties within them (Wellman, Carrington, and Hall, Chapter 6).

Structural analysts interpret all dyadic relations in the light of the two individuals' additional relations with other network members. "To discover how A, who is in touch with B and C, is affected by the relation between B and C ... demands the use of the network concept" (Barnes, 1972: 3). Analysts point out that dyadic relations can only be understood in the context of the structures formed by their linkages. Sociologists cannot discover such emergent properties as coalition formation or network density from the study of dyads. Nor can they study structural effects, such as the positive relationship between interlocking corporate ties and corporate profit levels (Carrington, 1981). This focus on structural form distinguishes structural analysis from other transactional approaches – such as "exchange theory" – which look primarily at structural patterns as they condition dyadic ties.[7]

Even nonhuman social systems have structural properties that are more than the sum of dyadic exchanges. Take the classic barnyard pecking order in which chicken A pushes chicken B away from the food, and chicken B, in turn, pushes chicken C away. Yet the overall social structure of the barnyard is not merely the aggregated sum of such dyadic dominance relationships. At times, chicken C may push chicken A away (i.e., a circle of dominance may prevail rather than a linear hierarchy); at times chicken B and C may form a coalition to push chicken A away from the food. It is the multiple-way relationships among chickens that make the barnyard pecking order a complex structural phenomenon (Landau, 1965; Chase, 1974, 1980). Like chickens, like people. Tilly (e.g., 1975, 1978) has shown that it is the linked relationships of interest groups that mobilize and structure political activity, and not individual grievances or simple contests between two groups.

Not only does network structure affect dyadic ties, there are times when the larger network itself is the focus of attention. The ties between two individuals are important not only in themselves but also as parts of the social networks in which they are embedded. Each tie gives network members indirect access to all those with whom their alters are connected. Social system members use a variety of direct and indirect ties to search for resources, often transversing several role relationships. Indirect ties link together in compound relationships (e.g., "friend of a friend") that fit network members into large social systems, transmitting and allocating scarce resources.

Thus, several structural analysts have charted the ways in which information – often a scarce resource – flows in structurally patterned ways through networks (e.g., Lee, 1969; Richardson, Erickson, and Nosanchuk, 1979; Delany, Chapter 16). Indeed, sometimes a dyadic success may have negative consequences as a result of the dyad partners' structural location. For example, interpersonal networks efficiently transmit information about job openings to women and subordinate minorities, but the jobs to which they direct persons often are entrapping cul-de-sacs because they are the only sorts of jobs about which network members know (Calzavara, 1982).

The world is composed of networks, not groups

Structural analysts try to avoid imposing assumptions about the boundaries of aggregates. They do not assume that analysis can proceed on the basis of a few discrete categories – such as proletariat and bourgeoisie or core and periphery. They do not assume that tightly bound groups are the fundamental building blocks of large-scale social systems – that communities, for example, are congeries of neighborhoods (Wellman and Leighton, 1979). Indeed, they caution that descriptions based on bounded groups oversimplify complex social structures, treating them as organizational trees, when it is the network members' crosscutting memberships in multiple social circles that weave together social systems (an argument dating back to Simmel).

By starting with networks rather than with groups, analysts are able to study both ties that do not form discrete groups and networks that are, in fact, sufficiently bounded and densely knit to be termed "groups" (Barnes, 1954; Boissevain, 1974; Doreian, 1981, 1982; Seidman, 1981; Seidman and Foster, 1981; McPherson, 1982; Wilson, 1982). What remains problematic is the existence of ramified, spatially dispersed networks of "community ties," even when they do not fit within bounded neighborhood or kinship solidarities. Nonetheless, this approach provides a structural basis for assessing the Durkheimian thesis concerning the integration of social systems through complex divisions of labor.

By treating the world as a structure of networks (and indeed, of "networks of networks") one is able to discover complex hierarchies of power, not merely discrete strata (Walton, 1976; Breiger, 1979; Miller, 1980). For example, structural analysis points a way out of the inevitably sterile debate over whether external linkages or internal class relations lead to colonial backwardness (Frank, 1969; Wayne, 1975; Carroll, 1985) by providing a mechanism for comprehending how internal and external relations intersect with and modify each other (see Bodemann, Chapter 8).

Structural methods supplement and supplant individualistic methods

Because of the linked nature of social structural phenomena, structural analysts have had to develop methods for analyzing networks of relationships among social system members. Developments have been most prominent in the domain of quantitative analysis.

Although statistical methods in sociology have grown increasingly sophisticated, they continue to treat individuals as independent units. The very assumption of statistical independence, which makes these methods so appropriate for an powerful in categorical analysis, detaches individuals from social structures and forces analysts to treat them as parts of a disconnected mass. Researchers following this tack can only measure social structure indirectly, by organizing and summarizing numerous individual covariations. They are forced to neglect social properties that are more than the sum of individual acts. Statistical packages such as SPSS (Nie, Hull, Jenland, Steinbrenner, and Bent, 1975) have become a worldview. As one review of social indicator research has noted:

> Social structure, social process, social institutions – all that
> which goes into a social scientific understanding of society – are
> all nearly absent. The society whose conditions we are to be
> informed about is one of atomistic individuals, grouped
> immutably by sex, race, and birth cohort. Their well-being
> comes in discrete little packages of disconnected benefits .... It
> is a world of work without dirty work, where there are unions
> and strikes, but no industrial conflict. It is an economy virtually
> without corporations, politics without either political parties or
> political power.   (Seidman, 1978: 718)

The shift away from methodological individualism toward structural analysis calls for the development of new relational methods and the redefinition of units of analysis:

> The unit is (now) a relation, e.g., the kinship relation among persons, the communication links among officers of an organization, the friendship structure within a small group. The interesting feature of a relation is its pattern: it has neither age, sex, religion, nor income, nor attitudes; although these may be attributes of the individuals among whom the relation exists. These fundamental definitions prevent structuralists from adopting measurement techniques and methodologies available to other sociologists (e.g., you cannot interview a friendship). A structuralist may ask whether and to what degree friendship is transitive or clustered. He may examine the logical consistency of a set of kin rules, the circularity of hierarchy of communication, or the cliquishness of friendship. We have, as yet, few tools for these tasks and almost none upon which there is universal agreement. Simply defining such terms as degree of transitivity has proven difficult.   (Levine and Mullins, 1978: 17)

To date there have been three associated thrusts in the development of structural methods:

1. Populations and samples have come to be defined relationally rather than categorically.
2. Categorical methods of description and analysis have been replaced by relational methods.
3. Individualistic statistical techniques are being used less and determinate mathematics more to study social structure directly.

Analysts have applied structural methods in a variety of ways. Several have used them to tackle statistical problems of analyzing social structure from samples of egocentric networks (Granovetter, 1976; Erickson, 1978; Frank, 1978; Erickson, Nosanchuk, and Lee, 1981). Some have used stochastic models to study search strategies, arguing that probabilistic judgments are intrinsic parts of social structures (Padgett, 1980; Delany, Chapter 16). Others have developed descriptive measures of social structures based, for example, on their clustering into relatively bound groups or on the extent to which resources diffuse through them (e.g., Shepard and Arabie, 1979; Hubert, 1980; White, 1980; Burt, 1980; Burt and Minor, 1982; Fienberg, Meyer, and Wasserman, 1985; Erickson, Chapter 5; McCann and White, Chapter 14). Thus, researchers have been able to analyze ruling groups in America by describing network clusters and social closeness among large corporations, state authorities, and elites (e.g., Alba and Moore, 1978;

Laumann, Galaskiewicz, and Marsden, 1978; Laumann and Marsden, 1979; Mintz and Schwartz, 1985).

One noteworthy technique, "blockmodeling," inductively uncovers underlying role structures in a social structure by juxtaposing multiple indicators of relationships in analytic matrices. Blockmodeling thus helps analysts to compare actual networks with hypothesized structures (Boorman and White, 1976; White et al., 1976; Arabie, Boorman, and Levitt, 1978; Levine and Mullins, 1978; Sailer, 1978; Breiger, 1979; Light and Mullins, 1979; Snyder and Kick, 1979; Carrington, Heil, and Berkowitz, 1980; Pattison, 1980; Panning, 1982; Heil 1983). Finally, some analysts use mathematical and statistical techniques to trace the course of social structure over time by modeling the interplay of relationships under specific analytic parameters (White, 1970a, b, 1981, Chapter 9; Howell, 1979, Chapter 3; Berkowitz, Chapter 18; Delany, Chapter 16).

These specialized methods have often been the most visible manifestations of structural analysis and may help to explain why structural analysts are often said to be a breed apart. Yet many quantitative analysts have continued to use standard statistical techniques in conjunction with measures of network properties (Wellman, Carrington, and Hall, Chapter 6; Howard, Chapter 7). Similarly, many analysts have continued to obtain powerful results from structurally informed fieldwork and archival research (Roberts, 1973; Lomnitz, 1977; Tilly, 1980; Salaff, 1981; Bodemann, Chapter 8; Brym, Chapter 13). What is distinctive about structural analysis is not the methods used, but the particular ways in which researchers pose questions and search for answers.

Some analytic principles

The principles in the working kits of many structural analysts are a mixture of definitions, assumptions, partially tested hypotheses, and empirical generalizations.

> 1. *Ties are usually asymmetrically reciprocal, differing in content and intensity.*

More than material goods flow through ties and networks. Flows can include resources such as information about one's environment and resources that are themselves a part of the ties – such as gratification obtained through being liked.

Ties between two persons are usually asymmetric in the amount and kinds of resources that flow from one to the other. Few ties resemble the link between Damon and Pythias – intense, comprehensive, and symmetric. Most are *asymmetric* in content and intensity. There is rarely a strict one-to-one correspondence between what two persons give to one another (Emerson, 1962; Macaulay, 1963; Kadushin, 1981; Cook, 1982; Wellman, Carrington, and Hall, Chapter 6; Bodemann, Chapter 8).

One study reports, for example, that only 36% of those named as close friends and kin feel symmetrically as close to the persons who named them. The ties they define as "close" are with others. They often have weaker, asymmetric ties to those who name them (Shulman, 1972, 1976). Many persons deliberately limit their claims for assistance from close ties in order to maintain the link (Wellman, Carrington, and Hall, Chapter 6). Yet such asymmetric ties crucially connect network members to each other, and, through the other's additional ties, indirectly connect them to larger social networks.

Although rarely symmetric, ties are usually reciprocated in a generalized way. For example, not only do clients send resources to patrons, but patrons usually send such resources as goods, information, and protection to clients. Further, the power of patrons is partly based on their ties with clients, as the ties themselves are a scarce resource. The ties are clearly not symmetric; nevertheless they are often stable parts of a social system (Wolf, 1956; Bodemann, Chapter 8; Howard, Chapter 7). Among the Ibadan Hausa in Nigeria, for example, reciprocal, asymmetric patron–client ties maintain complex trading networks over great distances (Cohen, 1969). Indeed, the most totalitarian social systems have not been able to function solely through one-way, coercive relations. Reciprocal ties between guards and prisoners permeate prisons and ensure compliance (Solzhenitsyn, 1968; Charrière, 1970).

2. *Ties link network members indirectly as well as directly. Hence, they must be defined within the context of larger network structures.*

The prevalence of asymmetric ties calls into question the voluntaristic assumption that ties exist because two members of a dyad want to interact with one another (Berscheid and Walster, 1978; Evans and Northwood, 1979). In practice, many ties are with network members whom one does not like and with whom one would not voluntarily form a twosome. Such ties are involuntary in that they come as part of the network membership package. They may be ties to persons who must be dealt with at work or in the neighborhood. They may be part of a solidary kinship group or friendship circle, or they may be patron–client ties. Despite their involuntary nature, such ties are often important in terms of the time spent on them, the resources that flow through them, the ways in which they constrain the activities of others, and the indirect access they give to the resources of third parties (Wellman, Carrington, and Hall, Chapter 6; Bodemann, Chapter 8; Howard, Chapter 7).

The possibilities for indirect ties are abundant because each direct tie links two concrete individuals and not just two roles. Jack and Jill are linked by more than a single pail of water. Although the role relationship between two members affects expectations for behavior, indirect ties are not necessarily restricted to a single role system: Network members typically use a wide variety of direct and indirect ties to search for resources, often traversing several sets of role relationships (Milgram, 1967; Lee, 1969; Travers and Milgram, 1969; Granovetter, 1974; Lin, 1983). For instance, one neighbor often asks another to approach a local politician for help in dealing with city hall. It is the overall *structural context* of network members that defines specific ties (Burt, 1980, 1982; Feld, 1981). Hence, such phenomena as patron–client ties must be treated as local manifestations of larger class structures (Bodemann, Chapter 8).

3. *The structuring of social ties creates nonrandom networks, hence clusters, boundaries, and cross-linkages.*

I start with two weak assumptions. The first is that ties in networks are often *transitive*. If there is a tie from A to B and from B to C, then there is an implicit indirect tie from A to C – and an increased probability of the formation of a direct tie at some time in the future. For example, friends of friends are more than randomly likely to be friends and not to be enemies or not directly linked (Davis, 1970; Holland and Leinhardt, 1977). This transitivity argument can apply to all networks and not just to ones composed of friendship ties. If there are transfer (or brokerage) costs, so that each node falling along a path through a network consumes some of the resource flow, then network members may often find it more efficient to maintain direct ties.

My second weak assumption is that there are *finite limits* to the number and intensity of ties that an individual can maintain (and that most individuals are near these limits). Consequently, most people cannot add many new ties (or add new strands to existing ties) without giving up some of their existing ties (Pool and Kochen, 1978).

Because of transitivity and reciprocity, two linked network members often draw on others with whom they are joined into a densely knit cluster (Abelson, 1979; Cartwright and Harary, 1979; Milardo, 1982). Finite limits operate so that involvement in dense clusters often entails the loss of other ties. Jointly, these structural processes encourage the formation of ties within clusters and few ties across boundaries. A clustered network of this kind contrasts markedly with a *random network* in which each member is equally likely to be linked with each other member, or with a clusterless *even network*, in which each member has the same number of links (Erdös and Spencer, 1974; Holland and Leinhardt, 1979b; Rapoport, 1979; Rytina and Morgan, 1982; Laumann, Marsden, and Prensky, 1983).

Transitivity is a weak assumption. If it were not, the world might well collapse into one giant cluster (Milgram, 1967). Network members often avoid some direct ties in order to maintain structural autonomy – for instance, when prodigal sons retain links to their parents through their brothers. Some direct ties are structurally difficult to maintain – such as friendships with feuding coworkers. *Intransitivity* helps to separate individuals from one another under these circumstances and to perpetuate discrete network clusters (White, 1966; Bernard and Killworth, 1973; Killworth, 1974).

Clustered networks have paradoxical implications for the integration of social systems: "At the level of the individual, the system is highly connected, for he lies at the center of a dense network of direct and indirect social relationships. At the level of the total system it is highly disconnected, for there are many pairs who have neither direct nor indirect relationships" (Davis, 1967: 186). This sort of pattern may well have been the principal structural reason why the Italian-American residents of Boston's West End were unable to form coalitions to defeat the massive "slum clearance" activities that destroyed their neighborhood in the late 1950s (Gans, 1982; see also Granovetter, 1973).

Yet not all network ties are bound up in clusters. Since both finite limits and reciprocity are weak assumptions, individuals are usually members of multiple social networks, and their ties can connect clusters. Both cross-linked "cosmopolitans" and internally linked "locals" transmit information, influence, and material resources through a network (and its cluster) in complementary ways (Gouldner, 1957; Merton, 1957). Cross-linkages give clusters within a network access to external resources and provide the structural basis for coalitions. Internal linkages within a cluster allocate resources and provide the structural basis for solidarity.

4. *Cross-linkages connect clusters as well as individuals.*

The nodes in a network do not have to be individual persons. They can be sets of nodes, groups, nation-states, or other discriminable units (Friedmann, Chapter 11; White, Chapter 9). The ties in such networks may result from individuals' membership in several clusters or because certain persons have "foreign relations" with other portions of the network. Although the observable ties may often be between individual persons, their importance lies in the fact that they form links between clusters (Bonacich and Domhoff, 1981; Breiger, Chapter 4). "The great promise of the network perspective is that micro and macro can be linked by examining the structural constraints imposed by relational configurations" (Rytina and Morgan, 1982: 90).

Consider the case of interlocking corporate directorates. What is usually more significant is that a director links two corporations, rather than that common board membership is shared by two directors. For example, if the officers of property development companies are also members of the board of a public housing agency, the links may enable the companies to acquire

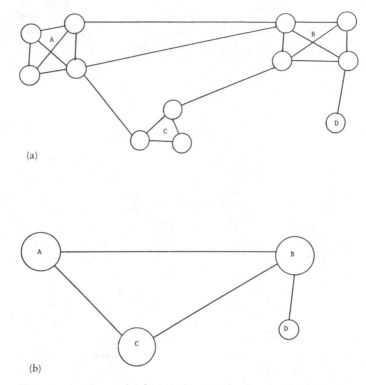

Figure 2.4. A network of networks. (a) Ties between individuals; (b) ties between network clusters.

"inside" information about public housing activities. When most of the major companies are represented on the public housing board, the links are likely to further the class interests of the industry rather than those of any particular company.

The ties give the managers of the public agency easy access to a "number of 'trusted' private firms to which it can subcontract its work. Here, the relevant links are clearly between the corporate entities, both public and private – although the specific linkages are people, who hold directorships on the boards of both" (Craven and Wellman, 1973: 81; see also Richardson, 1982; Berkowitz, Chapter 18).

When analysts focus on clusters and the ties between them, they are much less interested in internal ties within a cluster. If a tie between two clusters exists at all, then all members of one cluster are linked with all members of the other cluster through internal ties within clusters (see Figure 2.4). The link between General Motors and the Morgan Bank is more important analytically than ties between specific corporate directors or internal ties within the two corporations.

Some recent structural methods take into account the number of ties connecting two nodes or the proportion of all resources flowing between them. Yet some analysts argue that the most important information is whether or not any sort of tie exists between nodes. They suggest that, given the lack of connectivity in most social systems, any connection that facilitates flows of resources within a system is important (White, 1966; White et al., 1976).

5. *Asymmetric ties and complex networks differentially distribute scarce resources.*

Given asymmetric ties and bounded network clusters, resources do not flow evenly or randomly in a structure. The density of clusters, the tightness of boundaries between them, and the patterns of ties within and between clusters all structure resource flows. Because of their structural locations, members of a social system differ greatly in their access to these resources. Indeed, unequal access to scarce resources may lead to greater asymmetry in ties.

Asymmetric ties between nodes and clusters concatenate into hierarchical networks and engender cumulative differences in access to resources (Davis, 1970). In contrast to ideal models of hierarchies – such as those shown on organizational charts – actual networks often contain ties that transmit resources in two directions as well as complex structures with multiple and cyclical paths. Despite the fact that they are imperfectly hierarchical, actual networks are, however, *ultimately* hierarchical, and their cumulative effect is to distribute resources unevenly.

Researchers have used network-based notions of hierarchy to study the political economic development of nation-states. They have emphasized the importance of observing asymmetric ties *between* states, regions, and multinational interest groups to explain the nature of social structures *within* these states. Some researchers have suggested that the supposed "backwardness" of Third World societies is as much a matter of their ties with other social systems as it is of their internal rigidities (Wayne, 1975; Friedmann and Wayne, 1977). Others have shown the central importance of hierarchical networks in the formation of European nation-states (Wallerstein, 1974; Skocpol, 1979) and in the operation of international commodity markets (Friedmann, 1978, 1982; Chapter 11).

Positions as resources. Incumbency in a structural position is itself a scarce resource because it determines access to other resources. For example, many members of social systems profit from their positions as "gatekeepers" or "brokers." A gatekeeper controlling access to an organization's leader often gains wealth, flattery, influence, use of the organizational resources, and pleasure from exercising control. A broker linking two network clusters often takes a share of the resources passing through that position. Indeed, a canny broker may impede transitivity by working to prevent the formation of direct links between clusters. Brokers, by virtue of their structural location, cannot be full members of any one cluster. Often their very marginality means that they are not fully trusted because no one cluster can exercise effective social control over them (Goffman, 1963; Marsden, 1982, 1983; Brym, Chapter 13).

Flows through positions. Persons as well as resources flow through networks as they change structural positions. The flows of persons through positions and positions through persons are "duals" (Breiger, Chapter 4). Indeed, positions may experience social mobility when persons with different resources occupy them. Individual moves are part of linked "vacancy chains" (White, 1970a). Old incumbents vacate positions by moving to new ones. Hence, vacancies also flow through systems. Several structural analysts have used the flows of persons through positions to analyze mobility in occupations, organizations, and housing (White, 1970a, 1971; Mullins, 1972; Breiger, 1981; Aminzade and Hodson, 1982; Tolbert, 1982; Stewman and Konda, 1983; Levine and Spadaro, Chapter 17), and demographic constraints on flows of cohorts through social systems (Howell, 1979, Chapter 3; Tepperman, Chapter 15).

6. *Networks structure collaborative and competitive activities to secure scarce resources.*

Structured competition for scarce resources is inherent in social systems. In a system with limited resources, interest groups compete for access to them. In hierarchical networks with asymmetric ties, members must use collaborative or complementary ties to gain access to these same resources. Clustering within a network organizes these ties into more or less bounded coalitions and factions.

Network analysts have worked to show the structural basis of collective political activity. They have demonstrated how acts of collective violence, such as food riots or rebellions, are integral parts of broad contentions for power by different interest groups. Those engaged in collective violence are not the uprooted, disconnected individuals whose putative existence has fascinated "mass society" theorists.[8] On the contrary, those more deeply rooted and more densely knit into contending groups are more likely to be politically active – violently as well as nonviolently (Brym, Chapter 13; Tilly, 1967, 1975, 1979, Chapter 12; Feagin, 1973; Shorter and Tilly, 1974; Oberschall, 1978; Snyder, 1978).

Competition for resources may lead to change in social structure. Coalitions and factions shift in time, and network realignments can have broad systemic consequences (Nicholas, 1965; White and McCann, Chapter 14). For example, when local leaders in India transfer allegiance from one regional patron to another (in itself an outcome of the alternative sources of rewards available in a network), this causes profound shifts in the social interactions of all their clients, since these clients, themselves, form and relinquish network ties (Mayer, 1966; Pettigrew, 1975).

Although such network realignments redistribute access to resources, they do not cause major changes in the division of labor within a social system. Social scientists have had great difficulty explaining the conditions for such changes, either within single states or larger social units.[9] Since Marx, many have argued that structured competition for scarce resources creates conditions for large-scale social change, but they have not clearly set forth the mechanisms through which these changes take place.

Network modeling techniques may well provide useful tools for studying these mechanisms. Blockmodeling, for example, can provide a set of rules for the transformation of one structure's "image" – a simplified set of role relationships – into another (Boorman and White, 1976; Pattison, 1980). If analysts can integrate such rules with more strictly historical work by modeling the conditions under which system members mobilize to claim scarce resources (Tilly, 1978), the combination should improve our understanding of large-scale structural change.

The state of the art

Structural analysis has become self-conscious and organized. Intellectually, it has moved from a minimalist position, where "network analysis" was seen as a useful supplementary method, to a more maximalist, paradigmatic position, where its central concept – that all social phenomena are best studied through methods designed to uncover basic social structure – is seen as an important new approach to social inquiry. In addition to its critiques of other sociological approaches, structural analysis has now developed a coherent set of characteristics and principles backed up by a sizable body of empirical work. Institutionally, it is bolstered by a professional society, two journals, and frequent conferences.

The most significant substantive achievements of structural analysis have been to pose new intellectual questions, collect new types of evidence, and provide new ways to describe and analyze social structures. Structural analysts have mapped the interlocking ties of corporations, states, and world systems in understandable and useful ways, and they have found abundant evidence of "community" by looking for it in networks rather than in neighborhoods. The structural approach has revealed powerful ways of using consistent analytic frameworks in linking "micro" networks of interpersonal relations with "macro" structures in large-scale social systems.

Structural analytic thought has diffused widely in recent years among many sociologists (and other social scientists) who do not identify themselves as structural analysts. There is increasing recognition in mainstream work that the proper business of sociologists is the direct study of social structure and not indirect attempts to approach structure through the study of internalized norms, individual actions, and dyadic behavior.

The methodological advances of structural analysis have been impressive. Not only have structural analysts mounted an effective critique of the limitations of individual statistical techniques, they have produced a battery of concepts, methods, and techniques better suited to comprehending structures and relationships. To date, the strangeness and mathematical complexity of their approach has kept it from being widely adopted. Yet, its use is spreading widely, and many structural methods have worked their way into the tool-kits of those initiated into the higher mathematical arts.

The explanatory achievements of structural analysis have been more uneven. Although the general utility of its emphasis on studying social structures depends, to some extent, on one's aesthetic preferences, the specific utility of the more precise principles and methods of structural analysis depends to a greater extent on its success in providing more powerful analyses than other approaches to interpreting social phenomena. Here the results are not yet clear. This is because structural analysts often have not competed directly with other sociologists in explaining the same phenomena. Rather, they have been preoccupied with reformulating basic questions. They have proposed, for example, substituting world-systems analysis for single-state modernization theories, network communities for neighborhood communities, political networks for psychologistic interpretations of collective behavior, and vacancy-chain analyses for individualistic analyses of social mobility.

The current state of structural analysis is probably just a way station on the road to more comprehensive formulations. This chapter has reasoned upward, working from the characteristics of ties toward those of larger networks. By contrast, a more thoroughgoing structural formulation would have reasoned downward, working from the properties of large-scale "networks of networks" to the nature of clusters and ties. For example, such an approach might have systematically analyzed the nature of family and community networks within the constraints of capitalist or socialist economies. Sociologists are just beginning to advance beyond intuitive ways of doing such top-down analyses. To date, the success of their work has often depended heavily on the persuasiveness of their verbal descriptions. Here, too, the facility of structural analysts in posing questions would be enhanced by an increased ability to provide valid and reliable answers.

NOTES

1. Rosch and Mevis, 1975, have argued for the pervasiveness and usefulness of defining categories through "family resemblances." I follow their approach in this chapter by defining "structural analysis" in this fashion. Note that in stressing networks of linkages between categories, the family resemblances approach to cognition is itself analogous to some forms of structural sociology. Examples of recent efforts to provide a standard text are Leinhardt, 1977; Rogers and Kincaid, 1981; Berkowitz, 1982; Burt, 1982; Knoke and Kuklinski, 1982. Bibliographies include: Freeman, 1976; Feger, Hummel, Pappi, Sodeur, and Ziegler, 1982; Scherer, 1983. These works complement the present chapter, as do the discussions by Mullins, 1973; Howard, 1974; White, Boorman, and Breiger, 1976; Laumann, 1979; Berkowitz and Heil, 1980; Burt, 1980; Laumann et al., 1983; Pattison, 1980; Alba, 1981. *Connections,* the informal journal of the International Network for Social Network Analysis (INSNA), and *Social Networks,* a refereed journal, provide contemporary coverage.

2. I mean "British" in the intellectual sense; that is, most of the anthropologists were trained or based at British universities. Many of their origins (e.g., Australia, Canada, and New Zealand) and areas of study (e.g., Africa and India) were of the old and new Empire.

3. For summaries and reviews of this work see Srinivas and Béteille, 1964; Mitchell, 1969a, b, 1973b, 1974, 1979; Bott, 1971; Barnes, 1972; Boissevain, 1974, 1979; Whitten and Wolfe, 1974; Wolfe, 1978. Numerous case studies and analyses exist, e.g., Mitchell, 1956, 1961, 1969c; Gutkind, 1965; Wolf, 1966; Mayer, 1966; Liebow, 1967; Epstein, 1969; Parkin, 1969; Wayne, 1971: 51–2; Kapferer, 1972; Boissevain and Mitchell, 1973; Jacobson, 1973; Roberts, 1973; Mayer with Mayer, 1974; Boswell, 1975; Peil, 1978, 1981; Roberts, 1978; Peattie and Rein, 1979.

4. For example, analysts have mapped the structure of intercorporate relations in America (Levine, 1972; Soref, 1979; Burt, 1982; Mizruchi, 1982; Mintz and Schwartz, 1985); Canada (Berkowitz, Carrington, Kotowitz, and Waverman, 1978–9; Carrington, 1981; Carrol, Fox, and Ornstein, 1982; Ornstein, 1982; Richardson, 1985); Europe (Scott, 1979; Stokman, Ziegler, and Scott, 1985); and the entire western industrial world (Levine, 1984).

5. For studies of urban personal communities, see, Laumann, 1973; Shulman, 1976; Fischer, Jackson, Steuve, Gerson, Jones with Baldassare, 1977; Verbrugge, 1977; Wellman, 1979, 1985; Fischer, 1982; Greenbaum, 1982; Howard, Chapter 7; Wellman, Carrington, and Hall, Chapter 6. For studies of resource access, see Lee, 1969; Griffith and Miller, 1970; Granovetter, 1974; Boorman, 1975; Mullins, Hargens, Hecht, and Kick, 1977; Calzavara, 1982; Lin, 1983; Delany, Chapter 16. For studies of social support, see Gottlieb, 1981; Hirsch, 1981; Hammer, 1983; Kadushin, 1983; Brownell and Shumaker, 1984; Cohen and Syme 1985; Sarason and Sarason, 1985; Lin, Dean, and Ensel, 1986.

6. These seven points are based, in part, on Howard, 1974: chap. 1.

7. See Heath, 1976; Kapferer, 1976; Burgess and Huston, 1979. For work integrating exchange theory into structural analysis, see Emerson, 1981; Cook, Emerson, Gilmore, and Yamagishi, 1983; and Marsden, 1983.

8. For example, Davies, 1962; Kornhauser, 1968; Gurr, 1969. William Ryan (1971) calls such single-unit explanations of American race relations "blaming the victim."
9. For example, the development of the capitalist "world system," Wallerstein, 1974. Also see Friedmann, Chapter 11.

LITERATURE CITED

Abelson, Robert P. "Social Clusters and Opinion Clusters." In Paul Holland and Samuel Leinhardt (eds.), *Perspectives on Social Network Research*. New York: Academic Press, 1979.

Alba, Richard D. "From Small Groups to Social Networks." *American Behavioral Scientist* 24 (1981): 681–94.

"Taking Stock of Network Analysis: A Decade's Results." In Samuel Bacharach (ed.), *Perspectives in Organizational Research*. Greenwich, Conn: JAI Press, 1981.

Alba, Richard, and Gwen Moore. "Elite Social Circles." *Sociological Methods and Research* 7 (1978): 167–88.

Aminzade, Ronald, and Randy Hodson. "Social Mobility in a Mid-nineteenth Century French City." *American Sociological Review* 47 (1982): 441–57.

Anderson, Michael. *Family Structure in Nineteenth Century Lancashire*. Cambridge: Cambridge University Press, 1971.

Arabie, Phipps, Scott A. Boorman, and Paul R. Levitt. "Constructing Blockmodels: How and Why." *Journal of Mathematical Psychology* 17 (1978): 21–63.

Backman, Carl. "Attraction in Interpersonal Relations." In Morris Rosenberg and Ralph Turner (eds.), *Social Psychology: Sociological Perspectives*. New York: Basic Books, 1981.

Barnes, J. A. "Class and Committees in a Norwegian Island Parish." *Human Relations* 7 (1954): 39–58.

Three Styles in the Study of Kinship. London: Tavistock, 1971.

Social Networks. Reading, Mass.: Addison-Wesley, 1972.

Berkowitz, S. D. "Structural and Non-structural Models of Elites." *Canadian Journal of sociology* 5 (1980): 13–30.

An Introduction to Structural Analysis. Toronto: Butterworths, 1982.

Berkowitz, S. D., and Gregory Heil. "Dualities in Methods of Social Network Research." Working Paper 18 (revised), Structural Analysis Programme, University of Toronto, 1980.

Berkowitz, S. D., Peter J. Carrington, Yehuda Kotowitz, and Leonard Waverman. "The Determination of Enterprise Groupings through Combined Ownership and Directorship Ties." *Social Networks* (1978–79): 75–83.

Bernard, H. Russell, and Peter Killworth. "On the Social Structure of an Ocean-Going Research Vessel and Other Important Things." *Social Science Research* 2 (1973): 145–84.

"A Review of the Small World Literature." *Connections* 2 (1978): 15–24.

Berscheid, Ellen, and Elaine Walster. *Interpersonal Attraction*. Reading, Mass: Addison-Wesley, 1978.

Blok, Anton. *The Mafia of a Sicilian Village, 1860–1960*. New York: Harper and Row, 1974.

Bohannan, Paul. *Tiv Farm and Settlement*. Colonial Research Studies No. 15. London: Her Majesty's Stationery Office, 1954.

Boissevain, Jeremy F. *Friends of Friends*. Oxford: Blackwell, 1974.

"Network Analysis: A Reappraisal." *Current Anthropology* 20 (1979): 392–4.

Boissevain, Jeremy F., and J. Clyde Mitchell (eds.). *Network Analysis*. The Hague: Mouton, 1973.

Bonacich, Phillip, and G. William Domhoff. "Latent Classes and Group Membership." *Social Networks* 3 (1981): 175–96.

Boorman, Scott A. "A Combinatorial Optimization Model for Transmission of Job Information through Contact Networks." *Bell Journal of Economics* 6 (1975): 216–49.

Boorman, Scott A. and Paul Levitt. *The Genetics of Altruism*. New York: Academic Press, 1980.

Boorman, Scott A., and Harrison C. White. "Social Structure from Multiple Networks II: Role Structures." *American Journal of Sociology* 81 (1976): 1384–1446.

Boswell, David M. "Kinship, Friendship and the Concept of a Social Network." In C. Kileff and W. C. Pendleton (eds.), *Urban Man in Southern Africa*. Signal Mountain, Tenn.: Mambo Press, 1975.

Bott, Elizabeth. *Family and Social Network*. London: Tavistock, 1957; 2nd ed., 1971.

Breiger, Ronald L. "Toward an Operational Theory of Community Elite Structures." *Quality and Quantity* 13 (1979): 21–57.

"The Social Class Structure of Occupational Mobility." *American Journal of Sociology* 87 (1981): 578–611.

Breton, Raymond. "Institutional Completeness of Ethnic Communities and the Personal Relations of Immigrants." *American Journal of Sociology* 70 (1964): 193–205.

Brownell, Arlene, and Sally Shumaker (eds.). "Social Support: New Perspectives on Theory, Research and Intervention, I." *Journal of Social Issues* 40, 4 (1984).

Burgess, Robert L., and Ted L. Huston (eds.). *Social Exchange in Developing Relationships*. New York: Academic Press, 1979.

Burt, Ronald S. "Models of Network Structure." *Annual Review of Sociology* 6 (1980): 79–141.

Toward a Structural Theory of Action. New York: Academic Press, 1982.

Burt, Ronald, and Michael Minor (eds.). *Applied Network Analysis*. Beverly Hills, Calif.: Sage, 1982.

Calzavara, Liviana Mostacci. "Social Networks and Access to Job Opportunities." Ph.D. diss., University of Toronto, 1982.

Cancian, Francesca. *What Are Norms? A Study of Beliefs and Action in a Maya Community*. Cambridge: Cambridge University Press, 1975.

Carrington, Peter. "Horizontal Co-optation through Corporate Interlocks." Ph.D diss., University of Toronto, 1981.

Carrington, Peter, Gregory Heil, and Stephen D. Berkowitz. "A Goodness-of-fit Index for Blockmodels." *Social Networks* 2 (1980): 219–34.

Carroll, William. "Dependency, Imperialism and the Capitalist Class in Canada." In Robert Brym (ed.), *The Structure of the Canadian Capitalist Class*. Toronto: Garamond, 1985.

Carroll, William, John Fox, and Michael Ornstein. "The Network of Directors among the Largest Canadian Firms." *Canadian Review of Sociology and Anthropology* 19 (1982): 44–69.

Cartwright, Dorwin, and Frank Harary. "Balance and Clusterability: An Overview." In Paul Holland and Samuel Leinhardt (eds.), *Perspectives on Social Network Research*. New York: Academic Press, 1979.

Charriere, Henri. *Papillon*. New York: Morrow, 1970.

Chase, Ivan D. "Models of Hierarchy Formation in Animal Societies." *Behavioral Science* (1974): 374–82.

   "Social Process and Hierarchy Formation in Small Groups: A Comparative Perspective." *American Sociological Review* 45 (1980): 905–24.

Clement, Wallace. *Class, Power and Property*. Toronto: Methuen, 1983.

Cohen, Abner. *Custom and Politics in Urban Africa*. Berkeley: University of California Press, 1969.

Cohen, Sheldon, and S. Leonard Syme (eds.). *Social Support and Health*. New York: Academic Press, 1985.

Coleman, James S. "Relational Analysis." *Human Organization* 17 (1958): 28–36.

   The Adolescent Society. New York: Free Press, 1961.

   Introduction to Mathematical Sociology. New York: Free Press, 1964.

Coleman, James S., Elihu Katz, and Herbert Menzel. *Medical Innovation: A Diffusion Study*. Indianapolis: Bobbs-Merrill, 1966.

Cook, Karen S. "Network Structures from an Exchange Perspective." In Peter Marsden and Nan Lin (eds.), *Social Structure and Network Analysis*. Beverly Hills, Calif.: Sage, 1982.

Cook, Karen S., Richard Emerson, Mary Gilmore, and Toshio Yamagishi. "The Distribution of Power in Exchange Networks." *American Journal of Sociology* 89 (1983): 275–305.

Corman, June. "Control of Crown Corporations: A Case Study." Structural Analysis Programme Working Paper 51, University of Toronto, 1983.

Craven, Paul, and Barry Wellman. "The Network City." *Sociological Inquiry* 43 (1973): 57–88.

Davies, James C. "Toward a Theory of Revolution." *American Sociological Review* 27 (1962): 5–19.

Davis, James. "Clustering and Structural Balance in Graphs." *Human Relations* 20 (1967): 181–7.

   "Clustering and Hierarchy in Interpersonal Relations." *Sociological Review* 35 (1970): 843–52.

   "The Davis/Holland/Leinhardt Studies: An Overview." In Paul Holland and Samuel Leinhardt (eds.), *Perspectives on Social Network Research*. New York: Academic Press, 1979.

Davis, James, and Samuel Leinhardt. "The Structure of Positive Interpersonal Relations in Small Groups." In Joseph Berger, Morris Zelditch, Jr., and Bo Anderson (eds.), *Sociological Theories in Progress, II*. Boston: Houghton Mifflin, 1972.

Delacroix, Jacques, and Charles C. Ragin. "Structural Blockage: A Cross-national Study of Economic Dependency, State Efficacy, and Underdevelopment." *American Journal of Sociology* 86 (1981): 1311–47.

Deutscher, Irwin. *What We Say/What We Do: Sentiments and Acts.* Glenview, Ill: Scott, Foresman, 1973.

Doreian, Patrick. "Polyhedral Dynamics and Conflict Mobilization in Social Networks." *Social Networks* 3 (1981): 107–16.

"Leaving Coalitions as Network Phenomena." *Social Networks* 4 (1982): 27–45.

Durkheim, Émile. *The Division of Labor in Society.* New York: Macmillan, [1893] 1933.

Emerson, Richard. "Power-Dependence Relations." *American Sociological Review* 27 (1962): 31–41.

"Social Exchange Theory." In Morris Rosenberg and Ralph Turner (eds.), *Social Psychology: Sociological Perspectives.* New York: Basic Books, 1981.

Epstein, A. L. "The Network and Urban Social Organizations." In J. Clyde Mitchell (ed.), *Social Networks in Urban Situations.* Manchester: Manchester University Press, 1969.

Erdös, Paul, and Joel Spencer. *Probabilistic Methods in Combinatorics.* New York: Academic Press, 1974.

Erickson, Bonnie H. "Some Problems of Inference from Chain Data." In Karl F. Schuessler (ed.), *Sociological Methodology 1979.* San Francisco: Jossey-Bass, 1978.

Erickson, Bonnie H. and T. A. Nosanchuk. "The Allocation of Esteem and Disesteem: A Test of Goodes's Theory." *American Sociological Review* 49 (1984): 648–58.

Erickson, Bonnie H., T. A. Nosanchuck, and Edward Lee. "Network Sampling in Practice: Some Second Steps." *Social Networks* 3 (1981) 127–36.

Evans, R. L., and L. K. Northwood. "The Utility of Natural Help Relationships." *Social Science and Medicine* 13A (1979): 789–95.

Fararo, Thomas J. *Mathematical Sociology: An Introduction to Fundamentals.* New York: Wiley, 1973.

Feagin, Joe. "Community Disorganization." *Sociological Inquiry* 43 (1973): 123–46.

Feger, Hubert, Hans J. Hummel, Franz Urban Pappi, Wolfgang Sodeur, and Rolf Ziegler. *Bibliographie sum Project Analyse Socialer Netzwerke.* Wuppertal, W. Germany: Gesamthochschule Wuppertal, 1982.

Fienberg, Stephen, Michael Meyer, and Stanley Wasserman. "Statistical Analysis of Multiple Social Relations." *Journal of the American Statistical Association* 80 (1985): 51–67.

Feld, Scott L. "The Focussed Organization of Social Ties." *American Journal of Sociology* 86 (1981): 101–35.

Fischer, Claude S. *To Dwell among Friends: Personal Networks in Town and City.* Chicago: University of Chicago Press, 1982.

Fischer, Claude S., Robert Max Jackson, C. Ann Steuve, Kathleen Gerson, and Lynne McCallister Jones, with Mark Baldassare. *Networks and Places.* New York: Free Press, 1977.

Foster, John. *Class Struggle and the Industrial Revolution: Early Industrial Capitalism in Three English Towns.* London: Weidenfeld and Nicholson, 1974.

Frank, André Gunder. *Capitalism and Underdevelopment in Latin America.* New York: Monthly Review Press, 1969.

Frank, Ove. "Sampling and Estimation in Large Social Networks." *Social Networks* 1 (1978): 91–101.

"A Survey of Statistical Methods for Graph Analysis." In Samuel Leinhardt (ed.), *Sociological Methodology 1981*. San Francisco: Jossey-Bass, 1981.

Freeman, Linton C. *A Bibliography of Social Networks*. Exchange Bibliographies 1170–1171. Monticello, Ill.: Council of Planning Librarians, 1976.

Friedmann, Harriet. "World Market, State, and Family." *Comparative Studies in Society and History* 20 (1978): 545–86.

"Are Distributions Really Structures? A Critique of the Methodology of Max Weber." *Connections* 2 (1979): 72–80.

"Household Production and the National Economy." *Journal of Peasant Studies* 7 (1980): 158–84.

"The Political Economy of Food." *American Journal of Sociology* 88 (1982), Supplement: 248–86.

Friedmann, Harriet, and Jack Wayne. "Dependency Theory: A Critique." *Canadian Journal of Sociology* 2 (1977): 399–416.

Gans, Herbert. *The Urban Villagers*. 2d ed. New York: Free Press, 1982.

Godelier, Maurice. "Infrastructures, Societies and History." *Current Anthropology* 19 (1978): 763–8.

Goffman, Erving. *Stigma*. Englewood Cliffs, N. J.: Prentice-Hall, 1963.

Gold, Gerald. *St. Pascal*. Toronto: Holt, Rinehart and Winston, 1975.

Gottlieb, Benjamin. "Preventive Interventions Involving Social Networks and Social Support." In Benjamin Gottlieb (ed.), *Social Networks and Social Support*. Beverly Hills, Calif.: Sage, 1981.

Gouldner, Alvin. "Cosmopolitans and Locals." *Administrative Science Quarterly* 2 (1957): 281–306, 444–80.

Granovetter, Mark. "The Strength of Weak Ties." *American Journal of Sociology* 78 (1973): 1360–80.

Getting a Job. Cambridge, Mass.: Harvard University Press, 1974.

"Network Sampling." *American Journal of Sociology* 81 (1976): 1287–1303.

"The Strength of Weak Ties: A Network Theory Revisited." In Peter Marsden and Nan Lin (eds.), *Social Networks and Social Structure*, Beverly Hills, Calif.: Sage, 1982.

Greenbaum, Susan. "Bridging Ties at the Neighborhood Level." *Social Networks* 4 (1982): 367–84.

Griffith, Belver, and A. James Miller. "Networks of Informal Communication among Scientifically Productive Scientists." In Carnot Nelson and D. K. Pollack (eds.), *Communication among Scientists and Engineers*. Lexington, Mass.: D. C. Heath, 1970.

Gurr, Ted Robert. *Why Men Rebel*. Princeton, N. J.: Princeton University Press, 1969.

Gutkind, Peter. "African Urbanism, Mobility and the Social Network." *International Journal of Comparative Sociology* 6 (1965): 48–60.

Hagen, Everett E. *On the Theory of Social Change*. Homewood, Ill.: Dorsey, 1962.

Hall, Alan, and Barry Wellman. "Social Networks and Social Support." In Sheldon Cohen and S. Leonard Syme (eds.), *Social Support and Health*. New York: Academic Press, 1985.

Hammer, Muriel. "'Core' and 'Extended' Social Networks in Relation to Health and Illness." *Social Science and Medicine* 17 (1983): 405–11.

Harary, Frank, Robert Norman, and Dorwin Cartwright. *Structural Models*. New York: Wiley, 1965.

Heath, Anthony. *Rational Choice and Social Exchange*. Cambridge: Cambridge University Press, 1976.

Heil, Gregory. "Algorithms for Network Homomorphism: Block Modeling as a Structural Analytic Method for Social Structure." Ph.D. diss., University of Toronto, 1983.

Hirsch, Barton J. "Social Networks and the Coping Process: Creating Personal Communities." In Benjamin Gottlieb (ed.), *Social Networks and Social Support*. Beverly Hills, Calif.: Sage, 1981.

Holland, Paul W., and Samuel Leinhardt. "Transitivity in Structural Models of Small Groups." In Samuel Leinhardt (ed.), *Social Networks: A Developing Paradigm*. New York: Academic Press, 1977.

   (eds.). *Perspectives on Social Network Research*. New York: Academic Press, 1979.

Homans, George. *Social Behavior: Its Elementary Forms*. New York: Harcourt, Brace, 1961.

Howard, Leslie. "Industrialization and Community in Chotangapur." Ph.D diss., Harvard University, 1974.

Howell, Nancy. *Demography of the Dobe !Kung*. New York: Academic Press, 1979.

Hubert, Lawrence J. "Analyzing Proximity Matrices: The Assessment of Internal Variation in Combinatorial Structure." *Journal of Mathematical Psychology* 21 (1980): 247–64.

Inkeles, Alex, and David H. Smith. *Becoming Modern*. Cambridge, Mass: Harvard University Press, 1974.

Insurgent Sociologist. Special issue on "Marxism and Structuralism," vol. 9, no. 1, 1979.

Jacobson, David. *Itinerant Townsmen*. Menlo Park, Calif.: Cummings, 1973.

Kadushin, Charles. "Notes on Expectations of Reward in N-Person Networks." In Peter Blau and Robert Merton (eds.), *Continuities in Structural Inquiry*. Beverly Hills, Calif. Sage, 1981.

   "Mental Health and the Interpersonal Environment." *American Sociological Review* 48 (1983): 188–98.

Kapferer, Bruce. *Strategy and Transaction in an African Factory*. Manchester: Manchester University Press, 1972.

   "Introduction: Transaction Models Reconsidered." In Bruce Kapferer (ed.), *Transaction and Meaning*. Philadelphia: Institute for the Study of Human Issues, 1976.

Katz, Michael. *The People of Hamilton, Canada West*. Cambridge, Mass.: Harvard University Press, 1975.

Killworth, Peter D. "Intransitivity in the Structure of Small Closed Groups." *Social Science Research* 3 (1974): 1–23.

Knoke, David, and James Kuklinski. *Network Analysis*. Beverly Hills, Calif.: Sage, 1982.

Kornhauser, William. "Mass Society." *International Encyclopedia of the Social Sciences* 10 (1968): 58–64.

Landau, H. G. "Development of Structure in a Society with a Dominance Relation when New Members are Added Successively." *Bulletin of Mathematical Biophysics* 27 (1965): 151–60.

Laslett, Peter. *The World We Have Lost.* London: Methuen, 1971.

Laumann, Edward O. *Bonds of Pluralism.* New York: Wiley, 1973.

"Network Analysis in Large Social Systems: Some Theoretical and Methodological Problems." In Paul Holland and Samuel Leinhardt (eds.), *Perspectives on Social Network Research.* New York: Academic Press, 1979.

Laumann, Edward O., and Peter Marsden. "The Analysis of Oppositional Structures in Political Elites." *American Sociological Review* 44 (1979): 713–32.

Laumann, Edward O., Joseph Galaskiewicz, and Peter Marsden. "Community Structures as Interorganizational Linkages." *Annual Review of Sociology* 4 (1978): 455–84.

Laumann, Edward O., Peter Marsden, and David Prensky. "The Boundary Specification Problem in Network Analysis." In Ronald Burt and Michael Minor (eds.), *Applied Network Analysis.* Beverly Hills, Calif.: Sage, 1983.

Lee, Nancy (Howell). *The Search for an Abortionist.* Chicago: University of Chicago Press, 1969.

Leinhardt, Samuel. "Social Networks: A Developing Paradigm." In Samuel Leinhardt (ed.), *Social Networks: A Developing Paradigm.* New York: Academic Press, 1977.

Levine, Joel H. "The Sphere of Influence." *American Sociological Review* 37 (1972): 14–27.

Levine's Atlas of Corporate Interlocks. 2 vols. Hanover, N.H.: WORLDNET, 1984.

Levine, Joel H., and Nicholas C. Mullins. "Structuralist Analysis of Data in Sociology." *Connections* 1 (1978): 16–23.

Levine, Joel H., and William Roy. "A Study of Interlocking Directorates: Vital Concepts of Organization." In Paul Holland and Samuel Leinhardt (eds.), *Perspectives on Social Network Research.* New York: Academic Press, 1979.

Liebow, Elliot. *Tally's Corner.* Boston: Little, Brown, 1967.

Light, John M., and Nicholas Mullins. "A Primer on Blockmodeling Procedure." In Paul Holland and Samuel Leinhardt (eds.), *Perspectives on Social Network Research.* New York: Academic Press, 1979.

Lin, Nan. "Social Resources and Social Actions." *Connections* 6 (1983): 10–16.

Lin, Nan, Alfred Dean, and Walter Ensel. *Social Support, Life Events, and Depression.* New York: Academic Press, 1986.

Lomnitz, Larissa Adler. *Networks and Marginality: Life in a Mexican Shantytown.* Translated by Cinna Lomnitz. New York: Academic Press, 1977.

Lorrain, François, and Harrison C. White. "Structural Equivalence of Individuals in Social Networks." *Journal of Mathematical Sociology* 1 (1971): 49–80.

McClelland, David C. *The Achieving Society.* Princeton: Van Nostrand, 1961.

McPherson, J. Miller. "Hypernetwork Sampling: Quality and Differentiation among Voluntary Organizations." *Social Networks* 3 (1982): 225–49.

Macaulay, Stewart. "Non-Contractual Relations in Business." *American Sociological Review* 28 (1963): 55–70.

Marsden, Peter. "Brokerage Behavior in Restricted Exchange Networks." In Peter Marsden and Nan Lin (eds.), *Social Structure and Network Analysis.* Beverly Hills Calif.: Sage, 1982.

"Restricted Access in Networks and Models of Power." *American Journal of Sociology* 88 (1983): 686–717.

Mayer, Adrian."The Significance of Quasi-groups in the Study of Complex Societies." In Michael Banton (ed.), *The Social Anthropology of Complex Societies.* London: Tavistock, 1966.

Mayer, Philip, with Iona Mayer. *Townsmen or Tribesmen.* Capetown: Oxford University Press, 1974.

Maynes, Mary Jo. "Demographic History in the United States: The First Fifteen Years." *Historical Social Research* 19 (1981): 3–17.

Merton, Robert. "Patterns of Influence: Local and Cosmopolitan Influentials." *Social Theory and Social Structure.* Glencoe, Ill: Free Press, 1957.

Milardo, Robert. "Friendship Networks in Developing Relationships: Converging and Diverging Social Environments." *Social Psychology Quarterly* 45 (1982): 162–72.

Milgram, Stanley. "The Small-World Problem." *Psychology Today* 1 (1967): 62–7. *Obedience to Authority.* London: Tavistock, 1974.

Miller, Jon. "Access to Interorganizational Networks." *American Sociological Review* 45 (1980): 479–96.

Mintz, Beth, and Michael Schwartz. *The Power Structure of American Business.* Chicago: University of Chicago Press, 1985.

Mitchell, J. Clyde. *The Kalela Dance.* Manchester: Manchester University Press for Rhodes-Livingstone Institute, 1956.

"The Causes of Labour Migration." In *Migrant Labour in Africa South of the Sahara.* Abidjan: Commission for Technical Co-operation in Africa South of the Sahara, 1961.

"The Concept and Use of Social Networks." In J. Clyde Mitchell (ed.), *Social Networks in Urban Situations.* Manchester: Manchester University Press, 1969a.

"Preface." In J. Clyde Mitchell (ed.), *Social Networks in Urban Situations.* Manchester: Manchester University Press, 1969b.

(ed.). *Social Networks in Urban Situations.* Manchester: Manchester University Press, 1969c.

"Distance, Transportation and Urban Involvement in Zambia." In Aiden Southall (ed.), *Urban Anthropology.* New York: Oxford University Press, 1973a.

"Networks, Norms and Institutions." In Jeremy Boissevain and J. Clyde Mitchell (eds.), *Network Analysis.* The Hague: Mouton, 1973b.

"Social Networks." *Annual Review of Anthropology* 3 (1974): 279–99.

"Networks, Algorithms and Analysis." In Paul Holland and Samuel Leinhardt (eds.), *Perspectives on Social Network Research.* New York: Academic Press, 1979.

Mizruchi, Mark. *The American Corporate Network: 1904–1974.* Beverly Hills, Calif. Sage, 1982.

Moore, Wilbert E. *World Modernization: The Limits of Convergence.* New York: Elsevier North Holland, 1979.

Moreno, J. L. *Who Shall Survive?* Washington, D.C.: Nervous and Mental Disease Publishing, 1934.

Mullins, Nicholas C. "The Structure of an Elite: The Advisory Structure of the U. S. Public Health Service." *Science Studies* 2 (1972): 3–29.

Theories and Theory Groups in Contemporary American Sociology. New York: Harper and Row, 1973.

Mullins, Nicholas C., Lowell Hargens, Paul Hecht and Edward Kick. "The Group Structure of Cocitation Clusters." *American Sociological Review* 42 (1977): 552–62.

Nadel, S. F. *The Theory of Social Structure.* London: Cohen and West, 1957.

Nicholas, Ralph. "Factions: A Comparative Analysis." In Michael Banton (ed.), *Political Systems and the Distribution of Power.* London: Tavistock, 1965.

Nie, Norman H., C. Hadlai Hull, Jean G. Jenkins, Karin Steinbrenner, and Dale H. Bent. *SPSS: Statistical Package for the Social Sciences.* New York: McGraw-Hill, 1975.

Niosi, Jorge. *Canadian Capitalism.* Toronto: James Lorimer, 1981.

Oberschall, Anthony. "Theories of Social Conflict." *Annual Review of Sociology* 4 (1978): 291–315.

Ornstein, Michael. "Interlocking Directorates in Canada: Evidence from Replacement Patterns." *Social Networks* 4 (1982): 3–25.

Padgett, John. "Bounded Rationality in Budgetary Research." *American Political Science Review* 74 (1980): 354–72.

Panning, William. "Fitting Blockmodels to Data." *Social Networks* 4 (1982): 81–101.

Parkin, David. *Neighbors and Nationals in an African Ward.* Berkeley: University of California Press, 1969.

Parsons, Talcott. *The Social System.* Glencoe, Ill. Free Press, 1951.

"Pattern Variables Revisited." *American Sociological Review* 25 (1960): 467–83.

Pattison, Philippa. "An Algebraic Analysis for Multiple Social Networks." Ph.D. diss., University of Melbourne, 1980.

Peattie, Lisa, and Martin Rein. "Claims, Claiming and Claims Structures." Department of Urban Planning, Massachusetts Institute of Technology, 1979.

Peil, Margaret. "Research Roundup on African Networks, 1974–1978." *Connections* 2 (1978): 6–8.

Cities and Suburbs: Urban Life in West Africa. New York: Holmes and Meier, 1981.

Pettigrew, Joyce. *Robber Noblemen.* London: Routledge and Kegan Paul, 1975.

Pickvance, C. G. "Voluntary Associations and the Persistence of Multiplex Ties." University of Manchester, Department of Sociology, 1975.

Pool, Ithiel de Sola, and Manfred Kochen. "Contacts and Influence." *Social Networks* 1 (1978): 5–51.

Pye, Lucian W. *Politics, Personality and National Building.* New Haven, Conn.: Yale University Press, 1962.

Radcliffe-Brown, A. R. "On Social Structure." *Journal of the Royal Anthropological Society of Great Britain and Ireland* 70 (1940): 1–12.

Rapoport, Anatol. "A Probabilistic Approach to Networks." *Social Networks* 2 (1979): 1–18.

Richardson, R. J. "Perspectives on the Relationship between Financial and Non-financial Corporations: A Critical Review." University of Toronto, Structural Analysis Programme Working Paper 34 Toronto, March, 1982.

"A Structural-Rational Theory of the Functions of Directorship Interlocks between Financial and Non-Financial Corporations." In Robert Brym (ed.), *The Structure of the Canadian Capitalist Class.* Toronto: Garamond, 1985.

Richardson, R. J., and Barry Wellman. "Structural Analysis." *Canadian Review of sociology and Anthropology* 22 (1985): 771–93.

Richardson, R. J., Bonnie Erickson, and T. A. Nosanchuk. "Community Size, Network Structure and the Flow of Information." *Canadian Journal of Sociology* 4 (1979): 379–92.

Roberts, Bryan R. *Organizing Strangers*. Austin: University of Texas Press, 1973. *Cities of Peasants*. London: Edward Arnold, 1978.

Rogers, Everett, and D. Lawrence Kincaid. *Communication Networks: Toward a New Paradigm for Research*. New York: Free Press, 1981.

Rosch, Eleanor, and Carolyn Mervis. "Family Resemblances: Studies in the Internal Structure of Categories." *Cognitive Psychology* 7 (1975): 573–605.

Ryan, William. *Blaming the Victim*. New York: Pantheon, 1971.

Rytina, Steve, and David Morgan. "The Arthimetic of Social Relations: The Interplay of Category and Networks." *American Journal of Sociology* 88 (1982): 88–113.

Sailer, Lee Douglas. "Structural Equivalence." *Social Networks* 1 (1978): 73–90.

Salaff, Janet. *Working Daughters of Hong Kong*. Cambridge: Cambridge University Press, 1981.

Sarason, Irwin, and Sarason, Barbara (eds.). *Social Support: Theory, Research and Applications*. The Hague: Martinus Nijhoff, 1985.

Scherer, Jacqueline. "The Functions of Social Networks: An Exercise in Terse Conclusions." *Connections* 6 (1983): 22–31.

Schildkraut, Enid. "Ethnicity and Generational Differences among Urban Immigrants in Ghana." In Abner Cohen (ed.), *Urban Ethnicity*. London: Tavistock, 1974.

Scott, John. *Corporations, Classes and Capitalism*. London: Hutchison, 1979.

Seidman, David. "Picturing the Nation." *Contemporary Sociology* 7 (1978): 717–19.

Seidman, Stephen. "Structures Induced by Collections of Subsets: A Hypergraph Approach." *Mathematical Social Sciences* 1 (1981): 381–96.

Seidman, Stephen, and Brian Foster. "An Anthropological Framework for the Analysis of Social Networks." Paper presented at the annual meeting of the Society for Applied Anthropology, Edinburgh, 1981.

Shepard, R. N., and Phipps Arabie. "Additive Clustering: Representation of Similarities as Combinations of Discrete Overlapping Properties." *Psychological Review* 86 (1979): 87–123.

Shorter, Edward, and Charles Tilly. *Strikes in France*. Cambridge: Cambridge University Press, 1974.

Shulman, Norman. "Urban Social Networks." Ph.D. diss., University of Toronto, 1972.

"Network Analysis: A New Edition to an Old Bag of Tricks." *Acta Sociologica* 19 (1976): 307–23.

Simmel, Georg. *The Sociology of Georg Simmel*. Edited and translated by Kurt Wolff. Glencoe, Ill.: Free Press, 1950.

"The Web of Group Affiliations." Translated by Reinhard Bendix. In Georg Simmel, *Conflict and the Web of Group Affiliations*. Glencoe, Ill.: Free Press, 1955.

"Group Expansion and the Development of Individuality." Translated by Richard P. Alberes. In Donald N. Levine (ed.), *Georg Simmel on Individuality and Social Form*. Chicago: University of Chicago Press, 1971.

Skocpol, Theda. *States and Social Revolutions.* Cambridge: Cambridge University Press, 1979.

Snyder, David. "Collective Violence." *Journal of Conflict Resolution* 22 (1978): 499–534.

Snyder, David, and Edward L. Kick. "Structural Position in the World System and Economic Growth, 1955–1970." *American Journal of Sociology* 84 (1979): 1096–1126.

Solzhenitsyn, Alexander I. *The First Circle.* New York: Harper and Row, 1968.

Soref, Michael. "Research on Interlocking Directorates." *Connections* 2 (1979): 84–86, 91.

Srinivas, M. N., and André Béteille. "Networks in Indian Social Structure." *Man* 54 (1964): 165–8.

Stewman, Shelby, and Suresh Konda. "Careers and Organizational Labor Markets." *American Journal of Sociology* 88 (1983): 637–85.

Stokman, Frans, Rolf Ziegler, and John Scott (eds.). *Networks of Corporate Power.* Cambridge: Polity Press, 1985.

Sundt, Eilert. *Om Saedelighedstilstanden i Norge, I.* Oslo: Pax, [1857] 1968.

Tilly, Charles. *The Vendée.* New York: Wiley, 1967.

"Food Supply and Public Order in Modern Europe." In Charles Tilly (ed.), *The Formation of National States in Western Europe.* Princeton, N.J.: Princeton University Press, 1975.

From Mobilization to Revolution. Reading, Mass.: Addison-Wesley, 1978.

"Collective Violence in European Perspective." In Hugh Davis Graham and Ted Robert Gurr (eds.), *Violence in America: Historical and Comparative Perspectives.* Beverly Hills, Calif.: Sage 1979.

"Historical Sociology." In Scott G. McNall and Gary N. Howe (eds.), *Current Perspectives in Social Theory.* Vol. 1. Greenwich, Conn.: JAI Press, 1980.

As Sociology Meets History. New York: Academic Press, 1981.

Tilly, Louise A., and Joan W. Scott. *Women, Work and Family.* New York: Holt, Rinehart and Winston, 1978.

Tolbert, Charles, II. "Industrial Segmentation and Men's Career Mobility." *American Sociological Review* 47 (1982): 457–77.

Travers, Jeffrey, and Stanley Milgram. "An Experimental Study of the Small-world Problem." *Sociometry* 32 (1969): 425–43.

Verbrugge, Louis M. "The Structure of Adult Friendship Choices." *Social Forces* 56 (1977): 576–97.

Wallerstein, Immanuel. *The Modern World-System, I.* Library and text editions. New York: Academic Press, 1974, 1976.

Walton, John. "Community Power and the Retreat from Politics." *Social Problems* 23 (1976): 292–303.

Wayne, Jack. "Networks of Informal Participation in a Suburban Context." Ph.D. diss., University of Toronto, 1971.

"Colonialism and Underdevelopment in Kigoma Region, Tanzania." *Canadian Review of Sociology and Anthropology* 12 (1975): 316–22.

"The Logic of Social Welfare." University of Toronto, Structural Analysis Programme Working Paper 15. Toronto, 1980.

Wellman, Barry. "The Community Question." *American Journal of Sociology* 84 (1979): 1201–31.

"Domestic Work, Paid Work and Net Work." In Steve Duck and Daniel Perlman (eds.), *Understanding Personal Relationships, I.* London: Sage, 1985.

Wellman, Barry, and Barry Leighton. "Networks, Neighborhoods and Communities." *Urban Affairs Quarterly* 14 (1979): 363–90.

White, Douglas. "Material Entailment Analysis." University of California, School of Social Sciences Report 15. Irvine, 1980.

White, Harrison C. "Notes on the Constituents of Social Structure." Cambridge, Mass.: Department of Social Relations, Harvard University, 1965.

"Coupling and Decoupling." Cambridge, Mass.: Harvard University, Department of Social Relations, 1966.

"An Introduction to Social Relations." Harvard University, Social Relations 10: First Lecture, 1968.

Chains of Opportunity. Cambridge, Mass.: Harvard University Press, 1970a.

"Search Parameters for the Small World Problem." *Social Forces* 49 (1970b): 259–64.

"Multipliers, Vacancy Chains and Filtering in Housing." *Journal of the American Institute of Planners* 37 (1971): 88–94.

"Production Markets as Induced Role Structures." In Samuel Leinhardt (ed.), *Sociological Methodology 1981.* San Francisco: Jossey-Bass, 1981.

White, Harrison C., Scott A. Boorman, and Ronald L. Breiger. "Social Structure from Multiple Networks: I. Blockmodels of Roles and Positions." *American Journal of Sociology* 81 (1976): 730–80.

Whitten, Norman E., and Alvin W. Wolfe. "Network Analysis." In J. J. Honigmon (ed.), *The Handbook of Social and Cultural Anthropology.* Chicago: Rand McNally, 1974.

Wilson, Thomas. "Relational Networks: An Extension of Sociometric Concepts." *Social Networks* 4 (1982): 105–16.

Wolf, Eric. "Aspects of Group Relations in a Complex Society." *American Anthropologist* 58 (1956): 1065–78.

"Kinship, Friendship and Patron–Client Relations." In Michael Banton (ed.), *The Social Anthropology of Complex Societies.* London: Tavistock, 1966.

Wolfe, Alvin. "The Rise of Network Thinking in Anthropology." *Social Networks* 1 (1978): 53–64.

Wright, Erik Olin. *Class, Crisis and the State.* London: Verso, 1977.

"Class and Occupation." *Theory and Society* 9 (1980): 177–214.

3

Understanding simple social structure: kinship units and ties

Nancy Howell

Why study the kinship systems of simple societies?

Sociology ought to be a systematic exploration of social facts that leads to increased understanding of social processes. But often this goal seems far too ambitious. A typical research project involves identifying some phenomenon viewed as a dependent variable and then issuing a final report listing some 15 variables, each of which can be shown to account for 1–2% of the variance.

Results of this kind are not satisfying, either aesthetically or intellectually. All too often in sociology careful measurements and precise models of the interrelations among variables produce results that are statistically significant because we are so good at detecting weak relationships, but that are neither theoretically nor substantively important.

This discouraging state of affairs seems to be largely a result of the types of questions we ask and the perversely stubborn complexity of the realities we study. Forms of social organization too often lack the underlying simplicity that rewards theorists and empirical researchers with satisfying indications that their explanations are either right or wrong.

Network – as compared with categorical – models have clear explanatory advantages in that they incorporate individual perceptions of social structure into larger concepts that subsume these same individual perspectives. Network models have the advantage, on the one hand, of corresponding to, and resonating with, important concepts in sociology such as roles, statuses, and group boundaries and, on the other, of being consistent with dynamic, processual views of social structure as it is formed, maintained, and transformed over time. But network models, too, often fail to go beyond being suggestive to being explanatory. Network models of structures in modern societies are rarely simple enough to be comprehensible when the phenomenon under study is, itself, of ordinary complexity.

My own inclination when faced with puzzles that are too difficult to solve directly is to ask easier questions. Hence, when an opportunity arose to take a job as a demographer on an expedition to study the !Kung hunter–gatherers of the Kalahari desert in Africa, I was glad to take it. Examining the demography of a remote hunter–gatherer people – despite the obvious exotic and esoteric aspects of the Kalahari !Kung – promised to be far simpler, both theoretically and substantively, than understanding networks of friends, relations, workers, and strangers in industralized societies (Lee, 1969).

One source of this simplicity is theoretical: Demography is by far the simplest and most conceptually satisfactory topic in social science. The equations that relate the probabilities of birth and death by age to the size and age–sex composition of any population are a model of clear-cut explanation.

The other source is empirical: There is a real sense in which the !Kung and other hunter–gatherers are simpler than peoples living in industrial societies. This conclusion is based not on sentimentality or racism – and indeed not on the characteristics of individuals – but on properties of social structure. Hunter–gatherer societies always consist of relatively few people and are simple in that there is little role or task differentiation. Aside from the most elementary distinctions of sex and age, there are few sources of differences in power among individuals. The roles that do exist are not organized into social classes. Most important for present purposes, connections between one person and another in hunting and gathering societies are almost entirely based on kinship, so that individuals' ties are generated and constrained primarily by the demographic processes of birth, marriage, and death.

Demography and kinship

It is obvious, when you think about it, that demographic process generates kinship ties. Kin relationships are created by birth, not choice, and are terminated by death – the processes that demographers refer to as fertility and mortality. Conventional demographic models focus on the age–sex composition of the population as a whole and ignore the particular characteristics of individuals in their roles as parents and children: The models are simply designed to look at the replacement of one generation of a population by the next. Here we go beyond this and stress the *structural* dimensions of replacement by examining the relationship between births and deaths and the network of kinship ties formed among individuals.

Perhaps it is not as obvious that the existence of simple biological bases underlying kinship relations – that is to say, such relations are generated by birth and disconnected by death – considerably increases the analytic power of kin-models over those based on voluntaristic ties. Consider, too, that kinship ties are not only produced by birth and marriage, but are also created by adoption and other fictive relationships. We also know that kinship relations are not only disconnected by death and divorce, but can be totally disconnected or vaguely disregarded out of motives of mutual dislike or indifference. In fact, a major debate in anthropology has centered on the question of whether kinship systems are essentially social elaborations on biological phenomena (Hammel, 1965) or whether social and definitional characteristcs are foremost (Lounbury, 1965), and the biological correlates only incidental to the structure.

For the present purposes, we sidestep this debate by acknowledging that the considerations here apply only to kinship-based societies, inasmuch as the biological basis of kinship is operative, and do not apply where what looks like kinship is generated by choice rather than demographic events. Hence, in this case, whether we can gain analytic clarity and simplicity by focusing on kinship roles becomes an empirical question. Although one finds instances of fictionalized kinship relations among the !Kung (Marshall, 1976; Weissner, 1977), by assuming that kinship roles are generated demographically, we are able – as we shall see – to predict other important aspects of social structure. Our plea to the charge of "demographic reductionism" (Fallers, 1965), then, is "guilty, with empirical justification."

This chapter explores the causes and consequences of a particular type of social structure – the kinship-based systems of a hunter–gatherer society. Some features of these societies make them an ideal laboratory for such an enterprise. Hunter–gatherer societies are small enough to oversee and still maintain a focus on individuals. Moreover, since they are kinship-based, the allocation of personnel to roles in these societies – and the removal of both persons and role occupants – occurs almost entirely through birth and death and a marriage system that is only slightly more complex than our own.

The simplicity of hunter–gatherer social structures is slightly exaggerated here in that they are modeled entirely in terms of biological kinship, without regard for social inventions – such as fictive kin and adoption – which are often used to cope with an absence of kinsmen. All known hunter–gatherer groups ignore their own rules when it is convenient to do so (Fallers, 1965), but have general kinship rules that suit their needs well enough so that most social relations can be managed within the framework they provide. (We could, of course, model the exceptions to rules if we understood them unambiguously. In doing so, however, we would undercut the satisfying simplicity that led us to focus on hunter–gatherers in the first place.)

Rather than try to discuss the entire range of hunter–gatherer societies and the effects of various demographic schedules on their kinship networks, I use the !Kung as my only example and hope that readers understand that, by doing so, I do *not* claim that all hunter–gatherers are like the !Kung.[1]

The discussion opens with some observations about the general features of simple societies. Next, we see how the usual form of kinship analysis can be reconceptualized in network terms, and we consider some of the larger social units of the !Kung – households, families of procreation and orientation, lineages, and descent groups – as units that can be used at higher levels of analysis. The final section presents evidence that sibling groups – and the network of associations and relationships based upon them – provide the most useful higher-order units for kinship analysis.

Kinship-based societies

Hunter–gatherer societies are defined by both their economic basis (e.g., the collection of wild vegetable foods, fishing, and the hunting of wild animals) and their social organization. Information on contemporary hunter–gatherers, and on such societies in the past when they were more common, indicates that they consist of undifferentiated sets of small bands or living groups of 20–50 persons – each composed of several nuclear families with dependent children and their associated relatives. These groups, in turn, are and were clustered into larger units of some 200–800 persons, the mean being somewhere around 500. It is characteristic of hunter–gatherers that no group is dominant over the others and that relations among them are determined by proximity and kinship more than by special skills or preferences (Lee and DeVore, 1968).

Generally speaking, these larger units coincide with language or dialect groups that have a name for themselves – frequently one that translates as something like "real people." We loosely refer to these units as "tribes," but, since they lack chiefs and formal governing structures, we are not using the term in its technical sense (Lewis, 1968). Except in the special case of island populations, none of these groups are sharply bounded. If they have neighboring peoples, hunter–gatherers are likely to trade goods, services, stories and news, art and marriage partners with them. These trades are likely to be reciprocal and balanced if the neighbors are also hunter–gatherers, but unequal when the neighbors are agriculturalists, pastoralists, or more "advanced" peoples.[2]

Note that limits to the size of both local living groups and larger language units are largely a function of cultural and economic necessities and only marginally a direct result of demographic factors. Group size in any given year, it is true, can be expressed as some function of the previous year's size plus birth and immigration, minus deaths and emigration. But the "absolute size" of groups can only have an impact on demographic processes by first affecting people's behavior. Two common types of such behavior can be observed in simple societies.

The first of these is the *splitting* of groups into two distinct units when they grow too large. It is difficult to describe this process in hunting and gathering groups, since one of the characteristics of such groups is that they lack the centralized political organization that would permit them to make and carry out clear-cut decisions. Instead, splits "simply happen." To the people involved, splits almost always appear to be someone else's idea – to be the result of quarrels, migrations, or environmental crises. An unambiguous break can seldom be said to occur at a particular instant – although growing groups inevitably split, Chagnon (1980) is currently documenting and modeling these kinds of events in Yanomamo villages. Although splits are interesting and important in other contexts, for the present purposes we concentrate on groups that have no immediate need to subdivide.

The second set of observable behaviors – and the one most relevant here – is *density dependence*. When some groups reach a certain number, either absolutely or in relation to resources, this fact seems to feed back on their demographic schedules, causing them to lower their fertility (by increasing their age at marriage, increasing the length of their birth intervals, shortening the length of their reproductive span, etc.) or to increase the probabilities of death of their members at all or some ages (by infanticide, warfare, etc.).[3] Here we assume that hunter–gatherers' probability schedules of birth and death, marriage and divorce are fixed, varying only stochastically over time. In the long run, of course, we know that these schedules are variables, not constants, but this assumption enables us to focus more readily on the impact of demographic rates on kinship organization.

Kinship as a network of individuals

Let us review the ways in which kinship ties are created. When a person is born, he or she automatically acquires a mother and father as primary kin, along with indirect ties to siblings and other relatives. These indirect ties exist from birth, even though it is usually some time before they become recognized and cultivated. During childhood, kinship relations are severed through death (we are only interested in tracing ties among living people) and created through the birth of new siblings and cousins or through the marriage of kinsmen. For the !Kung, as for us, one can acquire a new uncle by having him marry an aunt, and the marrying uncle will, in turn, acquire not only a new niece or nephew, but a whole new group of "relatives-in-law."

Similarly, when a child grows up and marries, its kin inventory suddenly increases, not just by the spouse who will eventually link ego to children and grandchildren, but also by weaker but numerically important new affinal connections.

Both sets of events that generate new relationships – birth and marriage – are usually modeled as age-dependent probability processes (McFarland, 1972; LeBras, 1973; Goodman, Keyfitz, and Pullum, 1974). Similarly, the events that terminate relationships and disconnect previously tied people – death and divorce – can be modeled as probability processes. Most of Howell's book on the demography of the !Kung (Howell, 1979) is precisely this: an empirically based description of their probabilities of birth and death, marriage and divorce by age and sex – and the consequences of these rates. Given these probability schedules and a knowledge of how people describe and organize their kinship relations, it is not too difficult to construct a computer simulation that "gives birth to" fictional people according to the relevant fertility schedule, "kills" them according to their age-specific mortality schedule, and "marries" them when appropriate spouses are available according to local rules and age-specific marriage (and divorce) schedules.

A microsimulation program like this can be used to find out if a kin system that operates according to given rules and probability schedules is viable. It can also provide a tool with which to examine the range of expected stochastic fluctuations in small groups and societies, and to isolate and examine, experimentally, the independent effects of particular variables such as age at marriage or degree of permitted incest exogamy on that kin structure (Hammel et al., 1976). Once a simulation program is written – and writing one is not a simple task – it can also provide an easy way to make certain observations (here, lots of simple counts) that would be extremely tedious to carry out in a real population – and that in any case, could be expected to vary widely where groups are small.

This last feature of microsimulation provides a systematic framework with which to explore the consequences of demographic rules and probabilities for a kinship inventory. For instance, by using AMBUSH (a computer program designed for exploring the !Kung's demographic patterns), Howell and Lehotay (1978) found that it was possible to count the numbers of persons falling into each of the culturally defined types of relationships for egos of various ages and sexes.

Simulated results produced in this fashion can then be validated against observations taken on real populations. For example, AMBUSH might tell us that an average of 90% of !Kung children aged 0–9 at a point in time ought to have a living mother; about 80% of those 10–19 should have a living mother; and so on (see Figure 3.1).[4]

We could then estimate, in a similar fashion, the proportions of each age group who ought to have a living father (see Figure 3.2). These should be lower than the figure for mothers at each age – not only because !Kung males have a slightly higher probability of death at each age (as ours do) and because fathers have been at risk of death for some 9 months longer than mothers (a child can be born to a deceased father but not to a deceased mother), but primarily because !Kung fathers are, on the average, 7.5 years older than their wives. Hence the probability of death is higher for fathers than mothers throughout their children's lives. There ought to be, however, no differences between the probabilities of men or women having a living mother and father, because brothers and sisters are, on the average, younger than their parents by the same amount.

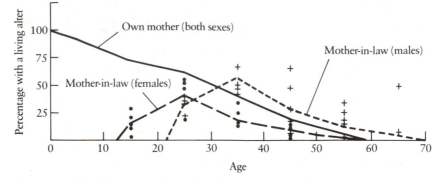

Figure 3.1. Percentage of people in age groups with a living mother and mother-in-law. (From simulations based on !Kung demographic parameters; see Howell, 1979: 310.)

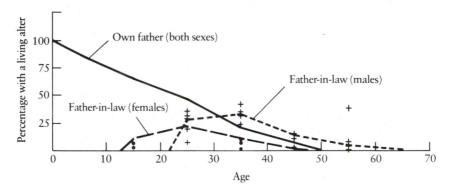

Figure 3.2. Percentage of people in age groups with a living father and father-in-law. (From simulations based on !Kung demographic parameters.)

When we compare results derived from this simulation to observed values in the real !Kung population, we find small, but systematic, differences between the proportions of persons with surviving parents in the real population and those predicted by simulation. These differences are probably largely due to improvements in mortality conditions in the Kalahari during the past several decades. But it is also true that the simulations are based on the assumption that the probabilities of survival of parents and their children are *independent*. In fact, both parents and children (or neither) are somewhat more likely to die than their age-specific mortality schedules would suggest. Accidents, contagious diseases, shared genes, and shared environments all make for a situation in which the probabilities of death of parents and children are linked to one another. Thus, in the real population death removes children whose inclusion in the simulation contributes to higher apparent parental mortality.

Kinship maps and distributions

The view of kinship proposed here is abstract and fully consistent with network concepts and terminology. Individuals are represented by nodes in a network, and parent–child relationships (mother–son, mother–daughter, father–son, father–daughter) by ties. These relationships are reciprocal, but not symmetric: You can have many children, but only one parent, of each sex. Nodes can be simultaneously defined as both "parents" and "children" to different alters.

In the static view, under the !Kung's fertility regime, nodes can have 0–2 ties to parents and 0–9 ties to children. The relative ages of ego and alters will assume a distribution that is the same as that familiar to demographers from observing the age of parents at the birth of their children, given particular age-specific fertility schedules. As we saw in Figures 3.1 and 3.2, the probabilities of having these will also fall into a characteristic pattern by age.

In a dynamic view, we see ties being created by the birth of children to parents and dissolved by the death of parents or children, who can range in age from 0 to 60 and over. If we watch this process of tie formation and dissolution over several generations, we see that parent–child ties involve *all* nodes in the role of child and some proportion of all persons in the role of parent. The form assumed by connections among members of the population is that which results from a classic branching process in that everyone is born to someone, but only some people have children. The large proportion of ever-born people who never have children can be seen as the end of their particular branch. This kind of process has been studied in the context of patrilineal inheritance models (Keyfitz, 1968; Wachter and Laslett, 1978) and genetics (Cavalli-Sforza and Bodmer, 1977; Howell, 1979).

"Bilateral descent" – which is the kinship term most appropriate to the !Kung – refers to a kind of branching process, but one that is more difficult to diagram clearly. A *minimum* of a three-dimensional space is needed to map clearly the relations generated by the simultaneous processes of descent and marriage that link adults as co-parents. A map of this kind that incorporated only the parent–child and husband–wife ties existing in a population at a given time would adequately model some of the realities of kinship, but would still require numerous inferences and filling in of roles by an observer. Instead of trying to read such a reduced map, we can "mine" the results of the AMBUSH simulations by examining the distributions of various types of dyadic ties (such as uncle–niece or nephew). In this way, we can obtain an "inventory" of expected numbers of people in each of several kin relationships for the various age and sex categories in the population. AMBUSH will

Table 3.1. *Expected numbers of kin in categories in older and younger generations, for males only, drawn from a single* AMBUSH *simulation based on !Kung demographic rates and subject to stochastic variation.*

Number of living	Age of ego		
	0–9	30–39	60–69
Grandfathers	0.075	0.000	0.000
Grandmothers	0.844	0.000	0.000
Fathers	0.872	0.281	0.000
Mothers	0.875	0.255	0.000
Uncles	2.737	0.708	0.020
Aunts	2.810	1.208	0.121
Sons	0.000	0.807	1.127
Daughters	0.000	0.720	1.172
Nephews	0.008	2.283	2.654
Nieces	0.006	2.438	3.000
Grandsons	0.000	0.000	1.332
Granddaughters	0.000	0.000	1.569
Totals	8.627	8.700	10.995

Note: Relationships omitted from this table are the same generation ones, spouse, cousins, and siblings (see Table 3.2).

count either the 28 types of relationships distinguished by the !Kung or the smaller number reflected in North American kinship terminology. For each form of kinship, AMBUSH will tell what proportion of, say, women 20–29 have zero, one, two, three ... up to a maximum of nine kinsmen in that relationship alive at any one time. There are 16 age–sex categories per relationship (8 ten-year age groups for the two sexes), so AMBUSH requires some 448 distributions to represent the detailed data on dyadic kinship relations generated by a given set of demographic parameters (Howell and Lehotay, 1978).

We can summarize this voluminous body of information in a number of ways. For instance, we can simply count the relatives of all types for each individual, summing them across relationship types and treating them as equally important. When we do this and cross-tabulate the resulting distribution by age and sex, we note some important and nonobvious features of the kinship system (Table 3.1).

One of these is the different length of the generations for men and for women. !Kung women start having children in their teens, but have few of them after age 35. Thus, the mean length of their generations is about

28 years. !Kung men marry, at the earliest, in their twenties and frequently have children through their forties – while married to considerably younger women. Thus, the mean length of their generations is about 35 years. Therefore women obtain their connections through marriage at a considerably younger age than their brothers, and women's "connectedness scores" peak at an earlier age than men's. Moreover, women are more likely than men to outlive their ties and become isolated, through the lack of surviving kin, in old age. This is true not only because women's age-specific mortality probabilities are slightly lower than men's, but because their kin relationships, formed earlier, have been at risk of termination for a longer period of time.

In quantitative terms, the !Kung's demographic probabilities and the kinship rules yield an average of about 16 relatives per person when double-counting of persons related to ego in several ways is eliminated. The distribution of the number of living kin of all kinds is almost symmetrical, the mean and mode being 16 and standard deviation about 5. Approximately 1% are really isolated (with zero or one relative), and about 1% have more than 40 relatives.

The implications of these observations extend beyond their importance for understanding the !Kung's kinship structure. Microsimulation is a simple, inexpensive method of drawing out and examining the consequences of *any* set of kinship rules and demographic probabilities. AMBUSH – and other microsimulation programs such as SOCSIM (Hammel et al., 1976) – provide a means of modeling kinship in any society for which we can specify those kinship rules and demographic parameters that generate and remove role occupants and connect them to or disconnect them from specific others. The theoretical generality of this method is considerable, even if, thus far, kinship theory per se has not been strongly influenced by results derived from simulations.

The limits to modeling dyads

The approach just described is essential in modeling kinship in small societies. By reporting on numbers and types of dyadic ties, the researcher is able to view a system in the way it is perceived by native informants and participant observers. Models that merely report results at higher levels of abstraction cannot be verified in this manner.

At the same time, despite satisfying conceptual simplicity, the sheer amount of information the model produces on dyadic ties is far too great to be easily used in comparing cultures. As we have seen, nearly 500 distributions are needed to describe the kinship inventory of individuals in a given society. This complexity is not an artifact of a particular computer program: The conception of a kin network that we have employed is, itself, very complex. Basically, we are modeling networks containing approximately 500 nodes (fluctuating between 200 and 800) and approximately 4,000 reciprocal ties at any one time, in which some 3–5% of the nodes and ties are created or disconnected annually. We can depict this complicated process satisfactorily, but to compare and express results is often clumsy or cumbersome.

Hence, in addition to the dyadic relationships, it is often useful to examine a kinship model in which individuals are aggregated together into larger groups. The nature of these larger groups and the balance among the various analytic criteria used in constructing them – such as permitted overlap in membership, degree of redundancy of ties, or the ethnographic importance of given units – can be assessed by analysts. Let us look at some of the available alternatives.

Larger units of analysis: households

!Kung households are stable units. A child (say, a girl) is born into her parents' household and lives in it until adolescence. For a period of some years, she may live with another adolescent or with a grandparent. She then joins a new household through marriage. The size of that new household will be increased by the birth of children and depleted by the death of those children or the marriage partners and, eventually, by the maturation of the children – until there are no members left. !Kung households, then, are what we refer to as *nuclear families* and *family fragments*. They usually share a little grass hut, a sleeping place, and a fire where their meals are cooked.

Over all ages, the mean expected household size would be 2.14 if the !Kung followed their own rules consistently. In fact, there are fewer observed one-member households than the simulations would lead us to expect. This is due, no doubt, to the minimum amount of work needed to maintain a !Kung household: in building the hut in the first place, but also, and more importantly, in collecting firewood, tending the fire, and collecting and cooking food. These tasks can be performed by a single individual or shared by members of multimember households.

Over a life span, the size of the household in which one lives shifts in predictable ways. Children are born into relatively large units (4 + members), as there will almost surely be two parents in the household and, on the average, a sibling or two as well. If a household contains at least one child, the probability that additional ones will be added in subsequent years is rather high. Thus, children tend to be born into households that are increasing in size. This pattern is also reflected in the mean age of parents at peak household size: 30–39, the prime reproductive years. When parents reach the age at which reproduction ceases, household size tends to contract. The probability of the loss of household members through death, maturation, and the marriage of the younger generation exceeds the probability of gaining new members for the rest of the life span. In old age, households in the simulations have only one or two members; occasionally, for reasons of convenience, they have three members in the real world.

Household composition is extremely important socially and is often useful for comparative purposes, especially when analysts wish to focus on economic and demographic decision making (Coale et al., 1965; Burch, 1980). However, rules of household composition vary so widely among societies that households, per se, are probably not the most useful units for exploring the structural consequences of demographic variation between societies. Moreover, households are not clearly related to one another in ways that would make them ideal units for constructing a society-wide network.

Families of orientation and procreation

During the course of a lifetime, one is ordinarily a member of two distinct nuclear families: a *family of orientation*, in which one is a child, and a *family of procreation*, in which one is a parent. We can count the number of living members of these groups and find their size distribution at a given time as follows.

For families of orientation, we use each living person as an ego and then count the number of living parents and siblings in addition to ego. We reckon people who have no living parents or siblings as a group of one. We then tabulate individuals by size of family and determine the number of families by dividing the number of reported egos by size of reported family.

Similarly, for families of procreation, we count everyone not yet married – as well as those who are widowed and have no surviving children – as groups of size 1. Others will be in groups of size 2–10. When this is done, we see that although a particular person may easily have two different scores, the distribution of the two kinds of nuclear families is the same. In fact, as implied earlier, families of procreation and orientation are the same units merely being reported by different egos. The different roles involved ("parent" vs. "child") are characteristics of the reporting egos, and not of the groups.

Families of orientation and procreation, then, are not the best units to use in summarizing the structural outcomes of demographic processes. Although nuclear families have characteristic patterns of stability and change over time that reveal a great deal about the dynamic processes that formed them, families of orientation and procreation cannot be easily differentiated; that is, it is difficult to determine when a new group has been created and an older one terminated.

Lineages and descent groups

Another possible unit we might employ at higher levels of analysis is what is called a *descent group*. When descent is traced only through maternal or paternal links, the resulting unit is called a "lineage": a multigenerational group whose members recognize a link to one another and who, consequently, marry outside that group. Where people, like the !Kung, trace descent through *both* maternal and paternal links (bilaterally), we can order them simultaneously into two nonoverlapping groups of living persons related to one another through common ancestors. Moreover, we can then count membership in various groups and generate size distributions for them – even when these units, themselves, are not socially important to the people in question.

AMBUSH, for instance, counts maternal descent groups by mapping a sibling group together with its mother and her siblings; the siblings group, in turn, is mapped together with its mother and her siblings, and so on. Everyone, male or female, is thus located in one and only one maternal descent group; males who have no living mother are necessarily assigned to groups of size 1. AMBUSH counts paternal descent groups – sibling group together with its father – in a similar fashion and assigns women who have no living father to groups of size 1. Each person, then, has a unique position in both a maternal and a paternal descent group. In fact, a society can be mapped into a three-dimensional space using time (year of birth) as the vertical dimension and maternal and paternal descent as two independent horizontal dimensions.

On occasion, given the demographic probabilities of the !Kung, these lineages may contain as many as 30–40 simultaneously living members. Their mean size, however, is much smaller. AMBUSH demonstrates that the size distributions of these groups are the most skewed of the units we have examined. Demographic parameters and precise marriage and kin allocation rules affect these distributions, but differences among them appear smaller, given their extreme skewness.

AMBUSH simulations also reveal characteristic differences between the size distributions of maternal and paternal descent groups and provide a method for exploring the sources of these differences. Paternal descent groups are typically larger than female ones, since males tend to have more offspring than women. (This is true despite the fact that males are more likely than females to have no children at all.) Fewer fathers than mothers actually participate in the production of each generation – even when polygamy is not permitted – provided both sexes are allowed to remarry after the loss of a spouse. When we control for age, men are also more likely than women to remarry after their spouse's death, because men have more *potential spouses* and because men's reproductive lives are longer.

In general, then, for groups similar to the !Kung, patrilineally connected descent groups are larger and fewer than matrilineally connected ones. It follows that patrilineal groups may be more effective structures for mobilizing group action. The larger the gap between the ages of marriage partners, the greater the differences in the size of male and female descent groups.

There are, however, several important disadvantages to employing lineage groups as units in comparative analyses of kinship systems. For one thing, descent groups often have complex internal structures. As a rule, we prefer to use small and homogeneous units as nodes in networks. Further, lineages may not be densely connected. Under these circumstances, some members of the same lineage may hardly recognize a kinship relationship, whereas others may see themselves as very close. This problem becomes particularly acute when the society being examined reckons kinship in terms of a unilineal descent system, but we classify its members into bilateral descent groups in order to make consistent comparisons across societies. Hence, although lineages are often important units in societies, their cultural definitions differ so widely that they can seldom be used in making useful comparisons.[5]

Sibling groups

On balance, sibling groups – the brothers and sisters born to a single mother – seem to be the large-scale units that best preserve detailed information, while permitting us to generalize it to levels that are useful for comparative purposes. Sibling groups are always (a) socially recognized as strong groups; (b) fully connected internally; (c) nonoverlapping in membership; and (d) stable over the course of an individual's life span – except for attrition. Siblings share at least all of those ties created by descent through their mother, and usually those from their father as well. In fact, the information on kinship relationships for a set of siblings is so redundant that Howell and Lehotay (1978) began using sibling groups as a time-saving device before fully recognizing the structural implications of this redundancy.

Figure 3.3 depicts an ordinary descent diagram that has been recoded into one that uses sibling groups rather than individuals as units. Note that many of the closest ties are absorbed within the units, so that only descent and marriage relations link sibling groups to one another. The pattern of linkage of sibling groups is the pervasive triad, which is formed when the sibling group of the father is linked to the sibling group of the mother by marriage,

Band 3-KAUTSA, by individuals

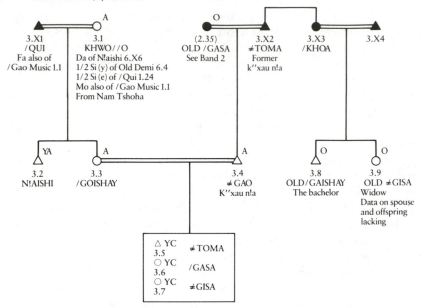

Band 3-KAUTSA, by sibling groups

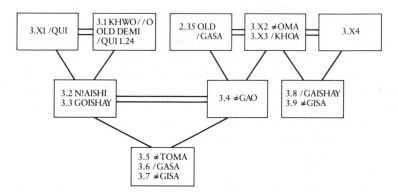

Figure 3.3. Kinship diagram comparing individual and sibling groups as units. Boxes enclose sibling groups; single lines indicate descent; double lines indicate marriage. Triangles = males; circles = females; black symbols = deceased persons. (Data and individual genealogy diagram from Marshall, 1976.)

and together they produce the new sibling group of the offspring of that marriage.

Marriage ties for members of a sibling group are not redundant for the members of the set. Note that in Figure 3.3 it is more difficult to represent marriage than descent ties, since there is no obvious place in the diagram to put the otherwise unrelated sibling group into which ego or siblings marry, and no neat way to show the links among these groups. Similarly, the relationship between in-laws – direct ties to one's spouse's consanguineal relatives and to one's sibling's spouse – is problematic in "social space" but recognized in virtually all societies.

Let us consider three dimensions of the network that are suggested by the probability processes that generate and disconnect the kin relations specific to given societies: (1) the size distribution and age composition of sibling groups (the "interior" of our units); (2) the number of links that emerge from each sibling group as a function of reproduction and marriage; and (3) the placement of the other end of those links, the pattern of connections between sibling groups. Each of these dimensions has its characteristic probabilities and can, therefore, be modeled in a straightforward fashion.

The size-by-age distribution

The size-by-age distribution of sibling groups is the easiest of these dimensions to calculate through a direct application of demographic theory and methods (see Table 3.2). All things being equal, a sibling set will be smaller while it is still being formed – that is, while its mother is still in childbearing years – than it will be when complete. The longer such sets have been exposed to the risk of mortality, however, the smaller their *expected* size.

Over the limiting period of 110 years – 30 years for the maximum difference in age between oldest and youngest siblings; 80 years for the maximum life span of the youngest member – sibling groups are created (by the birth of a first child), grow to their characteristic sizes, and are then increasingly trimmed back by deaths. For the purposes of our current simulation, we leave !Kung sibling group in existence until the youngest member of any group reaches a minimum age of 80, so that indirect kinship ties made through members of a sibling group can be maintained even if all members of that group are dead. The !Kung seem to do something similar: restricting kinship links among younger members to those made through the oldest living ancestral generation – although they readily use ties made through deceased members within that generation.

It is striking that the effects of the important biological processes of birth and death are almost entirely confined to their impact on the size and internal composition of the sibling group nodes of kinship networks. Cultural

Table 3.2. *Expected numbers of siblings for age classes, males only, from a single* AMBUSH *simulation based upon !Kung demographic rates and subject to stochastic variation*

Percentage with N living brothers and sisters	Age of male ego		
	0–9	30–39	60–69
0	19.0	20.1	59.1
1	29.3	27.1	27.5
2	29.3	28.5	9.1
3	13.3	17.4	4.0
4	6.3	5.3	0.0
5	1.9	1.3	
6	0.2		
Mean	1.659	1.645	0.0579
Standard deviation	1.259	1.207	0.817

Note: Results are subject to stochastic variation.

aspects of a population – such as marriage rules and types of kinship structures – affect the size of sibling groups through their impact on fertility and mortality probabilities, for example, through the age at marriage and intended fertility of parents, which, in turn, may influence the ultimate size of sib groups.

The first step in our analysis, then – determining the expected number and internal composition of the nodes in a given network – requires only that we know the probabilities of birth and death in a closed population.

Numbers of linkages

Each sibling group is linked to others by ties of descent and marriage. To count these ties, we do not need to distinguish among their "causes." But, for other purposes, we will find it useful to examine the dynamics of tie generation.

Each sibling group within a kinship network becomes the third element in a triad that consists of its mother's group, its father's group, and the offspring group itself. This triad almost invariably exists at the point where a new sib group is created and will persist throughout the "youth" of that group, even if the parents should die. Members of a sib group start forming ties to new groups only when their period of immaturity is over and they are ready to marry. Hence, the number of groups that will be linked to a given sib group depends, first, on the number of members of that group available for marriage and the number who actually do marry. It may also depend on whether multiple marriages are permitted in the society in question, which sex is permitted to make them, and how successful members of a particular sibling group happen to be in the multiple-marriage market. The timing of the formation of these new links to spouses' sibling groups will depend upon the marriage-by-age probability schedules for each sex. Moreover, with marriage, the opportunity arises for another set of links to new sibling groups created by the birth of offspring to a member of a sibling group and one of its member's new spouses.

Over its entire history, then, the number of ties between a given sibling group and others will reflect (a) its ties to the two parental groups, (b) the expected number of marriages made by its members, and (c) the expected number of offspring its members will have. In a classic stationary population with a net reproduction rate of 1.0, we would expect the mean distribution of ties to be close to 6, that is 2 to parents, 2 to spouses, and 2 to offspring groups. Population growth rates will, consequently, have far more effect on the size distribution within sibling groups than on the number of ties. But to the extent that the number of marriages in a sib group is a function of the number of siblings at risk of marriage, population growth will affect the numbers of ties per group. The maximum number of ties possible per sibling group is $2n + 2$, where n is the number of siblings in the group. For the !Kung, where the maximum size of a sibling group is 9, the maximum number of ties per group is 20. Most populations have higher maximum numbers of ties. The mean number of ties per group, in cross section at a point in time, will be lower than 6 because of ties to groups that have already been dissolved and ones that have not yet been formed.

Patterns of connection among sibling groups

The third dimension of a sibling group network that we can examine is the form assumed by ties among its nodes – especially where the placement of these ties is governed by cultural rules. Descent ties are not problematic because, initially at least, they always link a new group to two parental ones. Marriage links, however, are culturally defined, and indeed it is patterns of marriage ties that account for the important differences between social structures in kinship-based societies.

We classify societies as "elementary" precisely when they either prescribe marriage with a certain type of relative or divide all potential spouses into "prohibited" and "possible" classes (Lévi-Strauss, 1969). "Complex" systems limit themselves to defining a circle of "close relatives" about ego or leave the selection of spouses to other mechanisms. !Kung society, and probably all known hunter–gatherers, are considered elementary in this sense. Spouses are "possible" or "prohibited" depending on the kinship relationship between the pair, and some ties are valued more highly than others.

The !Kung prohibit marriage with members of one's own and one's two parental sibling groups. Such marriages are considered seriously incestuous not only by the !Kung, but by virtually all groups. Societies differ widely, however, in their attitude toward marriage with parents' siblings' offspring, that is, ego's first cousins. The !Kung prohibit such marriages, but they are preferred in many societies. Among the !Kung, preferred marriages are those for which we can trace a path of two or three links through intervening sibling groups between potential partners: for example, second cousins or siblings of spouses of close relatives. These persons are linked closely enough so that marriage arrangements can conveniently be made, but not so close that no new ties are formed by a marriage. It is striking, however, that in second- and higher-order marriages the preferred partner is often a same-sex sibling of the previous spouse. This is true for polygamous marriages – where second wives are often first wives' sisters in order to minimize conflict. In many societies, when a widow remarries – particularly a young widow with children who might otherwise have difficulty finding a new spouse – the spouse is often a brother or other close relative of her deceased husband. This pattern persists probably because sororal polygamy and levirate marriage require no rearrangement of the sibling group links formed by marriages.[6]

Preferences for spouses selected from among members of sibling groups with distinctive relationships to ego, when applied to all members of a particular society, create forms of alliance and affiliation that are characteristic not only of these societies, but of classes of societies with particular rules of preferential marriage.

Groups differ, however, in the extent to which they are able to conform to their own rules, and, hence, in the proportion of all marriages of the preferred type. Societies may also differ in the demographic parameters that affect sibling group size. Thus, they will vary in the extent to which they assume their characteristic structural form. "Pure types" are difficult to observe empirically.

Nonetheless, social anthropologists have long been aware that societies that follow the same rules of marriage choice have strong similarities in their role structure and in the types of group alliances they engender. It is striking that by restricting ourselves to the analysis of a few types of kin groups linked by simple ties, we are able to reach many of the same conclusions social anthropologists have reached on the basis of painstaking field observation. Whether their analyses would look different if they were explicitly based on the demographic generation of sibling group membership is a question best left for further research and consideration.

Conclusion

In the pursuit of parsimonious and testable structural models of real populations, we have considered the usefulness of several definitions of nodes and ties. The task in this chapter has been to strip away complexity to get at the simplest units and structures of units. The equally important and interesting job of looking at the implications and concatenations of simple processes as they sum to larger units and structurally equivalent categories remains a challenge for future structural analysis.

NOTES

1. The !Kung demographic structure used to model their kinship networks is that described in Howell, 1979.
2. A striking feature of the accounts of those studying hunter–gatherers and their neighbors is that marriages and sexual relations with neighbors take place between the hunter–gatherer women and "outsider" men, but that the reverse is not true; i.e., there is no corresponding contact between hunter–gatherer men and "outsider" women. This is consistent, of course, with the usual pattern of "hypergamy."
3. See Howell (1980) for a discussion of the motives, mechanisms, and consequences of density-dependent population control among hunter–gatherers.
4. See Figure 3.1 for the proportions for 10-year age group, in cross section.
5. The !Kung, for instance, hardly recognize lineage groups at all.
6. What is particularly striking is to see sororal polygamy and levirate preferred among the !Kung, where control of property and wealth play no role in marriage choices.

LITERATURE CITED

Burch, T. K. "The Index of Overall Headship: A Simple Measure of Household Complexity Standardized for Age and Sex." *Demography* 17(1) (1980): 25–37.

Cavalli-Sforza, L. L., and W. Bodmer. *The Genetics of Human Population.* San Francisco: Freeman, 1971.

Chagnon, N. A. "Mate Competition Favoring Close Kin, and Village Fissioning among the Yanomamo Indians." In N. Chagnon and W. Irons (eds.), *Evolutionary Biology and Human Social Behavior: An Anthropological Perspective.* North Scituate, Mass: Duxbury Press, 1980.

Coale, Anseley J., et al. (eds.). *Aspects of the Analysis of Family Structure.* Princeton: Princeton University Press, 1965.

Fallers, L. A. "The Range of Variation in Actual Family Size, a Critique of Marion J. Levy, Jr.'s Argument." In A. J. Coale et al. (eds.), *Aspects of the Analysis of Family Structure.* Princeton: Princeton University Press, 1965.

Goodman, Leo A., Nathan Keyfitz, and T. Pullum. "Family Formation and the Frequency of Various Kinship Relationships." *Theoretical Population Biology* 5 (1974): 1–27.

Hammel, Eugene A. "Formal Semantic Analysis." Special issue, *American Anthropologist* 67, no. 5, part 2 (1965).

Hammel, Eugene A., et al. *The SOCSIM Demographic-Sociological Microsimulation Program Operating Manual.* University of California, Institute of International Studies, Research Services 27. Berkeley, 1976.

Howell, Nancy. *Demography of the Dobe !Kung.* New York: Academic Press, 1979.
   "Demographic Behavior of Hunter–Gatherers: Evidence for Density-Dependent Population Control." In T. K. Burch, ed., *Demographic Behavior: Interdisciplinary Perspectives on Decision-Making.* AAAS Selected Symposium 45. Boulder, Colo.: Westview Press, 1980.

Howell, Nancy, and Victor A. Lehotay, Jr. "AMBUSH: A Computer Program for Stochastic Microsimulation of Small Human Populations." *American Anthropologist* 80 (1978): 905–22.

Keyfitz, Nathan. *Introduction to the Mathematics of Population.* Reading, Mass.: Addison-Wesley, 1968.

LeBras, Herve. "Parents, Grand-Parents, Bisaieux." *Population* 28 (1973): 9–38.

Lee, N. H. *The Search for an Abortionist.* Chicago: University of Chicago Press, 1969.

Lee, Richard B., and Irving DeVore (eds.), *Man the Hunter.* Chicago: Aldine, 1968.

Lévi-Strauss, C. *The Elementary Structures of Kinship.* Boston: Beacon Press, 1969.

Lewis, I. M. "Tribal Societies." *International Encyclopedia of the Social Sciences* 16: 146. New York: Macmillan, 1968.

Lounsbury, F. G. "Another View of Trobriand Kinship Categories." In E. A. Hammel (ed.), "Formal Semantic Analysis." Special issue, *American Anthropologist* 67, no. 5, part 2 (1965).

McFarland, D. D. "Comparison of Alternative Marriage Models." In T. N. E. Greville (ed.), *Population Dynamics.* New York: Academic Press, 1972.

Marshall, Lorna. *The !Kung of Nyae Nyae.* Cambridge, Mass.: Harvard University Press, 1976.

Wachter, K. W., and P. Laslett. "Measuring Patriline Extinctions for Modeling Social Mobility in the Past." In K. W. Wachter et al. (eds.), *Statistical Studies of Historical Social Structure.* New York: Academic Press, 1978.

Weissner, Polly W. *Hxaro: A Regional System of Reciprocity for Reducing Risk Among !Kung San.* Ph.D. diss., University of Michigan, 1977.

4

The duality of persons and groups

Ronald L. Breiger

Background

Consider a metaphor that has often appeared in sociological literature but has remained largely unexploited in empirical work. Individuals come together (or, metaphorically, "intersect" one another) within groups, which are collectivities based on the shared interest, personal affinities, or ascribed status of members who participate regularly in collective activities. At the same time, the particular patterning of an individual's affiliations (or the "intersection" of groups within the person) defines his or her points of reference and (at least partly) determines his or her individuality.[1]

The following discussion consists of a translation of this metaphor into a set of techniques that aid in the empirical analysis of the interpenetration of networks of persons and networks of the groups that they comprise. I use the term "group" restrictively to denote only those collectivities or social associations for which membership lists are available – through published sources, reconstruction from field observations or interviews, or by any other means. Such groups include corporation boards of directors (J. Levine, 1972), organizations within a community or national power structure (Perrucci and Pilisuk, 1970; Lieberson, 1971), cliques or organizations in a high school (Coleman, 1961; Bonacich, 1972), and political factions.

D. Levine (1959: 19–22) writes that "the concept of dualism" is a key principle "underlying Simmel's social thought." Levine explicates Simmel's dualism as "the assumption . . . that the subsistence of any aspect of human life depends on the coexistence of diametrically opposed elements." My own use of the comparable term "duality" is specified with respect to equations 4.3 and 4.4 below.[2]

For their criticism and encouragement, I am indebted to Harrison White, Gregory Heil, François Lorrain, and Scott Boorman. For seminars that first introduced me to Simmel's thought, I am indebted to Kurt H. Wolff. This work was supported through NSF Grant GS-2689. An earlier version of this chapter appeared in *Social Forces* 53 (1974): 181–90. It has been revised and reprinted here with the kind permission of that journal.

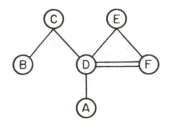

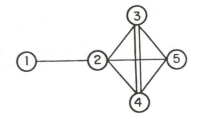

Figure 4.1. Graph of interpersonal network.

Figure 4.2. Graph of intergroup
network.

	A	B	C	D	E	F
A	0	0	0	1	0	0
B	0	0	1	0	0	0
C	0	1	0	1	0	0
D	1	0	1	0	1	2
E	0	0	0	1	0	1
F	0	0	0	2	1	0

Figure 4.3. Matrix representation (*P*) of Figure 4.1.

	1	2	3	4	5
1	0	1	0	0	0
2	1	0	1	1	1
3	0	1	0	2	1
4	0	1	2	0	1
5	0	1	1	1	0

Figure 4.4. Matrix representation (*G*) of Figure 4.2.

The basic conception

Consider a set of individuals and a set of groups such that the value of a *tie* between any two individuals is defined as the number of groups of which both individuals are members. The value of a tie between any two groups is defined conversely as the number of persons who belong to both groups. A fictitious example is provided in Figures 4.1 and 4.2, in which individuals are named by capital letters and their groups are named by integers. In concrete applications, we might take U.S. congressmen as the individuals and their committees as the groups, or schoolchildren as the individuals and their cliques as the groups, and so forth.

We may construct a matrix of interpersonal ties (denoted by *P*) and a separate matrix of intergroup ties (*G*) in the usual way (Figures 4.3 and 4.4): Let the (i, j)th entry of *P* indicate the number of groups to which both person i and person j belong, and let the (i, j)th entry of *G* indicate the number of persons who are members both of group i and of group j. Each matrix is square, having as row and column headings identical strings of the names of all persons (in the *P* matrix) or all groups (in the *G* matrix) under study. These matrices are mutually noncomparable in the following ways: They represent different levels of structure (persons and groups); they are not of the same dimension; and they differ in their cell-by-cell entries.

Although these differences between the interpersonal network and the intergroup network are quite evident, the *P* and *G* matrices nonetheless stand

(A)

	1	2	3	4	5
A	0	0	0	0	1
B	1	0	0	0	0
C	1	1	0	0	0
D	0	1	1	1	1
E	0	0	1	0	0
F	0	0	1	1	0

Figure 4.5. The binary adjacency matrix (A) of person-to-group affiliation.

in intimate relation to one another. Following Simmel (1955: 125–8, 147), think of each tie between two groups as a set of persons who form the "intersection" of the groups' memberships. In the dual case, think of each membership tie between two persons as the set of groups in the intersection of *their* individual affiliations.

Define a binary adjacency matrix A (Figure 4.5) whose (i, j)th entry is "1" if person i is affiliated with group j; "0" otherwise. Where there are p persons and g groups under consideration, A has dimension $p \times g$, and the P and G matrices have dimension $p \times p$ and $g \times g$ respectively.

Notice that if we intersect any rows i and j of the A matrix (i.e., lay one row atop the other, according the value "1" only to those entries that are "1" in the same column of *each* row) and count the number of ones in the intersection, we discover the (i, j)th entry of the P matrix of Figure 4.3 (and dually for the intersection of pairs of columns of A with respect to the G matrix of Figure 4.4). This result is purely definitional. As will be seen below, it will be useful to formulate the definition in matrix notation.

$$P_{ij} = \sum_{k=1}^{g} A_{ik} A_{jk} \tag{4.1}$$

and similarly for ties between groups:

$$G_{ij} = \sum_{k=1}^{p} A_{ki} A_{kj}. \tag{4.2}$$

The matrix A^T of group-to-person ties is equivalent to A except that its rows are transposed with its columns; that is, A^T is of dimension $g \times p$ and $A^T_{ij} = A_{ji}$ for any i and j. Hence we may rewrite the above equations using the person-to-group "translation" matrix A and its transpose to obtain the fundamental equalities:

$$P = A(A^T) \tag{4.3}$$
$$G = (A^T)A \tag{4.4}$$

where the multiplication is ordinary (inner product) matrix multiplication. Thus, two distinct matrices, one of person-to-person relations (P) and one of group-to-group relations (G), are uniquely defined by and derivable from a single translation matrix (A) of person-group affiliations.[3]

Comparison of membership nets and sociometric nets

There are crucial sociological and mathematical differences between the approach of this paper and that of conventional sociometry.[4] An elaboration of both types of differences will help to clarify the nature and potential utility of each approach.

Goffman (1971: 188), in his discussion of "tie signs," writes that "the individual is linked to society through two principal social bonds: to collectivities through membership and to other individuals through social relationships. He in turn helps make a network of society by linking through himself the social units linked to him."

I disagree with Goffman in that I see no reason why individuals cannot be linked to other individuals by bonds of common membership (as in interlocking directorates) or to collectivities through social relationships (as in "love" of one's country or "fear" of a bureaucracy). Moreover, Goffman's focus on the individual as his unit of analysis is a one-sided departure from Simmel's insight into duality. This demurral notwithstanding, I fundamentally agree that there are two types of social ties: membership and social relations. Following Goffman's terminology, I refer to my approach as "membership network analysis," in contrast to the conventional "social-relations network analysis" typified by sociometry. A similar vocabulary is hinted by the anthropologist S. F. Nadel (1957: 91, 95) in his discussion of "relational roles" and "membership roles":

> [B]elonging to a subgroup, being involved in its regular activities and rules of behaviour, has all the characteristics of role performance. Which means that the names describing persons in terms of the subgroups they belong to are true role names. And this means, further, that these membership roles, whether explicitly named or not, correspond to *relational* roles, since the very nature of groups depends on the relationships between the people comprising them. ... The two networks [membership and relational], in other words, can exist side by side and interpenetrate.

All sociometric approaches specify that the points or "nodes" of a graph are actors (persons or – much more rarely – collectivities) and that the lines or "ties" of the graphs are social relationships (affect, avoidance, "helping," influence, etc.). Actors and relationships are conceived as irreducible phenomena. When the relationships are those of membership, however, this conception is radically at odds with Simmel's image (Wolff, [1959] 1965: 350) in which "the fact of sociation puts the individual into the dual position...that he is both a link in the organism of sociation and an autonomous organic whole." With respect to the membership network, on the other hand, persons who are actors in one picture (the P matrix) are with equal legitimacy viewed as connections in the dual picture (the G matrix), and conversely for groups. Formally, we have two classes (one for all persons and one for all groups under consideration) of finite sets (each person is associated with the set of groups to which he or she belongs, and conversely for groups) and an axiom that the intersection of any two sets belonging to either class is contained in the power set of the other class.[5]

A second axiom of the membership network is symmetry: If person a is connected to person b by virtue of a shared membership, then b is connected to a as well. If two groups share at least one member, they are mutually related. This implies reflexivity: A person who belongs to any group is related to himself or herself by that fact, and similarly for any group with members.

The main diagonal of a sociomatrix consists solely of zeroes if irreflexivity has been imposed (as is usual). This absence of self-choice represents a crucial contrast with the membership network. As Harrison White (1971: 31) has stated, "whether to assign self-choices ('loops') in a generator graph...is a fundamental theoretical issue, not a technicality of computation, as it has often been regarded." One advantage of the membership net is the intuitively clear meaning of reflexivity: The number of ties between a person and himself or herself is the number of groups to which he or she belongs (and conversely in the dual matrix: The number of ties between a group and itself is the size of its membership), whereas to state in a sociometric analysis that a person "esteems" or "avoids" herself (say) three times has no meaning that has been developed. Moreover, the sum of the main-diagonal entries in P always equals the corresponding sum in G, as the affiliations not only *create* the differences between the two networks, but also *unify* them. (More formally: The sum of any row in the "translation" matrix A gives the number of groups to which a particular individual belongs; hence, by equation 4.3, the vector of row marginals of A is equivalent to the main diagonal of P; similarly, the vector of column marginals of A is equivalent to the main diagonal of G by equation 4.4; moreover, the sum of row marginals must equal the sum of column marginals.)

As a further theoretical implication of reflexivity, consider the group-to-group matrix G. A lower bound on the total number of *persons* who belong to all groups (i.e., a lower bound on the dimension of the P matrix) is given by the largest-valued cell on the main diagonal of G. An upper bound is given by the sum of main-diagonal cells in G. (That is, if all the persons belonging to all groups are found to belong to any *single* group, then the lower bound is the

	1	2	3	4	5	6	7	8	9	10	11	12	13	14
Eleanor	0	1	0	1	0	0	0	1	0	0	0	1	0	0
Brenda	0	1	0	1	0	0	1	1	0	1	0	1	1	0
Dorothy	0	0	0	0	0	1	0	0	0	0	0	1	0	0
Verne	0	0	0	1	1	1	0	0	0	0	0	1	0	0
Flora	1	0	0	0	0	1	0	0	0	0	0	0	0	0
Olivia	1	0	0	0	0	1	0	0	0	0	0	0	0	0
Laura	0	1	1	1	0	0	1	1	0	1	0	1	0	0
Evelyn	0	1	1	0	0	1	1	1	0	1	0	1	1	0
Pearl	0	0	0	0	0	1	0	1	0	0	0	1	0	0
Ruth	0	1	0	1	0	1	0	0	0	0	0	1	0	0
Sylvia	0	0	0	1	1	1	0	0	1	0	1	1	0	1
Katherine	0	0	0	0	1	1	0	0	1	0	1	1	0	1
Myrna	0	0	0	0	1	1	0	0	1	0	0	1	0	0
Theresa	0	1	1	1	0	1	1	1	0	0	0	1	1	0
Charlotte	0	1	0	1	0	0	1	0	0	0	0	0	1	0
Frances	0	1	0	0	0	0	1	1	0	0	0	1	0	0
Helen	1	0	0	1	1	0	0	0	1	0	0	1	0	0
Nora	1	0	0	1	1	1	0	1	1	0	1	0	0	1

Figure 4.6. The *A* matrix indicating presence (1) or absence (0) of each of 18 women at each of 14 social events. Row headings name the women; column headings name each event in chronological order. (Adapted from Homans, 1950: 83.)

actual number of persons; at the opposite extreme, if no groups overlap, the upper bound is the actual number of persons.) And conversely in consideration of the dual (*P*) matrix.

An application of dual analysis: social participation in "Old City"

In empirical work, we might define some minimal level of connectivity among (say) groups, excluding any group connected to at least one other by at least *k* links, and then examine the dual person-to-person matrix resulting from this selection. The goal is to look for patterned relations among persons; the strategy is to perform operations on the (group-to-group) matrix *dual* to our interest. The value of *k* is set according to the "graininess" or connectivity ratio (defined below) desired in the resulting matrix.

Consider the study by Davis, Gardner, and Gardner (1941) of the social participation of 18 women in "Old City." The method employed in their investigation is discussed in somewhat greater detail by Homans (1950). The researchers compiled a table with 18 rows, one for each woman, and 14 columns, one for each "event" (such as a club meeting, a church supper, a card party, and so on), held during the course of a year, for which it could be determined that various of the women were present. The goal of the study was to determine the clique structure among the women.

At the start of the analysis, the rows were arranged arbitrarily and the columns chronologically, as in the *A* matrix of Figure 4.6, which I have adapted from Homans's presentation, and in which the (i,j)th entry represents the presence or absence of woman i at event j. The reader will observe that the *A* matrix fits precisely my conception of a translation matrix. The researchers were aware that they could derive the woman-to-woman relations from *A*, but they chose not to do so. A glance at the *P* matrix of Figure 4.7 will, I believe, indicate why. The researchers were attempting to discover the clique divisions among the women; however, connectivity in the *P* matrix is 91%.[6] Since everyone was connected to virtually everyone else, identification of subgroupings became problematic. As Homans describes it:

> The chart in its rough form will not reveal very much. (If you do not believe this, try making such a chart for yourself.) For one thing, the columns are probably arranged in the chronological order of events, and the women are probably in no particular order at all. But then we begin to reshuffle lines and columns. As far as columns are concerned, we put in the center the columns representing the events... at which a large number of the women were present, and we put toward the edges the columns representing the events... at which only a few of the women were present. As far as lines are concerned, we put toward the top or bottom the lines representing those women that participated most often together in social events. A great deal of reshuffling may have to be done before any pattern appears. (Homans, 1950: 82–3)

There can be no doubt that the researchers were operating with an implicit conception of duality, although they were uninterested in event-to-event relations. A more explicit conception might have led them to a much less time-consuming approach (particularly as no computer was available), as follows. Begin with the unpermuted *A* matrix of Figure 4.6, even though it is in "rough form." By equation 4.4, create the matrix – call it *G* – of membership overlaps among events (see Figure 4.8). Impose the assumption that only those events that have *zero* overlap with at least one other event are likely to separate the women into socially meaningful subgroups. Therefore, by inspection of the *G* matrix (which is dual to the matrix of our interest), note each column that contains no zero entry (i.e., columns 4, 6, 8, 12) and eliminate the corresponding column in the *A* matrix, creating the modified translation matrix *A2* of woman-to-event relations. By equation 4.3, create *P2*, the new matrix of woman-to-woman relations (Figure 4.9), which may be thought of as the "skeleton structure" of the original *P* matrix. Inspection of *P2* will show that connectivity has been significantly reduced to 30% – but is this reduction *meaningful*? The answer is affirmative, with one minor

	El	Br	Do	Ve	Fl	Ol	La	Ev	Pe	Ru	Sy	Ka	My	Th	Ch	Fr	He	No
Eleanor	4	4	1	2	0	0	4	3	2	3	2	1	1	4	2	3	2	2
Brenda	4	7	1	2	0	0	6	6	2	3	2	1	1	6	4	4	2	2
Dorothy	1	1	2	2	1	1	1	2	2	2	2	2	2	2	0	1	1	1
Verne	2	0	2	4	1	1	2	2	2	3	4	3	3	3	1	1	3	3
Flora	0	0	1	1	2	2	0	1	1	1	1	1	1	1	0	0	3	2
Olivia	0	0	1	1	2	2	0	1	1	1	1	1	1	1	0	0	1	2
Laura	4	6	1	2	0	0	7	6	2	3	2	1	1	6	3	4	2	2
Evelyn	3	6	2	2	0	1	6	8	3	3	2	2	2	7	3	4	1	2
Pearl	2	2	2	2	1	1	2	3	3	2	2	2	2	3	0	2	1	2
Ruth	3	3	2	3	1	1	3	3	3	4	3	2	2	4	2	2	4	2
Sylvia	2	2	2	4	1	1	2	2	2	3	7	6	4	3	1	1	4	6
Katherine	1	1	2	3	1	1	1	2	2	2	6	6	4	2	0	1	3	5
Myrna	1	1	2	3	1	1	1	2	2	2	4	4	4	2	0	1	3	3
Theresa	4	6	2	3	1	1	6	7	3	4	4	4	2	8	4	4	2	3
Charlotte	2	4	0	1	0	0	3	3	0	2	3	2	0	4	4	2	1	1
Frances	3	4	1	1	0	0	4	4	2	2	1	1	1	4	2	4	1	1
Helen	2	2	1	3	1	1	2	1	1	2	4	3	3	3	1	1	5	4
Nora	2	2	1	3	2	2	2	2	2	2	6	5	3	3	1	1	4	8

Figure 4.7. The P matrix of woman-to-woman relations, derived from matrix A by equation 4.3. Each off-diagonal entry is the number of events at which two given women were jointly present; each main-diagonal entry is the total number of events attended by a single woman.

	1	2	3	4	5	6	7	8	9	10	11	12	13	14
1	4	0	0	2	2	3	0	1	2	0	1	1	0	1
2	0	8	3	6	0	3	6	6	0	3	0	7	4	0
3	0	3	3	2	0	2	3	3	0	2	0	3	2	0
4	2	6	2	10	4	5	4	5	3	2	2	8	3	2
5	2	0	0	4	6	5	0	1	5	0	3	5	0	3
6	3	3	2	5	5	12	2	4	4	1	3	9	2	3
7	0	6	3	4	0	2	6	5	0	3	0	5	4	0
8	1	6	3	5	1	4	5	8	1	3	1	7	3	1
9	2	0	0	3	5	4	0	1	5	0	3	4	0	3
10	0	3	2	2	0	1	3	3	0	3	0	3	2	0
11	1	0	0	2	3	3	0	1	3	0	3	2	0	3
12	1	7	3	8	5	9	5	7	4	3	2	14	3	2
13	0	4	2	3	0	2	4	3	0	2	0	3	4	0
14	1	0	0	2	3	3	0	1	3	0	3	2	0	3

Figure 4.8. The G matrix of event-to-event relations, derived from matrix A by equation 4.4. Each off-diagonal entry is the number of women who participated in both of two given events; each main-diagonal entry is the total number of women who attend a given event. Only columns 4, 6, 8, and 12 have no zero entries.

qualification: Although the two cliques (of sizes seven and five, respectively) that Homans describes[7] are contained person for person in the graph of P_2 (see Figure 4.10), each clique in the latter graph also contains one additional woman (Ruth and Verne, respectively), whom Homans (1950: 84) describes as "marginal" to both cliques. ("The pattern is frayed at the edges, but there is a pattern.")[8]

Duality and transitivity

Whereas the analysis of the previous section was predicated on knowledge of the translation matrix A, this section indicates that information about "reachability" in either the person-to-person or the group-to-group matrix may be derived from knowledge of its dual matrix. In the graph of person-to-person ties, two persons are mutually reachable along a path of length n if there exists a sequence of n contiguous ties between them (i.e., if there exist $n - 1$ intermediate persons on a connected path from one person to the other). The number of person-to-person ties of length n between all pairs of persons is given by entries of the binarized P matrix raised to the nth power (Harary, Norman, and Cartwright, 1965). With reference to the fictitious data of Figure 4.1, for example, persons B and D are connected by one 2-path (B-C-D; this is the shortest path), but also by all $(2 + 3k) =$ paths (k any positive integer), including two 5-paths (B-C-D-E-F-D and B-C-D-F-E-D; these are termed degenerate paths). Similarly for the group-to-group ties: The number of n-paths connecting groups is contained in the matrix G^n.

Suppose we know the G matrix but do not know the P matrix (e.g., suppose we are given information on director interlocks between corporations but

	El	Br	Do	Ve	Fl	Ol	La	Ev	Pe	Ru	Sy	Ka	My	Th	Ch	Fr	He	No
Eleanor	1	1	0	0	0	0	1	1	0	1	0	0	0	1	1	1	0	0
Brenda	1	4	0	0	0	0	3	4	0	1	0	0	0	3	3	2	0	0
Dorothy	0	0	0	0	0	0	0	0	0	0	0	0	0	0	0	0	0	0
Verne	0	0	0	1	1	1	0	0	0	0	1	1	1	0	0	0	1	1
Flora	0	0	0	0	1	1	0	0	0	0	0	0	0	0	0	0	1	1
Olivia	0	0	0	0	1	0	0	0	0	0	0	0	0	0	0	0	1	1
Laura	1	3	0	0	0	0	4	4	0	1	0	0	0	3	2	2	0	0
Evelyn	1	4	0	0	0	0	4	5	0	1	0	0	0	4	3	2	0	0
Pearl	0	0	0	0	0	0	0	0	0	0	0	0	0	0	0	0	0	0
Ruth	1	1	0	0	0	0	1	1	0	1	0	0	0	1	1	1	0	0
Sylvia	0	0	0	1	0	0	0	0	0	0	4	4	2	0	0	0	2	4
Katherine	0	0	0	1	0	0	0	0	0	0	4	4	2	0	0	0	2	4
Myrna	0	0	0	1	0	0	0	0	0	0	2	2	2	0	0	0	2	2
Theresa	0	3	0	0	0	0	3	4	0	1	0	0	0	4	3	2	0	0
Charlotte	1	3	0	0	0	0	2	3	0	1	0	0	0	3	3	2	0	0
Frances	1	2	0	0	0	0	2	2	0	1	2	2	2	2	2	2	0	0
Helen	0	0	0	1	1	1	0	0	0	0	0	2	2	0	0	0	3	3
Nora	0	0	0	1	1	1	0	0	0	0	4	4	2	0	0	0	3	5

Figure 4.9. The new matrix P_2 of woman-to-woman relations, formed by eliminating columns 4, 6, 8, and 12 of matrix A and then applying equation 4.10. (For the graph of P_2, see Figure 4.10.)

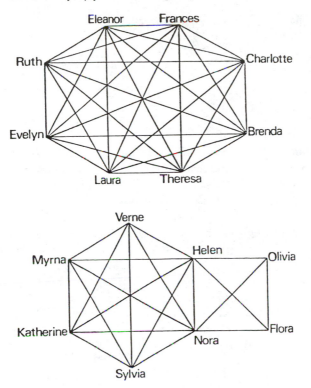

Figure 4.10. The graph of matrix P_2. For simplicity, the ties are shown in the binary form.

we have no knowledge of director-to-director ties). Suppose further that we have person-to-group information for only two (or several, say $p* \ll p$) of the p persons. We can find the 1-paths among these (two or several) persons by $A(A^T)$, where A has $p*$ rows and one column for each group in G. But it appears that we cannot find paths of length two or more among our $p*$ people because we do not know who the intermediate persons are or how these intermediaries are connected to others. In this case we are aided by

Lemma 1. $P^n = A(G^{n-1})A^T$: $G^n = A^T(P^{n-1})A$.

The proof follows from associativity and substitution of equations 4.3 and 4.4; for example,

$$P^n = (AA^T)^n = A(A^TA)^{n-1}A^T = A(G^{n-1})A^T.$$

In this manner, we can determine the number of paths of any length among our $p*$ people by examining the dual paths in G. What of the number of *groups* that a person can reach (and conversely the number of persons that a group can reach)?

Lemma 2. $P^n A = (G^n A^T)^T$

Proof:
$$P^n A = (AA^T)^n A = AG^n = ((AG^n)^T)^T$$
$$= ((G^n)^T (A)^T)^T = (G^n A^T)^T.$$

The assertion of Lemma 2 is that if we play out all chains of person-to-person ties as far as we like and then observe the groups that the last persons reach, we come out with the same endpoints as if we had played out all group-to-group chains to the same length and then looked at persons reached by the last groups.

The extension of lengths of paths in any graph has a natural limit; there exists some minimal m such that each node reaches all other nodes it will *ever* reach by paths of length m (at most): That is, converting the values of ties to their binary form and conceiving matrix multiplication as Boolean (Harary, Norman, and Cartwright, 1965), there is some minimal m for which the matrix P^{m+1} is contained in the union of the first m powers of P, and some minimal n for which G^{n+1} is contained in the union of the first n powers of G. The matrices P and G are then said to have reached transitive closure.

> **Theorem.** If P reaches transitive closure at the mth power and G reaches transitive closure at the nth power, then the absolute difference of m and n is at most 1.

Here is a sketch of the proof. It follows from Lemmas 1 and 2 that the matrix that is the union of the first k powers of $P^i A$ ($i = 1, \ldots, k$) specifies (for minimal k) all groups ever reached by each person if and only if the union of the first k powers of $G^i A^T$ specifies all persons ever reached by each group ($P^{k+1} A \subseteq \bigcup_{i=1}^{k} P^i A$ if and only if $G^{k+1} A^T \subseteq \bigcup_{i=1}^{k} G^i A^T$. Since the nodes on a path from a person to a group may be conceived as an alternating sequence of persons and groups, all persons reach all groups they will ever reach (by paths not exceeding length k, at most) *only* if they have just reached all *persons* they will ever reach (P reaches transitive closure at the kth power), *or* if they are about to do so at the next remove (P reaches transitive closure at the $k + 1$st power). And similarly for G (G reaches transitive closure only at the kth or the $k + 1$st power).

Primary affiliations and asymmetric ties

We have, until now, imposed symmetry on a network of membership ties; indeed, most writers (e.g., Perrucci and Pilisuk, 1970; Bonacich, 1972) conceive such ties as symmetric only. There are, however, cases (such as corporate interlocks or coalitions among parties or factions) in which it is more interesting to conceive of an asymmetric tie emanating from one person or group to another. This creation of asymmetric orientations out of the symmetry of group membership was formulated by Simmel (1955: 138, 155) in terms of primary and secondary affiliations.

> One group appears as the original focus of an individual's affiliation, from which he then turns toward affiliation with other, quite different groups on the basis of his special qualities, which distinguish him from other members of his primary group. His bond with his primary group may well continue to exist...An infinite range of individualizing combinations is made possible by the fact that the individual belongs to a multiplicity of groups.... The instinctive needs of man prompt him to act in these mutually conflicting ways: he feels and acts *with* others but also *against* others.

The generalization of this asymmetry occurs in Simmel's discussion (1955: 62) of competition. "Modern competition is described as the fight of all against all, but at the same time it is the fight of all *for* all" – and thus results not in the chaos of Hobbes (which necessitates external control), but in an intrinsically ordered interweaving of relations based on "the possibilities of gaining favor and connection."

Here is a method for building asymmetry into the basic approach of this chapter. Begin with p people, g groups, a $p \times g$ matrix F whose (i, j)th entry is "1" if person i has group j as his *primary* affiliation and is "0" otherwise, and a $p \times g$ matrix A (as above) showing all affiliations of each person. Partition the memberships in A among primary and secondary (i.e., all other) affiliations. Define the $p \times g$ matrix S of secondary affiliations by $S = A \cap \sim F$.

Let us say that two people mutually influence each other if they share a common primary affiliation. Our substantive conceptualization of a particular problem (e.g., influence among directors of corporations) might suggest specifying that an asymmetric tie exists from person i to person j ("i is influenced by j") if a group that is i's primary affiliation is a secondary affiliation for j (the assumption here being that directors of higher-status corporations are more sought after to lend their prestige to the boards of other corporations).[9]

Following from this conception is a matrix P' of asymmetric ties among persons:

$$P' = FF^T \cup FS^T = F(F^T \cup S^T) = FA^T.$$

By reasoning analogous to that of equation 4.3 and 4.4, we find the dual matrix G' of asymmetric ties among groups: $G' = A^T F$. Moreover, the above reasoning on duality and transitivity is easily extended to the asymmetric case; as the reader may verify, for example,

$$(P')^n = (FA^T)^n = F(A^TF)^{n-1}A^T = F(G')^{n-1}A^T$$

is the analogue to Lemma 1 for the asymmetric case.

NOTES

1. Simmel (1955) entitled one of his essays "The Intersection of Social Circles," but Reinhard Bendix changed the title in translation because "a literal translation of this phrase...is almost meaningless.... Simmel often plays with geometric analogies; it has seemed advisable to me to minimize this play with words" (Simmel, 1955: 125). For an assertion that Simmel's original title is not at all inappropriate, see Walter's essay in Wolff (1959). For a more complete explication of the "dualism" inherent in Simmel's thought, see the essays by D. Levine, Lipman, and Tenbruck in Wolff (1959). A similar metaphor was put forward in America by Charles H. Cooley ([1902] 1964: 148), who wrote that "a man may be regarded as the point of intersection of an indefinite number of circles representing social groups, having as many arcs passing through him as there are groups." Much later, Sorokin ([1947] 1962: 345) observed that "the individual has as many egos as there are different social groups and strata with which he is connected." On the "much neglected" development of the concept of "social circles" since Simmel's writings, see Kadushin (1966).
2. The "directional duality principle" enunciated by Harary, Norman, and Cartwright (1965) is to be distinguished from my conception. The former principle consists in reversing the directionality of lines in a graph; in the method of this paper, the lines in one graph are transformed into the points of its dual graph, and vice versa.
3. Notice that the products in equations 4.3 and 4.4 differ from the P and G matrices of Figures 4.1 and 4.2 in that the former have nonzero main diagonal entries. (The main diagonal of a square matrix consists of cells [1, 1], [2, 2], and so on to [p, p] or [g, g]). Implications of this difference are discussed in the following section.
4. For a review of sociometric and related methods, see Glanzer and Glaser (1959).
5. "Power set" denotes the set of all possible sets of the given elements; e.g., the power set of a set containing three objects consists of eight sets, including the empty and universal sets.
6. That is, of the $153 = (1/2)$ (18) (17) possible binary ties among the 18 women, we find by inspection of P that 139 ties actually existed. The ratio 139/153 is 0.91.
7. The clique membership reported by Homans (1950) is as follows. Clique 1: Evelyn, Laura, Theresa, Brenda, Charlotte, Frances, Eleanor. Clique 2: Myrna, Katherine, Sylvia, Nora, Helen. Women not clearly belonging to either clique: Pearl, Ruth, Verne, Dorothy, Olivia, Flora.
8. As Homans (1950) notes, the analysis of Davis, Gardner, and Gardner (1941) follows the logic of Forsyth and Katz, which – as several authors have observed – involved much awkward and tedious manipulation (see Glanzer and Glaser, 1959, for a review). More recent methods of clique detection (the methods of Festinger and of

Luce and Perry, reviewed by Glanzer and Glaser, 1959: 326–8; see also Alba, 1973) are applicable only to square sociomatrices: e.g., to the *P* matrix of Figure 4.7 rather than to the rectangular *A* matrix of Figure 4.6. Since connectivity in the *P* matrix approaches unity (91%), the problem for clique detection is the reduction of connectivity – hence, the concern for operations on the (group-to-group) matrix *dual* to the sociomatrix, rather than with powers of the latter. An algorithm (Breiger, Boorman, and Arabie, 1975) for detecting structure in multiple relational matrices combines the duality approach of this chapter with blocking and structural equivalence concepts (White and Breiger, 1975; White, Boorman, and Breiger, 1976). This algorithm has yielded highly interpretable results when applied to membership nets such as the one studied in this chapter, and also when applied to networks of social relations (see Breiger et al., 1975).

9. Mace (1971: 90) quotes this observation of a company official: "You want to communicate to the various publics that if any company is good enough to attract the president of a large New York bank as a director, it just *has* to be a great company."

LITERATURE CITED

Alba, Richard D. "A Graph-Theoretical Definition of a Sociometric Clique." *Journal of Mathematical Sociology* 3 (1973): 113–26.

Bonacich, Phillip. "Techniques for Analyzing Overlapping Memberships." In Herbert L. Costner (ed.), *Sociology Methodology*, pp. 176–85. San Francisco: Jossey-Bass, 1972.

Breiger, Ronald L., Scott A. Boorman, and Phipps Arabie. "An Algorithm for Clustering Relational Data with Applications to Social Network Analysis and Comparison with Multidimensional Scaling." *Journal of Mathematical Psychology* 12 (1975): 328–83.

Coleman, James S. *The Adolescent Society: The Social Life of the Teenager and Its Impact on Education.* New York: Free Press, 1961.

Cooley, Charles Horton. *Human Nature and the Social Order.* New York: Schocken Books, [1902] 1964.

Davis, Allison, Burleigh B. Gardner, and Mary R. Gardner. *Deep South: A Social Anthropological Study of Caste and Class.* Chicago: University of Chicago Press, 1941.

Glanzer, M., and R. Glaser. "Techniques for the Study of Group Structure and Behavior: I. Analysis of Structure." *Psychological Bulletin* 56 (1959): 317–32.

Goffman, Erving. *Relations in Public: Microstudies of the Public Order.* New York: Harper and Row, 1971.

Harary, Frank, Robert Z. Norman, and Dorwin Cartwright. *Structural Models: An Introduction to the Theory of Directed Graphs.* New York: Wiley, 1965.

Homans, George C. *The Human Group.* New York: Harcourt, Brace and World, 1950.

Kadushin, Charles. "The Friends and Supporters of Psychotherapy: On Social Circles in Urban Life." *American Sociological Review* 31 (1966): 786–802.

Levine, Donald N. "The Structure of Simmel's Social Thought." In Kurt H. Wolff (ed.), *Essays on Sociology, Philosophy and Aesthetics by Georg Simmel et al.*, pp.9–32. New York: Harper and Row, [1959], 1965.

Levine, Joel. H. "The Sphere of Influence." *American Sociological Review* 37 (1972): 14–27.

Lieberson, Stanley. "An Empirical Study of Military-Industrial Linkages." *American Journal of Sociology* 76 (1971): 562–84.

Mace, Myles L. *Directors: Myth and Reality*. Cambridge: Harvard Business School, 1971.

Nadel, S. F. *The Theory of Social Structure*. London: Cohen and West, 1957.

Perrucci, Robert, and Mark Pilisuk. "Leaders and Ruling Elites: The Interorganizational Bases of Community Power." *American Sociological Review* 35 (1970): 1040–57.

Simmel, Georg. *Conflict and the Web of Group-Affiliations*. Glencoe, Ill.: Free Press, 1955.

Sorokin, Pitirim A. *Society, Culture and Personality: Their Structure and Dynamics*. New York: Cooper Square Publishers, [1947] 1962.

White, Harrison C. "A Calculus of Social Networks." Harvard University, Department of Sociology unpublished working paper, Cambridge, Mass., 1971.

White, Harrison C., and Ronald L. Breiger. "Pattern Across Networks." *Society* 12 (1975): 68–73.

White, Harrison C., Scott A. Boorman, and Ronald L. Breiger. "Social Structure from Multiple Networks: I. Block Models of Roles and Positions." *American Journal of Sociology* 81 (1976): 730–80.

Wolff, Kurt H. (ed.). *Essays on Sociology, Philosophy and Aesthetics by Georg Simmel et al.* New York: Harper and Row, [1959] 1965.

5

The relational basis of attitudes

Bonnie H. Erickson

Background: Attributes and attitudes

Most social science studies explain individual attitudes in terms of individual attributes. For example, numerous election studies relate attitudes such as efficacy or party preference to variables such as income or sex. Typically, attributes explain only a small proportion of the differences in attitudes among people. The amount explained varies by time and place, and so does the identity of the more powerful predictor attributes. It is difficult to blame such problems on a poor choice of predictor attributes since the search for good ones has been conducted at length by highly competent people. It is equally difficult to blame methodology, per se, since studies of this type use some of the most sophisticated tools available. I suggest that the reason for these results is that the basic question has been posed in the wrong way:

(a) natural units of analysis for attitudes are *not* isolated individuals but social networks
and

(b) viable subjects for explanation are not individual attitudes, but degrees of attitude agreement among individuals in given structural situations.

People do not form attitudes in direct response to their attributes. Attitudes are made, maintained, or modified primarily through interpersonal processes.[1] Since these processes have little effect among strangers, they occur largely within the boundaries of social networks.[2]

For example, students interact far more with people on their own campuses than with others. Therefore, student attitudes are often generated almost independently on each campus. Whenever these networks are well

In writing this chapter, I had invaluable help from the Structural Analysis Programme, University of Toronto, and from several contributors to this volume. S. D. Berkowitz contributed useful editing of the final version. I am especially grateful for sustained help from Terry Nosanchuk and Barry Wellman.

bounded, that is, whenever there are few relevant ties extending beyond the network in question, both theory and research are greatly simplified. There are many substantively important examples of well-bounded networks, such as scientific communities (Breiger, 1976), some elites (Moore, 1979), and some subcultures (Fine and Kleiman, 1979).

Within a network, the effects of interpersonal *processes* depend both on the features of interpersonal relationships and on where these relationships fit into the structure of the network as a whole. For example, the closer two friends are to one another, the more likely they are to agree on intimate matters. In addition, if they belong to a tightly knit group, such as a fraternity, their attitudes are more likely to agree than if they do not (Wallace, 1966). The central concern in this chapter is how interpersonal processes are modified by structural location. The discussion opens with some observations on individual relationships, since this is a simple topic and will serve to develop some essential ideas.

Some theorists assume that the effect of a given type of tie is the same whatever its location within a network. Hence, a network's structure is important only as a map showing how individual ties and their effects fit together (Abelson, 1979; Doreian, 1979). Suppose, for example, that three people are all close friends. These researchers would expect all three to develop similar attitudes because the first would influence the second, who, in turn, would influence the third. By contrast, I argue that the chances of agreement are further increased by the fact that these three people form a small group.

More generally, I argue that interpersonal processes vary with the kind of larger structural unit within which individual ties are embedded. To identify potentially important kinds of structural units, I draw on three different families of models of network structure: clique, structural equivalence, and spatial models.

Network analysts often use these models to describe network structures, but they seldom employ them in predicting structural effects. Here I will develop predictions about attitudes by considering how social relationships and larger structural units affect the operation of one especially well researched interpersonal process, social comparison. Social comparison affects the degree to which people agree with each other, not *what* they will agree on. For example, our hypothetical group of three good friends might be three scientists who come to agree on research ethics and priorities, or three students who agree that sports are more fun than studies, or three other students who agree that studies are more interesting than sports. Each group can have equally homogeneous attitudes while agreeing on quite different topics, because each group began with a different mix of concerns and opinions. Such mixes are historically specific and, thus, we cannot hope to predict them. We can, however, understand them retrospectively if we have enough historical detail and analytic skill (as in Lipset, Trow and Coleman, 1956). Thus, I do not attempt to predict who will hold which attitudes. I attempt to predict only the extent of attitude agreement among people in different kinds of relationships and different kinds of structural locations.

Social comparison theory

When a new piece of work appears in my field I first develop a number of views on it by myself. But often there are points about which I am not sure, and I clarify my thinking by discussing such matters with close colleagues interested in the subject. As we continue to exchange views, we come to agree, and this support reassures us that we have taken the right positions. Processes like these, which are a familiar part of life for all of us, are what social comparison theory is all about. People feel uncomfortable when they are not sure that their attitudes are correct, especially if the attitudes are important in a particular context. Since there are no objective standards for attitudes, people can judge their own correctness only by comparison with the attitudes of others.

In general, people prefer to compare themselves with others who are similar in salient respects. Similar others are expected to have similar attitudes, and this expectation increases comparitors' confidence in others' views. Similar others also provide the most relevant information, since they are the people with whom comparitors feel that they ought to agree. Beyond this, comparison with similar others usually leads to agreement on stable attitudes. If people agree initially, comparison reinforces their views. If they disagree moderately, comparison increases their uncertainties and the resulting discomfort motivates them to reach agreement (Festinger, 1954). However, disagreement with similar others may not change a person's attitude if the disagreement is so extreme that the others are redefined as dissimilar, or if the person can obtain support for the initial attitude through comparison with even a few suitable others who do agree (Allen and Wilder, 1977).

Dissimilar others are not very useful in making comparisons. If they disagree, it can be attributed to their dissimilarities, rather than any incorrectness in comparitors' views. If they agree, comparitors will, if anything, be shaken by finding themselves in the wrong company. Comparisons with dissimilar others are, thus, not often desired nor consequential in attitude formation: although *dis*agreement with very *dis*similar others may reinforce the comparitors' confidence in their correctness (Goethals and Darley, 1977).

These basic arguments of social comparison theory are powerful, true, and incomplete: powerful in their implications, true in that each rests on a rich experimental literature, and incomplete in that they ignore broader features of long-term relationships. Except for Festinger's (1954) pioneering work, analysts have almost exclusively restricted themselves to laboratory subjects who do not know each other.[3] Consequently, they have paid attention to just one aspect of the dyads (or two people plus the relationship between them). Much work has dealt with the ways in which social comparisons vary with two people's attributes, but almost none has considered how comparisons vary with the types of relationships involved. Yet, this point is clearly important outside of laboratory settings. For example, earlier we noted that one tends to discuss doubtful points with *close* colleagues interested in a subject. Thus, the chance that someone will compare and come to agree with a person obviously depends on the nature of their relationship as well as similarity in their attributes, per se.

Dyads and attitude similarity

Frequency

The more frequently members of a dyad interact, the more opportunity they will have to learn to interpret each other's attitudes accurately. Thus, if social comparison takes place and one or both parties adjust their attitudes to agree with the perceived attitudes of the other, the more similar their actual attitudes will become. Further, if people believe frequency improves their ability to interpret others' beliefs accurately, they will find social comparison with more frequent interactants preferable. One's confidence in one's own opinion is not increased by the perception that a little-known other may, perhaps, agree. For instance, when freshmen first arrived at a small midwestern American campus, they rated grades as more important, and they aspired to go to graduate school less often than more advanced students. New students changed their orientation to grades more if the student contact included a larger proportion of more advanced students of the same sex, but their graduate school aspirations increased more if they met a larger proportion of more advanced male students planning to do graduate work. In both instances, freshmen's attitudes changed in response to some set of people they met. Influence did not come from strangers: Some nonzero frequency level is required. We further see that attributes such as sex play a part, but a variable one, among the particular nonstrangers used for comparison.

Multiplexity

People prefer to compare themselves with others who are similar in salient respects. Although the current experimental literature emphasizes similarity of personal attributes, similarity can also consist of sharing the type of relationship relevant to a given kind of attitude. For instance, one discusses local traffic patterns with neighbors, but academic matters with colleagues. The more different kinds of relationships a dyad includes – or, as we say, the more *multiplex* it is – the more relevant it is to different kinds of attitudes, and, hence, the more widely the dyad members agree. Thus, within more multiplex parts of the networks in a South African Coloured community, discussion was most wide-ranging, and behavioral norms (which sum up many specific attitudes) were fixed. Further, during a norm-related crisis, people were most responsive to pressures from others with whom they were multiply-tied (Wheeldon, 1969).

Strength

Strong ties lead to agreement between dyad members. For example, Kandel (1978) found that, once high school students became best friends, they developed increased agreement about marijuana use. This trend suggests that a strong shared tie may be a form of widely salient similarity that leads to frequent comparison and agreement. Conversely, a negative tie may be a form of salient *dissimilarity*, which either prevents social comparison or induces comparison that leads to disagreement. The effect of different degrees of positive feeling is hard to establish because very few studies have been done on weak as well as strong positive ties. Among the college students described above, grade orientations of freshmen changed in response to the orientations of upper-year acquaintances of the same-sex. The degree of change depended on the degree of liking if the acquaintances were rarely seen, but strength of feeling did not seem to matter if acquaintances were seen often (Wallace, 1966).

Asymmetry

A friendship may be much more important to one friend than to the other. A boss may give orders to an employee who gives no orders in return. In general, relationships may be asymmetric. I argue that asymmetry affects social comparison in different ways, depending upon the type of relationship involved and also the place of the relationship in a larger structure. First, asymmetry may have no effect on ties within a densely knit group of peers. In these settings asymmetry is both rare and short-lived, so there is little opportunity for distinctive patterns of social comparison to develop (Newcomb, 1961; Hallinan, 1978). Second, asymmetry may affect social comparison when the overall relationship between two groups is asymmetric. For example, management gives orders to labor, and less famous scientists know the work of more famous scientists, but not vice versa. Such asymmetries are likely to be both stable and consequential because they are rooted in and reinforce an inequality in resources.[4]

These effects may also vary by the degree to which the link is authority based, as in a workplace, rather than voluntary, as in a streetcorner gang (Homans, 1950). On the one hand, authority relationships are highly salient forms of dissimilarity, so that social comparison does not take place between groups, and these groups may disagree. The attitudes of subordinates are especially likely to differ from those of superiors when the subordinates are densely interrelated and can easily make social comparisons with one another (Marx, 1963). On the other hand, suppose that the asymmetric tie is essentially one of esteem and not authority, as in scientific specialties (Breiger, 1976). The subordinate group might well take the superior as a reference group, or as a group with such prestige that it gives a nearly objective validity to attitudes. In this case, asymmetrically linked cliques would tend to be similar in attitudes, although less similar than symmetrically linked ones because only one dyad member would try to adjust attitude discrepancies. If asymmetry can increase both agreement and disagreement, in the aggregate asymmetric pairs may not differ from symmetric ones. Thus, reciprocated friendships showed little if any greater agreement than unreciprocated ones in a recent urban sample (Laumann, 1973).

There are limits to structural effects and resulting exceptions to the generalizations we may wish to make about them. These discrepancies, however, are often comprehensible within the social comparison framework. People who are entirely certain of their attitudes, for instance, have no motive for social comparisons (Mettee and Smith, 1977). Hence, they may simply not try to make them. Beyond this, comparison may lag behind changes in the structure of relations because people cannot immediately learn and respond to all the attitudes of new contacts. Comparison may also extend beyond the network under investigation, whose boundaries will never be quite perfect. Thus, Newcomb (1943) found that Bennington College students with strong ties to their parents were less likely to change their political views to agree with the more generally liberal opinions of other Bennington students.

Within a network, members may choose comparitors on nonrelational grounds. For example, people prefer comparitors with attitudes generally similar to their own, even when told that the generally agreeing others disagree on the specific attitude to be compared (Castore and DeNinno, 1977). Of special interest here is similarity of personal attributes. If similarity with respect to an attribute facilitates social comparison, as the experimental literature repeatedly shows, then people alike on the attribute will tend to be alike on the compared attitude. Hence attributes and attitudes will be correlated. However, these correlations within a network are likely to be muted because persons of similar salient attributes may not be available. In addition, because the definition of saliency is social and varies from one network to another, attribute–attitude correlations will be weaker and more variable when aggregated over multiple networks. Thus, although attributes do play a part in attitude similarity, their role is limited and structurally constrained.

Network structure and attitude similarity

Beyond dyads

Large complex networks can be divided into subunits, or sets of people sharing similar positions within them. We can then predict the degree of attitude agreement for subunits, not just for dyads. At the very least, this approach provides a useful summary of the overall pattern of agreement. But even more important, this approach is theoretically essential if social comparison is affected by structural location as well as by characteristics of dyads. We have already seen one possible illustration of subunit effects in the discussion of asymmetry; asymmetric relationships, I maintained, will have different effects, depending on their place within a larger structure. The incoming college students provide others: Their attitudes were strongly influenced by membership in dense groups.[5]

One important purpose of this chapter is to describe network models that identify different kinds of subunits and to suggest how these subunits affect social comparison and hence levels of attitude similarity within subunits. Were it not for this concern with large complex networks, the previous discussion of dyads would be incomplete. Up to this point, we have described the effects of relationships on attitude agreement, not the converse. Social comparison theory itself predicts effects of both kinds. For example: People who agree provide each other with suitable and reassuring comparisons and hence are attracted (Newcomb, 1961; Kandel, 1978). Eventually we may be able to develop dynamic theories incorporating effects over time in both directions.[6] At present, we can afford to simplify our theoretical task by ignoring the effects of attitude similarity with regard to relationships. Such effects are most important when people can freely choose alters from a number of eligible others (e.g., those who are not too different from ego on salient attributes), and even in classrooms, which best exemplify this condition, relationships affect attitude similarity at least as much as the reverse (Kandel, 1978). More important, the choice of alters is not usually free. Relationships are largely constrained by impersonally determined opportunities to interact (Feld, 1981), such as those that arise in school systems in which peers are put in the classroom in the first place. Whenever we consider large complex networks – and not just small dense pockets of peers within – we can profitably assume that the overall structure of relationships is a given within which social psychological processes operate.

Clique models

Currently, there are three well-developed families of models of overall network structure. Each emphasizes a distinctive aspect of structure, and each includes a number of models that differ in detail. The first are clique models.[7] All clique models stress the identification of sets of people more densely tied to one another than to other people in their network, where density is the proportion of all possible ties that actually exist. Clique models can be thought of as ways of looking for the small groups in large networks. There are two major types of clique model, each having one clear-cut extreme version and a variety of modified ones. I first discuss these models in forms that use only the most simple kind of information about relationships, whether they exist or not.

By one extreme definition, a clique is a maximal set of density 1.0. Density 1.0 means all possible ties are present (everyone knows everyone else) and a maximal set is the largest possible one fitting the rest of the definition (here, if we have a maximal clique with N people in it, we cannot add anyone else without bringing density below 1.0). Empirically, a search for such perfectly dense cliques almost always produces a large number of very small cliques, including some sets of cliques that overlap so extensively that it is unreasonable to consider them separate entities.

Thus, although this extreme definition is clear and has some attractive technical features, it usually leads to results that analysts object to on substantive grounds. As a result, researchers usually employ one of two more flexible criteria. They may define a clique as either (1) a maximal set of persons with some minimal level of density or (2) a maximal set in which each member is linked to all but K of the others (Burt, 1980a). The smaller the K, or the higher the minimal level of density, the more the cliques will be dense, small, and numerous. Under such criteria, a given network may have levels of cliquing, depending on the strictness of the criteria used; and even at a single level, cliques may vary in density. Although some analysts see such variations as undesirable ambiguities, we can profitably analyze them as legitimate aspects of complex network structures.

By another extreme definition, a clique is a maximal set of people who can all reach each other directly or indirectly via others in the network. Although such a definition is sometimes useful (e.g., Laumann and Marsden, 1979), it is often too inclusive in that the resulting cliques may be very large, very low in density, and very clearly subdivided into groups with sparse interconnections. Thus, this approach also is usually modified, for example, by requiring that each clique member be able to reach each other via no more than n intermediaries within the clique itself (Alba, 1973). Again the modification can be more or less strict and cliques can vary in density.

Moore's (1979) analysis of an elite network in the United States illustrates some of the problems connected with extreme clique definitions and with efforts to modify them. The 941 network members had 442 completely connected groups of three or more people. Most of these groups were not very distinct. Merging the cliques that differed by only one person reduced the number of cliques dramatically to 46. On the other hand, 876 of the 941 members were connected by direct or indirect paths, so the alternative approach yielded one huge clique – with a density of 0.7%! Some modified strategy obviously was desirable. Moore began with fully dense groups; then she merged groups differing by one person; then merged groups if at least two-thirds of the members of a smaller group were included in a larger one. Each of these steps is plausible, but each is based on a somewhat different criterion, and the resulting 32 cliques varied greatly in density (0.038–1.0).

In general, many modifications are possible, and they can vary from study to study or even within a single analysis, so that results are difficult to compare. The analyst's choice of details should stem from theoretical goals. For example, Moore (1979) justifies her procedure by focusing on elite integration. In practice, however, analysts also use intuitive criteria with ambiguous theoretical implications.

In the U.S. elite study, respondents reported people with whom they had discussed the issue of most concern to them. The rest of the analysis was based on this simple measure of a tie: People had discussed an issue, or not. Neither the data collection nor the model dealt with possible variations in the strength of ties. This approach is understandable and widely used because it makes data collection and data collection and analysis much easier. However, we saw earlier that the strength of a relationship may make a difference to social comparison.

It is therefore important to note that some clique models use detailed variations in relational strength and that one can easily develop hypotheses for such models by recasting the same ideas discussed above. For example, one hierarchical clustering procedure begins with the strongest level of tie present and finds nonoverlapping cliques of people such that all clique members are tied to each other at that maximal level (Johnson, 1967). Then one moves to a somewhat weaker level and merges cliques or individuals from the first step if all the people involved are tied at or above the new level of strength. The process continues to the weakest level of strength. At each level, the cliques are fully dense in terms of the ties defined as present if and only if they exceed that level. This procedure parallels one extreme clique definition above, and the single-linkage procedure (Johnson, 1967) parallels the other. Hierarchical clustering is nonparallel in ruling out clique overlaps, although other procedures for nonbinary tie data allow them (Bailey, 1975).

Thus, we are left with the same crucial decisions, however detailed our measures of tie strength. We will need some compromise definition of cliques. Which is most appropriate? We can divide the network more or less strictly into more or fewer cliques of varying density. How can we incorporate these variations theoretically? In the next section, I propose some answers for the case of attitude similarity. For other purposes, other decisions might be more appropriate.

Implications for attitude similarity

The structural features emphasized by various clique models have different degrees of relevance for different processes. Defining cliques as sets of people all mutually reachable by, at most, n intermediaries is most relevant for processes that operate through intermediaries, such as the diffusion of clear-cut and widely salient information (Erickson, Nosanchuk, Mostacci, and Dalrymple, 1978). Social comparison does not operate at removes: People compare most often and most consequentially with those to whom they are directly connected. Thus, the relevant clique definitions stress density rather than reachability.

A densely knit clique will include many of a person's ties – indeed, probably many of his or her stronger ties and thus many of his or her preferred social comparitors. Moreover, the fact that density implies multiple redundant channels of communication increases the accuracy with which clique members perceive each other's attitudes. Redundant communication also increases the chances that attitude disagreements will become manifest and hence is more likely to be a source of uncomfortable comparisons. Denser cliques are more often recognizable as units by their members and may therefore be more attractive; this situation enhances the social comparison pressures toward uniformity. Density and attractiveness also increase the use of persuasion and rejection in the search for greater clique unanimity (Schachter, 1951; Festinger, 1954; Cartwright, 1968). These are often called aspects of conformity pressures, but the latter are indistinguishable from social comparison (Allen and Wilder, 1977). Thus, clique members have more attitude similarity than a random set of network members, and the greater the density, the greater the extent of this similarity (Festinger, Schachter, and Back, 1950; Homans, 1950). If relationships are measured by their presence or absence, a clique model includes levels from many very dense cliques to fewer less dense cliques. As already noted, the denser cliques should have greater attitude similarity. If strength of relationships is measured in degrees, the levels vary from many cliques knit internally by strong ties to fewer cliques knit by weaker ties. Attitude similarity should, on the whole, be greater for cliques with stronger ties, especially when the attitudes concern important topics for which comparison is limited to intimates.

Table 5.1. *A hypothetical sociomatrix*

	A	B	C	D	E	F
A	0	0	2	0	1	3
B	0	0	2	0	1	3
C	1	3	0	0	0	2
D	4	8	1	0	0	6
E	1	0	0	3	0	2
F	0	0	2	1	4	0

Some theoretical problems

Cliques including more multiplex ties should generate consensus on a wider range of attitudes. However, it is not clear how this prediction can be tested, given that clique models use just one kind of tie at a time. Every strategy raises some kind of theoretical difficulty.[8] Earlier, I argued that consistently asymmetric ties between cliques are related to attitude similarity between cliques. However, consistent patterns of external relationships are not part of clique models and may never be identified by them. Clique members can maintain attitudes different from the clique majority if even a few suitable comparison others support their views (Newcomb, 1943, 1947; Festinger, Schachter, and Back, 1950; Lipset, Trow, and Coleman, 1956: 167–80). However, clique models are not designed to distinguish clique members having different types of external relationships. Clique models do an excellent job of finding the small groups in large networks, and perhaps this is the only aspect of network structure that has systematic importance for attitude similarity. Small groups are clearly important sites of social comparison. Although comparison outside such groups clearly occurs, it may take place in terms of individual attributes. On the other hand, comparison outside and even within cliques may be affected by the wider structural context.

Models of structural equivalence

In a clique analysis, the important question about two people is whether they belong to the same relatively dense subgroup. In a structural equivalence analysis, the question is, to what extent do these people occupy similar places in the network as a whole? That is, to what extent are they tied to the same people by the same kinds of relationships? [9] For example, in the hypothetical network of Table 5.1, actors A and B are perfectly equivalent. Like A and B, people can have equivalent places in a network without having ties to each other. Actor D in Table 5.1 has ties that are a function of C's, $2(x + 1)$; the two sets of ties are identical in pattern but different in level and spread. Some measures of equivalence ignore scale differences; some do not.[10]

Table 5.2. *Four hypothetical blocks*

	a	b	c	d	e	f	g	h	i	j	k	l	m
Block 1													
a	o	o	o	o	o	o	1	o	o	1	1	o	o
b	o	o	o	o	o	o	1	o	o	1	1	o	o
c	o	o	o	o	o	o	1	o	o	1	1	o	o
Block 2													
d	o	o	o	o	1	1	o	1	o	1	o	1	1
e	o	o	o	1	o	1	o	1	o	1	o	1	1
f	o	o	o	1	1	o	o	1	o	1	o	1	1
Block 3													
g	o	o	o	1	1	1	o	1	1	1	1	1	1
h	o	o	o	1	1	1	1	o	1	1	1	1	1
i	o	o	o	1	1	1	1	1	o	1	1	1	1
j	o	o	o	1	1	1	1	1	1	o	1	1	1
Block 4													
k	1	1	1	o	o	o	1	1	1	1	o	1	1
l	1	1	1	o	o	o	1	1	1	1	1	o	1
m	1	1	1	o	o	o	1	1	1	1	1	1	o

Some procedures go on to find sets of structurally equivalent actors called blocks (White, Boorman, and Breiger, 1976). For example, one could apply the hierarchical clustering described above (Johnson, 1967) or variations on factor analysis (Schwartz, 1977) to the structural similarities among actors. Again such procedures give levels of results, from many blocks of highly equivalent people to a few blocks of people whose ties are only roughly similar. Blocks differ from cliques in two crucial ways: Block members must have similar patterns of ties, and they need not have any ties to each other. Consider the four hypothetical blocks in Table 5.2, all (for simplicity) composed of perfectly equivalent members. Block 2 is a clique with perfect internal density, but block 1 has no internal ties at all. Blocks 3 and 4 would be one perfectly dense clique in a clique analysis, but in structural equivalence terms they are distinct because of their very different ties to the actors in blocks 1 and 2.[11]

Implications for attitude similarity

Structurally equivalent people tend to have similar attitudes because they "tend to interact with the same types of actors in the same way" (Burt, 1978: 199). In present terms, they have approximately similar sets of available social comparitors. They are likely to agree with these comparitors, and hence to agree with each other, because they agree with the same or similar third parties. Note that such attitudinal agreement does not depend on direct ties nor on direct social comparison between the structurally equivalent people themselves.

Measures sensitive to level and spread differences are suitable for some kinds of problems. For example, suppose that the hypothetical ties in Table 5.1 are frequencies of interaction and the dependent variable of interest is similarity of information level. C and D obtain their information from the same sources in the same proportions, but D is likely to obtain considerably more, so their information levels will not be as similar as they would be if the two sets of ties were alike in level and spread as well as pattern. Measures sensitive to pattern, but insensitive to level and spread, are more suitable for studying social comparison. Social comparison takes place in terms of relative, not absolute strength of ties. C's ties appear weaker than D's in Table 5.1, but this is of no consequence for C, who engages in social comparison only in his or her own dyads. Since C is exposed to the same pattern of influences as D, C is likely to hold views very like D's. Note that ties weak in absolute terms can produce very strong attitude changes if these weak ties are the strongest that a person has, as in religious recruitment of social isolates through a few new ties to members of the religious group (Stark and Bainbridge, 1980).

The second theoretically important decision is whether to find blocks of equivalent actors and develop block hypotheses. Although this has usually been done, Burt and Doreian (1982) take a different view for attitudes: They predict that attitude similarity is a function of structural equivalence, so that dyadic analysis suffices, and blocks need not be found at all. This approach is correct for any processes that operate in a fully uniform manner for a given level of equivalence. Although such processes may exist, they do not include social comparison.

Minimally, social comparison processes will lead to different levels of attitude similarity for blocks of equally equivalent actors, but different levels of internal density. Consider the example in Table 5.2. Blocks 1 and 2 both consist of perfectly equivalent actors. Block 1 will have internal similarity of attitudes, because a, b, and c all are limited to social comparison with g, j, or k. Block 2 will also have internal similarity because d, e, and f share the same set of available social comparitors. But the internal similarity will be higher for block 2 than for block 1 because block 2 members are densely tied to each other and thus compare directly to each other socially, for reasons similar to those argued for cliques. Comparison within the block is an added source of similarity on its own account; it may also lead to greater similarity in response to external ties as well, since block members can generate a consensus concerning the most suitable comparison others among outsiders. Without direct intrablock ties (as in block 1) block members have similar sets of potential comparitors but may choose from this set quite differently in response to relational factors such as attribute similarity or overall attitude agreement.

Thus, the combination of social comparison theory and structural equivalence models leads us to two basic predictions. The greater the structural equivalence within a block, the more similar the attitudes; and the greater the internal density of ties between block members, the more similar the attitudes. However, the importance of density should not blind us to the consequential differences between block and clique predictions. Two differences are clear enough to be the basis of critical tests. First, a zero-density block should have more attitude similarity than a random selection of network members, whereas clique analysis would not consider such a set of persons to be a unit at all. It is interesting to note that students who do not appear to have been a clique, but rather to have shared marginality in a student network, may have similarly conservative attitudes (Newcomb, 1943). Second, a clique with high density may be split into different blocks because of differing external ties see blocks 3 and 4, Table 5.2. The more attitudinal difference between these blocks, the more support for the structural-equivalence approach. The possible importance of external ties is suggested by the early clique-oriented analyses cited above that often found attitudinal deviance to be related to external sources of support for the deviant opinion.

We must also consider whether attitude similarity within blocks is related to the level of the blocking. If blocks of more highly equivalent people are more similar in attitudes, then agreement is greatest within blocks at finer-grained levels with more, smaller, more equivalent blocks. This may hold especially for those attitudes on which people compare most widely so that they tend to agree with any others who have the same set of contacts. For topics on which people limit comparison to strong ties, the block model analysis should be based on strong ties, but the prediction would otherwise be the same: Greater equivalence gives greater similarity.

Recall that systematic asymmetry between two sets of people may lead to greater agreement between them (if the link is esteem) or greater disagreement (if the link is authority). Consistent asymmetry is readily detected by block analysis. In Table 5.2, for example, the links from block 4 to block 1 are almost unreciprocated, in contrast to the fully symmetric ties between blocks 3 and 4. One can also readily see whether block members have more or less multiplex ties, and hence agreement on a wider or narrower range of attitudes. Structural equivalence can be measured over several kinds of relationship at once, so that block members have similar patterns of ties for each kind of tie.[12] One would expect wider agreement if block members were tied in more ways to the same other blocks, and especially wide and consistent agreement if they were tied in many ways to each other.

Some theoretical problems

Structural equivalence models give us effective summaries of the overall pattern of ties in a network in the form of ties within and between blocks. They have already been used for important forms of structure that other models cannot reliably detect, such as structures with a dense core of elite actors and an internally unconnected periphery asymmetrically dependent on the core (Breiger, 1976; Snyder and Kick, 1979). But we have no idea how overall network structure may be related to attitude similarity. Social comparison theory gives no guidance for topics of this complexity, there is virtually no empirical evidence, and we do not yet know which kinds of structure are common enough to be worth serious theoretical speculation. It is possible, of course, that overall network structure is too remote from the experience of network members to have any emergent effect on their comparisons, that is, any effect beyond interpersonal and interblock ties taken a few at a time, as above. But given the pervasive importance of overall structure in sociological theory, its possible emergent effect should be investigated.

Spatial models

A spatial model assumes that members of a network are arranged in a social space such that spatial closeness corresponds to closeness of relationship. Such a model estimates that underlying space from measures of pairwise strength of relationship. The resulting map of social structure has great practical advantages: ready visibility, intuitive appeal, and realistically weak assumptions about the accuracy of relational data. Most data on interpersonal ties come from respondent reports, and respondents are often not fully aware of the exact strength of their ties. For example, one apparently objective and straightforward aspect of a tie is the frequency of communication. In one study of four different kinds of groups, there was only a weak relationship between the real frequency (recorded by trained observers or automatic devices) and the frequency reported by respondents (Bernard and Killworth, 1977). In addition, some data collection procedures are crude, for example, when respondents are asked to list a few of their closest ties in rank order.

In the light of such measurement problems, most current methods require only a monotonic relationship between pair distances in space and pair relational strength as recorded. That is, if the pair (a, b) is more strongly related than the pair (c, d), then a should be closer in space to b than c is to d, although their distances need not be in exactly the same proportion as their measures.

Table 5.3. *A hypothetical space*

Pairs	Distances	Hypothetical social distances		
		Consistent with space		Inconsistent
AC	2.83	1	1	2.8
CD	3.00	2	13	3.0
BC	4.47	3	62	1.0
AD	5.39	4	1000	5.4
AB	6.00	5	2000	6.0
BD	6.40	6	2001	6.4

For example, Table 5.3 shows points *A*, *B*, *C*, and *D* in a two-dimensional space. The distances between pairs of points are monotonically related to both of the first two hypothetical sets of social distance data, even though in one case the pair *CD* is twice as socially distant as the pair *AC*, whereas in the other case it is 13 times as socially distant. Thus, the space is a perfect representation of either data set, if we believe that detailed degrees of strength measurement cannot be taken too seriously. The third set of hypothetical data is partly inconsistent with the spatial model shown because the pair *BC* is the closest pair instead of the third closest, as in the space. If you try to arrange the points on paper so that interpoint distances are in the same order as pair social distances, you will find that there is no way to do so. For example, if we move *B* nearer to *C* to *B'*, we get a *B'C* distance smaller than any other, but then *B'A* is also smaller than *AD*, whereas in social distance *AB* is larger than *AD*. We can always find a space to fit any data if we add enough dimensions, but, if we have more than 2 or 3, we lose the simplicity and visibility that are a large part of a spatial model's appeal.

To find a spatial model of some social-distance data, the analyst chooses a space of given dimension and arranges people in it, often randomly to start with. Spatial pair distances are compared to the strength measures, the degree of departure from the ideal monotonic relationship is computed, and positions are shifted so as to improve the fit. After a number of iterations, one usually one usually obtain a good fit in two or three dimensions. The underlying dimensions may be thought of as the factors generating the distances, and the distances may be seen as a "cleaner" version of social distance than the original observations because pair distances are found subject to so many constraints.[13]

Spatial models contain a number of simplifying theoretical assumptions that do not hold in general. *Dyadically*, they assume that relationships are symmetric (as distance is). Most sociomatrices show only rough symmetry. *Triadically*, the models assume a weak form of transitivity. Since the distance from *a* to *b* cannot be greater than the distance from *a* to *c* plus the distance from *c* to *b*, the strength of a tie between *a* and *b* should not be very weak if *c* is strongly tied to both. Again, sociomatrices tend to have transitive trends while being far from perfectly transitive (Holland and Leinhardt, 1977). More *broadly*, the models assume that the whole network is included in the same, shared, continuous space. The models are not designed to highlight discontinuities in the structure of relationships, yet these discontinuities might include either the boundaries of cliques or the more complex cleavages defining sets of structurally equivalent people.

Implications for attitude similarity

People are most likely to compare with and come to agree with others to whom they are more strongly tied. Now, the closer two people are in a spatial model, the more strongly tied they tend to be. Moreover, two persons are more likely to agree if they have similar sets of potential comparitors and again closeness in a spatial model reflects strong ties to similar others. Thus, the smaller the spatial distance between two people, the more similar their attitudes. For some topics, social comparison is confined to close ties, so attitude similarity declines rapidly as spatial distance increases and levels off while distance is still fairly small. For other topics, social comparison includes weaker ties, so attitude similarity declines more slowly as spatial distance increases and levels off at a larger distance, if at all. At the same time, a spatial model implies that some features of network structure do *not* matter: neither asymmetry, nor intransitivity, nor cliques nor cleavages. Yet these features are of some importance for attitude similarity.

Asymmetry is most interesting in networks having marked internal stratification; intransitivity occurs most often in networks having marked internal cleavages (such as different interaction sites) that segregate some actors and hence interrupt the processes usually resulting in transitivity; cliques and blocks are of most interest when their boundaries are well defined, as they often are in large complex structures. These considerations suggest that spatial models are most suitable for networks without such features, that is, networks with high connectivity and a fairly diffuse pattern of ties, so that there is little structure to represent other than gradual shadings of relational closeness.

The networks most suitable for spatial models may usually be just parts of a complex network. It is perhaps suggestive that one productive use of spatial modeling is based on a small set of highly connected community leaders who may well form a structural subunit within the community as a whole (Laumann and Pappi, 1976). Applications in other disciplines often begin by using clustering to find domains of related objects and then apply spatial models within those domains (Burton, 1972). Spatial models of an entire complex network will not predict attitude similarity well unless structural features like asymmetry have no important consequences for social comparison.

Some theoretical problems

In general, a spatial model requires a number of assumptions and decisions on points as yet incompletely explored. The relative position of a pair of actors in space depends both on the strength of their direct tie to each other and on the similarity of strengths of their ties to third parties. These direct and indirect connections are combined in one particular way by the modeling procedure, although there are no clear theoretical reasons for thinking that this is the best way. Ties, often not symmetric as required, must be made so; again, it is not clear how this should be done. Most programs include some mechanical method such as averaging i's tie to j with j's tie to i, or taking the larger or the smaller of the two values. Any choice represents both a methodological and theoretical decision whose grounds are uncertain. For example, averaging assumes either that measurement error of basically symmetric ties is random or that asymmetric ties lead to social comparison of intermediate impact (perhaps because one person in the dyad considers it a more suitable forum for comparison than the other does), or both. A plausible case could be made for any choice. To complicate matters further, all the mechanical methods may be wrong because of the varying effects of asymmetry.

Conclusions

The three models of network structure have suggested three contrasting sets of predictions for the distribution of attitude similarity in a network. Perhaps the internal density, multiple communication channels, attractiveness, and other aspects of cliques make them attitudinal pressure cookers of much greater consequence than ties between cliques. If so, a clique model will best predict attitude similarity. Perhaps it is essential to consider the whole overall pattern of ties: external as well as internal, asymmetric as well as symmetric, multiplex as well as uniplex. If so, attitude similarity will be found within blocks of structurally equivalent people even if these blocks are not cliques, although the similarity will be still greater if internal density of ties is greater. Blocks internally multiplex will show similarity over a wide range of attitudes, and asymmetrically related blocks will be similar or dissimilar depending on whether the asymmetry is one of esteem or of command. Perhaps none of the structural features so far mentioned is very consequential, and all that really matters is gradual variations in pairwise strength of relationships; if so, attitude similarity will be a function of closeness in a spatial model.

Clearly, a comparison of the three sets of predictions would yield important information about both structure and process. On the structural side, we would learn what aspects of network structure matter most for attitudes. For other topics, of course, a different set of structural features might be more important, and each of the models may have its uses for certain dependent variables or certain types of network. I have suggested that information may flow rather differently than the way in which attitudes are shaped, even given the same network, because different processes are involved. Thus, the analysis of attitude similarity is but one part of the analysis of structural effects, although it is a part of considerable importance. On the process side, by comparing the predictions of the three models, we might learn how social comparison works in real-life networks and how social comparison theory should be revised and extended to accommodate the results. The results would tell us how people are actually chosen for comparison in networks, by telling us what kinds of structural features lead to attitude similarity. This approach would address the critical, as yet rather vague, problem in current versions of social comparison theory: How do people choose among their contacts in ongoing social life, as opposed to choosing among hypothetical strangers in a laboratory?

NOTES

1. Attitudes are also subject to impersonal processes, such as mass media exposure, and intrapersonal processes, such as cognitive balance. These processes are of less importance than, and are themselves affected by, the interpersonal processes dealt with here. (See Robinson, 1976, on interpersonal ties and media exposure.)
2. It is possible for attitudes to be affected by strangers. For example, a person may infer the attitudes of strangers from their behavior. Such effects are rare enough to be neglected here.
3. See Suls and Miller (1977) for recent trends.
4. See Snyder and Kick (1979) on the world system; Breiger (1976) on a scientific specialty, or Laumann and Senter (1976) on social status.
5. Fraternities and sororities, see Wallace, 1966.
6. For preliminary work, see Coleman (1957) and Abelson (1979).
7. Here I use "clique" as an umbrella term for small groups of various kinds, in line

with usage in much of the literature. In some of the more technical modeling literature, the broad term is "cluster," and a clique is one specific type of cluster with a density of 1.0. I also discuss clique and other models entirely in terms of people and interpersonal relationships, as this application is of interest here. The same models can be applied much more generally, for example, to nations and international relationships such as trade.

8. For example, one might combine a number of observed ties by summing them; but this confounds strength of tie with multiplexity, so that cliques will tend to be multiplex by construction, a situation that is especially undesirable if one hopes to analyze the effects of varying multiplexity within cliques. A different family of strategies arises if one tries to combine results after separate clique analysis of each type of tie. Here, the main problem is how to compare cliques that may be quite different from one analysis to another.

9. There are other possible definitions of equivalence. Most notably, some scholars define equivalence as similar ties to equivalent (not the same) others. For example, children are said to be equivalent because they are all tied to parents, though not to the same parents (e.g., Sailer, 1978). This definition is not useful for the problem in this chapter, however. Note that children equivalent in this sense, but without shared contacts, have no interpersonal route by which social comparison can take effect.

10. For example, Euclidean distance (Burt, 1980a) is sensitive to scale differences, whereas a product-moment correlation (White et al., 1976) is not. Both are nonresistant.

11. See White et al. (1976) for a further comparison of blocks and cliques.

12. Take the sociomatrix for each kind of relationship, stack one on top of the other, and correlate the columns or use some other measure of association to find out how similar each pair is over all the kinds of ties. Then find blocks as usual. Experience has shown (e.g., White et al., 1976) that one can find blocks of people who are equivalent in all of several, rather different kinds of relationships.

13. For more detailed information on various models, see Shepard, Romney, and Nerlove (1972). For network applications see Laumann and Pappi (1976).

LITERATURE CITED

Abelson, Robert P. "Social Clusters and Opinion Clusters." In Paul W. Holland and Samuel Leinhardt (eds.), *Perspectives on Social Networks Research*. New York: Academic Press, 1979.

Alba, Richard D. "A Graph Theoretic Definition of a Sociometric Clique." *Journal of Mathematical Sociology* 3 (1973): 113–26.

Allen, Vernon L., and David A. Wilder. "Social Comparison, Self-evaluation, and Conformity to the Group." In Jerry M. Suls and Richard L. Miller (eds.), *Social Comparison Processes*. New York: Hemisphere, 1977.

Bailey, Kenneth D. "Cluster Analysis." In David R. Heise (ed.), *Sociological Methodology 1975*. San Francisco: Jossey-Bass, 1975.

Bernard, H. Russell, and Peter D. Killworth. "Informant Accuracy in Social Network Data II." *Human Communication Research* 4 (1977): 3–18.

Breiger, Ronald L. "Career Attributes and Network Structure: A Blockmodel Study of a Biomedical Research Specialty." *American Sociological Review* 41 (1976): 117–35.

Burt, Ronald S. "Cohesion versus Structural Equivalence as a Basis for Network Subgroups." *Sociological Methods and Research* 7 (1978): 189–212.

"Models of Network Structure." *Annual Review of Sociology* 6 (1980a): 79–141.

"Innovation as a Structural Interest: Rethinking the Impact of Network Position on Innovation Adoption." *Social Networks* 2 (1980): 327–55.

Burt, Ronald S., and Patrick Doreian. "Testing a Structural Theory of Perception: Conformity and Deviance with Respect to Journal Norms in Elite Sociological Methodology." *Quantity and Quality* 16 (1982): 109–50.

Burton, Michael, "Semantic Dimensions of Occupational Names." In A. Kimball Romney, Roger N. Shepard, and Sara Beth Nerlove (eds.), *Multidimensional Scaling: Theory and Applications in the Behavioral Sciences.* Vol. II. *Theory.* New York: Seminal Press, 1972.

Cartwright, Dorwin. "The Nature of Group Cohesiveness." In D. Cartwright and A. Zander (eds.), *Group Dynamics.* New York: Harper and Row, 1968.

Castore, Carl H., and John A. DeNinno. "Investigations in the Social Comparison of Attitudes." In Jerry M. Suls and Richard L. Miller (eds.), *Social Comparison Processes.* New York: Hemisphere, 1977.

Coleman, James S. *Community Conflict.* Glencoe, Ill.: Free Press, 1957.

Doreian, Patrick. "Structural Control Models for Group Processes." In Paul W. Holland and Samuel Leinhardt (eds.), *Perspectives on Social Networks Research.* New York: Academic Press, 1979.

Erickson, Bonnie H., T. A. Nosanchuck, Livianna Mostacci, and Christina Ford Dalrymple. "The Flow of Crisis Information as a Probe of Work Relations." *Canadian Journal of Sociology* 3 (1978): 71–87.

Feld, Scott L. "The Focused Organization of Social Ties." *American Journal of Sociology* 86 (1981): 1015–35.

Festinger, Leon. "A Theory of Social Comparison Processes." *Human Relations* 7 (1954): 117–40.

Festinger, Leon, S. Schachter, and K. Back. *Social Pressures in Informal Groups.* New York: Harper, 1950.

Fine, Gary Alan, and Sherryl Kleiman. "Rethinking Subculture: An Interactionist Analysis." *American Journal of Sociology* 85 (1979): 1–20.

Geothals, George R., and John M. Darley. "Social Comparison Theory: An Attributional Approach." In Jerry M. Suls and Richard L. Miller (eds.), *Social Comparison Processes.* New York: Hemisphere, 1977.

Hallinan, Maureen T. "The Process of Friendship Formation." *Social Networks* 1 (1978): 193–210.

Holland, Paul W., and Samuel Leinhardt. "Transitivity in Structural Models of Small Groups." In Samuel Leinhardt (ed.), *Social Networks: A Developing Paradigm.* New York: Academic Press, 1977.

Homans, George C. *The Human Group.* New York: Harcourt Brace, 1950.

Johnson, Stephen C. "Hierarchical Clustering Schemes." *Psychometrika* 32 (1967): 241–54.

Kandel, Denise B. "Homophily, Selection and Socialization in Adolescent Friendships." *American Journal of Sociology* 84 (1978): 427–36.

Laumann, Edward O. *Bonds of Pluralism: The Form and Substance of Urban Social Networks*. New York: Wiley, 1973.

Laumann, Edward O., and Peter V. Marsden. "The Analysis of Oppositional Structures in Political Elites: Identifying Collective Actors." *American Sociological Review* 44 (1979): 713–32.

Laumann, Edward O., and Franz Urban Pappi. *Networks of Collective Action*. New York: Academic Press, 1976.

Laumann, Edward O., and Richard Senter. "Subjective Social Distance, Occupational Stratification and Forms of Status and Class Consciousness." *American Journal of Sociology* 81 (1976): 1304–38.

Lipset, Seymour Martin, Martin A. Trow, and James S. Coleman. *Union Democracy*. Glencoe: Free Press, 1956.

Marx, Karl. *Eighteenth Brumaire of Louis Bonaparte*. New York: International Publishers, 1963.

Mettee, David R., and Gregory Smith. "Social Comparison and Interpersonal Attraction: The Case for Dissimilarity." In Jerry M. Suls and Richard R. Miller (eds.), *Social Comparison Processes*. New York: Hemisphere, 1977.

Moore, Gwen. "The Structure of a National Elite Network." *American Sociological Review* 44 (1979): 673–92.

Newcomb, Theodore M. *Personality and Social Change: Attitude Formation in a Student Community*. New York: Dryden, 1943.

"Attitude Development as a Function of Reference Groups." In Eleanor E. Maccoby, Theodore M. Newcomb, and Eugene L. Hartley (eds.), *Readings in Social Psychology*. New York: Holt, Rinehart, and Winston, 1947.

The Acquaintance Process. New York: Holt, Rinehart and Winston, 1961.

Robinson, John P. "Interpersonal Influence in Election Campaigns: Two-step Flow Hypotheses." *Public Opinion Quarterly* 40 (1976): 304–19.

Schachter, Stanley. "Deviance, Rejection and Communication." *Journal of Abnormal and Social Psychology* 40 (1951): 190–207.

Schwartz, Joseph. "An Examination of CONCOR and Related Methods for Blocking Sociometric Data." In David Heise (ed.), *Sociological Methodology 1977*. San Francisco: Jossey-Bass, 1977.

Shepard, Roger N., A. Kimball Romney, and Sara Beth Nerlove. *Multidimensional Scaling: Theory and Applications in the Behavioral Sciences*. New York: Academic Press, 1972.

Synder, David, and Edward L. Kick. "Structural Position in the World System and Economic Growth, 1955–1970: A Multiple-network Analysis of Transnational Interactions." *American Journal of Sociology* 84 (1979): 1096–1126.

Stark, Rodney, and William Sims Bainbridge. "Networks of Faith: Interpersonal Bonds and Recruitment to Cults and Sects." *American Journal of Sociology* 85 (1980): 1376–95.

Suls, Jerry M., and Richard L. Miller (eds.). *Social Comparison Processes*. New York: Hemisphere, 1977.

Wallace, Walter R. *Student Culture*. Chicago: Aldine, 1966.

Wheeldon, P. D. "The Operation of Voluntary Associations and Personal Networks in the Political Processes of an Inter-ethnic Community." In J. Clyde Mitchell (ed.), *Social Networks in Urban Situations*. Manchester: Manchester University Press, 1969.

White, Harrison C., Scott A. Boorman, and Ronald L. Breiger. "Social Structure from Multiple Networks. I; Blockmodels of Roles and Positions." *American Journal of Sociology* 81 (1976): 730–80.

Part II
Communities

Although most people know that they, themselves, have abundant and useful community ties, they often believe that many others do not. As evidence, they invoke such common images as masses of individuals pushing and shoving their way along crowded streets, lonely people sitting by themselves in front of television sets, mobs running down streets during riots, or rows of office or factory workers at their separate machines or desks.

Until the 1960s, most sociologists shared this folk belief in the disappearance of "community" in large cities and spent a great deal of energy trying to explain why it had occurred. Most of their efforts centered on the seemingly cataclysmic changes associated with the Industrial Revolution during the past two centuries. Consequently, they wondered if such major social changes as the rise of capitalism, bureaucratization, industrialization, and accelerated technological growth had led to an erosion of the intimate, broadly based relationships that had traditionally formed the basis for communities. They feared that the specialized, hierarchical bureaucratic structures of contemporary large-scale societies had been producing specialized, segmented communities.

These analyses reflected the negative aspects of the ambivalence that many leading nineteenth-century sociologists felt about the impact of large-scale changes on interpersonal relations. On the one hand, they observed that the large-scale reorganization of production had created new opportunities for social development: the elimination of want (Marx and Engels), the extension of universalism (Weber), the breakdown of parochialism (Durkheim), and the encouragement of individual freedom and rational thought (Simmel). On the other, they feared that the Industrial Revolution had led to new types of exploitation (Marx and Engels), the weakening of communal bonds and the emergence of new forms of social pathology (Durkheim), and the loss of personal identity (Simmel).

Ambivalence about these dual aspects of the Industrial Revolution has continued well into the twentieth century, as evidenced in studies of families, work groups, neighborhoods, and other naturally occurring sites for informal or intimate ties. Have things in fact fallen apart? Are interpersonal ties now likely to be few in number, short in duration, and specialized in content? Have personal networks so withered away that the few remaining ties serve only as the basis for disconnected two-person relationships, rather than as the foundation for more extensive and integrated communities?

Many current analyses suffer from a "pastoral syndrome," nostalgically comparing contemporary communities with the supposedly good old days when villagers danced around maypoles, families brought in the hay, and artisans whistled while they worked. This work has a strongly normative tone:

- *Urban* sociologists have announced the loss of community. They say that the size, density, and heterogeneity of contemporary cities has fostered superficial, transitory, specialized, disconnected ties in local neighborhoods and on city streets (e.g., Wirth, 1938; Stein, 1960; Nisbet, 1969).

- *Family* specialists argue that high rates of social and geographical mobility – coupled with a capitalistic sensibility about "making it" on one's own – have weakened extended family ties and thrown individuals back on the resources of their households and a few transitory, uncertain, occupationally similar friends (e.g., Parsons, 1943; Sennet, 1970; Lasch, 1977).

- *Medical* sociologists worry that isolated individuals will be more likely to experience illnesses – and to suffer more seriously from them – because of their lack of social support from friends and relatives (e.g., Faris and Dunham, 1939; Jaco, 1954).

- *Gerontologists* fear that old age brings "disengagement" from supportive others – a process heightened by the disappearance of stable, solidary communities (e.g., Cumming and Henry, 1961).

- *Organizational* analysts lament the easy way in which the specialized, standardized, formally hierarchical nature of large-scale institutions weakens informal contacts between coworkers. Along with the urban sociologists, they think that the spatial segmentation of workplaces and residential areas separates workmates' ties from community ties (e.g., Whyte, 1956; Blauner, 1964; Slater, 1970).

- *Political* analysts worry about the effects of large-scale migration from rural villages to large, densely packed, modernizing cities and workplaces. They warn that the uprooting of migrants and their failure to integrate into neighborhood and work communities create "mass societies" of disconnected, discontented individuals, ripe for riotous mobilization by political agitators (e.g., Kornhauser, 1959; Davies, 1962; Gurr, 1969).

Such fears and beliefs have not stood up well under the scrutiny made possible by more systematic data-gathering techniques developed since the 1950s and wielded by a generation of sociologists born, raised, and comfortable in large cities and organizations. A major sociological industry has emerged, discovering community in places where it had been pronounced "lost": in rich and poor neighborhoods (in rich and poor countries), among extended kin, in workplaces, and among migrants and rioters. Sociologists have gathered so much evidence for it that the "persistence of community" has now become the prevailing orthodoxy.

At about the same time that researchers were showing that contemporary communities were not nearly so lost as had been thought, two other sets of researchers were demonstrating that preindustrial communities were not nearly as solidary as had been thought. Studies of contemporary Third World societies reveal that many localities do not have the supportive, broadly based, densely knit communities upon which the supposed contrast with industrial societies has rested. These studies show that relationships within such preindustrial societies are often hierarchical, specialized ties of exploitation, with sharp cleavages separating factions (see Bodemann, Chapter 8). Moreover, historians have systematically used demographic and archival sources to demonstrate that many pre–Industrial Revolution communities were less solidary than had once been thought. The supposed communalism of the preindustrial past now appears to be in large part an artifact of the focus of early scholars on localism and solidarity rather than on internal cleavages and external ties (see Tilly, Chapter 12).

By redefining the problem in structural terms, researchers have been able to demonstrate that the fears of a former generation of sociologists about the loss of community were, if not simply incorrect, at least incomplete. Community, structural analysts argue, has rarely disappeared from urban industrial societies. It has been *transformed*: New forms of community have come into being to replace older ones. They can be seen if analysts focus on social ties and systems of informal resource exchange rather than on people living in neighborhoods and villages.

This transmutation of "community" into "social network" is much more than a linguistic trick. It frees analysts from searching for Brigadoons: vestigial traditional solidarities hanging on into the twentieth century. Treating communities as networks makes such solidarities only one among many possible patterns. Rather than looking to see if what they find measures up to the traditional ideal of densely knit, tightly bounded, broadly based solidarities, analysts can evaluate the ways in which alternative structural patterns affect flows of resources to community members.

This shift in perspective from community to network allows analysts to examine the extent to which large-scale social changes have simultaneously created new forms of association and altered the structure of older interpersonal bonds such as kinship. It leaves open the extent to which such ties are intimate, frequent, or broadly based. It facilitates the analytic linkage of community networks to other structures of interaction – such as relations on the job and in the household – or links with bureaucratic institutions.

Carried to extremes, structuralism can become formalism: using the morphological pattern of ties to explain all processes. The three chapters in this part of the book avoid such formalism by also taking into account community members' unequal access to resources. The authors use a common set of structural analytic concepts and techniques to interrelate what they have found at different analytic levels. They are keen to trace the ways in which the pressures, opportunities, and constraints of large-scale social systems condition the nature of contemporary communities. Thus, they portray these communities as being situated in societies with unequal resources, the members in each community having differential access to these resources, and the structure of the communities allocating these resources in unequal, cumulatively hierarchical ways.

"The community" in such cases is largely a matter of how analysts define ties, where they draw boundaries, and how high they raise the level of analytic magnification in order to take into account internal links within clusters. It is possible that the same ties may be components of densely knit and tightly bounded networks at one level of analysis and components of sparsely knit and loosely bounded networks at a higher level of analysis.

Thus, *Barry Wellman, Peter J. Carrington*, and *Alan Hall* regard each person as the central node of a potentially complex network of community ties. Their approach leaves open the possibilities that all such "personal communities" are not structurally integrated – and indeed may have competitive or antagonistic elements; that community ties may well stretch beyond local boundaries; that individuals may often have to deal with the competing claims and obligations of the complex networks in which they are enmeshed; and that the overall structure of ties within a community may be a web of partly solidary, partly ramified relationships.

Wellman, Carrington, and Hall find that residents of East York – a homogeneously British-Canadian, densely settled residential area of central Toronto – usually have only a few specialized contacts with their immediate neighbors. This is the sort of observation that has led analysts to conclude that community is being "lost." But the authors discover that East Yorkers continue to garner a wide range of support from friends, kin, and workmates. As a rule, the "personal communities" in which the East Yorkers are involved are large and ramified, stretching throughout the metropolitan areas and beyond. They are sustained through visits, telephone calls, and gatherings that are made possible by rapid and inexpensive forms of transportation and communication.

The multiple worlds with which most East Yorkers are engaged (work, home, kin, leisure) are reflected in the multiple clusters in their networks. Most of their personal community members are not directly linked with one another. Moreover, the ties are often specialized in content, the East Yorkers using different relationships to obtain companionship, emotional aid, information, or a variety of small and large services. Thus, although some patterns of interaction are not as prevalent among these urbanites as they ought to be according to traditional conceptions of community, they have been supplemented and, to some extent, supplanted by others.

In his chapter, *Leslie Howard* also finds that community has been transformed when he compares the community ties of factory and nonfactory workers in the Indian industrial city of Ranchi. Howard directly confronts the loss-of-community assertion that large, specialized work organizations (such as factories and offices) are reproduced in their workers' specialized, unsupportive ties on and off the job. He argues that the organization of work – the ways in which workers depend on their superiors and workmates for their means of subsistence – crucially affects the nature of communities in Ranchi. Indeed, it is more important than caste or ethnicity.

Howard points out that factory workers depend on institutional relations with formal bureaucracies for their jobs, whereas nonfactory workers depend on interpersonal relations with their patron-employers. Working together to deal with the bureaucracy, factory workers are apt to form egalitarian relationships with coworkers. By contrast, nonfactory workers compete among themselves for their patrons' favors in securing and retaining jobs. Howard's findings are the direct opposite of romantic notions of communally integrated artisanal workshops and alienated, disconnected factories. Although nonfactory workers rarely form supportive, densely knit communities, the factory workers – jointly subject to standardized bureaucratic rules and less dependent on competitive patronage – readily maintain supportive, densely knit communities.

Whereas Howard concentrates on relations of power and exchange in the workplace, *Y. Michal Bodemann* argues that seemingly local patron–client relations are nothing more than a visible manifestation of large-scale systems of class relations. Bodemann uses both fieldwork and archival data to trace shifts during this century in the patron–client relations of a Sardinian village, "Telemula." Bodemann shows that far from being open and egalitarian – as the nostalgic view of preindustrial society would have it – village life is tightly bound in a system of production and a web of family ties that reinforce the class basis of social interaction. By personalizing class relationships in intimate two-person exchanges, patron–client ties hide underlying class antagonisms. Yet patron-clientage is much more than a series of dyadic exchanges in isolated pastoral villages. The patrons' power rests on their quasi-monopolistic external ties to state and church resources. Ultimately, patron-clientage is a network of asymmetric ties unequally transmitting power, economic goods, and other resources through relations that maintain, reproduce, and extend class structures in local, regional, and world systems.

Bodemann situates two successive Telemulese patterns of community ties within local and national relations of production. In the early twentieth century, Telemula had a traditional pastoral economy in which some of

the former bases of communal organization – age cohorts and special
solidarities – had withered away, in part because of out-migration to
industrializing areas. Only kinship remained. The emerging dominant clique,
the Sannas, used their socially and spatially close kin to forge a densely knit,
tightly bounded cluster of relations. With these ties, they controlled not only
the village's resources, but all access to outside sources of power. They were
politicians first, and landowners and entrepreneurs second.

The Sannas's control did not withstand changes in Italian and Telemulese
political economy. Their successors, the Taulas, were better able to function
in a new situation in which the demands of national capitalism called for
more differentiated and flexible divisions of labor and more far-ranging
relationships. The Taulas accomplished this by becoming regional brokers.
They developed specialized ties with socially and spatially distant kin in order
to access a broad range of political and economic institutions and
entrepreneurs.

Although Bodemann's account is confined to one village, it may well be
that the Sanna and Taula patterns suggest fundamental structural alternatives for the ways in which communities can either control existing resources
or gain access to additional ones (Wolf, 1966; Wellman and Leighton, 1979;
Granovetter, 1973). Certainly these two structural alternatives influence
much of the reasoning throughout this book, including all of the chapters in
this section.

Thus, although analyses of communities, families, health care, informal
organizational relations, and the like often operate within different research
traditions, many of the issues they deal with are quite similar. They are all
addressing the *community question* of how, on the one hand, large-scale
divisions of labor affect the structure and contents of community ties and
how, on the other hand, the structure and contents of these networks affect
large-scale divisions of labor. It is a question that in the nineteenth century
fascinated both Durkheim, with his emphasis on organic solidarity as
interdependence between community members, and Marx, with his concepts
of classes "in themselves" and "for themselves." Setting the agenda for a
good part of social thought from the times of Machiavelli and Hobbes until
today, the community question has posed the central twofold problem of the
lack of structural integration of social systems and the uneven distribution of
resources to their members.

Treating social structures as a network of networks is appealing because it
provides a way of going from small-scale to large-scale phenomena without
imposing a radical discontinuity in analytic approach. Capitalism, urbanization, and other "isms" and "zations" are not just abstract forces, acting and
being acted upon only in transcendentally diffuse ways. Rather, as all three
chapters in this part demonstrate, they are summary terms for patterns of
concrete relations between such social entities as individuals, clusters,

groups, and organizations. Viewed in this fashion, communities are no longer merely passive recipients of the forces of large-scale social systems. They are active arrangements by which members of that world engage with larger systems, accessing and modifying external resources in order to survive and reproduce their social contexts.

LITERATURE CITED

Blauner, Robert. *Alienation and Freedom*. Chicago: University of Chicago Press, 1964.

Cumming, Elaine, and William Henry. *Growing Old: The Process of Disengagement*. New York: Basic Books, 1961.

Davies, James C. "Toward a Theory of Revolution." *American Sociological Review* 27 (1962): 5–19.

Faris, Robert, and H. Warren Dunham. *Mental Disorders in Urban Areas*. Chicago: University of Chicago Press, 1939.

Granovetter, Mark. "The Strength of Weak Ties." *American Journal of Sociology* 78 (1973): 1360–80.

Gurr, Ted Robert. *Why Men Rebel*. Princeton, N. J.: Princeton University Press, 1969.

Jaco, E. Gartly. "The Social Isolation Hypothesis and Schizophrenia." *American Sociological Review*, 19 (1954): 567–77.

Kornhauser, William. *The Politics of Mass Society*. Glencoe, Ill.: Free Press, 1959.

Lasch, Christopher. *Haven in a Heartless World*. New York: Basic Books, 1977.

Nisbet, Robert A. *The Quest for Community*. New York: Oxford University Press, 1969.

Parsons, Talcott. "The Kinship System of the Contemporary United States." *American Anthropologist* 45 (1943): 22–38.

Sennett, Richard. *Families against the City*. Cambridge, Mass.: Harvard University Press, 1970.

Slater, Philip. *The Pursuit of Loneliness*. Boston: Beacon Press, 1970.

Stein, Maurice. *The Eclipse of Community*. Princeton, N. J.: Princeton University Press, 1960.

Whyte, William H., Jr. *The Organization Man*. New York: Simon and Schuster, 1956.

Wirth, Louis. "Urbanism as a Way of Life." *American Journal of Sociology* 44 (1938): 3–24.

Wellman, Barry, and Barry Leighton. "Networks, Neighborhoods and Communities: Approaches to the Study of the Community Question." *Urban Affairs Quarterly* 15 (1979): 363–90.

Wolf, Eric. "Kinship, Friendship and Patron–Client Relations." In Michael Banton (ed.), *The Social Anthropology of Complex Societies*. London: Tavistock, 1966.

6

Networks as personal communities

Barry Wellman, Peter J. Carrington, and Alan Hall

Toward a network conception of community

Searching for community

When our research group first started studying East York in 1968, we wondered why the empty streets gave little public evidence of community life. East York is a homogeneously British-Canadian, densely settled residential area of central Toronto in which much of the working-class and lower middle-class population owns small homes. It has a long tradition as a tranquil, cohesive place, insulated from the hurly-burly of urban life. We expected to see visible, almost palpable communities: neighbors chatting on front porches, friends relaxing on streets corners, cousins gathering for Sunday dinners, and storekeepers retailing local gossip. But wherever we looked, we found few signs of active neighborhood life.

We eventually realized that we were only seeing part of the picture. We had only been looking for the obvious physical signs of local community – on front porches and street corners – without noticing the more subtle reality of community ties. Although the streets of East York were usually empty, the residents were heavily involved in community networks. They had persons with whom they could visit, commune, share information, and exchange help. Community, like love, is where you find it. East Yorkers were finding it in ties, not in public places.

This presented us with a dilemma. Finding so many community ties, we could not say that East Yorkers were without community. Yet the ties we found did not fit neatly into the standard sociological criteria for community: densely knit neighborhood solidarities filled with mutual aid (Hillery, 1955;

Our deepest thanks go to Jenny Gullen, Robert Hiscott, and Ignacio Llovet, who ran many of the computer analyses reported here, and to Bonnie Erickson, Claude Fischer, A. Ron Gillis, Mark Granovetter, Robert Hiscott, Susan Hodgson, Charles Jones, Lorne Tepperman, and Beverly Wellman for their comments on earlier drafts. Our research has been supported by grants from the Social Sciences and Humanities Research Council of Canada; the National Welfare Grants Directorate of Health and Welfare Canada; the Joint Program in Transportation, York University–University of Toronto; and the Structural Analysis and Gerontology programmes, University of Toronto. Throughout the long course of the East York research, the Centre for Urban and Community Studies, University of Toronto, has been a sociable and supportive base.

R. Warren, 1978). Yet only some of the East Yorkers' ties seemed to provide strong support, only a few were local, and only some were part of densely knit solidarities. We needed a way to think about the kinds of communities in which East Yorkers were involved without insisting that these communities look like traditional solidarities.

Our solution has been to treat East Yorkers' networks as *personal communities*. We look for the social essence of community in neither locality nor solidarity, but in the ways in which networks of informal relations fit persons and households into social structures. Our approach focuses attention on the characteristics of "community ties" – informal links of companionship and aid between individuals – and on the patterns formed by these links.

Although others had studied such community ties before we did, they had usually looked at them only as indices of potentially solidary neighborhood, kinship, or interest groups. In contrast, our approach has not been limited by considerations of locality, kinship, or group solidarity: Rather than study communities defined by neighborhoods, we have examined communities defined by networks. To be sure, this approach has deemphasized the role of neighborhoods as real ecological arenas in which all inhabitants must rub shoulders and compete for scarce, territorially based resources. But it has given us the flexibility to discover both local solidarities and far-flung, ramified communities. Most important, the network approach has enabled us to see which attributes of ties and networks best foster sociable relations, interpersonal support, informal social control, and a sense of personal identity – the traditional output variables of community studies.

Treating communities as networks also moves "community studies" out of its role as an academic sideshow and into the heart of sociology: the systematic examination of how small-scale social structures, such as interpersonal networks, fit into large-scale division of labor. This approach concentrates attention on how networks channel resources to their members, locates them in small-scale social structures, and links them to large-scale institutions. Viewing these phenomena in network terms also makes it possible to link community studies analytically to other studies of small-scale structures such as kinship systems (Bodemann, Chapter 8), work groups (Howard, Chapter 7), and interest groups (Brym, Chapter 13; Tilly, Chapter 12).

By recasting the community question in this way, we have been able to enter the continuing debate about the extent to which sociologists can adequately analyze dyadic interpersonal ties without taking into account how such ties fit into larger social networks (Homans, 1961, vs. Simmel, [1908] 1971): In effect, it allows us to see how the large-scale division of labor in a social system affects the organization and content of interpersonal ties within that system.[1]

Community: causes and effects

Pundits have probably worried about the impact of social change on communities ever since human beings ventured beyond the vicinity of their caves. It is certain that many leading social commentators have earned their bread during the past hundred years by suggesting various ways in which the Industrial Revolution may have affected the structure and operation of communities. They have noted that

- National governments and multinational corporations now control activities previously run by local governments and small enterprises. This change may have caused a decline in local communal solidarity, for instead of hanging together to decide their common fate, each interest group now tries to make separate deals with these external agencies (Tilly, 1973, 1975).
- Capitalist modes of behavior have affected how people deal with each other in everyday life. In addition to treating their goods and services as commodities to be exchanged for the best bargains, they treat their community lives as a series of separate deals. This is quite different from a situation in which community members help each other because of their commitment to the well-being of the community as a whole (Polanyi, [1944] 1957; Titmuss, 1970; Shorter, 1975).
- Large bureaucratic organizations now employ many people in specialized jobs: blue, pink, and white collar. This bureaucratization of work can narrow the scope of workers' relationships on the job and disconnect their ties to workmates from their ties to kinfolk and neighbors (Stein, 1960; Braverman, 1974).
- The large scale and diversity of cities nourish the growth of many different interest groups. Whereas small-town folks tend to deal with the same interconnected web of persons throughout the day, big-city folks tend to leave their neighborhoods to work, stay at home at night, chat with neighbors on weekends, and take weekly fitness classes with yet another group of people. Such variety gives urbanites more choice about what they do and with whom they do it, but it can also fragment their lives into many social worlds (Simmel, [1902–3] 1950; Kadushin, 1966; Fischer, 1975).
- Large bureaucratic institutions now perform many of the reproductive tasks that families and communities used to do for themselves. Community members now purchase clothing, food, and emotional comfort and hire large institutions to care for their young and infirm. This "McDonaldization" of life may have reduced the number and scope of things that community members do for each other. Hence, the combination of increasing

bureaucratic centralization and specialization may have actually reduced interdependence between individuals (contra Durkheim, [1893] 1933).

- Cheap, efficient, and widespread means of transportation and communication have made it easier to sustain long-distance ties. People routinely telephone across the continent or drive across the metropolis to contact friends and relatives. Yet their communities may be dispersed and fragmented: At times they cannot see community members easily and they have even greater difficulty visiting a whole community at the same time (Webber, 1964; Hiltz and Turoff, 1979).

These large-scale changes have been clear and widespread. Few would deny that bureaucratization and capitalism are significant forces in almost all societies. And few searchers for community would come up empty-handed if they set out to look for evidence of lonely people, of people snuggled warmly in the bosoms of "urban villages" (Gans, 1962), or of cosmopolitans maintaining long-distance ties by means of expressways, telephones, or airplanes. The problem comes when analysts try to agree about (a) which large-scale changes have had the most powerful impact on community; (b) just what the effects have been; and (c) what structural mechanisms link particular large-scale causes with particular smaller-scale community effects. Indeed, even those who agree on the same cause often disagree on its *effects*: They debate whether a specific factor has destroyed communities, transformed them, or encouraged them to hang on as sheltering havens. Because of such uncertainties, many analyses have been like the results of projective tests in which scholars attribute alleged deficiencies (or triumphs) of contemporary communities to the particular large-scale cause of which they are most fond.

Debating community

Until the 1960s, debates about the overall tenor of community life were focused on the extent to which neighborhoods and kinship groups had remained solidary and supportive. Many scholars feared that large-scale social changes had created an environment in which community could not survive. They looked out their windows and saw the same sort of empty streets and bureaucratic services that we found in East York. They believed that community ties were now few in number, weak, narrowly specialized, transitory, and fragmented. They argued that individuals had become isolated atoms in a "mass society" – dependent on large bureaucracies for care and control (Kornhauser, 1959). These scholars feared that community had been "lost," and they worried that antisocial people would injure themselves and others when freed from nurturing and restraining communal bonds.[2]

Others argued that people gregariously form and retain communities in all social settings. They went out to look for community: hanging out on street corners, ringing doorbells for surveys, and sipping tea while conducting interviews. By the 1960s, their "Community Saved" argument had had much the better of the debate empirically. Hordes of social scientists had demonstrated convincingly that neighborhood and kinship groups continued to be abundant and strong. Rather than withering away in the face of the Industrial Revolution, such groups had acted as buffers against large-scale forces, filled gaps in contemporary social systems by providing flexible, low-cost aid, and provided secure bases from which residents could powerfully engage the outside world.[3]

This demonstration that communities have persisted has been convincing but not complete. Both the "Lost" and the "Saved" arguments define community as a solidary, local, kinshiplike group. They disagree only about whether or not such communities still flourish. Thus, both assume that a flourishing community can only be one that replicates the standard image of preindustrial communities: densely knit, tightly bounded, and mutually supportive villages. But such bucolic imagery not only disregards widespread preindustrial individualism, exploitation, cleavage, and mobility (see, for example, Laslett, 1971; Mayer with Mayer, 1974; Williams, 1975; LeRoy Ladurie, 1975; Macfarlane, 1978), it also restricts the criteria by which analysts can evaluate contemporary communities. For if neighborhood and kinship ties make up only a portion of community ties, then studies restricted to neighborhood and kinship groups give a distorted picture of community that can lead analysts to label people as "lost" if they have many far-flung, sparsely knit, community ties.

Scholars who have avoided this mislabeling have been fascinated by the possibilities offered by cheap, effective, long-distance transportation and communication facilities for maintaining relationships beyond local areas. Such scholars argue that large-scale specialization and personal mobility have "Liberated" community – encouraging membership in multiple, interest-based communities predominantly composed of long-distance friendship ties.[4] Their argument implies that people are not so much antisocial or gregarious beings as they are *operators* who are willing to forego a secure source of fruit for a chance to connect with more of the world. Perhaps East York's streets were deserted because East Yorkers were driving to friends' homes or were on the telephone chatting with physically distant, but socially close kinfolk!

Whatever side they take in this debate, most commentators have seen the Lost, Saved, and Liberated arguments either as alternative "true" descriptions of contemporary life or as evolutionary successors – with preindustrial Saved communities giving way to Lost, superseded by postindustrial

Liberated. By contrast, we see them as alternative structural models. Each model speaks to a different means of obtaining and retaining resources: direct use of formal organizations (Lost); membership in densely knit, all-encompassing, solidary groups (Saved); or selective use of specialized, diversified, sparsely knit social nets (Liberated). Although one or the other may predominate in a social system, all three models are likely to be reflected in current realities to some extent. Indeed, a single personal community may well be a composite of a densely knit core cluster and some more sparsely knit ties reaching out to connect with other groups and their resources.

Clearly, we cannot use our East York data to sort out the impact of various large-scale factors on community. However, we can use them to paint an accurate picture of networks as communities in order to assess the viability of these three structural alternatives in a contemporary Western context. Moreover by turning up our analytic magnification a bit, we can also zoom in on different parts of these personal communities. We believe that such structural pictures can help to explain how large-scale forces have affected everyday lives. Hence, although much of this chapter consists of sheer description, it is by no means intended as mere description.

Studying personal communities in East York

The first East York survey

We first surveyed a random sample of 845 adult East Yorkers in 1968 and gathered information about their socially close ("intimate") ties outside their households. We found that East Yorkers had many intimate ties. Most ties were with kin and friends (and a few with neighbors and coworkers) and most networks were sparsely knit. Most East Yorkers received emergency and everyday aid through their networks even though most ties did not provide such aid (Coates, Moyer, and Wellman, 1969; Gates, Stevens and Wellman, 1973; Wellman et al., 1973; Wellman, 1979).

Although this study addressed some important parts of the Community Question, we were still dissatisfied. The data were thin. We had asked about six intimates at most, and personal communities were larger and more complex than that. Brief answers to closed-ended survey questions had told us little about the subtleties and details of interaction. For example, we did not know what kinds of supportive resources network members supplied to each other or the ways in which strong, intimate ties differed from weaker ones.

The second East York study

We designed the second East York study with a view to obtaining richer, more comprehensive information about these kinds of issues. We decided to reinterview, in depth, a small subsample (33) of the original East York respondents. This enabled us to back up the statistically more reliable information obtained in the original survey with more detailed and valid information gained through 10 hours of interviewing. Instead of asking about only six intimates, we asked about all persons with whom East Yorkers were significantly "in touch." We obtained much more information about more ties in their networks: how persons first met one another, the circumstances of their jobs and home lives, their present joys and pains, and the kinds of things they did for each other. We were also able to obtain what are, to our knowledge, the first detailed structural descriptions of a sizable sample of personal communities, including information about the number and composition of components and clusters within these networks. However, we found that although these interviews yielded rich information about network dynamics, they did not provide systematic data about specific types of aid. Therefore, we used a follow-up mail questionnaire to find out which of fifteen types of aid each East Yorker gave to – and received from – each network member.[5]

In 1968, all 33 respondents lived in East York; by 1978 most were living elsewhere in southern Ontario. They were typical of East Yorkers and Torontonians in general (Table 6.1). In comparison with the 1968 survey sample, however, a larger proportion were divorced or single parents, and more women were employed outside their homes – all changes consistent with larger social trends.

Almost all the respondents were steadily employed (or, in some cases, were homemakers with steadily employed husbands) in occupations such as "electrician" or "dental technician" for the men, and "secretary" or "insurance claims examiner" for the women. All but two worked for others (mainly large corporations), one was a self-employed upholsterer, and one owned and operated a small store. Although few of the respondents had much discretion in the use of capital or over other employees' lives, most were skilled workers with some say about how they did their job – even if not about when, where, and to what purpose they did it.

The predominant British-Canadian ancestry of the sample reflects "old" East York. It was settled heavily between the World Wars by migrants from Yorkshire and Lancashire in search of a good job and a sturdy, detached home. East York was changing rapidly in 1968 when we chose our original sample. By 1978, it contained large numbers of Italian-, Greek-, and East Indian-Canadians, and many high-rise apartment towers looking down on the older red brick homes. Many longtime residents (or their adult children) had moved out to the more spacious suburbs.

In this chapter, we do not dwell on differences within our sample but use both quantitative and qualitative information to provide a broad overview of the composition, structure, and contents of our respondents' social networks.

For convenience, we refer to the respondents as "East Yorkers," and although this designation is more strictly true for 1968 than for 1978, Table 6.1 shows how closely respondents fit East York and metropolitan Toronto's profile. We describe these East Yorkers' ties and networks in two complementary ways:

- Our analysis by ties combines all of the 33 East Yorkers' significant ties into one data set. This allows us to describe community ties in the aggregate.[6]
- Our analysis by networks treats the 33 personal communities, themselves, as units of analysis. This allows us to describe variations in the personal communities.

The boundaries of personal communities

Personal communities seldom have well-defined boundaries. Because there are no gates (or gatekeepers) to divide members from nonmembers, analysts must always derive a sharp picture from a fuzzy reality. Such fuzziness is a fact of life, and not a methodological distortion. Although planners and politicians often draw sharp lines on neighborhood maps, neither friendship ties nor local services are so neatly clustered (Taub et al., 1977). Even supposedly stable and solidary preindustrial communities had fuzzy boundaries – with work, trade, migration, extra-local marriage, wars, and governments linking villagers to other worlds. In personal communities, friends come and go, their importance varying by the hour, day, and year. Thus, even though our interviews froze the East Yorkers' networks in brief, cross-sectional snapshots, we did not find single, all-purpose communities. For example, socially close network members were usually different persons from those who were in frequent contact.

Several analysts have estimated that people like the East Yorkers should in some way know 1,000–2,000 persons (Boissevain, 1974; Pool and Kochen, 1978), but we did not try to produce such comprehensive lists. Instead, we questioned respondents about all the people with whom they were currently "in touch." Collectively, they told us about 403 *significant* ties: relationships they actively think about and maintain (although not necessarily through frequent contact). We describe only these *significant* ties here, in part because they are more significant to the East Yorkers, and in part because we have much more confidence in reports about such ties. In particular, we focus on

- Intimate ties (164): all significant ties that East Yorkers identify as socially close
- Routine ties (96): all significant ties with whom East Yorkers are in contact at least three times a week – in person, or by telephone, letter, or CB radio.[7]

Table 6.1. Background characteristics of East Yorkers and Torontonians

Sample characteristics	1978 Interviews	1968 Survey	Population characteristics	East York 1971 (& 1981) Census	Toronto CMA[a] 1971 (& 1981) Census
Size (number)	33	845		104,785 (101,974)	2,628,045 (2,998,947)
Demographics					
Female	53	55	(Of persons 20+)	53 (51)	51 (51)
Median age	44	46		44 (43)	41 (41)
Reproduction					
Household composition					
Couples with resident children	50	43		— (29)	— (43)
Childless couples	12	21		— (14)	— (12)
Couples with absent children	12	21		— (14)	— (12)
Single parents	9	0.4		— (8)	— (9)
Singles	12	11	1-Person households	18 (30)	14 (22)
Median household size	3.0	2.1	Persons per household	2.7 (2.5)	3.3 (2.8)
Median number of children at home	1.0	0	Children per family	0.9 (1.0)	1.5 (1.3)
Married	76	74	Married (of persons 20+)	71 (66)	75 (70)
Divorced, separated	12	3	Divorced (of persons 20+)	12 (4)	3 (3)
In single-family houses	67	70	In single dwellings	55 (49)	64 (59)
Median length of residence in home (years)	4.5	5.2	(Estimated years of occupancy)	4 (5)	5 (4)
Born in Canada	88	62		64 (60)	66 (61)
Speaking English most often at home	100	—		84 (82)	82 (82)
British Isles ethnicity	65	57		65 (51)	57 (46)
Protestant	85	72		57 (47)	50 (43)
Living in East York	38	100		100 (100)	4 (3)

	Production			
Living eslewhere in metro Toronto	35	—	—	75 (68)
Living elsewhere in CMA	15	—	—	21 (29)
High school graduates (Of persons 15 +)	35	24	42 (54)	41 (56)
Employment status				
Employed full-time (Of persons 15 +)	64	55	67 (68)	66 (71)
In labor force	79	63		
Homemakers (Females 15 + not in labor force)	12	22	25 (41)	26 (39)
Retired	9	11		
Median Blishen score[b]	52	50		
Median family income (C$)	16,000	8,000	10,132 (24,363)	10,644 (27,775)
Class location				
Casual proletariat	7	—	—	—
Regular proletariat	36	—	—	—
Skilled worker	18	—	—	—
Semi-autonomous employee	18	—	—	—
Manager, foreman	11	—	—	—

[a] Census Metropolitan Area.
[b] Occupational status as per Blishen (1967); Blishen and McRoberts (1976).
Note: Figures denote percentages except where otherwise indicated. The dashes indicate that data are not available.

Ties, like networks, are fuzzy. For example, ties between married couples pose major definitional problems. What appears at first to be a single tie between two persons can often be a complex social relationship involving three or four persons. Is a tie to a married couple one tie or two? In most cases, there is really only a single tie to either the husband or the wife, the other person being only a background figure. In a few cases, husbands and wives each have distinctive relationships with respondents, and we recorded each as a separate tie. But for 35% of the ties to a married person (23% of all significant ties), the East Yorkers insisted that their tie was to the wife and husband jointly: They interacted with them as a unit and thought of them that way. Are these ties to one or to two persons? There is no single answer. For many purposes, husbands and wives can be thought of as one unit, and the relationship with them is similar to that with a single person. But it is quite possible that couples tend to provide most companionship, emotional aid, and material resources than single persons.

Ties: size, composition, and accessibility

Much of the debate over the three models of community has centered on the size, composition, and accessibility of contemporary communities. Whereas proponents of the Lost argument assert that most personal communities now contain only a few, transitory friendship ties, those supporting the Saved argument insist that most communities continue to consist of neighbors and kin living near one another and in frequent face-to-face contact. Those making the Liberated argument, although they agree that communities remain sizable, suggest that most contemporary ties are with residentially dispersed friends who are bound together through mutual interests and who often reach each other by telephone or expressway.

The size of networks

The results clearly show that the vast majority of East Yorkers are not lost and tieless. Most have at least 11 active ties in their networks – 14, if "couple ties" are counted as two (Table 6.2). This is more than enough for a boisterous birthday party. Most have at least 4 ties with socially close *intimates* – enough to fill the dinner table – and at least 3 ties with persons routinely contacted three times a week or more. Moreover, most have at least 1 socially close, routinely contacted tie: a "best friend" or "close sister" who is a reliable source of companionship and aid.

On the other hand, several East Yorkers are quite isolated from their networks. As one interviewer reported about Eddie Palmer (a pseudonym):

Table 6.2. *Number of ties in East Yorkers' networks*

By networks	Significant	Intimate	Routine	Intimate routine
Extreme upper network	27.0 (29.0)[a]	10.0 (14.0)	10.0 (15.0)	5.0 (7.0)
Upper quartile	15.5 (20.0)	6.0 (9.0)	4.0 (5.0)	3.0 (3.0)
Median	11.0 (14.0)	4.0 (6.0)	3.0 (3.0)	2.0 (3.0)
Lower quartile	9.0 (9.5)	3.0 (4.0)	1.5 (2.0)	1.0 (2.0)
Extreme lower network	3.0 (6.0)	1.0 (1.0)	1.0 (1.0)	1.0 (1.0)
Mean	12.5 (15.0)	5.0 (6.3)	3.3 (4.2)	2.1 (2.8)
Standard deviation	5.2 (6.6)	2.5 (3.1)	2.3 (3.3)	1.1 (1.5)

Composition of typical network of 11 significant ties:

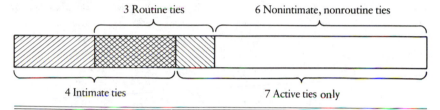

[a]Numbers in parentheses count couple ties as two persons.

I had the feeling that he keeps himself pretty much aloof from day-to-day close contact with these people. He made it clear that he considers himself to be extremely independent, that he has his own way of looking at things, and that he is not the kind of person that interacts a lot with anyone else.

Four East Yorkers are especially isolated. They do not have routine contact with any network member. The overall active networks of two respondents contain fewer than six members. These four are all married, working-class people; either retired (Jenny Draper, Gerald Hopkins) or in socially isolating jobs (Stan Walker, truck driver; John Williams, self-employed upholsterer). All stay at home at night or on weekends, believing in "keeping to ourselves."

Yet more East Yorkers have large rather than small networks. Three have a score or more of significant ties. If we count couple ties as two, nine networks have a score or more of significant members. Lurking in the background are even more ties: One East Yorker wanted to talk about all 84 of his kin, and another has a nodding relationship with every neighbor in the surrounding "seven blocks."

All East Yorkers with large networks are heavily involved with at least one large, densely knit social circle; some have links with two. Usually these are kinship circles ("my kin are my life," Patricia Fairgray says), but one retired couple maintains active ties with a large circle of old friends, and one single parent and actress is a member of three support groups of neighbors, coworkers, and friends.

Community roles

When asked to describe network members, East Yorkers almost always start by giving them a kinship label (e.g., "my sister-in-law") or by calling them "friend," "neighbor," "someone who works with me," or "a person I see at the church choir," and so on. To East Yorkers, these labels connote the social and sociophysical contexts from which they draw their ties and in which such ties operate, the expectations that network members have regarding others' behavior, and the contents of these ties. East Yorkers interviewed generally recognize six distinct types of these "roles," all capable of being subdivided more finely or of being cross-classified in terms of intensity, specificity, supportiveness, and frequency of contact: immediate kin, extended kin, neighbor, friend, coworker and organizational tie.[8]

Kin. Traditional roles – kin and neighbor – still make up the majority of ties in most East Yorkers' networks (Table 6.3). All the East Yorkers interviewed have at least some kin in their networks – except for one retired plumber who has cut his ties with relatives because they "expect more of you than natural friends do" (Gerald Hopkins). Indeed, kin comprise almost half of the East Yorkers' active and intimate ties (Table 6.4). Whereas immediate kin are likely to be intimates, extended kin usually have more limited contact with the East Yorkers. (Many other extended kin are latent or filler ties.) Most of the networks with high proportions of kin are large, supportive family groups. However, three networks with a high proportion of kin are quite small. These East Yorkers rarely see their kinfolk or exchange aid with them: They are persons who report they "keep to themselves," retaining kinship ties because they take less effort to maintain than ties to friends, neighbors, or coworkers.

Neighbors. Neighbors predominate among routine ties – making up almost half of the total if couples are counted as two (Table 6.4). Neighbors are rarely intimate: Their relationships are based upon quick physical access for companionship and small amounts of aid. Only a minority of currently active neighbors have anything to do with East Yorkers outside of their immediate neighborhoods (Table 6.5).

Neighboring tends to be a woman-to-woman or couple-to-couple affair. Homemakers usually have higher proportions of neighbors in their networks than women (or men) who are engaged in paid labor (Wellman, 1985; Luxton, 1980). Indeed, neighbors constitute one-third to one-half of four women's networks. In these situations, they work together in child care: exchanging goods, services, information, and emotional support.

Table 6.3. *Distribution of community roles in East Yorkers'*
ties (percent)

	Significant (N = 403)		Intimate (N = 209)		Routine (N = 99)	
Immediate kin	24	(21)[a]	30	(28)	15	(12)
Extended kin	23	(22)	18	(17)	13	(11)
Friend	24	(25)	39	(39)	8	(7)
Neighbor	18	(22)	9	(12)	39	(49)
Coworker	7	(6)	4	(3)	25	(20)
Organizational tie	4	(4)	1	(0)	0	(0)
	100	(100)	99	(99)	100	(99)

[a]Numbers in parentheses count couple ties as two persons.

Table 6.4. *Kin in each network (percent)*

	Significant (N = 33)		Intimate (N = 33)		Routine (N = 29)[a]	
Extreme upper network	100	(100)[b]	100	(100)	100	(100)
Upper quartile	67	(62)	67	(65)	50	(47)
Median network	42	(40)	50	(43)	0	(0)
Lower quartile	29	(27)	17	(19)	0	(0)
Extreme lower network	0	(0)	0	(0)	0	(0)

[a]Four networks have no routine ties.
[b]Numbers in parentheses count couple ties as two persons.

By contrast, 10 East Yorkers – all engaged in paid labor – have no ties
with neighbors. Six report that they avoided such ties in order to preserve
their household's privacy and autonomy:

> I don't become involved, and they don't become involved. It's
> an independent neighborhood here, although I do know the
> guy's name next door. (Eddie Palmer, an electrician)

> Mostly the neighbors around here all keep to themselves.
> Hello and goodbye, and that's it. The neighborhood kids used to
> be standing in the driveway waiting for me to open the pool so I
> just put a stop to it. I just told them it was put in for my family
> and not for all the other kids in the neighborhood. (Lisa Foster,
> a waitress)

In four households, although the male East Yorker respondents do not
neighbor, their wives maintain local contact. "My wife has friends all down
the block, but I don't go looking for them," Douglas Freedman, a business
machine technician, says.

Table 6.5. *Significant network members in each role interacting with East Yorkers in specific contexts (percent)*

Context	All	Immediate kin	Extended kin	Friend	Neighbor	Coworker	Organization tie
(Number)	383	88	88	96	68	28	(15)
Home[a]	88	97	94	91	88	54	47
Cottage[a]	18	17	26	25	7	7	0
Work[a]	14	10	1	11	5	96	11
Neighborhood[a]	24	11	5	14	87	4	17
Informal interest activity centers (e.g., skiing, pool)[a]	33	28	18	43	43	36	22
Organizations	16	9	6	14	25	25	72
Telephone[a]	85	96	76	91	74	72	80
Letters and cards	62	69	58	69	52	48	47
Mean number of contexts[a]	3.1	3.2	2.4	3.3	3.3	3.2	2.5

[a]Chi-square significant at .05 level.

Friends. Although friends are rarely routine contacts, they are often considered intimate and active ones. Friends tend to be persons with whom East Yorkers voluntarily feel intimate, rather than those they just interact with through juxtaposition at work, in the neighborhood, or in kinship groups. Thus, East Yorkers tend to interact with friends in a wider variety of social contexts than they do with network members in other community roles (Table 6.5). Yet friendship, too, arises from social structure and not sheer interpersonal attraction. Whereas only 2% of all significant friendship ties arose from direct, one-on-one encounters, 21% began as neighbors and 18% as coworkers. Former neighbor and coworker ties changed into friendships as greater intimacy and more diversified strands of relationship developed. Some friendships endured when former neighbors and coworkers changed homes and jobs.

Friends are members of 82% of the East Yorkers' networks. Those East Yorkers – mostly men – with a high proportion of friends in their networks actively recruited them. For example, Tom Robinson (a young printer) found most of his intimate male friends through ham radio; only later did these friends start getting together at their homes and summer cottages. Graham Hearst, a 30-year old unemployed student, had acquired men and women friends through traveling and active participation in downtown Toronto street life. One woman (Robina Cook) found comfort from her divorced women friends when she broke up with her first husband. These women became most of her intimates when she reconstructed her social life.

Coworkers. Although 64% of the currently employed East Yorkers have active coworker ties, these ties are always a minority of those in their networks and never more than one-third. However, coworkers do make up a sizable minority (26%) of East Yorkers' routine contacts, although few intimates are coworkers (Table 6.4).

Dick Johnson, the person with the highest proportion of coworker ties in the sample, is an ambitious young marketing manager for a large corporation. (Not only does he enjoy socializing with his colleagues and superiors, his job demands it.) Three other middle-class East Yorkers also use their coworker ties extensively in their careers.[9] For one of these East Yorkers, Mark Haines, the hierarchical nature of his corporation has constrained who he does – and does not – have in his network (see also Howard, Chapter 7). On the one hand, he has formed a close friendship with an older manager who has been teaching him the ropes and sponsoring him. On the other hand, his work has cut him off from sociable ties with other coworkers:

> My work is a manager's work. You obviously don't go out
> and do things yourself. You have to get your work done through
> other people. You never hear anything good from them. You
> never see them if there's no problems. There's obviously

problems. Therefore you see them, and you don't like to see
them! It's part of the job.

Although those working-class East Yorkers with a relatively high proportion of coworker ties (17–25% of their networks) are not interested in
corporate achievement, they do enjoy their workmates' companionship and
help. Indeed, Chris Armstrong, a firefighter, Stan Walker, a tow-truck driver,
and Diane Cressy, an actress, depend on these ties for their physical
survival. However, most East Yorkers limit the contexts in which they dealt
with their workmates: usually leaving their ties behind at 5 o'clock, with
occasional visits after work to a pub or each other's homes. As Chris
Armstrong put it: "I don't like bringing too much home. It's nice just to see
them at work."

Organizational ties. Organizational ties, the least common community role,
are present in only 30% of the networks and usually comprise only one or two
ties in these networks (5% of all significant ties). Very few are intimate and
none are routine.

Yet, organizational ties play a central role in four East Yorkers' lives. Jane
Hazlett's network is built around the friendships she and her husband found
through their active involvement in a Toronto yacht club and East York
politics. Many of Dick Johnson's friends came from his weekly hockey games
and much of Helen Troy's time has been spent in church activities. Betty
Lancaster's passionate concern for animal welfare has pulled her out of
her suburban home. Together with several comrades-in-arms, she pickets
furriers, heckles fashion shows, and works to arouse public concern about
cruelty to animals.

Duration. Whatever the roles involved, East Yorkers' ties are long-standing.
Their active and intimate ties have lasted a median of 19 years. Only one-
quarter of active ties have lasted less than 9 years. To be sure, many of these
are kinship relations into which the two parties were born. But the long
duration of these ties is not an artifact to be explained away. In any event, the
median length of ties with active nonkin is 8 years.

Routine ties – primarily with neighbors and coworkers – have also lasted
a median of 8 years. The shorter length is strongly related to the frequent
disruption of these ties by changes in homes and jobs. Only two unemployed
young men (Graham Hearst and Harry Warner) exhibit the rapid creation
and destruction of ties among young unemployed American black men found
by Liebow (1967). In the few other cases in which East Yorkers have many
new ties, a divorce, remarriage, or long-distance moves have encouraged
them to recreate much of their networks with apparently durable relations.

Diversity. The diversity of these quite stable relations suggests why analysts
have difficulty agreeing about whether contemporary communities are Saved

or Liberated. All the networks contain members from at least two roles (out of the six listed in Table 6.3); all but five of the networks contain at least three roles. The median for all East Yorkers is four – even though eight house-wives, unemployed or retired, have no current coworker ties.

Yet this diversity does not necessarily mean variety. Coworkers and neighbors dominate the small routine networks, and intimate networks are composed mostly of kin and friends. Most commonly, the only network member who is both an intimate and routinely in touch with an East Yorker is one immediate kinfolk – a parent, (adult) child, sister or brother. In short, East Yorkers spend much of the week interacting with a few network members with whom they did not feel very close, and are in less frequent contact – in person or by telephone – with almost all of their close intimate ties.[10]

Contexts. Although East Yorkers' personal communities are sizable and diverse, their operation was largely hidden from public view. When we first looked at the empty streets of East York, we were not just *not* seeing things. East Yorkers are part of "private home society," not "street corner society" (Whyte, 1981). The great majority of network members meet inside each other's homes – by far the most prevalent physical context used (see Table 6.5 above). Telephones provide the second most widely used context. Like the homes, they foster small-scale, voluntary, private interactions usually involving only two households at a time. Many community members also meet at rural Ontario "cottages," second homes whose primary purpose is for recreation on weekends and holidays.

East Yorkers interact much less often in contexts that would expand their networks or forge new ties among network members. Less than one-quarter of all network members ever interact with East Yorkers on neighborhood streets and verandas. Few East Yorkers are active in voluntary organizations. Those groups in which they are active tend to be built around informal get-togethers of a few intimate and routine contacts for sports, social visits, hobbies, and child care. Like most other Torontonians, they seldom acknowledge strangers on the street, and Toronto itself has few pubs and cafes to facilitate casual meetings.

This privatization of community life is accompanied by a fair amount of specialization in the kinds of activities that network members share. East Yorkers only deal with their median, significant, intimate, and routine contacts in three to four types of contexts out of the eight we studied (Table 6.5). Two of these contexts are almost always homes and telephones. As for the rest, coworkers tend to be limited to the workplace, neighbors to the neighborhood, extended kin to cards and letters, and friends to informal activity centers (such as skiing), as well as to cards and letters.

Clearly, East Yorkers' interactions are specialized by context. Few networks contain many ties in which network members interact in many contexts. Rather than deal with the same persons in a series of contexts, East Yorkers move from network member to network member as they move from context to context.

Access to network members

Distance. The spatial dispersion of network members confirms what the data on roles and contexts suggest: Networks are not local residential groups. Most active members live more than 9 miles from the East Yorkers. Only 22% live within 1 mile (Table 6.6). To be sure, these data exaggerate the distances that coworkers must travel or telephone to interact – many meet on the job and almost only there. Nevertheless, it takes a short drive or a local telephone call for East Yorkers to keep in touch with most network members. Moreover, about one-third of all their active and intimate contacts live more than 30 miles away, so that a long drive or a long distance call is necessary to keep in touch.[11]

We have not found any truly Saved local networks, in which most members live within walking distance of each other and the East Yorker. Even the four personal networks heavily laden with neighbors and local kin have a median residential distance of 2 miles; that is, they contain members beyond walking distance. To be sure, three women who both work and raise children have the majority of their ties close at hand – either at work or within a mile of their homes – but this is not nearly the same thing as a local residential community.

By contrast, the networks that contain the most spatially *distant* networks are not the most spatially dispersed. Whereas Jenny Draper, Teresa Kidd, and Stan Walker must travel and phone 5,500, 420, and 250 miles, respectively, to visit kin and friends in Germany and rural Ontario, their network members all live in densely knit hometown social circles. However, the members of most networks live at a variety of residential distances from the East Yorkers. This diversity may help explain why networks tend to interact in small groups rather than as wholes. It is difficult to get them together at the same time and – except for families gathering at "mother's house" – there is no East York tradition of meeting in public or ceremonial spaces.

Distance is strongly related to the amount of contact between network members. Thus 41% of the routine ties live within 1 mile of the East Yorkers – 66%, if we treat coworkers as "local" (Table 6.6). Moreover, when "couples" are counted as two, such local ties are weighted even more: up to 52% and 71%, respectively. Only 4% of routine contacts live more than

Table 6.6. *Network members living at different distances from East Yorkers (percent)*

Distribution by ties	Significant		Intimate		Routine	
	RD	CWD	RD	CWD	RD	CWD
Same building, block (0–0.1 mile)	17	24	10	13	36	61
Same neighborhood (0.2–1 mile)	5	5	8	8	5	5
Metro Toronto (1.1–30 miles)	45	38	50	47	54	30
South Central Ontario (31–100 miles)	13	13	17	17	4	4
Further away (more than 100 miles)	21	21	15	15	0	0
	101	101	100	100	99	100
Median mileage	10	9	10	10	2.8	0.1
Number of ties	403	403	164	164	95	96

Note: RD = residential distance; CWD = treats coworkers as "living" in the same building.

Table 6.7. *Frequency of contact by mode (days per year)*

	Significant ties (N = 402)			Intimate ties[a] (N = 162)		
	FTF[b]	Phone	All[c]	FTF[b]	Phone	All[c]
Lower quartile of contact	6	2	15	12	6	26
Median contact	21	12	48	24	24	66
Upper quartile of contact	52	52	128	59	52	209

[a] Routine ties omitted from table as all are in frequent contact.
[b] FTF = face to face.
[c] Includes contact by letter, card and CB radio, as well as face-to-face and telephone contact.

30 miles away (usually 1 hour's trip) – despite the availability of telephone calls for routine interaction.

Frequency of contact. The median network member is in touch with the East Yorkers about once every 2 weeks and uses face-to-face encounters somewhat more frequently than telephone contact (Table 6.7). Intimates keep in somewhat more frequent touch – a median of nearly once per week – using telephone contact as much as face-to-face contact. Intimates use the telephone more, in part because they are less often next-door neighbors and coworkers and in part because telephone contact is more voluntary than many face-to-face work, neighboring, and kinship encounters. Nevertheless, frequency of interaction varies enormously for intimates as well as other active contacts: from thrice daily visits with invalid mothers, best friend neighbors, and workmates to less-than-yearly contact with best friends who have moved overseas, kinfolk left behind in Germany, and temporarily absent lovers.

Only when ties stretch over long distances does telephone contact replace face-to-face encounters: Face-to-face and telephone contact are positively correlated. Network members use whichever means is handiest to contact one another. Moreover, the use of one medium often stimulates the other member – as when one sister calls the other to make a date for a social visit.

Most East Yorkers are well connected into their networks. For example, the median East Yorker is in touch with three active ties in an average day – including one or two intimates. Indeed, 5 East Yorkers are in touch with an average of 7–10 active ties per day: Two men (Andy Capp, a maintenance mechanic; Chris Armstrong, a firefighter) often see many coworkers and kin. Two women (Patricia Fairgray, secretary; Teresa Kidd, boutique owner) are deeply involved with large kinship groups. Patricia's kinfolk are from the local area, while Teresa frequently travels 485 miles to her northern Ontario hometown for extended visits. The third woman (Betty Lancaster, homemaker) sees a large, densely knit circle of neighbors at least three times a week, and she also spends a great deal of time, in person and on the telephone, with fellow animal welfare activists: "I'm constantly meeting new people in all sorts of places. There's lots of people I would like to see more often – or spend more time with – and you just don't have the time or opportunity or whatever."

The four East Yorkers previously identified as quite isolated are at the other extreme. Each is in touch with less than one active network member in an average day. In at least two cases, these East Yorkers appear to have deliberately chosen to limit their social contacts. The most disconnected, Jenny Draper, is in touch with less than one active contact in an average week. Most of her ties stretch back to the north German hometown she left in 1954. Retired to rural Ontario, she and her husband live self-contained lives. Although they are close only with their daughter and two old friends, they value and use these relations while guarding against new ones: "Sometimes you have to discuss things with somebody else that you don't want to discuss with your husband. You have to have someone. You can't stay alone, yet you can't do this with everybody – that's where I learned my lesson."

Thus, although not as visible as an "urban village" (Gans, 1962) to the casual observer, East Yorkers are in most cases embedded in networks composed of strong ties. These networks, moreover, are not homogeneous or dull grey. Ties are made with different colors. Kin, friends, neighbors, and coworkers often cohabit within the same network and are sometimes even connected to one another. The colors of the ties glow with different intensities: strong to weak. Although neighbor and coworker ties rarely glow strongly, they are more often thick through frequent contact. All East Yorkers have a fabric of ties. Most are strong, well-made coats of many colors. But, like Joseph, they have moved beyond the old neighborhood.

Ties: a summary

The composition of East Yorkers' ties provides a good indication of why analysts have been unable to decide whether contemporary communities are Lost, Saved, or Liberated. There is no one correct view. Rather, the view analysts hold depends on where they focus their attention in a complex, three-dimensional picture of East Yorkers' ties (see Table 6.8).

To some extent, the foreground of the picture supports contentions that many urbanites have lost community. Most East Yorkers have only a few ties with whom they are routinely in touch – by telephone or face to face. In their day-to-day lives, most deal only with three or fewer ties – only one of whom is a socially close intimate – and have less frequent contact with other network members. Although they may encounter many acquaintances, only a small proportion of East Yorkers are in routine touch with more than a handful of significant ties.

Yet, to look only at the foreground is to ignore most of the picture: most East Yorkers have a good number of stable, traditional ties at the core of their networks. Most ties have endured for 19 years or more. Even routine ties – primarily with neighbors and coworkers – have usually lasted for at least 8 years. About two-thirds of the ties have developed from traditional communal sources – kin, childhood friends, the neighborhood – and almost all were formed under the auspices of some social institution. Kin loom large in East Yorkers' worlds by all criteria except frequency of contact, and ties with parents and siblings are especially important for socially close intimate relations. Most network members are readily at hand, if not in the neighborhood or at work, then by a quick, low-cost drive or telephone call in the metro Toronto area. Although some East Yorkers are socially isolated – their small networks do not keep in touch very much – they seem more assuredly self-reliant than abandoned or lost.

The stable ties at the center still do not complete the picture. In some important ways, these networks provide support for the Liberated argument. Many ties have formed within the past decade, most since adulthood. Only a minority of ties are with kin. Friends are present to a significant degree in almost all networks. Almost all networks contain a variety of friends, kin, neighbors, coworkers, and, perhaps, organizational ties. More than three-quarters of all active network members live more than a mile away in walking distance, and intimates are even more likely to live outside the neighborhood. Indeed, network members tend to use telephones more often than face-to-

Table 6.8. *Three expectations for the size, composition, and accessibility of ties compared with the East Yorkers' data*

	Lost	Saved	Liberated	East Yorkers
Size of network	Very small	Very large	Large	1 active, 3 routine, 4 intimate
Origins	Friends, organizations	Kin, neighborhood	Friends, workplace	Kin, neighborhood, workplace
Duration	Short	Long	Mostly short	8–20 + years
Roles	Acquaintances	Kin, neighbors	Friends, coworkers	Kin, friends
Sociophysical context	Public, private	Communal spaces	Private spaces	Private (home, phone)
Residential separation	Somewhat dispersed	Local	Highly dispersed	10 miles; 1/4 within 1 mile, 1/3 more than 30 miles
Frequency of contact	Low	High (much in person)	High (much phone use)	Once a week; equal phone and face to face

face encounters to maintain contact – although they spend more time interacting face to face.

Networks, however, are more than the sum of discrete two-person ties, floating free in physical and social space. They are structures that help to determine which persons are available for interaction, what resources are available for use, and the extent to which these resources can flow to network members. In the next section, we examine the extent to which the East Yorkers' networks resemble disconnected sets of isolates predicted by the Lost argument, the densely knit solidarities foreseen by the Saved argument, or the multiple sets of specialized clusters implicit in the Liberated argument.

The structure of personal communities

Structural embeddedness

The many links between network members means that East Yorkers must deal with network structures and not just juggle sets of disconnected ties. Indeed, significant members of the median East Yorker's network are directly linked with a mean of four other network members in addition to being directly tied with the East Yorker. In three large, densely knit networks with a high volume of contact with the focal East Yorkers, members have an average of 7–10 links with one another. In two of these networks (those of Teresa Kidd and of Patricia Fairgray), a large group of kin often visit and help each other. In the third, a gregarious firefighter (Chris Armstrong) actively connects clusters of friends, neighbors, coworkers, and kin.

Most networks are not as densely connected. Indeed, in seven of the average-to-small ones, the mean number of links between members (mean "degree") is between one and two (Freeman, 1979). The four East Yorkers with no routine ties also have the networks with the lowest mean number of links. Yet they do not totally conform to the Lost model since the mean degree of their networks (1.0) shows that network members retain some capacity for coordinated action on their behalf.

The dozen or so significant members of East Yorkers' networks form only a small proportion of their ties. Hence, the impact of network structures on the East Yorkers' relationships with network members is far more pervasive than the mean degrees of 1.0–10.0 might imply. Indeed, four-fifths (81%) of the ties between East Yorkers and their network members are "structurally embedded," that is, their interaction is conditioned by the two persons' mutual links with others (Table 6.9). Proportions are higher (93%) for the predominantly neighbor and coworker routine ties and lower (73%) for the more voluntaristic intimate ties. Moreover, although East Yorkers enjoy almost all of their ties to some extent, they maintain a sizable minority of their ties mainly because they are mutually embedded in the same social

Table 6.9. *Structural embeddedness of ties (percent)*

Distribution	Significant (N = 391)	Intimate (N = 164)	Routine (N = 89)
Not structurally embedded	19	27	7
Structurally embedded, but also voluntarily tied	35	52	56
Structurally embedded; involuntarily tied	42	19	35
Structurally embedded; disliked	4	2	2
	100	100	100

Table 6.10. *Usual network context of interactions between East Yorkers and network members (percent)*

Distribution	Significant (N = 381)	Intimate (N = 164)	Routine (N = 92)
East Yorkers with network member	35	41	42
At least one of the two parties to the tie interacts as a married couple	23	25	23
Other network members are involved	42	34	35
	100	100	100

structures (Table 6.9). Indeed, they relate in this way to one-fifth (21%) of all their intimates.

Although interactions between these structurally embedded network members usually take place in private spaces, several persons are normally party to the interactions. More than one-fifth (23%) of all significant ties are actually made between two married couples rather than between two individuals (30% of the ties, if we count couples as two persons). Two-fifths of the ties usually operate in the presence of others to whom the East Yorker and the network member are mutually linked (Table 6.10). Indeed, in 76% of the networks a majority of members interact with the East Yorkers as couples or in the presence of such mutually linked others.

Isolates are quite rare in the East Yorkers' networks: only 12% of the network members are not directly linked with any other network member. (All "isolates" are, of course, linked to networks owing to their direct ties with the focal East Yorkers.) Indeed, 19 networks (58%) contain no isolates, and only 6 (19%) contain more than one or two. The extreme is accountant Henry Harrison's discreetly discrete ties with seven younger men.

Integration and fragmentation

East Yorkers' networks rarely correspond to the densely knit solidarities suggested by the Saved argument or to the disconnected fragments envisioned by the Lost argument. The median density of all networks is 0.33 (Table 6.11); that is, of 90 possible links between 10 network members, 30 actually existed. Such links are neither evenly nor randomly distributed: They clump together within the denser-knit networks roughly corresponding to such principal foci of East Yorkers' lives as kinship and work (Feld, 1981).[12]

Note that the structures described here omit the East Yorkers who are, after all, directly tied with all of their network members. Thus, we describe the networks as the East Yorkers saw them, rather than as a view from above. Including the East Yorkers would have raised the connectivity of all networks. For example, each network would have become one all-inclusive component and the density of the median network would have risen from 0.33 to 0.36.

Despite the sparseness of most networks, they are well connected in certain respects. In addition to one or two isolates or dyads, there is typically one large core *component* of about eight members, all of whom are directly or indirectly linked with one another, for example, as "friends of friends." These components form the boundaries of the channels through which information and other resources can flow without involving the focal East Yorkers. (If we had included the East Yorkers in the networks, then all members would have belonged to the same component, since the East Yorkers indirectly connect them all.) The structural opportunities for coordinate activity are high in most components: Their median density of 0.67 means that at least two-thirds of all possible links between component members are actually made.

Two persons may be within the same component and yet be three or more links removed from one another. *Clusters*, by contrast, are structures with higher proportions of direct links and, hence, more potential for coordinated, cohesive action. Almost all possible direct links among members are actually made. These clusters correspond to the parts of their networks that East Yorkers think of as "groups." All but two East Yorkers have at least one cluster in their networks; most of these range in size from four to eight members (Table 6.11). The mean size of these clusters tends to reflect the fact that they contain a high proportion of all the links in the network ("cluster dominance" in Table 6.11). Moreover, many network members belong to more than one cluster. Hence, these densely knit clusters tend to organize and dominate East Yorkers' networks, and their overlapping membership facilitate the coordination of activity between groups.

The appreciable amount of local integration within these networks does not mean that they are highly integrated *as a whole*. These networks tend to

Table 6.11. *Structural characteristics of East Yorkers' networks*

	Upper extreme	Upper quartile	Median network	Lower quartile	Lower extreme
Mean number of direct links between network members (mean degree)	10.4	5.5	3.2	1.9	0.4
Density – all active ties	1.00	0.56	0.33	0.25	0.04
Density of largest component	1.00	0.80	0.67	0.42	0.26
Size of largest component	25	13	8	5	2
Mean size of all clusters	15	8	5	4	0
Cluster dominance[a]	1.00	0.75	0.50	0.31	0.00
Mean-cluster overlap[b]	0.71	0.61	0.43	0.22	0.00
Mean clique size	15	5	4	3	0
Number of components	4	2	1	1	1
Number of isolates	7	1.50	0	0	0
Number of clusters	5	2.50	1	1	0
Number of cliques	18	6	3	1	0

[a] Mean size of all clusters/mean size of network.
[b] Mean of the extent to which two clusters within the largest component share a common membership.

contain numerous small *cliques* (in which all are directly linked with all) rather than one large clique embracing most members. In addition to the isolates and dyads present in all of them, many (39%) contain several components and clusters. Indeed, core components themselves are split into two clusters in one-quarter (24%) of the networks. In short, network members from various foci in the East Yorkers' lives are usually linked into dyads and densely knit clusters that are, in turn, knit into components by those few network members who belong to several clusters – usually persons from one focus who have gotten to know persons in another.

There are several clear variations in this general structural pattern. We have already discussed two: the small, sparsely knit networks of those East Yorkers who "keep to themselves" and the few networks with a great many isolates. Toward the opposite end of the spectrum, there are seven large Saved networks in which almost all members are in clusters. Although five of these networks are based on large kinship groups, in two cases (Tom Robinson, a printer; Jane Hazlett, the socially active wife of a retired insurance executive and political figure), the densely knit networks are social circles composed of "good friends."

Seven other large networks with sparser overall density more closely fit expectations under the Liberated argument: In them, East Yorkers move between multiple, thinly connected circles of kin, neighbors, coworkers, and friends. Five of seven of the East Yorkers tied in with both these large Saved and Liberated networks are women who are heavily involved in maintaining ties among kin and other community members.

Structures: summary and discussion

The ways in which most ties are structurally embedded in clusters and cliques greatly facilitates group support and social control. The fact that so many ties are structural in origin – and some not even sources of individual satisfaction – calls into question the social psychological assumption that community ties are formed and maintained through "interpersonal attraction" between parties (Berscheid and Walster, 1978; see also Erickson's critique, Chapter 5). Many East Yorkers are tied to persons with whom they have to deal in their neighborhoods, kinship groups, or on the job – whether they are attracted to them or not. Such ties are maintained by general social networks, or formal organizations that constrain network members to be parties to relationships. In these situations, interpersonal attraction may sometimes affect the intensity of ties, frequency of contact, and the number of strands in the relationship, but not the existence of these ties, themselves.

The structures themselves tend to complement the analytic patterns we found above at the level of ties (see Table 6.12). Only two networks are so fragmented that they lack clusters, and only three are simply one large cluster. Instead, East Yorkers are members of networks that are simultaneously decentralized into several clusters, dyads, and isolates and are centralized through high-density clusters and links between clusters. Their overall decentralization means that East Yorkers must obtain assistance from distinct, somewhat disconnected sources within their networks and cannot assume that information about their needs flows easily to all members. However, the high density of clusters and the moderate density of the large core components facilitates a substantial coordination of activity within most networks.

The information on the nature of East Yorkers' networks tends to resolve the paradox of community ties manifestly visible in surveys and interviews but not visible to the naked eye. Certainly these ties exist and are well structured. But they exist in small clusters – through meetings in private homes and on the telephone – and not in large, palpable bodies gathering in public squares, cafes, and meeting halls. Indeed, the very privacy of their operation may help to account for the stability of these networks: It is quite difficult for East Yorkers to meet many new persons unless they change homes, jobs, or spouses.

The contents of personal communities

Networks are not just structures without content. They convey resources. Indeed, the resources they carry largely determine the nature, and very existence of, ties. East Yorkers report that ties that do not do anything quickly fade into faint memory.

Table 6.12. *Three expectations for network structure compared with the East Yorkers' data*

	Lost	Saved	Liberated	East Yorkers
Structural embeddedness	None	Very high	High	High
Network context	Dyads	Large group	Small clusters	Clusters, dyads, couples
Density	Very low	Very high	Moderate overall, with dense clusters	Moderate overall, with higher density component, and even higher density clusters
Cluster overlap	Low	1 big cluster	Low	Moderate (0.43)
Number of network pieces (components + isolates)	Many small fragments and isolates	1 big cluster, no isolates	Several small clusters and isolates	1 big component containing 1 cluster; 1 isolate
Cluster dominance	No	Yes, by 1	Yes, by several	Moderate (0.50)

Most East Yorkers say they want their networks to bring them two sorts of resources (Leighton, 1986): companionship ("people who I enjoy being with"), and aid ("people who understand me, who I can count on in a crisis"). But what do East Yorkers actually get from their ties and networks? Although the Lost argument holds that they do not get much of anything, the Saved argument maintains that most ties in most networks provide a wide spectrum of companionship and aid, and the Liberated argument implies that people can get a wide spectrum of aid, but only by selectively using specialized ties. In this section, we describe the various contents, or *strands*, of East Yorkers' ties and networks.

The resources of personal communities

The principal strands of ties and networks. Ten of the 19 strands we studied dominate the East Yorkers' networks, providing them with various forms of companionship, emotional aid, and small-scale services (Table 6.13). Together, these 10 strands account for 86% of all strands actually flowing between active network members and East Yorkers. Hence, they represent the kinds of resources that most East Yorkers can reasonably expect to get from many – if not most – of their significant network members (Table 6.14).

Four strands involve forms of *companionship*. Indeed, one strand, "sociability" – that is, getting pleasure from being in one another's company – is present in nearly three-quarters of the active and routine ties and almost all of the intimate ones (Table 6.13). (The few intimate ties that do not involve sociability are almost always with disliked, structurally embedded, immediate kin.) Other more focused forms of companionship, although not as prevalent as sociability, are present in many ties: doing things together, discussing interests and ideas, and participating together in formally organized groups (outside of work). These shared activities – from discussing baseball to going away on joint vactions – are often important foci for ties and networks, bringing members together to reaffirm, readjust, and sustain their relationships.

In the midst of such abundant companionship, those who lack friends are noticeable, Four East Yorkers we have repeatedly identified as isolated have only two to four sociable relations in their networks (Jenny Draper, Eddie Palmer, Stan Walker, John Williams). Moreover, Stan and Eddie as well as Betty Lancaster and Leonard Dobson despite their larger networks lack companionship in most of their ties. All four have strained, cool relationships with most of their structurally embedded kin, and Betty is also "strictly business" with three of the four animal welfare activists who are important members of her network.[13]

Table 6.13. *Significant ties having specific strands (percent)*

Strand type	Companionship (33 networks)		
	Significant, EY↔	Intimate, EY↔	Routine, EY↔
Sociability	72	92	70
Discussing things	47	64	58
Doing things together	39	55	51
Impact in formal groups	18	16	20
[Number of ties]	374	163	91]

Strand type	Aid (29 networks)								
	Significant			Intimate			Routine		
	EY→	EY↔	EY←	EY→	EY↔	EY←	EY→	EY↔	EY←
Minor emotion aid	10	40	7	12	53	7	12	42	7
Family problems advice	10	29	10	13	38	9	13	33	8
Major emotion aid	10	25	8	11	36	8	10	31	2
Minor services	15	32	7	19	36	9	21	35	3
Minor household aid	12	26	9	20	33	12	14	28	12
Lend/give items	7	32	5	9	39	8	9	43	6
Aid with organizations	7	6	4	7	7	4	7	8	6
Major services	4	4	3	6	6	5	7	5	2
Major household aid	6	9	4	9	12	5	7	10	5
Lend/give large amounts $	2	0.3	4	4	0.7	5	1	1	8
Lend/give small amount $	8	8	5	13	9	6	9	9	6
Lend/give housing $	1	0.3	3	2	0	4	2	0	3
Housing search aid	5	1	3	8	2	4	6	3	3
Job opening information	5	1	5	6	1	8	5	5	2
Job contacts	3	0.6	4	3	0.7	6	6	2	10
Number of ties		336			137			82	9
Median of aid strands in a tie		2			3			3	
Median of all strands in tie		3			5			4	

Note: EY↔ = exchange of aid; EY→ = aid from East Yorker only; EY← = aid from network member only.

Table 6.14. *Networks in which at least one tie (and half of all ties) give a specific resource (percent)*

Strand type	Companionship		
	Significant, EY↔	Intimate, EY↔	Routine, EY↔
Sociability	100[a]	100	90
	(73)[b]	(97)	(83)
Discussing things	94	94	86
	(45)	(82)	(75)
Doing things together	91	85	76
	(45)	(70)	(65)
Interact in formal groups	48	45	35
	(6)	(12)	(17)
Number of networks	33	33	29

	Aid					
	EY →	EY ←	EY →	EY ←	EY →	EY ←
Minor emotional aid	86	83	86	83	79	67
	(48)	(45)	(72)	(69)	(62)	(54)
Family problems advice	83	76	79	69	75	58
	(35)	(28)	(55)	(52)	(46)	(33)
Major emotional aid	76	69	69	62	75	54
	(24)	(31)	(52)	(48)	(33)	(38)
Minor services	90	83	79	79	83	71
	(48)	(38)	(59)	(55)	(67)	(46)
Minor household aid	97	90	90	83	71	71
	(31)	(31)	(59)	(55)	(46)	(50)
Lend/give items	93	83	90	79	79	79
	(45)	(45)	(62)	(55)	(67)	(54)
Aid with organizations	38	38	34	34	29	25
	(14)	(3)	(21)	(10)	(21)	(17)
Major services	41	45	31	28	25	21
	(3)	(0)	(14)	(3)	(8)	(4)
Major household aid	59	55	48	48	37	46
	(14)	(3)	(17)	(17)	(17)	(17)
Lend/give large amount $	17	28	14	17	8	25
	(0)	(0)	(3)	(3)	(4)	(4)
Lend/give small amount $	72	62	55	45	50	37
	(7)	(10)	(24)	(21)	(17)	(17)
Lend/give housing	17	28	10	21	8	8
	(0)	(0)	(0)	(0)	(0)	(0)
Housing search aid	35	35	28	28	21	17
	(3)	(0)	(10)	(0)	(8)	(4)
Job opening information	35	48	21	31	25	42
	(3)	(0)	(7)	(3)	(12)	(12)
Job contacts	28	31	17	21	29	25
	(0)	(0)	(0)	(0)	(8)	(12)
[Number of networks	29	29	29	29	24	24]

[a] Percentages in the top row are for networks in which at least 1 tie provides that resource.
[b] Percentages in parentheses are for networks in which at least half of the ties provide that resource.
Note: Ey↔exchange of aid; EY → aid from East Yorker only; EY ← aid from network member only.

The most widespread strands of aid in these ties and networks are

> *Small services:* "minor household aid" (e.g., minor repairs to the
> house or car; occasional help with housework); "minor services"
> (e.g., errands, driving person to the doctor, occasional childcare);
> "lend/give household items" (e.g., food, tools, washing machine)
> *Emotional aid:* "family problems advice" (e.g., marriage problems,
> raising children); "minor emotional aid" (during a routine or
> minor upset); "major emotional aid" (during a major crisis or
> long-lasting problem).

Most East Yorkers obtain small services and emotional aid (major as well as minor) from at least one network member. Many obtain such aid from at least half their active ties (Table 6.14). Eighty-eight percent of ties contain at least one strand of aid; 93 percent contain either aid or companionship. Table 6.13 shows the percentage of ties that provide each type of aid and whether it is provided symmetrically (by both parties to the tie) or in one direction only (to or from the East Yorkers). The table shows, for example, that whereas 47% of the East Yorkers' active ties provide "minor emotional aid" (40% both ways plus 7% one way to the East Yorker only), as many as 60% of their intimates (53% plus 7%) provide such aid.[14] This means that, on the average, East Yorkers obtain minor emotional aid from two or three intimates and two or three other active network members (and probably from one or two more persons, if couples are counted as two). In general, intimates are much more likely than other network members to provide small services and emotional aid, while routine network members are also somewhat more likely. Thus, social proximity appears to be a more important determinant of getting help than physical closeness.

Employed men specialize in using job-related skills to perform small services for network members. Thus Douglas Freedman (a business machine technician) phoned his best friend to say: "I need your help. I'm doing aluminum siding. What are you doing this weekend? He said 'Fine. I'm on holiday this week and I'll earmark the weekend for you.' He stayed to Monday."

Not only do men fix machines, but they put in siding, wiring, and plumbing. Even if working at middle-class jobs, they put a special premium on handiness, often combining it with sociable companionship (Wellman, 1985). Thus Jane Hazlett says of her friend Phil (a businessman): "Phil's a very ambitious person. His idea of relaxing when he comes up here is doing things, so he'll be out digging in the garden. I'll say I wish I could get that done, and next thing he'll be doing it."

Homemakers exchange not only material services, but are also the East Yorkers who give and get the most emotional support. Although some of this support is related to major family and health crises, most comes in smaller, routine doses as fellow homemakers help each other to get through the child-care day and the husband-care night. As Eve Spencer says of her closest friend (and former neighbor): "We sometimes just go for walks around the block. We don't always talk even. We might just sort of look at the sky together. It's calm."

Despite the pervasiveness of small services and emotional aid among network members, some East Yorkers strictly limit their use of networks. For example, although Douglas Freedman exchanges many services, he avoids all emotional entanglements. He states flatly: "I don't have crises or emergencies. If I had a serious illness, I would handle it very gingerly. I would learn to live with it. I think we would probably manage on our own."

Five other relatively isolated East Yorkers exchange only a small amount of emotional support (Jenny Draper, Gerald Hopkins, Eddie Palmer, Stan Walker, and John Williams), and one of these (John Williams, a determined loner) does not exchange any small services. Yet the isolation of this small group makes even clearer the continued, widespread flow of emotional aid and small services through all the other networks.

Thus, companionship, emotional aid, and small services form the continuing basis of East Yorkers' ties and networks; they are what East Yorkers routinely expect to get from their ties – in daily life and in crises.

Both supply and demand help explain why these types of resources are so abundant in the networks. Companionship, emotional aid, and small services are easily supplied and require only small, widely available skills and services. On the one hand, the suppliers of these services do not have to have many material resources at their disposal. On the other hand, most find it easy to be buddies empathic listeners, and helpers. Moreover, these are not zero-sum relationships: Supplying these services does not necessarily cost the giver. Indeed, to give companionship – or even emotional aid and small services – may be to gain in companionship as well.

With respect to demand, companionship, emotional support, and helping hands are the resources that most East Yorkers want from network members. Although they could purchase such services, it is unlikely that they could get the same combination of frequent, flexible, nuanced, inexpensive services that network members supply. Hence, East Yorkers are more willing to invest in the time and effort necessary to maintain their ties (and their services) than they are to spend the money for equivalent services. Thus, although, like all Canadians, they can obtain low-cost psychiatric and medical care, the East Yorkers rely on network members, not professionals, for emotional aid in major crises as well as in routinely stressful situations. As Patricia Fairgray (a widowed secretary) says: "I might talk it over with someone, but no, I wouldn't go to a doctor. All he'll do is stick you on tranquilizers, and you'll be going around with your feet on the ground and your head up in the air, and it doesn't help."

Less common strands. Other strands are almost always optional extras in these ties, combined with companionship, small services, and emotional aid. These are the strands that call for (a) time and effort (major services, major household aid, romantic involvement); (b) money (minor financial aid, major financial aid, financial aid for housing); and (c) specialized information (aid in dealing with organizations, information about job openings, job contacts, housing search aid).

Each of these strands is present in only 3%–13% of the active ties (Table 6.13), and many East Yorkers have not yet received any of these resources from another network member (Table 6.14). To the extent that these strands exist, they tend to be part of intimate and routine ties.

There are several reasons for the comparative absence of these strands from the East Yorkers' ties. In some cases, East Yorkers do not want the specialized resources these strands deliver. In many others, when East Yorkers do want such resources, they purchase them on the open market or obtain them through formal bureaucracies. Often, East Yorkers do not even think of asking network members for this sort of help: They do not consider getting such resources to be part of their relationships. Often network members do not have such specialized resources available in the necessary qualities, such as time for long-term health care, money for mortgages, or the ability to deal with government bureaucracies. At other times, East Yorkers want to avoid the increased reciprocal obligations that would come if they draw such resources from network members. For example, some prefer to obtain mortgage money from banks rather than intimates.

Yet, even if the number of persons in a network who give such aid is limited, the accessibility of such aid from somewhere in the network is often crucial to East Yorkers' well-being. For example, consider the impact of such aid on two areas of Wendy Sherwin's life:

> Currently a suburban homemaker, she left a well-paying job to have a son. However, her son's chronic hyperactivity made family life very difficult for 10 years. After fruitless searches for useful medical help, she finally learned from a friend about the causal link between food additives and hyperactivity. Her son's diet now carefully controlled, Wendy's family leads an active, normal life. Although finding the proper additive-free foods still takes much time, Wendy had become active in an allergy information group. She writes letters to newspapers, distributes "Dr. Feingold's diet" to Canadians who have heard about her from other people, and spends a good deal of time giving advice to people on the telephone. Moreover, she has become a close friend of another homemaker whose hyperactive daughter also has been helped by the diet.

Wendy – and her household – also got a good deal of help with their current "dream house." They found the land it was built on through a close friend, who was also looking for a house. Wendy's mother gave her the mortgage money necessary to buy the land, and Wendy's father-in-law and brother-in-law came up on weekends and holidays to help her husband build the house: doing carpentry and putting up drywall. During the year the family spent building the house, friends would frequently drop by on weekends to help out in any way they could. This has been just one of such projects: Wendy and her husband helped her parents build a rural summer home a few years ago. [Interviewer's note.]

Considered as a property of ties, these less common forms of aid are rare (see Table 6.13). But considered as a network property, the aid that many East Yorkers obtain from their networks has been crucial in seeing them through a major illness or nervous breakdown, or has been the key to getting the right job or house.

Specialized and multistranded ties

Network analysts expect that more *multistranded* ties – ones containing several kinds of resources – will be more durable and intimate than specialized ties. This is because a wider range of contents binds together the two parties to a multistranded tie, so that each is involved in more of the other's life and the tie is able to endure the rupture of a specific strand.[15] The Saved argument has made the persistence of such broadly based multi-stranded ties and networks a central tenet; the Lost and Liberated arguments, by contrast, expect most contemporary ties to be quite specialized.

In fact, most East Yorkers' ties are fairly specialized. The median significant tie contains three strands from an East Yorker to a network member and three strands going from a network member to an East Yorker. Moreover, the same strands tend to be packaged together in the same specialized ties. Thus, significant ties going in each direction are likely to contain two strands either of emotional aid or of other small services, in addition to one strand of companionship.[16] Only 4% of active ties are multistranded enough to send as many as 10 different types of resources to the East Yorkers (out of the 19 we studied).

Thus, most East Yorkers and network members exchange only a narrow range of resources (see Table 6.15). They may not be called upon to give any more, they may not have it available, they may not deem it appropriate to give that sort of aid to the other party, or, indeed, they may not believe that aid of that sort is appropriate for any network member under any circumstances.

Table 6.15. *Means (and sums) of strands by network type*

	Significant (N = 29)		Intimate (N = 29)		Routine (N = 25)	
	EY →	EY ←	EY →	EY ←	EY →	EY ←
Upper extreme network	9	8	11	11	13	14
	(144)	(135)	(59)	(60)	(53)	(51)
Upper quartile	6	6	8	8	8	6
	(74)	(68)	(36)	(41)	(28)	(28)
Median network	5	4	7	6	6	5
	(54)	(50)	(28)	(31)	(18)	(15)
Lower quartile	3	3	4	4	4	4
	(36)	(29)	(16)	(19)	(8)	(7)
Lower extreme network	1	1	1	1	0	0
	(5)	(4)	(3)	(4)	(0)	(0)

Note: Numbers in parentheses denote sums. EY → from East Yorkers; EY ← to East Yorkers.

Several East Yorkers were shocked when asked if they received financial aid when they bought their homes.

Intimates – and, to a lesser extent, routine contacts – tend to have less specialized ties than other network members (see Table 6.13). Intimates tend to give each other two or three different types of small-scale aid, usually varieties of emotional aid and small services. Moreover, they are the only network members apt to transfer some large-scale aid, if only a median of one strand in each direction.

Thus, most East Yorkers' networks reflect a division of labor. Most ties in most networks contain less than six strands in each direction (Table 6.15). Indeed, several networks contain quite specialized, often single-stranded, ties. Consistent with our previous findings, "loners" Jenny Draper, Douglas Freedman, Eddie Palmer, and John Williams all give and get tiny amounts of resources from their networks. Yet some networks are full of multistranded ties conveying many resources. Thus, Wendy Sherwin's plump network of neighbors, friends, and kin provides her with 126 strands of companionship, child care, emotional aid, financial aid, important job contacts, and so on. The mean is 7 strands from each active tie.

Such broad service "general stores" are rare, and most networks are more like specialized "boutiques." The many specialized ties fit expectations under the Liberated argument better than under the Saved. The East Yorkers are not usually the calculating manipulators of their environments foreseen by the Liberated argument. Rather, like many North American managers, they are "satisficers" (March and Simon, 1958): taking what will suffice (and what is given to them unbidden) from their networks without too much planning or searching for optimal solutions (Lee, 1969).

Reciprocity

Whatever is given ought to be repaid, if only to ensure that more is available when needed. Repayment might be in the form of *specific exchange*, in which the same kind of aid is returned by the recipient to the person who originally helped out; *generalized reciprocity*, in which the aid given is returned by the recipient giving the original helper other kinds of aid; or *network balancing*, in which aid given by one network member is balanced by the recipient providing aid for other network members, not necessarily the person who originally helped out or the same kind of help (see Gouldner, 1960; Sahlins, 1965; Kadushin, 1981; Cook, 1982).

The Lost argument suggests that none of these forms of reciprocity are prevalent any more, for in a war of all against all, people take short-term advantage of each other. However, both the Saved and the Liberated arguments suggest that reciprocity still flourishes. The emphasis in the Saved argument on group solidarity and social control suggests that network balancing is the most prevalent form of reciprocity, whereas the emphasis in the Liberated argument on multiple social circles and specialized ties predicts that ties will reflect levels of both specific exchange and general reciprocity.

Specific exchanges. The more abundant strands of aid – emotional aid and small services – usually flow in both directions (Table 6.16). When network members give these kinds of aid, they usually recieve the same sort of aid in return from the same person, sooner or later.[17]

Network members are much less likely to reciprocate in the exchange of the less common strands of aid (Table 6.16). These resources tend to flow in one or another direction, but not both. Thus, persons who have lent mortgage money or have provided long-term, intensive health care rarely get back that sort of aid from those they helped.[18]

These types of resources are less often sought by network members and less often proffered by others. But the extent to which these exchanges take place depends on the *particular* networks in which East Yorkers are embedded. If, for example, most members of a network give emotional aid to others, then it is quite likely that any two given network members will be tied in this way. Thus, the neighboring homemakers in Martha Ellis's network are constantly giving each other emotional support. With so much support floating around the network, it is often the person who helped out the previous month who is being helped this month. By contrast, intensive, long-term health care is so rare that even if there are two strands of such aid in the same network, it is unlikely that the same two persons are involved in both cases.

This means that abundant types of aid are more likely to be exchanged even if no norm of reciprocity operates to encourage network members to "repay" them. In fact, a norm of reciprocity does appear to be at work: At

Table 6.16. *Percentage of ties containing specific strands of aid flowing in both directions*

	Significant	Intimate	Routine
Minor emotional aid	70	74	69
Family problems advice	59	63	61
Major emotional aid	58	65	72
Minor services	59	56	58
Minor household aid	55	51	52
Lend/give items	73	72	74
Aid with organizations	35	39	38
Major services	36	35	36
Major household aid	47	46	45
Lend/give large $	5	7	10
Lend/give small $	38	32	38
Lend/give housing $	7	0	0
Housing search aid	11	14	33
Job opening information	9	6	25
Job contacts	8	7	12

Note: % of both directions $= \left(\dfrac{EY \leftrightarrow}{EY \leftrightarrow + EY \rightarrow + EY \leftarrow} \right) \times 100.$

$EY \leftrightarrow$, $EY \rightarrow$, $EY \leftarrow$, taken from Table 6.13.

least twice as much aid is exchanged through significant and routine ties than we would expect from knowing the amount of aid flowing in one direction.

Although levels of exchange are somewhat lower in intimate ties, they are still higher than we would expect just from knowing the amount of aid flowing in each direction. The social closeness of intimates often weakens their concern about specific resources. Margaret Baillie (an insurance claims examiner with many kinfolk) explains her calculations:

> If it was somebody that I am really close to – like my sister – and if they did something for me, I don't think it would be that important that I return the favor. If it's an acquaintance, though, it depends on what it is. If it's just asking for something, like a ride, I would feel I had to give them a ride in return. But if they lent me a dime, I don't think I'd return it.

Generalized reciprocity. To study generalized reciprocity, we count the number of strands of aid sent and recieved in each tie. Thus, if an East Yorker sends all 15 types of aid to a specific person, the tie receives an "overall" sending score of 15. By correlating the sending and receiving scores of ties, we can see if the extent to which East Yorkers send many (or few) strands of aid to particular members is matched by the extent to which they receive strands of aid from them.

Table 6.17. *Correlations between aid given to and received from East Yorkers, by ties and by networks*

	Significant		Intimate		Routine	
	Ties	Nets	Ties	Nets	Ties	Nets
[Number	337	29	137	29	86	25]
Minor emotional aid	.67	.85	.58	.73	.63	.91
Family problems advice	.58	.79	.56	.76	.58	.75
Major emotional aid	.61	.77	.62	.78	.74	.90
Minor services	.56	.90	.46	.71	.56	.80
Minor household aid	.55	.86	.38	.71	.47	.77
Lend/give items	.75	.96	.65	.87	.70	.88
Aid with organizations	.47	.91	.49	.70	.48	.93
Major services	.48	.89	.43	.87	.47	.64
Major household aid	.57	.82	.53	.74	.58	.81
Lend/give large $	.07[a]	.04[a]	.10[a]	− .06[a]	.22	.08[a]
Lend/give small $	.47	.66	.36	.33[a]	.47	.50
Lend/give housing $	.11	.22[a]	− .03[a]	.11[a]	− .03[a]	− .08[a]
Job opening information	.15	.52	.10[a]	.54	.31	.54
Job contacts	.11	.71	.11[a]	.63	.16[a]	.57
Housing search aid	.25	.55	.20	.38	.43	.71
Overall aid	.78	.93	.73	.86	.73	.90

[a]Not significant at .05.

A comparison of these overall correlations (for significant, intimate, and routine ties) with the correlations for exchanges of specific types of aid suggests that generalized reciprocity does exist, over and above specific exchanges. The "overall aid" correlations in the "ties" columns of Table 6.17 are much higher than any of the (usually substantial) specific exchange correlations in the same columns – even after we discount the tendency for correlations of dichotomous variables to be lower than variables with more extended ranges. The very high overall correlations mean that even if two parties to a tie are not exchanging the same sort of resource with each other, they are sending about the same number of resources to each other. The few non-significant specific exchange correlations – for sending large sums of money and job information or contacts – indicate that truly one-way resources are asymmetrically possessed only by one party to a tie and are hardly ever reciprocated.

This does not mean that East Yorkers exchange the same range of resources with all of their network members.[19] It does mean that network members to whom they send many resources are quite likely to send many back to them, and that those to whom they send few resources send little to them. Hence, both Martha Ellis's multistranded neighbor tie and John Williams's single-stranded neighbor tie show generalized reciprocity:

> They can call on us for anything and we can call on them for anything. It would be done just like that. . . . I feel a sense of security. If there's any problem here and Les isn't home, all I have to do is ring that number and they'd be here in a flash. (Martha Ellis, homemaker)

> We don't bother them and they don't bother us. (John Williams, upholsterer)

Network balancing. Although there is evidence of general reciprocity at the level of ties, this phenomenon is even clearer at the network level. To study network balancing, we sum the strands of aid that East Yorkers send and receive in all ties within their networks. Hence, they receive two scores for each type of aid, indicating the number of network members to which they send or receive it. By correlating these scores we can tell the extent to which "sending" and "receiving" are balanced across entire networks, even if the persons to whom the East Yorkers send a type of aid are different from those from whom they receive it (see the "nets" columns in Table 6.17). To study overall network balancing, we take this procedure one step further and sum all the strands of aid (of any type) that East Yorkers send and receive in all ties. Overall correlations among these measures indicate the extent to which the strands of aid in the East Yorkers' network are balanced, that is the extent to which they are getting as many strands as they are giving (see Table 6.17).

No matter which analytic stance we adopt, network balance exceeds tie reciprocity. The "nets" correlations are almost always higher than corresponding "ties" correlations for each specific strand of aid, and usually markedly so. Only the weak-to-negative correlations for lending large amounts of money and for the job-search variables indicate that East Yorkers are likely to be senders or receivers of such aid, but not both. Moreover, not only is there a strong tendency for East Yorkers to have balanced books for specific strands of aid, but the overall measures are even more highly correlated, reaching 0.93 for all active ties. Thus, network balancing is the result of much more than exchanges and reciprocity between ties.

Three phenomena seem to be associated with network balancing. First, the *structural embeddedness* of many ties fosters balancing directly. East Yorkers report that network members acknowledge reciprocity even when aid is sent to another member of the same social circle and not to the original donor. Thus Mark Haines's father helped him to get settled. Every time Mark helps his ill sister, he remembers his father gratefully.

Second, East Yorkers who do not receive much aid also do not give out much of it. They prefer to stand on their own two feet, with networks *balanced at a low level* of activity. As Gerald Hopkins (a retired plumber) reports: "I am a very independent sort of guy. I can do a heck of a lot of work myself even if it takes two or three times the length of time to do it. I was using the shovel for three hours last Friday and five hours the week before, and I liked it."

Third, East Yorkers who are *active senders* of aid also tend to be *active receivers*. Their entire networks are built around sending and receiving resources over and above exchanges within specific social circles. To people such as Patricia Fairgray (a widowed secretary), this is a central moral tenet:

> People are put on this earth to do the best they can for other people, and we should not expect anything in return for it. Yet I am a firm believer that you get out of life what you put into it, and if you don't put anything into it, you can't expect much out of it.

Indeed, when all network members reciprocate heavily, networks become balanced almost automatically. This has been Chris Armstrong's experience: "I always feel I should do something for somebody who does something for me. I just feel better not owing anybody or thinking that I owe. Of course, all my friends are the same as me."

It is clear that the more bread East Yorkers cast upon the waters, the more floats back. Do unto others as you would have your network do unto you.

Summary

Our findings clearly take issue with the large health care literature that assumes that all interpersonal ties provide a generalized something called "support."[20] Most East Yorkers' ties are quite specialized in the kinds of resources they carry, and the kinds of supportive resources vary greatly between ties (see Table 6.18). Thus, East Yorkers often obtain even the most widely available resources – forms of emotional aid and small services – from different ties, and they are fortunate if any of their ties give them large services, amounts of money, or specialized information for dealing with organizations, jobs, and housing. Nor is support always a two-way street: Many strands flow only in one direction, especially those that transfer significant amounts of material resources or services.

Yet, overall, these networks are reciprocal and supportive. The few East Yorkers who do not get – or give – much help are making a virtue of self-reliance rather than being involuntarily disconnected. Although East Yorkers do not get many kinds of resources from most ties, almost all can get a wide range of help from somewhere in their network (Wellman and Goldman, 1986). Their diversified portfolios of ties provide access to a wide range of network members and resources. The ramifying, multiple pieces of their networks means that network members, in the aggregate, have further access to the resources of other social circles.

Table 6.18. *Three expectations for the contents of ties and networks compared with the East Yorkers' data*

	Lost	Saved	Liberated	East Yorkers
Abundance of aid	Low	High	Moderate	Moderate to low
Variety of aid	Low	High	High	Low to moderate
Articulation with large-scale social system	Little (companionship only)	Defensive coping with demands; companionship	Ways of accessing resources; companionship	Companionship; use of emotional aid; small services as defensive coping; some external articulation
Specialization	Specialized ties	Multistranded ties	Specialized ties	Specialized ties; somewhat more multistranded for intimate, routine ties
Reciprocity	Low; only dyadic	High; communal	High within circles	High; communal, dyadic

A network is a complex thing

Lost, Saved, or Liberated?

Like many sociologists, almost all of the East Yorkers value the pastoral ideal of community: They prefer to be members of densely knit, local networks, filled with emotionally compatible persons exchanging a wide range of aid. But almost all East Yorkers also say that they are satisfied with their current networks, even though most of these do not come close to reproducing the pastoral ideal (Leighton, 1986). They appear to have almost as much trouble as sociologists do in reconciling the ideal of community with the reality.

Is the East Yorkers' confusion false consciousness? We think not. Like sociologists, East Yorkers are not able to decide if contemporary communities are Lost, Saved, or Liberated because there is no one correct picture. What they see depends on where they focus their attention in a complex, three-dimensional world. Consider some of the contradictory phenomena we observed among the East Yorkers:

- The smaller the number of routine and intimate ties, the larger the number of active ties.
- The greater the paucity of neighborhood activity, the higher the

amount of metropolitan-wide activity (not to mention the high level of neighboring among homemakers).

- Although kin are a minority of the members of most networks, most ties in most networks still come from traditional origins.
- Although most ties are structurally embedded, they have a strong impact on East Yorkers' private domains.
- Although clusters and components at the center of most networks are dense, most are fractured into multiple pieces.
- Although the density of most networks is low, the density of their constituent clusters is high.
- Although most ties are specialized, almost all provide sociability and some form of either emotional aid or small services.
- Many types of resources in East Yorkers' networks are rare, but most types of resources are available from some network member.
- Although there is a lack of reciprocity among a large minority of ties – especially those that convey substantial amounts of money, goods, and services – there is also extensive mutual exchange of emotional aid and small services and, overall, a high level of network balancing.

East Yorkers' ties and networks, taken as a whole, clearly do not conform to the Lost model, but the complexities we have observed make it difficult to pronounce them unambiguously either Saved or Liberated. There are significant elements of both models in the total picture. Moreover there are significant differences between East Yorkers. Hence one way of assessing the adequacy of the Saved and Liberated models is to zoom in from a wide-angle view of the overall pattern of ties and networks to portraits of individual East Yorkers' networks.

These portraits show that the nature of individual networks varies greatly according to the ways in which East Yorkers are located in large-scale divisions of labor. For instance, about half a dozen East Yorkers have small networks, in which there are few links between members and low levels of aid exchanged. However, of these, only two unemployed single young men appear to be Lost: drifting through short-term ties and getting most of their resources from government and commercial organizations. They lack the kinship ties that marriage brings, the coworker ties a job brings, and the neighborhood ties child care brings. The others with small networks are skilled tradesmen (and one woman married to such a person) who value an "inner-directed" (Riesman, Glazer, and Denny, 1950), self-reliant life-style. Their life, like their work, is based on the exchange of artisanal skills and services. They look forward to retirement in a rural cottage where they can putter around endlessly, without "disturbing" social obligations.

Even more of the East Yorkers' personal networks closely correspond to what we would expect given the Saved model of densely knit, traditional community solidarities. Several are working-class people, heavily involved with hometown kin and workmates. Their kin tend to live near one another – thus, group contact is facilitated – and their jobs tend to foster contact with coworkers. In all cases, it is the women who maintain relations with kin (their own families and their in-laws) and the men with workmates.

Several other women's personal networks fit the Saved model by being heavily involved with neighborhood support groups. They are all home-makers who have changed neighborhoods and lifestyles as their husbands have changed jobs. Upon arriving in a new neighborhood, these suburbanites plunge heavily into local ties and institutions in order to obtain companion-ship and aid (Clark, 1966; Gans, 1967). Their community ties are more local in origin than in practice, since they have kept some long-distance ties with friends in their former neighborhoods.

Several middle-class men have personal networks that fit with the Liberated model: They are heavily involved in multiple clusters of ties and use their coworker ties for job survival, advancement, and sociability. Three of these men have moved quickly up occupational ladders, in large part because patrons have shown them the ropes and sponsored their advancement.

Yet even those networks that best epitomize the Lost, Saved, and Liberated models do not fit these types exactly, and many networks contain elements of both models. This is because the diversity of the overall patterns of East Yorkers' ties and networks is a product of diversity within individual networks as well as of differences between them. Most networks contain kin and friends, local and long-distance ties, clusters and isolates, multistranded and specialized ties, and so on. Indeed, close scrutiny of these networks often reveals the comfortable coexistence of Saved kinship clusters and Liberated friendship ties. Although this diversity makes for low communal solidarity, it has its own payoffs: Densely knit clusters within networks provide bases for cooperative activity, and the variety of ties organized into multiple clusters gives East Yorkers direct and indirect access to a wide spectrum of resources.

Little networks in a big world

East Yorkers' networks reflect both passive reactions to the pressures of large-scale divisions of labor and active attempts to gain access to – and control of – the resources of these differentiated social structures. First and foremost, the networks provide *havens*: a sense of being wanted and belonging, and readily available companionship (Sennett, 1970; Suttles, 1968). Second, they provide many *"band-aids"*: emotional aid and small services to help East Yorkers cope with the stresses and strains of their current structural locations. Third, the outward linkages of networks provide the

East Yorkers with *ladders* to change their situations (jobs, houses, spouses) and *levers* (animal welfare, local politics, food additives) to change the world Although this sort of resource is less common than the other two, we note that the everyday companions, stresses, and strains with which East Yorkers have to deal are an outcome of their current and past social situations. Moreover, even the most dedicated social climbers and world changers spend most of their time engaging in routine sociability and coping with everyday problems (cf. Podhoretz on himself, 1967; Kapp on Karl Marx's household, 1976).

Not only does the outer world create many of the problems with which East Yorkers – and their networks – have to deal, it also creates the contexts in which they have to deal with them. Thus all of the large-scale changes we discussed at the beginning of this chapter affect East Yorkers' lives:

1. A minority are politically active. Two have been active in East York politics, and a few homemakers have worked hard to make their neighborhood schools better places for their children. Two of the most politically active East Yorkers, who are passionately concerned about animal welfare and food additives, are involved in nonlocal, interest-group affairs. Thus only a small number of East Yorkers have worked to affect their local environments.

2. For the most part, East Yorkers do not regard exchanges of aid with network members as reciprocal contracts. They see giving and getting help as part of their diffuse commitment to the well-being of their contacts and networks. However, the weaker their ties, the more likely they are to expect reciprocity. Moreover, despite what they say, the East Yorkers' reciprocity with *specific* network members tends to be balanced, and their exchanges with their overall *networks* tends to be very much in balance.

3. Ties with workmates tend to be confined to the worksite, and job-related contacts are only weakly connected to the rest of the networks. However, workers in artisanal jobs – not in bureaucratic or industrialized ones – tend to be most cut off from other workers and, indeed, to have the smallest networks.

4. Although several East Yorkers especially the political activists have strong outside interests, the lives of most are confined to home and cottage, neighborhood, kin, and work. Most have used the diversity of the city only to secure more occupational and housing choices.

5. Not only have large bureaucratic institutions taken over many of the services that community members used to do for each other, they are often the only perceived choices by East Yorkers. For example, many East Yorkers have mortgages from banks rather than kin and friends who might have had the necessary funds. The domain of

most networks is now largely restricted to companionship, mental and physical health, and small services around the home, cottage, and neighborhood.

6. Cars are the key to most intimate and many other active ties. Most network members are a drive away, and many East Yorkers maintain close relations with hometown folks. Telephones, although often used, are only complementary: Few relationships survive by calls alone. Dependence on cars and phones help privatize relationships. East Yorkers deal with each other indoors, in small preselected groups, and not in village squares.

7. One nonchange is also relevant: Despite the much ballyhooed rearrangements of men's and women's rights and responsibilities, women remain much more responsible than men for maintenance of community. In the continuing sexual division of labor, men provide network members only with job-related skills and services, whereas women provide network members with companionship and emotional aid as well (see also Wellman, 1985).

East Yorkers are clearly coping and, to some extent, thriving in modern times. But do they have community? We have called their networks "personal communities" to demonstrate that they do many of the things that communities are supposed to do. But, in the traditional sense, these networks are not communities: Only those East Yorkers who spend a good deal of time around the house – homemakers and retirees – tend to know many of the people in their neighborhoods. Only a minority are members of densely knit solidarities. Thus, we have not found communities in the traditional sense. But we have surely found networks, and they seem to have satisfied most East Yorkers.

NOTES

1. This *Community Question* has been a continuing, central concern since at least the time of Machiavelli (1532) and Hobbes (1651). Recent contributions include Tilly (1974), Hunter (1975), Gusfield (1975), Pocock (1975), Poggioli (1975), Fischer (1976, 1982a), Warren (1978), and Wellman and Leighton (1979). Now, instead of only wondering about whether communities exist, we can start to wonder about the circumstances under which different types of personal communities flourish.

2. The classic arguments are in Tönnies ([1887] 1955), the first two-thirds of Simmel ([1902–3] 1950), and Wirth (1938). For more contemporary statements, see Stein (1960), Kornhauser (1968), Nisbet (1969), and Slater (1970).

3. Key early works include Jacobs (1961), Gans (1962, 1967), and Greer (1962, 1972). For more contemporary statements, see Bell and Newby (1971, 1976), Frankenberg (1966), Palm (1973), Craven and Wellman (1973), Wellman and Whitaker (1974), R. Warren (1978), D. Warren (1981), and Greenbaum (1982).

4. Some key works are Webber (1964), Kadushin (1966), Wellman (1972), Granovetter (1973), Fischer (1975, 1976, 1982a), Fischer et al. (1977), and Hiltz and Turoff (1979).

5. Our interviews are not a strict random subsample of the original survey sample. We chose a longitudinal sampling design, emphasizing differences in residential mobility, to facilitate the research of a member of our group (Crump, 1977). We believed at the time that such a purposive design was better than either starting over again with a small new random sample or just analyzing a 1978 random subsample of those who had lived in East York in 1968.

Our design selected randomly from the original East York survey respondents within four residential mobility categories: living in the same household as in 1968; living elsewhere in East York or its borderlands; living elsewhere in the municipality of metropolitan Toronto; living elsewhere in southern Ontario. This somewhat overrepresents residentially mobile persons in the interview subsample as compared with the original random sample. The overrepresentation helps explain why the median age of our 1978 interview sample is approximately the same as that of our 1968 survey sample instead of being 10 years older: The "movers" tend to be younger.

The mail questionnaire went to the 33 East Yorkers in the interview sample. We received 29 responses. One man in his sixties had died, and we could not find three physically mobile younger adults. To preserve anonymity, we changed all names of East Yorkers and network members, their home addresses, and the names of the businesses that employ them. In addition, we changed a few sensitive details in ways that should not weaken the validity of the examples and discussions. All quotations are from the East Yorkers' transcripts, edited for conciseness.

6. In tie-wise analyses, the ties are not independent of each other, as they all come from the same 33 networks. Moreover, the variation in size of these networks (from 3 to 27 ties) means that some networks are more heavily represented than others.

We describe our procedures for collecting and analyzing these data more fully in Wellman (1982). For our interview guide, see Leighton and Wellman (1978); for our codebooks, see Wellman et al. (1981). Note that all of our data are reports by East Yorkers about their community members and hence may vary in perception, recall, reporting, and interpretation.

7. In addition to reporting on the 403 significant ties, the East Yorkers also told us incompletely and inconsistently about two other types of ties: 66 *latent* ties (formerly significant ties who are now seldom contacted or thought of) and 48 *filler* ties (neighbors and coworkers with whom they only exchange pleasantries and the kinfolk they only see at large family gatherings).

Our data in this (and subsequent) studies differ somewhat from those presented in earlier papers because we recently cleaned up the tie coding.

Those 45 ties that are both intimate and routine are counted both ways. Although some unreliability can be expected when the respondents alone are allowed to define socially close intimates, in our own analysis we found that we would have coded the intimate ties differently only 8% of the time. Under the circumstances, we decided to let the respondents speak for themselves.

8. We derived our definitions of these roles from the East Yorkers' usage. "Immediate kin" are parents, sisters, brothers, and (now-adult) children (by birth or adoption). "Extended kin" are all other kin by birth or adoption; including in-laws, grandparents, aunts, uncles, and cousins, but not including godparents or "fictive kin" ("she's like an aunt"). "Kin" is a term that preempts all other roles; i.e., kin are kin even when they live nearby or work on the same job.

   "Neighbors" are nonkin living in the same (self-defined) neighborhood. The East Yorkers' definitions of "neighbors" are based principally on access via short walks or very brief drives. East Yorkers do not neighbor by car over widespread areas. Most neighbors live on the same block (or in the same high-rise building); almost all live within one mile.

   "Coworkers" are nonkin in paid employment at the same workplace as East Yorkers. (We did not encounter any situations in which people at different workplaces – e.g., academic colleagues at different universities – interacted heavily on the basis of work but if we had, we would have classified them as "coworkers".)

   "Friends" are neither kin, neighbors, coworkers, nor organizational ties. East Yorkers tend to use "friend" as a catchall, somewhat residual term for persons not interacted with in the social context of other roles (see also Feld, 1982; Fischer, 1982a).

   "Organizational ties" are maintained primarily through mutual participation in nonwork formal organizations, such as churches, hockey teams, unions, and voluntary organizations.

9. This pattern is analogous to that reported by Bell (1968) with respect to British "spiralists."

10. In one very crucial sense, these communities lack diversity. They tend to be composed of persons whose gender and social status are similar to those of the East Yorkers. This is less true for kin. Our findings about roles are roughly comparable to those concerning the analogous "primary social contexts" reported by Fischer (1982a, b; see also Feld, 1981, on "foci"). Although different methods of data definition, collection, and reporting preclude exact comparisons, Fischer's "metropolitan" networks seem to be somewhat larger and to contain more friends and coworkers. Thus, our findings confirm the popular stereotypes of traditional, kin-centered Torontonians and modern, friend-centered Californians.

11. Thirty (91%) East Yorkers have good access to automobiles. Public transportation is excellent in central Toronto, good in the suburbs, and poor to fair elsewhere in southern Ontario. Toronto area residents pay a flat monthly rate for unlimited metropolitan telephone service: It does not cost them any more to call someone frequently or to call someone 30 miles away. Nevertheless, the correlations between residential distance and the frequency of both telephone and in-person contact are quite high.

12. To cluster these ties within the thirty-three communities, we used the SOCK/COMPLT computer package (Alba, 1973). We thank Richard Alba for his generosity in making these programs available and his advice when we were using them. This is the first time to our knowledge that this sort of clustering has been done for such a large, naturally occurring sample of egocentric networks.

(Because of the time and cost involved, we have not clustered the less inclusive intimate and routine subsets of these networks.)

We caution that these are respondent-reported data. The problem is compounded here because the East Yorkers are reporting about ties between two other persons. For that reason, we did not ask them to report about the directionality of the tie; i.e., we assumed all ties were symmetric. We did not ask them to report about any subtle qualities of the relationship other than that the two persons were "in touch" with each other, the same phrase we used to define the East Yorkers' own nonintimate ties.

13. East Yorkers reported so little about their "romantic involvements" – another area of companionship we studied – that we omitted this area from our analysis.

14. To simplify matters, in this section we concentrate on the East Yorkers' "support systems," i.e., the strands of aid going to the East Yorkers from network members. (These are the EY $\leftrightarrow$ and EY $\leftarrow$ columns in Table 6.13). The strands of aid going in each direction, to and from the East Yorkers, are roughly symmetrical: Compare the EY $\rightarrow$ and EY $\leftarrow$ percentages in Table 6.13. However, a comparison of these two columns also reveals that East Yorkers believe that it is somewhat more blessed to give than to receive; they say that they give slightly more of most specific types of aid to network members than they receive from them.

15. However, Liebow (1967) shows that the growth of multistranded ties among young poor black American men can easily lead to the destruction of the tie. In the Washington, D. C., street corner he studies, the men relied so heavily on each other that the strandedness of the ties expanded rapidly. In their impoverished situations – when the principal resources they had were each other – the increased demands made by the two parties on their newly multiple strands were more than the ties could bear.

16. Wellman with Hiscott (1985) finds that the strands cluster into five "dimensions":

- companionship (sociability, discussing things, doing things together, interaction in formal groups outside of work)
- emotional aid (minor emotional aid, family problems advice, major emotional aid, large services)
- domestic services (small services, small household aid, large household aid, lend/give household items, help in dealing with organizations)
- financial aid (small amounts of money, large amounts of money, financial aid for housing)
- specialized information (information about job openings, important job contacts, information about housing vacancies).

17. We calculated the percentage of exchange for each strand by dividing the percentage of aid going in both directions by the sum of the percentage of aid going to the East Yorker only, from the East Yorker only, and in both directions (see the formula in the note to Table 6.16).

18. The variation in the percentages of specific exchanges does not seem attributable to the form of the questionnaire East Yorkers used to report these data. Each page on the form was devoted to a specific tie. The 15 types of aid were listed on each page, and the East Yorkers were asked to check off in two columns whether they

had given such aid to – or received such aid from – the community member noted at the top of each page. If any norm of specific exchange was operating, it would have been easy for the East Yorkers to balance their books by quickly checking the two adjacent columns, which would show that they had both sent and received a specific form of aid from a specific person. It would have taken more work to scan the rows and columns and balance the books on one page in order to show generalized reciprocity with a specific person. It would have taken even more work to scan the rows and columns and flip all 15 or so pages to show overall community balance in reciprocity.

19. We also caution that we refer here only to the number of kinds of aid, and not to the volume of aid, other than crude "major"/"minor" distinctions.

20. The "support system" literature is reviewed and critiqued in Gottlieb (1983), Cohen and Syme (1985), and Sarason and Sarason (1985).

LITERATURE CITED

Alba, Richard. "A Graphic-Theoretical Definition of a Sociometric Clique." *Journal of Mathematical Sociology* 3 (1973): 113–26.

Bell, Colin. *Middle-Class Families*. London: Routledge and Kegan Paul, 1968.

Bell, Colin, and Howard Newby. *Community Studies*. London: Allen and Unwin, 1971.

"Community, Communion, Class and Community Action." In D. T. Herbert and R. J. Johnson (eds.), *Social Areas in Cities II – Spatial Perspectives on Problems and Policies*. London: John Wiley, 1976.

Berscheid, Ellen, and Elaine Walster. *Interpersonal Attraction*. Reading, Mass.: Addison-Wesley, 1978.

Blishen, Bernard. "A Socio-Economic Index for Occupations in Canada." *Canadian Review of Sociology and Anthropology* 4 (1967): 41–53.

Blishen, Bernard, and Hugh McRoberts. "A Revised Socio-Economic Index for Occupations in Canada." *Canadian Review of Sociology and Anthropology* 13 (1976): 71–9.

Boissevain, Jeremy F. *Friends of Friends*. Oxford: Basil Blackwell, 1974.

Braverman, Harry. *Labour and Monopoly Capital*. New York and London: Monthly Review Press, 1974.

Clark, S. D. *The Suburban Society*. Toronto: University of Toronto Press, 1966.

Coates, Donald, Sharon Moyer, and Barry Wellman. "The Yorklea Study of Urban Mental Health: Symptoms, Problems and Life Events." *Canadian Journal of Public Health* 60 (1969): 471–81.

Cohen, Sheldon, and S. Leonard Syme (eds.). *Social Support and Health*. New York: Academic Press, 1985.

Cook, Karen. "Network Structures from an Exchange Perspective." In Peter Marsden and Nan Lin (eds.), *Social Structure and Network Analysis*. Beverly Hills, Calif.: Sage, 1982.

Craven, Paul, and Barry Wellman. "The Network City." *Sociological Inquiry* 43 (1973): 57–88.

Crump (Leighton), Barry. "The Portability of Urban Ties." Paper presented at the annual meeting of the American Sociological Association, Chicago, 1977.

Durkheim, Émile. *The Division of Labor in Society.* New York: Macmillan, [1893] 1933.

Feld, Scott. "The Focussed Organization of Social Ties." *American Journal of Sociology* 86 (1981): 1015–35.

"Interpersonal Comparability of Reported Friendships." Stony Brook, N. Y.: Department of Sociology, State University of New York, 1982.

Fischer, Claude S. "Toward a Subcultural Theory of Urbanism." *American Journal of Sociology* 80 (1975): 1319–41.

The Urban Experience. New York: Harcourt Brace Jovanovich, 1976.

To Dwell among Friends. Chicago: University of Chicago Press, 1982a.

"The Dispersion of Kinship in Modern Society." University of California, Institute of Urban and Regional Development Working Paper 382. Berkeley, 1982b.

Fischer, Claude S., Robert Max Jackson, C. Ann Steuve, Kathleen Gerson, and Lynne McCallister Jones, with Mark Baldassare. *Networks and Places.* New York: Free Press, 1977.

Frankenberg, Ronald. *Communities in Britain.* Harmondsworth, England: Penguin, 1966.

Freeman, Linton C. "Centrality in Social Networks: Conceptual Clarification." *Social Networks* 1 (1979): 251–39.

Gans, Herbert. *The Urban Villagers.* New York: Free Press, 1962.

The Levittowners. New York: Pantheon, 1967.

Gates, Albert S., Harvey Stevens, and Barry Wellman. "What Makes a Good Neighbor?" Paper presented at the annual meeting of the American Sociological Association, New York, 1973.

Gottlieb, Benjamin. *Social Support Strategies.* Beverly Hills Calif.: Sage, 1983.

Gouldner, Alvin W. "The Norm of Reciprocity." *American Sociological Review* 25 (1960): 161–78.

Greenbaum, Susan. "Bridging Ties at the Neighborhood Level." *Social Networks* 4 (1982): 367–84.

Greer, Scott. *The Emerging City.* New York: Free Press, 1962.

The Urbane View. New York: Oxford University Press, 1972.

Gusfield, Joseph R. *Community: A Critical Response.* New York: Harper & Row, 1975.

Hillery, George A., Jr. "Definitions of Community: Areas of Agreement." *Rural Sociology* 20 (1955): 111–23.

Hiltz, S. Roxanne, and Murray Turoff. *The Network Nation.* Reading, Mass.: Addison-Wesley, 1979.

Hobbes, Thomas. *Leviathan.* 1651.

Homans, George. *Social Behavior: Its Elementary Forms.* New York: Harcourt, Brace, 1961.

Hunter, Albert. "The Loss of Community: An Empirical Test through Replication." *American Sociological Review* 40 (1975): 537–52.

Jacobs, Jane. *The Death and Life of Great American Cities.* New York: Random House, 1961.

Kadushin, Charles. "The Friends and Supporters of Psychotherapy: On Social Circles in Urban Life." *American Sociological Review* 31 (1966): 786–802.

"Notes on Expectations of Reward in N-person Networks." In Peter Blau and Robert Merton (eds.), *Continuities in Structural Inquiry*. Beverly Hills, Calif.: Sage, 1981.

Kapp, Yvonne. *Eleanor Marx*. New York: Pantheon, 1976.

Kornhauser, William. "Mass Society." *International Encyclopedia of the Social Sciences* 10 (1968): 58–64.

Laslett, Peter. *The World We Have Lost*. London Methuen, 1971.

Lee, Nancy (Howell). *The Search for an Abortionist*. Chicago: University of Chicago Press, 1969.

Leighton, Barry. "Experiencing Personal Network Communities." Ph.D. Thesis, Department of Sociology, University of Toronto, 1986.

Leighton, Barry, and Barry Wellman. "Interview Guide Schedule: East York Social Networks Project Phase IV." University of Toronto, Centre for Urban and Community Studies Resource Paper 1. Toronto, 1978.

LeRoy Ladurie, Emmanuel. *Montaillou*. Translated by Barbara Bray. New York: Braziller, [1975] 1978.

Liebow, Elliot. *Tally's Corner*. Boston: Little, Brown, 1967.

Luxton, Meg. *More than a Labour of Love*. Toronto: Women's Press, 1980.

Macfarlane, Alan. *The Origins of English Individualism*. Oxford: Basil Blackwell, 1978.

Machiavelli. *The Prince*. 1532.

March, James, and Herbert Simon. *Organizations*. New York: Wiley, 1958.

Mayer, Philip, with Iona Mayer. *Townsmen or Tribesmen*. 2nd ed. Capetown: Oxford University Press, 1974.

Nisbet, Robert A. *The Quest for Community*. New York: Oxford University Press, 1969.

Palm, Risa. "Factorial Ecology and the Community of Outlook." *Annals of the Association of American Geographers* 63 (1973): 341–6.

Pocock, J. G. A. *The Machiavellian Moment: Florentine Political Thought and the Atlantic Republican Tradition*. Princeton, N. J.: Princeton University Press, 1975.

Podhoretz, Norman. *Making It*. New York: Random House, 1967.

Poggioli, Renato. "The Oaten Flute." In *The Oaten Flute: Essays on Pastoral Poetry and the Pastoral Ideal*. Cambridge, Mass.: Harvard University Press, 1975.

Polanyi, Karl. *The Great Transformation*. Boston: Beacon Press, 1944 (1957).

Pool, Ithiel de Sola, and Manfred Kochen. "Contacts and Influence." *Social Networks* 1 (1978): 5–51.

Riesman, David, with Nathan Glazer and Reuel Denny. *The Lonely Crowd*. New Haven, Conn.: Yale University Press, 1950.

Sahlins, Marshall D. "On the Sociology of Primitive Exchange." In Michael Banton (ed.), *The Relevance of Models for Social Anthropolgy*. London: Tavistock, 1965.

Sarason, Irwin, and Barbara Sarason (eds.). *Social Support: Theory, Research and Applications*. The Hague: Martinus Nijhoff, 1985.

Sennett, Richard. *Families against the City*. Cambridge, Mass.: Harvard University Press, 1970.

Shorter, Edward. *The Making of the Modern Family*. New York: Basic, 1975.

Simmel, Georg. "Group Expansion and the Development of Individuality." Translated by Richard P. Albanes. In Donald N. Levine (ed.), *Georg Simmel on Individuality and Social Forms*. Chicago: University of Chicago Press, [1908] 1971.

"The Metropolis and Mental Life." In Kurt Wolff (ed. and trans.), *The Sociology of Georg Simmel*. Glencoe, Ill.: Free Press, [1902–3] 1950.

Slater, Philip. *The Pursuit of Loneliness*. Boston: Beacon Press, 1970.

Stein, Maurice. *The Eclipse of Community*. Princeton, N. J.: Princeton University Press, 1960.

Suttles, Gerald. *The Social Order of the Slum*. Chicago: University of Chicago Press, 1968.

Taub, Richard P., George P. Surgeon, Sara Lindholm, Phyllis Betts Otti, and Amy Bridges. "Urban Voluntary Organizations: Locality Based and Externally Induced." *American Journal of Sociology* 83 (1977): 524–41.

Tilly, Charles. "Do Communities Act?" *Sociological Inquiry* 43 (1973): 209–40.

"Introduction." In Charles Tilly (ed.), *An Urban World*. Boston: Little, Brown, 1974.

"Reflections on the History of European Statemaking." In Charles Tilly (ed.), *The Formation of National States in Western Europe*. Princeton, N. J.: Princeton University Press, 1975.

Titmuss, Richard. *The Gift Relationship*. London: Allen and Unwin, 1970.

Tönnies, Ferdinand. *Community and Association*. Translated by Charles Loomis. London: Routledge and Kegan Paul, [1887] 1955.

Warren, Donald. *Helping Networks*. Notre Dame, Ind.: University of Notre Dame Press, 1981.

Warren, Roland. *The Community in America*. Chicago: Rand McNally, 1978.

Webber, Melvin. "The Urban Place and the Nonplace Urban Realm," in Melvin Webber et al. (ed.), *Explorations into Urban Structure*. Philadelphia: University of Pennsylvania Press, 1964.

Wellman, Barry. "Who Needs Neighbourhoods?" In Allan Powell (ed.), *The City: Attacking Modern Myths*. Toronto: University of Toronto Press, 1972.

"The Community Question: The Intimate Networks of East Yorkers." *American Journal of Sociology* 84 (1979): 1201–31.

"Studying Personal Communities." In Peter Marsden and Nan Lin (eds.), *Social Structure and Network Analysis*. Beverly Hills, Calif.: Sage, 1982.

"Domestic Work, Paid Work and Net Work." In Steve Duck and Daniel Perlman (eds.), *Understanding Personal Relationships I*, pp. 159–91. London: Sage, 1985.

Wellman, Barry, and Paula Goldman. "The Network Basis of Support." Paper presented to the Annual Meeting of the American Sociological Association, New York City, September 1986.

Wellman, Barry, with Robert Hiscott. "From Social Support to Social Network." In Irwin Sarason and Barbara Sarason (eds.), *Social Support*, pp. 205–22. The Hague: Martinus Nijhoff, 1985.

Wellman, Barry, and Barry Leighton. "Networks, Neighborhoods and Communities: Approaches to the Study of the Community Question." *Urban Affairs Quarterly* 15 (1979): 363–90.

Wellman, Barry, and Marilyn Whitaker (eds.). *Community-Network-Communica-*

tion: An Annotated Bibliography. University of Toronto, Centre for Urban and Community Studies Bibliographic Paper 4. Toronto, 1974.

Wellman, Barry, Brenda Billingsley, Christina Black, Sharon Kirsh, and Edward Lee. "East York Social Network Study Codebooks." University of Toronto, Centre for Urban and Community Studies Resource Paper 5. Toronto, 1981.

Wellman, Barry, Paul Craven, Marilyn Whitaker, Harvey Stevens, Ann Shorter, Sheila DuToit, and Hans Bakker. "Community Ties and Support Systems." In L. S. Bourne, R. D. MacKinnon, and J. W. Simmons (eds.), *The Form of Cities in Central Canada*. Toronto: University of Toronto Press, 1973.

Whyte, William Foote. *Street Corner Society*. Rev. ed. Chicago: University of Chicago Press, 1981.

Williams, Raymond. *The Country and the City*. London: Paladin, 1975.

Wirth, Louis. "Urbanism as a Way of Life." *American Journal of Sociology* 44 (1938): 3–24.

7

Work and community in industrializing India

Leslie Howard

The issues

According to a long tradition in sociology, large bureaucratic organizations necessarily generate personal atomization for their members, clients, and other implicated populations (Wellman, Carrington, and Hall, Chapter 6). Those who advance this argument contend that work and nonwork relationships are more distinct from each other for workers in large-scale, bureaucratically organized industries than for workers in small-scale, more personal settings. They further contend that both work and nonwork relationships in large bureaucracies are more specialized, thinner in content, and more culturally heterogeneous than are the relationships of workers in small-scale settings. Hence, they maintain that involvement with large bureaucracies separates the person – as well as his or her labor – from involvement in communities of complex, convoluted ties. In such settings, people's ties, as well as their work, will be specialized and thin in content, and these ties will not fit together into homogeneous, densely knit communities.

A good deal of contemporary research has challenged this argument. Researchers have demonstrated that people in urban environments and employment – even in bureaucratically organized factory jobs – often remain involved in complex communities (Benyon, 1973; Craven and Wellman, 1973; Kornblum, 1974; Roberts, 1978). These analysts have further shown that the separation of work from its embeddedness in communities does not necessarily entail the isolation of workers from meaningful relationships.

We now know that communities endure in the midst of cities and bureaucracies. Their persistence, abundance, and importance further suggest that they are intrinsic components of the urban industrial bureaucratic milieu, and not just tenacious remnants of earlier, preindustrial, forms of social organization. Bureaucratized urbanites heavily use community ties – on the job as well as at home. Indeed, recent research suggests that

This chapter is revised version of a paper presented at the annual meeting of the American Sociological Association, San Francisco, 1977. My thanks to Barry Wellman for editing this version to the point of accessibility.

involvement in a more personalistic organization of work does not necessarily ensure warm, supportive communities of complex bonds (Casagrande, 1965).

Clearly, it is no longer news that participation in urban industrial society does not mean divorce from close interpersonal relationships or even from communities defined by networks of such relationships, any more than participation in peasant agriculture or small-scale productive units ensures involvement in such supportive communities. My task here is not to herald this rediscovery, but to suggest the factors that constrain the nature of interpersonal bonds and the organization of communal structures for workers standing in different relationships to industrial organizations. I suggest that theories of a bipolar, *Gemeinschaft/Gesellschaft* transition were concerned with the wrong things in the right places when they considered the impact of workplace organization on community. Neglecting power, they concentrated on how specialized, segmented divisions of labor separated workers from each other. Yet we now know that broad structures of interdependence link workers in large bureaucracies. For example, superiors have discretion in the allocation of all sorts of resources to workers: jobs, favors, information, material goods, and the like. Not only do such vertical discretionary ties constrain interactions between superior and subordinate, but they can significantly affect relations between persons of the same occupational status who compete or form coalitions to gain discretionary resources from their superiors.

This chapter traces some relationships between the organization of structures of interdependence at work and the organization of local communities. It uses data from a study of Indian factory and nonfactory workers to argue that the organization of access to resources within the workplace significantly affects the nature of workers' community ties – both on the job and at home. To do this, I contrast the interdependencies between workers and superiors in large, bureaucratic factories and in small, informal workplaces (e.g., shops, rickshaw stands, and domestic employment). The factory workers studied were employed in manufacturing in firms of 50 or more employees. These firms, by contrast to the work setting of nonfactory workers, were organized into sets of "positions" or "offices" in which discretion to hire, immediate supervisory authority, and ultimate discretion over appeals were invested in *different* positions or offices. By contrast, the nonfactory workers studied worked in units of four or fewer persons. In this situation, they depended directly on the person employing them or providing them with capital equipment. For these workers, there was typically a fusion in *one person* of hiring discretion, immediate supervision, and ultimate discretion in the case of appeal.

My general concern is how the organization of work affects the communities of factory and nonfactory workers. Theories of bipolar transition would expect the nonfactory workers – who are less bureaucratized, albeit urbanized – to be more intensely involved in rich, complex, communal bonds. Yet the data indicate that it is the factory workers who are better able in many ways to build broadly based communities permeated with mutual support.

The setting and the data

The interviews on which this analysis is based were conducted in the city of Ranchi, India, in the mid-1960s.[1] During this period, government and private industry made major investments in the industrialization of the area, and the city's 1961 population of 140,000 increased by 44% in a decade. The workers interviewed were males, 18 years or older, from rural origins. Both the factory ($N = 100$) and nonfactory ($N = 101$) samples were evenly divided among persons living in Ranchi and persons living in their natal villages around the city, and between "tribals" and "caste Hindus," as defined in the 1961 Census of India for Bihar State. The subsamples referred to below are defined by these occupational, residential, and ethnic dichotomies.

The data available for the present analysis include information on a variety of interpersonal bonds:

1. "Workmates" are the three persons with whom the worker must cooperate most closely in doing his job or the three persons typically in closest proximity while he is working independently.
2. "Neighbors" are the heads of the three households closest to his own.
3. "Leisure companions" are persons with whom the worker has engaged in specific past nonwork activities.
4. "Brokers" are persons on whom the worker would rely for information or assistance in meeting certain hypothetical contingencies in his environment.
5. "Community contacts" is used as a collective term for friends, leisure companions, and brokers.

As the primary indicator of *relational specialization* (or "differentiation") I use the absence of overlap in the lists of persons named as workmates, neighbors, and community contacts. Specifically, I look at the overlap of workmates with other lists, as this indicates whether work is freed from embeddedness in complex communities. I also consider the overlap among types of community contacts, such as friends, leisure companions, and brokers.

My primary indicator of *relational richness* (or complexity) is *workers'* identification of the relationship as one of "kinship" or "friendship," as

Table 7.1. *Characteristics of workmates of nonfactory and factory workers*

	Nonfactory	Factory
Mean number workmates named	2.3	3.0
Homogeneity (mean % workmates):		
Same job label (as respondent)[a]	58	36
Same natal village[a]	28	4
Same present neighborhood[a]	38	16
Same ethnic group (caste or tribe)[a]	34	17
Same supervisory level[a]	65	34
Complexity (mean % workmates):		
Kin or friends (vs. acquaintances)[a]	53	42
Seen daily outside of work[a]	42	17
Overlap (mean % workmates):		
Also named as community ties[a]	34	10
Also named as neighbors[a]	7	2

[a]Indicates significance at the .05 level. Note that the quota design of the sample limits the applicability of significance tests to the interpretation of factory/nonfactory differences. Significance tests, based on confidence limits on differences between proportions, are included in these tables only for assistance in locating trends.

opposed to "acquaintanceship."[2] Regular contact outside of work is used as a supplementary indicator of the complexity of work and neighbor relations, and reports of specific kinds of past interactions are used as indicators of the complexity of friendship ties.

Lacking direct, rich information about on-the-job interactions, I offer here no rigorous tests of hypotheses. Rather, I present a plausible argument based on the survey data, my participant observation in Ranchi, and relevant arguments in the structural analytic literature.

Factory and nonfactory workers' communities

Interpersonal bonds

The observed pattern. In general, factory workers are more relationally specialized in their interpersonal bonds than nonfactory workers. Factory workers' work and nonwork relationships overlap less, and there is relatively less overlap among the different kinds of nonwork relationships (Tables 7.1, 7.2, and 7.3). Moreover, factory workers report a lower incidence of complex bonds (e.g., kinship or friendship vs. acquaintanceship) with their immediate workmates than their nonfactory counterparts in less bureaucratic and hiererchical work settings (Table 7.4). Factory workers' mates are more occupationally diverse in terms of job labels and authority levels. Further,

Table 7.2. *Characteristics of neighbors of nonfactory and factory workers*

	Nonfactory	Factory
Mean number neighbors named	3.0	3.0
Homogeneity (mean % neighbors):		
Same job label (as respondent)	6	3
Same natal village	51	50
Same work location or firm	9	11
Same ethnic group[a]	29	45
Complexity (mean % neighboring households):		
Containing kin or friends[a]	51	70
Containing persons spoken with daily[a]	54	65
Overlap (mean % neighbors):		
Also named as community ties	19	14

[a]Significant at the 0.5 level.

Table 7.3. *Characteristics of community contacts of nonfactory and factory workers*

	Nonfactory	Factory
Mean number community contacts named	7.0	7.3
Homogeneity (mean % community contacts):		
Same job label (as respondent)[a]	22	11
Same natal village	46	50
Same present neighborhood	46	47
Same work location or firm[a]	26	35
Same ethnic group[a]	47	59
Complexity (mean % community contacts who are):		
Kin or friends (vs. acquaintances)[a]	84	92
Overlap (mean % overlap in lists of):		
Friends, leisure companions, and brokers[a]	28	20
How met (mean % community contacts met in):		
Community contexts[a]	62	74

[a]Significant at the .05 level.

factory workers' mates are more heterogeneous in their ethnicity, birth-place (same natal village), and present residence. In sum, there is greater distinction between work and nonwork relationships for factory workers than for nonfactory workers in terms of specific personnel, the complexity and richness of their relationships, and ethnic and regional homogeneity.

What runs counter to the simple traditional–modern polarities are the

Table 7.4. *Complexity of relations with friends*

	Nonfactory	Factory
Mean number of friends named	2.8	2.9
Mean % friends with whom respondent has		
Exchanged loans[a]	43	59
Discussed religion[a]	64	74
Discussed family problems[a]	74	85
Attended cinema, fairs, etc.	76	83
Observed domestic commensality[a]	80	90

[a]Significant difference in percentages at the .05 level.

relationships away from the job. Tables 7.2 and 7.3 show that factory workers have higher incidences of complex ties with neighbors and community contacts (i.e., friends, leisure companions, and brokers) than nonfactory workers. Further, factory workers' nonwork relationships are more often bounded, ethnically homogeneous ties than is the case for nonfactory workers.

The relatively greater distinction between work and nonwork relationships for factory workers is also shown in the higher proportion of community contacts that they have formed in communal contexts (Table 7.3) – contexts such as kinship, natal villages, neighborhoods, schools, or other organizations in which persons who encounter one another can reasonably presume that they already have multiple indirect ties through mutual friends (see Feld, 1981). On the other hand, relatively more of the nonfactory workers' community contacts have grown out of introductions or juxtaposition in work or exchange, that is, contexts in which persons who encounter one another are less likely to presume that they have multiple links through mutual friends or kinfolk. Indeed, for both occupational groups, strong "friendship" ties form disproportionately in communal contexts whereas weaker "acquaintanceship" ties form disproportionately in noncommunal contexts, for example, out of introductions and encounters in the economy.

Friendship choice. The observed difference between strong friendships formed in communal contexts and weaker acquaintanceships formed through economic associations (e.g., on the job, in market relations) leads us to closely examine friendship "choice" within the work situation. Using a series of variables measuring qualities and locales shared, I correlated expressed friendship (vs. acquaintanceship) with a series of variables measuring the extent to which workers and their (nonkin) workmates share the same backgrounds and have symmetrical work relationships.

Table 7.5. *Prediction of expressed friendship with workmates*

	Correlation with friendship
Social background	
Same ethnic group	.12
Same caste level	.12
Also tribal or caste Hindu	.07
Same religion	.07
Similar birthplace	
Same natal village	.16
Same natal district	.20
Co-residence	
Same neighborhood	.17
Same city or village	.02
Work relationships	
Same job label	.13
Same supervisory level	.28
Same occupational status	.23
Same work group	.09
Social position	
Same educational level	.02
Same perceived social position	.17

Note: $\sum R = .40$; $r^2 = .16$. Shared social qualities as predictors of "friendship" (as opposed to "acquaintance") in nonkin work relations, each quality being treated here as one of a series of dichotomous variables characterizing the 373 workmate ties examined.

Two shared qualities predict consistently and significantly the strength of friendship among workmates (Table 7.5).[3] The first is *symmetry of control*: Friends are more likely than acquaintances to be at similar levels in work structures, as indicated by the similarity of occupational status or supervisory level. Friendships in work situations form disproportionately between persons who are symmetrically interdependent rather than between persons who are linked by asymmetric authority relations. The second quality is living in the *same neighborhood*: Juxtaposition in a common neighborhood implies high probabilities of both direct and indirect ties outside and independent of the work situation.

The criteria of friendship formation operative here seem to be transactional and structural rather than categorical; that is, they seem to reflect sensitivities to flows of resources, relative mutuality of dependency vis-a-vis each other and work situations, indirect ties, and the extent to which workmates are in situations where they are juxtaposed with each other.

By contrast, the data do not reflect consistent preferences for association in terms of the cultural categories of Indian society. The categories of caste and religion – which most Indians and Indianists take to be a pervasive influence on social structure and interaction – are weak here in their power to predict the emergence of friendships out of juxtaposition in the workplace. The symmetry or asymmetry of the work relationship and the probability of unintended contact outside the work situation are much more powerful than these categories in predicting the elaboration of work bonds into friendships and other nonwork ties of activity and interdependence.

The data suggest that the criteria for the development of complex bonds are structural rather than categorical, depending on multiple juxtapositions and indirect ties. If this is so, then transformations in the communities defined by such complex bonds should develop more out of structural changes than out of *Gemeinschaft* to *Gesellschaft* changes in the value systems presumed to give the rules for such bonding. Hence, it is to structural differences in the organization of interdependencies at work that we must look for an understanding of the differences in the organization of factory and non-factory workers' personal communities.

Constraints on community

Nonfactory workers. For nonfactory workers much more frequently than factory workers, interdependence on the job is organized around structures of patronage. Often, the nonfactory worker's patron is his or her employer – or is located in chains of patronage involving the employer. More generally, higher proportions of nonfactory than factory workers report reliance on brokers higher than themselves in caste level, occupational status, education, and perceived social position (Table 7.6). Routinized reliance on a particular higher-position broker is the localized expression of a patronage system. Looked at from below, such structures seem to be chains, and labor services and loyality in factional conflict appear to flow up these chains. Looked at from above, such structures seem to be inverted trees, and sponsorship in access to means of subsistence or to centers of discretion over the distribution of scarce resources seems to flow down the branches.

The nonfactory workers' relative integration of work and nonwork relationships integrates the interpersonal dependency implicit in the organization of their work into their personal communities. It thus constrains the form of that community and the strength of relationships within it. Patronage becomes not only the basis of organization of work life, but also the organizing principle for relational structures in general.

As a form of organization of interdependence, patronage goes beyond particular patron–client ties in its constraint on the qualities of interpersonal bonds. Patron–client ties tend to link up into hierarchical structures that

Table 7.6 *Channels of information and influence for nonfactory and factory workers (percent)*

	Nonfactory	Factory
Vertical reach of personalistic brokerage relations (persons named as potential sources of information or assistance in dealing with hypothetical environmental contingencies such as emergency loans, theft, tax problems, or family problems)		
Mean number of brokers named	3.1	2.8
Respondents for whom named brokers include		
Respondent's employer[a]	29	0
A person older than the respondent	78	81
A person of higher caste level[a]	45	22
A person of higher occupational status[a]	84	63
A person of higher education[a]	72	46
Articulation with institutional channels of information and influence		
Respondents who report		
Some institutional sources of potential emergency credit, theft assistance, and/or tax information	76	83
Some formal education[a]	60	80
Some secondary education[a]	10	60
Voluntary organization membership[a]	48	67
Reading newspapers[a]	56	78
Listening to radio[a]	77	95

[a]Significant at the .05 level.

contain few loops.[4] Yet such loops are the indirect ties that structural analysts believe provide the structural grounds for trust in two-person bonding (Davis, 1970; Nadel, 1957). Thus, hierarchical, loopless structures not only inhibit the multiplicity of indirect ties between juxtaposed parties, but they also build the basis for *dis*trust and for limiting the complexity of bonds among juxtaposed persons at the same "levels" of structures. The same informants who told me, "I love my boss more than my father," also told me it was dangerous to let any given friend know too much about you because he could use it against you in competition with a common patron or in broader factional conflicts.

Factory workers. Factory workers are less dependent upon particular patrons for access to critical resources than nonfactory workers. They rely more on reciprocal assistance with comparably, but differently, situated friends and acquaintances, and more on such institutional channels of resource access as education, organizational membership, radio listening, and the newspapers (see Table 7.6).

Factory workers, like most nonfactory workers, lack control over their means of subsistence. But their dependence on employment for subsistence is located within an *institutional* nexus rather than an *interpersonal* nexus. This separates their dependency as workers from the relationships that define their communities. Such separations free factory workers to develop their communities with those who are juxtaposed with them in several social contexts and who provide them with reciprocal assistance. Furthermore, the presence of large numbers of status-equals in the larger work situation of the factory – in contrast with the small, hierarchically organized work situations of nonfactory workers – encourages friends of friends to develop multiple indirect ties in factories.

Conclusions

Although both factory and nonfactory workers in Ranchi, India, are heavily involved in community relationships, these differ markedly in character. Factory workers draw more of their relationships from communal contexts apparently conducive to the formation of richer, more complex bonds. The symmetric interdependence of these bonds – which form communities with collateral (nonhierarchical) structures – seems to rest on whether their participants each have some relatively secure resource base: For example, whether their land or jobs are not subject to patrons' favor or they can influence others' exercise of discretion in allocating resources. The participants in these collateral community structures deal with their environment through these relatively symmetrical relationships. In turn, involvement in symmetrical relationships reinforces participants' investment in collateral structure and dependence on its continued operation.

The situation is quite different for persons in the types of patronage structures commonly found among nonfactory workers. Persons in these structures must invest their labor and discretion in the service of the patron – the source of sustenance – rather than in the service of reciprocal assistance within communal contexts. Their competition for patron's scarce resources inhibits their development of interpersonal bonds to others with whom they are juxtaposed in these contexts. Moreover, the hierarchical nature of patronage structures further inhibits the development of elaborate structures of supportive interpersonal bonds.

It is not likely that these differences in factory and nonfactory workers' communities are attributable to differential recruitment, since similar proportions of factory (60%) and nonfactory (64%) workers used personal contacts to acquire jobs. In fact, factory workers more frequently used contacts that they perceived as higher in social position (68% of those using personal contacts) than did the nonfactory workers (58%). What is significant is that for factory workers – with their relative security of job tenure in the expanding industrial system and the decentralization of discretionary power over them – these sponsorship ties have not been routinized into stable patterns of patronage and dependency. Rather, factory workers have been able to invest their resources in collateral interdependence.

Thus, the observed patterns defy understanding in terms of bipolar ideal types of traditionalism and modernity. Face-to-face societies and work situations do not necessarily breed cozy community, nor does bureaucratic impersonalism necessarily breed anomic isolation of the individual. Rather, we ought to look to the specifics of the organization of *interdependence* – to determine who is reliant on whom for what – for an understanding of observed differences in solidary relationships.

The immediate relations of production, the work group, have been the point of departure for this examination. Nonfactory workers are located in small-scale *work structures of interpersonal dependency* that permeate and constrain their lives. Factory workers, although dependent on *impersonal industrial firms* for employment, are less often embedded in patron–client structures of interpersonal dependency – either in work or in other relationships – than nonfactory workers. Moreover, factory and nonfactory workers' similarities in the use of patronage to obtain jobs suggests that differences in their current community relationships emerge from their current work situations rather than from differences in their personal or cultural predispositions.

Thus, differences in the personal communities of factory and nonfactory workers at the time of the study apparently rest on the differing degrees of centralization of resource access in their *work situations*. We need not turn to differences in the *prior socialization* of future factory and nonfactory workers, as the bipolar modernization literature has been wont to do (Hagen, 1962). For the most part, the culturally focused traditional–modern polarities that underlie the modernization theories of the 1960s paid scant attention to how new forms of productive organization provide structural sources of variation for those involved.[5] Thus, I came away from my study convinced that changes in the form and content of interpersonal communities were a product not so much of a cultural modernization flowing from industrialization, but of changes in the ways in which interdependence was organized among workers at a relatively microscopic level. I had set out on my quest in the company of Talcott Persons (1960), Alex Inkeles (1969), and Cyril Black (1966), and I returned home with Abner Cohen (1969), Joseph Casagrande (1965), and F. G. Bailey (1969). S. F. Nadel (1957) had provided guidance for the whole adventure, especially in his reminder that it is the process of abstraction, rather than its product, that tells you what you know.

My findings suggest the more general proposition that the form of personal communities – and the complexity of the relationships that define them – are constrained by the degree of centralization of access to resources in the structures of interdependence with which they interpenetrate. Hence, an understanding of the organization of interdependence in communities is essential to an examination of the occupationally specific impact of industrialization on the relationship between ethnicity and communities, and on the relationship between objective class relations and the effective lines of social cohesion and cleavage.[6]

NOTES

1. These data were collected by me while working in Ranchi on the Harvard University Project on Socio-Cultural Aspects of Development under the directorship of Alex Inkeles and under the guidance in India of A. K. Singh. The sample is a subsample from that study and follows its basic quota design (Inkeles and Smith, 1974). The questionnaire is included in Howard (1974). I would like to thank the above mentors along with Harrison White, who guided my earlier treatment of this material; the people who cooperated with me in the study; and Harriet Friedmann, Max Heirich, Nancy Howell, Walter Phillips, Jack Wayne, and Barry Wellman, with whom I have had extensive discussions of the issues treated in this paper.

2. What I here call "relational richness" is closely related to what other analysts have called relational "multiplexity," "intensity," or "strength" (see Granovetter, 1983).

3. These are the only shared qualities that are consistent among the subsamples of respondents (defined by the occupational, residential, and ethnic dichotomies) and statistically significant for the aggregate of respondents in predicting the direction of expressed friendship.

4. A loop is a structure in which A has some control over B, B has some control over C, but C has some control over A.

5. Such modernization theories married economists' concerns with self-sustaining growth to the premises of sociological functionalism (see Hermassi's review, 1978). The pivotal question for these theories was how innovation and growth became institutionalized within particular societies. An influential subset of this work used industrialism as its organizing concept and focused specifically on the ways in which factory organization of production, once introduced, created and sustained its own requisite conditions. The conditions considered by the model were primarily the qualities of individual participants in the emerging industrial order – the modernist economic rationality of all, the entrepreneurship of new industrialists, the labor commitment of new wage laborers, and everyone's greater universalism and capacity for empathy. Socialization was the primary process accounting for social order within the functionalist perspectives of the period, and adult socialization was the process through which these theories sought to account for social transformation.

6. Ironically, such an understanding may also make sense out of the experiences of academics – certainly the most "modern" of men and women – who often find themselves involved in precisely the kinds of patronage structures that their ideologies have relegated to the distant past.

LITERATURE CITED

Bailey, F. G. *Stratagems and Spoils: A Social Anthropology of Politics*. Oxford: Basil Blackwell, 1969.

Benyon, Huw. *Working for Ford*. London: Allan Lane, 1973.

Black, C. E. *The Dynamics of Modernization*. New York: Harper & Row, 1966.

Casagrande, Joseph B. "Strategies for Survival: The Indians of Highland Ecuador." In *Contemporary Cultures and Societies of Latin America*. New York: Random House, 1965.

Cohen, Abner. *Custom and Politics in Urban Africa*. Berkeley: University of California Press, 1969.

Craven, Paul, and Barry Wellman. "The Network City." *Sociological Inquiry* 43 (December 1973): 57–88.

Davis, James A. "Clustering and Hierarchy in Interpersonal Relations: Testing Two Graph Theoretical Models on 742 Sociograms." *American Sociological Review* 35 (1970): 843–52.

Feld, Scott L. "The Focussed Organization of Social Ties." *American Journal of Sociology* 86 (1981): 1015–35.

Form, William. "Comparative Industrial Sociology and the Convergence Hypothesis." *Annual Review of Sociology* 5: 1–25, 1979.

Granovetter, Mark. "The Strength of Weak Ties: A Network Theory Revisited." *Sociological Theory*. San Francisco: Jossey-Bass, 1983.

Hagen, Everett E. *On the Theory of Social Change*. Homewood, Ill.: Dorsey, 1962.

Hermassi, Elbaki. "Changing Patterns in Research on the Third World." *Annual Review of Sociology* 4 (1978): 239–57.

Howard, Leslie. "Industrialization and Community in Chotanagpur." Ph.D. diss., Harvard University, 1974.

Inkeles, Alex. "Making Men Modern: On the Causes and Consequences of Individual Change in Six Developing Countries." *American Journal of Sociology* 75 (1969): 208–25.

Inkeles, Alex, and David H. Smith. *Becoming Modern: Individual Change in Six Developing Countries*. Cambridge, Mass.: Harvard University Press, 1974.

Kornblum, William. *Blue Collar Community*. Chicago: University of Chicago Press, 1974.

Nadel, S. F. *The Theory of Social Structure*. London: Cohen and West, 1957.

Parsons, Talcott. "Pattern Variables Revisited." *American Sociological Review* 25 (1960): 467–83.

Roberts, Bryan R. *Cities of Peasants: The Political Economy of Urbanization in the Third World*. London: Edward Arnold, 1978.

8

Relations of production and class rule: the hidden basis of patron-clientage

Y. Michal Bodemann

> It is always the immediate relationship of the owners of the conditions
> of production to the immediate producers...which reveals the
> innermost secret, the hidden basis of the entire social construction, and
> with it, the political form of the sovereignty and dependency relation, in
> short, the respective specific forms of the state.
>
> Karl Marx, *Capital*

Issues

There have now been nearly two decades of debate on patron–client
relations. This debate has reached the point where three substantial
anthologies have appeared on the subject (Schmidt et al., 1977; Gellner and
Waterbury, 1977; and Eisenstadt and Lemarchand, 1981), and an ency-
clopedic essay with hundreds of references has attempted to synthesize the
swelling literature surrounding this newly developed central concern,
particularly in anthropology (Eisenstadt and Roniger, 1980). Nevertheless,
one might question whether there has been a debate at all, given the rather
minor disagreements between the principal writers on the subject.

Despite this apparent unanimity, some troubling questions remain. On the
one hand, a number of non-Marxist scholars have expressed serious doubt
about the utility of the concept as a whole. On the other, Marxist scholars,
with few exceptions,[1] have failed to enter the debate – this fact is especially
astonishing because the patron-clientage described in the literature is most
prevalent in dependent, "misdeveloped" societies, a basic focus for Marxist
debates.

The failure of Marxist writers to enter into the debate is best attributed to
the ambivalence of Marxist theory in relation to all types of "primordial
loyalties," a category in which patron-clientage has often been placed (Alavi,
1973). Patron–client relations have been of great interest to non-Marxists

This chapter has been adapted for this volume with the assistance of Barry Wellman and S. D.
Berkowitz. See Bodemann (1982) for a more detailed discussion.

because they resemble voluntary exchange relations and, at the same time, involve unequals. They are personal in nature, are defined as friendships, and entail loyalty, yet they bar one of the partners from the resources and political ties that the other partner monopolizes. Patron–client ties (Alavi, 1973: 50) appear in all human societies, yet seem to be characteristic of backward societies in particular.

An essay by Eisenstadt and Roniger (1980) expresses the current scholarly consensus so well that it is a good starting point for a critique of work in this area. Therefore I deal with it first and then outline the direction a structurally oriented Marxist analysis of patron-clientage would take.

From their broad survey of the literature, Eisenstadt and Roniger (1980: 49) draw out what they call "core analytical characteristics" of patron-clientage. These include its particularistic–diffuse nature, the expression of loyalty along vertical lines undercutting horizontal solidarities, and the exchange of different types of resources in a framework of "inequality and asymmetry in power." The authors assert (1980: 50) that patron–client relations include long-range credit and obligations, are entered into voluntarily, "at least in principle," and are not fully contractual, but are based on informal, yet "tightly binding understandings."

Universalism

The list of "core characteristics" points to a number of serious problems. First, patron–client relations, as defined here, are practically universal, can occur at various levels of the class structure, and transcend historically specific constraints. This ubiquity (Waterbury, 1977) is further emphasized by the authors' exchange theory framework, which views patron–client relations as "not... types of social organizations," but rather as "models structuring the flow of resources and of interpersonal interaction and exchanges in society" (1980: 56).

However, the analytic power of this concept is curtailed if patron–client relations are taken to be a universal characteristic of all human societies. This assumption puts the authors at odds with the underlying premise of the patron–client literature, which is that these relations are characteristic of specific types of dependent societies. The authors resolve this problem by distinguishing societies in which patron–client relations are "predominant" or "full-fledged" from those societies (e.g., centralized imperial systems and advanced capitalist states) in which patron clientage is "an addendum-type of relation" (1980: 74).

Where patron-clientage assumes a peripheral role, it appears to be limited to certain societal sectors, is generally weaker and less stable than in societies where it is prominent, and is usually nonlegitimate. Eisenstadt and Roniger thus find a broad consensus in the literature that patron–client relations are aggregative, exist in varying degrees, and may be prevalent or absent – much like a "Protestant ethic" or "backwardness." As such, this approach describes and classifies what is visible on the surface, but fails to deal with the causes, or hidden basis of this form of social organization. Instead, in line with the approaches taken by Parsons, Lipset, McClelland, Banfield, and others, it blames the backwardness of backward societies on the ways in which their "particularism" and "ascriptive characteristics" are expressed in patron–client relations.

Class

A second major problem in the literature which Eisenstadt and Roniger only exacerbate is that it fails to deal with the class nature of patronage. Instead, many works downplay the class factor, mistakenly assume that patron–client relations are relatively isomorphic within given societies, and conform with the authors' voluntaristic bias.

First, although Eisenstadt and Roniger admit, as virtually all writers on the subject do, that patron–client relations are based on "inequality and differences in power" (1980: 50), they consistently refuse to acknowledge that these power differentials are rooted in class antagonisms. Classes, themselves, are replaced here by "semi-ascriptive hierarchical subcommunities," "major social actors," or "major social groups" that are characterized by a "low degree of internal solidarity and... organizational... autonomy" (1980: 64). Although Eisenstadt and Roniger recognize "ladders of social hierarchy" (1980: 66), they weaken the notion of classes into "highly elaborated hierarchies of ranks and positions" (1980: 67).

Second, Eisenstadt and Roniger see patron–client ties in ahistorical terms; these relations may be predominant in some societies and marginal in others, but they are ubiquitous. Since these authors conceptualize ladders or hierarchies of ranks and positions on one hand and rather vague "markets of resources" on the other, patron–client relations must be ubiquitous within the class structure as well, and cannot be said to epitomize specific class relations – such as those between landowners and landless peasants – in given societies. In their view, the mechanisms of patron-clientage and all its concomitant characteristics appear to exhibit congruent features, whether we are dealing with, say, the relationship between national politicians and landowners or the local bureaucrats and the peasantry. The patron role of a bureaucrat in the national capital, then, appears to correspond structurally to that of the principal party boss or local entrepreneur. The great problem with this abstract and formalistic conception of patron-clientage is that it denies qualitative differences between positions and relations.

Third, the authors' voluntaristic bias is also problematic. The bias is evident in terms such as "market" and "exchange" which imply an encounter of free and independent actors pursuing mutually beneficial relationships (see also Hall, 1974). The authors find that a basic characteristic of patron–client relations is that they are "entered into voluntarily and can...in principle" and "officially at least" be "abandoned voluntarily" (1980: 50). In such relations, "different concrete services, goods or resources" are "exchanged" (1980: 70). In that case, how do these authors reconcile a notion of free agency with the monopolistic and coercive character of patron–client relations? They assert that clients abdicate "their potentially autonomous access to major markets to positions of control over use of resources or to the center" (1980: 59). This "abdication" occurs because "the client 'buys,' as it were, protection against the *exigencies* of the markets or of nature or of the arbitrariness of weakness of the center, against the demands of other powerful groups or individuals" (1980: 71, my emphasis). These "exigencies," which are not elaborated further, induce the client to abandon "his control of his [the client's] access to markets" (1980: 71) to the patron.

The voluntaristic position adopted by these writers raises a number of questions, which remain unanswered: What is the structure of markets and the source of "natural" exigencies that act, a priori, against the client and only then lead to monopolization of resources in the hands of patrons? Why do these exigencies act agaist the client and in favor of the patron, given that "a certain balance of power" (1980: 73, my emphasis) is allegedly inherent in properly functioning patron–client systems? And what is the original source of inequality in the patron and client relationships?

Since the authors' approach is basically ahistorical, we cannot locate the factors that elevate the clients' weakness to a quasi-eternal principle. We are also not able to find out why a market that presupposes unequal, yet autonomous actors – patron and client – only leads to a relationship of monopolistic control of the patron over his client – a "core characteristic" of patron-clientage in the first place. These flaws derive from the authors' complete disregard of the class nature of patron–client relations – which is somewhat astonishing given the stark class inequality in the societies in question. These flaws also derive from the authors' ahistorical and restricted conception of patron–client ties, which fails to place these ties in historically specific relations of production.

Both of these problems – the ahistorical-phenotypical approach to patron–client relations and the absence of class analysis – are widespread in the literature on patron–client relations. Let us examine them more closely.

Relations of production

As we have seen, much of the literature on patron-clientage is fundamentally unable to establish causality. If we want to investigate causality in political-economic relations, we must deal with the concrete relationship between basis and superstructure. In this context, it means that we must first explain the relations of production contained in patron–client ties.

Scott (1977: 22) provides an imaginative new approach to the type of analysis: He sketches a model of clientelism as it occurs in noncapitalist relations of production in agrarian societies. He argues that his narrow focus on the rural sector, "is not entirely one of analytical convenience and interest. Throughout much of the Mediterranean world the relations between the tillers of land and its owners have represented the locus of livelihood and materials well-being for a large share of the population."[2]

Indeed, one could go even further and argue that throughout large areas of the Mediterranean, the climate and certain historical conditions dating back to antiquity have created what is, with local variations, one specific form or type of agrarian mode of production. This form was dominant within the region even before the dawn of capitalism and has continued to impose a distinctive character on the capitalist social and political relationships that have arisen subsequent to it.

Scott argues that this Mediterranean variant of the precapitalist agrarian mode of production has several distinctive characteristics: (a) the crops produced must be low-risk varieties because of the precarious climate; (b) the landlord owns or controls a large part of the means of production (land, seed, equipment, etc.); (c) the system of labor is based on the family, and the peasantry is tied, de facto, to the land owing to such factors as the absence of new arable land; and (d) surplus is appropriated in kind or in cash from *mezzadri*, or tied laborers.

Scott's key point is that the precise form assumed by this appropriation of the surplus product is a result of the irregular climatic conditions character-istic of the Mediterranean region. Suppose that a landowner extracts a constant share from the peasant's crop. Suppose further that the harvests therefrom vary such that, in one year, peasants produce crops beyond what is minimally necessary for the reproduction of their labor (Scott's "subsistence danger line"), and in another year they produce either at the danger level or below it. It is easy to see that a small surplus may be left to the peasant in the first year, but that in the second taxation paid to the landowner will either force him below the subsistence level or, if the harvest was already below that level to begin with, will lead him into catastrophic ruin.

In the "clientelist" form of surplus appropriation, on the other hand, landlords would not only be prepared to forego their rent payments, but would actually subsidize peasants in order to bring them above the danger line. Thus, in contrast to a system in which the landlord stabilizes his income at the expense of the peasant, the peasant's income in this system is considerably stabilized at the landlord's expense. But, as Scott points out

(1977: 33), in this system the ratio of exploitation might well be higher than under a fixed levy and yet be resented less, "inasmuch as it avoids the outcomes which peasants fear most" – which is that they may be deprived of their livelihood.

In contrast to a fixed levy system, this clientelistic mode of surplus appropriation *personalizes* the relationship between lord and peasant. The lord is personally interested in the welfare of his tenant (1977: 34), and instead of engaging in an impersonal form of taxation, he extracts surplus through negotiations between himself and the peasant, whenever the latter experiences crises. Naturally, negotiations regarding the landlord's take are extended from crises based upon fluctuation in crop yields to ones arising from other economic and noneconomic factors, for example, the quantity and quality of family labor or illness. Other factors – such as other concrete forms of protection provided by the landlord or the peasants' loyalty, especially in the form of willingness to provide extraordinary services – obviously enter into these negotiations as well.

Scott only discusses clientelistic relations from the peasant's perspective, however, and assumes his underlying rationality. The peasant is seen as "a cultivator who faces a set of continuing existential dilemmas over his physical security which he is often poorly equipped to solve by himself" (1977:34). "The reverence in which the institution of patronage is held thus ultimately depends upon how well it helps peasants survive the recurrent crises of food supply, defense, and brokerage which mark their life" (1977: 35). Scott is correct that the clientelistic mode of surplus appropriation amounts to a subsistence guarantee for the peasant. But an even more critical point emerges from this analysis. *By guaranteeing the peasant's subsistence, the patron actually guarantees his own survival as patron*; in other words, this form of surplus extraction assures the reproduction of the exploitative relation between lord and peasant in which both patron and client are embedded. If Scott's hypothetical model is supported by empirical evidence – the collection of which is not undertaken here but is necessary in order to advance this debate – we could argue that patron-clientage fulfills, in certain precapitalist agrarian economies, the same functions as social security systems in advanced capitalist countries: They ensure the reproduction of exploited classes and are, therefore, a crucial feature of their relations of production. At the same time, both are also a result of, and an advance in, class struggle between two antagonistic classes. But whereas, under capitalism, social insurance deflects the worker's class antagonism away from the exploiting class as class and to the state, the insurance function of patronage hides the class antagonism by personalizing the relationship between exploiter and producer.

According to Scott, then, the clientelistic form of the appropriation of surplus characterizes the agrarian sector in large areas of the Mediterranean region. It has long been the dominant form of agrarian production relations in these areas. *This specific form of exploitation,* as a dominant form, has given rise to corresponding social and political relationships and ideologies, most of which are.described in the literature in terms of patron-clientage. These social and political relationships stretch far beyond the local areas in which clientelistic production relations prevail. Where they are hegemonic, the clientelistic superstructure they generate becomes institutionalized not only throughout the countryside, but also in bureaucracies both in areas where the landlord–tenant system prevails and in marginal areas dominated by pastoral agriculture. This occurs not only where capitalist forms of agriculture have developed, but also where small industrial nuclei have actually been created. For the same reason, not only is the *democrazia cristiana* clientelistic in southern Italy, but the Communist Party is also clientelistic there.

As a surplus-appropriating class, patrons must develop coercive, political means to maintain their position. Yet the standard patron–client literature has failed to look beyond dyadic patron–client relations – individual "strong men" and their followers – to the underlying class structure. Instead of focusing on relations of production, this literature has addressed itself to the superstructural emanations of clientage, which it has suffused with social–psychological models of leader-and-followership. Given this idealistic approach, it is no wonder that we still lack sufficiently specific economic accounts of landlord–peasant relations in the Mediterranean area.

In contrast, most of the Marxist literature has dealt abstractly-globally with the mechanics of domination and exploitation, and has usually not studied relations of production in situ. The point is that the time has come to start from the microlevel – at the bottom. That is to say, in order to understand the peculiar nature of these class relations, we must treat them precisely as relations between people.

Class rule as patronage

Up to this point, I have focused on relations of production and on the mode of appropriation of surplus characteristic of patron-clientage. I will now focus on the structure of local units of the patron class, especially its kinship structure and its role in relation to the state. The case material presented in the next two sections is taken from the Sard village of Telemula. I compare the characteristics of its ruling elite around the turn of the century with those of the clique that emerged in the late 1960s. These characteristics are located in the local kinship system by virtue of the prevailing relations of production and the linkage between the local ruling class and the central bureaucracy of the Italian state.

The old ruling clique in Telemula, 1875–1945

The Sannas

Telemula (population = 610 in 1901 and approximately 1,500 in 1975) is a village in the *Barbagia*, the area surrounding the Gennargentu Mountains in central Sardinia. The village economy is predominantly pastoral. The area is one of densely clustered communities, each of which now has a population of anywhere from one to six thousand persons.

Telemula's local elite, the Sanna kin group, rose to power in the last quarter of the nineteenth century.[3] At the beginning of that period, several smaller families with some strategic resources developed an intensive pattern of cooperation. The *Lai–Mureddu family*, shown in Figure 8.1, owned a small store and received a double portion of land in the division of communal lands (see the discussion later in the chapter). The *Corrias–Balisai–Mongili* family stands out for two important reasons. It was closely tied to the church and as such later received title to prebendal land. Its members tended to be active in the politics of the village, and like the Lais, occasionally held the position of community elder. Moreover, for winter grazing they traditionally used communal land located near Sardinia's major road along the eastern coastline and thus the Sannas were able to function as important messengers and gatekeepers for Telemula.[4]

The *Bassu–Muscau* family originally stood out because Michele Bassu was an accomplished practitioner of folk medicine, had briefly attended a theological seminary, and was for a long time the only resident of the village who knew how to read and write.

These families developed intensive relationships of mutual cooperation cemented by intermarriages over several generations (see Figure 8.1). Successive strategic intermarriages, apart from excluding outsiders from access to family capital and other resources, counteracted – by means of the positive uxorial ties – the ordinary loss of solidarity among partilateral kin. With their personal ties to the church and the larger political structure, the Sannas emerged as the local elite, primarily as mayors and councillors in the village.

The formation of the Sanna kin group, in the years immediately after the foundation of the Italian state, occurred at a time when the Italian *mezzogiorno* experienced a serious disruption of its economy and saw great hardship among its rural populations.

A drastic rise in regional taxation during the last quarter of the nineteenth century led, first, to the depletion of local resources (especially lumber), and then to severe disruptions in the ecological balance. These upheavals were accompanied by the breakup of communally held land into individual

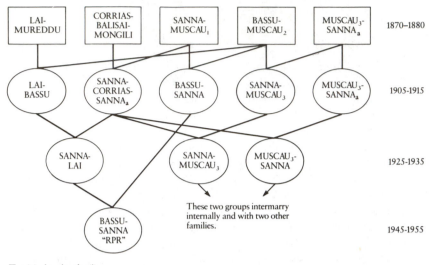

Figure 8.1. The formation of the Sanna kin group over four 10-year spans of principal family formation. Lines indicate origins of spouses in the principal intermarriages. MUSCAU$_1$, MUSCAU$_2$, and MUSCAU$_3$ are unrelated families with identical names; SANNA$_a$ are members of the SANNA kin group, but a separate branch.

parcels. The nature of agricultural activity changed, as the population's increasing need for cash during the disruptions transformed such locally consumed products as cheese into cash commodities.

At the time of this drastic transformation, the Sannas achieved an unprecedented degree of economic and political power in the village. Along with outsiders, they bought many parcels of formerly communal land, which they worked through heavily exploited day laborers. They were landlords to the *carabinieri*, the town hall, and the elementary school and monopolized access to church authorities. With the help of an uncle, a powerful priest in the area, one relative obtained a medical education and a daughter became the first local elementary school teacher. Their internal power and external connections gave them a continuing role in policing this major economic transformation.

These transformations occurred before 1922. The subsequent Fascist period was one of economic stagnation and harsh political repression. The Sannas' role as presiders over the economic transformation of the area disappeared, although they established themselves as the local representatives of the Fascist state.[5] The Sannas continued to marry among themselves (see Figure 8.1), and, in terms of kin ties, became increasingly isolated from the rest of the community. At the same time, they failed to establish ties to the ruling cliques of neighboring communities or with the upper class in the major towns. Thus, they became "lonely aristocrats" in Telemula. After 1945, they slowly began to lose the initiative in the political affairs of Telemula and were supplanted by new ruling clique, the Taulas.

Class

The beginnings of the economic transformation of Telemula coincided with the emergence of the Sanna kin group as an entity distinct from other village families. During this transformation, the Sannas acquired the lion's share of local land: over 600 hectares in contrast to an average of 3 hectares held by other village families. Evidence from the neighboring village of Orgosolo (Bodemann, 1982) suggests that the local populace regarded this wealth as illegitimate because it was derived from the massive expropriation, enclosures, and shady acquisitions of previously communal land. Throughout the Barbagia at this time, people were only beginning to treat land as an alienable commodity and to extract surplus value from it. In short, families like the Sannas had participated in transforming land from a communally owned means of production to a commodity. This permitted them to extract surplus from an emerging class of sharecroppers. The local system, which had been without class antagonisms, began to be replaced by an agrarian-based class structure.

The Telemulese case reveals the close interrelation of the economic and political activities of the ruling clique. Only their dominant political role allowed the Sannas to amass the vast amount of land and other resources they eventually came to own. The Sannas controlled the principal commercial resources: the government monopoly on salt and tobacco and a major share in the sale of liquor. Yet their economic role, as landowners and beneficiaries of the government monopolies, was precapitalist, and their economic behavior contrasted sharply with that of the charcoal manufacturers and prospectors, with whom they worked hand in glove. Their rentier activity has been perpetuated by their descendants as well, who have remained in the noncapitalist domain either as professionals, doctors and teachers, or as overseers of their basic domains – land and the state monopolies. (See Luxemburg, [1951] 1964; and Bodemann and Allahar, 1980, on the transformation from precapitalist to dependent social formations.)

Familism and kinship

In Telemula, the solidarity of cognatic kin, especially males, is precarious and usually superseded by close ties between affinal males. There are strong, positive ties between a woman and her married daughters, whereas parent–son, especially father–son, ties, are tension-ridden and highly conflictual (see Bodemann, 1979: chap. 4).[6] The strong affinal and weak patrilineal ties of males ensure a close interconnection between the various kin groups.

Traditionally, the relations of production in pastoralism and domestic production determine the regulatory function of the local kinship system, but, after the transformation, kinship preponderantly rules the course of local politics, and thereby its economy as well. The Sannas' monopolization of political and economic resources led, contrary to prevailing norms, to endogamous marriages. Affinal ties continued to be turned "inward," encapsulating the ruling clique, endowing it with strong internal solidarity, but slowly separating it from the rest of the community. In other words, the endogamous marriages sharply delineated the boundaries of the Sanna kin group and over time weakened the structural basis for coalitions with other village kin groups (Wolf, 1966; Wellman, 1981; Banfield, [1958] 1967). The use here of the concept of familism differs from that of Banfield in that I do not see familism as being tied to the nuclear family, nor as being distributed evenly throughout a given social structure. Rather, I see it as being class-specific. Even on an analytical level, Banfield's use of the term is problematic. If parents, for example, maximize the immediate material interest of their nuclear family, will they therefore act for their own benefit against the interests of their married child's in-laws? Will a young couple – that is, a newly formed nuclear family – act against the interests of their parents? Certainly the type of behavior Banfield describes is least likely in southern Italy, where resources are mobilized in the framework of elaborate kinship networks and patron-clientage. The fact that, as a practice, familism is linked to the local upper class does not mean that, as an ideology, it is not spread throughout the social structure at large, as Galtung (1971) attempted to show. Pinna (1971: 72, 75) essentially rewrote Banfield for the situation in Sardinia. The objections that apply to Banfield's "familism" therefore also apply substantially to Pinna's 'exclusivism," the class-specific usefulness of both concepts notwithstanding (see Bodemann, 1979c: 199 ff.).

In sum, the solidarities that come into play within the community – its political–legal superstructure – were governed by kinship ties that were in turn shaped by the relations of production. It is therefore not the peasant mode of production per se that explains this dominance of kinship (Bodemann, 1979a, 1979c; Meillassoux, 1973). What we find in Barbaricine communities is a form of social involution, a regressive intensification of kin ties. In the wake of the destruction of the traditional economy and social structure in the nineteenth century, other important relations, such as age cohorts and ceremonial solidarities, had withered away and kinship remained the major organizing principle at the local level.

The state

In Telemula, the local ruling clique established itself as the crucial link between the community and the state. This clique was characterized by three salient features:

1. In relation to the community, the clique was kin-based in nature. It was linked to the community primarily by ties of kinship and it constituted a kin group itself.

2. Members of the ruling clique were personally tied to state institutions as priests, lawyers, deputies, and the like. Conversely, the ruling clique was the embodiment of the local political and economic interests of the state. They were the state's local "organic" representatives because through their privileged access to local resources and kinship ties, they were anchored in the village and were in a position to mobilize substantial segments of the village for political purposes. Instead of the state being the highest social reality of the individual, a single individual represented the highest reality of the state.[7] Nonlocal landlords, however extensive their holdings, did not have the ties to others that would have allowed them to play such a part.

3. The local ruling class monopolized access to all important state institutions. Where it failed to do so, there was often conflict between competing groups. The extreme monopolistic character of the ruling clique and its role as accessory in the process of primitive accumulation was potentially explosive. The power of the Sannas was seriously challenged in Telemula and, indeed, was suspended for a number of years. Although the mode of mobilization in these conflicts was kinship-based, its substance was a primitive political revolt against the destruction of the traditional social and economic order and the imposition of the new state apparatus on the village. In the following section I try to show how this rigidity in the power structure was largely overcome with the rise of the new ruling class following the post–World War II economic boom.

The new ruling clique in Telemula since 1965

The Taulas

In Sardinia, as in other parts of the *mezzogiorno*, the restructuring of the capitalist state after 1945 was manifested in the closure of local coal mines in the early 1950s, which increased rural unrest, and in the establishment of the *Cassa per il Mezzogiorno*, a massive "modernization" program for the south, with new road construction, capital-intensive industries such as oil refineries, and a giant paper factory; the extension of port facilities; and a reforestation program. The local and regional economies became much more intensively integrated into Western European capitalism; in particular, there was large-scale emigration of Sardic labor to northern industrial centres and a massive inflow of industrial commodities and consumer goods.

In this period, a new local elite, the Taulas, began to emerge in Telemula quite independent of the Sannas. By 1970, this new group had used the new capitalist developments to achieve solid and unrivaled political power in the village (see Bodemann 1979a for a detailed description).

The meteoric rise of the Taula siblings – Bruno, Giovann' Antonio, and Iolanda – from an average-to-poor local family was set in motion by their abnormally structured kinship ties. Having lost their father in early childhood, they were cut off from tension-ridden relationships with agnatic kin, and they were soon alienated from the traditional herding environment. Their deviant network of kin ties, in turn, generated a host of other kinship abnormalities, starting with unconventional marriages of two sons – which, contrary to marriages of the normal pattern, did not undermine their close cooperative relationships.[8]

Owing to an unusual combination of circumstances, enormous drive, and great sensitivity for the new economic directions, the siblings managed to purchase a truck, and – with virtually no competition in Telemula and the neighboring villages – were able to develop a small trucking business. In the 1960s, they built a small hotel in Telemula, added a modern bakery, received a trucking monopoly for bottled beverages to the larger area, and later in that decade opened a furniture business.

These unprecedented activities were watched in Telemula with great diffidence and some open opposition. By the mid-1960s, the Taulas had become aware of their weak political position and the need to solidify their business ventures. They began to establish a political base in the village.

Between 1945 and 1970, the political situation in Telemula was fairly unstable, with weak and constantly shifting municipal administrations. On several occasions, prefectural officials took over the municipal offices because of continuous in-fighting and general administrative chaos. During much of this period, the Sannas, although they had lost the political initiative, were still able to block most political decisions that ran counter to their interests by means of their alliance with local priests.

In the late 1960s, the Taulas began a fierce campaign against the strongest nucleus of the then prevailing DC/PSI (Christian Democratic/Socialist) coalition and won the mayoralty in 1970. Virtually unchallenged, they held full and effective power throughout the following decade. Why were the Taulas successful when for 25 years other political groupings had failed?

In the early years of their business career, until approximately 1965, the Taulas gave short-term and long-term jobs to a particular segment of lower-ranking kin. These individuals were close affinal kin – mostly siblings or first cousins of two of the Taula siblings' spouses who were in a relatively inferior position vis-à-vis their employers. Since the three siblings and their families constituted an internally cohesive and strong kin group, these lower-ranking kin had no higher authority to appeal to in cases of unfair treatment, labor disputes, and the like. Until that time, the Taulas had virtually ignored their own cognatic kin entirely. Very few jobs or business favors were extended to their own relatives, even to first cousins.

After 1965, coincidental with the expansion of their business and the growing awareness that they were politically isolated in the community, a significant shift in their hiring practices took place. A large number of temporary jobs and favors were given to distant kin: second or third matrialateral and patrilateral cousins and relatives of the group of lower-level kin who at that time constituted the core of the Taula party.

With the further expansion of their business in the early 1970s, the Taulas also began to consider their own close cognatic kin. Several of the more dynamic individuals were encouraged to set up grocery stores, bars, and furniture businesses outside Telemula, where, as equal-ranking kin, they were no threat to the Taula siblings. They could even be trusted with investments made on their behalf, but to the benefit of the Taulas, as "satellites" outside Telemula.

Overtures to distant kin – to individuals often as closely related to the Taula opposition – were made to them precisely as distant kin. That is to say, the Taulas activated and gave concrete significance to distant kin ties by extending favors, especially jobs. Around the core of the Taula group, therefore, a wider sphere of kin could see themselves as "sib" and shifted their own political loyalty (and that of some of their own close relatives) to the Taulas, who could then mobilize majority support in the village and become the new local elite. These developments, to a greater degree than in the case of the Sannas, increasingly deformed the traditional structure and the role of kinship in the village.

To complete the picture, mention must be made of the local subelite, a group of three "lieutenants" to whom the Taulas have awarded the bulk of recent municipal contracts (e.g., for the construction of roads and transport of construction materials). These three men, directly or through their wives, are distant kin of the Taulas and are also directly related to each other. They have assumed important oligarchical roles in the village as seconds-in-command.

Although the Taulas have remained officially outside the framework of the DC and are antagonistic to the church, they have rapidly developed highly personalistic ties to important politician-technocrats who are themselves members of the DC. The Taulas have thus succeeded in circumventing the "official" DC patronage extended to the anti-Taula forces by more old-style notables and party functionaries. As a consequence, the older DC patronage in Telemula has become stagnant, being restricted to occasional patronage jobs in the road repair service, employment by a DC businessman-politician outside Telemula, and the like.

Qualitatively then, the patronage system of the DC in Telemula is at the level of the other parties, even though it is comparatively more resourceful: The Socialist, Neo-Fascist, and even the Communist electorate are embedded in ties to notables, particularly to lawyers, other professionals, and entrepreneurs in the major towns who provide occasional services in return for electoral support. But it is the Taulas who control the significant ties, for example, the financially potent bureaucrats who dispose of the major government funds for the improvement of tourism, the local economy, or other parts of the infrastructure. These funds flow into enterprises controlled by the Taulas, and their business ventures have received far more state funding, tax benefits, and so on than all other Telemulesi combined.

When the new local ruling clique (the Taulas) is compared to the clique that established itself in the early years of the Italian state (the Sannas), a number of interesting points emerge.

Class

The most striking difference between the old and the new local ruling clique is that the latter is a part of the capitalist class – albeit, a junior member. The Taulas import mass-produced commodities to the region and develop modest capitalist enterprises that employ wage labor. They are also the guarantors of "perpetualized primitive accumulation" – a system that does not separate, but only temporarily suspends, the tie between the rural producer and his land as means of production (see Bodemann and Allahar, 1980). Thus, the Taulas are hostile to modernized agriculture in the community, and their employment practices have launched the industrial career of many prospective labor migrants.

Familism and kinship

Given the relative immaturity of the new ruling clique, it is still too soon to document fully their exclusive familistic tendencies. On the other hand, the case of the Taulas clearly shows the capacity of these affinal ties to link wide segments of the village population to this clique. They consider carefully who should receive jobs and other favors, and the jobs are spread to distant kin throughout the community. In this way, the Taulas received the political support needed to expand their economic role. The manner in which economic decisions are now directed by considerations of kinship and the intensity in this new kinship network, developing to the detriment of other kinship loyalties in the community, is so striking that, to paraphrase Marx and Engels, the kin ties of the ruling class have become the ruling kin ties.

The state

In contrast to the old ruling cliques, this new ruling clique is not as visibly tied to the state and lacks one of the major characteristics of the old ruling clique: it does not personify the state, nor does it embody the state apparatus, properties that are focal in patron–client literature.

Although the Taulas' survival as the ruling clique depends upon their political predominance, they are first and foremost representatives of the capitalist economy and representatives of the capitalist class:[9] their political position is ancillary. As for the old ruling clique, the primacy of the economic role is at least in question: the Sannas are politicians first and landowners and merchants second.

Moreover, the old local elite in the rural area only rarely established lasting relations such as intermarriage with the Sardic ruling class in Cagliari or Sassari. There is therefore a peculiar contradiction in the position of this old elite. According to its relationship to the means of production, it is a class. But to the extent that class entails a measure of internal cohesion or at least social contact, the old elite comprises merely a series of isolated cliques, because their economic role was not conducive to collective action.

In contrast, the Taulas and similar groups in other villages have viable ties to each other, and especially to the upper class in the cities – ties that grew out of previous business contacts. These ties are being reproduced: The Taulas send their children to elite boarding schools in the Sard capital, Cagliari, instead of to the local *liceo* in a neighboring town, as the Sannas did in the past and continue to do.

In sum, the old local ruling class held an exclusive monopoly of access to the state. With the establishment of a party structure after 1945, other groups developed links to external political institutions through these parties. These institutions, however, dispense merely welfare (pensions, legal assistance, etc.) in exchange for votes, and the Taulas monopolize access to those political institutions that have a central role in the capitalist economy.[10]

The evolution of patron-clientage in Telemula strikingly shows the relationship between class position and kinship structure. The precapitalist Sannas avoided coalitions with other groups and built up a densely knit, tightly bounded cluster of ties through endogamy. Such a network structure worked well for conserving control over existing Telemulese resources as long as the larger structural conditions of Italian and Sardic society allowed the Sannas to monopolize and minimize external access to Telemula. Yet postwar capitalist conditions have demanded the integration of Telemula into larger social and economic systems. As the enterprises of the Taulas are based on economic relations with interests elsewhere, they must develop coalitions with other groups. Consequently, in contrast to the Sannas, their kinship ties are widely dispersed and lack the sharp demarcations noted in the kinship structure of the Sannas. These differences in kinship structure, then, have not been fortuitous or passive responses to conditions: indeed, a key to the Taulas' recent success has been their deliberate development of such ramified kinship networks to protect and advance their interests (see Wolf, 1966; Wellman, 1981).

The leaderless interregnum, 1945–1970

From the time that the autocratic rule of the Sannas came to a close to the time that the Taulas began to tighten their grip on the village – between about 1945 and 1970 – there existed a mildly chaotic interregnum in the village. Why was this possible, and why did no new ruling clique emerge from the groups that held nominal power during that period?

An analysis of the membership of the municipal council and a review of the background of the various mayors during that time – who were far more representative of the ordinary Telemulese than either the Sannas or the Taulas – clearly brings out one point: As agriculturalists or herders, these individuals all belonged to the traditional, paralyzed economic sector of the community.

Some of these individuals had indeed attempted to break with traditional attitudes. Some had tried their hand, without the luck of the Taulas, at new entrepreneurial activities. Some of them were active in left-wing parties or the left wing of the DC. Some were more conservative. However, none of their particular attitudes or activities enabled them to form a stable new ruling clique. The fact alone that they were tied to the stagnant means of production – herding and agriculture, sectors that had received little or no government assistance while billions of lire were being poured into others – made it impossible for any group in the traditional sectors to achieve firm political control.

Only in the late 1960s, during a short period in which an agricultural technician who was of Telemulese background but who resided out of town had been elected mayor, did it seem that a new ruling clique might emerge from this traditional sector to form around two agricultural cooperatives that this mayor had proposed. But the cooperatives did not receive the government backing necessary for success. Also by that time, the Taulas were already too powerful and, setting popular opinion against such "favoritism," eventually blocked the success of these plans. The prospective members of these two cooperatives were all linked by kin ties, and the Taulas clearly sensed that such economic cooperation within a network of kin would have set up a serious and sustained opposition to their own political goals. The Taulas have therefore systematically attempted to deactivate these kin ties in order to block a resurgence of this alliance.

Conclusion

Patron-clientage and class relations

This discussion has made a number of interrelated points. What appears as patronage, as "lopsided friendship," and indeed entails a form of reciprocity is not an independent phenomenon. It is a form of class rule and class struggle and at the same time its concealment. Owners of the key means of production confront nonowners, but this conflict is hidden by, in the words of the Communist Manifesto, the "patriarchal, idyllic relations" between the oppressed and their "patrons" – particular individuals of the dominant class.

These patrons – whether they be lawyers, priests, contractors, or politicians – must be identified in terms of the means of production (e.g., land) of which their status or principal activity (e.g., as priests or physicians) is only a derivative. Such identification, which involves an analysis of the kin ties into which these patrons are embedded, establishes not only the key means of production, but the sum of resources that such kin groups regulate and that they tend to monopolize as a collectivity.

Such resources range from access to the state apparatus outside the village, town, or region to their skills as professionals or secondary commercial activities (e.g., landowners who also operate a quarry). This identification allows us to describe them as the "local elite" or "ruling clique."

As a class, then, this assemblage of patrons can be identified regionally or nationally in terms of the means of production they typically control. However, in order to understand this class as a ruling clique, we must also describe it at the local level, as the local apparatus of political domination, and its constituent features must be identified before we can draw inferences about the regional constitution of these cliques.

In the concrete case that I have analyzed, the old ruling clique was propelled to power by means of existing links to the state, usually via the church. These links permitted them to seize land and gave them privileged access to commercial activities (e.g., state monopolies of salt, tobacco, postage, liquor). It is not surprising, therefore, that in their overall emphasis and day-to-day concerns, members of these cliques were politicians first and landowners and entrepreneurs second. Because these cliques monopolized political power, the means of production (land), and commercial resources, they did not encourage intensive cooperation with other groups outside or inside the community; they therefore tended to become encapsulated and relied on ties with notables in the regional and provincial capitals.

The postwar ruling cliques, on the other hand, are entrepreneurs first and politicians second. They started out as independent entrepreneurs, then sought political support and financial backing from the state, and in turn assumed political functions in the local communities in order to guard their control over key resources. The nature of their commercial activities – small industry, transportation, tourism, and so on – defines their ties to the state as principally economic ones. These are integrative, not encapsulating ties. Their activities force these groups into perpetual cooperation with bureau-technocrats and other entrepreneurs, both at the supra-local level, and with a subservient collaborating class of minor entrepreneurs in the home community. In contrast to the old ruling cliques, which are the personified representatives of the state, the new elite appears as the representative and junior member of the capitalist class.

Whether we deal with the old or the new local cliques or with "patronage" in Sardinia or elsewhere, all of these local groups of powerful individuals who exert power over peasants or peasant proletarians have at their disposal diffuse political and economic resources. In order to mobilize these resources to their advantage, they must be embedded in hypostatized kinship structures, that is, involuted, cancerous ties exerting significant control over these resources. I describe such groups as local ruling cliques. These hypostatized kinship structures, as I have attempted to show, in turn affect the local relations of production and regulate the monopoly of access to key state institutions. In this sense, patron-clientage is not an anachronism and not a residual primordial relation.

Finally, we must ask how the social structure in these communities may evolve in the future. I have attempted to show that the social structure as a whole is not familistic, but is merely the social structure of the local ruling class; that is, kin ties, which once constituted the relations of production, have assumed a strength of their own and are concentrated in a small, powerful minority. Today, with the destruction of the traditional herding and peasant economy in southern Italy and the paralysis of the rural economy, kinship has begun to lose its significance as the organizing principle. Labor migrants marry into families that are anathema to their parents and siblings. Local students, teachers, and professionals who are marginal to the village no longer even know exactly who their second or third cousins are. The remaining mass of the underemployed in the village form ties regardless of kinship. They associate with or against the ruling clique, with or against their kin groups, depending on who is more likely to help them find a job or some marginal income.

There is a contrast, then, between the concentration of kin ties at the top and the negation of kinship solidarities at the bottom of the social structure. The erosion of kinship solidarities at the bottom may bring about broadly based solidarities of peasant and herder and thus do away with the familistic local ruling class, which has resisted attempts to transform the rural economy.

As long as we merely describe patron–client ties, we only elaborate on the local population's own ideological perception of the social order. Singelmann (1975: 402) has pointed out that a basic condition for the progress of rural political movements is the capacity of its members to perceive local "bosses" (in his case, landowners) collectively as members of an opposing class, rather than individually as "good" or "bad" patrons.

I see here an important task for social scientists who regard themselves as advocates of these exploited populations – for how can the peasantries of these regions deal with their opponents as a class as long as we, their historians, anthropologists, or whatever, fail to analyze them as such?

NOTES

1. See Flynn (1974), Gilmore (1977), Gilsenan (1977), and L. Guasti (1977). I am applying the Marxist label more liberally here than some of the authors in question may think appropriate.
2. For some earlier formulations in support of this position, see Hall (1974: 506) and Guasti (1977: 423). Hall speaks of the "original rural setting" of patronage.
3. All Telemulese proper names given here are fictitious. The rather loose term "kin group" is used to denote a group of cooperating households closely linked by kinship ties. In contrast, locally *ratza* denotes a group usually traced patrilineally through six or seven generations. For a more detailed comparison, including a parallel analysis of Orgosolo, a neighboring village, see Bodemann (1982).
4. Until 1865, all land, with the exception of the church prebends, was communally owned. Some parts of the communal land called *vidazzone* were periodically divided on a rotating basis and distributed to grow cereals. Between 1865 and 1881, much of the land previously used to produce cereals was subdivided equally among households and turned into private property.
5. In the period immediately before World War I, a serious revolt, called a *scioppero* (strike), had taken place in Telemula. The mayor at the time, a member of the Sanna kin group and a particularly incompetent and corrupt individual, was physically driven from the community. In the subsequent election, one leader of the revolt was elected mayor, seriously challenging the position of the Sannas. Moreover, the "popular" sentiments of this mayor made him an early supporter of Mussolini, thus outmaneuvering the Sannas in the first years of fascism. With its massive political support from the outside, its resources in the community, and its close alliance with the *carabinieri*, the Sannas gained the upper hand. The mayor was expelled from office and framed with trumped-up charges. He fled to the mountains as an outlaw, fell into a trap set by the Sannas, and was shot by the *carabinieri*.
6. I have dealt elsewhere with the economic basis of Sardic kinship structure (Bodemann, 1979c: 180 ff.). In summary form, the tension-ridden relationships of fathers and brothers and the relatively harmonious relationships of mothers and daughters might be explained as follows. In the pastoralist context of Sardinia, the father typically owns his herd. His sons work for him from childhood onward on a noncontractual basis. A great diversity of work and varying degrees of

drudgery are involved. In contrast to the work of *tharrakkos* (serfs) or *gumpanzos* (cooperating herders), a son's duties are diffuse, and work of varying desirability is age-graded between the father and his sons.

In contrast, in women's work (e.g., baking bread, cooking, weaving, etc.) the ownership of the instruments of production plays a subordinate role. The work is more egalitarian, drudgery tends to be distributed more evenly, and a number of tasks (e.g., bread baking, harvesting, making handicrafts) tend to involve women from more than one household. This situation by itself helps discharge possibly tense work relationships, since work is typically of a sociable cooperative nature in contrast to the isolation of the herders. As a result, despite attempts at counterbalancing the situation, for example, through the prevailing patrilocal residence, the relationship of cognatic males is usually tension-ridden and this antagonism is also transferred to brothers' spouses. Cognatic women, on the other hand, especially mother–daughter relationships, are very close and endure after marriage. This encourages husbands into cooperative relationships with their fathers-in-law, and possibly into an even deeper break with their parental family. Despite the importance of ties involving women, most portrayals of patron–client relations discuss only men. Very rarely (e.g., Gilmore, 1977; Silverman, 1975) do women enter the picture.

7. This is reminiscent of Marx's formulation, with reference to the Prince, in his "Critique of Hegel's Philosophy of the State" (*MEW*, [1843] 1961: 240).

8. The most important characteristic of these marriages was that they failed to generate the ordinarily strong affinal solidarity (see note 6). Bruno married a woman from outside Telemula, and his brother married a woman from a poor family who was adopted by the natural mother's sister. Thus, neither brother developed strong dependencies on their wives' families. Iolanda's husband, on the other hand, followed the traditional affinal dependency pattern and was drawn into the sphere of the Taulas, thus strengthening the family even further.

9. For example, the Taulas like to point out that they have been the first in the area to introduce particular types of advanced machinery and new trucks or automobiles. On the ideological level, they are virtually alone in Telemula in stressing capitalist virtues: private enterprise, a "Protestant ethic," and openness to the world.

10. Two examples illustrate this new quality of the monopolization of access that is so characteristic of patron-clientage. Members of the anti-Taula forces have had some success in the courts that repealed municipal decisions touching on some minor property questions; and others had the courts rule in their favor in a case where a close associate of the Taulas insulted a Taula opponent. On the other hand, the man who coordinated the planning of a new cooperative and who was closely tied to a pre-1970 mayor (who was opposed to the Taulas) found that after Bruno Taula's election as mayor, lawyers and administrators in Cagliari (the capital of the region of Sardinia) refused to have any further dealings with him.

LITERATURE CITED

Alavi, Hamza. "Peasant Classes and Primordial Loyalties." *Journal of Peasant Studies* 1 (1983): 23–62.

Banfield, Edward. *The Moral Basis of a Backward Society*. New York: Free Press, [1958] 1967.

Bodemann, Y. Michal. "Natural Development (Naturwüchsigkeit) in Early Society. A Note to Engels' Anthropology." *Critique of Anthropology* 15 (1979a): 15–83.

"Telemula: Aspects of the Micro-Organization of Backwardness in Central Sardinia." Ph.D. diss. Brandeis University, 1979c.

"Class Rule as Patronage, Kinship, Local Cliques and the State in Rural Sardinia." *Journal of Peasant Studies*. January (1982).

Bodemann, Y. Michal, and Anton Allahar. "The Micro-Organization of Backwardness in Central Sardinia: A Re-appraisal of Luxermburg's Phases of Underdevelopment." *Journal of Peasant Studies* 4 (1980): 458–76.

Eisenstadt, S. N., and Rene Lemarchand (eds.) *Political Clientelism, Patronage and Development*. Beverly Hills, Calif.: Sage, 1981.

Eisenstadt, S. N., and Louis Roniger. "Patron–Client Relations as a Model of Structuring Social Exchange." *Comparative Studies in Society and History* 1 (1980): 42–77.

Flynn, Peter. "Class, Clientelism and Coercion: Some Mechanisms of Internal Dependency and Control." *Journal of Commonwealth and Comparative Politics* 2 (1974): 133–56.

Galtung, Johan. *Members of Two Worlds*. New York: Columbia, 1971.

Gellner, Ernest, and John Waterbury (eds.). *Patrons and Clients in Mediterranean Societies*. London: Duckworth, 1977.

Gilmore, David. "Patronage and Class Conflict in Southern Spain." *Man* 3 (1977): 446–58.

Gilsenan, Michael. "Against Patron–Client Relations." In Ernest Gellner and John Waterbury (eds.), *Patrons and Clients in Mediterranean Societies*. London: Duckworth, 1977.

Guasti, Laura. "Peru: Clientelism and Internal Control." In Steffen W. Schmidt, (ed.), *Friends, Followers and Factions*. Berkeley: University of California Press, 1977.

Hall, Anthony. "Patron–Client Relations." *The Journal of Peasant Studies* 4 (1974): 506–8.

Hess, Henner. *Mafia and Mafiosi: The Structure of Power*. Westmead: Saxon House, 1977.

Luxemburg, Rosa. *The Accumulation of Capital*. New York: Monthly Review Press, [1951] 1964.

Marx-Engels-Werke (MEW). Vol. 1. Berlin: Dietz Verlag, [1843] 1961.

Meillassoux, Claude. "The Social Organization of the Peasantry: The Economic Basis of Kinship." *Journal of Peasant Studies* 1 (1973): 81–9.

Pinna, Luca. *La Famiglia Esclusiva: Parentela e Clientelismo in Sardegna*. Bari: Laterza, 1971.

Schmidt, Steffen W. (ed.) et al. *Friends, Followers and Factions: A Reader in Political Clientelism*. Berkeley: University of California Press, 1977.

Scott, J. C. "Patronage or Exploitation?" In Ernest Gellner and John Waterbury (eds.), *Patrons and Clients in Mediterranean Societies*. London: Duckworth, 1977.

Silverman, Sydel. *Three Bells of Civilization*. New York: Columbia University Press, 1975.

Singelmann, Peter. "The Closing Triangle: Critical Notes on a Model for Peasant Mobilization in Latin America." *Comparative Studies in Society and History* 17 (1975): 389–409.

Waterbury, John. "An Attempt to Put Patrons and Clients in Their Place." In Ernest Gellner and John Waterbury (eds.), *Patrons and Clients in Mediterranean Societies*. London: Duckworth, 1977.

Wellman, Barry. "The New East York Study." Department of Sociology, University of Toronto, 1981 (mimeographed).

Wolf, Eric. R. "Kinship, Friendship and Patron–Client Relations in Complex Societies." In Michael Banton (ed.), *The Social Anthropology of Complex Societies*. London: Tavistock, 1966.

Part III

Markets

As noted earlier, showing that communities can flourish without being rooted in long-lasting, densely knit solidarities has posed an important challenge for structural analysts. In contrast, the challenge facing those studying markets is to show that markets have inherent connectivity and structure.

Until now neoclassical economists have had a virtual monopoly over the study of markets. As a result, markets have by and large been seen as unstructured aggregations of individuals, the "buyers" and "sellers" coming together for only short-lived dyadic exchanges – an extension of the Lockean premise that socioeconomic systems arise out of the behavior of individuals independently pursuing their own ends. Hence, economists have usually ignored "social structure" in the sense that we use the term here. But even when they have not, they have treated it as an "externality" or a source of "market imperfection," relegated it to the back of the scholarly bus as a property of second-class "informal economies," or treated it through reference to a loosely articulated notion of "organizational culture."

Consider, for instance, how puzzled North American economists and business people have been about the West's failure to penetrate Japanese markets. Their explanations have usually been "culturally based," in the broadest and loosest sense. The Japanese, they argue, xenophobically reject foreign businesses, or Japanese business people "know how to cooperate" better than Westerners. These interpretations take as their normative baseline, the Western myth that markets consist of dyadic exchanges between buyers and sellers operating at arm's length. They regard the so-called "free market" as normal – and, hence, in little need of further explanation – and treat Japanese imperfect competition as an aberration that demands explanation for its stubborn persistence.

If we begin with the notion of *structure*, however, we can readily construct less patronizing analyses on the basis of long-term, complex networks allocating a variety of goods and services among structurally embedded participants. In this perspective, economic interchanges do not take place via some free-floating or abstract market, but through modifications in ties within concrete networks of exchange. Although economic competition requires actors to reexamine their market behavior constantly, in response to external constraints and the behavior of others, they do not do this in a vacuum.

221

To be sure, Western economists sometimes recognize long-lasting business relationships. But they treat these as special cases – as attempts to limit the effects of, or undermine, market forces. In contrast, structural analysts see the establishment of a set of *social* relationships among firms as an intrinsic part of the *formation* of concrete markets. Viewed from this vantage point, what needs to be explained in the Japanese case is not the persistence of dense economic ties that are resistant to foreign intrusion, but why an enterprise would cut itself loose from the established networks within which it operates in order to gain short-lived benefits from transactions with a structurally isolated Western business.

By approaching markets in this fashion, structural analysts are not only challenging the conventional economic wisdom, but they are reestablishing an important sociological tradition. Classical sociologists such as Marx and Weber were deeply interested in concrete economic mechanisms – including those through which markets are established. This historic interest in "economy and society" is reflected in contemporary analyses of such things as capitalism, urban development, and Third World societies.

Mainstream sociology, however, has always been ambivalent on this score. On the one hand, most sociologists have scorned economists' ignorance of the social consequences of markets and have done important work demonstrating the role played by markets in coordinating local and regional activity, diffusing innovation, and creating social groups. On the other hand, sociologists have largely ignored markets themselves – treating them as black holes in the social fabric. Most functionalists and Marxists, for instance, have implicitly accepted the economists' view that markets pursue their own logic independent of other aspects of social reality. Functionalists thus speak of markets as "adaptive" or "integrative," and traditional Marxists characterize them as "a means of realizing surplus value." In both cases, the predominant pattern has been to address the consequences of markets without examining their structure of operation in any concrete or detailed way.

Structural analysis, in contrast, begins with the premise that *markets are social structures* and not the spontaneous products of aggregated dyadic exchanges. Actors fit into, and structurally modify, positions within these markets. Thus, structural analysts contend that the ways in which actors observe and respond to others – the essence of a market – can be determined in the same fashion as any other socially structured activity.

Consider the microcomputer industry in the 1980s: a hot market, with rapid developments in hardware and software and a large number of buyers and sellers. On the surface, it ought to correspond closely to the kind of frictionless market economists have used as a standard. However, there is abundant evidence of structured interaction among participants. On the producers' side, manufacturers routinely steal personnel from one another in order to discover commercial secrets, devote much energy to attending trade shows, and read high-priced insiders' newsletters. On the buyers' side, participants are also well connected. Many fat-paged magazines keep them informed of new products, distributors selectively sponsor new types of technology, computer clubs help them evaluate what is available, and informal trading networks pass software and lore from one hand to another. Indeed, most software companies deliberately refuse to protect their products, reasoning in part that the best advertising is an endorsement by opinion leaders spreading tangible tokens of their approval through interpersonal networks.

Connectivity is clearly a pervasive characteristic of markets. But what sorts of structures are they and what consequences do they impart? In the first chapter in this part, *Harrison C. White* treats social structure as *simultaneously* growing out of – and constraining – role behavior. He argues that social structure is "both the trace and enactment of mutual perceptions feeding into practical choices by distinct actors." Just as Erickson has shown (Chapter 5) how structures shape perceptions, White demonstrates how perceptions feed back into the dynamic modification of structures.

White criticizes economists who assume that markets consist of actors engaging in transactions at arm's length. Instead, he argues, markets foster social control by juxtaposing and revealing sets of producers and buyers to one another. Two sorts of networks – those *within* sets of producers and buyers and those *between* producers and buyers – facilitate the actors' mutually aware calculations of options and constraints. Therefore, White maintains, it is important to explore the conditions under which buyers and sellers come together to sustain market transactions.

Unlike most economists, who assume that markets are inevitable, White considers the emergence of markets to be problematic: "The center of any concrete theory of markets should be on the tradeoff that must be made among firms' divergences in order to keep all of them viable within the same market." Mutual orientation and role taking markets allow buyers and sellers to interpret one another's actions. The key to understanding this process is the notion of a "market schedule" and how buyers and sellers cooperate to sustain it over time.

Neoclassical economics has treated variations in market form as anomalies, special cases generated by exogenous forces. Yet, White observes, there are strikingly different kinds of markets, and any theory of markets should be capable of coming to grips with this fact. He demonstrates how a variety of markets for different goods – from industrial products to professional theater – form around particular market schedules and how market players take on particular roles within each of them.

S. D. Berkowitz's chapter complements White's work by proposing a structural analytic strategy for constructing practical models of market structure. Berkowitz asserts that there has been a historic disjuncture between the kinds of units of analysis economists have used in modeling industrial organization and the ways in which they have collected their data. As a result, theoretically important results in the area have not been properly validated.

Yet, our ability to measure the structure and effects of markets substantially determines whether we see them as powerful, central parts of societies or as marginal holes in social structure. Berkowitz argues that we can reconstruct the units and bounded structures of markets in complex industrial societies by recasting problems of units and levels in structural analytic terms. His strategy for doing this involves the use of "enterprises" as actors and "market-areas" as tangible structures of interaction.

In her chapter, *Harriet Friedmann* places the discussion of markets in the context of broad international relations of domination and dependency. Like Berkowitz, she is primarily concerned with identifying the proper units and levels of analysis. To do this, she modifies the *world-systems* approach. World-systems analysis has been useful, she says, in that it provides a thoroughgoing critique of the *modernization* paradigm's treatment of nation-states as independent analytic units. In essence, the modernization approach – which treats economic development almost entirely in terms of the resources, infrastructure, and culture of nations – blames the weak for their poverty and congratulates the strong for their prosperity. This is both fatuous and inaccurate.

Friedmann appreciates the ways in which world-system analysts have demonstrated that a nation's *structural* location within a global pattern of relations crucially determines a wide range of its putatively "national characteristics" – such as its rate of economic growth, income distribution, and political regime. She asserts, however, that "grasping the notion that the world economy is based on a set of relations is only a start. The choice of units and relations greatly affects the kinds of analytic models we use and the conclusions we reach." World-systems analysts have chosen to study relations between geographic *regions*: the "core," "periphery," and "semi-periphery." But these are *spatial* units that are externally defined and have no natural validity as *social structural* units. Friedmann proposes that we study, instead, the relations between two inherently *social* units of analysis: enterprises and states. Her approach thus resembles that taken by community analysts in Part II who substituted networks for neighborhoods in their search for more meaningful analytic foci.

Friedmann goes on to provide a detailed case study of the world wheat market. She argues that the world-system approach ultimately fails because it intertwines economic with political relations. She suggests an approach that treats economic, political, and social relations as conceptually linked but analytically separate entities. She discovers that the world wheat market has historically taken two different forms: a "generalized exchange structure" approximating a world market and a "segmented exchange structure" of bilateral exchanges between nations. The wheat markets of both types have central mechanisms for establishing the roles of states in international divisions of labor. Generalized exchange has tended to reorganize the location of production along the lines of comparative advantage whereas segmented exchange has tended to reinforce existing distributions of production.

Thus, all three chapters in this part of the book argue forcefully that market structures are linked sets of social relations that are defined socially rather than spatially or in terms of the attributes of individual units. In each case, the authors maintain that this is accomplished dynamically through the interaction of the units involved and cannot be established a priori through formal boundary-making rules. Finally, each contends that the market behavior of actors is strongly constrained by the structures in which they are embedded.

9

Varieties of markets

Harrison C. White

Production markets as social structures

This chapter explicates production markets as particular kinds of social structures, which may be modeled in network terms. Aggregate and local niche aspects of markets are shown to mutually determine one another. On one side of the market, actors imitate one another. On the other, their only concern is to reach through the market to conclude transactions. Self-interest sustains a joint schedule of terms of trade among these actors and sides.

In other publications (e.g., White, 1981a, b; White and Eccles, 1987; Leifer and White, 1987), I have given a detailed technical account of this new theory together with an array of its applications to current U. S. industrial markets. Here I compare this approach to existing microeconomics and to network models within sociology. I begin by examining some underlying basic theory.

Social facts

A "social fact" is one that is created by the joint action of many individuals, but that is inexorable for any one of them. Social facts are the basis of sociology, but most of our methods establish and examine them only elliptically. Here I present a direct method and develop it in detail for one context: the production of goods for cash sale within a tangible social structure conventionally referred to as a "market."

Markets have two "sides" – a "buyers" and a "sellers" – so it may seem odd to choose such an apparently complex setting for elucidating the construction of social facts. Consider an obvious alternative:

Ross (1921), following Tarde (1895), identifies "imitation" in customs or convention as the fundamental aligning process that produces social facts. Ross sharply distinguishes, however, between the social psychological

Financial support under grants SER76-17502, SOC76-24394 and SE580-08658 is gratefully acknowledged. Ronald L. Breiger, Robert G. Eccles, Eric M. Leifer, John F. Padgett, and Arthur L. Stinchcombe made helpful suggestions, as did George Von Deventer in his statement on the market for Ayrshires. I am indebted to S. D. Berkowitz and Barry Wellman for shaping this chapter.

dimensions of the establishment of social facts – through the creation of "planes" of commonality via imitation – and those growing out of the groups and structures that men devise and into which they unite. The latter are usually seen as the proper province of sociology. Ross leaves vague, however, how the former contribute to the latter. Indeed, he only discusses how "the social environment is moulded by the extraordinary person" (Ross, 1921: 5). Furthermore, he neither posits a general theory of role frames nor explains how they relate to one another. Most modern theories ignore this issue as well (Nadel, 1957; White, 1965).

Social structure summarizes tangible process, so even a minimal unit must include all actors who have a direct impact on the context for any given actor. Social structures must therefore include at least one "interface" – or arena of mutually recognized perceptions marking a transition from one social formation to another (White, 1982) – so that markets are among the simplest structures we could examine. Imitation can only be one component of even partial social structures because the processes that reproduce role structures and niches require more complex patterns of interaction and tradeoffs. A complete and consistent theoretical framework must be capable of dealing with both the actor-orienting processes described by Ross and the forces shaping the larger structures in which they are bound up or embedded.

Markets as social structure

Markets are useful and relatively simple settings in which to observe social facts. Industrial markets each contain one set of actors, "producers," who invest in the equipment and lead time needed to manufacture a product for a buyer side. But what is the *setting* for these actors, the "market" itself? At first glance, *actual* markets are bewilderingly complex: Each embodies a number of independent actors – some individual and some corporate – engaged in a variety of transactions involving both money payment, received or given, and some other form of valuation (e.g., "Taste for a particular product" or "costs of production"). Somehow, through congeries of myopic, self-interested actions, out of this chaos must be created a market setting in which each actor may find a footing and contribute to the context perceived by others.

Although microeconomics has devoted considerable attention to the theoretical and practical consequences of different market contexts for the behavior of given firms, it has by and large ignored the key issue: How are markets able to reproduce themselves over time? Yet this question is interesting and useful to explore in its own right, and by doing so we can grasp certain aspects of the market behavior of firms that would otherwise be intractable. Industrial markets – falling, as they do, between bureaucracies, on the one hand, and the macro-processes of political economy, on the other – provide examples of a crucial intermediate level of social structure that most sociologists have virtually neglected. By examining these markets, we may be able to enlarge our understanding of how social structure and processes operate in more general cases.

Models of markets

Most theories or models of competitive markets assume that the producing firms within a market are, for all intents and purposes, isolated from one another; that is, under normal circumstances they act independently, and, because of the sheer number of actors involved, they are unable to interpret the *particular* activities of their competitors in any meaningful way. In effect, they are only indirectly associated with one another through their perception of and acts within the same abstract arena.

I propose that we interpret a market as a *tangible clique of producing firms, observing one another in the context of an aggregate set of buyers*. From this perspective:

   a. Market actors, and many potential entrants into markets, are known to one another.
   b. They take the perceived actions of others into account in formulating market strategies and in acting.
   c. Market actors are keenly interested in one another and in how each producing firm relates to the buyers' side.
   d. They normally share a great deal of information about the style of behavior each firm adopts vis-à-vis the others, that is, the social context in which they operate.

There are strikingly different kinds of markets. This observation naturally leads us to ask if there are historical peculiarities in one setting – if something "cultural" about particular products leads to divergent forms – or if these differences are due to small variations in the ways in which actors' attributes intermesh to sustain a market. Instead of making observed variations in markets important to their theories of market organization, economists put forward theories that may work for any conceivable array of costs and tastes. Furthermore, they often treat markets as settings for deep gaming, and, hence, heavy psychologizing. Economists, as a rule, have tended to see "rational" and "personal" behavior as something quite different – and have avoided examining concrete social structure and behavior by expressing a fondness for cultural glosses or psychologism in depth.

By contrast, I hope to provide one example of the parsimony of focusing on tangible social structure as both the trace and enactment of mutual perceptions feeding into practical choices by distinct actors. My approach accommodates both the calculating and affective sides of social life – in fact, it sees them as complementary. Viewed in this way, social roles emerge as the natural progeny of "hardheaded" rationalistic behavior in a particular *social* context. In turn, actions and mutual perceptions of participants create and sustain this context. In other words, what is proposed here is an approach to the construction of formal theory that is necessary if we are fully to understand how markets and other intermediate levels of structure can be sustained as social productions. Historically, neither sociology nor economics has addressed this problem in precisely this way.

In the next few pages I briefly explain how my approach appears to improve on existing ones. Then I show how market schedules articulate producers' perceptions and choices. In order to do so, I lay out the measurement framework. Next, I define cases and work out exemplary markets in a typology, "the tradeoffs plane." I also demonstrate explicit aggregation by feedback processes, bringing buyers into clearer focus. Finally, I generate results on stability and change in market types over time.

Conventional approaches

Both sociology and economics incorporate existing specialties that bear on the issues dealt with here. Within sociology, network (or structural) analysis is probably the most directly relevant because more conventional approaches to role theory have been either too "macro" or too "micro" (social psychological) to be useful in examining tangible social structure. Within economics, the relevant specialties already come wrapped in a package called "microeconomics," or price theory.

Relationship to network modeling

Although much current network research explores problems of imperfect connectivity or irregularity in network topologies, this analysis presupposes complete connectivity and, hence, pure cliques. Like earlier work on ecological metaphors (Hannan and Freeman, 1977), it develops ideas of differentiated niches and hierarchy. Thus, although this chapter falls squarely within the network tradition that emphasizes the regularized construction of mutual perceptions among conscious actors (Granovetter, 1978), it goes beyond the main thrust of this tradition in certain important ways. In particular, it extends previous observations about the role structures that emerge crescively in everyday life (White, 1965) to include the special case in which actors' attributes induce differences among them.

The concepts and methods of blockmodeling also deal with induced, everyday role structure (White, Boorman, and Breiger, 1976; Pattison, 1980; Breiger, 1981). Blockmodeling ultimately rests on the concept of structural equivalence: It partitions actors into blocks on the basis of similarity in the overall patterning of their ties to *others*. Thus, like the market theory developed here, blockmodeling focuses on the "knittedness" of patterns of interconnection within networks and on how this knittedness reflects the overlying choices and tasks of distinct actors.

There are three specific similarities between the market model developed here and blockmodeling:

First, both reject prior, imposed specification of cultural structure (White et al., 1976; 733) and, instead, presuppose processes of simultaneous, self-consistent search and choice.

Second, both assume that actors share the same perceptions and, hence, proceed from the same, socially induced, motivational logic. Therefore, both models assume homogeneity across a given population at a specified level of abstraction. Although they accept that actors may have different tastes and locations, they assume that all are rationally motivated and sensitive to reinforcement of ties by supporting acquaintanceships.

Third, both use comparative statics as a core method: They only informally treat detailed paths of change in structure over time. I suggest, but do not formally specify, that there are self-acting disciplinary mechanisms that erase violations of equilibrium.

The two models also differ in several basic ways:

First, in the market model, *actors* are "marked," in linguistic terms. That is, there are two sides to the market, and actors are assigned ex ante to one or the other. There is no such a priori marking in blockmodeling as it has developed so far. In blockmodeling, it is *ties* that are marked or permanently segregated by type.

Second, differing roles are induced in the market model by virtue of differences in actors' attributes vis-à-vis others. By contrast, blockmodels of positions and roles in networks are induced from the simple pattern of ties between nodes, without regard to node attributes. (Later in the chapter, I show, through asymptotic special cases, how market structure is shaken by a collapse in differentiation.) Blockmodels presuppose particular processes of systemic resonance (through indirect ties) that initially tend to amplify slight differences among patterns (Boorman and White, 1976).

Third, in the market model, any specific population of market actors is said to emerge out of some general population through a process of mutual recognition and accommodation. Markets can fall apart or be impossible to form. By contrast, blockmodeling takes preexisting populations as given and has no way of predicting, a priori, which specific blockmodels will never be observed or which sets of actors cannot sustain interaction.

Fourth, in the market model, role behavior is entirely oriented toward satisfying *material* goals. By contrast, blockmodeling assumes that actors are principally motivated by social rewards and reinforcements. This is why the market model emphasizes how distinctive "tastes" (analogous to ties) can be converted into comparable footings.

Fifth, in the market model, metric variables identify attributes and actors' choices. In blockmodeling, choices and locations are discrete, though possibly multivalent.

Sixth, typical actors in the market model are either large organizations or other aggregated composite actors. To date, blockmodeling has been used primarily to induce aggregates (blocks) from networks of ties among individual persons.

In sum, both methods infer role structures from a homogeneous social logic applied by individuals at different locations to an observable set of transactions. Both emphasize reinforcement and resonance in a final pattern, either with respect to ties or to volumes of flows. Blockmodeling emphasizes permanent differences in types of ties, whereas the market model assumes a fundamentally asymmetric relationship between "decider" and "accepter," at the level of the actor and in the aggregate.

Relationship to business and microeconomics

Business consultants have a keen interest in facts about actual markets – which they well know are highly competitive, even when a "Big Four" have a predominant share of the total. But it is not practical for them to expend much effort on rigorous – and hence idealized – theories of markets. Business advisors know full well that *markets are tangible social structures encompassing sets of producers that have evolved specific role behaviors toward one another and toward an accustomed set of buyers.* They also know that firms orient themselves primarily toward tangible market schedules and act accordingly – rather than haring off after theorists' speculations. Although businessmen also usually know these facts, they have little motivation to put them together into a general theory.

Very few social scientists have conceptualized competitive markets as tangible joint constructions of reality, and these few have only dealt with markets that are monopolistic or strongly oligopolistic. Under these circumstances they often abandon general economic theory in favor of game theory or other "strategic" models of decision making.

Arthur Stinchcombe is one of the very few sociologists who recognize the problem: "A new product inherently has a highly unpredictable market, because neither the past experience and present feelings of buyers as determined by market research, nor the past experience of the seller of the product, are reliable guides to the size of the market" (Stinchcombe, 1965: 272–3; see also Barber, 1977). Yet even Stinchcombe, although he is consciously theoretical, repeats the neoclassical economists' ideology of markets. This is also true of Peter Blau, who goes so far as to ignore the social construction of reality inherent in the notion of an exchange in favor of a naive reification of economists' notions of demand (Blau, 1964; 154). Even his hesitations are confined to extensions to social situations (Blau, 1964: 96).

Thomas Schelling, an economist, comes much closer to reality when he argues that "People are responding to an environment that consists in other people responding to *their* environment, which consists of people responding to an environment of people's responses" (Schelling, 1978: 14). But with some notable exceptions (Bator, 1961; Muth, 1961), economic theorists have been timid in developing these basic insights from sociology in their own context. The really odd aspect of microeconomic theory is its refusal to examine markets as concrete structures composed of a large number of independent actors. Instead, economic theorists have been obsessed with flows; both individual and aggregate. Consequently, they have shied way from explicit treatments of structure of the kind provided in social network models.

It follows from these observations that much standard microeconomic theory is not very useful (Stigler, 1946; Wilson and Andrews, 1951). The master theorists who pioneered in the modeling of individual markets – notably, Jevons, Marshall, and Chamberlin – conveyed an ebullient desire to achieve striking empirical confirmations of their theories. They used the comparative-statics method common to all branches of science, but with such ingenuity that they managed to cast light on process as well. Unfortunately, their early insights have not been systematically developed within economics proper, and new work in their spirit has only recently begun (Winter, 1971; Spence, 1974; Grossman, 1975; Rothschild and Stiglitz, 1975).

Since the publication of Samuelson's disastrous *Foundations of Economic Analysis* (1947), mainstream economics has lost its nerve. Underneath the spell of Jacobians and other glittering techniques – borrowed as if by a cargo-cult from advanced sciences – many theorists reveal a complete lack of faith and a disinterest in new or old aspects of observable markets. The actual gap in serious applications of theory in microeconomics is obscured – as elsewhere in the social sciences – by the fact that analysts rely almost exclusively on statistical techniques and strategies of data analysis: When suitable labels are applied to common statistical terms, many social scientists deceive themselves into believing that some theory is being applied (Leamer, 1978).

Economic theorists have been largely caught up in psychological speculation. This is as much an effect as a cause of their abandoning the attempt to construct a phenomenology of markets as tangible, if idealized, structures. The truth is that market activity is intensely social – as social as kinship networks or feudal armies – with only modest room for speculation.

The hold of psychologism on economics has become so powerful that even the great reform – Simon's behaviorism – often deteriorates into simply another way of overemphasizing cognitive process. My approach makes minimal changes in older Marshallian assumptions about behavior in markets. It aims, however, to put these assumptions together into a social framework: a feedback mechanism for role maintenance.

New approach: market schedules

Thus far, contemporary industrial markets have been used to illustrate the new theory outlined here. Hence, in the treatment that follows the actors will be "firms." However, since I suppress internal detail entirely and treat firms as role-taking, integral actors, precisely the same formalizations can be applied to markets consisting of individuals (e.g., producer craftsmen).

In some sense it may seem to be an oversimplification to treat firms as if they were individual people. Apart from the fact that this kind of assumption is conventional when dealing with markets or marketlike phenomena at this level of abstraction, there are important substantive reasons for doing it here.

Businessmen know all about markets as role structures. They become upset when a given firm does not hew to the style of behavior – the role – imputed to it. Their first question about a new *firm* has to do with what they call its "politics": its accustomed structure of deference and differentiated behavior. Similarly, their first question about a new *industry* does not have to do with engineering or accounting, but with the major roles played by big firms and their style of dealing with smaller ones. Businessmen typically assimilate information such as this so quickly that they must be applying principles that they can transpose to other settings. That is, they must be assimilating and using information about "roles," generally.[1]

Creating a market schedule

The key to understanding how this can come about is the notion of a *market schedule*. The side of a market that makes active decisions consists of *producers*. Since each producer has a different cost structure, each must choose a volume of production that is optimal for it, given its requirements. Consequently, each producer finds itself in a quandary as to what options – what terms of trade – are available to it. The other side of the market – which consists of buyers – is able to differentiate among producers on the basis of the *volume* each ships relative to the others. Hence, each producer is seen as "distinct," and each firm's shipments are seen as occupying a particular place in an array – a *schedule* – of prices and volumes of product being offered.[2]

Both producers and buyers, then, expect variations in the terms of trade to occur as a function of producers' volumes and they expect to orient themselves accordingly. Only in the asymptotic limiting case, pure competition – where all firms' goods seem indistinguishable – can one lump all flows together into a generalized "supply." Moreover, only under these conditions is there any common clearing price and a basis to talk about supply and demand in the most general terms. Even then, each producer selects an optimal volume of production from a *schedule* of payments that has the *same* constant slope of revenue by volume.[3]

Taken together, these observations suggest a simple new way to construe the process of price formation, which remains a sore point in the economics literature. My idea is that under normal circumstances producers extend this process of reading schedules of possible payoffs by interpolating among revenue-volume outcomes achieved by all competitors in the market. Producers continue to watch producers, as they do in pure competition, but they are not so foolish as to suppose that the interpolated terms of trade are a constant slope. This implies that producers are searching to find and maintain a niche in a continuing social structure consisting of other producers and those buyers attracted by some of their wares.

The observed points on the perceived terms of trade are there only because buyers have bought particular packages of products. So the shape of the terms-of-trade curve depends on relative valuations by buyers, on their saying "yes" to given volume-revenue matches. At the same time, the shape must also reflect cost pressures seen by producers, so that the terms of trade take shape as an interface reflecting competing pressures from two sides, together with dispersions within each separate side.

If the observed schedule of results for producers does not induce each to choose again so as to continue sustaining the schedule, it will change and may disappear – *no market may be constructible* for a given set of producers and buyers. But the schedule may reproduce itself, and keep on doing so, in a shape characteristic of the dispersions on the two sides that are rubbing up against each other in maintaining it. What this generates is a role structure in which each niche occupant positions itself optimally in terms of its own needs played off against a publicly observable schedule of payoffs from buyers to producers.[4]

Sustaining a market schedule

The formalization presented here traces equilibrium conditions for cases where such note-taking and role-assimilating behavior cumulates in a market schedule, $W(y)$. As we observed earlier, active decision makers view a market schedule as a continuous array of possible choices. The schedule connects the resulting set of actual choices made, which, in turn, defines niches, roles for firms. Given the long lead time needed to buy materials, lay out labor commitments, keep machinery in shape, and so on, the firms that make up a production market must continually decide, well in advance, how much product to offer. Thus, they face a double problem in making these production decisions: Each producer is *different* from the others, yet the market is viable and sustainable only if, in some sense, all are on the *same* footing.

Buyers' actions in markets effectively solve this intricate double problem all the time. Buyers are the agents who are most insistent that firms be on an equivalent footing, that is, that a deal offered by one firm be just as good as any of those offered by others. *Somehow tradeoffs are made between divergences among firms on cost and on taste for their outputs.* This tradeoff must rest on and sustain the possibility of choosing a range of different volumes, and thus distinctive niches or roles. In short, the tradeoff is effected through the market schedule.

Producers see the market schedule as a continuous frame for choice, whereas buyers see it as a menu of dishes and prices; that is, as *ex ante* as opposed to *ex post*. This multiplicity of complementary perspectives is essential to the realization of an interface in any social structure. Market schedules are both a mirror in which producers observe each other and a manhole through which buyers may reach. Thus a market is, by analogy, a kind of one-way mirror.

Two ideal types

The Market Schedule yields the tradeoff. Hence, it ultimately depends on schedules of cost of production by volume *and* of buyers' valuation by volume for each firm. The tradeoff problem can be solved precisely *because* one factor can be played off against the other. But it follows that not just any set of firms or products can sustain a market.[5]

This can best be explained by beginning with two extreme cases (1 and 2 in Table 9.1) where one side of the double problem evaporates. Under "perfect competition" buyers are absolutely indifferent between firms' products. If, moreover, buyers are indifferent as to how much of the available product comes from different sources – that is, they have no taste for either sheer diversity or ensuring a broad spread of supplier firms – then the familiar notion of a price as the market schedule emerges. (Or, in the terminology used here, price as the slope of the market schedule, which is now a fixed multiple of volumes.) The familiar feedback process, "supply and demand," comes into play to establish a price in terms of the actual firms and volumes offered and the given buyers.

It is important to note in this first extreme case that the shape of a schedule depends on the shape of buyers' tastes, and not on producers' cost structures. All the producers perceive and decide volumes in terms of *the same* market schedule: a fixed price times amount sold. Then each firm chooses a different volume – the size of which depends on the contextual effect of which (and how many) other producers are in the market – since each firm has a different cost structure by volume.

The second extreme case is generally treated as a form of imperfect competition. The term itself indicates that this is not thought of as a special extreme case on the same level as perfect competition, but as a vague residual category. Here it is defined in terms of a market in which buyers evaluate one

Table 9.1. *Aggregate sales, at break-even for buyers,* W_0, *in seven limiting types of markets and for various levels k of shift in the market schedule W(y)*

1. *Perfect competition:* $b \to 0$; $a < c$

$$W_0 \to \left(\frac{r}{q^{a/c}} \left(\frac{a}{c} \right)^{a/c} \#^{1-(a/c)} \right)^{\gamma/(1-(a/c)\gamma)}$$

2. *Pure taste:* $d \to 0$. When $k = 0$:

$$W_0 \to \left(\frac{r}{q^{a/c}} \#^{1-(a/c)} \right)^{\gamma/(1-(a/c)\gamma)}$$

3. *No tradeoff leverage:* $a/c \to b/d$

$$W_0 \to 0 \quad \text{and} \quad k \to 0$$

4. *Identical variability with quality of cost and valuation:* $b \to \delta$

$$k \to 1 \quad \text{and} \quad W_0 \to \left[\frac{1-k}{1-\delta/b} \frac{1-a/c}{q} \frac{r^{c/a}}{\#^{c/a-1}} \right]^{1/(c/a\gamma-1)}$$

5. *Borderline of runaway markets:* $c \to a\gamma, c < a$, *and* $b \to \delta$

$$W_0 \to \exp\left\{ \frac{k-1}{b/\delta-1} \right\} \Big/ \exp\left\{ \frac{q\gamma}{1-\gamma} \#^{1-\gamma}/r^{1/\gamma} \right\}$$

6. *Combination of 3 and 4 simultaneously:*

$$W_0 \to \left[\frac{r}{q}(1-k) \right]^{\gamma/(1-\gamma)}$$

7. $a \to c$, *with* $d < 0$:
   Same, but $k \to 0$.

firm's products differently from the same volume of output generated by any other, but where each firm experiences the same cost structure by volume. This case immediately suggests a flavor of hokum – TV ads and the like – since common sense says that higher-quality goods are harder and more expensive to make. Chamberlin (1954), who pioneered the study of imperfect competition a half-century ago, focused on such "flavors" in an economy. Chamberlin, however, overshot the mark: in his famous "symmetric case," not only costs but also tastes for products are the same across firms. The one distinction left is a taste for diversity in and of itself!

Let us refer to this second case as "pure taste." Here, all firms have the same schedule of production cost by volume, but each yields a distinct schedule of contribution-to-buyers'-evaluations by volume. If, in addition, the common cost schedule is linear by volume, the situation is the formal converse of perfect competition (with no pure taste for diversity).

The remaining asymmetry between dual cases is now forced into view: Producing firms make the main (volume) decisions open to actors in a market. Buyers have the important, but passive, role of saying yes or no to packages producers offer them. A firm cannot change or control the overall market context, the schedule of possibilities that are presented to it as an objective and overwhelming social fact, but it can choose from that menu so as to maximize its net benefit. As a rule, buyers are numerous, diverse, and uncoordinated. But collectively they have great force: Woe to the producers who overcharge relative to the perceived quality and commonness of their products in the market, for they may not be able to sell any of it. However, buyers *react*: They do not act. They do not make the advance decisions on production volumes that shape the market. Buyers also are not in a position to maximize their net self-interest, given the market context, since they can only react to the menu it provides.

This asymmetry between these two groups of actors also explains why Chamberlin may have pushed the pure taste extreme onto the symmetric case (taste for pure diversity among products otherwise equally valued). Valuation schedules are shadowy compared with a factory's cost schedules, and they cannot be attributed to independent active choosers maximizing individual benefits. So it is attractive not to have to model differences in valuation of firms' products.

The trouble is that, when pushed this far, the extreme case collapses into an undifferentiated single outcome. With costs *and* attractiveness the same, each firm should do exactly the same thing. But under these circumstances today's outcomes cannot guide tomorrow's choices. Thus, this lock-step decision can only be assessed theologically.

Strategy of analysis

An important point emerges here: *Somehow it must be divergences, dispersions, deviations of one firm's outcomes from another's that provide the cognitive grist needed for the firms' decision mills.* But if decisions are all to be validated in the market, they all, in some sense, must be equivalent. Divergences must not *only* supply clues for actors, but the resulting decisions must also diverge so as to exploit the underlying differences in actual collective market behavior. *In short, the market not only has an aggregate-level feedback loop (supply and demand), but a micro-level feedback process at the level of individual firms that must guide and confirm one another in a market schedule with a definite shape.*

For linear cost schedules, the pure taste extreme can also lead to constant price being the market schedule – just as in perfect competition with no pure taste for diversity. Again, the schedule is not confirmed unless each firm chooses a different volume appropriate to its circumstances. But under perfect competition known cost structure guides firms toward their appropriate levels, whereas under pure taste firms must rely entirely on peering into the complexities of putative consumer taste. *I argue (dual to the case of perfect competition) that, just because there is no spread on cost structures, it is they, and not the shape of demands with volume, that determine the shape of the market schedule.* In fact, the market schedule is cost-based in pure taste. It is a cost-markup schedule.

The perfect competition schedule – unique price in absence of taste for diversity – is the dual extreme that is purely demand-based, that is, derived from the shape of dependence of valuation on volume supplied.[6]

Hence, it seems sensible to reduce greatly the attention given to the platitudinous aggregate level in feedback – supply and demand – in favor of a focus on the real feedback issue: *How are aggregate concepts like "supply" and "demand" embodied in a real market where each firm and each product is distinctive?* In the aggregate outcome formulae derived below, their dependence on tactical maneuvering by firms for a schedule should become clear.

Any concrete theory of markets should be centered on the tradeoff that must be made among firms' divergences in order to keep all of them viable within the same market. Here I propose a theory that focuses on precisely this and illustrate it with the simplest framework that contains basic divergences among firms (see Table 9.1). Particular attention is paid to seven limiting cases in which one or more of these divergences simply disappear.

Self-selection indexed by quality

Here each firm perceives an array of recent performances in its market: the revenue-volume pairs for all producing firms as its own array of possible choices. Thus, this represents a generalization of the situation in perfect competition where all the revenue-volume pairs lie on a straight line drawn through the origin – the unique market clearing price as the slope. As in that case, the producer sticks with observables that can be related to its own situation. Each eyes all others. The buyers' side of the market will turn away from a given firm's offering if it is overpriced relative to its perceived quality and availability (a producer could only see this rejection emerge after the fact from disaggregated decisions). It is even hard to determine firms' *relative* standing in terms of quality, since standing is strongly affected by the volume of production offered.

Rather than dream about buyers, firms watch their competitors. To understand whether and how this mutual watching on the surface of the market works out, we must specify the underlying facts of taste and cost, although they are mostly unknown to the market participants themselves. We need schedules that describe these facts according to volume for distinctive products.

The simplest schedules that can yield the dispersions and tradeoff on which a market is based are just power functions: Take the contribution of a volume, y, of a given firm's product to the valuation by the buyer side as y raised to the power a. Take the cost imposed on a firm by production as volume y as y raised to the power c. Buyers' evaluations of a given firm's output must depend not only on its volume but also on what other firms are producing and at what volumes. Again, simplify by assuming there is only an overall interaction among firms, in the form of a saturation effect (parameterized by gamma in this discussion), rather than specific interactions between individual pairs of products.

The model presented here hews to neoclassical economic orthodoxy in asserting that firms are maximizers, so that the relevant cost is the so-called variable cost.[7] Each firm chooses its volume to maximize the excess of payment received over this cost modeled by y^c: In usual business parlance, it is maximizing its cash flow. In principle, fixed costs – whether for equipment or TV campaigns – should come from this cash flow plus net profits for the stockholders, governments, and so on. The model also requires cash flow to be nonnegative.[8]

So far, so good. But how can it be that firms making recognizably different products can all confirm the same observed market schedule? Not just any set of firms and products can do so.

Divergence among firms as producers must be represented by shifts in the cost-versus-volume schedule of one firm relative to another. Divergence among firms' products, as evaluated by the buyer side, will also be represented by shifts in valuation-versus-volume schedules of one firm versus another. A market can be sustained only if there is a *mutual ordering, as between these two sets of schedules, in order to permit a tradeoff* that will simultaneously confirm the wisdom of each firm's volume choice. To proceed, each set of schedules is parameterized in terms of a quality index that can provide the basis for parameterizing the other set. For simplicity's sake, the model uses the same forms of the power function adopted to describe variation with volume, y.

The proportionality constant in a given cost schedule is parameterized in terms of an index – call it n – identifying a particular firm. This reflects the "quality" of that firm's product and orders all firms along a dimension. Any proportionate constant can be represented as n raised to a power – which I define as d – and the other firms are then spaced so that their own cost factors are given by their index values to that same power. The crucial assumption here is not the particular values of the proportionality constants, but the fact that the cost curves of the various firms are nested inside one another with no

cross-overs. This is a severe simplification, but it permits simple parameterization of cost so that tradeoff versus dispersion in evaluations of products can
be examined. In short, the variable cost

$$C(y; n) = qy^c/n^d, \tag{9.1}$$

where q is a positive constant defining the overall cost level, and the volume
exponent, c, is necessarily positive.

Calibration of evaluation contributions from different firms' products
must be made in terms of the same index, n. Indeed, the index is defined and
its scalar ordering assumed on the basis of *buyers'* reactions to differentiated
products. If it leads to a one-dimensional ordering of cost schedules, in
order to permit a market, n must also yield a one-dimensional ordering of
valuation contributions. Designate these contributions by $S(y; n)$. Assume
a parameterization of dispersion parallel to (9.1):

$$S(y; n) = ry^a n^b, \tag{9.2}$$

where r is a positive constant identifying an overall monetary level, a is
positive since additional volume enhances evaluation at least somewhat, and
b can be taken as positive as a matter of definition, given increasing quality.
However, these valuation contributions are not fully parallel to costs. All
buyers have been aggregated, and this aggregate is merely assumed to accept
or reject the volume–value pair offered by each firm. The contributions are
defined only as parts of the aggregate valuation function for the full menu of
purchases, $y(n)$, from firms designated by values of n:

$$V(\#) = (\Sigma S(y(n); n))^\gamma, \tag{9.3}$$

where $\#$ is the count of the firms purchased from, designated by a set of index
values, n, included in the summation.[9]

Sustainable market schedules

The pieces of the market puzzle are now ready to be fitted into place.
Designate as $W(y)$ money payment by the buyers' side for volume y of a firm's
product. Plot the pair $W(y(n))$ versus $y(n)$ for each firm in the market. A
market will only be sustained if interpolation through these points yields a
mapping of dollar value onto physical volume. Each firm views this function,
$W(y)$, as its best estimate from tangible data of the schedule of of possibilities
open to it. Each firm will then choose that value of y which will maximize its
cash flow – that is, the difference between W and C. To be accepted, its
contribution to the valuation of the buyers' side must be as high as that from
any other firm.[10] A market that will reproduce itself – an equilibrium
market – is one in which the offer function $W(y)$ perceived by all firms is such
that each firm, in choosing the $y(n)$ optimal for it, will be induced to offer a

volume-value pair as desirable to the buyers' side as that from every other firm.

This is a feedback loop, at the level of individual firms, which determines the allowable shape of an equilibrium market schedule $W(y)$. As we shall see later ("Range and Aggregation"), this loop is embedded in the more familiar macro-feedback that equates aggregate supply with aggregate "demand." Specifically, $W(y)$ must be such that a firm chooses that volume (its $y(n)$) which maximizes $W(y(n)) - C(y(n); n)$, and which, at the same time, yields

$$S(y(n); n) = \theta W(y(n)),\tag{9.4}$$

where θ is a positive constant (the size of which is determined by an aggregate feedback loop). It is then straightforward to show that a family of shapes, $W(y)$, satisfy this feedback loop for a given factual context (cost schedules and valuations specified by equations 9.1–9.3), namely,

$$W(y) = (Ay^{(bc + ad)/b} + k)^{b/(b+d)}.\tag{9.5}$$

Here A is specified in terms of θ and the parameters (see equation 9.6 below), but k is an arbitrary constant, positive or negative, which measures how far the schedule is from going through the origin.

For the moment (until the "Range and Aggregation" section), put aside k; take it as zero. Then, the form of $W(y)$ makes much intuitive sense: Like cost schedules and valuation contributions, it is a power of y, and has an exponent, $(bc + ad)/(b + d)$, which is a weighted mean of the cost exponent c and of the valuation exponent a. These weights derive, as we expect, from the respective dispersions over the quality index, n, of cost schedules, on the one hand, and of valuation schedules, on the other. That is, one weight is the ratio of b to the sum $b + d$, and the other is $d/b + d$. By parameterizing variation with quality, n, in terms of a power of n, variation with quality is put on the same footing as variation with volume in the notation, with resulting help to intuition.

But note that the proportionate slope of cost schedules with volume (the exponent c) is weighted by the proportionate slope, b, which makes valuation changes with quality. Similarly, the contribution of proportionate slope, a, of valuation with volume y to the basic market payment schedule, $W(y)$, is weighted by the ratio of d to $b + d$, that is, by the proportionate rate of change of cost schedules across quality. This explains my earlier use of the tradeoff metaphor. This also suggests how the market schedule works out in the two basic limiting cases that we have emphasized – all products the same to buyers $(b = 0)$, and all costs schedules the same $(d = 0)$.

In perfect competition, $b = 0$, and the exponent a becomes the slope of $W(y)$. If different firms' products look the same and in addition buyers have no liking for diversity in sources of supply, then $a = 1$ and the familiar fixed price (linear $W(y)$) market emerges. Now we see the inverse as characterizing pure taste markets: With $d = 0$, the exponent c of the cost schedule becomes the volume dependence in $W(y)$. Furthermore, if costs are linear in volume, $c = 1$, fixed price schedule again results (with $k = 0$ still imposed). Pure taste markets, or ones close to them, should tend to have equilibrating market schedules that are cost based – and perhaps resemble the familiar business idea of using markups on cost to determine market price. Perfect competition markets should have market schedules whose shape depends mostly on how taste for a firm's product changes with volume – surely the salesman's predilection, and one that has grown more common since early in the century.

The tradeoff comes in when firms really do diverge from one another, both in their cost schedules and in consumers' tastes for their products. Does a or c contribute more to the shape of the market schedule $W(y)$? Well, a has more leverage when the variation of cost schedules d is greater than those of the valuation schedules b across quality. But the larger a itself is relative to c, the more dominant it will be. One can efficiently think in terms of tradeoff between the two relative sizes, the ratios a/c for volume and b/d for quality in variation of valuation over variation of cost.

Cases and examples arrayed by tradeoffs

Other special cases can now be dealt with. When $a = c$, that is, when cost increases by volume by an amount equal to valuation, strange results may appear. But such special cases are not as basic as perfect competition and pure taste because they are brought about by the deliberate simplification of the families of functions that we use to lay out costs and tastes for the various firms in the market. Not only do we assume that cost schedules for different firms (and different quality levels) are nested inside one another, but we also assume that one schedule is a fixed multiple of another. In short, we suppress interaction effects between change in quality (identity of firm) and change in volume of production. With such simple functional forms, there are, naturally, many special cases – each of which will prove intuitively instructive, but which one need not expect to encounter very often in reality. Instead, we are far more interested in whole classes or regions in tradeoff ratios.

The tradeoff plane

I define a plane, where any market is located at a point, by two tradeoff ratios. One special feature of this construction is important – an apparent paradox emphasized by my specialized choice of functional forms. I assume an ordering of firms by quality. This is one simple specification of how firms dispersed in terms of both cost and taste structures can, nonetheless, gain

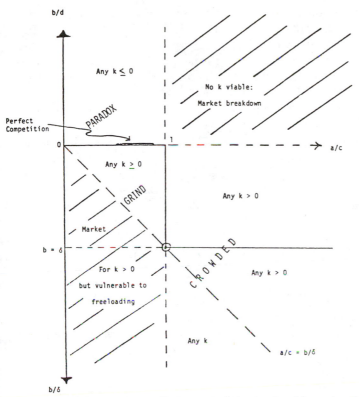

Figure 9.1. Tradeoff plane: A market is placed by ratio of volume variabilities (*a/c*) and by ratio of quality variabilities (*b/d*); each ratio is from an evaluation schedule over a cost schedule.

footings in the same market as defined by their adherence to the same market schedule. But the way these firms are ordered on cost may be precisely opposite to the way they are ordered on valuation: Products more attractive to buyers may come from firms that actually spend less to make the same volume! Indeed, this is the baseline convention adopted by equation (9.1). It is the paradoxical case, the kind of wry situation that Chamberlin tried so hard to bring to the attention of mainline economists.[11] The upper half of the tradeoff plane will represent such paradoxical cases.

The central issue is the existence and shape of a viable equilibrium schedule $W(y)$ for a market. This depends essentially on the four exponents a, b, c, d, as demonstrated by (9.5). Further, because of the tradeoff, the mutual ratios are important. I choose a/c, the ratio of dispersions over volume for evaluation and cost, and b/d, the parallel ratio over quality index n.

Figure 9.1 is the "tradeoff" plane since it is defined by the ratio of volume nonlinearities (a/c) and the ratio of quality dispersions (b/d) on the two sides of a market. The horizontal x-axis is a/c, and the ordinate is the b/d. The upper half corresponds to the Chamberlin-type situation in which better-liked products cost less to make. There is no "left" half to the plane, since there is no meaningful interpretation for a product that costs less or is valued less the larger the volume being produced by the firm.[12]

It is the bottom half of Figure 9.1 that contains the greatest variety of market situations and apparently the greatest number that can be matched to currently observable markets (White, 1981b). For convenience, the magnitude of d, a negative quantity there, is separately designated as delta. Here, the meaning of "tradeoff" and "averaging" exponents changes: The exponent of y in equation (9.5) can be rewritten as $(bc - a\delta)/(b - \delta)$. In this new convention, the expression for A is given as

$$A = [(b - \delta)c \cdot q/(bc - a\delta)](\theta/r)^{\delta/b}. \tag{9.6}$$

This formula suggests an important special case when the two ratios are equal:

$$a/c = b/\delta.$$

Where there is no basis for tradeoff, the market is caught on a frictionless slope. Another special case is that in which the ratio of valuation to cost dispersions over quality is unity:

$$b = \delta.$$

Figure 9.1 shows these various special lines on the plane, and Table 9.1 collects outcomes for special cases.

I pause here to show some interesting applications before returning to additional aspects of complete modeling for markets. First, I show, by explicit calculation, how one important aspect of markets – profit – depends on tradeoffs. Then I describe qualitatively how a whole family of special markets can be located in a tradeoffs plane.

Profit level

Unlike microeconomic theory, the current model has profit flowing to firms in equilibrium. Firms find stable positions in a mutual structure of niches, and they establish levels of volume and revenue through a process of interactive search in the common market environment. If a new firm can find a niche for itself, this does not "squeeze" the market schedule to some determinate lower level of richness. Aggregate volumes follow from the terms of trade that establish themselves as market volume, and not the reverse. *Differential profits are a normal by-product of the very mechanism through which a market schedule establishes itself.*

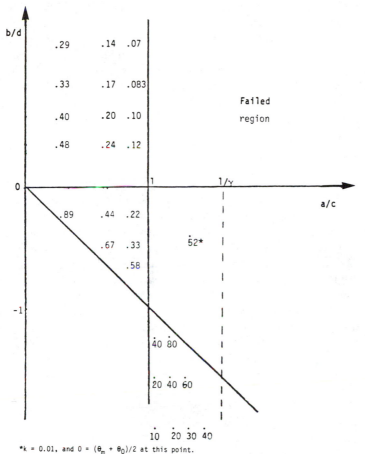

b/d

.29	.14	.07
.33	.17	.083
.40	.20	.10
.48	.24	.12

Failed
region

0 ————— 1 ————— 1/γ —————————→

a/c

.89	.44	.22
	.67	.33
		.58

52*

-1

40 80

20 40 60

10 20 30 40

*k = 0.01, and 0 = (θ_m + θ_0)/2 at this point.

Figure 9.2. Profit as percentage of revenue, in aggregate, with shift $k = 0$.

How does level of profitability in a market shift between one major region and another in Figure 9.1, and how does it shift with smaller or more manipulable changes of parameters? Figure 9.2 supplies illustrative results for profit (that is, cash flow $W - C$) as a percentage of total revenue or sales. Within the PARADOX region, the aggregate rate of profit increases with a decrease in the ratio of product differentiation (b) to cost differential ($|d|$). The same is true in the CROWDED region. In striking contrast, overall profitability in the GRIND region increases as product differentiation increases (as $b \to |d|$).

In the other dimension, profitability is enhanced the further a is from c. If $a < c$, then average profitability is higher if buyers value most small amounts of each good. If $a > c$, profitability is implied by buyers favoring concentration of purchases from one firm.

Only in the special cases of market schedules with a shift $k =$ zero do all firms in a market have the same profitability so that the level can be given unambiguously by one parameter. When k is unrestricted,[13] profit level varies sharply with size or quality of firm. Even so, variation is reduced by my approximations, by simple power functions, of the facts for costs and tastes (equations 9.1 and 9.2).

Professional theater markets

Up to now I have confined my argument to markets composed of industrial firms either producing for other firms or for customers. Yet I do not restrict the theory proposed here to production markets in a narrow sense. For example, one can visualize at least six or seven distinct professional theater markets in terms similar to those developed for industrial markets (see Figure 9.3). Such an analysis is empirically supported by a recent large-scale study (Anderson et al., 1978), as well as by earlier economic analyses (Poggi, 1968), institutional assessments (Engel, 1967; Goldman, 1969; Greenberger, 1971), and case studies (Zeigler, 1973; Prince, 1974). Still, my goal here is illustrative and didactic: to encourage facility in working with the regions of Figure 9.1 and to provide substantive content for the tradeoff ratios.

The "producers" in any one of these theater markets should be thought of as continuing nuclei, teams of producer-directors who produce a continuing series of plays in their own distinctive style for the market. The market for each is exactly the other nucleii whom they eye as they plan productions for their shadowy population of potential playgoers (see Faulkner, 1982, on film production). As Figure 9.3 shows, I assert that the playgoing population is *not* subject to contagion, that is, to explosive growth ($\gamma > 1$) in its overall valuation of the theater.[14] In the producers' terms there is some overlap between playgoers' reactions to one and another of these markets, but my model insists on independence among them.

First I locate each market on the figure from the tradeoff over volume nonlinearity (a/c) and the tradeoff over quality dispersion (b/d) between valuation and cost. Both costs and valuation by audiences of Broadway musicals go up with quality and at about the same rate. (American audiences are as accurate with musicals as Italian ones are with operas.) So b/d is about -1. A show designed for a longer run and a bigger theater (higher volume y) than another has a more than proportionate increase in relative valuation by the audience $a > 1$, and somewhat less than proportionate increase in cost ($c < 1$). So although musicals are in the CROWDED region, they are in the wealthy reaches of it. Broadway drama (which is a *separate* market) is similar except for one sad difference: Quality does not enhance audience appreci-

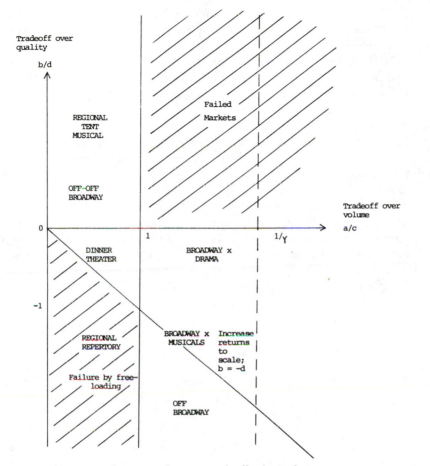

Figure 9.3. Theater markets on tradeoffs plane of Figure 9.2.

ation so much as it does cost. The Off-Broadway market, where drama is not so distinct from musicals (and sometimes neither are apparent!), has the reverse and happy difference (although the reason is the low level and lack of a contingency component to actors' pay).

In "dinner theater,"[15] perceived evaluation of the performance does not go up as fast as cost does with enhanced quality (n). Thus $b/\delta < 1$, and $a/c < 1$ because cost of production goes up faster with volume (chair-days) than valuation does. Off-off Broadway has a similar tradeoff over volume, but now the cost actually declines over quality (of play, not dinner) vis-à-vis higher evaluation by the (highbrow) playgoer population ($d > 0$, because of greater eagerness by actors and other personnel). Ironically, the highly commercialized "tent musicals," fairly common in the summer in the Midwest and South, are rather similarly placed – the key being the slickness of the bigger and more profitable chains compared with the independents in these markets.

These map locations yield sensible insights. Dinner theater is right in the GRIND region, along with dreary industries such as cement (White, 1981b). Off-off Broadway appears in Spence's "signaling" subregion of PARADOX markets (Spence, 1974). Broadway musicals, however successful, fall in the CROWDED region where the addition of further "firms" (e.g., new Harold Princes) actually cuts the *overall* rewards – not just a competitor's.

I make one additional qualitative prediction concerning serious local theater markets outside New York (each mainly centered on repertory companies). Such markets should fall in the lower-left region, as shown in Figure 9.3. Although tradeoffs over quality are not so different from the situation on Broadway, there is a penalty, rather than a reward, for running shows longer and larger ($a < 1$), and costs are actually exacerbated ($c > 1$). In the model developed here, a market cannot be sustained under such conditions. Further, it is the biggest firms (here the big local rep) that will "freeload" and thus drive smaller, but higher-quality, competitors out of existence.[16]

Ranges and aggregation

The theater examples bring vividly to mind the *particularity*, the distinctive identity, of each market. But they further suggest the spread of outcomes that can become established by chance in a particular arena of actors – a spread that is somewhat paradoxical in that a given market schedule outcome sharply defines optimal niches for various producers. (This range of possible outcome schedules suggests the considerable scope to possible manipulation and gaming in my perspective.) What must now also be made explicit is how the specific population of firms in a market affects the context seen by each member firm, whose response, in turn, helps determine the level of a market schedule observed and sustained by that population. In short, we will be able to analyze ranges and aggregation in a market.

In order to do this, we must examine the robustness as well as the existence of the putative market schedules given in equation 9.5. We must first discover what values of the schedule shift, k, are feasible, and what factors may determine them, given each firm's need to have a determinate optimum volume that yields a positive cash flow and at the same time offers the buyers' side as good a bargain as any other. We can then examine the aggregate feedback loop through which the number and types of firms in a market determine the actual numerical level of the schedule and of the volumes produced. From time to time these results will be developed further through solution formulas that apply in five asymptotic limiting cases (de Bruijn, 1961).

Let us begin by summarizing earlier findings as to how firms maneuver for niches within a market schedule. As we noted before, a market can only be formed by a set of firms whose cost structures and appeals to buyers are integrated in such a way that they sustain the volume decisions made by each firm. By implication, only a relatively small number of firms may exist in any one market – a dozen or a score rather than the hundreds or thousands vaguely implied by textbook rhetoric (Berkowitz, Chapter 10). A production market is a social structure that evolves so as to sustain, through the joint outcomes of myopic activities, the tangible regularities that bring order and a measure of predictability to firms. But up to this point we have left aside questions of the indeterminacy of "the" market schedule and the actual aggregate size of all market sales.

Shifts of market schedules

The constant k in the equilibrium form of the schedule in equation (9.5) reflects the fact that there is no authoritative planner and organizer of a production market. Since Walras, economic theorists have postulated a counterfactual auctioneer who receives and collates bids so as to clear the market without recourse to actual actors in actual networks. In reality, the market schedule is an affair of circumstance: It is the trace, in equilibrium form, of jockeying by firms and other actors at risk. The value k reflects in particular the actions of those producers who end up contributing smaller amounts to the market. If some of them cut prices for the same volume to enhance the "deal" they offer, shifts of purchases can force other producers to follow suit to a limited extent. The net result is the same as if some Walrasian auctioneer had issued a new formula for $W(y)$ with a lower value for k. The point, of course, is that no firm, big or small, has reason except error (or "speculation" or "gamesmanship" left outside this model) to shift terms away from the point it has found on an existing equilibrium schedule. Hence, one usually expects *any* of a range of possible schedules to succeed in establishing itself in any given factual context. When exogenous change occurs – whether in engineering, in the entry or exit of actors from the market, or in the price of supplies – then the actual market may well end up in a new schedule that reflects not only the shift mandated by that exogenous change, but a change in k as well.

In limiting cases, the scope for k can disappear. Under perfect competition ($b = 0$), firms have no room to maneuver their volume–value pairs, so that k is treated as zero.[17] Such cases lie along the x-axis of Figure 9.1.

The dual extreme, pure taste, is shown by the horizontal line at infinity.[18] Here, by contrast, k seems to get full scope: According to equation (9.5), it is simply added to the volume-dependent term – the common cost schedule – to make up $W(y)$. This appears to be the businessman's familiar cost-plus-markup pricing, although there is the oddity that k is a fixed markup and not a percentage.

Under pure taste, k is permitted no scope, but on quite different grounds. Asymptotic analysis indicates that low-quality firms (i.e., ones with low values of n, assuming they happen to be part of the set forming this market) are unable to find distinctive individual volume niches that satisfy the buyers' side demand for parity; even though they could achieve positive cash flow. The two inequalities just applied can be stated for the general case as

$$\frac{(a/c) - 1}{(b/\delta) - 1} A y^{c - a(\delta/b)} > \frac{a/c}{b/\delta}(-k) \tag{9.7}$$

and

$$\frac{(a/c) - 1}{(b/\delta) - 1} A y^{c - a(\delta/b)} > (-k). \tag{9.8}$$

These inequalities – which guarantee unique individual optimal niches and nonnegative cash flow at optimal niche – explain the forbidden regions in Figure 9.1. The upper-right quadrant, beyond $a = c$ and above $d = 0$, corresponds to factual circumstances that can never sustain a market. The lower-left region, where a is less than c and their ratio less than b over delta, depicts situations that can sustain markets only if there are no low-quality firms in the market that are unable to find distinctive niches. If there are, we *call the flaw freeloading.* The significant point in the latter case is that the scope for a freeloader goes up as k increases. Each region in Figure 9.1 indicates the range of schedules (in terms of k-values) that can be sustained, whatever the quality range among firms in the market.

Supply and demand

Aggregation presupposes another feedback loop: The average size of the payment schedule $(W(y))$ sustained depends on the number of characteristics of the firms, on the size r, and the saturability (γ) of the buyers' side. This loop, in turn, depends on the micro loop, since the issue is where on the schedule of a certain height a firm will locate. The second "wild card" constant now appears: the level of theta. The buyers' side can insist on equally good deals from every firm, and so a sharp numerical value is given for theta. But since they form parts of a dispersed aggregate, buyers have no mechanisms for choosing the unique ratio, θ, so the maximum net benefit is $(V - \Sigma W)$.

It is easier to understand how theta is determined if one holds the other shift constant, k, fixed. By inspection (Figure 9.1), the value $k = 0$ is the single most commonly allowed value across various sorts of markets. This zero value for k was assumed in deriving the explicit formulas for θ from aggregate feedback.

The feedback loop can be schematized as the perceived offer schedule, $W(y)$, which elicits its optimal production level $y(n)$ and thereby sales volume $W(y(n))$ from each firm. Optimal sales from the # of firms accumulate together into aggregate sales W. W is sustained only if the various firms' relative volumes have satisfied buyers' perceptions of their relative worth through the shape of $W(y)$ and the aggregate valuation V seen by the buyers' side is greater than what they are paying, (W), by a determinate fraction given by θ: the equal marginal ratio imposed on the valuation/cost of all firms' products. Formally:

$$W(y) \to y(n) \to W(y(n)) \to W \to \theta \to W(y) \cdots$$

Hence, the ratio, θ, on which $W(y)$ depends must itself be dependent on the sum over the # firms of their choices from $W(y)$. No Walrasian auctioneer is there to choose θ. Like k, θ is a value that emerges in equilibrium after a period of backing and filling. Consequently, it is a value affected by accidents in initial conditions.

We must calibrate this ratio, which has neither a natural zero nor unity. The obvious calibration level, denoted by the subscript zero, is *break-even* by the buyers' side:

$$V_{o} = W_{o}. \tag{9.9}$$

Substitute from equations (9.3) and (9.4) to derive the general relationship between these two aggregates:

$$V = \theta^{\gamma} W^{\gamma} \tag{9.10}$$

(which holds for any k value). Thus the break-even value of θ is

$$\theta_{o} = W_{o}^{(1-\gamma)/\gamma}. \tag{9.11}$$

From here on, θ will be measured in units of this break-even value. Define this ratio as t

$$\theta \equiv t\theta_{o}. \tag{9.12}$$

Break-even θ can then be computed by simply summing the chosen values $W(y(n))$ for a break-even schedule. When $k = 0$, the chosen volumes $y(n)$ take a simple form and the sum is

$$W_{o} = \left(\frac{r}{W_{o}^{(1-\gamma)/\gamma}} \right)^{c/(c-a)} \left(\frac{bc - a\delta}{(b - \delta)cq} \right)^{a/(c-a)} \sum_{\#} n^{(bc - a\delta)/(c - a)}$$

After the terms in W_{o} are collected, we have

$$W_{o} = \left[\frac{r}{q^{a/c}} \left(\frac{b/\delta - a/c}{b/\delta - 1} \right)^{a/c} \left(\sum_{\#} n^{(bc - a\delta)/(c - a)} \right)^{1 - (a/c)} \right]^{\gamma/(1 - a\gamma/c)} \tag{9.13}$$

from which θ_o is determined by using equation (9.11). Cycling back to equation (9.10) and repeating the derivation of equation (9.13) for general θ, we compute that, for $k = 0$,

$$V = W_o/t^{a\gamma/(c-a)} \tag{9.14}$$

and

$$W = W_o/t^{c/(c-a)}. \tag{9.15}$$

Straightforward calculation established that the market aggregates, V and W, must always be less or equal to their sizes at break-even. In particular, if the market ended up by chance at a level of θ that yielded the maximum net benefit (largest $(V - W)$) to the buyers' side, then

$$V_{\text{optim}} = W_o \left(\frac{a\gamma}{c} \right)^{1/((c/a\gamma)-1)} \tag{9.16}$$

and

$$W_{\text{optim}} = W_o \left(\frac{a\gamma}{c} \right)^{1/(1-(a\gamma/c))}. \tag{9.17}$$

Similar conclusions may be obtained for general k.[19]

A number of major findings are implicit in equation (9.13), for the aggregate sales volume for a market at break-even, even before specializing to various asymptotic cases (and generalizing to nonzero k). The exponent on the overall brackets, $(1/(1 - (a\gamma/c)))$, must be positive to yield sensible markets, for example, those in which volume grows with consumer demand. When, instead, a/c exceeds the reciprocal of γ, there is no stable equilibrium schedule, the reason being that, if any firm raises its price and others follow suit, the explosive buyers' demand just accepts the increase and draws out more net benefit. There is no finite aggregate size of market that is the unique optimum for the buyers' side. An additional bounding line can be entered onto the tradeoff plane shown in Figure 9.1: the vertical with $(a/c) = 1/\gamma$. To the right of this line, equilibrium notions are inapplicable: It can be denoted the EXPLOSIVE region.

Analytic results for five asymptotic limiting cases

Table 9.1 presents aggregate sales in markets in the five limiting cases shown by lines drawn onto Figure 9.1. The guide for schedules $W(y)$ with $k = 0$ is equation (9.13). The complex dependence on the sum over the n-values for firms in that equation suggests a further simplifying clarification to uniform quality.[20]

Even before asymptotic cases are examined, the basis for the designation of the CROWDED region is clear: If cost's proportionate variability with volume (the exponent c in the cost schedule) is actually less than the valuation schedule's proportionate volume variation exponent a, then the equilibrium aggregate sales of all firms (including a new one) are actually decreased by raising the number of firms, #, in the market.

The most striking results in Table 9.1 are implicit in the feedback result for aggregate sales in equation (9.13) and are counterintuitive from equations (9.5) and (9.6) for the tangible offer schedule, $W(y)$, itself. The market vanishes when there is no divergence between quality ratio b/δ and volume ratio a/c. And W_0 in equation (9.13) is proportionate to a power of the difference between these two ratios. Equation (9.13) does not provide sufficient guidance to the sales aggregates for the cases with b approaching delta. Asymptotic analysis is essential there to identify the limit when the denominator in equation (9.13) is approaching zero.

The last five of the seven special limiting cases shown in Table 9.1 are instructive, but not fundamental, since they critically depend on choice of power function families to approximate cost and valuation schedules (equations 9.1 and 9.2). The general feature of these five solutions for aggregate market volume is that they DECREASE when the shift constant k increases. In those limiting cases where b approaches delta, k is constrained to take a value near unity. Thus, the solutions for $k = 0$ developed earlier are not applicable at all. In the others, k is constrained to approach zero to permit a market schedule in equilibrium: so that in all these limiting cases k is limited to unity or less. Elsewhere I have shown that in *just those cases where aggregate sales go to zero, there tends to be greater equality in market shares* among firms (once one reintroduces a distribution over quality values, n) (White, 1981a, b). In other cases where aggregates do not tend to zero, a tendency toward equality in market shares does not appear.

The first two limiting cases are the most robust and important. The most interesting aspect of their aggregate outcomes is just how close they come to the general case given in equation (9.13). That is, in either of these dual limiting cases of competition, there are smooth and minor adjustments of aggregate volumes of the competitive markets as one or the other of the differentiating parameters (b or d) disappears. Further, observe that in these two cases, as opposed to 4 or 5, aggregate sales increase as the number of firms increases (# goes up). Note that in perfect competition the shift constant k simply does not appear: The schedule does not depend upon its value, and, hence, neither does the aggregate. The only remaining shift parameter for perfect competition is theta (or its t value); and only break-even ($t = 1$) is treated here for simplicity's sake.

By contrast, pure taste competitive markets directly depend on the shift constant k (only the result for $k = 0$ is shown in Table 9.1). The market schedule itself, $W(y)$, is simply the cost schedule plus k in this limiting market

254   *Harrison C. White*

form. The distinctive aspect of the pure taste market cannot be seen from aggregate predictions: It is implicit in the inequalities given in 9.7 and 9.8. Detailed calculation shows that

- when *a* is less than *c*, the only *k* values allowed are positive, and even they are subject to freeloading by any firms present with small quality levels *n*.
- when *a* is greater than *c*, if *d* is also positive, no *k* will do; for *d* negative, any positive *k* will do.

The implication is that, in this limit of common costs among producers of differentiated products, one should expect to see signs of outside-the-market social organization to combat freeloading. By the same logic, in other regions of the tradeoff plane, such as PARADOX, one may expect to find *k* other than those stated in the figure associated with organizational attempts to try to capture some of the extra cash flow available from such schedules for producers (White, 1976). Further, from inequality 9.7, the differences between net revenues at various volumes chosen by any firm are so minimal that direct market observation provides the firm with little guidance toward its appropriate niche. This is what really distinguishes this model from perfect competition and is the source of the striking differences in tone between Chamberlin's microeconomics and textbook versions.

Conclusion

As envisioned here, markets are a distinctive form of social control as well as particular tangible structures within monetary economies. Asymmetry between the producers' and buyers' sides is permanent and flows from asymmetry in valuation. Individuation takes place mainly on one side, and actors (firms) are disparate in size relative to the other. A market gears (down or up) a set of one sort of actors into another, disparate set. The market's "trick" is that it mainly shows the firms each other. How else can actors be subject to social control except through a process of comparison with *comparable* others, those on the same side (Erickson, Chapter 5)?

To me, the market seems to be a marvelous social mechanism, as it does to economists. But I see its marvel in the social intercalation of perceived options and constraints rather than in feats of psychological computation, gaming, and speculation. Social psychologists such as Sherif (1965) – as well as some analysts with other union cards, such as Schelling (1978) – also tell us about "emergent" properties of groups. But they do not embed them in the gripping logic of a larger social setting such as an economy.

In place of a summary, let us examine some contrasts between predictions based on the model presented here and those that can be derived from either mainline economic theory or from the work of Chamberlin and his successors. I use a recent paper by Spence (1976b) as the canonical formulation of a Chamberlinian theory of competition.

Contrast 1. When both the model developed here and Chamberlinian ones agree on the existence of a market, their numerical predictions differ as to volumes and payments across the spectrum of products (White, 1979: Table 1, panel A).

Contrast 2. A wide range (indexed by k and θ) of volume-payment schedules can sustain the sociologically conceived market, which discounts various claims by mainline economists of efficiency and social optimality for the market institution.

Contrast 3. Mainline economists call on entry and exit of firms from the market to rescue claims of optimality by transferring them to a "long run." A tangible market in which each particular producer has buyers partly shaped by the whole context of other producers with their established volumes and customers denies the possibility of across-the-board predictions for entry and exit. *Entry and exit are now to a social structure and not to a collection of isolates.* For one major class of facts as to costs and consumer values, it turns out that entry of more firms decreases the market's aggregate cash volume.

Contrast 4. The most dramatic differences between the perspective presented here and Chamberlin's can be seen at the naturalist's level: I have found markets in a wide range of factual situations where neoclassical economists deny they could exist. All the economists' markets explode if there are increasing returns to scale in the observed range of production volume and cost. Economists simply sweep this problem away by claiming that decreasing returns to scale are self-evident. The present model, by contrast, links increasing returns to scale – one can think of operations well below capacity where volume savings in cost are not at all exhausted – with consumers who see considerable interchangeability between products of different firms.

Contrast 5. On the other hand, the present model denies the likelihood of viable markets over most of the decreasing-return, classical-consumer factual situations that are identified as markets by economists of all stripes. The instabilities here are subtle and not universal: They depend upon the range of qualities present in firms. "Freeloading" is the summary term used in Figure 9.1 (White 1981a, and b).

There is an amusing quirk in these contrasts. Both our perspective and the economists' agree on viable markets for modern consumers, who, perversely, value more highly those goods that were produced more cheaply; but only given declining returns to scale in production. This rather unclassical and unbecoming type of market (PARADOX) looms larger in the economists' theory than in ours, where returns need not be decreasing.

In conclusion, consider an irony: *All of the major technical pieces of the model presented here were already in the economics literature.* Indeed, the irony reaches further: Two of the very same younger economists who independently updated Chamberlin's market theory – Spence and Stiglitz – also, and again independently, created the complete technical base for the model of self-fulfilling perceptions (Spence, 1974; Rothschild and Stiglitz, 1975). And they did so without even thinking of the Chamberlin theory (or at least those papers are not cited).

   Why? I suggest that we can find the root in the intense psychologizing of economists. Even this new breed, in their latter feedback-type models, were trapped within a psychologistic framework of reference by Simon's notion of imperfect information (Spence, 1976b).

Appendix: Derivation of Table 9.1

Let every $n = 1$. Then $W_o = \# W_o$. Equation 9.4 specializes to

$$y(1) = \left(\frac{\#^{(1-\gamma)/\gamma}}{r} W_o^{1/\gamma} \right)^{1/a}$$

at break-even level. Substitution into equation 9.5 yields

$$W_o^{1-(\delta/b)} = k + q \frac{1 - \delta/b}{1 - (a/c)(\delta/b)} \left(\frac{\#^{(1-\gamma)/\gamma}}{r} \right)^{c/a} W_o^{c/a\gamma - \delta/b}.$$

The seven limiting results emerge from straightforward asymptotics. For example, let $1 - \delta/b \equiv \varepsilon$ and $\varepsilon \to 0$. Then

$$(1 - k) \to \varepsilon \frac{q}{1 - a/c} \left(\frac{\#^{(1-\gamma)/\gamma}}{r} \right)^{c/a} W_o^{c/a\gamma - 1}$$

defines case 4 in Table 9.1. It is clear that $k \to 1$ or else $W_o \to \infty$; so define z by

$$(1 - k) \equiv z\varepsilon.$$

Thus,

$$W_o^{c/a\gamma - 1} \to z \left(\frac{1 - a/c}{q} \right) \left(\frac{r}{\#^{1/\gamma - 1}} \right)^{c/a}.$$

   NOTES

1. See Berkowitz, Chapter 10, for a discussion of effective decision-making units within industrial markets.
2. See Corey (1978) for an example of how this schedule works for "requests for quotations."

3. In fact, actual producers would know they are in perfect competition by noting that all their competitors' volume-revenue pairs lie on the same straight line.
4. Note that the superrationality of the producer-as-social-isolate, as is intrinsic to much neoclassical microeconomic theory, is replaced here by the social conformity of the firm as a seeker of stable market position.
5. One interesting example is limiting case 3 in Table 9.1, where the two actors are exactly matched and cannot be played off.
6. I wonder whether the total predominance of this extreme case in the microeconomics of the past generation may account for the disdain of economic theorists for cost-markup concepts. It seems much more appropriate to develop a market-schedule theory that reduces either to demand-based prices or to cost-based prices, depending on the facts of the situation for a concrete market and its members.
7. To my axiom on how firms perceive schedules I have simply adjoined standard neoclassical economic axioms (e.g., Mansfield, 1975) of optimizing by choice "at the margin" to obtain determinate predictions of any given firm's decisions, which are its self-selections.
8. *Or,* the firm will not remain in the market. But I make no attempt at modeling long-range constraints required to keep the firm viable it its overall macroenvironment, fiscal and otherwise (cf. Caves and Porter, 1977).
9. The exponent γ is less than 1 when the market buyers (as one would usually expect) are less keen on adding volume to their purchases as volume increases.
10. Thus, every firm in the market in equilibrium must have the same ratio between the W paid to it and $(\gamma/V(\#)^{1-\gamma}$'s.
11. Ironically, it is *only* in this paradoxical Chamberlin region that the standard microeconomic dictum holds good that a market cannot be sustained unless firms face declining returns to scale, that is, c greater than a in my terms. With a unity, as is commonly supposed, this becomes c greater than unity, or a cost schedule that is concave upward. The "paradox" is more feasible than it might seem since in our definition cost refers only to the additional or "variable" costs associated with choice of volume to produce in the next period. Thus, for example, a massive TV advertising program undertaken a year before or a long-standing patented invention that may have cost a huge amount will not enter into the cost schedule at all, but may have convinced buyers of superior quality.
12. I continue to put aside, until the next section, the arbitrary shift constant k, and I ignore parameters r and q, which, though important in scaling results, do not affect their structure. And until the second section, below, I ignore θ and the saturation parameter γ, which, together with the number of firms, $\#$, and their particular values on the quality index, n, determine the aggregate level feedback.
13. Treated in the section "Ranges and Aggregation." For numerical examples, see White (1981a, b).
14. Perhaps in a past era, such as the early 1920s, the arrival of many successful plays would breed audiences for yet larger volumes, described by > 1.
15. Performance at a restaurant, often suburban, usually for a fixed price exclusive of drinks.
16. Freeloading is a kind of contextual effect, defined and briefly discussed after equations (9.7) and (9.8). Detailed treatments can be found in White (1981a, b).

The essential point is that with each of several kinds of customer-taste patterns, it can happen that firms in some particular range of quality or size can spoil the possibility of any equilibrium schedule. In the upper PARADOX region of Figure 9.1, for example, freeloading can occur to bar high (and highly profitable) price structures in the presence of small, low-quality, high-cost firms.

17. As can be seen, formally, from asymptotic analysis of equation 9.5 (de Bruijn 1961).

18. Either plus or minus infinity on Figure 9.1, so that it may be easier to think of Figure 9.1 as rolled up on a horizontal cylinder.

19. Parallel computations at other values of k are straightforward but do not yield closed-form results as do equations (9.13) through (9.15). The general results can be construed in terms of a calibration level, together with the t that gives the common ratio (θ) of valuation over payment to firms in units of the break-even theta. It makes sense to focus for calibration on the sales volume itself at break-even, W_o, since that is directly interpretable. I give much attention to equation (9.13) to disentangle analytically the various kinds of influence on aggregate size. Computations from equations (9.14) and (9.15) suggest that net benefit to buyers' side is quite insensitive to changes in t, and numerical calculations for other values of k support this. The likely range of the ratio t (or, equivalently, theta), between unity for break-even and the optimal value just quoted, is itself not large. It is important to establish by calibration the overall size of the market, but significant *shifts* in market schedule are associated with the shape constant k rather than the height scaling t for the schedule.

20. Although in a real case there must be at least some spread of firms across quality levels to generate the outlying points that establish $W(y)$ as a schedule perceived by firms, I assume a further specialization to the point where nearly all the firms have the same quality value, say n^1, which, for further simplicity, I take to be unity. Then in equation (9.13) the sum over n terms contributes the factor $(\#)^{1-(a/c)}$ to the bracketed expression; in W_o.

LITERATURE CITED

Anderson, Robert J., H. Baumol, S. O. Maltezon, and R. Wuthnow, et al. *The Condition and Needs of the Live Professional Theater in America*, Phase 1 (Data Collection Analysis); Report to the National Endowment for the Arts. Princeton, N. J.: MATHTECH, 1978.

Barber, Bernard. "Absolutization of the Market." In G. Tworkin et al. (eds.), *Markets and Morals*. Washington, D. C.: Hemisphere, 1977.

Bator, F. "The Anatomy of Market Failure." *Quarterly Journal of Economics* (1961): p. 351ff.

Blau, Peter. *Exchange and Power in Social Life*. New York: John Wiley, 1964.

Boorman, Scott A., and Harrison C. White. "Social Structure from Multiple Networks. II Equations". *American Journal of Sociology* 81 (1976): 1384–1446.

Breiger, Ronald L. "Structures of Economic Interdependence among Nations." In Peter M. Blau and Robert K. Merton (eds.), *Continuities in Structural Inquiry*. Beverly Hills, Calif.: Sage, 1981.

Caves, R. E., and M. E. Porter. "From Entry Barriers to Mobility Barriers: Conjectural Decisions and Contrived Deterrents to New Competition." *Quarterly Journal of Economics* (1977): 241–61.

Chamberlain, Edward. *Toward a More General Theory of Value*. Oxford: Oxford University Press, 1954.

   The Theory of Monopolistic Competition. Cambridge, Mass.: Harvard University Press, 1956.

Corey, E. Raymond. *Procurement Management*. New York: Van Nostrand Reinhold, 1978.

de Bruijn, N. G. *Asymptotic Methods in Analysis*. Amsterdam: North-Holland, 1961.

Engel, Lehmann. *The American Musical Theater*. New York: Macmillan, 1967.

Faulkner, Robert. *Music on Demand*. New Brunswick, N. J.: Transaction Books, 1982.

Geanakoplos, J. D., and H. M. Polemarchakis. "On the Disaggregation of Excess Demand Functions." Economics Department, Harvard University, 1978.

Goldman, William. *The Season*. New York: Harcourt Brace World, 1969.

Greenberger, Howard (ed.). *The Off-Broadway Experience*. Englewood Cliffs, N. J.: Prentice-Hall, 1971.

Grossman, S. "Rational Expectations and the Economic Modeling of Markets Subject to Uncertainty." *Journal of Econometrics* 3 (1975): 255–72.

Granovetter, Mark S. "Threshold Models of Collective Behavior." *American Journal of Sociology* 83 (1978): 1420–2443.

Hannan, Michael, and John Freeman. "The Population Ecology of Organizations." *American Journal of Sociology* 82 (1977): 929–65.

Leamer, Edward E. *Specification Searchers: Ad Hoc Inference with Non-Experimental Data*. New York: John Wiley, 1978.

Leifer, Eric M., and Harrison C. White. "A Structural Approach to Markets." In Mark Mizruchi and Michael Schwartz (eds.), *The Structural Analysis of Businesses*. Cambridge: Cambridge University Press, 1987.

Mansfield, Edwin. *Microeconomics: Theory and Applications*. New York: W. W. Norton, 1975.

Muth, John F. "Rational Expectations and the Theory of Price Movement." *Econometrica* 29 (1961): 331–35.

Nadel, S. F. *The Theory of Social Structure*. London: Cohen and West, 1957.

Pattison, Philippa. "An Algebraic Analysis for Multiple Social Networks." Ph.D. diss., University of Melbourne, 1980.

Poggi, Jack. *Theater in America*. Cornell University Press, 1968.

Prince, Harold. *Contradictions*. New York: Dodd Mead, 1974.

Ross, Edward Alsworth. *Social Psychology*. New York: Macmillan, 1921.

Rothschild, Michael, and Joseph Stiglitz. "Equilibrium in Competitive Insurance Markets: An Essay on the Economics of Imperfect Competition." *Journal of Political Economy* (1975): 629–49.

Samuelson, Paul A. *Foundations of Economic Analysis*. Cambridge: Harvard University Press, 1947.

Schelling, Thomas C. *Micromotives and Macrobehavior*. New York: W. W. Norton, 1978.

Sherif, Muzafer. *Psychology of Social Norms*. New York: Octagon 1965.

Spence, A. Michael. *Market Signalling: Informational Transfer in Hiring and Related Screening Processes*. Cambridge, Mass.: Harvard University Press, 1974.

——— "Product Selection, Fixed Costs, and Monopolistic Competition." *Review of Economic Studies* 43 (1976a): 217–35.

——— "Informational Aspects of Market Structure: An Introduction." *Quarterly Journal of Economics* 91 (1976b): 591–7.

Stigler, George. *The Theory of Price*. New York: Macmillan, 1946.

Stinchcombe, Arthur L. "Social Structure and Organizations." In J. G. March (ed.), *Handbook of Organizations*. Chicago: Rand-McNally, 1965.

Tarde, Gabriel. *The Laws of Imitation*. 2d ed. Translated by Elsie Clews Parsons. New York: Henry Holt [1895] 1903.

White, Harrison C. "The Cumulation of Roles into Homogeneous Structures." In W. W. Cooper et al. (eds.), *New Perspectives in Organization Research*. New York: John Wiley, 1965.

——— "Everyday Life in Stochastic Networks." *Sociological Inquiry* 43 (173): 73.

——— "Subcontracting with an Oligopoly: Spence Revisited." RIAS Program Working Paper 1, Harvard University, 1976.

——— "On Markets." RIAS Program Working Paper 16, Harvard University, 1979.

——— "Production Markets as Induced Role Structures." In Samuel Leinhardt (ed.), *Sociological Methodology 1981*. San Francisco: Jossey-Bass, 1981a.

——— "Where Do Markets Come From?" *American Journal of Sociology* 87 (1981b): 517–47.

——— "Interfaces." *Connections* 5 (1982): 11–20.

White, Harrison C., Boorman, Scott A., and Breiger, Ronald, L. "Social Structure from Multiple Networks: I. Blockmodels of Roles and Positions." *American Journal of Sociology* 81 (1976): 730–80.

White, Harrison C., and R. G. Eccles. "Production Markets." In John Eatwell, Murray Milgate, and Peter Newman (eds.), *The New Palgrave: A Dictionary of Economic Theory and Doctrine*, New York: Stockton Press, 1987.

Wilson, T., and Andrews, P. (eds.). *Oxford Studies in the Price Mechanism*. Clarendon Press, 1951.

Winter, S. "Satisficing, Selection and the Innovating Remnant." *Quarterly Journal of Economics* 85 (1971): 237–61.

Zeigler, Joseph W. *Regional Theater*. University of Minnesota Press, 1973.

10

Markets and market-areas: some preliminary formulations

S. D. Berkowitz

Markets, market-areas, and enterprises

Over the last several years social scientists have become increasingly interested in the role played by larger-than-firm groupings of companies – or "enterprises" – within advanced capitalist economies.[1] Recent technical developments have made it possible to begin rigorously exploring the behavior of these units under a variety of circumstances.[2] For instance, our research group has demonstrated that the density of director–officership ties *among enterprises* is an important intervening variable in the relationship between corporate concentration and profit margins.[3] Related work on multinational, multifirm corporations suggests that at least two important aspects of market conduct – transfer pricing and capital investment – are strongly affected by the internal organization of enterprises (Aharoni, 1966; Greene and Duerr, 1970; Kopits, 1972; Adams and Whalley, 1977; Booth and Jensen, 1977; Burns, 1980; Lessard, 1979). Factors operating at the enterprise level may also play an important role in determining the kinds of transfers of technology that take place among firms

I am greatly indebted to P. J. Carrington and G. Heil, whose intellectual contributions to the course of the research reported here are far too numerous to acknowledge in detail. Y. Kotowitz and L. Waverman, together with the author, were the principal investigators during an earlier phase of this study. We are collectively grateful to the Department of Consumer and Corporate Affairs, Ottawa, and to the Royal Commission Corporation Concentration for supporting this earlier work. The present research has been facilitated by computer funds provided by the Structural Analysis Programme and the Social Sciences and Humanities Research Fund, University of Toronto, and by the Academic Computing Center, University of Vermont. Additional research support was provided by the Royal Commission on Economic Union and Development Prospects for Canada. An earlier version of this chapter appeared as part of a report to that body. Their assistance is gratefully acknowledged. The final revisions of the theoretical framework and data analysis employed here and in subsequent work on market areas were made possible by an award from the Faculty and Institutional Grant Programme, Canadian Studies Programme, Government of Canada. The timely and generous support of this program was essential to continued work in the area and is gratefully acknowledged as well. Linton Freeman, Nancy Howell, Stanley Lieberson, Beth Mintz, Frank Sampson, Lorne Tepperman, Leonard Waverman, Douglas White, Harrison White, Thomas Wilson, and Barry Wellman are to be thanked for their timely scholarly criticism and continuing support for this work during its various phases.

261

(Baranson, 1970, 1978; Globerman, 1975), in fixing the constraints under which market pricing occurs (Burt, 1979), and in establishing the division of decision-making responsibility within corporations (Williamson, 1970, 1981; Caves, 1982).

Although it is clear that research on enterprise structure and behavior has the potential to provide us with a far more realistic picture of the operation of a complex, modern economy than we have had in the past, this work has also sensitized us to a number of closely related problems in industrial organization that must be addressed before much of this earlier research can be of direct use in concretely interpreting economic structures. An important example of such a problem is the need to recast the ways in which we go about conceptualizing and measuring the boundaries between "markets."

In the course of research on corporate concentration it became clear that, for a variety of reasons, conventional methods of assigning establishments – and, hence shipments – to various "standard industrial classification" groupings did not allow analysts to examine important dimensions of market structure. The principal statistical system used by most Western countries to represent their economies is designed to reflect the *production*, and not the sale and distribution, of commodities. In effect, it ignores buyers' sides of markets. This schema works reasonably well where industries produce relatively simple goods for sale into final consumption markets – e.g., fruit farms with roadside stands. Under these circumstances, there is a close fit between classifications of "industries" and classifications of their "outputs." Where there is not so close a fit – where, for instance, sellers are heavily involved in a number of different producers' markets or in providing a range of services – this schema is less effective.[4] This is significant because (a) all higher-level market analyses – for example industrial concentration, capital investment by sector – ultimately depend on this schema, and (b) it is most problematic when applied to the more dynamic parts of modern industrial economies.

Although at least some of these difficulties are widely recognized, there is no clear consensus as to how they can best be overcome. Most researchers studying market structures have simply assumed that there is a close correspondence between the "industries" in which producers compete in maximizing the benefits from similar productive facilities and the markets in terms of which these same producers compete in satisfying the demand for similar commodities. Since this is often not true, studies have historically underestimated relationships between factors such as corporate concentration and net profits owing to large random errors associated with their calculations. This has been especially true of studies based on fine-grained four-digit Standard Industrial Classifications (SICs) (Statistics Canada, 1980; Carrington, 1981a:40), but the source of the problem is intrinsic to the measurements themselves. Government censuses have attempted to solve the problem by reckoning shipments at the level of a single productive facility – or establishment – and then aggregating upward (Dominion Bureau of Statistics, 1970: 9; U.S. Office of Management and Budget, 1972: 583–5). Since a single establishment often produces goods for only a limited range of markets – and since these censuses assign establishments, not firms, to SICs – this reduces some difficulties on the sellers' side. However, both price theory and the methodological apparatus designed to interpret markets require that sellers *and* buyers be "on the same footing." Thus, a more robust solution to the problem demands that we deal with the issue of buyer as well as seller "substitutability": In systems terms, we must devise a way of empirically detecting boundaries between markets and describing the relationship between market definitions and the conventional assignments of production to industries and industrial sectors.

Here we review and extend one set of solutions of this boundary problem, which is based upon, and consistent with, the use of *enterprises* as market actors and *flows of commodities* as measures of market activity. First we examine the relevant literature on markets, enterprises, and market activity and describe the market boundaries problem. Next we introduce the concept of a "market-area" and show some of the implications of market-area–like definitions for the description of market structure. Finally, we point out some directions in which research in this area is likely to go.

Markets, enterprises, and boundaries

The concept of a market has a long and varied history in the social sciences. Early theoretical work on the subject – in the eighteenth and nineteenth centuries – often dealt with markets for particular goods, the roles played by actors within them, and the observed or inferred consequences of specific market arrangements for the welfare of given participants or the economic system as a whole (Smith, [1776] 1937; Ricardo, 1817). Thus, although abstract, these early notions of a market were clearly tied to – or generalizations from – palpable realities.

Since the birth of modern neoclassical economics early in this century, however, there has been an increasing tendency for economists to move away from particular or concrete formulations of the concept – or even general formulations associated with particular cases – toward the notion of a "market" as an abstract arena or set of processes for determining the price and allocation of goods and services. Although Marshall and others of his generation recognized that real-world markets were "imperfect," they were content to use the "average behavior" of "representative firms" and "typical consumers" in constructing their models (Marshall, 1920). Friedman (1976) and other economists in this genre have arrived at the point where they use the notion of a market as a pure construct that can only be validated with reference to other concepts isomorphic to concrete "observables."

Work running counter to this trend, although important, has become increasingly rare over the years. Despite the foundations laid by Mason, Berle, and Means in the 1930s (Mason, 1939; Means, 1932; Berle and Means, [1932] 1969) and the heroic attempts of Chamberlin (1933) to revivify general interest in the subject, the study of concrete market conditions has become increasingly divorced from mainline economic theory construction and model-building.

This trend has been particularly clear in the development of the subfield known as industrial organization: Apart from generally adhering to the structure-conduct-performance paradigm (Caves, 1977), work in the area has not been well articulated with a broad theoretical base but, instead, has centered around sets of empirical generalizations drawn from a number of different contexts.[5] Consequently, the fit between well-developed, rigorous model-building and the statistical apparatus used in studies of industrial organization has often been poor.

The most obvious problems have to do with units of measurement or analysis. In theory, markets consist of *independent* economic actors engaging in arm's-length exchanges mediated only by general conditions of supply and demand. Where there are large numbers of buyers and sellers, the argument goes, no actor can earn monopoly rents because the obtained market price will not allow a seller or buyer to earn profits disproportionate to its contribution to these factors (Vickery, 1965).

Where there are few buyers or sellers, however, actors can, and do, exercise market power. In order to gauge the extent to which given market conditions depart from this "ideal," it is necessary to establish (a) the number of independent units involved and (b) the intensity of their transactions with one another, that is, the extent to which they attempt to offer the same goods or services to, or buy the same goods or services from, other participants.

Enterprises

Considerable headway has recently been made in tackling the first of these problems. Students of industrial organization have traditionally used *firms* – usually legally incorporated, limited liability joint stock companies – as their ultimate units of analysis. Bain (1968), for instance, simply *assumes* that "firms" are the loci for decision making within an industrial system.[6] However, in recent years there has been a significant and growing tendency in advanced capitalist economies for firms to acquire control over other firms through the purchase of shares, the exercise of warrants or convertible debentures, loan arrangements, or other mechanisms leading to the domination of their boards of directors. In some cases, firms have deliberately created separately incorporated subsidiaries as vehicles for engaging in particular activities. Thus, many researchers argue, we can no longer assume that separate incorporation implies independent action and, hence, that firms, per se, can be used in this way.[7]

One solution, of course, is to devise some means of identifying those forms of social organization that now play the roles that were attributed to firms in the past (i.e., that act as independent units for decision making, optimization, etc.). Given the structural variability in any large economy, this task is not simple. In some cases, firms may be entirely independent. In others, several hundred firms may serve as vehicles for one capital pool. Thus, any method of detecting or uncovering "actual" decision-making units must be capable of accommodating both extremes and a variety of intermediate cases.

The first step in finding this solution is to devise an organizational typology consisting of mutually exclusive and exhaustive units. In a study undertaken for the Canadian Royal Commission on Corporate Concentration (Berkowitz, Kotowitz, Waverman, et. al., 1976; Berkowitz, Kotowitz, and Waverman, 1977; Berkowitz, Carrington, Corman, and Waverman, 1979), we propose a threefold categorization of the components of complex economic systems into *establishments, firms,* and *enterprises.* Within this schema, the focal (but not ultimate) units are large, usually bureaucratically organized, industrial, or financial organizations – public or private – that are incorporated as limited liability joint stock companies (Berkowitz, 1975). Each of these firms encompasses a collection of assets (capital and other) held in a common name, "and consists of a plant, or series of plants, located at different geographic locales, in which the production of goods takes place, around which services are organized, and through which business is conducted" (Berkowitz, Carrington, Kotowitz, and Waverman, 1978–9: 394). These actual productive units are referred to as *establishments.* Sets of firms operating under common control – the actual decision-making units in which we are ultimately interested – are called *enterprises.* Hence, the limiting cases in the model we propose would be the single establishment, firm, enterprise and the multi-establishment, multifirm, enterprise (see Table 10.1).

Understood in this way, the critical problem in *mapping* a complex industrial system is the assignment of establishments to firms, and firms to enterprises. This task, once again, is not simple, but it is at least do-able; that is, consistent and rigorous operational definitions of these three types of units will permit investigators to discriminate, simultaneously, between *levels* within an industrial system and the *functions* of units at each level. Previous operationalizations of the concepts of establishments, firms, and enterprises in the industrial organization literature often confused these uses (Bain, 1959; Caves, 1977). Critically, the three-tiered typology proposed by our research group eliminates a certain amount of confusion by, in a given case, leaving the

Table 10.1. *Relationships between levels of modern corporate systems*

Level	Unit	Basis of definition	Function
1	Establishment	Physical or geographic contiguousness of capital assests.	Physical locus for production, provision of services, employment, etc.
2	Firm	Legal requirements for a corporate persona through which business can be organized.	Holding of capital or other assets; party to contracts; incur debts; acquire and dispose of assets, etc.
3	Enterprise	Some measure of power or, in the limiting case, control exercised between and among firms.	Allocate capital among alternative uses; garner and assign credit; coordinate management or production.

Source: Berkowitz, Carrington, Kotowitz, and Waverman 1978–9: 395.

question of the *control* exercised by firms over one another – and, by extension, the relationship between firms and enterprises – as problematic rather than determining it a priori.

Berkowitz, Kotowitz, Waverman, et al. (1976) put forward a method of making these assignments that utilizes combined ownership and directorship ties as a measure of intercorporate control (see also Berkowitz, Carrington, Kotowitz, and Waverman, 1978–9). In the mid-1960s, central statistical bureaus began to recognize that certain of their calculations – for example, market concentration – were meaningful only if done on an "enterprise consolidated" basis. Hence, they began to experiment with the use of nonmarket ties as a means of establishing intercorporate domination – and, hence, the boundaries between enterprises (Department of Consumer and Corporate Affairs, 1968, 1971; Statistics Canada, 1973, 1978).

The real difficulties have to do with instances of minority control: most analysts are willing to recognize that majority ownership of voting stock conveys control over the board of directors of a held firm. But it is also widely recognized that one firm can exercise effective control over another through ownership of a considerably smaller proportion of its voting shares. There is no broad agreement, however, on what proportion is needed to do this. Berle and Means (1969 [1932]), for instance, maintain that a firm or group of business associates can enjoy effective control over a held firm with 20% of its stock if other ownership is scattered. In 1963, Larner reviewed the evidence with regard to the U.S. case and concluded:

> In view of the greater size of the 200 largest nonfinancial corporations in 1963 and the wider dispersion of their stock, this lower limit [20%] to minority control seems too high. In the present study, a firm is classified as immediately controlled by a

minority stock ownership if 10% or more of its voting stock is held by an individual family, corporation or group of business associates. (Larner, 1966: 779)

By contrast, we submit that (a) the actual proportion of minority ownership needed for control cannot be determined a priori, but must be established empirically, and that (b) this can only be done properly through the analysis of some form of data other than those related to ownership, itself. We argue that the ultimate objective of an external minority stockholder seeking to control a firm is to dominate its board of directors. Thus it seems likely that the actual exercise of minority control – as opposed to attempts at control – would be reflected in the composition of the board of the controlled firm and, hence, in the pattern of ties between dominant and subordinate units within a network of corporate interlocks. By combining ties reflecting proportionate minority ownership with those indicating a pattern of substantial directorship overlap, we contend it is possible to distinguish between linkages that are indices of control by parents over subsidiaries and those that are made for noncontrol related purposes, such as pure investment or diversification of risk.[8]

Given this interpretation, there are a variety of mathematically consistent ways in which dissimilar ties can be combined to form a single common measure of control. We do this in a series of steps.[9] First, we map together all firms joined by directed majority ownership ties, both transitively and additively, within successive stages (degrees of remove) from an ultimate owner or parent. This is accomplished by multiplying, under Boolean arithmetic, powers of the matrix of ownership ties, summing together the results of each multiplication in stepwise fashion, and binarizing the results, that is, assigning the value 1 to a tie meeting the majority control criterion and 0 to a tie that does not. Thus, given this procedure and the pattern shown in Figure 10.1, A is deemed to control D since A controls B and C and these, taken together, control D.

Here the circled letters (nodes) in the graph represent firms and the arrows (relations) the direction of ownership. The valence associated with each directed ownership tie shows the proportion of voting stock held by the sender in the receiver firm. Note that neither the B-D nor C-D relation, by itself, reflects majority control. However, by mapping firms together in successive stages from the ultimate owner, A, it becomes possible to take into account the indirect domination exerted by A over D.[10]

Next, we examine the directorship ties that "map over" or correspond to less-than-majority ownership relations. Treating all such ties as *binary* that is, either as "made" or "not made," we discovered that in the Canadian case the general pattern of ownership ties was random within tolerable limits (Rapoport and Horvath, 1961).[11] In practical terms, this means that these ties would add no information if they were combined with the majority

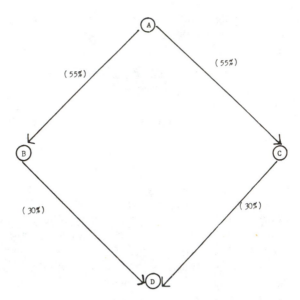

Figure 10.1. Hypothetical pattern of indirect ownership ties between firms. The arrows represent the direction of ownership, the numbers the percentage of voting stock held.

ownership measures. All single-stranded director–officership ties were then eliminated and the procedure repeated. Once again, in the Canadian case the result was a random graph – but less random than the first.

From a series of these experiments, our research group concluded that, for our data, a 15% minority ownership tie, when combined with three connected director–officership interlocks, yielded the most consistent and interpretable arrays. To avoid the anomalies that would have been generated if no attempt had been made to combine measures directly,[12] each director–officership tie greater than 2 was reckoned as the equivalent of a 12% ownership tie. Firms mapped together on this basis – transitively and additively within stages – were then added to the sets generated by majority ownership linkages.

Although this method of determining – or, more properly, detecting – the boundaries of enterprise groupings appears to be well adapted to the Canadian case, there are, of course, a variety of similar procedures that might work as well or better if a given economy were organized somewhat differently. Moreover, despite the fact that a number of other researchers have used the arrays generated by our research group and have found that they yield consistent results (most recently, Shapiro, Sims, and Hughes, 1983), it is quite conceivable that another method of combining ownership data with some other measure would be more suitable for certain applications.

The chief advantage of these kinds of procedures is that they lead to greater commensurability among units. Although most analysts would agree that, in principle, this is important, most seem reluctant to do much more than strive for rough comparability among units within the context of a single study. This means that, in practice, even the best-conceived and systematic research in the area tends to be difficult to evaluate. Caves, for instance, recognizes the utility of the notion of an "enterprise" ("rather than a company") in that it directs attention "to the top level of coordination in the hierarchy of business decisions" since "a company ... may be the controlled subsidiary of another firm" (Caves, 1982: 1). He reserves the term, however, for entities that manage at least two establishments[13] and excludes establishments not directly involved in production. In practice, both of these restrictions limit the generality of his use of the term and generate problems in assignment. In regard to the multinational enterprise, he notes that "the transition from an overseas sales subsidiary or a technology licensee to a producing subsidiary is not always clearcut. ... What constitutes 'control' over a foreign establishment is another judgmental issue. Not infrequently a ... [multinational enterprise] holds a minor fraction of the equity of a foreign affiliate" (Caves, 1982: 1).

Since Caves is primarily interested in transfers of technology, ideas, and the like between *production-based* establishments, these restrictions are not particularly germane in his particular case. However, note that, in general, he would be forced to discriminate between single firm and multifirm enterprises, to decide, in each instance, which establishments to include in his calculations, and so on. With even a moderately sized study population, this could lead to difficulties. With one as large as ours (5,306 firms), these problems would become almost insuperable. Most important, extensions of Caves's work that dealt with other aspects of within-enterprise behavior would require a redefinition of the study population.

Boundaries

The second of these general problems – establishing the intensity of interaction among market actors – has been less well explored. Classical notions of markets assumed that participants were either "in" or "out" of a given market and, if in, that they had equally good opportunities to directly interact with one another. Modern research recognizes that these stipulations are unrealistic and even mainstream economics has begun to deal with departures from "ideal" market conditions – such as the existence of marginal actors or lack of effective competition – under rubrics such as "barriers to entry" or "market segmentation" (Scherer, 1980: 10–12). But, until quite recently, apart from bread-and-butter technical work – such as measuring its effects on pricing behavior or innovation – conventional treatments have paid relatively little attention to systematic variations in market form or structure.

The research most germane to this problem grew out of what is referred to as the transaction cost approach. During the 1930s and 1940s, institutional economists made important contributions to the formulation and use of the concept of market structure. But because most early researchers in the area were preoccupied with immediate applications of their work to antitrust or anticombines policy, their findings tended to be more descriptive than analytic and, often, concerned with particular contexts. Those with broader interests, such as Coase (1937), Chamberlin (1933), and Commons (1934), while important, were the exceptions. For the most part, institutional economics of the 1930s and 1940s did not encourage the development of alternative theoretical frameworks, and, as a result, its practitioners tended to couch their findings in the somewhat inappropriate language of price or value theory (Massel, 1963). It was not until the 1960s and 1970s that a "new" institutional economics began to emerge that was, at once, more broadly focused and more attentive to larger theoretical issues.

For present purposes, the key difference between the "older" and "newer" forms of institutional economics is that, because the latter has tended to follow Coase in focusing on transactions and alternative means of economizing on them, its adherents are able, in principle, to deal with structure at each of several orders of generality simultaneously: at the level of *actors* (e.g., firms, enterprises), at the level of *markets or industries*, and at the level of *the economy* as a whole. Thus, rather than starting with the conventional imagery of frictionless markets or with a restricted range of cases (e.g., monopoly, duopoly, etc.), analyses in this vein are free to examine empirically all the types of structure that may grow up under a variety of constraints. Specifically, what is called the "market failures" literature has treated the formation of markets, themselves, as problematic since they represent only one of several alternative mechanisms for minimizing transaction costs under conditions of uncertainty and bounded rationality (Williamson, 1975: 4).

As Coase observes, "firms" – and here he means something akin to what we imply by the term "enterprises" – attempt to capture a set of transactions that will integrate and sustain activities (e.g., industrial processes, exchanges, service functions) that will allow a given firm to maximize revenues, minimize costs, or both. Which transactions a firm internalizes and which it affects through markets thus becomes the subject of an economic decision.

For instance, given the high fixed costs associated with maintaining machinery, small and medium size publishers often contract-out the actual printing of the books they produce. The transaction costs associated with this strategy tend to be high: Manuscripts can be misplaced or damaged in transit, production of a particular book may be delayed by extraneous factors, and terms of contract are notoriously difficult to enforce; thus, high investments in personnel are necessary to monitor contractors' performance. But, unless publishers produce a large number of books each year, they are generally willing to bear these costs in preference to those associated with establishing and maintaining their own printing plant; in institutional terms, the organizational costs associated with recourse to the market via contract are less than those they would incur by producing the books themselves. If, however, these costs-of-contract were to rise precipitously – as a result, for instance, of very long delays – publishers might consider internalizing the production process and shifting these transactions out of the market context. By extension, very large publishers may print books themselves – trading off intraorganizational transaction costs against the costs and uncertainties of mediating these exchanges through the marketplace – or they may pursue a mixed strategy: Where external costs are likely to be high (e.g., with math texts), print the books in-house; where low, contract-out. Hence, from the point of view of the observer, which transactions take place within markets – and which potential markets are actually formed – would depend, in a given instance, on the gradient of costs actors encounter in the course of affecting exchanges.

The chief difficulty with the transaction cost approach is, of course, that since the notion of a "transaction" implies nothing about the levels of the units or types of goods and services involved, it provides few guidelines as to (a) which transactions are important to model, (b) which costs ought to be taken into account, and (c) how to establish tradeoffs among them.[14] These specifications are critical because which of several possible factors analysts use in constructing a *cost gradient* will, in large measure, determine (a) the forms of interaction that can be observed and (b) the effective boundaries between firms and markets and among market segments.

Fortunately, these developments in institutional economics have been paralleled by theoretical and technical work with regard to what structural analysts refer to as "the boundary question" (Berkowitz, 1982; Laumann and Marsden, 1982). Since most have backgrounds in sociology and anthropology, few structural analysts have explicitly looked at market boundaries or the conduct of market actors, per se.[15] But as recent work by Arrow (1975), White (1981a), and Williamson (1981) illustrates, there is a natural fit between the transaction cost approach and the conceptualizations and modeling techniques structural analysts have developed to represent complex systems. In fact, Ouchi's (1980) formulation of the problem of establishing "efficient boundaries between operating units" represents an explicit bridge between the two.

Theoretically and practically, the "boundary question" has three major dimensions. First, beginning with a structure represented by a network of ties, is it possible to define levels of detail within that network that correspond to levels of organization in the real-world phenomena it is intended to model? Put another way, are there clear, reasonably self-defined limits to the activities of units of varying size and complexity that are implicit in graphic representations of transactional data? Second, given a positive answer to this first question, can we then specify reasonably reliable boundaries between sets of closely related elements *within* each of the levels so defined? Can we, in effect, detect "naturally occurring units" within levels? Finally, given a knowledge of these layers and the boundaries between sets of elements within them, can we draw inferences about the kinds of constraints that would have engendered the forms of organization we observe? In other words, can we reconstruct the fundamental morphogenic processes that produced this structure?

Thought of in this way, working solutions to one aspect of the boundaries question are at least partly dependent upon solutions to the others. As noted earlier, we found that in defining or detecting enterprise groupings – an example of the "boundaries within levels" problem – we had to draw on network-wide information about the organization and distribution of director–officership and ownership ties. Similarly, in order to establish empirically the major boundaries between levels within some larger structure, one must have at least a tentative mapping of the effective units, that is, bounded sets of elements, within each level. Ultimately, mappings neither within nor between levels can be validated unless they can be incorporated into a falsifiable model of the social processes that underlie and sustain a particular structure.

During the course of the last two decades, structural analysts have developed a series of tools – such as clustering, multidimensional scaling, and algebraic modeling – that can be employed in operationalizing tentative solutions to two or more aspects of this boundary question. Which tool one may apply depends, in large measure, on the characteristics of the system being examined: all these techniques deal with structures holistically and were designed to evaluate the relationships between units or elements in terms of the ways in which they are embedded within the larger structure. Although they recognize that organizations and their environments are interdependent (Williamson, 1970) and that these interdependencies determine, in large measure, the types of accommodations that may occur between the two (Williamson, 1975; Williamson and Ouchi, 1981), even economists pursuing the transaction cost approach have made little use of these kinds of tools and, consequently, have put most of their effort into the highly specialized and limiting case in which actors are *assumed* to function autonomously and to form only episodic linkages during the bargaining process (Laumann and Marsden, 1982: 336).

What is clearly needed, then, is a method of dealing with different aspects of this boundaries question that (a) will accommodate all forms of interaction among market actors likely to be present in modern industrial economies and (b) will utilize data on systemic properties in determining the scope and intensity of market transactions. The next section examines one approach that allows us to do this.

Markets and market-areas

The structures that sustain the production, sale, and distribution of goods in modern industrial economies are extremely varied and complex. For this reason, producers operating within different sectors and industries perceive these structures very differently and act accordingly. At one extreme, large multifirm enterprises produce a wide range of goods that they sell to a variety of other producers or directly to final consumers. At the other, small single-firm enterprises produce an extremely limited range of goods for a narrowly defined group of customers. Both types of producers must, of course, face the same general problem of attracting a group of buyers with whom they can sustain a series of transactions over time (White, 1981a; Chapter 9). But because the technologies they use, the organizational forms they adopt, and the ways in which they go about garnering capital and recruiting a labor force are, in many cases, so different, the strategies that different producers follow in solving this general problem often have little or no bearing on one another.

For instance, a small specialized wire manufacturer in Iowa or Saskatchewan may, for all practical purposes, have only one or two potential buyers for its product. These buyers, in turn, may produce an extremely limited range of goods for only a half-dozen or so large consumers. By contrast, the wire division – or wire subsidiary – of a large multifirm, multinational enterprise may produce everything from fine computer wire to long-distance transmission cable. For instance, it may sell the wire it produces either by itself or as part of electrical equipment installed by its construction subsidiary in a generating station built for a power company it owns in South America. Under these circumstances, the small single-firm producer in Iowa or Saskatchewan would probably know all the downstream uses to which its product was being put and, consequently, would see no need for advertising its wares in trade journals. The large multifirm enterprise probably would not be aware of all of its downstream buyers and, except in the limiting case where it absorbed all of its product itself, would, in all likelihood, find it necessary to maintain a sales force and to advertise widely. Thus, although in the abstract both producers could be considered part of the "wire manufacturing industry," the specific markets they encounter and the attendant market strategies they pursue would be quite different (White, 1976).

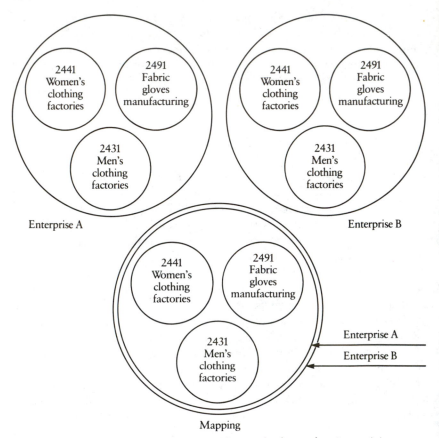

Figure 10.2. Two enterprises with completely overlapping activity sets.

Yet, at another level, both small single-firm and large multifirm enterprises exist within the same general economy and, therefore, must confront one another – albeit indirectly. Even specialized producers in geographically isolated areas must contend with the possibility that some large diversified enterprise may decide to enter their particular market. Thus, locally struck bargains cannot vary a great deal from those that would obtain if transaction costs were the same for all producers; that is, local producers must not strike bargains that will encourage "outsiders" to enter their territory. Similarly, since locally produced and traded goods frequently enter wider markets later in the production process,[16] it would be unrealistic to think of local and national or international market structures as wholly discrete. In fact, many small specialized producers ultimately depend on one or two subsidiaries of large enterprises for the majority of their sales and, in this sense, are probably

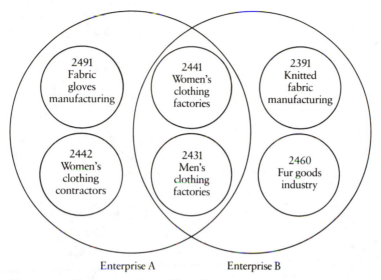

Figure 10.3. Two enterprises with partly overlapping activity sets.

more vulnerable to higher-order structural changes than more diversified producers.

Viewed in this way, a given product normally moves through a series of interfaces during the course of its transformation from a raw material to a finished good (Coase, 1937). At each point in this flow where a technological break or transfer occurs, some kind of transaction must take place. Some, perhaps many, of these are negotiated within markets of various kinds. Others are arranged between firms or divisions within enterprises. Since any given interface may be bridged either within or between enterprises, the *span* of the internal and external transactions in which an enterprise normally engages is an important indication of its specific location within this production system. By extension, if two or more enterprises participate in precisely the same activity sets, we can say that they focus on structurally equivalent locations in the production process.[17] Where they engage in some – but not all – of the same activities, we can measure the degree of *overlap* between sets[18] and, given some criterion of tolerance, say that they address *structurally similar* locations. Thus, in Figure 10.2 enterprises *A* and *B* can be said to be focused on structurally equivalent positions in the production process because there is a one-to-one correspondence between the activities (women's clothing manufacturing, men's clothing manufacturing, and fabric gloves manufacturing) in which they both engage. In Figure 10.3, no one-to-one correspondence exists, although there is a 50% overlap between the two, and we may decide to treat their locations as structurally similar.

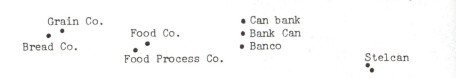

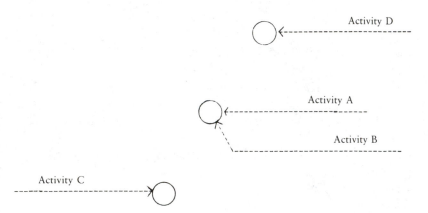

Figure 10.4. A hypothetical example of a mapping of between-enterprise distances based on similarities in activity sets.

Figure 10.5. A hypothetical mapping of between-activity distances.

Although this concept of structurally equivalent or similar locations is interesting and useful, only when it is generalized to the *system* level can we really begin to make use of it in interpreting market structure. Consider a matrix in which the rows and columns are enterprises and the cells indicate the number of activities that each *ij* entry has in common, that is, the intersection of their activity sets. Call this a "similarity matrix." By computing the reciprocal of the entries in this matrix we can then derive a "dissimilarity" matrix in which each *ij* referent corresponds to a "distance" between enterprises. By plotting or reconciling these distances,[19] we can then produce a mapping in which like-located enterprises appear close to one another and others are shown further apart. A hypothetical example of such a map is given in Figure 10.4.

We can, however, follow the same logic but reverse the roles of nodes and ties, that is, use activities as units and calculate distances by calculating the number of enterprises that participate in any *pair* of activities.[20] A hypothetical example of such a mapping is shown in Figure 10.5.

Here activities *A* and *B* are plotted at the same point because all enterprises hypothetically involved in *A* (men's clothing manufacturing) are also involved in *B* (women's clothing manufacturing). Note that activities *C* (fabric glove manufacturing) and *D* (fur goods industry) appear close to this point but do not fully coincide with it because only some enterprises involved in *A* and *B* are also involved in *C* and *D* – and no enterprise involved in *C* is also involved in *D*.

This mapping comes closer to representing what we understand as a "market location," that is, a point of confluence in the production process, but it fails in three important respects. First, although it represents production locations on the basis of similarities in the activity profiles of *different* enterprises, it ignores joint activities that exclusively take place between units *within* them. Since interfaces may be bridged within as well as between enterprises, paired or combined activities that only occur within multifirm enterprises must also be taken into consideration. Second, although Figure 10.5 illustrates similarties on the sellers' side, it ignores the buyers' side entirely. Ideally, both sides of an interface ought to be taken into account. Finally, this mapping accepts whatever artificial distinctions have been introduced through the coding of the industrial activities of enterprises. A more robust method of depicting interfaces would try to offset these effects.

These problems in representing market structure can be overcome by (a) utilizing a measure of similarity that includes within- as well as between-enterprise overlaps, and (b) clustering together only those productive activities that are homogeneous on the buyer's as well as seller's side, that is, if their downstream effects are the same. This can best be accomplished in two stages. In the first, one maps all industrial activities into a matrix whose rows and columns correspond to SIC areas. Cells reflect the number of pairwise combinations that occur within enterprises.

In our study of the Canadian economy, for instance, we found 47 pairwise overlaps between SIC 286 (commercial printing) and SIC 288 (publishing, not printing). This suggests that an appreciable number of Canadian enterprises involved in commercial printing in 1972 also engaged in publishing. We also noted that there were 41 and 44 pairwise overlaps, respectively, between SICs 286 and 288 and SIC 289 (publishing *and* printing). Therefore, at least some enterprises containing firms exclusively engaged in printing or publishing also contained firms engaged in both. Figure 10.6 represents these data in the form of a set diagram.

Such patterns of overlapping, if they meet some previously established criterion, indicate that the activities designated by separate SIC codes occur at the same location in the production process and, therefore, ought to be grouped together *if* they also meet the homogeneity criterion. The second step is summarized in Table 10.2: (a) the same activities in the Royal Commission study were next grouped together into larger units (supernodes) on the basis

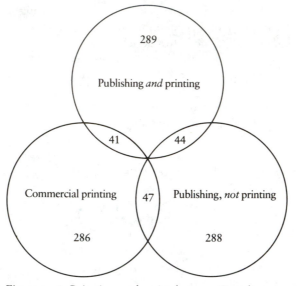

Figure 10.6. Pairwise overlapping between Canadian commercial printing, publishing, and printing *and* publishing SICs in 1972.

of proportionate overlaps in their joint occurrences within enterprises; and (b) the SICs with radically different downstream shipments, that is, those shipping a large proportion of their goods to buyers in SICs different from those of the core group, were eliminated. Note, for instance, that although SICs 376, 378, and 379 (soap and cleaning compounds, industrial chemicals manufacturing, and miscellaneous chemical industries) overlap to a consider- able extent in our data, they are *not* grouped together here because their downstream effects are so different; that is, they deal with different buyers, trade into both producers' and final consumption markets, and so on. Also note that although SIC 064 (crude petroleum production) overlapped appreciably with SICs 365 (petroleum refineries), 378 (industrial chemicals), 502 (services incidental to air transport), 507 (truck transport), and 515 (pipeline transport), only SICs 365 and 369 have effects that are sufficiently homogeneous to allow us to group them together.

We refer to these groups of industrial activities ordered together on the basis of their structurally equivalent or structurally similar locations within the production process as "*market-areas.*"[21] In practice, the SICs included within market areas are similar to those falling into some conventional industrial sectors, except in two key respects. First, market areas are homogeneous in the sense that all producers on the seller's side confront the same buyers – or at least buyers within the same SIC. This is important

Table 10.2. *Definitions of market-areas*

2 [a]Logging
031[b]

3 Metal mines (excluding gold quartz mines)
053, 054, 055, 056, 057, 058, 059

4 Gold quartz mines
052

5 Meat and dairy products
101, 103, 105, 107

6 Fish products, fruit, and vegetable canners
111, 112

7 Feed, flour, and bakery, products
123, 124, 128, 129

8 Miscellaneous food processors
131, 133, 139

9 Beverage manufacturing
141, 143, 145, 147

10 Rubber industries
163, 169

11 Textiles and knitting mills
212, 213, 218, 219, 229, 231, 239

12 Clothing industries
243, 244, 245

13 Wood industries
252, 254, 256, 259

14 Sawmills
251

15 Furniture industries
261, 264, 266

16 Pulp and paper mills
271

17 Paper box and bag manufacturing
273

18 Miscellaneous paper converters
274

19 Printing and publishing
286, 288, 289

20 Primary iron and steel industries
291, 292, 294, 295

21 Miscellaneous primary metal industries
296, 297, 298

22 Metal fabricating
301, 302, 303, 304, 305

23 Miscellaneous metal fabricating
309

24 Miscellaneous machinery and equipment manufacturing
315

25 Automobile, truck, and parts manufacturing
323, 324, 325

26 Aircraft and parts manufacturing
321

27 Shipbuilding and repair
327

28 Appliance, radio, and TV manufacturing
331, 332, 334

29 Communications equipment manufacturing
335

30 Nonmetallic mineral products
351, 352, 354, 355

31 Petroleum and coal products
365, 369

32 Mixed fertilizers manufacturing
372

33 Paint and varnish manufacturing
375

34 Industrial chemicals manufacturing
378

35 Miscellaneous chemicals industries
379

36 Sporting goods and toy manufacturing
393

[a]Market-area number.
[b]Standard Industrial Classification code number.

because, if we are to use the usual econometric tools in interpreting industrial organization data, they should be organized in such a way that they conform, as much as possible, to the assumptions on which these tools are based.[22] Second, since market-areas are defined in terms of common locations within a production chain and sectors are not, the fit between the two is greatest where sectors include both highly substitutable and vertically related activities. Market-area definitions are transaction-based. Thus, they only approximate sectoral designations where, for a variety of reasons, the core activities in sectors reflect transactions taking place around a particular interface or set of interfaces.

Definitions of market-areas can be augmented in various ways for particular purposes. For instance, given the extremely large entries in the columns corresponding to the 700 series in our Canadian data (financial and business service SICs), portions of this sector heavily tied to core activities were also defined as falling within industrial market areas – even though 700 series activities did not involve production in the normal sense of the term (Carrington, 1981).[23] This procedure reflected the idea that market definitions ought to embody *all* the activities involved in bridging a given interface – and financing or facilitating the financing of transactions is one of the most important of these.

Different methods of measuring or clustering joint activities will, of course, yield somewhat different market-area arrays. The procedures used in generating boundary definitions for the Canadian study, for instance, were sensitive to ties in receiving (column) as well as sending (row) SICs and, thus, were able to detect ties between downstream SICs in the petroleum product industries even though there were no direct connections between them. Since branching can occur at any point in a production chain, it is obviously important that the algorithms used in detecting joint activities in producers' markets be able to do this. However, researchers examining other kinds of issues can use different clustering techniques where these are more consistent with other theoretical concerns and problems.[24]

This flexibility in designating the SICs – and hence firms – involved in particular production locations is both the chief strength and principal source of difficulty in the use of transaction-based measures of market activity. Given the wide variety of clustering methods currently available, it is possible to define market-areas in such a way that the criteria one uses will closely reflect the particular conditions of specific market locations and industries, that is, to "fine-tune" clustering techniques to meet the special conditions present in one part of a production chain. At the same time, to be consistent, criteria used to designate one market location must be applied to all parts of a system. Thus, there is an inherent tension between methods that most accurately portray the conditions faced by buyers and sellers whose activities are concentrated around one particular interface and the kind of techniques that are more appropriate for modeling the circumstances faced by actors operating at several discrete locations in the production chain.

Extensions

Apart from its theoretical consequences, this dual aspect of markets – that they are, at once, highly local and specific for one set of producers and highly global and general for others – has important practical implications for the ways in which we look at any economy. Since, by definition,[25] single-firm enterprises can fall into only one SIC, the global structure and content of market-areas within a given system is largely determined by the mix of activities in which its multifirm enterprises typically engage.[26] This is not an artifact: *Any* study of market domains utilizing transaction-based measures must come to the same general conclusion. In effect, whenever a multifirm enterprise contains two firms involved in activities with structurally similar downstream effects, we are justified in assuming that a decision has been made to create a division of labor in production around a particular market location. Whenever enterprises contain pairs of firms both sending (selling) and receiving (buying) the same goods, we can infer that the enterprises involved have decided to bridge these transactions internally. Hence, it is interesting to note, apart from any specific empirical findings, that the most salient aspects of market structures in advanced capitalist economies will tend to be an outgrowth of particular combinations of multifirm enterprise activities, since these will necessarily reflect deliberate attempts to span the markets within which single-firm enterprises operate.

Despite the fact that considerable attention has been paid to these kinds of spanning relations in other contexts, few systematic attempts have been made to use set–subset or overlapping relationships among domains as a basis for the creation of global measures of market structure. Given current operationalizations of the notion of a market-area, however, several indices of structural change can be derived in a straightforward fashion.

Consider, for instance, a series of directed graphs in which nodes represent market locations – each acting as a focus for production by sets of enterprises – and ties depict shipments of goods between them. Each path (distinct sequence of steps) through each of these graphs corresponds to a "production chain." In Figure 10.7, for instance, path *A-B* represents a flow of goods from "sellers" at market location *A* to "buyers" clustered around *B*.

This representation is quite general and may be applied to markets of varying degrees of complexity. Classic forms of market relationships can then be represented in a straightforward fashion. A monopoly, for instance, can be depicted as in Figure 10.8. Figures 10.9 and 10.10 extend this to monopsony (monopoly on the demand side) and duopoly.

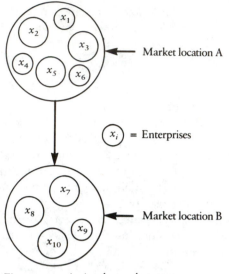

Figure 10.7. A simple market-area.

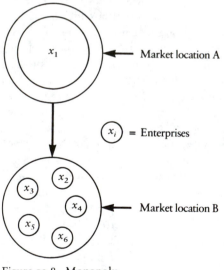

Figure 10.8. Monopoly.

Note here that the only imposed limits on this modeling technique have to do with (a) the number of distinct participants associated with a given market location and (b) the number of locations to be mapped. If we are unable to establish the boundaries between collective actors (in this case, enterprises) or locales, this mapping would reduce to a simpler form.

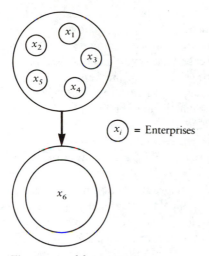

Figure 10.9. Monopsony.

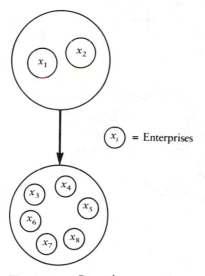

Figure 10.10. Duopoly.

Given this mapping – and given a conventional set of network modeling tools – it then becomes possible to describe market structure in much the same way that one might describe a friendship group or the structure of citations among scientists. One can, for instance, calculate *overlaps* – or points of convergence – within production chains. This is useful in determining such things as "bottlenecks" in the transactional structure of an economy. *Centrality* measures can be calculated on graphs showing extended (more than one step) production paths and from these we can identify points of high integration between market-areas. The simple *indegree and outdegree* at a given market location can be used as a measure of the intensity of transactions at that point (Freeman, 1977, 1979). *Reachability* can be interpreted as a measure of the social distance between market locations, that is, the directness of the interdependence between transfer points. In sum, mapping market locations – and the relations between them – in this fashion allows us to reduce the problem of describing market organization to ones we have encountered in the past.

Structural analysts have only just begun making use of network tools to look at markets in this way, but some of the results to date have been striking. Carrington (1981a, b), for instance, used the 1972 market-area mappings shown here to examine the effects of interlocking director–officerships on conventional measures of corporate concentration and profits. He hypothesizes that director–officership ties "are one method by which enterprises co-opt one another, or co-ordinate their actions, in oligopolistic markets. [Hence] operationally, the degree of interlocking is hypothesized to explain part of the association between concentration and profits" (Carrington, 1981a: 180–1). He models these relationships in terms of a series of path equations[27] that stipulate that interlocking among the core enterprises within a market-area has a residual effect on profits over and above that of interlocking in general and that, consequently, as overall interlocking increases, profits increase. But as the size of central market-area cliques increases – and, hence, coordination becomes more problematic – interlocking and profits decrease.

Carrington tests these hypotheses using two different measures of concentration and examines differential associations in market-areas where vertical, horizontal, or bank-related interlocking predominate. He concludes that "interlocking does indeed explain a considerable amount of the effect of concentration on profit margins":

> In the 22 market-areas where directly and indirectly horizontal ties exist between enterprises, these kinds of ties explain one-third to one-half of the relationship between concentration and profit margins. ... Over all 30 market-areas, directly and indirectly horizontal interlocks alone account for only about one-quarter of the relationship between concentration and profits. However, when directly horizontal interlocks are combined with bank ties with firms in the market-area, the relationship between concentration and profit margins is *entirely explained*.   (Carrington, 1981a: 205–6)

Apart from their larger theoretical and methodoligical implications, the sheer magnitude of these results is striking in an area of research where explained variance of .04 to .09 is common (Waverman and Baldwin, 1975). Three factors appear to contribute to the strength of Carrington's associations. First, his units of analysis are enterprises, not firms. This is especially important since there seems to be a marked tendency toward separate incorporation of operating subsidiaries in Canada (Berkowitz, Kotowitz, Carrington, and Waverman, 1978–9). Second, Carrington has used market-areas, rather than SICs or sectors, as domains for bounding market activity. This has reduced the within-variance among his economic domains and has thus enabled him to predict the consequences of actor's market conduct more precisely. Finally, his measure of "interlocking" – graph density[28] – is more appropriate under the circumstances than simple numbers of ties. Most earlier studies of this kind were based on grosser hypotheses and, thus, did not recognize the theoretical importance of systemic, rather than local, measures of interlocking (Clement, 1975, 1977; Waverman and Baldwin, 1975; Berkowitz, 1980).

A variety of extensions of these basic ideas are possible. In a study completed for the Canadian Royal Commission on Economic Union and Development Prospects for Canada, for instance, Berkowitz et al. (1985) demonstrate ways in which dynamic changes in the definition of market-areas can be used to identify shifts in the organization of production within an economy over time. They accomplish this, in the first instance, by generating a market-area array at time t_1. This is then used to modify an input–output table for the economy by grouping market locations together. Values for shipments are then aggregated. A second input–output table is then generated by using the structure implicit in the first. Values at t_2 are then compared to the first, and differences calculated. The results can be used as a measure of commodity flows from t_1 to t_2. Actual changes in market-area arrays could have been obtained to look at structural changes in market locations, themselves. Work of this kind is currently under way.

Implications

Recent structuralist studies have greatly extended our ability to represent and interpret the intricate patterns of interconnection between corporations typical of advanced capitalist systems. Most research to date, however, has focused on the overall *morphology*, or form, taken by these systems as opposed to either (a) the observable economic *behavior* of their constituent parts, or (b) their explicit *structure*, that is, the way in which transactions between or among economic actors are constrained by systemic organization. Consequently, with rare exceptions, the results reported in studies of corporate interconnection, although useful and interesting in their own right, cannot be directly juxtaposed to expectations derived from explicit and detailed models of economic activity.

Moreover, although this emphasis on morphology is quite understandable given the sheer complexity of the patterns of ties among even highly restricted samples of corporations (Levine, 1972; Carroll, Fox, and Ornstein, 1982; Mokken, 1978), there has been an observable gap in these studies between the theoretical concerns that led to structuralist work on corporate structure in the first place and the kinds of rigorous conclusions that researchers have been able to draw from them, given the nature of their data and the broad-gauged approach they have adopted.[29] Researchers have assumed, for instance, that ties between firms or enterprises generate anticompetitive effects; that is, they lead to the establishment of "tacit agreements" to restrict economic competiton. But "competition" in terms of what? Morphological studies of corporate structure seldom, if ever, utilize data either about the industries or sectors within which firms or enterprises operate, or about transactions or flows of resources between them. The concept of an anticompetitive effect, therefore, is without context since there is no meaningful way to measure it: There is an important difference between showing that ties – or even a pattern of ties – exists between sets of corporations and demonstrating that these have some palpable effect on the behavior of economic actors. This is why, in our view, it is important to develop models that bring notions of system morphology together with behavioral contexts within which its impact can be shown. Hence our emphasis here on market-areas.

Unfortunately, the current literature contains only the barest beginnings of a structural theory of market behavior. Granovetter's 1974 pioneering research on job information networks lays the groundwork for assessing the strategic choices of actors within one type of market structure. Boorman's (1975: 220–7) formalization of this work clarifies its implications and allows it to be extended to a range of similarly structured N-person games, but only in the case of one-stage information transfers with qualitatively distinct kinds of inputs, that is, "strong ties" and "weak ties." The interpretive range of existing models is thus highly circumscribed (Kaplan, 1964: 274–5). Although seminal in many ways, for instance, Boorman's work – or extensions of it by Delany (see Chapter 16) – cannot be directly or easily generalized to those complex exchanges within advanced capitalist economies in which corporate researchers are primarily interested. The morphological studies already undertaken by some analysts (Levine, 1972; Bearden, Atwood, Freitag, Hendricks, Mintz, and Schwartz, 1975; Berkowitz, Kotowitz, Waverman, et al., 1976; Carroll, et al., 1977; Mokken and Stokman, 1978; Richardson, 1982; Mintz and Schwartz, 1985) provide a basis for doing this, but the detailed formal modeling simply has not been done.

What is really needed, of course, is some general method for specifying and elaborating the structural constraints under which market behavior occurs. Here, once again, despite highly suggestive theoretical beginnings (White, 1976, Chapter 9) and some important testing of empirical generalizations about linkages among different types of market participants (Burt, 1979, 1983; Carrington, 1981a, b), the work is still in its infancy.

Two important streams of structuralist research – on corporate systems and on market behavior – have emerged in the past decade. They have not been forced to converge, however, and it would require, in the first instance, more detailed attention to substantive economic problems and issues for this confluence to occur. White's studies of competition under conditions of monopoly or oligopoly, reported in detail in Chapter 9, provide an impressive formal framework for examining interactions among market participants under these conditions. White has been able to accomplish this because of his success in specifying a theoretically germane context in which his results can be tested for consistency. More work in specifying specific contexts for interaction – that is, in our terms, different types of market-area structures – must be done before his impressive formal results can be generalized to them.

Conclusion: Market-areas and economic structures

Changes in the organization of advanced industrial economies during the past several decades have forced social scientists to begin examining the roles played by larger-than-firm groupings – or enterprises – within economic structures. Although recent technical developments have now made it possible to define these groupings more or less rigorously, industrial organization economists have not followed through on many of the theoretical and methodological implications of this change in focus or perspective.

The most important of these has been the need to develop a view of the domains within which market transactions take place that is consistent with the use of *collective corporate actors* – ones that have the potential for operating within several market locations simultaneously – as decision-making units. We have examined one solution to this problem: an operationalization of the concept of markets-areas based on groupings of market domains within which structurally similar sellers engage in transactions with like buyers. Although only one of several such possible solutions to the market-boundary problem, this approach enables analysts to begin reformulating the notion of market structure in such a way that it becomes possible to experiment with a variety of measures and techniques for representing change in them.

Research, such as Carrington's, that explicitly uses structural analytic tools to increase the congruence between units and the conventional measures designed to interpret them clearly has important immediate implications for the formulation of economic theory. Although, for instance, neoclassical theory suggests that there ought to be a strong and unequivocal relationship between the simple number of core participants with a market domain and profit margins – since fewer participants will tend to lead to higher concentrations of economic power – there has been little direct empirical evidence of this. Carrington has shown that, in market-areas where there are dense linkages between participants, anticompetitive effects are enhanced and, hence, there are stronger relationships of the kind economic theorists anticipate. This is especially true, Carrington has discovered, where conventional horizontal linkages are supplemented by other nonmarket ties made indirectly through banks.

Further research in which structural indices, themselves, are used as principal explanatory variables is likely to yield similarly interesting results. Centrality, density, and other systemic measures[30] have proved to be extremely useful in illuminating otherwise intractable aspects of other forms of social organization. There is no reason, in principle, why they should not prove as useful as measures of economic structure. Moreover, if the results derived from the application of these indices to markets are consistent with those from other contexts, extrapolations to other theoretically germane substantive problems should be quite straightforward. Market-areas that are highly "central" according to some version of the Mintz-Schwartz (1985) measure, for instance, should probably come under special scrutiny when an attempt is being made to assess the impact of taxes or tariffs. Market-areas with low "betweenness" are likely to be much more easily affected by economic change than those with low scores on this measure. Enterprises in market-areas in which participants are densely connected are more likely to respond to changes in fiscal policy in predictable and collective ways than those in which participants are not.

Although it is difficult to gauge how particular market structure indices might be applied without direct empirical trials, recent work by Burt (1983) suggests that we can construct measures of the constraints that different sectors exercise on one another's profits. If similar techniques can be used in analyzing market-areas, it might be possible to identify the interdependencies between market locations in a more explicit and detailed way.

Various operationalizations of the concept of market-areas, in general, have strong implications for how we might go about identifying the most dynamic portions of an economy. Ceteris paribus, market-areas that are growing – that is, incorporating new SICs, increasing the value of their shipments, and generating greater downstream effects – are likely to occur around market locations where corporate actors perceive advantages to internalizing transfers. Theoretically, this should happen where resort to contract is most problematic or where internal organizational costs are minimal. Growth in a market-area, then, can be either positive or negative: positive in that it reflects more efficient productive arrangements, or negative in that it arises out of attempts to minimize losses due to chaotic market conditions. Structural analytic indices can thus be used to identify high-growth areas, and more traditional methods can then be employed in differentiating these conditions.

Beyond this, something like the longitudinal analysis of shipment values we alluded to earlier can clearly be used to identify market-areas in which shifts in technology or organization are likely to have long-term consequences for the economy. Given successive market-area arrays based on recalculations of enterprise boundaries – or given arrays generated using slightly different algorithms – it should be possible (a) to predict those new market-areas that are likely to emerge as a result of market failure or decreased internal organizational costs; (b) to specify interfaces that are being reconstituted owing to shifts in technology or terms of trade; and (c) given sufficient detail in data regarding assignments of establishments and firms to SICs and sufficient disaggregation in corresponding input–output tables, to identify instances in which current classifications obscure important features of the economy in general.

In broad perspective, then, although the changes that have led to a greater role for larger-than-firm groupings in post–World War II economies have made it difficult to assess certain kinds of events and trends, they have also opened up new possibilities for analysis. Given the state of the art, many of the techniques that are being developed to exploit these possibilities should be treated with caution. Some, because of the nature of the calculations involved, are perhaps best implemented by central statistical bureaus. Others can only be developed in concert with more intensive theoretical model-building.

In the final analysis, these developments necessitate a great deal of practical empirical research into the global dynamics of economic structures. Structural analysts have already made important contributions to this task. But a more general notion as to how participants' market conduct is limited or constrained by the systemic contexts in which they operate is needed before we can enjoy the full fruits of their labors to this point.

Appendix

1970 Three-digit SICs

011: Livestock and livestock combination farms
013: Field and field crop combination farms

015: Fruit and vegetable farms
017: Other crop and livestock combination farms
019: Miscellaneous specialty farms
031: Logging
051: Placer gold mines
052: Gold quartz mines
053, 054, 055, 056: Metal mines (excluding gold quartz mines, etc.)
057: Uranium mines
058: Iron mines
059: Miscellaneous metal mines
061: Coal mines
064: Crude petroleum and natural gas industry
071: Asbestos mines
072: Peat extraction
073: Gypsum mines
079: Miscellaneous nonmetal mines
083: Stone quarries
087: Sand pits or quarries
096: Contract drilling for petroleum
098: Other contract drilling
099: Miscellaneous services incidental to mining
101: Meat and poultry products industries
102: Fish products industry
103: Fruit and vegetable processing industries
104: Dairy products industry
105: Flour and breakfast cereal products industry
106: Feed industry
107: Bakery products industries
108: Miscellaneous food industries
109: Beverage industries
109: Wine, spirits manufacturing
151: Leaf tobacco processors
153: Tobacco products manufacturing
162: Rubber products industries
165: Plastics fabricating industry
172: Leather tanneries
174: Shoe factories
175: Leather gloves factories
179: Luggage, handbags, and small leather goods manufacturing
181: Cotton yarn and cloth mills
182: Wool yarn and cloth mills
183: Man-made fiber, yarn, and cloth mills
184: Cordage and twine industry

185: Felt and fiber-processing mills
186: Carpet, mat, and rug industry
187: Canvas products and cotton and jute bags industries
188: Automobile fabric accessories industries
189: Miscellaneous textile industries
231: Hosiery mills
239: Knitting mills (excluding hosiery)
243: Men's clothing industries
244: Women's clothing industries
245: Children's clothing industry
246: Fur goods industry
248: Foundation garment industry
249: Miscellaneous clothing industries
251: Sawmills, planing mills, and shingle mills
252: Veneer and plywood mills
254: Sash, door, and other millwork plants
256: Wooden box factories
258: Coffin and casket industry
259: Miscellaneous wood industries
261: Household furniture manufacturing
264: Office furniture manufacturing
266: Miscellaneous furniture and fixtures manufacturing
268: Electric lamp and shade manufacturing
271: Pulp and paper mills
272: Asphalt roofing manufacturing
273: Paper box and bag manufacturing
274: Miscellaneous paper converters
286: Commercial printing
287: Platemaking, typesetting, and trade bindery industry
288: Publishing only
289: Publishing and printing
291: Iron and steel mills
292: Steel pipe and tube mills
294: Iron foundries
295: Smelting and refining
296: Aluminum rolling, casting, and extruding
298: Metal rolling, casting, and extruding (excluding aluminum)
301: Boilerplate works
302: Fabricating structural metal industry
303: Ornamental and architectural metal industry
304: Metal stamping, pressing, and coating industry
305: Wire and wire products manufacturing
306: Hardware, tool, and cutlery manufacturing

307: Heating equipment manufacturing
308: Machine shops
309: Miscellaneous metal fabricating industry
311: Agricultural implement industry
315: Miscellaneous machinery and equipment manufacturing
316: Commercial refrigeration and air conditioning equipment manufacturing
318: Office and store machinery manufacturing
321: Aircraft and aircraft parts manufacturing
323: Motor vehicle manufacturing
324: Truck body and trailer manufacturing
325: Motor vehicle parts and accessories manufacturing
326: Railroad rolling stock industry
327: Shipbuilding and repair
328: Boat building and repair
329: Miscellaneous vehicle manufacturing
331: Manufacturing of small electrical appliances
332: Manufacturing of major appliances
333: Manufacturing of lighting fixtures
334: Manufacturing of household radio and TV receivers
335: Commercial equipment manufacturing
336: Manufacturing of electrical industrial equipment
338: Manufacturing of electric wire and cable
339: Manufacturing of miscellaneous electrical products
351: Clay products manufacturing
352: Cement manufacturing
353: Stone products manufactuirng
354: Concrete products manufacturing
355: Ready-mix concrete manufacturing
356: Glass and glass products manufacturing
357: Abrasives manufacturing
358: Lime manufacturing
359: Miscellaneous nonmetallic mineral products industries
365: Petroleum refineries
369: Miscellaneous petroleum and coal products industries
372: Manufacturing of mixed fertilizers
373: Manufacturing of plastics and synthetic resins
374: Manufacturing of pharmaceuticals and medicines
375: Paint and varnish manufacturing
376: Manufacturing of soap and cleaning compounds
377: Manufacturing of toilet preparations
378: Manufacturing of industrial chemicals
379: Miscellaneous chemical industries
391: Scientific and professional equipment industries

392: Jewelry and silverware industry
393: Sporting goods and toy industries
397: Signs and display industry
399: Miscellaneous manufacturing industries not otherwise specified
404: Building construction
406: Highway, bridge, and street construction
409: Other construction
421: Special-trade contractors
501: Air transport
502: Services incidental to air transport
503: Railway transport
504: Water transport
505: Services incidental to water transport
506: Moving and storage
507: Other truck transport
508: Bus transport, interurban and rural
509: Urban transit systems
512: Taxicab operations
515: Pipeline transport
516: Highway and bridge maintenance
517: Miscellaneous services incidental to transport
524: Grain elevators
527: Miscellaneous storage and warehousing
543: Radio and TV broadcasting
544: Telephone systems
545: Telegraph and cable systems
572: Electric power
574: Gas utilities
576: Water systems
579: Other utilities
602: Wholesalers of farm products
606: Wholesalers of coal and coke
608: Wholesalers of petroleum products
611: Wholesalers of paper and paper products
612: Wholesalers of general merchandise
614: Wholesalers of food
615: Wholesalers of tobacco products
616: Wholesalers of drug and toilet preparations
617: Wholesalers of clothing and drygoods
618: Wholesalers of household furniture and furnishings
619: Wholesalers of motor vehicles and accessories
621: Wholesalers of electrical machinery equipment and supplies
622: Wholesalers of farm machinery and equipment
623: Wholesalers of miscellaneous equipment and machinery

624: Wholesalers of hardware plumbing and heating equipment
625: Wholesalers of miscellaneous metal and metal products
626: Wholesalers of lumber and building materials
629: Wholesalers not otherwise specified
631: Food stores
642: Department stores
652: Tire, battery, and accessory shops
654: Gasoline service stations
656: Motor vehicle dealers
658: Motor vehicle repair shops
663: Shoe stores
665: Men's clothing stores
667: Women's clothing stores
669: Other clothing and dry goods stores
676: Household furniture and appliance stores
678: Radio, TV, and electrical appliance repair shops
681: Drugstores
691: Book and stationery stores
692: Florists' shops
694: Jewelry stores
695: Watch and jewelry repair shops
696: Liquor, wine, and beer stores
697: Tobacconists
699: Miscellaneous retail stores
712: Chartered banks*,[31]
714: Trust companies*
715: Mortgage and loan companies*
723, 725: Sales finance and consumer loan companies*
741: Securities brokers*
751, 752: Mutual funds*
769: Miscellaneous financial agencies*
771: Life insurance carriers*
781: Insurance and real estate agencies*

Market-areas and their corresponding SICs

Market-area: 1970 SICs; 1980 SICs[32]

(2) Logging: 031; 0311, 0319.
(3) Metal mines excluding gold quartz: 053–059, 0580, 0591, 0592, 0593, 0594, 0599
(4) Gold quartz mines: 052; 0520
(5) Meat and dairy products: 101, 103, 105, 107; 1011, 1012, 1040
(6) Fish products, fruit and vegetable Canners: 111, 112; 1020, 1031, 1032

(7) Feed, flour, and bakery products: 123, 124, 128, 129; 1050, 1060, 1071, 1072

(8) Miscellaneous food processors: 131, 133, 139; 1081, 1083, 1089

(9) Beverage manufacturing: 141, 143, 145, 147; 1091, 1092, 1093, 1094

(10) Rubber and allied industries: 163, 169; 1620

(11) Textiles and knitting mills: 212, 213, 218, 219, 231, 239

(12) Clothing industries: 243, 244, 245; 2431, 2432, 2441, 2442, 2450

(13) Wood industries: 252, 254, 256, 259; 2520, 2541, 2542, 2543, 2544, 2560, 2591, 2592, 2593, 2599

(14) Sawmills: 251; 2511, 2513

(15) Furniture industries: 261, 264, 266; 2611, 2619, 2640, 2660

(16) Pulp and paper mills: 271; 2710

(17) Paper box and bag manufacturing: 273; 2731–2733

(18) Miscellaneous paper converters: 274; 2740

(19) Printing and publishing: 286, 288, 289; 2860, 2880, 2890

(20) Primary iron and steel industries: 291, 292, 294, 295; 2910, 2920, 2940, 2950

(21) Miscellaneous primary metal industries: 296, 297, 298; 2960, 2970, 2980

(22) Metal fabricating: 301–305; 3010, 3020, 3031, 3039, 3041, 3042, 3050

(23) Miscellaneous metal fabricating: 309; 3090

(24) Miscellaneous machinery and equipment manufacturing: 315; 3150

(25) Automobile, truck, and parts manufacturing: 323–325; 3230, 3241, 3242, 3243, 3250

(26) Aircraft and parts manufacturing: 321; 3210

(27) Shipbuilding and repair: 327; 3270

(28) Appliance, radio, and TV manufacturing: 331, 332, 334; 3310, 3320, 3340

(29) Communications equipment manufacturing: 335; 3350

(30) Nonmetallic mineral products: 351, 352, 354, 355; 3511, 3512, 3520, 3591, 3599

(31) Petroleum and coal products: 265, 369; 3651, 3652, 3690

(32) Mixed fertilizers manufacturing: 372; 3720

(33) Paint and varnish manufacturing: 375; 3750

(34) Industrial chemicals: 378; 3781–3783

(35) Miscellaneous chemicals industries: 379; 3791, 3799

(36) Sporting goods and toy manufacturing: 393, 3931, 3932

NOTES

1. This use of the term follows that in Berkowitz, Kotowitz, and Waverman et al. (1976) and Berkowitz, Carrington, Kotowitz, and Waverman (1978–9). Thus, an

"establishment" is, in these terms, a single productive unit; a "firm" a collection of assets held in a common name; and an "enterprise" a group of firms operating under common control. This typology extends and clarifies the definitions and operationalizations in the traditional industrial organization literature. See the discussion of these terms later in the chapter.

2. See Berkowitz (1982), Burt (1978–9, 1979), Fennema and Schijf (1978–9), Carroll et al. (1982), Ornstein (1980, 1982).

3. The discussion in this paper draws on earlier work reported in Berkowitz, Kotowitz, and Waverman et al. (1976), Berkowitz, Carrington, Kotowitz, and Waverman (1978–9), Carrington (1981a), and Berkowitz et al. (1985).

4. Dominion Bureau of Statistics (1970); U.S. Office of Management and Budget (1972).

5. Sherman's statement on the subject is indicative: "So although to a degree industrial organization can claim respectable theoretical origins, the subject matter does not rest firmly on a broad theory. All empirical efforts have not used theory; empirical work frequently was undertaken to pursue in measurable terms relationships thought to be important because of previous observations, or due to some perceived social problem or great public policy concern. In the USA, where I think it is fair to say this empirical work in industrial organization started, two forces can be seen posing problems and issues. One is a traditional academic one, where implications from the body of economic theory, largely deterministic neoclassical theory, were to be tested. The other is the world of affairs where public disputes simply had to be settled, disputes such as whether the Alcoa aluminum company was a monopoly in violation of antitrust law, whether the marketing of milk was to be regulated, or more recently whether government certification of safety is to be required and if so whether to stop with food and drugs, rotary lawnmowers, toilet seats, or whatever" (Sherman, 1977: 3).

6. "By an enterprise we refer ... to a privately owned business *firm* ... which engages in productive activity of any sort with the opportunity of making a profit. Enterprises defined thus include private firms engaged in manufacturing, wholesale and retail trade, supplying gas and electricity, construction, banking, and so forth" (Bain, 1959: 5; emphasis mine).

7. By using "firms" as units of analysis, researchers implicitly accept whatever variability in form lawyers and their clients have wished to introduce through the mechanism of incorporation. This is a serious error since there is no empirical evidence to support the belief that most officers and directors principally see given corporations as anything other than vehicles through which decisions may be carried out. In much of the theoretical literature in economics the term "firm" is used as a surrogate for the notion of some kind of decision-making unit. This usage poses no real difficulties here as a long as one bears in mind – as many economists do not – that these theoretical "firms" have little if anything to do with the ones we can observe in the real world.

8. Some analysts draw a sharp distinction between "portfolio" and "direct investment" capital. For an elaboration of the issues involved, see Park and Park (1962).

9. For a description of this procedure in mathematical and algorithmic form, see Berkowitz, Carrington, Kotowitz, and Waverman (1978–9).

10. The technical procedures proposed by Berkowitz, Kotowitz, Waverman, et al. (1978–9) are sufficiently general to allow them to do this, moreover, with all ownership patterns that can be represented as acyclic directed graphs.

11. For the general interpretation of randomness in graphs and its application in this instance, see Berkowitz, Carrington, Kotowitz, and Waverman (1978–9: 401).

12. If the criterion of majority ownership or 15% ownership plus three directorship ties was applied blindly to the data – and no tie that failed to meet this criterion was allowed – then one would be faced with situations in which one accepted ties that barely met this criterion, but rejected ones in which a substantial proportion of majority ownership, say 45%, was involved, but only two directorship ties linked the firms in question. By, in effect, reckoning directorship ties as a surrogate for ownership, this type of anomaly can be avoided.

13. Since Caves is concerned with multinational enterprises, he stipulates that these two establishments must be located in two different countries. See Caves (1982: 1).

14. In this sense, the transaction cost approach ought to be thought of, at present, as more of an analytic strategy than a fully developed framework.

15. See Boorman (1975), Granovetter (1974), Friedman (1976, 1978), White (1981a, b).

16. See White (1976) for a description of the implications of this.

17. Note here that enterprises are said to focus around structurally equivalent or structurally similar locations. Two nodes are deemed to be structurally equivalent in the roles they play if they are connected to others in the same or equivalent ways. Nodes are said to be structurally similar if they are connected to others in similar ways. Obviously, the way in which one defines equivalent or similar is critical to how one operationalizes these concepts. Here we designate locations as structurally equivalent or similar in terms of (a) their common ties and (b) their downstream connections. This is somewhat different from, but consistent with, the ways in which it is often done in the literature. See Lorrain and White (1971), Arabie and Leavitt (1978), Sailer (1978), Berkowitz and Heil (1980), and Berkowitz (1982).

18. In mathematical terms, this would be their intersection.

19. The class of techniques for doing this is called "multidimensional scaling" or MDS. See Shepard, Romney, and Nerlove (1972).

20. This second network, in which the role of nodes and arcs is reversed, is referred to as the "dual" of the first. See Berkowitz (1982) for a discussion of the technical issues involved in the relationships between networks and their "duals." Also see Breiger (1974).

21. An Appendix provides a list of market areas and the corresponding SICs used in our study of Canadian economic structure.

22. The most important of these are that (a) units affecting choices are independent and (b) all such units have access to the bargaining process, i.e., sellers confront the same buyers and *vice versa*. When these conditions are not present, some sort of "special condition" must be stipulated, e.g., "imperfect information," "nonmarket barriers to entry," and so on.

23. Whether or not this is done, depends, of course, on the theoretical uses to which market-areas are being put. In some uses, financial enterprises tied to producers

have been assumed to fall within market areas. See Carrington (1981a).

24. The purpose of clustering is to discover sets of nodes that are relatively internally coherent and externally isolated (Davis, 1967). A clique is the form of a cluster in which all potential ties are made. This is too restrictive a type of structure to be useful for our purposes here (Glanzer and Glaser, 1959; Epstein, 1969; Mitchell, 1969). For a good general overview of clustering procedures, see Cartwright and Harary (1979). Shepard and Arabie (1979) propose a different approach to clustering than that conventionally used, which may well also have applications to the market-boundary problem.

25. For these purposes, firms are assigned to SICs on the basis of the area in which the majority of shipments by their establishments fall.

26. Single-firm enterprises play an indirect role in fixing the boundaries of market-areas since SICs engaged in transactions with radically different downstream SICs or into final consumption markets are excluded from producers' market-areas – and these may include market locations dominated by single-firm enterprises.

27. This term refers to a series of techniques for representing and testing causal relations among aggregate variables and should not be confused with the term "path" as it is used by graph theorists. See Wright (1960), Duncan (1966), and Blalock and Blalock (1968).

28. $D = 2A/N(N-1)$,
where D = density, N = the number of nodes, A = the actual ties made.

29. These difficulties in understanding corporate systems are, moreover, not wholly a consequence of either the purely technical problems involved, or even of the intractability of the empirical world. Structural models usually demand highly detailed information at the level of specific node-pairs (Berkowitz, 1982). However, detailed data about corporate transactions are often either not gathered or are treated as confidential where they exist.

30. See Berkowitz (1982), Burt (1982), and Burt and Minor (1983) for examples of applications of these.

31. Asterisks indicate interim classifications used by Statistics Canada at the time our 1972 data were compiled.

32. Numbering follows Carrington (1981a) to allow for comparison. Four-digit SICs are extensions of corresponding three-digit SICs.

LITERATURE CITED

Adams, J. D. R., and J. Whalley. *The International Taxation of Multinational Enterprises in Developed Countries.* Westport, Conn: Greenwood, 1977.

Aharoni, Y. *The Foreign Investment Decision Process.* Harvard University, Division of Research, Graduate School of Business Administration. Boston, 1966.

Arabie, P., S. A. Boorman, and P. R. Leavitt. "Constructing Blockmodels: How and Why." *Journal of Mathematical Psychology* 17 (1978): 21–63.

Arrow, K. J. "Vertical Integration and Communication." *Bell Journal of Economics* 6 (1975): 173–83.

Bain, J. S. *Industrial Organization.* New York: Wiley, 1959.

Baranson, J. "Technology Transfer through the International Firm." *American Economic Review* 60 (1970): 435–40.

"Technology Transfer: Effects on U.S. Competitiveness and Employment." In U.S. Department of Labor, *The Impact of International Trade and Investment on Employment*. Washington, D. C.: U.S. Government Printing Office, 1978.

Bearden, J., W. Atwood, P. Freitag, C. Hendricks, B. Mintz, and M. Schwartz. "The Nature and Extent of Bank Centrality in Corporate Networks." Paper presented at the annual meetings of the American Sociological Association, 1975.

Berkowitz, S. D. *The Dynamics of Elite Structure: A Critique of C. Wright Mills' "Power Elite" Model*. Ph.D. diss., Brandeis University, 1975.

"Structural and Non-Structural Models of Elites: A Critique." *Canadian Journal of Sociology* 5 (1980): 13–30.

An Introduction to Structural Analysis. Toronto: Buttersworth, 1982.

Berkowitz, S. D., P. J. Carrington, Y. Kotowitz and L. Waverman. "The Determination of Enterprise Groupings through Combined Ownership and Directorship Ties." *Social Networks* 1 (1978–9): 391–413.

Berkowitz, S. D., P. J. Carrington, J. Corman, and L. Waverman. "Flexible Design for a Large-Scale Corporate Data Base." *Social Networks* 2 (1979): 75–83.

Berkowitz, S. D., D. Costello, E. Nunez, S. Tron, and D. Wiesner. "Enterprise Activity and Market-Area Structure: A Technical Report to the Royal Commission on Economic Union and Development Prospects for Canada." Burlington, Vt.: Department of Sociology, University of Vermont, 1985.

Berkowitz, S. D., and Greg H. Heil. "Dualities in Methods of Social Network Research." University of Toronto, Structural Analysis Programme Working Paper 18 (rev.). Toronto, 1980.

Berkowitz, S. D., Y. Kotowitz, and L. Waverman. "A Design for a Large-Scale Data Analysis System for Corporate Information." University of Toronto, Institute for Policy Analysis. Toronto, 1977.

Berkowitz, S. D., Y. Kotowitz, and L. Waverman, with B. Becker, R. Bradford, P. J. Carrington, J. Corman, and G. Heil. *Enterprise Structure and Corporate Concentration*. Royal Commission on Corporate Concentration Technical Study 17. Ottawa: Supply and Services Canada, 1976.

Berle, A. A., and G. C. Means. *The Modern Corporation and Private Property*. New York: Harcourt Brace and World [1932] 1969.

Blalock, H. M., and Ann Blalock (eds.). *Methodology in Social Research*. New York: McGraw-Hill, 1968.

Boorman, Scott A. "A Combinatorial Optimization Model for Transmission of Job Information through Contact Networks." *Bell Journal of Economics*. 6 (1975): 216–49.

Booth, E. J. R., and O. W. Jensen. "Transfer Prices in the Global Corporation under Internal and External Constraints." *Canadian Journal of Economics*. 10 (1977): 434–6.

Breiger, R. L. "The Duality of Persons and Groups." *Social Forces* 53 (1974): 181–90.

Burns, J. O. "Transfer Pricing Decisions in U.S. Multinational Corporations." *Journal of International Business Studies* 11 (1980): 23–39.

Burt, R. S. "A Structural Theory of Interlocking Corporate Directorships." *Social Networks* 1 (1978–79): 415–35.

"Disaggregating the Effect on Profits in Manufacturing Industries of Having Imperfectly Competitive Consumers and Suppliers." *Social Science Research* 8 (1979): 120–43.

Toward a Structural Theory of Action: Network Models of Social Structure, Perception, and Action. New York: Academic Press, 1982.

Corporate Profits and Cooptation. New York: Academic Press, 1983.

Burt, R. S., and M. J. Minor (eds.). *Applied Network Analysis: A Methodological Introduction.* Beverly Hills, Calif.: Sage, 1983.

Canada, Government of. *Foreign Direct Investment in Canada* [Gray Report]. Ottawa: Information Canada, 1972.

Carrington, P. J. "Horizontal Co-optation through Corporate Interlocks." Ph.D. diss., University of Toronto, 1981a.

"Anticompetitive Effects of Directorship Interlocks." Paper read at the annual meeting of the Canadian Sociology and Anthropology Association, Halifax, 1981b.

Carroll, W., J. Fox, and M. Ornstein. "The Network of Directorate Interlocks among the Largest Canadian Firms." *Canadian Review of Sociology and Anthropology* 19 (1982): 44–69.

Cartwright, Dorwin, and Frank Harary. "Balance and Clusterability: An Overview." In Paul Holland and Samuel Leinhardt (eds.), *Perspectives on Social Network Research.* New York: Academic Press, 1979.

Caves, R. E. *American Industry: Structure, Conduct, Performance.* 4th ed. Englewood Cliffs, N. J.: Prentice-Hall, 1977.

Multinational Enterprise and Economic Analysis. Cambridge: Cambridge University Press, 1982.

Chamberlin, E. H. *The Theory of Monopolistic Competition.* Cambridge, Mass.: Harvard University Press, 1933.

Chase-Dunn, C. "The Effects of International Economic Dependence on Development and Inequality." *American Sociological Review* 40 (1975): 720–38.

Clement, Wallace. *The Canadian Corporate Elite.* Toronto: McClelland and Stewart, 1975.

Continental Corporate Power. Toronto: McClelland and Stewart, 1977.

Coase, Ronald H. "The Nature of the Firm." *Economica* 4 (1937): 386–405.

Commons, John R. *Institutional Economics.* Madison: University of Wisconsin Press, 1934.

Davis, James A. "Clustering and Balance Theory in Graphs." *Human Relations* 20 (1967): 181–7.

Department of Consumer and Corporate Affairs. *Concentration in the Manufacturing Industries in Canada.* Ottawa, 1968, 1971.

Dominion Bureau of Statistics. *Standard Industrial Classification Manual.* Ottawa: Information Canada, 1970.

Duncan, O. Dudley. "Path Analysis: Sociological Examples." *American Journal of Sociology* 72 (1966): 1–16.

Epstein, A. L. "The Network and Urban Social Organization." In J. Clyde Mitchell (ed.), *Social Networks in Urban Situations.* Manchester: Manchester University Press, 1969.

Fennema, M., and H. Schijf. "Analyzing Interlocking Directorates: Theory and Methods." *Social Networks* 1 (1978–79): 297–332.

Freeman, Linton C. "A Set of Measures of Centrality Based on Betweenness." *Sociometry* 40 (1977): 35–41.

"Centrality in Social Networks: Conceptual Clarification." *Social Networks* 1 (1979): 215–39.

Friedman, Milton. *Price Theory*. Chicago: Aldine, 1976.

Friedmann, Harriet B. "The Transformation of Wheat Production in the Era of the World Wheat Market, 1873–1935: A Global Analysis of Production and Exchange." Ph.D. diss., Harvard University, 1976.

"Simple Commodity Production and Wage Labor in the American Plains." *Journal of Peasant Studies* 6 (1978): 71–100.

Glanzer, M., and R. Glaser. "Techniques for the Study of Group Structure and Behavior: I. Analysis of Structure." *Psychological Bulletin* 56 (1959): 317–32.

Globerman, S. "Technological Diffusion in the Canadian Tool and Die Industry." *Review of Economics and Statistics* 57 (1975): 428–34.

Granovetter, Mark. *Getting A Job*. Cambridge, Mass.: Harvard University Press, 1974.

Greene, J., and M. G. Duerr. *Intercompany Transactions in the Multinational Firm*. New York: Conference Board, 1970.

Kaplan, Abraham. *The Conduct of Inquiry: Methodology for Behavioral Science*. Scranton, Pa.: Chandler, 1964.

Kopits, G. F. "Dividend Remittance Behavior within the Industrial Firm: A Cross-Country Analysis." *Review of Economics and Statistics* 54 (1972): 339–42.

Larner, R. J. "Ownership and Control in the 200 Largest Non-Financial Corporations, 1929 and 1963." *American Economic Review* 56 (1966): 777–87.

Laumann, Edward O., and Peter V. Marsden. "Microstructural Analysis in Interorganizational Systems." *Social Networks* 4 (1982): 329–48.

Lessard, D. G. "Transfer Prices, Taxes, and Financial Markets: Implications of Financial Transfer within the Multinational Corporation." In R. G. Hawkins (ed.), *Research in International Business and Finance: An Annual Compilation of Research*. Greenwich, Conn.: JAI Press, 1979.

Levine, Joel H. "The Sphere of Influence." *American Sociological Review* 37 (1972): 14–37.

Lorrain, François, and Harrison C. White. "Structural Equivalence of Individuals in Social Networks." *Journal of Mathematical Sociology* 1 (1971): 49–80.

McManus, J. C. "The Theory of the International Firm." In G. Paquet (ed.), *The Multinational Firm and the Nation State*. Don Mills, Ont.: Collier-Macmillan Canada, 1972.

Marshall, Alfred. *Principles of Economics*. 8th ed. London: Macmillan, 1920.

Mason, E. S. "Price and Production Policies of Large-Scale Enterprises." *American Economic Review* 29 (1939): 61–74.

Massel, Mark S. "Models of Value Theory and Antitrust." In Alfred R. Oxenfeldt (ed.), *Models of Markets*. New York: Columbia University Press, 1963.

Means, Gardiner C. *Structure of the American Economy*. Washington D.C.: National Resources Committee, 1932.

Mintz, Beth, and Michael Schwartz. *The Power Structure of American Business*. Chicago: University of Chicago Press, 1985.

Mitchell, J. Clyde. *Social Networks in Urban Situations*. Manchester: Manchester University Press, 1969.

Mokken, Robert. "Traces of Power III: Corporate-Governmental Network in the Netherlands"; "Traces of Power IV: The 1972 Intercorporation in the Netherlands." Joint Sessions of Workshops of the European Consortium for Political Research, Grenoble, 1978.

Mokken, Robert, and Frans Stokman, "Corporate Governmental Networks in the Netherlands." *Social Networks* 1 (1978): 333–58.

Ornstein, M. "Assessing the Meaning of Corporate Interlocks: Canadian Evidence." *Social Science Research* 4 (1980): 287–306.

"Interlocking Directorates in Canada: Evidence from Replacement Patterns." *Social Networks* 4 (1982): 3–35.

Ouchi, William G. "Markets, Bureaucracies, and Clans." *Administrative Science Quarterly* 25 (1980): 129–42.

Park, Libbie, and Frank Park. *Anatomy of Big Business.* Toronto: Progress, 1962.

Rapoport, Anatol, and William J. Horvath. "A Study of a Large Sociogram." *Behavioral Science* 6 (1961): 279–91.

Ricardo, David. *On the Principles of Political Economy and Taxation.* London: J. Murray, 1817.

Richardson, R. J. "'Merchants against Industry': An Empirical Study of the Canadian Debate." *Canadian Journal of Sociology* 7 (1982): 279–95.

Sailer, Lee D. "Structural Equivalence: Meaning and Definition, Computation and Application." *Social Networks* 1 (1978): 73–90.

Scherer, F. M. *Industrial Market Structure and Economic Performance.* (2d ed.) Chicago: Rand McNally, 1980.

Shapiro, Daniel M., William A. Sims, and Gwenn Hughes. "The Efficiency Implications of Earnings Retentions: An Extension." *Review of Economics and Statistics* 65 (1983): 327–31.

Shepard, R. N., and Phipps Arabie. "Additive Clustering: Representation of Similarities as Combinations of Discrete Overlapping Properties." *Psychological Review* 86 (1979): 87–123.

Shepard, R. N., A. Kimball Romney, and Sara Beth Nerlove (eds.). *Multidimensional Scaling: Theory and Applications in the Behavioral Sciences.* New York: Seminar Press, 1972.

Sherman, Roger. "Theory Comes to Industrial Organization." In A. P. Jacquemin and H. W. de Jong (eds.), *Welfare Aspects of Industrial Markets.* Leiden: Martinus Nijhoff, 1977.

Smith, Adam. *An Inquiry into the Nature and Causes of the Wealth of Nations.* Edited by Edwin Canaan. New York: Modern Library, [1776] 1937.

Statistics Canada. *Industrial Organization and Concentration in the Manufacturing, Mining and Logging Industries.* Ottawa: Information Canada, 1973.

Domestic and Foreign Control of Manufacturing Establishments in Canada, 1972. Ottawa: Information Canada, 1977.

Structural Aspects of Domestic and Foreign Control in the Manufacturing, Mining and Forestry Industries, 1970–1972. Ottawa: Information Canada, 1978.

Standard Industrial Classification, 1980. Ottawa: Ministry of Supply and Services, 1980.

U.S. Office of Management and Budget, Statistical Policy Division, *Standard*

Industrial Classification Manual. Washington: U.S. Government Printing Office, 1972.

Vickery, W. S. *Microstatistics.* New York: Harcourt, Brace and World, 1965.

Waverman, L., and R. Baldwin. "Determinants of Interlocking Directorates." University of Toronto, Institute for Policy Analysis Working Paper 7501. Toronto, 1975.

White, Harrison C. "Subcontracting with An Oligopoly: Spence Revisited." Harvard University, RIAS Working Paper 1. Cambridge, 1976.

"Where Do Markets Come From?" *American Journal of Sociology* 87 (1981a): 517–47.

"Production Markets as Induced Role Structures." In Samuel Leinhardt (ed.), *Sociological Methodology, 1981.* San Francisco: Jossey-Bass, 1981b.

Williamson, O. E. *Corporate Control and Business Behavior.* Englewood Cliffs, N. J.: Prentice-Hall, 1970.

"The Economics of Organization: The Transaction Cost Approach." *American Journal of Sociology* 87 (1981): 548–611.

Markets and Hierarchies: Analysis and Antitrust Implications. New York: Free Press, 1975.

Williamson, Oliver E., and William G. Ouchi. "The Markets and Hierarchies Program of Research: Origins, Implications, Prospects." In William Joyce and Andrew Van de Ven (eds.), *Organizational Design.* New York: Wiley, 1981.

Wright, Sewall. "Path Coefficients and Path Regressions: Alternative or Complementary Concepts?" *Biometrics* 16 (1969): 189–202.

11

Form and substance in the analysis of the world economy

Harriet Friedmann

The conceptual units of the world economy

In the 1960s, sociological studies of the world economy broke with the modernization paradigm's use of nation-states as independent analytic units. Researchers working in the new tradition sought to recognize the complexity of the relations that constitute the world economic order. They argued that relations among parts of the "world-system" determined its units, and they conceived of process as inherent in the whole but reflected in its changing constituent elements (Wallerstein, 1979). Using this world-systems approach, analysts demonstrated that a nation's *structural* location within a pattern of relations crucially determined a wide range of its putatively national characteristics, for example, economic growth (Snyder and Kick, 1979), urbanization (Kentor, 1981), income distributions (Rubinson, 1976), political regimes (Goldfrank, 1978), and revolutionary transformations (Skocpol and Trimberger, 1978).

World-systems analysis has been useful in that it has led us away from the sort of studies of single countries that pronounced them backward because they had supposedly traditional social structures, a population that lacked achievement orientation, or parents who practiced inappropriate child-rearing behavior. Most scholars are now far more willing to interpret what happens within a country in terms of its location within networks of political and economic relations than they were a decade ago. Yet, grasping the notion that the world economy is based on a set of relations is only a start: One still has to determine the *units* between and among which these relations take place. Both "nations" and "regions" have been proposed. Another problem is how to characterize the relationships among these elementary units. In particular, can relations of political domination and market exchange be consistently analyzed together? In this chapter, I argue that the choice of units

This chapter benefited from discussion of an earlier draft by a working group of authors contributing to this collection. Special thanks go to Charles Tilly for his useful suggestions and to Barry Wellman for organizing and inspiring everyone.

and relations greatly affects the kinds of analytic models we use and the conclusions we reach. I examine Wallerstein's world-systems approach to studying the world economy as a hierarchy of regions (Wallerstein, 1974a), and I evaluate his approach by using as a case study global trade in the basic foodgrain commodity, wheat. I propose an alternative, structural approach that promises to help researchers better explain political and economic relations within the foodgrain sector.

Nation and region

Although most analysts agree that studies of world political economy ought to focus primarily on relations, they have had trouble deciding on appropriate units of analysis. Nations are obvious candidates, but many processes that analysts wish to treat as internal to their units cross national boundaries, which, moreover, shift over time. Many analysts believe that regions are less ambiguous units than nations because the term "nation" denotes both a geographic and a political entity. The term "region" is more purely geographic and, hence, fits better with the spatial metaphor of "center" and periphery" inherent in the concept of world-systems. For example, Wallerstein's (1974a;b) starting point for his world-system model was the trade-induced specialization of Western Europe in manufactures and Eastern Europe in grains. He used these *regional* units to explain the formation of nations within each region – as well as the internal economic organization of given nations.

Despite the preliminary usefulness of this kind of regional analysis, "regions" cannot stand as sound building blocks for a model of world economic structure: They have no inherent internal validity as units. Seemingly natural geographic boundaries are externally defined: A region is simply the bounded area identified at certain historical moments by the intersection of political and economic networks.

Although nations, like regions, are embedded in networks of external relations, they are not wholly defined by these external relations. First, nations are better defined empirically. There is the reality of states as ruling organizations whose jurisdictions define national territories. Nation building and state formation are complementary processes (Tilly, 1975). Thus, states define the boundaries of national politics and are the units of the international state system.

Second, national *economies* are realities, not statistical artifacts. To varying degrees, national boundaries mark real differences between the economic transactions that occur within them and those that cross them. National economies are the central units used in analyses of international trade and, as such, are a useful addition to the classic units of economic theory. Of course, money in practice takes the form of national currencies.

Moreover, nations constitute the bounded arenas for markets in land and labor and can thus be compared to one another in terms of the proportions between these specific factors of production.

Thus nations are useful units of analysis if we can avoid treating them as *independent* (the modernization problem) or as a *geographic* subset of a region (the world-system problem). A nation is an *arena* in and across which various social networks exist. A nation's characteristics, including its boundaries, are the result of the formation and dissolution of economic and political networks in specific geographic locations. For example, the borders, cultures, and economic activities of African nations – as well as the patterns of domination within them – have much to do with the intertwined histories of colonial rule and export production.

Indeed, all analysts attempting to understand world economies use nations in empirical studies because they tend to be the units for which data exist. Sometimes relations among nations become reduced to a national variable as they do when analysts use foreign trade or similar measures to situate nations in the purely conceptual regions of "center" and "periphery." Strictly structural studies, which look for networks of *international* relations, also use nations as analytic units (Breiger, 1981; Krasner, 1976; Chase-Dunn, 1978; Snyder and Kick, 1979; Friedmann, 1983). Yet, used in this way, nations are not independent units of analysis, but units of *aggregation* defined both by the internal systems of relationships and by the structure of the world economy in which they are embedded.

Domination and exchange

Wallerstein's world-systems model is based on the spatial metaphor of dominance due to centrality. It is structural in that it defines the position of each geographic zone (or region) by the totality of its relations to other zones. It groups these regions into three strata according to the similarity of ties within and across them:[1] the core, the periphery, and the semiperiphery. The core benefits from transfers of value produced in the other two. Regions of the periphery have their product appropriated from above, and regions in the semiperiphery both appropriate value from the periphery and have value appropriated by the core.

The model has two central features: (a) it is holistic – it defines the world system as the bounded arena encompassing the geographical division of labor, and (b) it incorporates *a set of relations* defining and connecting constituent regions. This set of relations, which Wallerstein understands as "transfers of surplus," is ambiguous and needs unraveling. It involves a substitution of spatial relations – that is, the core–periphery metaphor – for at least two distinct networks of social relations: domination among states and circulation among enterprises. This conflation causes problems: The model has operational difficulty in reducing both economic and political relations to one formal system. But the question is not only whether Wallerstein has failed or succeeded in this attempt, but whether in principle he has properly defined the task.

In Wallerstein's original statement of his methodological position (1974a: 2–11), he explicitly denies the use of any unit of analysis smaller than the whole. This leaves his actual use of regions, states, classes, "ethno-nations," and so on, unexplained. By denying that he employs units of analysis, Wallerstein attempts to shunt the problem aside. He argues that analysis must proceed from smaller structures to the system as a whole, and he uses a posteriori arguments, phrased in terms of the logical necessity of specific social relations antecedent to the one now thought to exist.

Despite these precepts, in practice the regions of his world-system are not generalizations of observed local structures: They do not arise either from the division of labor within or between enterprises, or from domination within bureaucracies or by states. At best, his system is a generalization of a geographic specialization of activity such as that between town and country (Wallerstein, 1979). This is a much less grand level of generalization, which by no means implies inherently "unequal relations of exchange." Moreover, by introducing a teleology in place of a historical analysis, Wallerstein feeds data into a mill that always grinds out three regions.[2]

The regions of Wallerstein's world-system are not really analytic units: Regions do not occupy positions in the core, periphery, or semiperiphery by virtue of their relations to others. Instead they are geographically bounded territories that contain the "activities" of "different bourgeoisies" in relation to each other (Wallerstein, 1979: 221). These bourgeoisies, in turn, have specific exploitative relations to producing classes within their respective regions, in contrast to the universal wage relations posited by Emmanuel (1973). Thus, "unequal exchange" between regions reduces to unequal redistribution of surplus products collected on the spot by each "regional bourgeoisie."[3]

For Wallerstein, not only classes, but states, are nodes in networks crosscutting regions. In the original model (Wallerstein, 1974a, b), unequal exchange was facilitated, if not engineered, by stronger states over weaker ones on behalf of their own bourgeoisies (Wallerstein, 1979: 274–5). But Wallerstein's conception of the state seems to have withered under the mortal blows of its critics (Skocpol, 1977; Block, 1978): It is far less central to his account of the consolidation of the world economy in the seventeenth century than to its rise in the sixteenth. Yet nothing in his revised model has replaced the crucial role of the state as a mechanism of unequal exchange distorting the world market and enforcing the resulting continuum of "freedom" in relations of production (from greatest in the core to least in the periphery, with the semiperiphery, as always, falling between).

Thus relations among regions seem to derive from relations among two different types of units: enterprises and states (Friedmann, 1982). The former includes the notion of class in a sense adequate for Wallerstein's model,[4] which focuses on "the view from the top" (Kaplan, 1978): The owners of enterprises are the bourgeoisies, by Wallerstein's loose definition. He uses relations of production within enterprises to define different types of proletariats with different degrees of "freedom" – from contractual sellers of labor power through sharecroppers to slaves.

The use of states and enterprises logically defines four categories of relations: state-to-state; enterprise-to-enterprise; state-to-enterprise; and enterprise -to-state.[5] In Wallerstein's model, the last two are duals: States act on behalf of their entrepreneurs, and are, in general, subordinate to them. Similarly, entrepreneurs who are more successful than those in other zones provide the economic basis for greater state strength relative to other states and enhance their capacity to serve the interests of their respective bourgeoisies.

The relation between states and classes is hotly disputed, but is not germane here. The different relations linking each unit to others of its kind are more directly relevant to the measurable structure of the world economy: that is, *domination* of one state over another and *exchange* among enterprises.

Domination and exchange are complementary dimensions of structure. For both Marx and Weber, competitive relations within markets are the anonymous counterpart to direct command within organizations (Marx, 1967: 184–5; Lindblom, 1977; Collins, 1980). True, they assign different weights to each relation within their theories and treat the conceptual basis of the two relations differently. Yet Marx and Weber crucially agree on the specificity of domination and exchange in modern society: For Marx the most important aspect of domination is the capitalist's command over labor once the wage contract is put in motion. This substantive inequality, underlying the formal equality of contracts struck in the marketplace, is for Marx the real basis of social organization. For Weber, domination and exchange have equivalent conceptual status since each derives from legal–rational social action and complements the other formally and substantively. Thus, Marx sees contradiction where Weber sees complementarity. Yet, in either case, relations of domination and exchange imply distinct units in distinct social arenas.

In classical sociology exchange is *external* and domination is *internal* to the enterprise (and to other organizations, such as state agencies).[6] Thus, within capitalism, the labor process requires that individuals occupying one position dominate the occupants of another. This ability of one person to command another derives from the authority vested in the positions arranged in a pattern of super- and subordination. Moreover, in contrast to the anonymous and formally equal encounters of the market, domination consists of a hierarchy of formally specified and unequal relations (Weber, 1968: 469). Whereas markets are self-regulating mechanisms, hierarchies have no intrinsic dynamic: Change either comes from external markets or from informal relations established within the formal hierarchy.

Wallerstein's world-system, however, is a coterminous market and hierarchy. He achieves this structural coincidence by substituting *one geographic unit* for two types of *social* unit: Instead of analyzing legally equivalent actors (market units) and ranked positions of command and obedience (hierarchy units), he ranks *regions* into a global hierarchy connected by unequal exchange. Domination, in this sense, corresponds to the notions underlying central place theory in geography: Networks of influence extend outward from metropolitan centers through hierarchies of regional domination (Berry, 1967; Skinner, 1972; Friedmann and Wayne, 1977; Friedmann, 1982, 1983). For Wallerstein, however, the core, semiperiphery, and periphery are ranked through unequal exchange. Thus, regional inequality is a peculiar case of domination through exchange.

But can the geographical region adequately stand in for the two social units of analysis appropriate to markets and hierarchies (Wellmann, Hall, and Carrington, Chapter 6)? In other words, does any version of the region coincide with the social boundaries defined by independently determined networks of states and enterprises?

Hierarchies and markets: the case of wheat

Although Wallerstein's later modifications have reduced the formalism of the original model somewhat, tension still remains between interregional hierarchies and global economies.[7] In this section, we examine some hypotheses derived from Wallerstein's model in order to see how valid they are when applied to specific trade and productive relations. I focus on the analytic connections among states, relations of production (what Wallerstein calls "modes of labor control"), and regional specialization of commodity production. Since wheat is crucial to each of the phases of Wallerstein's world-system, it is a good case study: The origins of the modern world-system in the sixteenth century lay in the grain trade between Eastern and Western Europe (Wallerstein, 1974a), and the relocation of cereal production from periphery to core was important during the second phase in the seventeenth century (Wallerstein, 1980: 84–5; 268). The data used here will not cover so long or so early a period. In order to evaluate the hypotheses in the light of these data, I provisionally adopt Wallerstein's units of analysis, clarifying, as much as possible, relations among states, enterprises, and regions.

Table 11.1 *Wheat export shares of major export countries, 1828–1969 (percentage of total of major exporters in each period)*

	United States	Canada	Australia[a]	Argentina[a]	Russia/Soviet Union	Prussia[a]	France[a]	India[a]	Danube basin and North Africa[a]	Total (million bushels)
1828–47	4.4	10.7	—	—	22.4	62.7	—	—	—	5.48
1848–67	26.4	4.2	—	—	34.2	35.2	—	—	—	25.40
1875–94	50.0	1.5	—	2.3	29.8	—	—	8.2	8.2	277.63
1895–1914	33.3	7.2	3.9	13.6	25.7	—	—	5.6	10.7	507.70
1920–34	21.1	36.7	14.6	21.8	3.4	—	—	0.7	1.7	691.36
1950–69	40.8	27.1	12.9	7.0	6.5	—	5.8	—	—	11,258.47

[a]Dash (—) indicates "not applicable."
Note: Gaps in time periods indicate different series after 1867 and 1934. Based on annual averages. First series, U. K. imports only. Data from Friedmann (1983), Tables 1 and 6; 1982, Table 1.

> Hypothesis 1. The degree of regional specialization of a given commodity in the international divison of labor varies directly with the basic (as opposed to the luxury) character of that commodity. Since wheat is undoubtedly a staple, it should be highly specialized within the international division of labor.

Wheat has certainly been one of the earliest and most significant products in interregional and international trade. However, complexity of measurement precludes quick evaluation of wheat in relation to other commodities. Table 11.1 suggests a high concentration of exports since the early nineteenth century. For a commodity so widely produced, a relatively small number of countries have dominated wheat exports. Between the two 20-year periods beginning in 1875, the total exports of the major countries increased more than tenfold. A growth in the number of sources accompanied this growth in exports, despite the end of previously important Prussian exports. Even so, the combined shares of the two largest exporters – the United States and Russia – remained well above 50%. Although export shares were more equally distributed, the number of significant exporters declined with the stabilization and contraction of world trade in the interwar period. With the postwar expansion of the wheat trade, exports were increasingly concentrated in North America, particularly in the United States. Therefore, commodity production of wheat took place in ways predicted in the first hypothesis.

> Hypothesis 2. Specialization in specific commodities corresponds to cumulative differences in regional wealth. Specifically, regions specializing in wheat production should show an increasingly homogeneous level of wealth within a given historical range.

During the nineteenth century, and increasingly between 1873 and 1914, there were three categories of countries in the wheat trade: export countries, import countries, and basically self-sufficient countries (whether through trade policy or unrestricted economic conditions). Kuznets's (1966: 64–5) calculations of the long-term rate of growth of total and per capita product for selected countries make it possible to compare within and across these categories (Table 11.2). The most important and obvious conclusion is that there is no pattern.

In the column showing the growth rate of total national product by decades, the lowest rates are those for Germany before protection in the 1870s and the United Kingdom (import countries), France (self-sufficient), and – after a large gap – European Russia (including the period before 1928 in which it shared the vast bulk of world exports with the United States). The highest rates (apart from the Soviet Union) are those of Japan (self-sufficient), and the United States and Canada (exporters). These data belie any supposed association between wheat exports and national growth.

Table 11.2. *Growth rate by decade of national product, population,
and per capita product, selected countries, by position in wheat trade,
long periods (product in constant prices)*

	Total product	Population	Product per capita
Importers			
United Kingdom			
1885–59 to 1957–59	21.1	6.1	14.1
Germany			
1851–55 to 1871–75	17.6	7.7	9.2
1871–75 to 1960–62	31.1	11.2	17.9
Denmark			
1870–74 to 1960–62	31.8	10.4	19.4
Exporters			
United States			
1839 to 1960–62	42.5	21.6	17.2
Canada			
1870–74 to 1960–62	40.7	19.1	18.1
Australia			
1861–65 to 1959-60–1961-62	34.1	24.2	8.0
European Russia			
1860 to 1913	30.2	13.8	14.4
U.S.S.R (present)			
1928 to 1958	53.8	6.9	43.9
Sufficient			
Sweden			
1861–65 to 1960–62	36.9	6.7	28.3
France			
1841–50 to 1960–62	20.8	2.5	17.9
Japan			
1879–81 to 1959–61	42.0	12.3	26.4

Source: Kuznets (1966: Table 2.5).

Perhaps more revealing are the rates of growth per capita shown in the last
column: The lowest rates are for an exporter (Australia) and an importer
(Germany before 1875), and the highest rates are for the self-sufficient
countries (Sweden and Japan); furthermore, the highest rate among the
exporters (Canada) is quite similar to the highest among the importers
(Denmark). Thus, exporting and importing wheat seem to have no
relationship, in themselves, to levels of economic growth.

Indeed, in contrast to the general thrust of Wallerstein's model, trade in
this basic commodity has not independently affected development or
underdevelopment. For example, economic historians studying late
nineteenth-century Europe have concluded that protection (that is, state
policy) affected growth quite apart from the quantity of trade (Kindleberger,
1951), and that rapidly expanding exports of wheat corresponded to vastly
different patterns and rates of growth, especially for such important

exporters of the period as the United States and India (Olson, 1974). These results would be still stronger if the full range of important and expanding wheat export countries in the late nineteenth century were included in Table 11.1: Between 1885 and 1889, the combined exports of Austria-Hungary, Romania, India, and North Africa accounted for just under a quarter of annual average world totals, whereas the growing exports of Canada, Argentina, and Australia accounted for only 2.3% (Friedmann, 1983: Table 6). Although data for the period after World War II are more consistent with the hypothesis that concentration of wheat exports is associated with a uniform (high) level of national wealth (Friedmann, 1982), the evidence of the earlier period is sufficient to reject it.

> **Hypothesis 3.** Each type of regional specialization corresponds to a specific state strength relative to states in other regions. Thus state strength should be equal among specialized wheat regions.

Here the correspondence between nations and regions becomes difficult to accept, even provisionally. The noncorrespondence between economic zones of production and state jurisdictions in the original model was unidirectional: The dependence of the model of the sixteenth-century grain trade between Eastern and Western Europe and the inclusion within each region of several states allowed for the loose assertion of a relationship. However, when states later came to organize grain exports through the colonization of newly conquered lands, the relationship between wheat-producing regions and nation-states became reversed: Wheat exports developed as part of the extension of existing national economies that included other activities. Thus, the United States, which was eventually to become the leading wheat export country, became a leading manufacturing nation at the same time. Moreover, dependence on wheat imports characterized both a growing manufacturing economy (Great Britain) and an increasingly prosperous agricultural economy (Denmark), but not many of the other industrializing countries of Europe. When states contain various specialized regions instead of existing within them, analysts have difficulty operationalizing the relationship between each type of region and state strength (itself an ambiguous idea). When such difficulties are true for so basic and locationally specific a commodity as wheat (see Hypothesis 1 above), they pose quite serious problems for the model.[8] However, we can restate this hypothesis more modestly to assert that a relationship exists between wheat exports and state strength. In this case, specialization in wheat production enters into the complex of determinants of political and economic structure within national economies. Presumably those states that combined specialization in wheat with specialization in manufacturing would have different strengths from those that specialized only in one. This approach reformulates the hypothesis in the language of variables measured on nations rather than relations and

Table 11.3. *Selected countries by specialization and position in*
international state system, late nineteenth century

Strength of state	Export specialization		
	Manufactured goods only (A)	Wheat only (B)	Both A and B
High	United Kingdom, Germany	Russia[a] Austria-Hungary[a]	United States
Low		Canada Australia Argentina India Romania	

[a]Categorized as "high" because they were Great Powers.

thus poses difficulties for the model as a whole. However, since it makes some
sense, the relation is illustrated in Table 11.3 for the expansive period 1873 to
1914, when changes in both specialization and state building were proceeding
apace.

Few countries have both low state strength and high manufacturing
exports, whether combined with wheat exports or not. But what of the many
countries that have low state strength but specialize in wheat exports? In
practice, a few countries exported most of the wheat – a fact sufficient to cast
doubt on correlations that treat all exporting countries equally. Thus the
United States alone accounted for almost one-quarter of world wheat exports
in the decade before World War I, and the combined exports of the United
States, Russia, and the Danubian region (including Austria-Hungary and
Romania) accounted for well over half of world wheat exports in the prewar
decade.

Thus even the more modest proposition will not stand. Nor does it help to
take into account the direction of movement in the statistics. The two states
generally agreed to be rising most rapidly – the United States and
Germany – were the largest wheat exporter and an important importer,
respectively. The declining Great Powers of Eastern Europe – Russia and
Austria-Hungary (together with Romania) – were important and expanding
regions of wheat export. Other European powers, declining only relative to
the rise of America and Germany, were England (the largest wheat importer)
and France (largely self-sufficient). A nation such as Denmark, which
specialized in other agricultural production and sacrificed its wheat production to cheaper imports, had a state hardly worthy of consideration in the

nineteenth century. And colonial India, which rapidly expanded its wheat exports, did not even govern itself.

The narrower question of hegemonic states is, however, interesting. The wheat trade was important to both of the hegemonic powers of the past two centuries. England, the hegemonic power of the nineteenth century, sacrificed domestic agriculture, encouraged a regime of free international trade, and developed foreign as well as domestic markets for her expanding industries. Indeed, the complementary specialization of other regions in the export of food and raw materials became the principal historical referent for the concept of underdevelopment at the heart of the world-system model. Challenge to British hegemony (as to earlier and later hegemonies) is generally understood in terms of competitive exports of manufactures, and even import substitution – in other words, a move away from specialized export agriculture. The United States, the hegemonic power of the twentieth century, has had a different relation to trade in general and wheat in particular: Trade has been a smaller proportion of its national product than that of either core competitors or peripheries. Moreover, the proportion of exports accounted for by manufactures is much smaller than for any core competitors. As its hegemony has declined, agricultural exports have become increasingly important in international competition for the United States and also for Europe (Chombart de Lauwe, 1979: 338). Although American policy, like that of Britain in its period of hegemony, has been to support liberalization of trade, until the 1980s wheat was consistently treated as an exception at American insistence. Although wheat has not been the source of American strength, its increasing domination of world grain markets has been an aspect of American hegemony, and decreasing domination has accompanied the decline of American hegemony. Although the contrast between nineteenth-century Britain and twentieth-century America suggests a slim basis of support for the relationship between specialization and hegemony, the relationship is in the opposite direction from that predicted. Thus, it seems dangerous to assume that commodities have essential characteristics, endowing their creators with wealth or poverty, strength or weakness.[9]

> **Hypothesis 4.** Regional specialization corresponds to geographical concentration of relations of production appropriate to the commodities exported. Thus, specialized wheat export regions should show increasingly homogeneous relations of production.

Wheat commerce expanded throughout the nineteenth century – spectacularly so in the last decades. A simultaneous homogenization of productive organization accompanied the increase in world trade between the 1870s and 1920s. Simple commodity production – fully commercial family farming – became the rule throughout the world wheat market.

Coincidentally, both unspecialized peasant households and highly elaborated capitalist enterprises declined both in number and importance. Indeed, many peasant households and capitalist enterprises gave way to commercial family farming.[10] Despite the increasing integration of the various stages of food production since World War II – from fertilizers to processed foods – simple commodity production has continued to characterize grain production in major export countries: Argentina, Australia, Canada, France and the United States (Mann and Dickinson, 1978). Hence, the history of wheat production supports Hypothesis 4.

Summary

Thus, an analysis of the wheat market supports two of the four relationships examined. The first relationship supported (Hypothesis 1) is between the staple character of a commodity and specialization within the international division of labor. The second relationship supported (Hypothesis 4) is between specialization and uniformity of relations of production. Of course, a positive formulation of the place of wheat in the modern world economy is considerably more complex than these hypotheses would suggest (Friedmann, 1982, 1983). Nonetheless, these two hypotheses seem plausible, but not those relating specialization to relative state strength and relative wealth. By examining these hypotheses, we should be able to answer, tentatively, the question posed at the end of our critical discussion of Wallerstein: Do regions, as analytic units, coincide with the social boundaries defined by independently determined networks of states and enterprises? The answer seems to be no. By themselves, economic relations produce comparative advantages among regions and ways of organizing production. Both specialization in wheat production and the worldwide prevalence of family farms producing wheat for export can be explained without reference to inequality, domination, or hierarchy. Thus, these propositions, by themselves, do not improve on the theory of international trade. The problem remains unformulated in Wallerstein's world-systems model: how to reconcile economic theory with unequal power among states.

Toward a structural analysis: the case of wheat

If the world-systems model fails to provide adequate content for a spatial unit of analysis, it is because the model is designed to accomplish the difficult task of combining political networks with economic theory. In this chapter I have focused on economic relations in the world-systems model, highlighting those aspects of the model that touch on the theory of international trade. But since the world-systems model sacrifices the elegance of comparative advantage, it is disappointing to find that economic explanations arising from the model do not substantially differ from – or improve upon – explanations stemming from the economic theory of international trade.

Like the world-systems model, the theory of international trade explains differences among national economies. International trade theory super-imposes these national economies on economic theories that use commodity owners as the units of analysis for examining circulation. It cannot account for the specifically *sociological* dimensions of the world order: power relations among states and relations of production within enterprises. Hence the unit of analysis issue remains. As with the world-systems model, its resolution depends on understanding the international division of labor as the result of independently conceptualized relations of commodity circulation and power. National economies and policies must have a place in the theory, but they cannot serve as substitutes for the analysis of multiple relations and distinct units. The world economy consists (at least) of state-to-state relations and enterprise-to-enterprise relations. The former are by definition *international*: The nation-state has progressively replaced the old imperial powers in Central Europe and Asia, and the European colonies in Africa and South America. Although relations among enterprises are often *transnational*, each enterprise must mobilize labor, technology, and raw materials in specific locations and consequently under the jurisdiction of specific states, however temporarily. A theory of the mutual effects of states and enterprises presupposes an independent conceptualization of each, both in relation to one another and in relation to the national economy.

This section considers some of the basic components of a coherent conceptualization of economic and political relations *within* the world economy. Rather than rely on spatial metaphors (e.g., core–periphery) and spatial propinquity (e.g., regions), the proposed approach remains *structural*, emphasizing patterns of specific relations in the larger world economy. Whereas I used the case of wheat in the preceding section to criticize the world-systems model, here I use it more positively to guide the analysis of that *sector* of the world economy that has to do with basic foodgrains. I expect the economics and politics of food to be specific: The structure of the wheat economy should be, at once, particular to foodgrains and part of the larger dynamics of accumulation.

At different periods in time, the world wheat economy has had two different types of *exchange structures*.[11] One, a *generalized exchange structure*, approximates what is generally meant by the term "world market": that is, there exists an effective world price, and all national prices are functions of the world price. This does not mean that all national prices are *the same*: It implies that supply and demand are generalized throughout the structure, such that frosts, bumper harvests, wars, or new inventions have the same effects in both direction and degree in all national economies. It follows that state policies may modify, but not determine, patterns of production and trade. Comparative advantage should be realized in general, subject, of course, to the distortions introduced by tariffs and the like.

Thus, the unit of analysis in generalized exchange structures is the commodity owner: National boundaries serve mainly to demarcate the arenas in which land and labor are mobilized and regulated and comparative advantage in factor proportions may be realized.

The second type, *segmented exchange structure*, is a network of bilateral exchanges between countries. There is no world price in an effective sense: Prices in different national economies do not necessarily move to the same degree, or even in the same direction, despite trade. Indeed, national prices for domestic buyers may not move in relation to export prices, or even sometimes import prices. However, networks of trade connect these national economies without integrating them into a world market. The unit of analysis is the national economy, and each price corresponds to national circulation. Enterprises in different national economies are not in direct competition with one another, nor are buyers in different national economies. The existence of multiple national sources of supply sets an upper limit to prices for buyers abroad, and similarly sets a lower limit for multiple national buyers. Segmented exchange may be the result of natural or technical barriers to trade or of state policies of sufficient scope and intensity to prevent global circulation. But even when segmented international exchange is not the result of aggregate trade policies, global circulation does not greatly constrain the state. The state plays a crucial role (even passively) in determining the quantity and character of production within its territory.

Wheat prices in all important trading countries are the empirical basis for identifying generalized or segmented exchange structures. Since most countries have only one harvest a year, shifts in supply and demand from one year to the next should produce similar price shifts in each trading country when generalized exchange is present. Negative correlations, or the absence of correlations, among national price movements would indicate that a situation of segmented exchange prevails. By experimenting with different breaks in the price series, one can establish shifts in exchange structures. This enables analysts to establish historical periods systematically through procedures that can be generalized to test other propositions about the interactions between exchange structures, state policies, and productive relations.

The structure of wheat commerce shifted twice between 1815 and 1973. There was a segmented exchange structure in wheat from 1815 until 1873.[12] Using a price series beginning in 1847, we find the correlation between United States and English price movements was .29. Lest it be thought that transport delayed the price relation, the correlation of the one-year lagged price is only slightly higher, at .35. Although these correlations might not seem low by normal standards, they are low as an indicator of generalized exchange. On the other hand, generalized exchange had begun to characterize wheat commerce *within* Europe, so that the correlation between English and Prussian prices in most of the same period (1847–61) was .91. Correlations of lagged price movements between 1873 and 1896 (when shipping was revolutionized) and correlations of simultaneous price movements thereafter show the emergence, particularly after 1884, of generalized exchange between England and the United States ($r = .83$), which was sustained until the mid-1930s.

After World War II, a new segmented exchange structure took shape; it was based not on transport limitations, but on aggregate state policies – particularly food aid – that shaped trade into politically determined quantities and directions. Finally, recent price data indicate that a new generalized exchange structure may be emerging. If so, this gives empirical grounding to the popular impression of a "food crisis," namely, a turning point in the structure of world wheat commerce. These periods generally correspond to those used in a more ad hoc fashion by historians who have studied the wheat trade. Once they are identified, it is possible to examine the effects of each exchange structure using other data on international specialization, productive relations, and state policies. Briefly, there is some support for the following hypotheses. First, state policies, such as tariffs, have different effects within each structure. In generalized exchange a tariff affects the national price as a function of the world price. However, tariffs in the aggregate may be sufficiently high to separate national prices and create segmented exchange globally. In this case, they constitute a segmented exchange structure.

Second, generalized exchange tends to undermine noncommodity production, whereas segmented exchange reinforces it. Generalized and segmented exchange have corresponding effects on the international division of labor: Generalized competition reorganizes the location of production along the lines of comparative advantage, whereas segmented exchange tends to reinforce the existing distribution of production internationally.

The above approach makes use of economic data (prices) systematically to examine political and social relations along with commodity relations. Clearly it needs methodological development and must be grounded in relation to the world economy as a whole. Yet the particular sequence of wheat exchange structures has a great deal to do with its use to people dependent on local, national, or global *markets* in basic foodgrains. Even the more refined aspects of the history – such as the convergence in time of English and American price movements *within* the generalized exchange structure of the late nineteenth century – have to do with the specific natural features of grain, namely, that it is not highly perishable and that it is bulky in relation to its value. In other words, although the analysis of generalized and segmented exchange may be useful for the historical analysis of other commodities, and perhaps even of labor and money markets, I do not expect historical periods to coincide in this sense. Nor do I expect analysts to use the concepts readily to characterize the structure of the world economy as a whole.

Conclusion

Theories of international power and world economics have yet to reach a synthesis. In general, economists have ignored power (Strange, 1975), and political scientists have subordinated economic tendencies to state policies (Krasner, 1976; Friedmann, 1982). The result tends to leave economics with its logical rigor intact, but with its assumptions rather distant from realities. The reverse side of the coin is that realistic attempts to reckon with observed inequalities in economic relations have so far failed to achieve a comparable rigor.

The question for structural analysis is whether formal models might solve the problem. Clever methodologists might devise a formal solution for multiple units of analysis. However, the solution probably cannot be purely formal. Beside treating historical issues, a solution requires a second level of analysis, situating global economics and international power relative to the national economy. The national economy is not comparable to states and enterprises; it is an arena rather than a complex organization. Wallerstein attempted a simultaneous methodological and substantive solution by using the region as a surrogate for other relations.[13] The disentangling of enterprises, states, and national economies reveals that the problem is substantive: If the other relations cannot be reduced to international hierarchies nor national economies used to represent other relations, then a theoretical conceptualization of the national economy is as important as a formal analysis of economic and political relations across its boundaries.

As capital becomes more and more global in its various forms – commodity capital, money capital, and productive capital – it increases the transnational character of enterprise-to-enterprise relations and changes the relation of these to states (Fröbel, et al., 1980). The effects on national economies of the changing complex of relations, however, is not an outcome of these changes alone (Palloix, 1973; Michalet, 1976). The need for capital to produce commodities (and to reproduce its own conditions of existence) ties it to a material locale. At the same time, states exist in relation to the territories they govern. Thus, Wallerstein's focus on the "region" is grounded in material reality. Yet the regional or national economy must be conceptualized independently and not derivatively, precisely because it is so basic a condition of existence for states and enterprises. Whatever the mobility of capital or the migration of labor, production remains geographically rooted for a given round of production, even if factories may move after the round is complete. Therefore, capitalist reproduction at any moment depends on conditions determined by the regional (or national) economy. As commodity and money circuits become increasingly global, capital tends to become less bound by national limits although this may be offset by other factors.

Yet labor must be organized for production within a complex of social and cultural institutions that encompass the whole round of daily life and generational reproduction, even if people migrate in considerable numbers. People must live the day and year round in stable material and cultural settings. Hence, the limiting condition for capital is the geographic bounds imposed by the human needs that must be met if people are to be continually available for employment. Labor markets are different from other markets. People are available with respect to their energy, skills, and culture only through the social structures, including states, that make possible their existence outside the factory and office.

The material basis of social life is a theoretical assertion. It underlies classical political economy and suggests that the development of concepts such as accumulation and class formation are a useful substantive complement to formal analysis of structures linking enterprises and states. Whether this theory is best or not, the special status of the national economy seems to require some theory to link it to states and enterprises. It would remain the arena for the reproduction of labor even if all other aspects of capital were somehow to transcend national boundaries. Indeed, because the national economy is an arena – a complex of social relations simultaneously underlying and limiting both enterprises and states – analysts cannot treat it as a unit of structure in the same way that they treat organizations. Moreover, the structures of enterprises and of states can exist only within and across these arenas. This is the substantive clue to the formal mystery of the world economy.

NOTES

1. This critique does not reflect Wallerstein's writings since 1981. See also the "blockmodeling" discussions in White, Boorman, and Breiger (1976) and Breiger (1981).
2. This correlation is less clear as Wallerstein (1979) emphasizes process over structure, particularly in the form of cyclical expansions. On one side, regions are infinitely divisible and geographically noncontiguous. Thus, core regions contain peripheral regions, and unequal exchange characterizes not only core–periphery relations, but also urban–rural relations (Wallerstein, 1978). On the other, proletarianization and the commercialization of land are increasingly global phenomena in Wallerstein's later writings (Wallerstein, 1979). Without national

classes, the earlier concomitants of state strength and mode of labor control are ambiguous. The basic feature of Wallerstein's system, however, remains an interregional division of labor, featuring characteristic commodities, productive relations, and state organizations in each region.

3. This is clear from Wallerstein's account of rivalry among core countries (1980: chap. 3). Its consequences are suggested by his first question concerning the periphery in a time of systemic contraction: why they "do not drop out" of the world economy (1980: 129). This is astonishing in the light of the original model's assertion that regions are core or peripheral by virtue of the ability of the former to plunder the latter. What might core competition be, if not over the ability to participate most favorably in the unequal exchange with the periphery? And what choice might peripheries (states, classes, enterprises) have in a world system structured around their giving up of their products? Since he does not offer new definitions of the zones in his revised accounts, his deemphasis of the state adds confusion without substituting the crucial role of the state in the original model.

4. For an elaboration of the consequences of using the nation or the enterprise as the unit of analysis of world commerce, especially in contrast to the theory of international trade, see Friedmann (1983).

5. For a similar schema of logical possibilities that employs three rather than two variables and is directed toward an analysis of politics, see Therborn (1979).

6. Of course states dominate individuals as citizens or subjects and the universality and anonymity of this domination resembles that of the market. The argument here applies only to the narrow sense of "domination" in Weber's theory of bureaucracy.

7. Revisions of the model in more recent essays (e.g., Wallerstein, 1979) and in the analysis of the second phase of the world economy (Wallerstein, 1978) have used more dynamic concepts. The emphasis on long cycles of expansion and contraction is most evident. Accompanying it is an apparent shift of units of analysis, "dichotomies" basic to "the operation of the system," class, and region (Wallerstein, 1979: 155). "Global spatial hierarchialization," including core and periphery and unequal exchange (Wallerstein, 1979: 284) and global class formation, reflect Wallerstein's growing determination to understand the processes by which capitalist relations of production (in the "strict sense," i.e., wage labor) penetrate or are resisted by political and economic relations in different parts of the world economy. Yet "class" and "region" (or "states" and "enterprises") remain slippery constituents of the model. Although formalism no longer dominates, distinctions between economic and political concepts are no less blurred.

8. This essay cannot address the still deeper ambiguity in the concept of state strength: between internal cohesion and control of its regions and populations, on one side, and effective politico-military domination over other states on the other. This ambiguity permeates the discussion of the changing core status of the Netherlands in the seventeenth century, which consequently verges on tautology (Wallerstein, 1980; 244–89). I use state strength here coincidentally with international military position.

9. I use this phrase, rather than "modes of labor control," because it is more general. Since wheat – like many commodities – is often produced through family labor in

family-owned enterprises, any control analogous to serfdom or use of purchased labor-time is external to the enterprise. There is considerable debate about exploitation and control of simple commodity production (Servolin, 1972; Foster-Carter, 1977; Vergopoulos, 1978; Bernstein, 1979; Friedmann, 1980b; Chevalier, 1982). This is not to deny partriarchal control within family enterprises, but to mark its difference from class relations (see Friedmann, 1978a).

10. See Friedmann (1978b) for a more complete discussion of the rise of simple commodity production.

11. Friedmann (1983), develops this argument and the empirical analysis underlying it, especially statistical tests of the effects of state policies on national and world prices within each exchange structure.

12. These data come from Friedmann (1983).

13. The use of the word "region" instead of "national economy" would not affect the argument's validity. The same arguments hold for nonnational, regional economies such as the postbellum American South (See Friedmann (1980c).

LITERATURE CITED

Bernstein, Henry. "Concepts for the Analysis of Contemporary Peasantries." *Journal of Peasant Studies* 6 (4) (1979): 421–43.

Berry, Brian J. L. *Geography of Market Centers and Retail Distribution.* Englewood Cliffs, N. J.: Prentice-Hall, 1967.

Block, Fred. "Marxist Theories of the State in World Systems Analysis." In Barbara Hockey Kaplan (ed.), *Social Change in the Capitalist World Economy*, pp. 27–37. Beverly Hills, Calif.: Sage, 1978.

Breiger, Ronald. "Structures of Economic Interdependence among Nations." In Peter M. Blau and Robert Merton (eds.), *Continuities in Structural Inquiry*, pp. 353–80. Beverly Hills, Calif.: Sage, 1981.

Chase-Dunn, Christopher. "Core-Periphery Relations: The Effect of Core Competition," pp. 159–76 in Barbara Hockey Kaplan (ed.), *Social Change in the Capitalist World Economy*. Beverly Hills, Calif.: Sage, 1978.

Chevalier, Jacques. "There Is Nothing Simple about a Simple Commodity Production." *Studies in Political Economy* 7 (1982): 89–124.

Chombart de Lauwe, Jean. *L'Aventure agricole de la France de 1945 à nos jours*. Paris: Presses Universitaires de France, 1979.

Collins, Randall. "Weber's Last Theory of Capitalism: A Systematization." *American Sociological Review* 46 (6) (1980): 925–42.

Emmanuel, Arghiri. *Unequal Exchange: A Study of the Imperialism of Trade*. New York: Monthly Review Press, 1972.

Food and Agriculture Organization. *Trade Yearbook*. Rome: Food and Agriculture Organization (annual).

Foster-Carter, Aiden. "The Modes of Production Controversy." *New Left Review* 107 (1978): 47–77.

Friedmann, Harriet. "Simple Commodity Production and Wage Labour in the American Plains." *Journal of Peasant Studies* 6 (1978a): 71–100.

"World Market, State, and Family Farm: Social Bases of Household Production in an Era of Wage Labor." *Comparative Studies in Society and History* 20 (1978b): 545–86.

"Review of *The Capitalist World Economy* by Immanuel Wallerstein," *Contemporary Sociology* 9 (1980a): 71–100.

"Household Production and the National Economy." *The Journal of Peasant Studies* 7 (1980b): 158–84.

"Economic Analysis of the Postbellum South: Regional Economics and World Markets." *Comparative Studies in Society and History* 22 (1980c): 639–52.

"State Policy and World Commerce: The Case of Wheat, 1815 to the Present." In Charles Kegley and Pat McGowan, (eds.). *Foreign Policy and the Modern World System*. Beverly Hills, Calif.: Sage, 1983.

"The Political Economy of Food: The Rise and Fall of the Postwar International Order." *American Journal of Sociology* 88 (Supplement, 1982): 248–86.

Friedmann, Harriet, and Jack Wayne. "Dependency Theory: A Critique," *Canadian Journal of Sociology* 2 (1977): 399–416.

Fröbel, Folker, Jurgen Heinrichs, and Otto Kreye. *The New International Division of Labour*. Cambridge: Cambridge University Press, 1980.

Goldfrank, Walter, "Fascism and World Economy." In Barbara Hockey Kaplan (ed.), *Social Change in the Capitalist World Economy*. Beverly Hills, Calif.: Sage, 1978.

Kaplan, Barbara Hockey (ed.). *Social Change in the Capitalist World Economy*. Beverly Hills Calif.: Sage, 1978.

Kentor, Jeffrey. "Structural Determinants of Peripheral Urbanization: The Effects of International Dependence." *American Sociological Review* 46 (1981): 201–11.

Kindelberger, Charles. "Group Behavior and International Trade." *Journal of Political Economy* 59 (1951): 30–46.

Krasner, Stephen D. "State Power and International Trade" *World Politics* 28 (1976): 317–47.

Kuznets, Simon. *Modern Economic Growth. Structure and Spread*. New Haven: Yale University Press, 1966.

Lindblom, Charles E. *Politics and Markets*. New York: Basic, 1977.

Mann, S. A., and J. M. Dickinson. "Obstacles to the Development of a Capitalist Agriculture," *Journal of Peasant Studies* 5 (1978): 466–81.

Marx, Karl *Capital*, I. New York: International Publishers, 1967.

Michalet, Charles-Albert. *Capitalisme mondiale*. Paris: Presses Universitaires de France, 1976.

Olson, Mancur. "The United Kingdom and the World Market in Wheat, 1885–1914." *Explorations in Economic History* 11 (1974): 333–55.

Palloix, Christian. In *Les fermes multinationales et le procès d' internationalisation*. Paris: Maspero, 1973.

Rubinson, Richard. "The World-Economy and the Distribution of Income within States: A Cross-National Study," *American Sociological Review* 41 (1976): 638–59.

Servolin, Claude. "L'absorption de l'agriculture dans le mode de production capitaliste." In Yves Cavernier, Michel Gervais, and Claude Servolin (eds.), *L'univers politique des paysans dans la France conetmporaine*. Paris: Librairie Hermand Colin et la Fondation Nationale des Sciences Politiques, 1972.

Skinner, G. William. "Marketing and Social Structure in Rural China." In P. W.

English and R. C. Mayfield (eds.), *Man, Space and Environment*. New York: Oxford University Press, 1972.

Skocpol, Theda. "Wallerstein's World Capitalist System: A Theoretical and Historical Critique." *American Journal of Sociology* 82 (1977): 1075–90.

Skocpol, Theda, and Ellen Kay Trimberger. "Revolutions and the World-Historical Development of Capitalism." In Barbara Hockey Kaplan (ed.), *Social Change in the Capitalist World Economy*. Beverly Hills, Calif.: Sage, 1978.

Snyder, David, and Edward L. Kick. "Structural Position in the World System and Economic Growth, 1955–1970: A Multiple Network Analysis of Transnational Interactions." *American Journal of Sociology* 84 (1979): 1096–1126.

Strange, Susan, "What Is Economic Power, and Who Has It?" *International Journal* 30 (1975): 207–24.

Therborn, Goran. "Enterprises, Markets and States. A First, Modest Contribution to a General Theory of Capitalist Politics." University of Toronto, Structural Analysis Programme Working Paper 9. Toronto, 1979.

Tilly, Charles (ed.). *The Formation of National States in Western Europe*. Princeton: Princeton University Press, 1975.

Vergopoulos, Kostas. "Capitalism and Peasant Productivity." *The Journal of Peasant Studies* 5 (1978): 445–65.

Wallerstein, Immanuel. *The Modern World-System. I Capitalist Agriculture and the Origins of the European World-Economy in the Sixteenth Century*. New York: Academic Press, 1974a.

"The Rise and Demise of the World Capitalist System," *Comparative Studies in Society and History* 16 (1974b): 387–415.

The Capitalist World Economy. Cambridge: Cambridge University Press, 1979.

The Modern World-System. II Mercantilism and the Consolidation of the European World Economy. New York: Academic Press, 1980.

Webber, Max, *Economy and Society*. Edited by Guenther Roth and Claus Wittich. New York: Bedminster Press, 1968.

White, Harrison C., Scott A. Boorman, and Ronald L. Breiger. "Social Structure from Multiple Networks. I. Blockmodels of Roles and Positions." *American Journal of Sociology* 81 (1976): 730–80.

Part IV
Social change

They're rioting in Africa,
There's strife in Iran.
What nature doesn't do to us,
Will be done by our fellow man.

(Harnick, 1961)

These Kingston Trio lyrics are as relevant today as they were two decades ago – although some would now insist that the last line should be gender-neutral. Scholars, policymakers, and people, in general, are fascinated by strife. Strife makes for vivid television images and appears to affect national interests mightily. In contrast, stability tends to be taken for granted, even when it is oppressive or exhilarating. Scholars have seriously studied collective political upheavals, violent and nonviolent, since at least the time of Machiavelli. Their work has been an important part of research on social change: fundamental alterations permeating structures of relationships between individuals, groups, and organizations in social systems.

Studies of social change, like studies of community, have historically concentrated on the effects of those large-scale processes associated with the Industrial Revolution. As Tilly points out in the first chapter in this part of the book, until recently most analysts have associated the dramatic changes in the nature of political activity since the early 1800s with "modernization": the rapid shift from a traditional, agrarian, homogeneous, solidary world to one that is fast changing, urban, postindustrial, heterogeneous, fragmented, and filled with conflict. Most analyses of modernization have attributed political strife to the uprooting of large masses from their traditional homes, villages, families, and work groups. The reasoning behind such analyses has run parallel to that underlying warnings of the "loss of community." It has pointed to the migration from villages to giant cities, the replacement of small enterprises by large industries, the loss of local communal autonomy to remote central bureaucracies, the replacement of religious belief by secular and scientific authority, and the easy movement of people and ideas due to modern means of transportation and communication.

Most of those who look at modernization in this way worry that such social changes have been cataclysmic, cutting people loose from the communal ties that integrated and restrained them. Recalling Tocqueville and Durkheim, they fear that the masses, adrift in cities and large bureaucracies, lack communal social control and normative guidance. Hence, they believe that the members of "mass societies" are ripe for mobilization by political movements that promise new purpose and social attachments. All that would be necessary, they reason, would be a sudden gap between material well-being and "rising expectations," coupled with the appearance of canny, demagogic leaders who know how to recruit them.

Scenarios of this kind continue to capture the minds of journalists, policymakers, and the public. These scenarios have been used to explain such disparate phenomena as riots by blacks in the United States, demonstrations by French students, the overthrow of the Shah of Iran, intercommunal conflict in Lebanon, and uprisings by black South Africans. The modernization analysis has often persuaded policymakers to implement "community development" programs – such as the American War on Poverty and the Peace Corps – aimed at ending alienation and strife by creating new communal roots.

Despite its continued popularity, the modernization argument has been severely criticized on both empirical and theoretical grounds by structural analysts who contend that it (a) inaccurately describes the nature of pre- and (post-)industrial communities and the nature of politically active groups within these communities, and (b) asks misleading questions about social change in general and the nature of political activity in particular. The modernization argument rests on a contrast between supposedly solidary preindustrial communities and supposedly lost postindustrial ones. Yet, as we have already seen in Part II, ties and networks remain strong and useful in contemporary communities. Far from falling apart, they continue to provide crucial interpersonal resources and positioning for individuals within larger social structures.

Part IV opens with *Charles Tilly*'s analysis of one side of this argument: He questions whether preindustrial social systems were "a closed, traditional, unconnected, immobile set of social worlds." Tilly argues that far from being isolated pastoral backwaters, rural European communities were open, connected, and mobile social systems. By the end of the eighteenth century, "major shares of the rural and small-town population were involved in various forms of manufacturing." In many parts of Europe, mercantile capitalism had penetrated deeply into village life. The rural population already produced heavily for the market, responding to socioeconomic changes in supply and demand both locally and far from home.

Thus, Tilly points out, nineteenth-century changes in capitalism and the growth of nation-states transformed communal relations but did not demolish them. With the concentration of capital in large trade and manufacturing organizations, migrants moved to the large cities – so much so that rural manufacturing was much more prevalent *before* large-scale

industrialization than *after* it. Moreover, many migrants were rural industrial workers whose jobs had been displaced by the growth of large urban
factories and who were already used to wage labor, specialized work, and job
mobility. They were rarely traditional peasants ignorant of market labor.

Tilly contends that the concentration of capital and the growth of national
states substantially changed the nature of collective political activity in the
nineteenth century. In an analysis echoing Howard's (Chapter 7) and
Bodemann's (Chapter 8), he argues that "local" and "patronized" collective
activity gave way to "national" and "autonomous" activity. There were
much more sharply defined cleavages and contentions between powerholders
and the quickly growing proletariat. New kinds of interest groups became
prominent and national in scope reflecting large-scale coalitions and
cleavages, for example, business firms, trade associations, political parties,
and labor unions. Thus it is unlikely that nineteenth-century collective
political disturbances were a destructive, alienated response to the strains of
rapid, uneven social change. "It is more plausible," concludes Tilly, "that
those who struggled were coherent actors pursuing well-defined interests."

Thus, structural analysts criticize the modernization argument for taking
the quiet stability of a social system for granted and only seeking to explain
disturbances in it. The implicit ideology of modernization, they contend,
treats sociopolitical integration as normal and protest and conflict as
aberrations. Its explanations for participation in such strife are patronizing,
rooted in abnormal psychology. They assume that stresses and strains of rapid
change will unsettle the masses, and that loss of communal control will
unleash their base instincts to rape, rob, and riot. Structural analytic research,
however, has shown that active participants in all kinds of political activity
tend to be the comparatively well-connected and not rootless, isolated,
normless masses. Black American ghetto rioters, for instance, are more likely
than nonrioters to be employed, settled, and have well-developed communal
ties. Merchants in their bazaars played central roles in overthrowing the
Shah, linking together politically active groups through their central access to
information, goods, and money. Those most active in contemporary
Lebanese struggles seem to be the communally connected rather than the
disaffected.

Hence, structural analysts see political strife as growing out of routine
political activity and embedded in the broader structures of everyday life. In
their view, large-scale social changes have not destroyed communities but
have transformed the conditions under which coalitions and competitions
operate between interest groups. Tilly points out that "most of the time
ordinary people have an idea, more or less, of their short-run interests, but
vary enormously in their capacity and opportunity to act on these interests."
A key analytic task, then, is to study "the ways in which large social changes
alter the interests, capacities, and opportunities of ordinary people."

Such a stance permeates *Robert J. Brym*'s chapter. He wants to know why various sorts of Jewish intellectuals affiliated with different political groups in turn-of-the-century Russia engaged in revolutionary activities. He notes that the traditional explanations for their revolutionary political activities have been based on their "rootlessness." Intellectuals are alienated from society, the traditional argument asserts, because they find it difficult to find suitable jobs and because established political parties rarely recruit them. Since Jewish intellectuals tend to be especially marginal in many societies, they were significantly "malintegrated" into late nineteenth-century Russia.

This "rootlessness" argument clearly has a great deal in common with the mass-society perspective since its theme is that disconnections caused by large-scale social changes led the socially isolated actors to latch onto the new social movements. In contrast, Brym offers a "rootedness" explanation: He observes that new intellectual currents do not simply spring into existence in response to the severing of traditional bonds. Turn-of-the-century Russian-Jewish intellectuals did not affiliate randomly with revolutionary groups. The specific form of the ties among these intellectuals and between them and the larger social structure strongly affected the disproportionate role played by Jews in Russian revolutionary movements as well as their specific ideological attachments.

Major uneven social changes in Russia during the eighteenth and nineteenth centuries meant that Jews living in different areas were subject to a variety of assimilatory pressures. In a significant minority of cases, they became less dependent on their ties to fellow Jews and more structurally embedded in Russian society. Brym demonstrates that Jewish intellectuals undergoing such experiences were apt to join the Bolsheviks and Mensheviks, revolutionary groups arguing "that the only reasonable solution to the Jewish problem was the complete assimilation of the Jewish people within a country rid of autocratic rule." In contrast, those intellectuals who remained structurally embedded in Jewish social life were more apt to become involved with the Labor Zionists who sought a Palestinian Jewish homeland or with the Bundists seeking Jewish cultural autonomy within Russia. Brym's analysis is not limited to questions relevant to a specific interest in Jewish circumstances at the time: He argues that the kinds of social networks in which the intelligentsia were involved greatly affected their relations with workers, peasants, and non-Jewish intellectuals.

Douglas R. White and *H. Gilman McCann* examine a different kind of revolution in their chapter: a scientific revolution or shift away from the practices and beliefs associated with one paradigm and toward another. Like other authors in this section, they argue that revolutionary changes in attitudes or practices are strongly influenced by shifts in the structure of social relations among the concerned actors (see also Erickson, Chapter 5). Their data consist of journal references that chemists made to one another's work during the period when a major paradigmatic shift was taking place from phlogiston- to oxygen-based chemistry. White and McCann use these data to demonstrate how a new technique, "material entailment analysis", provides a useful way to study transitive relations between network members. In this case, they show that material entailment analysis can be used to represent detailed patterns of relations among chemists and to trace changes in these relational networks through the 1780s. They are thus able to show that the "chemical revolution" was associated with a fundamental reorganization in the structure of a scientific community.

The three chapters in this part thus provide a structural analytic basis for studying social change at levels ranging from global transformations to shifting patterns of interpersonal relations. Tilly's chapter traces the large-scale context of social change, showing that it has been based on the transformation of connectivity rather than on the chaos of disruption. Brym looks within a specific context to show how the domestic affiliations of Jewish intellectuals affected the form and content of their revolutionary activities. White and McCann demonstrate a powerful way of tracking structural shifts in relations between individuals and groups. A key message of this section, then, is that social change is really social structural change and can be usefully and concretely studied on that basis.

LITERATURE CITED

Harnick, Sheldon. "The Merry Minuet." In *The Kingston Trio from the Hungry i.* Hollywood, Calif.: Capitol Records, 1961.

12

Misreading, then rereading, nineteenth-century social change

Charles Tilly

Leitmotifs

The discipline of sociology grew from the encounter between worried bourgeois and the massive changes of the European nineteenth century. For the most part, both the bourgeois and the sociologists constructed faulty pictures of those changes. Examining a world that had long been mobile, interdependent, heavily involved in manufacturing, strongly oriented to cities, and full of conflict, what did they see? They imagined a past world that was immobile, fragmented, agrarian, rural, homogeneous, and integrated. Surrounded by a world in which whole regions were deindustrializing, work was proletarianizing, capital was concentrating, power was nationalizing, the scale of formal organization was expanding, and capitalists were seizing control of the entire productive process, how did they theorize? They created models of social change that ignored most of these monumental processes. A Tönnies or a Durkheim could represent the basic changes as a rapid shift from an integrated past to a disintegrated present and could portray crime, conflict, and personal malaise as consequences of the individual disorientation and weakened social control produced by rapid change. Customary small-scale social life, went the tale, dissolved in the rising waters of urbanization, industrialization, and secularization.

The view of social change as the dissolution of customary small-scale social life is familiar. It became the dominant bourgeois analysis of the nineteenth century. It knits nicely with the notion that wealth, mobility, and urban experience corrupt virtuous peasants. It fits just as well, paradoxically, with the call for a civilizing mission on the part of schools, local government, and military service. The former is the conservative, nostalgic version, the latter the liberal, progressive version, of the same theory.

The bourgeois analysis gave rise to the great nineteenth-century dicho-

This chapter is a revised version of Charles Tilly, "Did the Cake of Custom Break?" in John Merriman (ed.), *Consciousness and Class Experience in Nineteenth-Century Europe* London: Hutchinson, 1979. I am grateful to Hutchinson for permission to revise and reprint the article.

tomies: *Gemeinschaft* and *Gesellschaft,* status and contract, mechanical and organic solidarity. It also helped form the presumptuous social sciences, whose objects were to document, to explain, and perhaps to guide the transition from one side of the dichotomy to the other.

Nor did the ideas die with the nineteenth century. On the contrary. They became the basis of standard twentieth-century conceptions, both academic and popular, of large-scale social change. Although the particular variants called modernization theory rose and fell in the quarter-century after World War II, the general idea of modernization as dissolution and integration has survived from the nineteenth century to our own time. In one form or another, it appears widely in North American analyses of Europe, including those of such widely read authors as Black (1966), Gillis (1970), Shorter (1975), and Stearns (1975). Recently, it has surfaced in Weber's widely acclaimed *Peasants into Frenchmen* (1976), a book that portrays France before about 1870 as a congeries of isolated, autonomous, traditionalist, and miserable societies that only the stirred-up communication of the late nineteenth century drew into national life. The difference between Weber and his colleagues does not lie in the novelty of his basic argument. It lies in his insistence on the period from 1870 to 1914 and, more important, in his extraordinary use of ethnographic detail to present the argument.

Familiarity is not truth. Is it *true* that the dominant social changes in nineteenth-century Europe comprised (or resulted from) the displacement of traditional, localized, immobile cultures by industrialism, urbanism, and expanding communication? That is doubtful. It is doubtful on two rather different grounds: (1) because many of the most important concrete changes in the social life of nineteenth-century Europe did not follow the paths required by theories of modernization; (2) because the massive industrialization, urbanization, and communications shifts – which did, indeed, occur – grew from the interaction of two deeper and wider processes: the growth of national states and the expansion of capitalism.

My discussion dwells on the first point: the failure of important processes to follow the courses charted by theories of modernization. That is the easier of the two points to establish. It also leads naturally to consideration of the reasons for the failure of the theories, then to reflection on alternative general accounts of social change in nineteenth-century Europe. Those alternatives will easily take us back to capitalism and state making.

The issues matter in their own right: We are asking, after all, how the world changes and how the world we know came into being. The issues also matter in another way: theories of modernization underlie many accounts of nineteenth-century conflict, consciousness, and collective action. Conservative modernization models nest neatly with interpretations of protest, conflict, and collective action as irrational responses to the stresses and strains of rapid change. Progressive modernization models, on the other hand, articulate plausibly with a vision of awakening consciousness, of increasing integration into cosmopolitan worldviews that guide collective action on a large scale. If the underlying models prove incorrect, we shall have to consider another alternative more seriously: that most of the time ordinary people have an idea, more or less clear, of their short-run interests, but vary enormously in their capacity and opportunity to act on those interests. If that is the case – as, obviously, I think it is – the proper substitute for the study of modernization is likely to be the study of the ways in which large social changes alter the interests, capacities, and opportunities of ordinary people.

Notions of modernization

Whether theories of modernization are worthless or merely cumbersome depends, however, on how much we ask of them. In an undemanding version, the notion of modernization is simply a name for general features of contemporary life: intense communications, big organization, mass production, and so on. If our program is simply to inquire whether those features of social life were already visible in the nineteenth century and to search for their origins, then the analysis of modernization is no more misleading than most other retrospective schemes.

In a somewhat more demanding guise, modernization becomes a label for dominant patterns of change. Lepsius (1977: 24–9), for instance, breaks modernization into these elements:

1. differentiation
2. mobilization
3. participation
4. institutionalization of conflict.

The fit between these terms and the main trends in nineteenth-century Europe depends on their specification: which units are supposed to be differentiating, who is supposed to be mobilizing with respect to what end, and so on. It also depends on our vantage point. From the perspective of the national state and the national elite, differentiation, mobilization, participation and institutionalization summarize many of the changes going on in nineteenth-century Europe. From the perspective of the local community, many of the same changes involved dedifferentiation, demobilization, perhaps even deinstitutionalization: Rights, rituals, and rounds of life that had previously prevailed now lost their strength. Nevertheless, any model of social change requires us to take some vantage point, and the center is as permissible a vantage point as any other. Thus, we can make it a question of fact whether differentiation, mobilization, participation, and institutionalization do, indeed, describe the main trends in nineteenth-century Europe, as seen from its central locations.

The real difficulties with modernization theories only begin when we move from simple inventories of common themes to the analysis of what sorts of structures changed and why. Did urbanism, industrialism, and expanding communications dissolve previously stable, small, self-contained structures; release people from their control; generate disorder as a consequence; and finally produce a new, complex, large-scale set of connections to replace the old? Such an account, to my mind, has far too little power, interest, and conflict in it. But even if it were sometimes a plausible account of social change, it would be an unlikely model for the European nineteenth century. Its most important weakness as a guide to the nineteenth century is its starting point: a closed, traditional, unconnected, immobile set of social worlds. In the remainder of this chapter, I spend a major part of my effort in demonstrating the openness, connectedness, and mobility of the European world as it faced the nineteenth century. Because the rural world is the one in which modernization models should apply most clearly, I concentrate on changes in Europe's rural areas.

What will we find in the countryside? We will find a mobile, differentiated population heavily involved in different forms of production for the market and responsive to changes occurring far from home. We will find varying forms of mercantile capitalism penetrating deep into village life. We will find agents of national states intervening actively in local organization in order to extract the men, food, and money required for armies and other expensive governmental activities. We will find a sensitive interplay between economic structure and family life – between the organization of production and of reproduction. We will find few traces of the isolation and autarky that are dear to theorists of modernization.

None of this means that the nineteenth century was a time of stability or of trendless turbulence. Industrial capitalism took shape in important parts of Europe. Capital concentrated and the scale of production rose. The working population, urban and rural, proletarianized. Firms, parties, trade unions, and other specialized associations assumed much more prominent roles in public life. National states continued to gain power by comparison with any other organizations. Capitalism and state making, in short, transformed social life. That includes the social life of the countryside.

We can have no hope of enumerating, much less of analyzing, the full range of nineteenth-century change in one brief chapter. After a look at broad patterns of nineteenth-century change over the continent as a whole, let us close in on the nature of employment in Europe's rural areas.

Population growth and vital rates

A glance at the elementary statistics of the period gives an immediate sense of the nineteenth-century's dynamisms. The European population of 1800 stood

Table 12.1. *Annual growth rates and vital rates for major world areas, 1960–8*

Area	Annual growth rate %	Crude birth rate	Crude death rate
Africa	2.4	45	21
North America	1.4	21	9
Latin America	2.9	40	12
Asia	2.0	38	17
Europe	0.9	18	10
Soviet Union	1.3	20	7
Oceania	2.1	26	10
World	1.9	34	15

Source: Annuaire Statistique de la France 1970-71: 7.

in the vicinity of 190 million, that of 1900 around 500 million. The increase of more than 300 million people implies a growth rate around 1% per year. Such a rate is not sensational by twentieth-century standards: As Table 12.1 indicates, Europe is still growing at about that rate, and all other continents are growing faster. But for a whole continent to grow so fast for so long was an extraordinary event in the history of the world up to that time (Durand, 1967; McKeown, 1976).

The increase occurred, furthermore, despite a probable net loss through migration on the order of 35 million people. For the century as a whole, a reasonable guess is that 45 million Europeans left the continent, and 10 million returned home. Close to half the century's emigrants left from Britain and Ireland, and three-quarters of the British and Irish went to North America. The vast majority of emigrants from all parts of Europe sailed to the Americas; the transatlantic movement was one of the grandest migrations of all time. In sheer numbers and distances, it was probably unprecedented in human history.

If the estimates of migration are correct, Europe's excess of births over deaths during the century as a whole totaled close to 350 million. With a plausible crude birth rate of 35 for the whole continent and the whole century, that figure implies a crude death rate in the vicinity of 25. In the world of the later twentieth century, a crude birth rate of 35 and a crude death rate of 25 could only occur in a poor country. For purposes of comparison, Table 12.1 presents continental rates from the 1960s. No continent now approximates the European nineteenth-century situation; all continents now have lower mortality rates, and the poorer parts of the world all have larger gaps between birth rate and death rate; that means, of course, that the rates of natural increase are higher today than they were in nineteenth-century Europe. The closest approximations of Europe's situation a hundred years ago are contemporary Africa and Asia.

Table 12.2. *Vital rates for selected European areas in 1800, 1850, and 1900*

Country	Crude birth rate[a]			Crude death rate[a]		
	1800	1850	1900	1800	1850	1900
Austria	n.a	39.6	35.0	n.a	32.9	25.2
Belgium	n.a.	30.0	28.9	n.a.	21.2	19.3
Bulgaria	n.a.	n.a.	42.3	n.a.	n.a.	22.6
Denmark	29.9	31.4	29.7	28.5	19.1	16.8
Finland	37.6	35.7	32.6	25.5	26.3	21.9
France	32.9	26.8	21.3	27.7	21.4	21.9
Germany	n.a.	37.2	35.6	n.a.	25.6	22.1
Hungary	n.a.	n.a.	39.4	n.a.	n.a.	27.0
Ireland	n.a.	n.a.	22.7	n.a.	n.a.	19.6
Italy	n.a.	n.a.	33.0	n.a.	n.a.	23.8
Netherlands	n.a.	34.6	31.6	n.a.	22.2	17.9
Norway	22.7	31.0	29.7	27.6	17.2	15.8
Portugal	n.a.	n.a.	30.5	n.a.	n.a.	20.3
Romania	n.a.	n.a.	38.8	n.a.	n.a.	24.2
Russia	n.a.	n.a.	49.3	n.a.	n.a.	31.1
Serbia	n.a.	n.a.	42.4	n.a.	n.a.	23.4
Spain	n.a.	n.a.	33.9	n.a.	n.a.	29.0
Sweden	28.7	31.9	27.0	31.4	19.8	16.8
Switzerland	n.a.	n.a.	28.6	n.a.	n.a.	19.3
England, Wales	n.a.	33.4	28.7	n.a.	20.8	18.2
Scotland	n.a.	n.a.	29.6	n.a.	n.a.	18.5

[a] n.a. indicates "not available."
Source: Mitchell (1975: 105–20).

Within Europe, the nineteenth century brought pivotal changes in the character and geography of natural increase. Over the continent as a whole, the trend of nineteenth-century fertility was no doubt a gentle decline, as compared with a significant drop in mortality; the difference between the two rates of decline accounted for the continent's large natural increase. Table 12.2 presents some scattered observations of birth rates and death rates for 1800, 1850, and 1900. In general, the poorer parts of Europe (which were probably also, on the average, areas of higher fertility and mortality throughout the century) lack data for the early years; there was a rough correlation between prosperity and statistical reporting. As of 1900, the range of variation was large: crude birth rates running from 21.3 in France to 49.3 in Russia, crude death rates from 15.8 in Norway to 31.1 in Russia. As Ansley Coale (1969) and his collaborators have shown, a long frontier separated the high-fertility regions of Eastern and Southeastern Europe from the low- to medium-fertility regions of the north and west. In these statistics, Bulgaria, Hungary, Romania, Russia, and Serbia stand well above other countries.

The national units mask further diversity: Fertility and mortality correspond much more closely to economic and cultural regions than to political boundaries. Although Hungary shows up in these statistics as a high-fertility area, for example, Hungary actually included some of Europe's lowest-fertility regions. Andorka and his colleagues have done family-reconstitution studies of several villages in the Ormansag and Sarkoz regions of Hungary during the eighteenth and nineteenth centuries; there they have discovered marital fertility plummeting to remarkably low levels. In those areas an arrangement known as the "one-child family system" prevailed; by 1850 actual completed family sizes were running between 3 and 4 (Andorka, 1977). Plenty of other studies from elsewhere show significant village-to-village variation as a function of economic opportunity and family structure (e.g., Levine, 1977; Gaunt, 1977; Spagnoli, 1977).

Industrialization

One of the factors behind the changing microgeography of fertility in nineteenth-century Europe was the continent's industrialization. Industrialization has two dimensions: (1) a decrease in the proportion of economic activity devoted to agriculture, forestry, and fishing, and (2) an increase in the scale of producing units. Our twentieth-century prejudice – compounded by a sloganeering idea of the Industrial Revolution and a fixation on the factory as the vehicle of industrial growth – is to think of the two as tightly correlated. In fact, they have often varied quite separately from each other. Many regions of Europe were already relatively industrial with respect to the first dimension by the end of the eighteenth century: Major shares of the rural and small-town population were involved in various forms of manufacturing. But the scale remained very small: The household and the small shop were the typical producing units. The nineteenth century saw both a substantial decline in the share of agriculture, forestry, and fishing and a dramatic rise in the average scale of production.

No one has so far assembled comparable accounts of these nineteenth century changes for all regions of Europe. Some features of the changes, nevertheless, are fairly clear:

1. The areas that experienced major industrialization during the nineteenth century were basically of two kinds:
   a. areas in which small-scale manufacturing had already been important during the eighteenth century – the regions of Manchester, Lille, Milan, Barcelona, Moscow, and so on – and which experienced an urbanization and increase in the scale of that industry during the nineteenth century;
   b. areas in which coal deposits combined with water or rail transportation to facilitate the development of heavy industry: Yorkshire, much of Belgium, Silesia, and so on.

2. As this implosion of industry occurred, large parts of the European countryside deindustrialized, devoting themselves more exclusively to agriculture.

3. In absolute terms, agriculture, forestry, and fishing did not decline. They actually grew, but more slowly than manufacturing and services. In sheer numbers, the agricultural labor force reached its maximum some time around World War I.

4. Wage-laborers – proletarians in both agriculture and industry – increased far more rapidly than the rest of the labor force. One reasonable guess is that proletarians and their families comprised 90 million of Europe's 190 million people in 1800 and had grown to 300 million of the total of 500 million by the end of the century. After having occurred mainly in villages and small towns for centuries, most of the nineteenth-century increase of the proletarian population took place in cities. Urbanization and proletarianization were interdependent processes.

As a result of these changes, regional disparities in industrial activity, wealth, urban concentration, and population density increased through the nineteenth century. Around 1900 the major countries of Europe distributed themselves as in Table 12.3. The proportions rose, broadly speaking, with increasing distance from the English Channel.

The changing geography of wealth shows up in Bairoch's (1976) estimates of per capita gross national product. Table 12.4 shows the eight highest-ranking areas in 1830 and 1900.

Real GNP per capita, according to Bairoch's estimates, rose by about 90 percent over those 70 years. That is slow growth by twentieth-century standards, but extraordinary compared with anything that had happened before. Per capita GNP grew fastest in Denmark, Sweden, Switzerland, Germany, and Belgium – especially, that is, in the areas that saw the development of coal-consuming, metal-processing industries.

The map of urban population conformed more and more closely to the map of large-scale industry. Table 12.5 summarizes the changes. In 1800, close to 3% of the European population lived in cities of 100,000 or more. By 1850, the proportion had risen to around 5%, by 1900, 10%. That meant a rise from 5.4 million to 12.7 million to 50.1 million inhabitants of big cities – almost a quadrupling in the last half of the century. The combination of substantial natural increase within cities and massive rural-to-urban migration produced thunderous urban growth: about 0.6% per year from 1800 to 1850, about 2.1% per year from 1850 to 1900.[1]

The regional disparities were wide in 1800 and widened during the century. In 1800, the presence of giant Constantinople made the European segment of what was to become Turkey the most urban of the continent's major political units: 13.3% of European Turkey's entire population lived in that one city of

Table 12.3. *Regional disparities in Europe around 1900*

Over 70% of the labor force in agriculture, forestry, and fishing: Bulgaria 81.9, Romania 79.6
61–70%: Hungary 70.0, Portugal 65.1, Spain 68.1
51–60%: Austria 59.8, Finland 51.5, Italy 58.7, Russia 58.6, Sweden 53.5
41–50%: Denmark 46.6, France 41.4, Ireland 42.9, Norway 40.8, Poland 45.9
31–40%: Germany 39.9, Switzerland 34.2
Less than 31%: Belgium 27.1, Netherlands 30.8, United Kingdom 9.1

Sources: Mitchell (1975: 153–65) and Bairoch (1968: 83–120).

Table 12.4. *Per capita gross national product, Europe, 1830 and 1900 (in 1960 U.S. dollars and prices)*

1830		1900	
Netherlands	317	United Kingdom	881
United Kingdom	346	Switzerland	785
Belgium	295	Belgium	721
Norway	280	Germany	639
Switzerland	276	Denmark	633
Italy	265	Netherlands	614
France	264	France	604
Spain	263	Norway	577
Europe	240	Europe	455

Source: Bairoch (1976: 286).

600,000. Elsewhere, the range ran downward from the 10–11% for Denmark, England, and Wales to a number of countries with no city of 100,000 or more. By the end of the century, Finland was the only large political unit with no city of 100,000; Helsinki then had about 90,000 residents. But the range ran from less than 5% in Finland, Greece, Hungary, and Romania to more than 30% in Scotland, England, and Wales. The rank orders of urbanization and industrialization had converged.

Either because no one with the heroic statistical capacities of a Paul Bairoch has so far compiled the evidence or because the changes involved do not lend themselves to simple numerical summary, other major changes that were undoubtedly happening are harder to document. Roads, then railroads, proliferated; mail and telegraph communications multiplied; newspapers circulated as schooling and literacy increased; voluntary associations, trade unions, political parties waxed; and so on through the inventory of communications, organizations, and everyday routines.

Amid the great swirl of transformation, the expansion and reorganization of European states set some of the main currents of change. Perhaps the most dramatic feature of Europe's nineteenth-century state making was the consolidation of the state system into a smaller and smaller set of larger and

Table 12.5. *Number of inhabitants and percentage of population in cities of 100,000 or more, 1800–1900, in selected areas of Europe*

Area	Number of inhabitants (thousands)			Percentage of population		
	1800	1850	1900	1800	1850	1900
Austria	231.9	549.6	2462.4	1.7	3.0	9.5
Belgium	—[a]	326.7	1148.7	—	7.5	17.1
Denmark	105.0	142.0	491.3	10.7	9.4	20.2
Finland	0.0	0.0	0.0	0.0	0.0	0.0
France	852.4	2025.7	6005.4	3.2	5.8	15.4
Greece	0.0	0.0	111.5	0.0	0.0	4.4
Hungary	0.0	170.0	837.2	0.0	1.3	4.3
Ireland	165.0	258.4	722.1	3.0	3.9	16.1
Italy	1053.0	1607.5	3206.4	5.8	6.7	9.9
Netherlands	200.0	224.0	1137.5	9.3	7.2	22.0
Norway	0.0	0.0	227.6	0.0	0.0	10.1
Poland	100.0	160.0	989.8	3.3	3.3	9.9
Portugal	180.0	240.0	529.0	5.8	6.3	9.8
Prussia/Germany	272.0	799.0	9007.3	1.1	2.3	16.0
Romania	0.0	120.0	282.1	0.0	3.1	4.5
Scotland	0.0	490.7	1390.9	0.0	16.8	30.8
Spain	400.0	450.0	1676.3	3.3	3.1	9.0
Sweden	0.0	0.0	452.6	0.0	0.0	8.9
Switzerland	0.0	0.0	364.7	0.0	0.0	11.0
European Turkey	600.0	850.0	1230.0	13.3	15.2	20.0
England and Wales	959.3	3992.1	12806.2	10.5	21.7	39.0
European Russia	470.0	850.0	5012.5	1.3	1.5	5.0
Total Europe	5406.6	12656.9	50091.0	2.8	4.8	10.1

[a]Dash (—) indicates not available.
Source: Tilly, Fonde, and O'Shea (1972).

larger units: about 50 states of various sorts on the eve of the French Revolution; a radical reduction through French conquests to about 25 states in 1800 and about 20 in 1812; a temporary reversion to about 35 states with France's defeat, followed by a new consolidation process that left 20–25 independent states (depending on how we define "independent" and "state") at World War I. Although French imperialism cleared the way and nineteenth-century wars took their toll, the chief paths to consolidation passed through semivoluntary unions, notably those of Germany and Italy. Throughout the process, state structures expanded, centralized, and became the dominant organizations within their own territories. A number of innovations followed: uniformed professional police forces, national elections and referenda, censuses and statistical bureaus, income taxes, technical schools for specialists, civil service careers, and many other pieces of the state apparatus that have prevailed into our own time.

Can we reasonably apply the word "modernization" to this ensemble of changes? That depends on how demanding an idea of modernization we adopt. If all we require is that recognizable features of twentieth-century life emerge, then the urbanization, large-scale industrialization, fertility decline, and other changes portrayed by the statistics easily qualify as modernization. If we demand common paths of change – something like Lepsius's differentiation, mobilization, participation, and institutionalization of conflict – the question remains moot; observations at a national or European scale simply do not tell us how the changes occurred. And if we want to try a causal model of modernization (one in which, for instance, intensified communications produce new states of consciousness, which in turn make people more open to rational solutions for their problems), the hopelessness of approaching the analysis with hugely aggregated evidence becomes clear. We must look at evidence that comes closer to the experiences of individuals and small groups. Let us consider how work changed in Europe's rural areas.

Peasants and proletarians

In order to understand changes in the nineteenth-century European country-side, we must exorcise the ghosts in the word "peasantry." If all we mean by peasants is poor people who work the soil, then in 1800 most Europeans were peasants. Usually, however, we have something more precise in mind: something like agriculturalists organized in households that control the land on which they live, draw most of their subsistence from that land, and supply the bulk of their own labor requirements from their own efforts. By that definition, the bulk of the European rural population was already nonpeasant by the start of the nineteenth century. In much of Eastern and Southern Europe, large landlords made the basic agricultural production decisions and used a variety of devices to draw labor from a mass of agricultural workers who controlled little or no land. In much of Northern and Western Europe, a major share of the agricultural labor force consisted either of day laborers or of live-in servants and hands. Although the serfs of Eastern Europe and the day laborers of Western Europe often had garden plots or small fields of their own, they depended for survival on the sale of their household labor power. They were, in a classic Marxian sense of the word, proletarians.

Again a little exorcism is in order. Despite Marx's own clear concentration on changes in the rural labor force, the word "proletarian" has taken on an urban-industrial imagery as in *Modern Times* with Charlie Chaplin turning bolts on the assembly line. If we confine the proletariat to people working at subdivided tasks in large units under close time discipline, then that industrial proletariat certainly grew during the nineteenth century, but it probably did not approach a fifth of the European labor force in 1900.

If, however, we include all people whose survival depended on the sale of their labor power to holders of capital – which was, after all, Marx's basic idea of the proletariat – then by the end of the nineteenth century the great majority of the European labor force was proletarian. Agricultural wage laborers were probably the largest category, but industrial and service workers were then competing for the lead. Before the middle of the nineteenth century, most of the large increase in the proletarian population occurred in small towns and rural areas. By a rough computation from the figures presented earlier, perhaps 50 million of the 70 million increase in the European population from 1800 to 1850 occurred in places under 20,000. It is reasonable to suppose that at least 40 of that 50-million increase in smaller places consisted of wageworkers and their families. During the second half of the century, the smaller places may have grown by another 140 million, the great bulk of the increase having been proletarian. By then, however, the cities were beginning to take over: 100 million of the 240-million increase occurred in places of 20,000 or more, and many of the smaller settlements that grew were actually suburbs and satellites of major industrial centers. To be sure, in the present state of the evidence, any such numbers rest on a tissue of suppositions. Yet, the main point is firm: The patterns of urban growth and of total population growth imply a massive proletarianization of the European people during the nineteenth century. Contrary to common impressions, much of that proletarianization took place in smaller towns and rural areas.

The sketchy evidence I have presented leaves open the possibility that the places of fewer than 20,000 inhabitants in question were mainly seats of mines, mills, and other large-scale industrial establishments. Some were; the hinterlands of Manchester and Lille, for example, were full of smaller industrial centers. Even in those two quintessential manufacturing regions, however, agricultural proletarians and rural outworkers multiplied during the nineteenth century. Away from the major poles of industrial growth, much more of the expansion took place in agriculture and in manufacturing on a very small scale.

The earlier European experience provides numerous examples of proletarianization within rural areas. In fact, the rural versions of proletarianization were so visible at the middle of the nineteenth century that Karl Marx considered them the basis of primitive accumulation: "The expropriation of the agricultural producer, of the peasant, from the soil, is the basis of the whole process" (Marx, n.d., chap. 26). It would be useful, however, to differentiate among types of agricultural regions rather more than Marx did. At a minimum we need to distinguish:

1. areas, such as coastal Flanders, in which peasants specialized in cash-crop production, and nonproducing landlords were unimportant

Table 12.6. *Proletarianization of British agricultural families, 1831*

Occupying families employing labor	144,600
Occupying families employing no labor	130,500
Laboring families	686,000
	961,100

Source: 1831 Census Abstract, Vol. I: ix.

2. areas, such as East Prussia, in which large landlords produced grain for the market by means of servile labor, whose subsistence came mainly from small plots assigned to their households
3. areas, such as southern England, in which large landlords likewise produced grain for the market, but with wage labor
4. areas, such as western France, in which landlords lived from rents and peasants lived from various combinations of owned, rented, and sharecropped land.

Within category 1, proletarianization tended to occur as a consequence of differentiation within the peasantry: Extra children and households losing in the local competition moved into wage labor for other peasants. In Category 2, the redistribution of land that commonly accompanied nineteenth-century emancipations produced a temporary movement away from the proletariat, but the substitution of cash payments for access to subsistence plots created a far larger movement toward wage labor. Category 3 began with an essentially proletarian agricultural labor force and grew by adding more wage laborers. Category 4 sometimes transformed itself into Category 1 by means of the increasing involvement of peasants in cash-crop production, sometimes transformed itself into Category 3 as the landlords consolidated their control over production, but rarely created proletarians within the agricultural sector. (Category 4 was not, however, a bulwark against proletarianization; it was an especially favorable environment for cottage industry.) The European agrarian structure, then, provided multiple paths out of the peasantry and multiple paths into the agricultural proletariat. Over the nineteenth century, the net shift from one to the other was very large.

In Europe as a whole, the proletarianization of agricultural labor had begun well before the nineteenth century. Great Britain was one sort of extreme; except for some portions of its Celtic fringes, Britain had essentially eliminated its peasantry by the start of the nineteenth century. By the time of the 1831 census, the breakdown of agricultural families in Britain ran as in Table 12.6.

Table 12.7 presents the occupations of males 20 and over for 1831. Both the breakdown for families and the breakdown for adult males show about 71% of Great Britain's agricultural labor force to be essentially landless laborers.

Table 12.7. *Distribution of occupations of males 20 and older in Great Britain, 1831 (percent)*

Category	England	Wales	Scotland	Total
Agricultural occupiers employing laborers	4.4	10.1	4.7	4.7
Agricultural occupiers not employing laborers	3.0	10.3	9.8	4.3
Agricultural laborers	23.3	28.5	15.9	22.5
Employed in manufacturing	9.8	3.2	15.3	10.3
Employed in retail trade or handicraft	30.1	22.2	27.7	29.5
Capitalists, bankers, professionals and other educated men	5.6	2.7	5.3	5.4
Nonagricultural laborers	15.7	16.2	13.9	15.4
Servants	2.2	1.1	1.1	2.0
Others	5.9	5.7	6.4	6.0
Total	100.0	100.0	100.1	100.0
Number	3,199,984	194,706	549,821	3,944,511

Source: Great Britain, Census Office. Abstract of the answers and returns made pursuant to an act, passed in the eleventh year of the reign of His Majesty King George IV, instituted "An Act for Taking an Account of the Population of Great Britain, and of the Increase or Diminution Thereof" (Westminster: House of Commons, 1831), vol. I, p. xiii, "General Summary of Great Britain."

For England alone, the figure was 76%. Although the division between owners and wageworkers within the category "retail trade or handicraft" (in which the letter P, for example, includes paper maker; pastry cook, confectioner; pattenmaker; pawnbroker; poulterer; printer; printseller; publican, hotel or innkeeper, retailer of beer) is hard to guess, the figures suggest that in 1831 Britain's agricultural labor force was more proletarian than the rest. By 1851, laborers amounted to some 85 percent of all agricultural workers (Deane and Cole, 1967: 143–4). That was the peak; thereafter, hired labor began to desert British agriculture for industry, and machines began to replace or displace labor as never before (Jones, 1964: 329–44).

Although Britain was extreme, it was not unique. Much of Eastern Europe began the nineteenth century with the bulk of its agricultural population proletarians of a different kind from their English cousins: as servile landless laborers on large estates (Blum, 1978: 38–44). Although nineteenth-century emancipations eventually gave some of them title to land, the main trend ran toward the creation of a vast agricultural proletariat. Peasant property may have increased in absolute terms, but the rural population grew much faster. A common interpretation of those trends (Blum, 1978: 435–6) is that an exogenously generated population increase overran the supply of land; my own view is that proletarianization helped create the population increases. Whichever argument is correct, however, the correlation between proletarianization and rural population growth is clear. In such southern European areas as Sicily, the dispossession of feudal landlords likewise made property owners of some former tenants; but its main effect was to accelerate the expropriation of the land by large farmers and bourgeois, and thus to hasten the proletarianization of the remainder of the agricultural workers (Romano, 1963; Schneider and Schneider, 1976: 116–18). Again, a rapid population increase aggravated the process of proletarianization, and again the causal connections between proletarianization and population increase are debatable.

The cases of Eastern and Southern Europe are well known. Less known until recently was the extensive proletarianization of the Scandinavian rural population. Winberg (1978: 170) sums up the Swedish experience:

> Between 1750 and 1850 the population of Sweden doubled. The increase in population was particularly rapid after 1810. Throughout this period about 90 percent of the national population lived in rural areas. The increase was very unequally distributed among the different social groups of the rural population. The number of *bonder* (peasants) rose by c. 10 percent, while the number of landless – i.e. *torpare* (crofters), *inhyseshjon* (borders), *statare* (farm workers partly paid in kind) etc. – more than quadrupled.

Winberg attributes the rural proletarianization to two main processes: a capitalistic reorganization of large estates that squeezed out the tenants in favor of wage laborers, and an increasing integration of the peasantry into the national market economy, which in turn produced increased differentiation between landed and landless. If that is the case, Sweden combined the paths of Category 1 and Category 2 and ended with a combination of a small number of capitalist landlords, a larger number of cash-crop farmers, and a very large number of agricultural wageworkers.

Protoindustry and proletarianization

Sweden was unusual in one important regard: Unless we count mining and forestry, very few of Sweden's rural workers went into industry. Over Europe as a whole, manufacturing played a large part in the transformation of the nineteenth-century countryside. Economic historians have recently begun to speak of protoindustrialization: the growth of manufacturing through the multiplication of small producing units rather than through the concentration of capital and labor. Economic historian Franklin Mendels (1972) introduced the term into the literature in order to cope with the way that sections of rural Flanders made large shifts from agriculture to manufacturing without the development of factories, without important changes in production techniques, without large accumulations of capital, without substantial urbanization of the working class.

Older economic historians, back to Marx, knew about cottage industry and allied forms of production long ago. The advantage of the new term is to draw attention to the variety of ways in which European entrepreneurs of the seventeenth to nineteenth centuries organized networks of households to produce large volumes of cheap goods for national and international markets. In the process, they made manufacturing not a mere by-employment for farmers, but the dominant economic activity in important parts of the European countryside. *Industrialisierung vor der Industrialisierung*, by Kriedte, Medick, and Schlumbohm (1977), surveys the growing literature on the subject. The book emphasizes the ways in which protoindustrialization transformed the rest of the rural economy, established its own peculiar patterns of family structure, and cleared the way for large-scale industrialization. It makes clear the utter inadequacy of any portrayal of the nineteenth-century rural world as a territory essentially populated by peasants and fundamentally devoted to agriculture.

As Kriedte sums up the importance of protoindustrialization:

> Protoindustry stands between two worlds, the narrow world of the village and the boundary-breaking world of trade, between the agrarian economy and merchant capitalism. The agrarian sector produces a labor supply, a supply of merchant-entrepreneur knowledge and capital, supplies of products and markets. Merchant capital opens foreign markets to rural crafts, whose personnel thus become aware of the opportunity for expansion if they enter into protoindustrialization.... The unified symbiosis of merchant capital and peasant society thereby marks a decisive step on the way to industrial capitalism. (Kriedte et al., 1977: 88)

The general line of argument, in terms of "vent-for-surplus," goes back to Adam Smith (Caves, 1965, 1971). But Kriedte and his collaborators go on to point out the irreversible effects of the new symbiosis: commercialization of the entire rural economy, dependence on adjacent agricultural areas for subsistence, transformation of households into suppliers (and breeders) of wage labor, detachment of marriage and reproduction from the inheritance of land, acceleration of population growth, rising rural densities, the growth of an industrial proletariat in the countryside.

Kriedte et al. brush against, but do not quite state, a fundamental advantage of protoindustrial production over urban shops and factories: In a time of small-scale agricultural production with high costs for the transportation and storage of food, protoindustry kept the bulk of the labor force close to the food sources, and made industrial labor available, in odd moments and peak seasons, for food production. Up to a point, the individual merchant could assume that the workers would feed themselves. The logic of the system was, in short, a cheap, elastic, compliant labor force for merchants who are short on capital and technical expertise but long on knowledge of opportunities and connections.

Protoindustrial production and producers multiplied beginning well before 1800 and did not start to contract visibly until well into the nineteenth century. A labor force consisting largely of dispersed, part-time and seasonal workers resists enumeration; we are unlikely ever to have precise counts of the rise and fall of prodoindustrial workers. Nevertheless, we have enough evidence to be sure that protoindustrialization was not simply one of several known patterns of change. Before the middle of the nineteenth century, when manufacturing increased significantly in some part of Europe, it normally increased through the multiplication of households and other small, dispersed producing units linked to national and international markets by webs of entrepreneurs and merchants. It increased, that is, not through the concentration of capital, labor, and the scale of production, but through protoindustrialization.

That is notably true of textile production. As Milward and Saul (1973: 93–4) put it:

> It is impossible not to be struck by the extraordinary growth of spinning and weaving in the countryside of many European areas. In some areas the manufacture of iron products, toys or watches developed in the same way, but textiles, whether of linen, wool or the newfangled cotton were the typical rural product. The technological transformations which initiated the Industrial Revolution in Britain were heavily concentrated in these rural textile industries and their development on the continent may therefore be seen as the true precursor of the Industrial Revolution there rather than the older "manufacturers." But setting on one side the developments of the Industrial Revolution itself and looking at the matter simply from the point of view of employment in industrial activities whether those industries were "revolutionized" or not it would still be true to say that the most industrial landscapes in late eighteenth century Europe, for all their lack of chimneys, were the country areas around Lille, Rouen, Barcelona, Zurich, Basel Geneva.

The rise of coal-burning and metalworking industries during the nineteenth century eventually changed the picture. But it took a long time. The expansion of manufacturing continued to take a protoindustrial form well past 1800.

Because of Braun's (1960) rich, intensive analyses of the Zurich region, the Zuricher Oberland has become the locus classicus for students of protoindustrialization. In the Zuricher Oberland, the poor subsistence farming areas far from the city had been thinly settled exporters of domestic servants and mercenaries until the eighteenth century. Then the growth of an export-oriented cotton industry based in Zurich but drawing the bulk of its labor from the countryside transformed the uplands: Farm workers took to spinning and weaving, emigration slowed, population densities rose, and an essentially industrial way of life took over the villages and hamlets of the mountains. A rural proletariat took shape.

During the nineteenth century, as the scale of production in Zurich and its immediate vicinity rose, the process reversed. The hinterland deindustrialized, and migrants flowed toward Zurich. The Zurich region moved from (1) urban manufacturing fed by a largely agricultural countryside to (2) rural protoindustrialization coupled with expanded mercantile activity in the central city to (3) concentration of industry near the center, bringing hardship to rural producers, to (4) deindustrialization of the countryside. The Zurich sequence provides a paradigm for the regional history of protoindustry throughout Europe. The chief variables are when the sequence occurred, how extensive each stage was, and whether a significant industrial nucleus survived the final period of urban implosion and rural contraction.

Urbanization of industry, deindustrialization of the country

Properly generalized, Zurich's experience has significant implications for Europe's nineteenth-century experience as a whole. Protoindustry did finally give way to its urban competitors throughout the continent. If so, the rural workers involved disappeared. But only in the artificial world of statistics can workers simply vanish. In real life, Europe's protoindustrial workers either hung on unemployed, moved into other employment in the countryside, or followed industry to the city. They did all three, although in what proportions we do not know so far. In the region of Lyon, at midcentury, rural workers miles from the city lived in its long shadow. "For if we observe," comments Yves Lequin (1977: I, 43),

> the concentration of workers in urban centers which were
> seizing, to their advantage, declining rural industries, the latter
> held on to a considerable share; in some places, indeed, the
> spreading of work into the countryside had found its second
> wind and was promoting the expansion of other more dynamic
> branches of industry. The large shares of the districts of Saint-
> Etienne and Lyon should not mislead us: cities without

boundaries, they attracted people, to be sure, but even more so they projected their energy into distant villages: rather than men coming to industry, it was work that went to men.

The balance shifted in the next half-century. Despite a decline in the old handicraft manufacture of silk, despite a distinct suburbanization of Lyon's manufacturing, and despite some tendency for mills with power looms to head for the waterpower of the Alpine slopes, the industrial capital swelled. Lyon grew from 235,000 to 456,000 inhabitants between 1851 and 1906. The depression of the 1870s and 1880s first struck at the manufacturing population of the countryside and temporarily augmented the agricultural labor force. But the depression marked the end of a long expansion for the hinterland. The villages began to leak women and men to the cities.

Especially to Lyon. The changing relationship between Lyon and its hinterland had a paradoxical effect: the geographical range from which the city recruited its working population narrowed during the latter half of the nineteenth century. Instead of arriving from Switzerland, from Italy, from industrial centers elsewhere in France, they arrived increasingly from Lyon's own surrounding region. Within the region, however, Lyon and the other industrial cities did not simply attract a cross section of the rural population; they drew disproportionately from the old centers of rural industry (Lequin 1977: I, 239–46). The incomplete evidence suggests that they also drew disproportionately on the *people* of the hinterland who were already involved in their industrial networks.

The other side of this process was a wholesale deindustrialization of the countryside. Rural areas became more exclusively agricultural than they had been for centuries. Area by area, the homogenization of rural life was even greater, for the specialization in one cash crop or another tended to convert whole regions into vineyards, or wheat fields, or dairy farms. So we arrive at a set of unexpected consequences: an industrialization that recruited, not peasants, but experienced industrial workers from the countryside; a "ruralization" of that same countryside as a consequence of the increasing importance of the city; and an increasingly great contrast between the economic activities of city and country.

Rural exodus

In absolute terms, Europe's rural population kept growing until some time in the twentieth century. Its proportion declined only because the urban population grew faster than the rural. Nevertheless, the cloud of numbers through which we have made our way implies a huge nineteenth-century exodus from the European countryside. Let us take a very conservative assumption: that rates of natural increase were just as high in places above

20,000 inhabitants as in smaller places. Even on that assumption, the figures imply that the smaller places lost about 25 million people to net migration in the first half of the century, and about 90 million in the second half. A substantial number of those migrants went overseas, but the net movement to larger places within Europe must have been on the order of 80 or 90 million migrants.

Who left? That depended on the pattern of opportunities in country, city, and overseas area. Those patterns varied with time and place. As a working hypothesis, I suggest the following rough rank order for departures from the nineteenth-century European countryside:

1. rural industrial workers
2. agricultural wageworkers
3. tenants and sharecroppers
4. landowning farmers.

I suggest, but with greater hesitation, that their school-leaving children emigrated in roughly the same order: children of rural industrial workers first, and so on. The logic of hypothesis is simple: Having transferable skills promotes migration, but having a stake in the land impedes it. The same logic suggests that in the case of migration to farms elsewhere (as in much of the Scandinavian migration to the American Midwest), agricultural workers headed the list. But that was a secondary stream; most people who fled Europe's rural areas entered urban employment.

The consequence of such an order of departure would be first to deindustrialize the countryside, then to strip it of its remaining proletarians. At the logical end of such a process, family farms would predominate. For Europe as a whole, rural natural increase may well have exceeded out-migration – thus producing continued slow growth in the total rural population – until the end of the century. In the precocious case of rural France, however, large regions were losing population before 1900. In those regions, by and large, the remaining population was becoming more nearly peasant than it had been for centuries. There and elsewhere, deindustrialization and rural exodus had the ironic consequence of creating an agrarian world that resembled the traditional countryside postulated by simple models of modernization.

At first view, the rural exodus itself seems to fit one part of the modernization model: The presumed rise of mobility and of urban contacts breaks down rural isolation and opens the countryside to civilization. A closer look at nineteenth-century mobility patterns, however, gives a very different idea of what was going on. In the early nineteenth century and before, local markets for wage labor were very active, generally involved more than a single village, and commonly promoted widespread seasonal, annual, and lifetime migration from village to village. In areas of wage labor, mobility rates comparable to those prevailing in the contemporary United

States – a fifth of the population changing residence in an average year – seem to have been common (Eriksson and Rogers, 1978: 177–239). Temporary migration, over short distances and long, permitted millions of European workers to supplement the inadequate incomes available at their homes by meeting the seasonal demand for labor elsewhere (Châtelain, 1976). Some rural regions (upland Switzerland is a famous example) built their economic survival on the exportation of domestic servants and mercenaries, and the importation of remittances from the servants and mercenaries, until the expansion of cottage industry permitted excess hands to remain on the land (Perrenoud, 1971). Growing cities generated huge migration flows because cities both (1) recruited many of their workers as temporary migrants who moved on or returned home and (2) were death traps, especially for the migrants themselves. Both factors meant that the total numbers of migrants were far, far greater than net increases through migration (Sharlin, 1978).

All these features were true of European mobility patterns before the nineteenth century and continued well into the century. Yet, the nineteenth century did not simply bring more of the same. Overseas migration, as we have already seen, played an incomparably greater role than it had in previous centuries. The net flows of migrants to cities from rural areas rose far above earlier levels. The average distances people moved undoubtedly increased. The definitiveness of long-distance moves probably increased as well: fewer people spending their lifetimes in repeated migration from one distant location to another. Short-distance migration probably declined, at least relatively, as people began to substitute daily commutation by rail or bicycle for longer-term changes of residence. (For a general survey of these trends, see Tilly, 1978.) With one crucial exception – the influence of governments, wars, and political crises on international migration was to become preponderant during the twentieth century – the mobility patterns with which Europeans are familiar today were taking shape. The mistake is to think that those contemporary mobility patterns emerged from a previously immobile world.

Summed up, the nineteenth-century changes in work, mobility, and population distribution have another important implication. The locus of proletarianization was shifting radically. For a long time, most individuals and families who passed into the proletariat had made the fateful transition in villages and small towns. During the nineteenth century, the balance shifted toward cities. Within the city, and in the move to the city, people passed from having some control over their means of production to depending on the sale of their labor power to others. Those others were mostly capitalists of one variety or another. The work they offered consisted increasingly of disciplined wage labor in relatively large organizations: offices, stores, factories, railroads, hospitals, and so on.

Capitalists, managers, and large organizations took over the task of creating a compliant proletariat. Whereas the small entrepreneurs who preceded them had relied on cash payments, personal patronage, and community pressure to secure compliance, the nineteenth-century capitalist boldly undertook the creation of new kinds of people: tidy, disciplined, sober, reliable, and uncomplaining. That they did not succeed is a tribute to the staying power of the European working class.

The nineteenth century that played itself out in the process had plenty of drama, but departed radically from the script conventionally assigned to it. Instead of master craftsmen who invent or adopt new production techniques and thereby create the means for expanding their firms, building factories, drawing more and more peasants into new industrial work, and thus constructing an "industrial revolution," we find something quite different: capitalists who begin the nineteenth century knowing how to sell all sorts of goods, but not how to make them, and who spend much of the century struggling to seize control of the labor process from workers who *do* know how to produce, but have less and less ability to sell products to their own advantage.

In place of increasing mobility, we see a growing subordination of mobility to markets for wage labor. Where analysts have seen accelerating technological innovation as the stimulus to economic change, we discover capital accumulation and control of labor power as the motor. In cases where observers have talked about industrialization, we see extensive deindustrialization, at least in the countryside. As alternatives to a supposed modernization, we face very different processes, much less continuous and much more filled with conflict and power: capitalization, proletarianization, state making.

In that context, the struggles during the nineteenth century between powerholders and ordinary citizens also changed shape. The analysis of nineteenth-century change as modernization driven by technical innovation leads easily to an interpretation of conflict as a destructive response to the strains of rapid, uneven social change. The alternative I have sketched, in contrast, makes it more plausible that those who struggled were coherent actors pursuing well-defined interests. The great prominence of artisans and skilled workers – rather than newly minted proletarians – in nineteenth-century labor movements makes sense in the light of the effort of employers to transform artisans and skilled workers into obedient proletarians.

The same perspective reduces the paradox involved in saying that nineteenth-century workers developed class consciousness, while noting the large backward-looking components in nineteenth-century working-class ideologies. The alternative perspective, finally, helps us understand how the specific forms of popular collective action – the food riots, Rough Music, machine breaking, strikes, demonstrations, public meetings, and so on – could evolve systematically through interaction between challengers and authorities: An older repertoire of collective action that we might label *local and patronized* gave way to a newer repertoire that we might call *national and autonomous*. That shift corresponded to a net shift in people's interests toward organizations and actors operating on a national scale, and another shift toward direct representation of popular interests vis-à-vis the national state. In short, popular collective action underwent extensive organizational change in Europe during the nineteenth century, but not the change one would expect on the model of protest as a response to strain.

Did the cake of custom break?

Much more changed, to be sure, in nineteenth-century Europe. In order to build a comprehensive analysis of nineteenth-century social change, we would have to follow the expansion and elaboration of capitalism much farther. We would have to deal seriously with the concentration of power in national states. We would have to examine the changes in organization, productive technique, communications, and everyday experience that developed from the interaction of capitalism and state making. We would have to take account of the interdependent but distinct trajectories of center and periphery, of North, South, East, and West. The thin slice we have taken from the century is far from a cross section.

Nevertheless, the evidence we have reviewed is broad enough to make clear what did *not* happen. A congeries of isolated, immobile agrarian societies did not give way under the impact of industrialization, urbanization, and expanding communications. The isolated, immobile societies did not give way during the nineteenth century because they did not exist at the beginning of the century. The European world bequeathed to the nineteenth century by the eighteenth was actually connected and mobile. In its way, it was even industrial. There was no solid cake of custom to break.

What *did* change, then? The scale of producing organizations increased greatly. The average range of geographic mobility expanded. National states, national politics, and national markets became increasingly dominant. The population of Europe urbanized and proletarianized. The long transition from a high-fertility and high-mortality world began. Inanimate sources of energy started to play an indispensable role in everyday production and consumption. Capitalism matured. The European way of life we now know took shape.

So is there anything wrong with summing up those changes as the "modernization" of Europe? No, if the name is nothing but a convenient name. The errors only begin with the elevation of the idea of modernization into a model of change – especially as a model in which expanded contact with the outside world alters people's mentalities, and altered mentalities produce a break with traditional forms of behavior. That magic mentalism is not only wrong, but unnecessary. The analysis of capitalism and of state making offers a far more adequate basis for the understanding of change in nineteenth-century Europe.

NOTE

1. In Table 12.5, many states, e.g., Greece and Finland, did not exist for some or all of the nineteenth century; in those cases, the figures refer to the boundaries at the acquisition of independence. Others, e.g., Prussia/Germany, changed boundaries radically; in those cases, the figures refer to the boundaries at the date shown. The population estimates in Chandler and Fox (1974) yield slightly higher totals and slightly higher percentages, but the pattern is essentially the same as in my compilations.

LITERATURE CITED

Abel, Wilhelm. *Massenarmut und Hungerkrisen im Vorindustriellen Europa.* Hamburg and Berlin: Paul Parey, 1974.

Ågren, Kurt, et al. *Aristocrats, Farmers, Proletarians. Essays in Swedish Demographic History.* Studia Historica Upsaliensia 47. Uppsala: Almqvist and Wiksell, 1973.

Åkerman, Sune, Hans Christian Johansen, and David Gaunt (eds.), *Chance and Change: Social Economic Studies in Historical Demography in the Baltic Area.* Odense, Denmark: Scandinavian Universities Press, 1978.

Alapuro, Risto. "On the Political Mobilization of the Agrarian Population in Finland: Problems and Hypotheses." *Scandinavian Political Studies* 11 (1976): 51–76.

Andorka, Rudolf. "The One-child Family System in Two Microregions of Hungary in the 18th and 19th Century." Unpublished paper, Central Statistical Office, Budapest, 1977.

Bairoch, Paul (ed.). *La Population Active et Sa Structure.* Brussels: Institut de Sociologie, Université Libre de Bruxelles, 1968.

"Europe's Gross National Product, 1800–1975." *Journal of European Economic History* 5 (1976): 273–340.

Taille des Villes, Conditions de Vie et Développement Economique. Paris: École des Hautes Études en Sciences Sociales, 1977.

Bercé, Yves-Marie. *Croquants et Nû-pieds. Les Soulèvements Paysans en France du XVIe au XIX siècle.* Paris: Gallimard/Julliard; Collection "Archives," 1974.

Fête et Révolte. Des Mentalités Populaires du XVIe au XVIIIe Siècle. Paris: Hachette, 1976.

Black, Cyril. *The Dynamics of Modernization. A Study in Comparative History.* New York: Harper and Row, 1966.

Blom, Grethe Authén (ed.). *Industrialiseringens Føorste Fase.* Urbaniseringsprosessen i Norden, vol. 3 Oslo: Universitertsforlaget, 1977.

Blum, Jerome. *The End of the Old Order in Rural Europe.* Princeton: Princeton University Press, 1978.

Braun, Rudolf. *Industrialisierung und Volksleben.* Zurich: Rentsch, 1960.

Sozialer und Kultureller Wandel in einem Ländlichen Industriegebiet. Zurich: Rentsch, 1965.

"Early Industrialization and Demographic Change in the Canton of Zurich." In Charles Tilly (ed.), *Historical Studies of Changing Fertility.* Princeton: Princeton University Press, 1978.

Caves, Richard E. "'Vent for Surplus' Models of Trade and Growth." In Robert E. Baldwin et al. (eds.). *Trade, Growth, and the Balance of Payments: Essays in Honor of Gottfried Haberler.* Chicago: Rand-McNally, 1965.

"Export-led Growth and the New Economic History." In Jagdish N. Bhagwati et al. (eds.), *Trade, Balance of Payments and Growth. Papers in International Economics in Honor of Charles P. Kindleberger.* Amsterdam: North-Holland, 1971.

Chandler, Tertius, and Gerald Fox. *3000 Years of Urban Growth.* New York: Academic Press, 1974.

Châtelain, Abel. *Les Migrants Temporaires en France de 1800 à 1914: Histoire Economique et Sociale des Migrants Temporaires des Campagnes Françaises du XIXe Siècle au début du XXe Siècle.* Lille: Publications de l'Université de Lille, 1976.

Coale, Ansley. "The Decline of Fertility in Europe from the French Revolution to World War II." In S. J. Behrman et al. (eds.), *Fertility and Family Planning.* Ann Arbor: University of Michigan Press, 1969.

Deane, Phyllis, and W. A. Cole. *British Economic Growth, 1688–1959. Trends and Structure.* Cambridge: Cambridge University Press, 1967.

Dunbabin, J. P. D. *Rural Discontent in Nineteenth-Century Britain.* New York: Holmes and Meier, 1974.

Durand, John. "The Modern Expansion of World Population." American Philosophical Society *Proceedings* 52 (1967): 136–59.

Eriksson, Ingrid, and John Rogers. "Rural Labor and Population Change. Social and Demographic Developments in East-Central Sweden during the Nineteenth Century." *Studia Historica Upsaliensia 100.* Uppsala: Uppsala University, 1978.

Gaunt, David. "Familj, Hushall och Arbetsintensitet." *Scandia* 42 (1977): 32–59.

"Pre-industrial Economy and Population Structure: The Elements of Variance in Early Modern Sweden." *Scandinavian Journal of History* 2 (1977): 183–210.

Gillis, John. "Political Decay and the European Revolutions, 1789–1848." *World Politics* 22 (1970): 344–70.

Youth and History. Tradition and Change in European Age Relations, 1770–Present. New York: Academic Press, 1974.

Henning, Friedrich-Wilhelm. "Der Beginn der Modernen Welt im Agrarischen Bereich." In Reinhart Koselleck (ed.), *Studien zum Beginn der Modernen Welt.* Stuttgart: Klett-Cotta, 1977.

Jones, Eric L. "The Agricultural Labour Market in England, 1793–1872." *Economic History Review* 17 (1964): 322–38.

"The Agricultural Origins of Industry." *Past and Present* 40 (1968): 58–71.

Kälvemark, Ann-Sofie. "The Country That Kept Track of Its Population." *Scandinavian Journal of History* 2 (1977): 211–30.

Kellenbenz, Hermann. *The Rise of the European Economy. An Economic History of*

Continental Europe from the Fifteenth to the Eighteenth Century. London: Weidenfeld and Nicolson, 1976.

Kollman, Wolfgang. *Bevölkerung in der Industriellen Revolution.* Göttingen: Vandenhoeck und Ruprecht, 1974.

"Zur Bevölkerungsentwicklung der Neuzeit." In Reinhart Koselleck (ed.), *Studien zum Beginn der Modernen Welt.* Stuttgart: Klett-Cotta, 1974.

Kosinski, Leszek A. *The Population of Europe. A Geographical Perspective.* London: Longmans, 1970.

Kriedte, Peter, Hans Medick, and Jürgen Schlumbohm. *Industrialisierung vor der Industrialisierung. Gewerbliche Warenproduktion auf dem Land in der Formationsperiode des Kapitalismus.* Göttingen: Vandenhoeck und Ruprecht, 1977.

Kuhnle, Stein. *Social Mobilization and Political Participation: The Nordic Countries, c. 1850–1970.* Bergen: Institute of Sociology, 1973.

Landes, David S. *The Unbound Prometheus. Technological Change and Industrial Development in Western Europe from 1750 to the Present.* Cambridge: Cambridge University Press, 1969.

Lepsius, M. Rainer. "Soziologische Theoreme über die Sozialstruktur der 'Moderne' und die 'Modernisierung'." In Reinhart Koselleck (ed.), *Studien zum Beginn der Modernen Welt.* Stuttgart: Klett-Cotta, 1977.

Lequin, Yves. *Les Ouvriers de la Région Lyonnaise (1848–1914).* Lyon: Presses Universitaires de Lyon, 1977.

Lesthaege, Ron J. *The Decline of Belgian Fertility, 1800–1970.* Princeton: Princeton University Press, 1977.

Levine, David. *Family Formation in an Age of Nascent Capitalism.* New York: Academic Press, 1977.

Lundqvist, Sven. *Folkrörelserna i det Svenska Samhallet, 1850–1920.* Stockholm: Almqvist & Wiksell, 1977.

McKeown, Thomas. *The Modern Rise of Population.* New York: Academic Press, 1976.

Marx, Karl. *Capital. A Critique of Political Economy.* London: Lawrence & Wishart, n.d. 3 vols.

Mendels, Franklin. "Proto-industrialization: The First Phase of the Industrialization Process." *Journal of Economic History* 32 (1972): 241–61.

"Agriculture and Peasant Industry in Eighteenth-Century Flanders." In William N. Parker and Eric L. Jones (eds.), *European Peasants and Their Markets.* Princeton: Princeton University Press, 1975.

Merlin, Pierre, et al. *L'Exode Rural, Suivi de Deux Études sur les Migrations.* Paris: Presses Universitaires de France. Institut National d'Études Demographiques, Travaux et Documents, Cahier 59, 1971.

Milward, Alan S., and S. B. Saul. *The Economic Development of Continental Europe, 1780–1870.* London: George Allen and Unwin, 1973.

Mitchell, Brian R. *European Historical Statistics, 1750–1970.* New York: Columbia University Press, 1975.

Pellicani, Luciano. "La Rivoluzione, Industriale e il Fenomeno della Proletarizzazione." *Rassegna Italiana di Sociologia* 14 (1973): 63–84.

Perrenoud, Alfred. "Les Migrations en Suisse sous L'Ancien Régime: Quelques Problèmes." *Annales de Démographie Historique* 1970 (1971): 251–59.

Pitié, Jean. *Exode Rural et Migrations Intérieures en France. L'Exemple de la Vienne et du Poitou-Charentes*. Poitiers: Norois, 1971.

Redlich, Fritz, and Herman Freudenberger. "The Industrial Development of Europe: Reality, Symbols, Images." *Kyklos* 17 (1964): 372–401.

Romano, Salvatore Francesco. *Storia della Mafia*. Milan: Sugar, 1963.

Runblom, Harald, and Hans Norman (eds.). *From Sweden to America. A History of the Migration*. Minneapolis: University of Minnesota Press, 1976.

de Saint-Jacob, Pierre. *Les Paysans du Bourgogne du Nord*. Paris: Les Belles Lettres, 1960.

Saville, John. "Primitive Accumulation and Early Industrialization in Britain." *Socialist Register 1969* (1969): 247–71.

Schneider, Jane, and Peter Schneider. *Culture and Political Economy in Western Sicily*. New York: Academic Press, 1976.

Sharlin, Alan. "Natural Decrease in Early Modern Cities: A Reconsideration." *Past and Present* 79 (1978): 126–38.

Shorter, Edward. *The Making of the Modern Family*. New York: Basic Books, 1975.

Spagnoli, Paul G. "Population History from Parish Monographs. The Problem of Local Demographic Variations." *Journal of Interdisciplinary History* 7 (1977): 427–52.

Stearns, Peter. *European Society in Upheaval. Social History Since 1750*. New York: Macmillan, 1975.

Sundbärg, Gustav. *Aperçus Statistiques Internationaux*. Stockholm: Gordon and Breach, [1908] 1968.

Tilly, Charles. "Migration in Modern European History." In William H. McNeill (ed.), *Human Migration: Patterns, Implications, Policies*. Bloomington: Indiana University Press, 1978.

Tilly, Louise A., and Joan W. Scott. *Women, Work and Family*. New York: Holt, Rinehart, Winston, 1978.

Tilly, Richard, and Charles Tilly. "An Agenda for European Economic History in the 1970's." *Journal of Economic History* 31 (1971): 184–97.

Tilly, Charles, Karen Fonde, and Ann V. O'Shea, "Statistics on the Urbanization of Europe, 1500–1950." Unpublished paper, Center for Western European Studies, University of Michigan, 1972.

Tortella Casares, Gabriel. *Les Origines del Capitalismo en España: Banca, Industria y Ferrocarria en el Siglo XIX*. Madrid: Editorial Ternos, 1973.

deVries, Jan. "Barges and Capitalism: Passenger Transportation in the Dutch Economy, 1632–1839." *A. A. G. Bijdragen* 21 (1978): 33–398.

van de Walle, Etienne. *The Female Population of France in the Nineteenth Century. A Reconstruction of 82 Départements*. Princeton: Princeton University Press, 1974.

Weber, Eugen. *Peasants into Frenchmen. The Modernization of Rural France, 1870–1914*. Stanford: Stanford University Press, 1976.

Winberg, Christer. "Population Growth and Proletarianization. The Transformation of Social Structures in Rural Sweden during the Agrarian Revolution." In Sune Åkerman et al. (eds.), *Chance and Change. Social and Economic Studies in Historical Demography in the Baltic Area*. Odense, Denmark: Scandinavian Universities Press, 1978.

13

Structural location and ideological divergence: Jewish Marxist intellectuals in turn-of-the-century Russia

Robert J. Brym

The sociological problem of the intellectuals

The central tenet of the sociology of knowledge is that ideologies are formulated and accepted in accordance with the existential basis of the ideologist. People, it is held, do not think ideologically as individual atoms, but as members of structurally defined groups.

Since Marx's time, classes have deservedly received the greatest attention in the analysis of ideologies: The beliefs, symbols, and values that help direct political action are often viewed as "embodiments of particular class-relations and class-interests" (Marx, n.d.: vol. 1, 21). The trouble is that this argument is apparently confounded by a whole range of cases. One of the most important of these has to do with the participation of middle-class intellectuals in left-wing social movements. After all, if ideologies are class-based, why should members of the middle class align themselves with, and even articulate the ideologies of, wage laborers? If, as Merton (1968: 517–18) says:

> we cannot derive ideas from the objective class position of their
> exponents, this leaves a wide margin of indeterminacy. It then
> becomes a further problem to discover why some identify
> themselves with the characteristic class stratum in which they
> objectively find themselves whereas others adopt the
> presuppositions of a class stratum other than their own.

True, a partial resolution of Merton's dilemma may be found even in the corpus of Marx's writings. In *The Manifesto of the Communist Party*, he and Engels assert that men of letters may come to be associated with the socialist movement because the polarization of classes that accompanies capitalist development causes them to be "precipitated into the proletariat" (Marx and Engels, 1972: 343).

Elite theorists endorse a variant of this interpretation. Michels (1932) comments on how periods of heightened intellectual unrest have often been associated with the formation of an "intellectual proletariat" owing to an oversupply of intellectuals relative to job opportunities. Mannheim (1956: 145) and Brinton (1938: 782) concur.

The widespread view that economic malintegration within (or into) the middle class incites intellectuals to cross class lines ideologically has since been broadened. Several scholars have noted that *political* malinte- gration – caused by a scarcity of occupational positions in which intellectuals are allowed to exercise "bourgeois" freedoms or by low levels of intellectual recruitment to establishment political parties – has often had much the same effect (Jellinek, 1965: 27; Weinberg and Walker, 1970). The line of thought that has been proposed in answer to Merton thus holds that intellectuals who are marginal to middle class jobs, establishment insti- tutions, and liberal occupational roles become radicalized.

This, however, is an answer that does more damage than good, theoretically – not so much because it is inaccurate, but because it empha- sizes the social *rootlessness* of intellectuals (or malintegration or marginality or alienation), rather than their social *rootedness*. And the cost of directing our attention away from their structural rootedness has been high, indeed (Wellman, Hall, and Carrington, Chapter 6; Howard, Chapter 7).

To the degree that we ignore ties that bind intellectuals to social structure, we abrogate responsibility for developing the central tenet of the sociology of knowledge. How can one show precisely how the social positions of intellectuals determine their ideas – or even demonstrate the existence of an elective affinity between position and consciousness – if we have no sense of their social locations?

To concretize the issue, observe that left-wing intellectuals in given historical settings often associate with different or even opposing parties. Yet, we have no theory that explains why, from the vantage point of their social relations, intellectuals on the left become *divided* ideologically.

We have reached this juncture, I submit, as a result of having listened too intently to Marx, Michels, and others who maintain that left-wing in- tellectuals are malintegrated into or divorced from classes, institutions, and roles. As a result, the field has been left open to all kinds of psychologistic reasoning, voluntarist approaches, random-variation models, and cultur- ological argument. For instance, a leading student of the European left informs us that there "can be little doubt that the sociological approach to communism, while of cardinal importance in analysing proletarian or peasant behavior, is of strictly limited use when applied to intellectuals. ... The act of [intellectuals'] political affiliation remains one of personal conviction, personal psychology, personal choice" (Caute, 1964: 17–19). Avineri (1957: 277) writes that, as far as intellectuals are concerned, there "is no *a priori* determination [of ideas]" and that "choice is the very embodiment of the intellectual's determined social being." Hoffer (1951: 25) contends that when intellectuals "are ripe for a mass movement, they are usually ripe for any effective movement." And Parsons (1963: 4) asserts that intellectuals place "cultural considerations before social ones" – thus encouraging a retreat from the central problems of the sociology of knowledge and a plunge into the murky waters of cultural and intellectual history. This may represent the state of social scientific thinking on the subject of ideological divergence, but most of it is not sociology – let alone structurally based analysis.

This chapter reports on a preliminary structural theory of intellectual radicalism and ideological divergence (Brym, 1978; 1980; in press). It argues that the drawbacks of the arguments as to the social rootlessness of radical intellectuals and, concomitantly, the advantages to be derived from focusing on their rootedness, can best be displayed by analyzing a case where the intelligentsia is usually regarded as being especially rootless – the case of Russian Jews before the revolution.

Wolfe (1948: 33), for instance, agrees that members of the Russian intelligentsia were

> held together, neither by a common social origin and status, nor
> by a common role in the social process of production. The
> cement which bound them together was a common alienation
> from existing society, and a common belief in the sovereign
> efficacy of ideas as shapers of life. They lived precariously
> suspended, as in a void, between an uncomprehending autocratic
> monarchy above and an unenlightened mass below. ... They
> anticipated and supplied in advance the requirements of a world
> that was too slow in coming into being, and sought to serve a
> folk that had no use for their services. In the decaying feudal
> order they found neither scope nor promise; in the gross, timid,
> and backward mercantile bourgeoisie neither economic support
> nor inspiration; in the slumbering people no echo to their ardent
> cries.

If, on the whole, radical Russian intellectuals were rootless, alienated, functionally superfluous – and therefore easily swayed by ideological currents – then how much more true this was of the Jews among them. Conventional sociological wisdom locates Jews "on the margin of two cultures and two societies" during the early stages of capitalist development (Park, 1928: 892). Insulated from contact with gentiles in the pre-capitalist era, they were absorbed into European society only in the nineteenth century – and then only slowly and incompletely. This pace of absorption served to radicalize Jewish intellectuals in disproportionately large numbers. Thus, Michels, who followed this line of reasoning, located the chief cause of the Jewish intellectual's "predominant position" in working class parties in "the peculiar position which the Jews have occupied and in many respects still occupy. The legal emancipation of the Jews has not (in Germany and Eastern Europe) been followed by their social and moral emancipation" (Michels, 1962: 247–8).

In sum, the traditional argument is that middle-class Jewish intellectuals were, because of their socially disadvantaged position, unusually marginal to the middle class and were therefore transformed into radical men of ideas par excellence. Count Witte seems to have been not all that far off the mark when, in 1903, he informed Theodor Herzl that half the revolutionary intellectuals in Russia were Jews. What better case could one find than these "rootless cosmopolites" (as Andrei Zhdanov later called them) to demonstrate the importance of social roots in shaping intellectuals' ideologies?

Classification: The Jewish Question

Although prone to generalize well beyond the limits of historical accuracy, many thinkers – including Weber (1952: 336–55; 1961: 151–2, 263–5), Marx (n.d.: vol. 3, 330; 1972: 25–41), and Simmel (1971) – have hit upon the most striking fact concerning Jews in medieval Eastern Europe: that whereas lord and serf derived their existence from the land, Jews usually played the role of commercial intermediaries. They imported luxury goods, exported raw materials, ran liquor concessions, managed estates, collected taxes, made loans, and so forth. As late as 1818, roughly 85% of the Jewish labor force were so employed (Leshchinsky, 1928: 30). And although nearly 12% of Jews were artisans, they were bound to the merchant class by ties of economic dependence – just as petty merchants were bound to wealthier ones – insofar as they relied upon merchants for credit, tools, and raw materials, or markets (Wischnitzer, 1965: 226).

Especially in the nineteenth century, the expansion of a modern business class and state apparatus steadily undermined the economic position of the Jewish community, because its functions had been closely associated with feudalism. The nineteenth-century state in Eastern Europe came to monopolize tax collection and liquor production in order to finance increased fiscal expenditures. Intensified domestic production of many goods – aided by tariff barriers – ruined many importers. Non-Jews began to compete with Jews in several fields of business that had hitherto been almost exclusively in Jewish hands. Modern credit institutions obviated much of the need for petty moneylenders, and the capital, credit, and jobs formerly generated by the wealthiest elements of the Jewish community dried up as they mobilized funds for extra-community investment in banks, railway construction, sugar beet, and oil production (Rubinow, 1907; Dubnow, 1916–20; Mahler, 1971; Weinryb, 1972a, b; von Laue, 1974).

It was almost exclusively among those, such as the very wealthy, who cut their economic ties to the Jewish community and began to integrate into the Russian class structure, that one could detect the first significant movement toward ethnic assimilation in the nineteenth century (Grunwald, 1967). Admittedly, assimilation was restricted to a small group: The vast majority of Jews were transformed by these large-scale changes into a mass of impoverished merchants, owners of small and unmechanized factories, master craftsmen, and artisans. Squeezed, as they were, between two modes of production – the decline of feudalism having robbed them of their old functions and the advent of capitalism having provided them with no new ones that could survive the growth of modern capital-intensive industries, banks, and large state bureaucracies – most Jews remained ethnically cohesive. The fact remains, however, that some became less culturally Jewish to the degree that they became less structurally dependent on other Jews for their livelihood.

Therefore it is important to know the segments of the Jewish community in which members of the Russian-Jewish intelligentsia originated: Variations in the degree to which intellectuals' families of orientation were economically embedded in the community – that is, dependent on other Jews for a livelihood – had wide-ranging implications for the character of intellectuals' socialization and, consequently, their subsequent ideological orientations. Students of political culture maintain that the most fundamental component of political socialization is the sense of identity one develops as a child (Verba, 1965: 529). In the present case, a high degree of embeddedness in the class structure of the Russian community (i.e., a low degree of embeddedness in the Jewish community) led future intellectuals to receive a secular education and come to think of themselves as more Russian than Jewish. The opposite structural circumstance produced an unquestioned sense of Jewish identity. Intellectuals' attitudes towards the question of what ought to happen to the Jewish community now that the period of its economic usefulness had ended represented one of the three major ideological differences among the most important Marxist parties in Russia; and, for Jews, these attitudes were shaped by one's sense of identity.

When I collected biographical data on all the most important, and many of the less important, Jewish Marxist intellectuals born before 1891 in European Russia (N = 207), I discovered significant differences between mean degrees of embeddedness of each party's intellectuals. Bolsheviks' families of orientation had weaker structural ties to the Jewish community and stronger ties to the class structure of the Russian community than did those of members of other parties. Their mean degree of embeddedness was 3.5. Next came the Mensheviks (mean = 3.0), then the Bundists (mean = 2.0), and, finally, the labor Zionists (mean = 1.4). Cross-classifying each intellectual's degree of embeddedness by party affiliation, I found that the distribution could occur by chance less than once in a thousand times.[1]

Those whose youthful links to the Jewish community were strongest – the labor Zionists – generally received traditional, religious education in *heders* and *yeshivas* and developed the most Jewish-nationalistic answer to the Jewish question. They were oriented not only toward the furtherance of working-class interests in Russia, but also toward the establishment of a Jewish homeland in what was then Ottoman Palestine (Frankel, 1981). The Bundists, who occupied the next position on the continuum of embeddedness, sharply contested this program. They believed that all that was necessary for Jewish survival was the overthrow of the old regime, coupled with what they called "national-cultural autonomy": Jewish control over institutions capable of ensuring and encouraging the development of their secular culture (Tobias, 1972). Still further divorced from the Jewish community structurally, Mensheviks (some with reservations) and Bolsheviks (pretty well unanimously) contended that Jews should not survive as Jews. For them, ethnic particularism endangered the unity of the revolutionary movement. Moreover, they argued that the only reasonable solution to the Jewish problem was the complete assimilation of the Jewish people within a country rid of autocratic rule (Ascher, 1972; Deutscher, 1965; Getzler, 1967).

Declassification: Becoming radicals

If Jewish intellectuals in the Bolshevik, Menshevik, Bundist, and Labor Zionist parties differed from one another in terms of the extent to which they were rooted in the Jewish community in their youth, then they had in common the fact that they had all completed the Jewish or Russian school systems at least as high as the secondary level (and, in many cases, university). Regardless of their social origins, they were on their way to becoming members of what is now called the new middle class. Yet, instead of becoming solid middle-class citizens, they used the educational system as a platform for launching revolutionary careers.

The theory mentioned earlier that ascribes intellectual radicalism to poor middle-class integration applies reasonably well here. The problem was not one of scarce jobs – only in the 1860s and 1870s did the numerical expansion of employment opportunities in some fields fail to keep pace with the number of graduates (Brower, 1975: 141; Fischer, 1960: 259) – but was one of illiberal institutions. Because the Russian capitalist class was notoriously weak, the autocracy had a free hand in censoring publications, outlawing political parties of any stripe, and so on. Instead of employing intellectuals in institutions where liberal viewpoints could flourish, the autocracy often provoked them into open acts of rebellion (Berlin, 1948: 342; Tompkins, 1953, 1957; Kochan, 1962: 175; Eymontova, 1971: 152–4).

Moreover, it is clear that rates of radicalism among different intellectual groups varied in proportion to their degree of malintegration into the middle class. Students, for example, formed "the quintessence of the Russian intelligentsia" (Izgoev, 1969: 500), freed as they were of occupational, familial, and other ties and obligations that might constrain their thoughts and actions to a greater degree. Jews were greatly overrepresented in the revolutionary movement: Only about 4% of the Empire's population was Jewish, yet the proportion of Jewish revolutionaries increased steadily until 1905, at which time they composed 37% of all political arrests.

Part of the reason for their high rate of radicalism was that Jews entered that hothouse of radicalism, the Russian school system, in disproportionately large numbers. Until 1887 the growing ratio of Jewish students to the total number of students was roughly equal to the ratio of Jewish radicals to the total number of radicals. After that year, as part of a general anti-Semitic reaction, a quota system severely restricted Jewish enrollment in secondary and advanced schools. Yet, from then until 1905 the proportion of Jewish political arrestees increased from about 14% to 37% of the total. Thus, it was not education per se that radicalized Jews, but their low level of embeddedness in the middle class. The quota system radicalized even more Jews because it effectively threatened to block their entry into the middle class (Cherikover, 1939: 79; Greenberg, 1944–51: vol. 1, 149; Dinur, 1957: 114; Avakumovic, 1959: 182; Mosse, 1968: 148; Nedava, 1972: 143; Brym, 1977). Add to this the effects of job discrimination and other causes of blocked mobility and, as one Bolshevik remarked, it is difficult to imagine how a Jewish student could *not* become a radical (Aronson, 1961: 9–10).

But malintegration is not the whole story. For the capacity of intellectuals poorly embedded in middle-class jobs, establishment institutions and liberal roles to translate ire into action cannot be taken for granted. Such people may become disillusioned and cynical, they may join political sects that are substitutes for the world rather than a means of changing it, or they may temper their discontent with various philosophical rationalizations: Radical action and ideology constitute only one of several theoretically available alternative reactions to malintegration. I submit that only if malintegrated intellectuals are able to create a dense network of social ties among themselves will they experience sustained radicalism – a fact that has been overlooked by proponents of the malintegration thesis in their haste to establish that radical intellectuals typically have weak social roots.

For example, from the 1870s on some students *refused* to accept opportunities for professional employment or they accepted jobs and *remained* active in the revolutionary movement. These individuals were exceptions to the rule that the existence of opportunities for middle-class integration automatically results in decreased radicalism. Their actions must be explained on the basis of the fact that a radical counterculture had become a highly organized and institutionalized feature of Russian political life by the 1870s (Brower, 1975). This counterculture consisted of a most elaborate network of organizations: intellectual discussion circles, student communes, loan banks, journals, courts, libraries, cooperatives, public meetings, and so forth. In fact, it amounted to the existence of what Brower calls an independent "school of dissent," which functioned partly within and partly outside the official school system and provided a virtually uninterrupted supply of recruits to the revolutionary movement, independent of the lure of job opportunities. The possibility of forging new ties to the legitimate occupational world failed to deradicalize many activists who had forged strong ties with one another in the school of dissent: The institutionalization of a counterculture had provided them with a power base that ensured the sustenance of intellectual radicalism.

Thus, intellectuals' social rootedness during their youth and during the process of radicalization had a major impact on whether or not they remained radicals and on their affiliation with one party rather than another. But the consequences of embedding extended far beyond the period of radicalization. Radicalized intellectuals entertained few illusions about their ability to overthrow the old regime unaided and therefore sought to bind themselves to a historical agent of change: the working class. Contrary to the suggestion of many historians (e.g., Wolfe, 1948: 33), the intelligentsia did not always hang suspended between classes, but was tied, sometimes strongly, sometimes less so, to different strata of the Russian working class. Moreover, variations over time in the density of these ties, and in the exigencies resulting from having to organize different strata of workers, account substantially for major ideological differences among the important Marxist parties.

Reclassification, I: The agents and character of the revolution

Consider what at first appears to be a quite trivial incident. In 1905, Y. Sverdlov, a Jewish intellectual who headed the Bolshevik organization in the Urals, wrote a pamphlet entitled *What Is a Workers' Party?* It was apparently intended for distribution among backward first-generation workers who were fresh from the countryside and still owned small plots of land that they tilled on holidays and even weekends. Not only was its style simple, but its content was readily understandable to a factory worker with strong ties to the peasantry. This is evident from Sverdlov's definition of capitalist exploitation as "a new form of corvée" and his likening of workers to serfs (Sverdlov, 1957–60: 5). In order to propagandize among backward workers, intellectuals frequently had to talk in peasant terms and to some extent adapt to their way of thinking. In this case, this involved only an allusion to serfdom, the memory of which was kept very much alive in the mind of the "protoproletarian" (McGee, 1973) by the continued existence of various obligations dating back to the 1861 emancipation of the serfs. If one did Social Democratic work where the protoproletariat was particularly numerous, one had to think peasant.

Only the Bolsheviks tended to do so: Much more frequently than intellectuals in other parties, they were recruited to, and worked in, the revolutionary movement in the eastern part of European Russia, where protoproletarians predominated. Nearly half the Bolsheviks in my sample were recruited to the east of a line joining St. Petersburg and Astrakhan, compared with less than a quarter of the Mensheviks, 1% of the Labor Zionists, and none of the Bundists.[2]

At the beginning of their careers, future Bolsheviks subscribed to the traditional view that there would be a bourgeois revolution in Russia. They held that the middle class aided by the workers would seize state power, ushering in an extended period of capitalist development that eventually would culminate in a second, socialist revolution and the triumph of the working class over the bourgeoisie. But by 1902 – before the split between Bolsheviks and Mensheviks – their opinions had begun to shift, for the workers who moved back and forth between factory and village virtually led them to see the revolutionary potential of rural Russia. In some areas that were later to become Bolshevik strongholds, more than half the industrial labor force still lived in the countryside and took revolutionary ideas home with them. Intellectuals began to establish workers' groups and committees designed specifically for propaganda purposes among the peasants in semi-industrialized rural areas and in outlying settlements. Thus, when large-scale peasant uprisings in 1902 put an end to years of relative quiescence, those intellectuals who were most closely connected to the peasants started thinking about a strategically important role for the countryside. Vaguely by 1905, clearly by 1917, they envisaged an alliance between industrial workers and peasants in opposition to the bourgeoisie. The heretical idea of an immediate *socialist* revolution not preceded by a long period of capitalist development thus originated partly in the social ties that bound Bolshevik intellectuals to rural Russia (Morokhovetz, 1925a, b; Lyadov, 1926: 24–39, 184–92; Piatnitsky, 1933: 106; Dan, 1964: 256; Lane, 1969).

More than 77% of the Mensheviks and 99% of the Bundists and labor Zionists in my sample were recruited to the revolutionary movement in regions where highly urbanized workers predominated. Such workers could not expose the intellectuals to whom they were attached to the possibility of an alliance between the working class and peasants and the immediate establishment of a socialist regime: All intellectuals aside from the Bolsheviks continued to adhere to traditional viewpoints until 1917 and, in many cases, even later.

At least in their first years of party membership, intellectuals' ideologies were in a state of flux. Movement from one region to another often placed new demands on their strategic thinking and resulted in their switching from one party platform to another that was more appropriate to their changed circumstances. Indeed, the social character of workers to whom they were attached influenced not only their views about the expected agents and type of revolution, but even about something as fundamental as their own identity. For example, several of the top leaders of the Bund were assimilated intellectuals, from families that had had weak economic ties to the Jewish community. They first joined the revolutionary movement while at university in urban centers where there were next to no Jewish artisans. They were active in non-Jewish segments of Russian Social Democracy until apprehended by the police, who escorted them to exile in their home town of Vilna – which happened to be the center of the Jewish working class. There the intellectuals realized that in order to continue their radical work they would have to learn Yiddish, and after a time they began to identify so closely with the Jewish artisans that they became much less universalistic and argued for a separate Jewish workers' movement and "national-cultural autonomy." The opposite pattern was also evident: Unassimilated intellectuals were sometimes compelled to become Bolsheviks or, more frequently, Mensheviks when they began working among non-Jewish proletarians (Mishkinski, 1969; Tobias, 1972).

Social roots thus mattered greatly: Early variations in embeddedness in the Jewish community and later regional variations in working-class embeddedness helped shape party choice; firm embeddedness in the intellectual stratum itself ensured sustained radicalism. In addition, variations in working-class embeddedness were associated with variations over time in intellectual elitism – a third major ideological difference among the parties, to which we now turn.

Reclassification, II: The role of the intelligentsia

Russian Marxism, especially its Bolshevik component, is often criticized for playing down the decision-making role of the working class and magnifying that of the intelligentsia. There is much justice in this criticism. However, it fails to take into account variations over time in intellectuals' level of elitism and to locate the social forces underlying these variations. My reading of prerevolutionary Russian history leads me to conclude that when social ties between workers and intellectuals were relatively dense, intellectual elitism waned because workers' power in party organizations increased. When these ties were sparse, intellectuals' elitist attitudes strengthened as workers' power declined.

For example, the 1890s were years of heavy foreign investment, rapid industrial expansion, and relatively low unemployment. They witnessed not only a mounting wave of labor unrest, but also a concerted attempt on the part of many workers to have the intelligentsia help organize, educate, propagandize, and agitate. "This time," wrote one intellectual, "it was not us who sought out the workers, but the workers who sought out us." Intellectuals viewed with pride the "continuous growth of our connections to factories and workshops" and the rapidly increasing number of workers in party organizations (Gorev, 1924: 24, 33).

The strike movement increased the participation and influence of workers in the revolutionary movement. It originated in Poland, spread to the western part of European Russia, then moved further eastward. Significantly, a new strategic idea diffused along precisely the route blazed by the strikers. During the last years of the preceding populist era, radical intellectuals, ignored by the peasants, felt the need to "give history a push" and engage in individual acts of terror. But now things were developing quite nicely on their own. As workers' power in the revolutionary movement increased, the intellectuals played down their own role. The social democratic movement was to be, as its name implied, democratic; intellectuals, it was argued, must be careful not to take things into their own hands. Acceptance of the new idea was signaled by the publication in Vilna of Arkady Kremer's 1893 pamphlet *Ob Agitatsii*, which provided the whole social democratic movement with strategic foundations sound enough to last some 8 years. Kremer (1942: 293–321) admonished intellectuals not to hurry the unfolding of revolutionary consciousness among workers. Even Lenin, who would only a few years later argue the opposite, claimed in 1895 that the role of the intelligentsia is merely "to *join up with* the workers' movement, to bring light into it, to *assist* the workers in the struggle they *themselves* have already begun to wage" (Lenin, 1960–70: vol. 2, 112; my emphasis).

However, several factors caused many intellectuals to discard such opinions by 1901. Among the most important was the recession that struck late in 1899 with disastrous consequences, mainly for those strikers employed in large enterprises. It is not always the case that increased labor unrest is associated with upswings in the business cycle and calm with downswings. But very often they are, and Russia appears roughly to have followed that pattern (Johnson, 1975). During the boom of the 1890s, workers had increased resources, notably financial reserves and alternative job opportunities, and therefore more power to strike. But at the turn of the century few gains could be registered on the economic front since the depression compelled workers to concentrate more on survival than revolution, to give up participation in both strike and party activities for the more mundane goal of finding enough to eat (cf. Brym, 1986).

At least equally important a cause of the growing rift between workers and intellectuals involved increased party infiltrations, political arrests, and brutality on the part of the police. From 1899 to 1901 there evolved a cycle of repression leading to increased intelligentsia radicalism, leading to increased repression, and so on. This caused the intelligentsia's sense of self-importance to grow as its attention shifted away from workers to educated "society." As one historian notes, the "image of the worker's position at the forefront of the revolutionary movement began to fade into the background and in its place emerged the heroic radical intelligentsia" (Wildman, 1967: 209). Thus, the intelligentsia's self-esteem rose at precisely the same moment that the workers' movement declined.

Little wonder, then, that under the leadership of the editors of *Iskra*, those who in only a couple of years were to become Bolsheviks and Mensheviks built up a highly centralized organization in order to dominate Russian Social Democracy (Wildman, 1964). *Iskra*'s plan, worked out by Lenin in *What Is to be Done?* was based on the notion that workers by themselves were capable of developing only "trade-union consciousness" and could not reach the point of demanding the overthrow of the autocracy. The ideas of social democracy were thus to be brought to the workers completely "from without" by a centralized party of "professional revolutionaries" (Lenin, 1960–70: vol. 6, 236). The intelligentsia was not, in other words, to join the workers (as Lenin had claimed in 1895). Rather, a few of the more advanced workers were to join the intelligentsia in an organization in which there would be no institutionalized check on authority. In this manner, a relatively high concentration of power in the hands of intellectuals, caused by a weakening of social ties between them and workers, bred intellectual elitism.

What was the situation in some of the other parties at the time? The Jewish Bund – until 1905 the largest and best organized party on the left in the Empire – never reached the same heights of intelligentsia elitism and centralizing fervor, mainly because the party's mass base did not disappear from sight. In contrast to the strike movement among non-Jewish workers, employed mainly in large industrial enterprises, the movement among Jewish workers, who were employed chiefly in artisans' workshops, appears to have continued to grow, probably because the latter were better organized: Coming out of an urban craft tradition, they had a longer history of guild, mutual-aid, and political involvement, in contrast to first- and second-generation Russian workers. In any event, the number of Jewish strikers per annum increased steadily from 1895 to 1903, whereas the number of non-Jewish strikers per annum dropped quickly after 1899. In 1902 – the year *What Is to be Done?* was published – there seem to have been more Jewish than non-Jewish strikers, although Jews made up only 10% of Russian citizens engaged in "mechanical and manufacturing pursuits" (Rubinow, 1907: 500; Borokhov, 1923: 29, 41; Haimson, 1964: 627; Turin, 1968: 187). The continued prominence of artisans in the Bund indicated to intellectuals in the party that artisans were still very much a force to be reckoned with. Bundists therefore continued to argue, as had Kremer, that "it is better to go along with the masses in a not totally correct direction than to separate oneself from them and remain a purist" (Kosovsky in *Vladimir Medem ...*, 1943: 133). Before 1905 the actions that such words implied were anathema to Bolsheviks, Mensheviks – and Labor Zionists.

Until 1906, Labor Zionist intellectuals were not similarly affected by the wave of Jewish labor unrest because their leaders lived in the Ukrainian town of Poltava, which was nearly devoid of workers. The relatively high concentration of power in the hands of labor Zionist intellectuals, a function of weak working-class ties, permitted the development of elitist ideas in some ways reminiscent of Bolshevism. Borokhov, the chief theoretician of the Poalei-Zion ("Workers of Zion") Party, thus complained in late 1904 or early 1905 that "we are too much involved in pleasant and lofty discussions on Zionism as a 'movement of the people'" (1955: 52). Labor Zionism, he insisted, must be a movement of politically conscious pioneers drawn from the intelligentsia, prepared to undergo tremendous personal sacrifice readying Palestine for colonization.

But Borokhov (1972) forgot entirely about this elite vanguard in a year or so. Palestinian colonization was by 1906 viewed as the inevitable outcome of spontaneously developing socioeconomic forces affecting not intellectuals, but the Jewish masses. What prompted the about-face? Principally, the fact that the influence of workers in party organizations increased dramatically between early 1905 and 1906. During the 1905 revolution, intelligentsia elitism receded as worker militance surged ahead. In 1905 the party leaders became convinced that their headquarters should be transferred to Vilna, the center of the Jewish labor movement. One worker-leader who made the move from Poltava explained how in Vilna "there opened up a world with new impressions and influences. ... We felt the pulse and rhythm of the political movement" (Zerubavel, 1956: vol. 1, 122–3).

So did the Bolsheviks and the Mensheviks to the east and south. For 1905 was a year in which over 550% more workers went out on strike – to make first economic, then political demands – than during the whole preceding decade. By September of that year the Bolshevik and Menshevik parties ceased to be sect-like organizations, having once again sunk roots into the working class.

As in the 1890s, ideological accommodation to the exigencies of the moment now took place. By November, Lenin admitted that conditions had so changed that much of the analysis in *What Is to be Done?* was "outdated." He therefore called for the establishment of a political center with "deep roots in the people"; demanded "the full application of the democratic principle in party organization"; and even went so far as to claim that "the working class is instinctively, spontaneously Social Democratic" (Lenin,

1960–70: vol. 10: 22, 32, 33). To be sure, Bolshevism remained the most elitist form of Russian Marxism. Nevertheless, Lenin's position amounted to a major revision of earlier Bolshevik views. And Bolshevism was relatively democratic in practice when, in 1912–14 and in 1917, labor militancy once again surged ahead. It was only when civil war and foreign invasion combined to decimate the Russian working class after 1917 that the party once again substituted itself for the proletariat. The short-lived era of political democracy in the party thus came to an end (Carlo, 1973).

Structural and nonstructural analyses of intellectuals

I have presented a simplified explanation of a complex phenomenon – an explanation that, nonetheless, outlines the major structural forces that radicalized Jewish intellectuals in turn-of-the-century Russia and led them to diverse ideological viewpoints. In summary:

The families that comprised Russian Jewry in the middle of the nineteenth century were ranged along a continuum of embeddedness in the community; the greater the degree of embeddedness, the stronger the family members' sense of Jewish identity. Bolshevik intellectuals tended to be recruited to their party from the community segment with the weakest occupational ties to the community; Labor Zionists from the segment that was most firmly embedded in the community; Bundists and Mensheviks from segments that manifested intermediate degrees of embeddedness. Differences in attitude toward the Jewish question were largely a function of these variations in degree of embeddedness.

Regardless of social origin, intellectuals in all four parties were socially mobile. But, owing to the character of employment opportunities, they were unable to become firmly entrenched in the Russian middle class. They thus became part of that malintegrated segment of the middle class that was radicalized. Radicalization was ensured by their having forged a dense network of ties among themselves.

It stands to reason that the availability of mass movements in the immediate social environments of the intellectuals after they were radicalized structured opportunities for the formation of ties to potential agents of change. And since the character of mass movements varied over time and place, the practical problems that intellectuals had to face called forth a wide range of ideological responses. Which segment of the working class was available to the intellectual substantially affected his or her views concerning the likely agents and character of the impending revolution and even such fundamental questions as that of identity. Variations in availability over time were also important: When ties binding intellectuals to workers were strong, intellectuals were relatively democratic in their thinking; when such ties were weak, they were relatively elitist.[3]

Notwithstanding the evidence favoring this interpretation, many political historians of Russia have been unwilling to accept a structural explanation of intellectual radicalization and ideological divergence. This reluctance is, I believe, connected to the political historian's way of understanding social causation. Clarification of this issue is warranted because it highlights the difference between structural and nonstructural explanation in general.

In order to make my point I must distinguish among three terms: "motivation," "precipitant causes," and "structural causes." Motivations refer to the reasons people give for their attitudes and actions. They are subjectively constructed linkages between perceived cause and effect. Structural causes, on the other hand, are objective in the sense that they are located outside peoople's minds, in those patterns of social relations that render more or less likely their holding certain attitudes and taking certain actions. Finally, precipitants are proximate causes. They connect motivations with often remotely situated structural causes, to produce attitude and action, much like a spark combines oxygen and combustible material to produce fire. Beyond motivations lie a progression of social forces that render a given attitude or action more or less probable; when structural sociologists theorize about why people think and behave the way they do, I suppose they usually envisage a series of "whys," the answer to the first "whys" being the precipitants, the answer to the last, the fundamental structural causes (Zaslavsky and Brym, 1983).

Political historians typically work with a more attenuated model of causation. Consider, for example, an argument made in a recent history of a large segment of the Russian-Jewish intelligentsia (Frankel, 1981; cf. Brym, 1982). Frankel asks why some assimilated intellectuals, who had no knowledge of Yiddish and no special yearnings to work among or separately organize the Jewish working class, nonetheless took the lead in forming the Jewish Bund. He contends that a comparative analysis of Jewish labor movements in Poland, Galicia, Romania, England, and the United States prompts a political interpretation of the assimilated intellectuals' turn to Bundism: The Russian Social Democratic Party (RSDRP) was small, weak, and disorganized in the 1890s so it could not impose its internationalist will on the future Bundist intellectuals. Instead, the latter were pushed by competition for supporters from such popular movements as the Polish Socialist Party (PPS) and the Zionists to adopt a more nationalistic position: "Where there was an established socialist party ready to permit or even encourage the autonomy of a Yiddish-speaking section ... there the internationalist (in effect the assimilationist) tendency won out. However, where the Jewish socialists felt betrayed by the dominant party ... a reverse process was set in motion" (Frankel, 1981: 178).

Frankel's argument makes sense and is supported by solid evidence. But it does nothing to discredit the explanation of intellectuals' political behavior perhaps first suggested by Lamartine in 1848: "Je suis leur chef. Il faut que je les suive!" Frankel's explanation focuses on the level of motivations and precipitants, Lamartine's on the level of structural causes. Most assimilated intellectuals who did not work among Jewish artisans became Mensheviks or, less commonly, Bolsheviks. Surely without some intellectuals' becoming embedded in the Jewish working class, RSDRP, PPS, and Zionist influence would not have precipitated a move to nationalism and motivated them to create Bundist ideology. Frankel's explanation is not wrong. But it is partial since, like most political historians, he draws our attention toward immediate causes (motivations, precipitants) and away from the more remote constraints imposed by social structure on people's thoughts and actions.

Yet, by analyzing these constraints, structural sociologists have frequently incurred the wrath of political historians, who presumably feel that the structuralists are trying to make light of, and supplant, their explanations. In my opinion, the political historians' anxieties are misplaced. By locating motivations and precipitants in their structural contexts, structuralists usually seek merely to explain social phenomena more fully, to supplement rather than supplant. In some fields, such as French history, this appears to be appreciated, and we have the Albert Sobouls (e.g., 1977) and the Charles Tillys (e.g., 1978) to thank for that. In other fields, such as Russian history (and especially Russian-Jewish history), structural thinking has had practically no impact, and the introduction of that approach is bound to create some confusion and ill feeling until its claims are properly understood.

Opposition from some political historians notwithstanding, the plain theoretical implication of my analysis is that it serves no useful purpose to continue underlining radical intellectuals' social rootlessness. Radical intellectuals *are* generally divorced from middle-class jobs, establishment institutions, or liberal roles; but, if we hope to develop more sophisticated theories that specify precise linkages between social location and ideological proclivity, we would do well to emphasize intellectuals' *embeddedness*: their shifting social ties to changing social groups. Social structures evolve. So do intellectuals' careers. Match the two processes and, I submit, we can learn a good deal about intellectuals and their ideologies.[4]

NOTES

1. Most of these data were taken from four multivolume biographical dictionaries (*Deyateli* ... n.d. [1927–9?]; Hertz, 1956–8; Niger and Shatzky, 1956–8; Raizen, 1928–30). In addition, memoirs and biographies, a full list of which is found in Brym (1978: 133–53) were consulted. For details on the construction of these indices, see Brym (1978: 42–3, 65–6, 129–31).

2. Cross-tabulating the intellectuals by party and region of recruitment yielded $\chi^2 =$ 86.3 ($p < .001$, d.f. $= 12$). These were, of course, only tendencies. For example, work published after my 1978 study reveals that some relatively urbanized artisanal workers in Moscow were deeply involved in Bolshevik party organizations (Bonnell, 1978–9). But on the whole, subsequent research on working-class support for the Bolshevik and Menshevik parties confirms the analysis summarized here. See, especially, Koenker (1978).

3. Disentangling the separate effects of social origins and political opportunities on party choice is a difficult task requiring much additional work. For an initial attempt, see Brym (1978: 64–5).

4. For a more formal analysis of why structurally equivalent people share similar ideas, see Erickson, Chapter 5.

LITERATURE CITED

Aronson, Grigori. *Revolyutsionnaya Yunost': Vospominaniya, 1903–17.* New York: Inter-University Project on the History of the Menshevik Movement. (Russian: *Revolutionary Youth: Reminiscences, 1903–17*), 1961.

Ascher, Avram. *Pavel Axelrod and the Development of Menshevism.* Cambridge, Mass.: Harvard University Press, 1972.

Avakumovic, Ivan. "A Statistical Approach to the Revolutionary Movement in Russia, 1878–1887." *Slavic Review* 18 (1959): 182–6.

Avineri, S. "Marx and the Intellectuals." *Journal of the History of Ideas* 28 (1957): 269–78.

Berlin, Isaiah. "Russia and 1848." *Slavonic Review* 18 (1948): 341–60.

Bonnell, V. "Radical Politics and Organized Labor in Pre-Revolutionary Moscow, 1905–1914." *Journal of Social History* 12 (1978–9): 282–300.

Borokhov, Ber. *Di Idishe Arbeter Bavegung in Tzifern.* Berlin: Ferlag Ferdinand Ostertag. (Yiddish: *The Jewish Labor Movement in Figures.*) 1923.

    Ktavim, 3 vols. (Translated by M. Avidor; edited by L. Levita and D. Ben-Nakhum. Tel Aviv: Ha-Kibutz ha-Meukhad (Hebrew: *Writings.*) 1955.

    Nationalism and the Class Struggle. Westport, Conn: Greenwood, 1972.

Brinton, Crane. *The Anatomy of Revolution.* New York: Knopf, 1938.

Brower, David. *Training the Nihilists: Education and Radicalism in Tsarist Russia.* Ithaca: Cornell University Press, 1975.

Brym, Robert J. "A Note on the *Raznochintsy*." *Journal of Social History* 10 (1977): 354–9.

    The Jewish Intelligentsia and Russian Marxism: A Sociological Analysis of Intellectual Radicalism and Ideological Divergence. London: Macmillan, 1978.

    Intellectuals and Politics. London: Allen and Unwin, 1980.

    "Review: J. Frankel, *Prophecy and Politics.*" *American Historical Review* 87 (1982): 1431–2.

    "Incorporation versus Power Models of Working Class Radicalism: With Special Reference to North America." *Canadian Journal of Sociology* 11 (1986): 227–51.

    "The Political Sociology of Intellectuals: A Critique and a Proposal." In A. Gagnon (ed.), *The Role of Intellectuals in Liberal Democracies.* New York: Praeger, in press.

Carlo, Antonio. "Lenin on the Party." *Telos* 17 (1973): 2–40.

Caute, D. *Communism and the French Intellectuals, 1914–1960.* London: André Deutsch, 1964.

Cherikover, Eliahu. "Yidn Revolutzionern in Rusland in di 60er un 70er yorn." *Historishe Shriftn* 3 (1939): 61–172. (Yiddish: "Jewish Revolutionaries in Russia in the 60s and 70s.")

Dan, Theodore. *The Origins of Bolshevism.* Translated by J. Carmichael. New York: Schocken, 1964.

Deutscher, Isaac. *The Prophet Armed: Trotsky, 1879–1921.* New York: Vintage, 1965.

Deyateli SSSR i Oktyabr'skoy Revolyutzii, n.d. (1927–9?), n.p. (Moscow?): Granat. (Russian: *Makers of the USSR and the October Revolution.*)

Dinur, Ben-Tzion. "Dmuta ha-historit shel ha-Yahadut ha-Rusit u-ve'ayot ha-kheker ba." *Tzion* 22 (1957): 93–118. (Hebrew: "The Historical Image of Russian Jewry and Problems in Its Research.")

Dubnow, Simon. *History of the Jews in Russia and Poland.* 3 vols. Translated by I. Friedlander. Philadelphia: Jewish Publication Society of America, 1916–20.

Eymontova, R. "Universitetskiy vopros i russkaya obshchestvennost' v 50–60-kh godakh XIX v." *Istoriya SSSR* 6 (1971): 144–58. (Russian: "The University Question and Russian Society in the 50s and 60s of the 19th Century.")

Fischer, George. "The Intelligensia and Russia." In C. Black (ed.), *The Transformation of Russian Society: Aspects of Social Change Since 1861.* Cambridge, Mass.: Harvard University Press, 1960.

Frankel, J. *Prophecy and Politics: Socialism, Nationalism and the Russian Jews, 1862–1917.* Cambridge: Cambridge University Press, 1981.

Getzler, Israel. *Martov: A Political Biography of a Russian Social Democrat.* Cambridge, Mass.: Harvard University Press, 1967.

Gorev, Boris, *Iz partiynogo proshlogo: vospominaniya 1895–1905.* Leningrad: Gosvdarstvennoe Izdatel'stvo, 1924. (Russian: *From the Party's Past: Reminiscences, 1895–1905.*)

Greenberg, Louis. *The Jews in Russia: The Struggle for Emancipation.* 2 vols. New Haven, Conn.: Yale University Press, 1944–51.

Grunwald, Kurt. "Europe's Railways and Jewish Enterprise." *Leo Baeck Institute Yearbook* 12 (1967): 163–209.

Haimson, Leopold. "The Problem of Social Stability in Urban Russia, 1905–17 (Part One)." *Slavic Review* 23 (1964): 619–42.

Hertz, Y. S. (ed.). *Doires bundistn.* 3 vols. to date. New York: Farlag Unzer Tzait, vols. 1–2, 1956–8. (Yiddish: *Generations of Bundists.*)

Hoffer, E. *The True Believer: Thoughts on the Nature of Mass Movements.* New York: Harper and Brothers, 1951.

Izgoev, A. S. "On Educated Youth (Notes on its Life and Sentiments)." *Vekhi (Signposts): A Collection of Articles on the Russian Intelligentsia.* Translated by M. Schatz and J. Zimmerman. In *Canadian Slavic Studies* 3 (1969): 594–615.

Jellinek, F. *The Paris Commune of 1871.* New York: Grosset and Dunlap, 1965.

Johnson, Robert Eugene. *Peasant and Proletarian: The Working Class of Moscow in the Late Nineteenth Century.* New Brunswick, N. J.: Rutgers University Press, 1979.

Kochan, Lionel. *The Making of Modern Russia*. Harmondsworth, England: Penguin, 1962.

Koenker, D. "The Evolution of Party Consciousness in 1917: The Case of the Moscow Workers." *Soviet Studies* 30 (1978): 38–62.

Kremer, Arkady. "Vegn agitatzie." In *Arkady: zamlbukh tzum andenk fun Arkady Kremer*. New York: Farlag Unzer Tzait, 1942: 293–321. (Yiddish: "On Agitation." In *Arkady: A Compendium in Memory of Arkady Kremer*.)

Lane, David. *The Roots of Russian Communism*. Assen: Van Gorcum, 1969.

Lenin, Vladimir. *Collected Works*. 45 vols. Edited by C. Dutt and J. Katzer. Moscow: Foreign Languages Publishing House, 1960–70.

Leshchinsky, Yaakov. "Di antviklung fun Idishn folk far di letzte 100 yor." *Shriftn far ekonomik un statistik* 1 (1928): 1–64. (Yiddish: "The Development of the Jewish People over the Last 100 Years.")

Lyadov, M. *Iz zhizni partii: nakanune i v gody pervoy revolyutzii (vospominaniya)*. Moscow: Izdatel'stvo kommunistincheskogo un-ta imeni Ya. M. Sverdlova, 1926. (Russian: *Of Party Life: On the Eve and in the Years of the First Revolution (Reminiscences)*.)

McGee, T. "Peasants in the Cities." *Human Organization* 32 (1973): 135–42.

Mahler, Raphael. *A History of Modern Jewry, 1789–1815*. Translated by Y. Haggai. London: Vallentine Mitchell, 1971.

Mannheim, Karl. "The Problem of the Intelligentsia: An Inquiry into Its Past and Present Role." In E. Mannheim and P. Kecskemeti (eds.), *Essays in the Sociology of Culture*. London: Routledge and Kegan Paul, 1956.

Marx, Karl. *Capital: A Critical Analysis of Capitalist Production*. 3 vols. Moscow: Progress, n.d.

Marx, Karl, and Friedrich Engels. "Manifesto of the Communist Party." In R. Tucker (ed.), *The Marx–Engels Reader*. New York: Norton, 1972.

Merton, Robert. "The Sociology of Knowledge." *Social Theory and Social Structure*. Enlarged ed. New York: Free Press, 1968.

Michels, Roberto. "Intellectuals." *Encyclopedia of the Social Sciences*, 8. New York: Macmillan, 1943.

  Political Parties: A Sociological Study of the Oligarchical Tendencies of Modern Democracy. Translated by E. and C. Paul. New York: Free Press, 1962.

Mishkinski, Moshe. "Regional Factors in the Formation of the Jewish Labor Movement in Czarist Russia." *VIVO Annual of Jewish Social Science* 14 (1969): 27–52.

Morokhovetz, E. "Krest'yanskoe dvizhenie 1905-07 gg. i sotzial-demokratiya." *Proletarskaya revolyutziya* 39 (1925a): 41–83. (Russian: "The Peasant Movement 1905-07 and Social Democracy.")

  "Krest'yanskoe dvizhenie 1905-07 gg. i. sotzial-demokratiyaya." *Proletarskaya revolyutziya* 40 (1925b): 57–91. (Russian: "The Peasant Movement 1905-07 and Social Democracy.")

Mosse, W. E. "Makers of the Soviet Union." *Slavonic Review* 46 (1968): 141–54.

Nedava, Joseph. *Trotsky and the Jews*. Philadelphia: Jewish Publication Society of America, 1972.

Niger, Sh., and Shatzky, Y. eds. *Leksikon fun der naier Yidisher literature*. 6 vols. to date. New York: Cyco, 1956–8 (Yiddish: *Lexicon of the New Yiddish Literature*.)

Park, R. "Human Migration and the Marginal Man." *American Journal of Sociology* 23 (1928): 881–93.

Parsons, T. "The Intellectual: A Social Role Category." In P. Rieff (ed.), *On Intellectuals*. Garden City, N. Y.: Anchor, 1963.

Piatnitsky, O. *Memoirs of a Bolshevik*. London: M. Lawrence, 1933.

Raizen, Z. (ed.). *Leksokon fun der naier Yidisher literatur, prese un filologie*. 4 vols. Vilna: Vilner ferlag fun B. Kletzkin, 1928–30. (Yiddish: Lexicon of the New Yiddish Literature, Press and Philology.)

Rubinow, I. "Economic Condition of the Jews in Russia." *Bulletin of the Bureau of Labor* 72 (1907): 487–583.

Simmel, Georg. "The Stranger." In D. Levine (ed.), *On Individuality and Social Forms*, Chicago: University of Chicago Press, 1971.

Soboul, Albert. *A Short History of the French Revolution, 1789–1799*. Berkeley: University of California Press, 1977.

Sverdlov, Yaakov. *Izbranye proizvedeniya*. 3 vols. Moscow: Gosudarstvennoe izdatel'stvo politicheskoi literatury, 1957–60. (Russian: *Selected Works*.)

Tilly, Charles. *From Mobilization to Revolution*. Reading, Mass.: Addison-Wesley, 1978.

Tobias, Henry. *The Jewish Bund in Russia from Its Origins to 1905*. Stanford: Stanford University Press, 1972.

Tompkins, S. *The Russian Mind from Peter the Great through the Enlightenment*. Norman: University of Oklahoma Press, 1953.

   The Russian Intelligentsia: Makers of the Revolutionary State. Norman: University of Oklahoma Press, 1957.

Turin, S. *From Peter the Great to Lenin: A History of the Russian Labour Movement with Special Reference to Trade Unionism*. London: Cass, 1968.

Verba, Sydney. "Comparative Political Culture." In L. Pye (ed.), *Political Culture and Political Development*. Princeton: Princeton University Press, 1965.

Vladimir Medem: tzum tzvantzigstn vortzeit. New York: American Representation of the General Jewish Workers' Union of Poland, 1943. (Yiddish: *Vladimir Medem: On the Twentieth Anniversary of his Death*.)

Von Laue, Theodore. *Sergei Witte and the Industrialization of Russia*. New York: Atheneum, 1974.

Weber, Max. *Ancient Judaism*. Edited and translated by H. Gerth and D. Martindale. Glencoe, Ill.: Free Press, 1952.

   General Economic History. Translated by F. Knight. New York: Collier, 1961.

Weinberg, Ian, and Kenneth Walker. "Student Politics and Political Systems: Toward a Typology." *American Journal of Sociology* 75 (1970): 77–96.

Weinryb, Bernard. *The Jews of Poland: A Social and Economic History of the Jewish Community in Poland from 1100 to 1800*. Philadelphia: Jewish Publication Society of America, 1972a.

   Neueste Wirtschaftsgeschichte der Juden in Russland und Polen: von der I. polnischen Teilung bis zum Tode Alexanders II. (1772–1881). (*The Latest Economic History of the Jews in Russia and Poland: From the First Polish Partition to the Death of Alexander II (1782–1881)*.) Hildesheim: George Olms Verlag, 1972b.

Wildman, Alan. "Lenin's Battle with Kustarnichestvo: The Iskra Organization in Russia." *Slavic Review* 23 (1964): 479–503.

The Making of a Workers Revolution: Russian Social Democracy, 1891–1903. Chicago: University of Chicago Press, 1967.

Wischnitzer, Mark. *A History of Jewish Crafts and Guilds.* New York: Jonathan David, 1965.

Wolfe, B. *Three Who Made a Revolution.* New York: Dial, 1948.

Zaslavsky, Victor, and Robert Brym. *Soviet Jewish Emigration and Soviet Nationality Policy.* New York: St. Martin's Press, 1983.

Zerubavel, Y. *Bleter fun a leben.* 2 vols. Tel Aviv: Farlag Peretz-bibliotek, 1956. (Yiddish: *Pages from a Life.*)

14

Cites and fights: material entailment analysis of the eighteenth-century chemical revolution

Douglas R. White and H. Gilman McCann

The structural-analytic literature of the past decade indicates that transitivity in social networks is an important concern. However, existing structural analytic methods are frequently unable to deal directly with the substantive and methodological problems posed by transitive relations in social structures (Berkowitz, 1982). These difficulties typically surface in one of two contexts.

First, those who model structures through multiple graphs defined onto the same set of elements tend to assume either (1) global transitivity or intransitivity – that is, the same degree of transitivity obtains throughout the network (Johnsen and McCann, 1982), or (2) that there is a sharp and arbitrary limit to the graph theoretic distances over which effects travel (Berkowitz, Carrington, Kotowitz, and Waverman, 1978). Neither strategy allows analysts to examine transitivity, itself, empirically. Second, techniques for examining relations among sets of *overlapping* attributes or ties are still in their infancy. Once again, transitivity among these sets is typically treated a priori rather than as a substantive or empirical problem.

A new technique – *Material entailment analysis* – allows researchers to model concrete situations in which the degree of transitivity present within social structures defined in either of these ways may be investigated empirically. This chapter describes this new technique and outlines ways in which it can be applied to a variety of structural problems in the social sciences.

We address the transitivity problem as a special case of the more general issue of orders and partial orders of variables or attributes. Following Nadel (1957), sociologists and anthropologists are often concerned with clusters of attributes in which the presence of one implies the presence of others. To the extent that such an implication is not reciprocated (symmetrical), we have an ordering of the attributes or cultural values. Consequently, a variety of social and cultural domains may be modeled in terms of "if . . . then" or set–subset relationships among cultural items. One study, for instance, found a partial ordering of basic color terms of the form "if a language has color term X, then it also has color term Y" (Berlin and Kay, 1969); and another found a similar ordering in the sexual division of labor such that if women (men) perform certain tasks they also tend to perform specific other tasks (Burton, Brudner, and White, 1977). Similar orderings have been found by other anthropologists, sociologists, linguists, and psychologists (Nadel, 1957; Gagne, 1965; Greenberg, 1966; D'Andrade, 1976). Most of the methodological work on orderings has been done by educational statisticians who utilize only a single overall cutoff level for strengths of ties within a system and an overall test of significance; that is, they tend to focus only on global orderings (Bart and Krus, 1973; Bart and Airasian, 1974; Baker and Hubert, 1977).

A more general approach, which examines both local and global orderings – and which can be used with relational as well as attribute data – is necessary for structural analysis. From a methodological point of view there is a need for a method that can address both morphology (the overall structure) and attributes using the same rules, or language. Material entailment analysis is such a method. It models patterns of either structure (relational data) or attributes in terms of entailment chains or hierarchies. These structures reflect "if . . . then" relations: *If* some attribute or connection (tie) is present, *then* some other attribute or tie is also present. The fact that such implications can be extended to three or more attributes, thus implies transitivity. Entailments extended to further attributes, ties, or nodes form entailment *chains* (partial orders) or hierarchies.

In the following sections of the chapter we briefly explain the theory and methods of entailment analysis and then illustrate its applications through an examination of citation networks among eighteenth-century chemists. We also draw some general conclusions about its applications to a range of social scientific problems.

Entailment analysis

Entailment analysis detects tendencies toward set–subset relationships among binary variables.[1] Given a set of variables, if some attribute (or some score on a dichotomized variable) logically implies (entails) the presence of some other attribute – or if *cases* with one attribute (X) are a subset of *cases* with another (Y) – then X implies Y ("If X then Y" is true). If the cases having Y as an attribute are also a subset of cases having Z, then Y implies Z *and*, quite interestingly, X also implies Z, since the set–subset relation is transitive. Formally: if X implies Y and Y implies Z, then X implies Z. Transitive relations of this general kind may extend to any number of attributes. Other logical relations are also possible between two variables: for instance, the presence of one implying (being a subset of) the *non*-presence of another (X implies not-Y) or the absence of one implying the presence of a second (not-X implies Y). The relations are more complex among more than two variables.

In logic, set–subset relations are necessarily categorical: *All* of the cases with X also have Y. With real data, however, there may be some exceptions. That is, some cases may have X as an attribute, but not Y. The possibility of such exceptions to purely logical relations makes it necessary to examine empirical implications – that is, "material entailments" – statistically. We call an analysis that takes these factors into account "*material* entailment analysis." The consideration of higher-level entailments, those involving three or more attributes or ties, raises the problem of transitivity and complicates the statistical analysis since exceptions may cumulate among the chain of entailments.[2]

More formally, suppose we have n observations on m variables where observation N_i on variable M_j may take one of two values, X, or its complement $\overline{X}$. The *frequencies* of observations with values X, X and Y, X and Y and Z, and so forth, are respectively designated $.X, X.Y, X.Y.Z$. An implication is a statement of the form[3]

> "If X then Y,"

which has exceptions designated $X.\overline{Y}$. "If X *and* Y *then* X" and "If X *then* Y *or* Z" are the canonical forms of higher order and entailments, that is, they are standard forms or models to which other types can be reduced. Other forms, such as "If X *or* Y *then* Z," can be reduced to first-order entailments – in this case, "If X then Z" and "If Y then Z."

A system of entailments is a set of implications that meet the following criteria:

> **Criterion 1** (exceptions). For "If X then Y" to be true, but not its converse ("If Y then X"), there must be fewer exceptions to the former than to the latter. This criterion induces asymmetry (ordering) in the resulting system. In the case that the statements "X implies Y" and "Y implies X," both have the *same* number of exceptions, X and Y are considered equivalent (and they are set-theoretic equal if the number of exceptions is zero).

In addition to assuming the form "X implies Y," an entailment should give us some confidence that X and Y are *in fact* related, that is, that X has "relevance" (Salmon, 1971) for the existence of Y. This consideration leads to

> **Criterion 2** (material relevance of material correlation). For "If X then Y" and its converse to be true, X and Y must be positively correlated ($\phi_{xy} > 0$, for the phi coefficient[4]).

Table 14.1, using fictitious data, provides us with an example of a proposition with few exceptions, but in which the two variables are statistically independent. There are only 5% (5/100) exceptions to the

Table 14.1. *Corporate size and centrality*

Centrality	Corporate size		Total
	Large	Small	
Low	95	9,405	9,500
High	5	495	500
Total	100	9,900	10,000

$\phi(=r) = .00$

proposition that "large corporations have low centrality," and a miniscule 1% (5/500) to the (logically equivalent) proposition that "corporations with high centrality are small." However, being large does not entail having low centrality since the association between size and centrality is zero.

A material entailment thus not only requires relatively few exceptions, but also a positive correlation between variables.

> Criterion 3 (transitivity). For the statements "If X then Y" and "If Y then Z" both to be true, the statement "If X then Z" must be true, and the partial correlation between X and Z given Y must be nonnegative ($\phi_{xz.y} \geq o$).[5]

The requirement of transitivity in a chain of entailments is motivated by the tendency for sets of observations defined by particular values to form *transitive subsets.* "If X then Y" and "If Y then Z" are propositions about the tendency for observations with value X to form a subset of those with value Y, and those with Y to form a subset of those with value Z. If there were no exceptions, we could infer from these relations that those with X form a subset of those with Z; so we require such transitivity in cases with exceptions as well.

Figure 14.1 shows a case in which there are no exceptions in a three-set chain: One set (with 3 elements) has attribute X; another (with 6 elements) has attribute Y; the third (with 9 elements) has attribute Z. The set $\{X\}$ is contained in $\{Y\}$, $\{Y\}$ is contained in $\{Z\}$, and it follows that $\{X\}$ is contained in $\{Z\}$. The correlations between X and Y and Y and Z are equal, $\phi_{xy} = \phi_{xz} = 1/\sqrt{3}$. The correlation $\phi_{xy} = \frac{1}{3}$. The partial correlation $\phi_{xz.y} = o$ is given by the formula:

$$\phi_{xy.z} = \frac{\phi_{xz} - (\phi_{xy}\phi_{yz})}{(1 - \phi_{xy}^2)(1 - \phi_{yz}^2)}.$$

Thus condition (3) is satisfied.

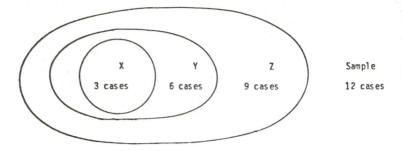

Figure 14.1. A three-set chain with no exceptions.

Condition (3) is *always* satisfied when set–subset relations or entailment chains contain *zero* exceptions. For those containing one or more exceptions, it is not necessarily satisfied, and potential entailments are regarded as valid in a system of entailments only if it is; that is, a tendency toward transitivity exists for all entailment chains in which the entailment is embedded.

These are the central criteria of entailment analysis. In addition, there are decision criteria for comparing a given *system* of observations to an expected distribution of entailments by levels of exception and degrees of correlation (under the null hypothesis) and for testing assumptions of no higher-order interactions.

> **Criterion 4** (rejection of total independence hypothesis). The probability that an observed entailment with a given level of correlation and exceptions will occur by chance under the assumption of total independence of the variables must be lower than some preset level for rejection.

This criterion is implemented through an application of signal detection theory (Coombs, Dawes, and Tversky, 1970) to the problem of whether observed entailments are likely or unlikely to be due to chance. This approach is explained later.

> **Criterion 5** (replication – lack of interaction). For entailments to be valid, interaction should not be present; that is, the measure of relevance (correlation coefficient) must not differ significantly across the categories of control variables.[6]

The significance of the difference can be expressed probabilistically by generalizing Fisher's exact test from the 2 × 2 case to the 2 × 2 × 2 case under the (null) hypothesis of no trivariate interaction with given bivariate distributions (White and Pesner, 1983). White, Pesner, and Reitz (1983) show how to derive a group significance for the hypothesis of no interaction for a system of binary variables.

Material and probabilistic entailments

The entailments we have been examining are material entailments associated with specific exceptions. These exceptions can also be expressed as *conditional probabilities* of exceptions to an entailment ("If X then Y") given either (a) the antecedent, $P(\bar{Y}|X)$, or (2) the complement of the consequent, $P(X|\bar{Y})$.[7] The same pair of conditional probabilities will obtain whether we consider the entailment or its *contrapositive*.[8] To obtain a single such probability for the comparison of entailments, we take the larger value of this pair. That is, in Table 14.1 we take .05 (5/100) rather than .01 (5/500). Given this, we can now reformulate criteria 1–3 for *probabilistic entailments*:

1. For "If X then Y" (but not its converse, "If Y then X") to hold, there must be a lower probability of exceptions to the former than to the latter.

2. For "If X then Y" and/or "If Y then X" to hold

$$d_1 = \max\left[(P(\bar{Y}|X) - P(Y|X)), (P(X|\bar{Y}) - P(\bar{X}|\bar{Y}))\right] \text{ and/or}$$
$$d_2 = \max\left[(P(\bar{X}|Y) - P(X|Y)), (P(Y|\bar{X}) - P(\bar{Y}|\bar{X}))\right]$$

must be positive.

3. For both "If X then Y" and "If Y then Z" to hold, "If X then Z" must hold (by 1 and 2) and

$$P(\bar{Z}|X) \leqslant P(\bar{Z}|Y)P(Y|X) + P(\bar{Z}|\bar{Y})P(\bar{Y}|X)$$
$$P(X|\bar{Z}) \leqslant P(X|Y)P(Y|\bar{Z}) + P(X|\bar{Y})P(\bar{Y}|\bar{Z})$$

must both be true.

These criteria are logically equivalent to the original criteria 1–3.

Several interesting consequences flow from these criteria. Most basic is that for an entailment to be valid, both antecedent and consequent must vary; that is, both column marginals and both row marginals in our basic 2 × 2 table must be greater than zero, so that we must work with variables (not constants). Second, a material entailment logically implies its contrapositive, which is important since in ordinary logic an implication is equivalent to its contrapositive. Third, we cannot obtain contradictory conclusions;[9] that is, if "X entails Y" is valid, then neither "X entails not-Y" nor "not-X entails Y" can be valid. Finally, two technical consequences follow that are important for the logical status of entailment analysis: "X entails X" (given that X varies), and "X entails Y" logically implies both "X entails X" and "Y entails Y."

Material or probabilistic entailment analysis, therefore, has the properties of a formal logic (noncontradiction, restricted identity, transitivity, contraposition, etc.) comparable to structures of logical entailment (Anderson and Belnap, 1975).[10]

Methods

Material entailment analysis of a system of binary variables is dependent upon two *constructive* procedures. One involves signal detection (Coombs et al., 1970): the comparison of the potential entailment relationships within an actual data set to a simulated (Monte Carlo) distribution of potential entailments.[11] This serves to separate those entailments that might occur randomly from those that are not likely to occur by chance. Once entailments that are considered to be signal are determined, they are then *ordered* by level of exception and, within each exception level, by strength of correlational relevance.

The second procedure begins by accepting the strongest entailment (fewest exceptions, strongest relevance) and then adds successive entailments to the structure only if they satisfy criteria 1 through 5, including transitivity with respect to entailments previously admitted to the entailment structure. For example, if "X entails Y" is the strongest entailment, it is selected first. "Y entails Z" will be added to the structure – assuming it has passed the signal detection test (which implies that it passes criteria 1, 2, 4) – only if "X entails Z" also passes and all three entailments satisfy criteria 3 and 5 as a system. Furthermore, the investigator can place additional constraints on admissible entailments, such as a maximum (number or percentage) of exceptions or a minimum level for correlational relevance.

Representing entailment structures

There are three types of forms of entailment between two variables (sets of ties).

1. *Inclusion* refers to the inclusion of one set in another; that is, ties to X are a subset of (included in) ties to Y (cases with X are a subset of those with Y) or vice versa, or both: "If X then Y" or "If Y then X," or both. The inclusion with the *lesser* number of exceptions is called a "strong" inclusion and that with the greater number of exceptions is called a "weak" inclusion.

2. *Exclusion* refers to the exclusion of one set by another; that is, the presence of one attribute (set of ties) entails the absence of another: "If X then not-Y" or "If Y then not-X" (which are contrapositives and, therefore, equivalent).

3. *Coexhaustion* refers to the situation in which two ties (attributes) exhaust the possibilities; that is, if a case does not have a tie to X then it will have a tie to Y: "If not-X then Y" (equivalent to "If not-Y then X").

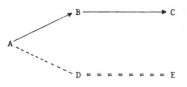

Figure 14.2. An entailogram.

Inclusion, exclusion, and coexhaustion are entailment relationships between antecedents and consequents that we can designate by different types of symbols for pictorial representation. Inclusion is an asymmetric relationship unless accompanied by its converse. Exclusion and coexhaustion are symmetric relationships:[12]

1. Inclusion $\qquad$ $X \longrightarrow Y$
2. Exclusion $\qquad$ $X ---Y$
3. Coexhaustion $\qquad$ $X = = = Y$

"Complementation" provides a number of ways of expressing the same entailment; and it is always possible to express an entailment by complementing the antecedent, the consequent, or both (the contrapositive). In general, either the three types of entailment or two of them plus complementation of some elements are necessary and sufficient to represent all possible entailment structures in a graphic form called an entailogram. Let us say that we have found that if people choose *A* they also choose *B*; that is, *A* entails *B*, and that *B* entails *C* (this implies that *A* also entails *C*). Also, those who choose *A* do not choose *D* (*A* entails not-*D*), and those who do not choose *D* choose *E* (not-*D* entails *E*). We can represent this pictorially (Figure 14.2).

An illustration: structure among citations of revolutionary chemists

The chemical revolution that we focus on here is a classical example of a "paradigm shift" (Kuhn, 1962; McCann, 1978). Kuhn argues that science may assume two forms: "normal" and "revolutionary." Normal science is based upon a *paradigm*: a matrix of accepted "beliefs, values, techniques," as well as concrete examples, which bind together a scientific community. The paradigm guides scientists in the community in choices of problems and methods and provides clear expectations about solutions. Normal science, thus, takes on the character of puzzle solving: data that apparently conflict with the reigning theory are not viewed as counterexamples, but as anomalies or puzzles that a scientist can solve (Kuhn, 1962: 5).

In contrast, a revolution, in which a new paradigm replaces an old one, occurs at times when such anomalies are incorrigible, and new or different explanations of some observed phenomena are advanced by one or more scientists. The result is a crisis in the community that can only be resolved by the defeat of one of these alternatives.

The issues raised during the chemical revolution centered around experiment and theories concerned primarily with the chemistry of gases ("airs") and the phenomena surrounding burning and other forms of what is now called oxidation. The existing paradigm, which had dominated for some 25 to 30 years in France and Great Britain (Guerlac, 1959; Rappaport, 1961; Schofield, 1970) and even longer in Germany, was based on the phlogiston theory of combustion and related phenomena. Bodies, phlogistonists thought, were combustible because, and to the extent that, they contained phlogiston, the matter of fire. They contended that when something burns, it gives up its phlogiston. Substances such as coal or oil were thought to be full of phlogiston; and hydrogen, when it was discovered, was thought by many phlogistonists to be this substance itself.

During the 1770s the discovery of "airs" led to the rapid growth of chemistry (McCann, 1978: chap. 3), intensive work on combustion (Perrin, 1969), and to widespread interest in it within fashionable circles in Paris and London. Thorough examination of the weight relations during combustion led Antoine Lavoisier to question the phlogiston explanation.[13] During the 1780s, Lavoisier developed a countertheory and undertook supporting experiments to a point where he was able to convert the leading chemists of France (including most of his colleagues in the Paris Academy of Sciences, the world's leading scientific institution at the time) to it. By the end of the 1790s, most British and European chemists had converted as well.

The context in which these changes were taking place becomes clear when we examine citations, that is, references that one scientist makes to another's work in his or her published writings. Citations reflect their purpose[14] and the structure of the disciplines in which scientists are embedded. We expect, for instance, that subject areas will hang together such that if one member of a specialty is cited, then others in the same group will also be cited.

These specialties may be thought of as information pools: Some members of a given pool will contribute more to it than others and, hence, will be cited more often by both those in the pool and those outside it. If, for instance, *A* and *B* are two members of a given pool, and *A* contributes more (is more "important"), then those who cite *B* should also tend to cite *A*, whereas those who cite *A* may not cite *B*.

Thus, specialties tend to have hierarchical structures: For one thing, more productive, prestigious, and visible scientists are likely to be cited more often. These scientists would then appear at the "top" of entailment chains, and those who are less productive, prestigious, and visible would only appear at

(a) Normal Sociogram

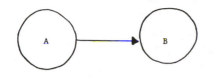

(b) Entailogram

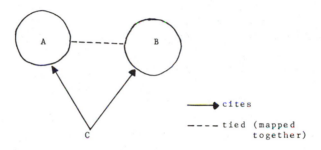

Figure 14.3. Comparison of a normal sociogram and an entailogram.

the bottom. Thus, a scientist's location within an entailment chain of citations is a good indication of his role within the overall structure.

Because entailment analysis involves set–subset relations, if a given discipline or specialty is structured in this fashion (i.e., citing of one person leads to the citing of another), the citations to the first will form a subset of those to the second, and so on. Further, to the extent that the second is cited more often, his or her citations can be only a superset of those to the first. Therefore, entailment analysts view the data somewhat differently from the usual sociometric conception (Figure 14.3). A "link" exists between A and B not when *A* cites *B* but when one or more chemists who cite *A* also cite *B*. Since there may be more than one problem area in a discipline, we would expect more than one entailment chain to surface.

Data

The data we examine here come from a study by McCann (1978) and consist of *all* references to chemists in scientific papers published by British and French nationals in Great Britain and France from 1760 through 1795. There were a total of 3311 citations in 858 papers in which 219 authors referenced

591 chemists. Elimination of those not cited or not citing (including all scientists outside the sample owing to nationality) yields a structure containing 758 links (multiple citations ignored) among 115 authors.

In the eighteenth century, references rarely specified particular works (papers, books, talks) but merely mentioned names. Consequently all citations take the form "person A cites person B." Thus, our data reflect only the number of persons who cite a given person; that is, a citation from A to B exists if there is at least one paper in which A cites B.

For purposes of illustration we consider the sets composed of links to the 48 chemists most often cited between 1760 and 1795. We use the following cutoff values: (1) two exceptions – the first because we do not include self-citation, and the second to allow for random variation or noise; (2) ϕ (relevance) of .3 to eliminate weak relations (1 or 2 exceptions but a small set); and (3) a reasonably conservative signal-to-noise ratio of 1 to 1 (White, 1980; White and McCann, 1981).

We consider all ties to the top 48 chemists among chemists publishing in each period. We first figure out the sets of citations – that is, the subset of citers that is tied to each top man. We then look for set–subset relations by considering each of the $[N(N-1)/2]$ possible pairs among the 48 and calculating both the percentage of exceptions and the correlation. For example, suppose chemists A, B, and C cite 1; A, B, C, and D cite 2; and B, C, and D cite 3. Then 1 entails 2 (since those who cite 1 are a subset of those who cite 2) and 3 entails 2 – both with no exceptions.

This case shows a convergence of two subgroups. A chain may also split if those who cite 1 are a subset of those who cite 2 and are also a subset of those who cite 3, but some of those who cite 3 (and do not cite 1) do not cite 2.

Once all of the coefficients and exception levels have been calculated for each of the pairs, the entire system of exception levels and the coefficients are compared against a randomly generated set. Then we start with the strongest one and add those that meet all of the criteria, in particular, those that satisfy the transitivity criterion. For example, assume that 4 entails 5 with no exceptions and a correlation coefficient of 1.0, and 5 entails 8 with no exceptions and a correlation coefficient of 1.0. Then 4 must entail 8 (since there are no exceptions). If 8, in turn, entails 20 with 2 exceptions and a coefficient of .8, for example, then before 8 entails 20 can be added to the structure 4 and 5 must also entail 8 (pass the signal-detection test), and the appropriate partials must be positive (e.g., $\phi_{48.5} \geqslant 0$).

Thus, in the following analysis, a chain leading up to Priestley, for instance, will mean that some group of chemists who cited a man lower in the chain also cited every person higher, with less than the cutoff level of exceptions, and that all of the partial correlations were positive. Priestley will not only be cited by everyone who cites anyone else in the chain (not counting exceptions), but he will also have the highest total number of citations.

Results

Figures 14.4 through 14.7 depict the entailment structure of the chemists' network over time. Each entailogram corresponds to an important phase in the chemical revolution. In general we see a picture of growth in structure: from almost none in the earliest years (Figure 14.4), to great complexity during the period of dispute and conversion (Figure 14.6) to a simpler pattern in the last, consolidation phase (14.7)). In detail, these entailograms both support and add important dimensions to the discussion in McCann (1978).

Figure 14.4 shows the entailment structure for 1760–71, a period during which chemistry was in its infancy and in which, consequently, there were relatively few journals or chemists. There is no evidence of an overlap in citations: Although 24 chemists cited one or more of the 48 leaders during these years (16 of 48), the only set overlap that met the criteria was the citing of Lassone and Montet by Cadet.

The period 1772–84 was the one in which the chemistry of airs became popular, and Lavoisier recognized various anomalies and then launched his attack on phlogiston theory. The entailogram (Figure 14.5) shows a distinct structure: a small number of generally short chains leading from less prominent, primarily young, chemists to recognized leaders in the community (Priestley, Black and Cavendish in England, the leaders in gas chemistry; and Baume, Lassone, and Lavoisier in France). Priestley clearly links two large groups whereas Lavoisier appears somewhat peripheral, a result that reflects the roles of Priestley as the primary exponent of the phlogiston theory – vocal, prolific, working in the "hot" area (airs) – and Lavoisier as a critic attacking the accepted model. We also note that, with the exception of Cavendish, the eminent men tend to head separate subgroups rather than being cited by identical followers (or outsiders).

In 1785 Lavoisier won his first major convert, Claude Berthollet, who was followed by Antoine Fourcroy in 1786 – both members of the Paris Academy of Sciences. By 1789 the battle had been won in France, and a new journal, devoted to the oxygen paradigm (the *Annales de Chimie*), was established. The entailogram for this period (Figure 14.6) exhibits the sort of structure one would expect: a complex and dense network with many chains, representing the great publishing activity resulting from paradigm dispute and the shifting alliances and arguments (McCann, 1978: chap. 3). The structure is complicated by the fact that both positive and negative citations are included,[15] so that Priestley, for example, appears at the top of both French and British phlogistonist and oxygenist chains. New French chemists, notably Berthollet, Morveau (coauthor of the new chemical nomenclature based on oxygen and cofounder of *Annales de Chimie*), and Macquer (older, author of the dominant phlogiston textbook, and defender of phlogiston), rise to the top, or close to the top, of entailment chains. As in the preceding period, we find

Lassone ←————————→ Montet

Figure 14.4. Entailment structure of network of chemists, 1760–71. $\phi \geqslant .3$; 0 exceptions; signal-to-noise ratio, 1:1.

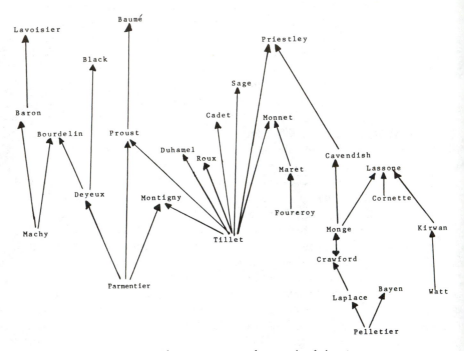

Figure 14.5. Entailment structure of network of chemists, 1772–84. $\phi \geqslant .3$; exceptions $\leqslant 2$; signal-to-noise ratio, 1:1.

that the most prominent men tend to fall into distinct, although often highly connected, chains; that is, they specialize enough to remain the heads of slightly different subgroups. This separation may help to account for the tendency of disputants to talk past one another (Kuhn, 1962; Hufbauer, 1982) as well as reflect, in part, the tendency for paradigms under attack to fragment (Kuhn, 1962; McCann, 1978).

Finally, in the last entailogram (Figure 14.7) we see a period of consolidation in which the new paradigm has succeeded and the battle is over (at least in France). Almost all French chemists have converted or have stopped publishing: Only two men, one a mineralogist (Sage) and one an editor (Delametherie), published pro-phlogiston articles in France after 1790 (McCann, 1978: 81). This period exhibits a clear and relatively simple structure: a major chain leading to Lavoisier, the instigator of the revolution, with lesser and connected chains leading to other oxygen chemists.[16] The

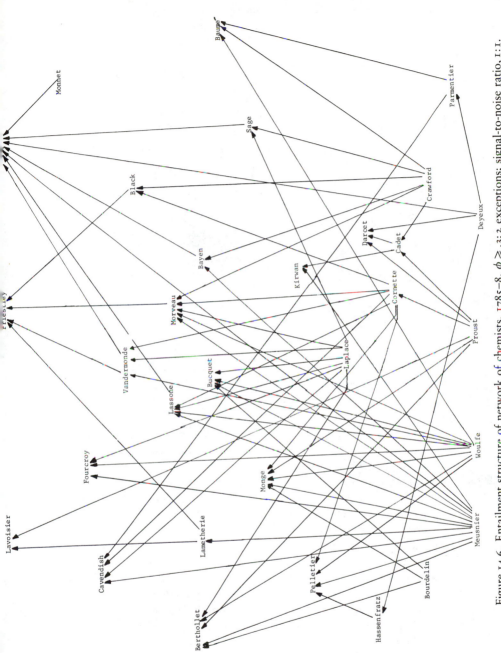

Figure 14.6. Entailment structure of network of chemists, 1785–8. $\phi \geqslant .3$; 2 exceptions; signal-to-noise ratio, 1:1.

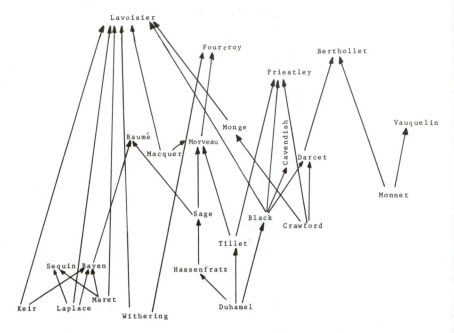

Figure 14.7. Entailment structure of network of chemists,
1791–5. $\phi \geqslant .3$; I (= 2) exception; signal-to-noise ratio, 1:1. [Note:
Vertical placement determined by number of citations, horizontal by
ease of reading (i.e., by "eyeball").]

picture is one of normal science: the leading expert of the paradigm
(Lavoisier) at the top, with other experts at the tops of their subspecialties.

In sum, the changes in structure over time show an early period with little
coherence,[17] followed by a period in which clear subareas appear and experts
take their positions at the heads of these subareas and in which a young Turk
begins the fragmentation process with an attack on the guiding paradigm.
During the period of most intense conflict, the structure is highly interconnected, exhibiting overall coherence, but with internal divisions reflecting
various camps in the dispute; that is, both the prime revolutionary and the
major defenders of the faith take their positions at the top. Finally, as the
conflict subsides and the research questions guided by the new paradigm
come to the fore, the structure becomes simpler, more orderly, and closer to a
single paradigmatic hierarchy, with the leading revolutionary at its head.

The analysis refines Kuhn's (1962, 1970) broad description of the process of
paradigmatic change: breakdown in a given paradigm, a period of crisis and
conflict during which the supporters of each view contend with one another,
and the triumph of the new paradigm. It elaborates his view that revolutions
will be reflected in shifting distributions of cited literature (1962: ix), which

themselves reflect changes in the formal and informal communication networks of scientific communities (1970: 178) by providing details of the structure of the communities and revealing changes in the structures that accompany revolutionary change. Consonant with previous literature on science, the analysis shows a center–periphery pattern (McCann, 1974; Burt, 1978), or what has been called an "invisible college" (Crane, 1972), with the experts who are most often cited sitting at the heads of entailment chains. An interesting refinement, however, is the discovery that the most prominent scientists do not appear in a single chain or as structurally equivalent (in the sense of being linked to the same others), but each seems to carve out his own niche.

In addition we get a dynamic picture of the changing roles of important scientists as the process of revolution unfolds. Older scientists fall away and newer ones take their place, a process that is, of course, inevitable but that is undoubtedly speeded up by a revolution, during which role players rapidly change.

Conclusion

This chapter has described a new technique that allows researchers to model concrete situations in which the degree of transitivity present within social structures may be investigated empirically. As we have seen, the transitivity problem is a special case of the more general issue of orders of variables or attributes. Entailment analysis represents a very general approach that simultaneously examines both local and global orderings present within relational and attribute data. Entailment structures reflect "If ... then" relations that can be extended to three or more attributes; the fact that they can be expended implies transitivity.

We have discussed and illustrated the use of five criteria to examine the empirical relations in a social network: number of exceptions, relevance, transitivity, independence, and interaction. The number of exceptions in set–subset relations and the relevance of one set for another were used to define local structure. The criteria of transitivity, independence, and lack of interaction were used to determine global structure. The use of these criteria, with varying values or cutoffs, permits us to look at the global and the local structure simultaneously and to discover the empirical connections in the network in a subtle, rather than heavy-handed, manner. The exceptions to entailments can also be expressed as conditional probabilities, and as a result, the first three criteria can be viewed probabilistically.

We then described a means of representing these entailment structures in a diagram, the entailogram. Entailograms were constructed for four periods representing a paradigmatic shift from normal to revolutionary and then again to normal chemistry: what is known as the chemical revolution of the eighteenth century. This revolution, as we have seen, was primarily concerned with the chemistry of gases and the phenomena now known as oxidation.

We found that the entailment structure of citation groups during the chemical revolution revealed new information that extended the historical and sociological investigation carried out by McCann (1978). The new analysis presented here revealed details of the *process* of structural development of a scientific specialty and the varying roles played by members of its community during a period of revolutionary change. It further showed that entailment analysis, while preserving a global center–periphery pattern (McCann, 1974: chap. 7; Crane, 1972: chap. 3) was also able to depict the *internal* structure of specialty groups in fine detail.

From a theoretical standpoint material entailment analysis, because of its set–subset orientation, may force us to reconceptualize the way networks and similar phenomena have traditionally been represented. Further, entailment analysis focuses on relations and demands transitivity, and consequently is able to make fine separations and exhibit both orders and partial orders. Thus, it incorporates hierarchical and quasi-hierarchical structures that may be implicit in the data.

More generally, material entailment analysis can be used to complement other structural analytic techniques. It provides, for instance, a fine-grained image of potential roles played by actors in a concrete system that could be used in constructing more precise blockmodels. Similarly, the structure represented by an entailogram might be clustered or the entailogram itself could be superimposed upon a clustering (White, 1981), providing internal structure to clusters. Other methods of network analysis, such as multidimensional scaling or cliquing, may also be profitably supplemented in this fashion.

In sum, material entailment analysis promises to add to our "bag" of methodological equipment and to enrich substantive thinking. It is useful for detecting ordering or transitivity in both relational and attribute data and may therefore help integrate the two.

NOTES

1. For a discussion and example of nonbinary variables, see Burton et al. (1977).
2. The transitivity problem for material entailment analysis may be stated as follows: If we allow a given number (level) of exceptions to an entailment (i.e., if we assume the validity of an entailment although there are (some small number of) exceptions to it), then if X entails Y and Y entails Z, it may not be the case that X entails Z because the exceptions to Y entails Z may be different from those to X entails Y so that their sum, which is the number of exceptions to X entails Z, may exceed the allowed cutoff level. In other words, the exceptions may cumulate

along the chain of entailments; and although transitivity always holds for purely logical entailments, it may not hold for material (empirical) ones.

3. The element "X" may be replaced by a *conjunctive* series (e.g., *A and B and* C) and the element "Y" may be replaced by a *disjunctive* series (e.g., *D or E or F*). It is sometimes necessary for convenience of discussion or representation to refer to the complement of an attribute or to look at contrapositives. To form the contrapositive of an implication (which is always equivalent to the given implication and has the same exceptions), reverse the antecedent and consequent, interchange "ands" and "ors," and complement all elementary terms. For example, the contrapositive of "If X then Y" is "If not-Y, then not-X."

4. Although we use the phi coefficient in this discussion because of its symmetric character and its relation to conditional probabilities other coefficients can obviously be used.

5. In longer chains, such as "if W then X then Y then Z," the fact that all first-order partials ($\phi_{wy.x}$, $\phi_{wz.x}$, $\phi_{wz.y}$, etc.) are positive does not imply that second-order partials will be positive. This may be required in stronger tests of transitivity.

6. Failure to satisfy the criterion of no interaction is not necessarily a serious problem in entailment analysis. If only first-order entailments (two place: "If X then Y," for example) are examined where higher order interactions are present, the common effect is not to create spurious entailments, but simply to miss the higher-order ones. However, higher-order entailments may be theoretically important.

7. This notation is a standard way of stating conditional probabilities, where "X" is the presence of value (event), X, as above, and "$\bar{X}$" represents the absence of X (nonoccurrence of X). Thus, $P(\bar{Y}|X)$ is to be read as "the probability of not-Y (or of not observing Y) *given* X," which is equivalent to the probability of an exception, $\bar{Y}$, to the entailment "If X then Y."

8. Consider "X entails Y." X is called the antecedent (because it logically comes before Y) and Y the consequent. The contrapositive of an entailment is obtained by negating (taking the complement of) both the antecedent and the consequent and interchanging them. For example, the contrapositive of "X entails Y" is "not-Y entails not-X" and the contrapositive of "X entails not-Y" is "Y entails not-X."

9. The first and third consequence (theorems 1 and 3) rule out the type of possible contradiction where "If X then Y" and "If X then not-Y" both could occur with zero exceptions due to the nonoccurrence of X ($\cdot X = 0$). Similarly, "If X then Y" and "If not-X then Y" could otherwise occur owing to the universal presence of Y ($\cdot Y = N$). These kinds of contradictions are standard in ordinary implicational logic, where the falsity of an antecedent implies the truth of contradictory consequences and the truth of the consequent implies the truth of propositions with contradictory antecedents (Anderson and Belnap, 1975).

10. The strengthening of material implication by the criterion of relevance directly parallels Anderson and Belnap's (1975) restriction of logical entailment to a stronger case of logical implication with the added criterion of logical relevance (derivation by proof). The axioms of logical entailment are identity, transitivity, restricted assertion, and self-distribution (Anderson and Belnap, 1975: 24).

11. The decision to accept or reject a given entailment is based on a signal-to-noise ratio used in this comparison. For details, see White and McCann, 1981.

12. There are further logical combinations possible, some of which may be useful in simplifying the presentation of complex systems.

13. There were a very few others (e.g., Bayen, an apothecary with the army, and Turgot) who raised doubts about phlogiston, but only Lavoisier created an alternative.

14. We realize that reasons for citations are diverse and that their exact import is problematic. Scientists presumably cite one another to acknowledge influence or ideas, and they also use citations to indicate knowledge of a field. For these reasons citations usually lead to recognition and prestige for those cited (Hagstrom, 1965; Blume and Sinclair, 1973; Gustin, 1973). Since citations lead to recognition, scientists may also cite their friends or others they wish to promote (or denigrate in the case of negative citations). The place of friendship ties in science is little studied, although some work has been done by networkers on networkers (Freeman and Freeman, 1979, 1980). Nevertheless, most theory and findings support the view that scientists tend to cite disproportionately the leaders of a field or specialty.

15. Negative citations, those in which a scientist disagrees with the person being cited, are almost entirely ignored in the literature. Their recognition and coding might clarify and extend results of citation analyses – the blind counting of citations without taking into account their valence may easily bias interpretations. For the case here, we note that Priestley, the leader of the phlogistonists, received more citations from oxygen chemists than did Lavoisier. Lavoisier and Priestley also, not surprisingly, cited each other frequently.

16. Among these other oxygen chemists were Fourcroy and Berthollet, the most eminent, who dominate French chemistry after Lavoisier's death by guillotine in 1793, and Baume, an older man and a late convert. Another chain leads (through phlogiston chemists only) to Priestley.

17. The lack of structure is not due to the lack of a paradigm. However, there were many reactions for which phlogiston was not relevant, and chemistry as a profession was only weakly institutionalized (McCann, 1978: chap. 3).

LITERATURE CITED

Anderson, A. R., and N. D. Belnap. *Entailment: The Logic of Relevance and Necessity.* Princeton, N. J.: Princeton University Press, 1975.

Baker, F. B., and L. Hubert. "Inference Procedures for Ordering Theory." *Journal of Educational Statistics* 2 (1977): 217–33.

Bart, W. M., and P. W. Airasian. "Determination of the Ordering among Seven Piagetian Tasks by an Ordering Theoretic Method." *Journal of Educational Psychology* 55 (1974): 277–84.

Bart, W. M., and D. J. Krus "An Ordering-Theoretic Method to Determine Hierarchies Among Items." *Educational and Psychological Measurement* 33 (1973): 291–300.

Berkowitz, S. D. *An Introduction to Structural Analysis.* Toronto: Butterworths, 1982.

Berkowitz, S. D., P. J. Carrington, Y. Kotowitz, and L. Waverman. "The Determination of Enterprise Groupings through Combined Ownership and Directorship Ties." *Social Networks* 1 (1978): 291–413.

Berlin, B., and P. Kay. *Basic Color Terms: Their Universality and Evolution.* Berkeley: University of California Press, 1969.

Blume, S. S., and R. Sinclair. "Chemists in British Universities: A Study in the Reward System of Science." *American Sociological Review* 38 (1973): 126–38.

Burt, R. "Stratification and Prestige among Elite Experts in Methodological and Mathematical Sociology Circa 1975." *Social Networks* 1 (1978): 105–58.

Burton, M., L. Brudner, and D. White. "A Model of the Sexual Division of Labor." *American Ethnologist* 4 (1977): 227–51.

Coombs, C. H., R. M. Dawes, and A. Tversky. *Mathematical Psychology: An Elementary Introduction.* Englewood Cliffs, N. J.: Prentice-Hall, 1970.

Crane, D. *Invisible Colleges: Diffusion of Knowledge in Scientific Communities.* Chicago: University of Chicago Press, 1972.

D'Andrade, R. G. "A Propositional Analysis of U.S. American Beliefs about Disease." In K. H. Basso and H. A. Selby (eds.), *Meaning in Anthropology.* Albuquerque: University of New Mexico Press, 1976.

Freeman, L., and S. Freeman. "A Semi-Visible College: Structural Effects on a Social Networks Group." In M. Henderson and M. J. McNaughton (eds.), *Electronic Communication: Technology and Impacts.* Boulder: Westview Press, 1980.

Freeman, S., and L. Freeman. "The Networkers' Network: A Study of the Impact of a New Communications Medium on Sociometric Structure." University of California, School of Social Sciences, Research Reports 46. Irvine, 1979.

Gagne, R. M. *The Conditions of Learning.* New York: Holt, Rinehart, and Winston, 1965.

Greenberg, J. H. *Language Universals, with Special Reference to Feature Hierarchies.* The Hague: Mouton, 1966.

Guerlac, H. "Some French Antecedents of the Chemical Revolution." *Chymia* 5 (1959): 73–112.

Gustin, B. H. "Charisma, Recognition, and the Motivation of Scientists." *American Journal of Sociology* 78 (1973): 1119–34.

Hagstrom, W. O. *The Scientific Community.* New York: Basic Books, 1965.

Hufbauer, K. G. *The Formation of the German Chemical Community.* Berkeley: University of California Press, 1982.

Johnsen, E., and H. G. McCann. "Acyclic Triplets and Social Structure in Complete Signed Digraphs." *Social Networks* 4 (1982): 251–72.

Kuhn, T. S. *The Structure of Scientific Revolutions.* Chicago: University of Chicago Press, 1962.

The Structure of Scientific Revolutions. 2d ed. Chicago: University of Chicago Press, 1970.

Lorrain, F., and H. C. White. "Structural Equivalence of Individuals in Social Networks." *Journal of Mathematical Sociology* 1 (1971): 49–80.

McCann, H. G. *The Development and Reception of the Chemical Revolution by the Chemical Communities of France and Great Britain, 1760–1795.* Ph.D. diss., Princeton University, 1974.

Chemistry Transformed: The Paradigmatic Shift from Phlogiston to Oxygen. Norwood, N. J.: Ablex, 1978.

Nadel, S. F. *The Theory of Social Structure*. London: Cohen and West, 1957.

Perrin, C. E. "Prelude to Lavoisier's Theory of Calcination: Some Observations on *Mercurius Calcinatus Per Se*." *Ambix* 16 (1969): 140–51.

Rappaport, R. "Rouelle and Stahl – The Phlogistic Revolution in France." *Chymia* 7 (1961): 73–102.

Salmon, W. C. *Statistical Explanation and Statistical Relevance*. Pittsburgh: University of Pittsburgh Press, 1971.

Schofield, R. E. *Mechanism and Materialism: British Natural Philosophy in an Age of Reason*. Princeton, N.J.: Princeton University Press, 1970.

White, D. R. "Material Entailment Analysis: Theory and Illustrations." University of California, School of Social Sciences, Research Reports 15. Irvine, 1980.

   "American Beliefs About Disease: Material Entailment Analysis of D'Andrade's Data." University of California, School of Social Sciences working paper. Irvine, 1981.

White, D. R., and H. G. McCann. "Material and Probabilistic Entailment Analysis: Methods for Multivariate Analysis." University of California, School of Social Sciences working paper. Irvine, 1981.

White, D. R., and R. Pesner. "Internal Replication, the Systems Concept, and Sources of Validity in Nonexperimental Research." *Behavior Science Research* 18 (1983): 26–44.

White, D. R., R. Pesner, and K. Reitz. "An Exact Significance Test for Three-way Interaction." *Behavior Science Research* 18 (1983): 103–22.

Part V
Social mobility

American sociologists are as fascinated as the rest of their countrymen with achievement at work or at school. They study "occupational mobility" – shifts in job status by individuals during their lifetimes or between generations – as if it were the only kind of change in structural position that mattered. Indeed, American sociologists first developed one of their more elaborate statistical techniques, path analysis, to trace the impact on work and school achievement of factors such as gender, parents' education and occupations, and the achievement and aspirations of friends.

Almost all of these efforts have been directed toward the study of individual mobility: How high can a given person with given characteristics go up the social ladder? Although conservative and Marxian analysts have disagreed about whether occupational status or social class is the relevant analytic category for studying mobility, both have treated mobility as an individual race to the top, albeit a complex race with different starting points, finish lines, snakes, and ladders along the way. True, some nonstructuralist scholars have studied the social determinants of mobility, and some have taken into account gross characteristics of the opportunity structures in which jobs are located. But the focus of their analyses has been on the study of individuals with similar attributes, each making his or her own separate way to jobs.

Structural analysts contend that it is more fruitful to view mobility as a general, overarching process rather than as a series of isolated rat races. Consider universities, a key element in the mobility marathon. Universities operate as arenas for the exercise of individual merit and achievement, where a grade of B+ is supposed to be not only more meritorious than a B, but a greater aid to future occupational achievement. But academic achievement is also a collective phenomenon. Universities differ significantly in their access to resources, so that the students at elite universities receive better training than those at others. They offer substantially different opportunities for young adults to form supportive networks with future "old boys" and "old girls." Nor does this collective experience end with graduation. Academics are asked where and with whom they studied – not what grades they received. Every Ph.D. turned out by an elite university, for instance, has a stake in the continued success of his or her department – even 20 years later.

Lorne Tepperman's chapter, the first in this part, is an extended argument for studying mobility structurally. Tepperman believes that the traditional use of individuals ("particularly the adult male") as units of analysis in mobility studies overemphasizes the importance of personal attributes such as merit, ambition, intelligence, and personality in occupational careers. He notes that social structures set important constraints on the information individuals have about social systems and the freedom they have to move about within them.

Tepperman argues, in a manner reminiscent of White's discussion of markets (Chapter 9), that the internal differentiation of labor markets – an inherent social structural phenomenon and not a bothersome "imperfection" – restricts the number and types of opportunities available to given actors. Portuguese-Canadian women in Toronto, for example, guide one another into low-paying, dead-end jobs. To some extent, *dual labor market* studies have tried to take such structural phenomena into account, distinguishing between the formal sector of bureaucratic employment and the informal sector of more personalized job networks. But the notion of dual labor markets, as developed in much of the literature, still implies that individuals are moving as individuals within separate sectors. "Social mobility is not the random nor even the meritocratic selection of individuals for higher rewards," asserts Tepperman. "It is primarily the movement of collectivities relative to one another." Hence *groups* are the appropriate units of analysis here, since individual opportunities depend on those opportunities accessible to the groups to which these individuals belong. Tepperman points out that dynasties – successions of rulers from the same family or line – are a special type of collective mobility. Families provide a basis for enhancing the mobility of their members, and dynastic families, such as the Hapsburgs and the Rothschilds, have historically been very conscious of their collective role in doing this.

Although often powerful collective actors, dynasties and elite groups are not omnipotent. As in Howell's studies of the !Kung (Chapter 3) and Tilly's studies of the transformation of nineteenth-century Europe (Chapter 12), Tepperman is deeply aware of how demographic factors affect social structures. He notes that upper-class survival is part of the broader problem of the extent to which groups can maintain their social positions over time. Even in stable, conservative Toronto, dynasties rarely persisted since they tended to be demographically "inundated." In the long run, the best schools and old boy networks, he notes, were overwhelmed. Thus Tepperman's chapter is as much about the impact of social change on social mobility as it is about mobility itself. Indeed, change and mobility are dual to one another in some important ways: by altering the relationship between individuals and groups, social change alters the paths by which people move into social positions. However, mobility into new social positions creates possibilities for individuals to link new relationships with old – thereby creating new coalitions and cleavages.

John Delany's chapter considers in more detail one of the social processes to which Tepperman refers: how the nature of ties and networks affects the movement of individuals through social systems. Delany is principally concerned with how individuals secure information about job opportunities and the implications of this process for the operation of social structures. He is particularly interested in Granovetter's idea (1973, 1982) that socially "weak" ties are especially useful for acquiring new information because they are more heterogeneous than socially close, "strong" ties. They reach into otherwise inaccessible neighborhoods within networks and, hence, provide network members with novel information.

Delany says we ought to alter radically our mental image of social mobility. Do people find jobs or do jobs find people? Instead of starting with individuals seeking out new positions, we must start with networks flooding individuals with information about the outside world even before they consciously start looking for it. He argues that weak ties are efficient sources of job information for individuals and efficient mechanisms throughout social systems for allocating insider information and scarce economic resources.

Unlike most sociologists, Delany does not employ "real" data – that is, those based on observation – but simulations designed to mimic various aspects of the process of locating jobs through networks. "A dynamic simulation," he points out, "affords the network modeler a way to preserve the formal assumptions of a theoretical model while sidestepping cumbersome mathematical expressions. Instead, one analyzes a set of statistics from a Monte Carlo simulation of network allocation performance." These simulations can then be compared to actual observations of the real world.

Delany's simulations suggest that networks are efficient conduits for information: little news about job openings goes to waste. Even when simulated individuals put little effort into maintaining their ties – as is usually the case with weak ties – their networks yield bountiful returns on limited investment. Indeed, low-density networks are as efficient in minimizing the length of job searches as are high-density ones. Nor are these findings restricted, in principle, to job searches: Delany concludes that microsimulations of the kind he has performed have broad implications for understanding how resources and needs are matched within social structures.

In the final chapter in this part *Joel H. Levine* and *John Spadaro* use information about how people move through a social system to explore its class structure. The trick, they contend, is to choose occupational categories for analysis that illuminate class structure and not obscure it. Wright (1980), for example, has argued that traditional studies of mobility have ignored the extent to which different occupations have control over their own work and the work of others. Wright's argument usefully introduced the structural analysis of social classes into the hitherto primly status-bound study of occupational categories. But his approach still defines, a priori, the occupational categories to be analyzed.

By contrast, Levine and Spadaro use their own data reflexively to discover a set of occupational categories. They liken their work to that of a physician using a barium X ray to trace the otherwise invisible structure of the body parts through which the radioactive barium is moving: "Men and women moving from one job to another are like the barium" they say. "They provide a trace of the occupational structure that guides and restricts their mobility." An approach, such as the one they have adopted, defines groups in terms of the relations between occupations: If members of two occupations tend to have similar patterns of movement, then they belong in the same category.

Thus Levine and Spadaro's model uses individual movement to discover the structure of intergenerational change. Their analysis reveals that in the United States, both status (prestige levels) and class (relationships to the ownership of the means of production) are structurally relevant dimensions by which adult children differ from their parents. The net effect of this analysis is that Levine and Spadaro produce a better delineation of the parameters that govern social mobility than those traditionally obtained by methods that use a priori categorizations. By varying these parameters, they are able to predict the effects of structural shifts on patterns of mobility across generations. Thus, they are able to transmute structural mobility from a shadowy figure lurking in the wings to an evolving, reflexive, concretely studiable phenomenon.

LITERATURE CITED

Granovetter, Mark. "The Strength of Weak Ties." *American Journal of Sociology* 78 (1973): 1360–80.
Wright, Erik Olin. "Class and Occupation." *Theory and Society* 9 (1980): 177–214.

15

Collective mobility and the persistence of dynasties

Lorne Tepperman

This chapter deals with the persistence, or survival, of upper classes. Many sociologists favor voluntaristic explanations of elite behavior, dynastic persistence, social stratification, and mobility. Yet, their explanations ignore major issues that we must address in order to get around the present impasse in social mobility research. I begin by indicating the nature of this impasse, to show how it results from the use of an inadequate voluntarist paradigm, and then discuss some research on dynasties that emphasizes a structuralist paradigm that comes to grips with these problems.

What is mobile?: Units of analysis

What should be the unit of analysis in studies of social mobility? In conventional American sociology the unit of analysis has been the individual, particularly the adult male. The primary datum has been the father-by-son mobility matrix (Breiger, 1981; Levine and Spadaro, Chapter 17) or the multivariate correlation matrix (Blau and Duncan, 1967; Featherman and Hauser, 1978). The preferred analytic technique is to decompose this matrix in order to measure the magnitude of direct, indirect, and interaction effects.

These models have provided many insights but they have also presented many difficulties. First among their shortcomings is that they ignore social context. Much effort has been expended, not always successfully, to adjust for the effect of changing marginals on this matrix (Lipset and Bendix, 1967; Tepperman, 1976a). The aim is to model, or control for, one simple fact: Mobility varies with the number and types of opportunities available. Their second shortcoming is that they ignore internal differentiation or multiple markets. Yet we can scarcely measure mobility within and across classes without a better notion than we presently have about what constitutes a class in which mobility takes place, that is, a notion about equivalence classes.

I am grateful for the critical comments of Michal Bodemann, Nancy Howell, and Barry Wellman, and for painstaking editorial work by Steve Berkowitz.

Thus, we still need to discover a social mobility metric (Breiger, 1981; Levine, 1972, Chapter 17).

The existence of multiple markets leads us to ponder the existence of multiple labor forces. Individuals do not compete against all others for every position. Rather, they complete against *some* others for *some* positions. A prime example is the secondary labor market filled largely by women and ethnic or racial minorities. Another is the presence of multiple career and mobility experiences (Edwards, 1979; Smith and Tepperman, 1974).

The model of multiple markets that has so complicated mobility studies in the United States is further complicated in Canada by the "vertical mosaic," a conception of Canadian society developed by Porter (1965). The Canadian class structure is crosscut by ethnic differentiation that results from a combination of selective immigrant recruitment and the maintenance of ethnic community cohesion. Thus Reitz, Calzavara, and Dasko (1981) have found that men and women in Toronto typically have different jobs, just as the dual labor market theory would predict. But Italian-Canadian men and Jewish men have different jobs from one another, and Italian-Canadian women and Jewish women have jobs different from one another and also from the men in their respective ethnic group. An analysis of careers in Toronto would, therefore, have to specify at least sex and ethnicity as the parameters of interclass mobility.

Such career differentiation points to an ethnic mobility trap: the coexistence of parallel career structures within ethnic communities (Wiley, 1967). Moreover, ethnic career structures not only differ between the sexes, they also vary from one city to another (Reitz, 1980).

Conceivably, ethnic groups, not individuals, are the appropriate units for studying social mobility. Ethnic groups create and maintain structures within which individual mobility takes place. They may mount campaigns to upgrade the general standing of their members vis-à-vis outsiders. In this way, individual members benefit.

The fact of collective mobility by ethnic groups reminds us of other forms of collective mobility. For example, within the business community, firms compete for a greater share of the market. When firms change their position in the market, employees of upwardly mobile firms benefit more than the employees of downwardly mobile firms, even if no employees change their position *within* their respective firms. Similarly, highly organized occupational groups – for example, teamsters or physicians – enjoy collective mobility vis-à-vis other occupational groups, thereby bringing their individual members more benefits than the members of less highly mobilized groups receive.

Broader still, citizens of entire nations or empires experience collective mobility. Imperialist nations often deal with such internal problems as poverty or unemployment by exploiting other, less developed or weaker nations. As a result, members of that society experience collective upward mobility in the world stratification system, even without changing places in their own internal stratification system.

On a smaller scale, being a corporate lawyer in New York City is not the same as hanging out a shingle in a small city. It makes no sense to speak of legal careers that include both cases – nor to treat two cases of mobility with these as end points (that is, classes of destination) as equivalent. It is equally wrong, by contrast, to ignore the conditions under which people can or cannot move from one stream to the other, although these positions are, by a gross standard, the same.

Thus the stratification system within any society is a collection of larger and smaller islands, with different kinds and degrees of internal differentiation, somewhat different patterns of internal mobility, and relatively unknown patterns of competition and flow between one position and another.

Within this complex set of sets, we find multiple collectivities: individuals operating simultaneously as individuals and as members of personal acquaintance networks (Granovetter, 1974), regional or linguistic groups (Breton and Breton, 1980), ethnic groups (Reitz, 1980, 1981), and professions (Larson, 1977), among others. We find business firms, nations, and even empires competing. From all of these collective competitions result what we call social mobility.

Family dynasties

"Dynasties" are successions of rulers from the same family or line. Family dynasties may best be thought of as a special case within this context of collective mobility through multiple milieux. Families, like other groups, help their members achieve mobility. They are special in that they are more conscious, typically, of both their existence as a nameable collectivity – more so than an acquaintanceship network, for example – and they have historically committed themselves to the advancement of their members more firmly than other collectivities. Thernstrom (1971) was the first, though not the last, quantitative historian to demonstrate that immigrant families mobilize their collective resources to further the careers of one or more family members.

The historical analysis of inheritance rules reveals a long-standing bias in favor of close kin, hence in favor of maintaining wealth within kin groups. Marriage rules often demonstrate the same thing. For example, marriage rules in Arab peasant groups traditionally precluded the possibility of outmarriage, hence the loss of rights to land or cattle (though also, of course, loss of the opportunity to add to the stock by a fortunate marriage). Even our society, which claims to attach relatively little formal importance to the family, follows a long-established pattern by devolving wealth to closest kin in the absence of a written will or testamentary deposition.

The word "dynasty" comes from a Greek root and connotes special ability. It is most associated with ruling *families* in feudal social relations, where the idea is to hold property together. Kinship structures within the bourgeois *class* under capitalism pose a somewhat different problem. For the bourgeoisie, "weak ties" are essential. The nature of the *resources*, the nature and different forms of surplus appropriation, shape kinship and friendship ties.

Yet kin groups remain important units of wealth acquisition even in bourgeois society. This should lead us to conclude that families, not individuals, are the appropriate units of analysis in a social mobility study; especially one that includes preindustrial or early industrial periods. This conclusion is further strengthened by several recent developments. First is the large-scale entry of women into the labor force, and their increasingly important contribution to a family's social and economic position. The social status and economic well-being, in short, the life chances of a child from a family with two professional-class parents, is probably twice as good as a child's from a family with only one professional-class parent. However, most analysts of social mobility continue to ignore mothers' contributions to a family's social status and influence by focusing only on *father*–son mobility.

Along these lines, studies that focus on father–*son* mobility fail to consider the mobility experiences of daughters. This is true, in part, because women have only recently entered the work force or begun careers in large numbers. But this has also been true because of methodological difficulties in dealing with the complicated interactions of influences within families. A given child, whether male or female, benefits from the income, status, and encouragement of mother, father, sister, brother, sister-in-law, brother-in-law, uncle, and so on. Sociologists have confined their attention largely to fathers as the source of income, status, and encouragement. Current lifestyles – for example, two-career marriages – are now forcing sociologists to attend to women's achievements. We must also take into account their contribution to the collective social mobility of families and the individual mobility of family members. From here we may extend our interest to the possible indirect influences of fathers on sons, of fathers on daughters, mothers on sons, mothers on daughters, brothers on sisters, and so on. As was the case in defining the structure within which mobility takes place, defining the unit that is mobile – the mobile family – raises many unanswered questions.

The claim by some that families have a declining influence on social achievement rests on the undeniable importance of formal education and credentials over social inheritance. Yet the evidence remains strong that family status largely determines the acquisition of education and credentials, which in turn make the apparent decline of social inheritance possible. Although some societies have tried, none has found a way to remove this influence of family on both educational aspiration and achievement – short of, of course, removing children from their families at birth. Thus, families are important in the mobility of their members, and we can meaningfully speak of collective family mobility (Bodemann, Chapter 8).

By studying dynasties of important families we can gain insight into the collective mobility of families. Eminent families, like eminent individuals, leave sociologists a trace of their achievements. Books, articles, even songs and poems may be written about them. As rulers, they make wars and cause wars. They are remembered in glory or infamy, but they are remembered. We can trace their rise and fall much more readily than that of ordinary families. Dynasties are simply an extreme version of the collective behavior of ordinary families. They stand in the same relationship to the ordinary family as a professional sportsman stands to an amateur.

The proper unit of analysis in mobility studies, as we have argued, is not individuals, but the collectivity. But which collectivity is relevant where so many are involved? For example, many collectivities such as families, ethnic groups, and occupational groups, may act similarly and cooperatively within the construction trades during a generation of urban expansion. How do we analyze this phenomenon? Only by studying mobility collectively can we successfully deal with the complexity of real life, and especially with the role of invisible members of these collectivities, for example, women. Moreover, only by studying larger-than-individual units can we hope to understand patterns of cross-generational mobility. Finally, only by proceeding in this way can we bring the study of mobility together with an analysis of class and societal transformation over long periods.

Two approaches to studying mobility

The failure of conventional social mobility studies to address the individual–collectivity issue arises out of a commitment to what can be called the voluntarist outlook. Voluntarist ideas underlie most conventional research on mobility, dynasties, classes – indeed, on all social order. They are ubiquitous in North American social science. These ideas lead us to ignore the reliance of individuals on others for their well-being and their capacity for sharing and cooperation. They also inflate the capacity of the individual to determine his or her own fate and overcome obstacles single-handedly. Voluntarism is, in some sense, more of a moral precept than a sociological paradigm: It posits a world of rational choosers possessing both complete freedom and information. It is more than methodologically individualistic because it is insensitive to the ways in which systems of past or simultaneous choices constrain subsequent choices and outcomes.

Much modern sociology insists on believing that people are well informed and choose freely. Impediments to free selections of alternatives, to perfect information, and systemic consequences of past choices are largely ignored and are considered, if at all, remediable deviations from a norm. Given this notion of rational choosing, we should not be surprised that voluntarists *assume* that the future is largely predictable and controllable. What *is*, they seem to say, will continue to be, unless interrupted by choice or unanticipated cataclysm.

In fact, most social scientists lack principles for interpreting structures over time and for aggregating individual choices into collective ones. This results from the poverty of our verbal models and from our lack of skills in mathematical modeling. For instance, time spans in most theories of social organization (e.g., epochs, such as Judeo-Christian civilization or late capitalism or postindustrialism) are so gross that they yield an imagery that is virtually ahistorical. Although this style of modeling deals only with real-time variation in a vague way, it is *overly* precise in its treatment of time-independent differentiation. Large structures are portrayed as constituting the most delicately variegated role systems.

One school of sociology – symbolic interactionism – has been almost completely absorbed in creating taxonomies of roles. Worse still, this interpretive school suggests that roles, not people, are important. People are interchangeable, it argues. Structures survive because roles and role definitions exist independently of the actors involved.

The reputational method, employed by W. Lloyd Warner and his students (Warner, Meeker, and Eells, 1960) located as many classes as there are discriminable groupings of individuals (or families) in a community. But they rarely made clear how they established these classes or how families fit into them. Is a class structure merely created by the perceptions of freely choosing respondents? Or do classes, with their own dynamics and internal organiz-ations, really *exist* independently of Warner's respondents. If the latter is the case, what processes govern changes in a class system?

Too often in this sort of work, abstraction is mistaken for reality. Take the notion of an upper class itself. According to much of the literature,[1] one would imagine that, on any given day, an upper class can be found lunching at particular clubs, roaming the corridors of power, or spending scarce resources to achieve desired ends. This voluntaristic notion of an upper class is close to that implied in an increasing number of novels and journalistic accounts of family dynasties whose readers want to romanticize and idealize dynastic continuity. (This explains, I think, the popularity of television programs such as "Dynasty.") It tends to trivialize the mechanisms of class continuity and wealth acquisition in several important ways.

First, voluntarists are naive about the relative role of individual enterprise or merit and larger social dynamics in the winning and keeping of wealth. They overemphasize the importance of ambition, intelligence, and other personal qualities in social mobility and stratification. As a result, they tend to make unwarranted moral assumptions about the deservingness of the rich.

Second, voluntarists tend to treat upper-class social relations, within private schools, clubs, summer camps, private resorts, and so on, as no more than conspicuous consumption: a *lifestyle* to which others might aspire because of its obvious attractiveness. It is better, Podhoretz says, to be rich than poor, powerful than powerless (Podhoretz, 1969: ii). This ignores the survival value of such lifestyle behaviors.

Third, voluntarists suppose that the kinds of qualities that are needed to make a fortune are needed to keep it. Yet keeping wealth is probably much easier than making it, and requires fewer, and certainly different, degrees of effort and intelligence. Even by chance, a competitive lead is preserved for a very long time (Feller, 1968: 78–88). Social processes are even *more* likely to preserve inequalities. The social and economic position of the rich in capitalist societies is maintained by a legal system committed to the sanctity of private property, a tax system sympathetic to capital gains, and a government reluctant to alienate or endanger the powerful. Interpersonal relations among the powerful, based on a generally shared commitment to private property and the status quo, also maintain the position of upper-class individuals.

Thus, for example, it is difficult to earn $1,000,000 legally by working at almost any kind of job. However, this amount is a mere 10% interest on an investment of $10,000,000. Anyone with $10,000,000 to invest can earn this money without risk, talent, or effort. Since wealth can be inherited and invested, children of the wealthy routinely receive huge sums without effort, assisted when necessary by highly skilled legal and financial advisors.

A structuralist approach

What all of these voluntarist frameworks have in common is that they ignore the larger, systemic effects of these patterns of behavior: the ways in which they tend to increase the likelihood that a given dynasty will survive and the ways in which they support and maintain the dynastic system as a whole.

First, as we shall see, family discipline is very important in helping dynasties to persist. Families enforce discipline to hold on to family wealth. Similarly, public service has a clear payoff for the upper classes today, quite apart from any moral or humanistic concerns. Such civic activity is publicly approved and makes the maintenance of the established class structure more acceptable. Moreover, it is an important means by which the powerful can meet and communicate with one another. The flow and interlocking of elites through various kinds of public and private corporate concerns is the structure of what Mills (1956) called the "power elite." As much as the prevailing, pro-establishment ideology, this interlocking of elite roles and interelite communication keeps the powerful in power. It also helps them to protect their wealth and to hear about new opportunities for making money. Public service exercises social control, appears virtuous, makes one famous, and is often tax deductible.

These behaviors are not merely conspicuous consumption or conspicuous virtue. They are the means by which a ruling class maintains and extends its rule. Unlike voluntaristic explanations, structural approaches lead us to examine sets of both external and internal processes that affect the persistence of dynasties. The first of these includes (1) circulating succession, which minimizes intraclass conflict; (2) family support and endogamy, which maximizes the sharing of resources; and (3) continuous differentiation of functions, which enables elites to adapt effectively to the modern corporate world.

The second set of processes relates changes in dynastic structure to those in the surrounding society and economy. In particular, the likelihood of dynasties persisting is affected by (1) changes in societal class structure, which constrain existing ruling families, and (2) demographic inundation, a significant change in the relationship of numbers of upper-class heirs to ruling positions and competitors for positions.

To sum up thus far: Social mobility research cannot proceed without taking into greater account collective mobility. Family mobility is a historically important form of collective mobility and our best evidence of family mobility comes from the study of dynasties. Yet the study of dynasties has been hindered by the voluntarist perspective. In contrast, the structuralist study of dynasties enables us to advance beyond voluntarist, ahistorical studies of elites. This advance suggests how we might proceed in studying ordinary mobility.

It is unnecessary to present purposes to refute romantic popular conceptions of dynastic persistence – those having to do with personal qualities of ambition and effectiveness or moral qualities of public service and family discipline. They will prove redundant when we demonstrate the impact of structural forces. Therefore, we shall examine a less idealistic way of thinking about the preservation of wealth and power. Particular dynasties persist for certain reasons, and these reasons tell us a great deal about the functioning of the social system as a whole.

Earlier research on the persistence of dynasties in Ontario has shown that dynasties are affected by a variety of structural factors. First, some processes that affect dynastic persistence are *external* to individual families. They derive from the structural evolution of a national or international economy and the balance of forces under which ruling families must operate. These include changes in the class structure due to commercial or industrial revolutions and changes in the relative sizes of social classes through differential reproduction.[2] Second, we can identify three *internal* processes that are critical to maintaining upper classes or elites: circulating succession, family support, and dynastic endogamy.

External factors affecting elite continuity

If they are to persist, dynasties must accommodate to changes in the scale and complexity of elite organization. They must deal with new demands for resources, skills, and strategies that may not be immediately available within the dynasty, as well as the need to recruit, coopt, and otherwise control new entrants into the elite, especially during periods of rapid growth, when numerical inundation of old elites by new is a strong possibility.[3]

Changes in class structure

This point is often easiest to see in a concrete context. After the rebellions of 1837 in Upper and Lower Canada (today, Ontario and Quebec, respectively), the British government send Lord Durham to investigate the political discontent. In his report, Durham described an Upper Canadian "Family Compact," consisting of the Governor's advisors linked together by party interests, personal ties, and family connections. By filling almost all high public offices from among its members, the Compact was able to wield governmental power, distribute patronage as it pleased, and bring successive governors under its sway. Yet the descendants of these families are not powerful today. How could this have happened?

The evidence suggests an inability on the part of these upper-class families to adapt to changes in the socioeconomic order. The source of families' status naturally changes over time. Over the generations since the Family Compact held power, the source of class and family wealth has changed radically: In 1830, high status was associated with landholding and officeholding. Later it was associated with commerce and banking, then industry. Different sources of wealth have different implications for the stability of family wealth and thus for the transmission of family status.

By 1848, Ontario had gained responsible government and elective local government (Durham, 1963).[4] This reduced the hegemony of the Family Compact and other aristocratic elements and placed greater control into the hands of the classical petite bourgeoisie: the farmers, small businessmen, skilled tradesman, and more prosperous craft workers. The Family Compact could no longer control elite recruitment, nor depend upon its friends in government for monopolies and protection. As a result, it could not defend itself against competition from increasing numbers of power seekers drawn from other groups and strata (Johnson, 1972).

Saunders (1957: 178) notes that "it was largely their too-marginal interest in business that led to the Family Compact's downfall. The rise of a new business class that could combine business with politics, and conservative ideas with political connections, tolled their passing."

In the 1880s, this new triumphant *petite bourgeois* commercial elite began a struggle for power with an emerging industrial elite. Only a small portion of this elite came from old Canadian industrial and commercial families (Acheson, 1972: 171). The largest group consisted of the offspring of British, American, or German families who had brought some of their families' industrial or commercial wealth to the New World.

This horizontal mobility through immigration was extremely important in establishing an industrial elite, but vertical mobility was also possible. Many Scottish immigrants and native Canadians of farm or minor industrial origins rose to elite status by means of gradual upward mobility.

This new industrial elite could neither overthrow nor join the commercial ruling class – nor even contend with it for power to a meaningful degree (Clement, 1975: 71). By the start of World War I, immigrants with skills and some capital were kept from pursuing their earlier opportunities for upward mobility through the manufacturing sector. The ruling commercial class, made up of financiers, railway magnates, and members of the state elite, had transformed the economy from entrepreneurial to corporate capitalism.

Yet, by the mid-twentieth century, this trend had seemingly reversed again, and almost half of the Canadian corporate elite had risen from middle- or working-class origins (Porter, 1965).

To explain this reversal, I studied a sample of men prominent in Toronto in the 1920s (Tepperman, 1976b). My goal was to understand the social processes that admitted largely unwanted people into what had been believed to be a highly controlled elite world. Two in every five of these prominent men were financiers or manufacturers; another quarter were educators, lawyers, and judges. About 30% held one or more directorships or high management positions in smaller enterprises.

To devise a measure of economic power, I factor-analyzed the highly intercorrelated data on directorships (Tepperman, 1979). A single factor accounted for just under half of the variance. Using weights determined by this factor, I assigned each member of the study population an economic power score. Sixteen men in the sample had factor scores two or more standard deviations above the mean. They proved almost all to be financiers, rather than industrialists or merchants.

More interesting, not one of these men bears a surname that belongs to one of the few dynasties that had survived from the Family Compact period: no Robinsons, Powells, Boultons, Baldwins, Cartwrights, Hamiltons, Ridouts, or Shaws. Indeed not a single patrilineal descendant of any Compact family remained in the Toronto elite sample of the 1920s. Instead, about half of the known descendants of surviving Family Compact dynasties lived outside Toronto: in Ottawa, Kingston, or elsewhere. Many practiced a profession or served in government. Although parts of dynasties, they were simply not as prominent or powerful as the members of the 1920s Toronto elite (Tepperman, 1972).

Demographic inundation

Descendants of the Family Compact have been inundated by new men, outnumbered as well as forced out. Porter showed that, in the mid-1950s, persons who originated below the elite or upper class held about half of the positions in the Canadian economic elite. Under conditions of elite control over recruitment, this can happen *only if* available elite positions increase more rapidly than the elites can have children to fill them. And this is precisely what had happened between 1925 (the Toronto elite study) and the 1950s (Porter's study). It probably had happened in earlier generations as well.

Between 1925 and 1955, the number of persons listed in the Financial Post's *Directory of Directors* increased at slightly more than 3% per annum. The population of metropolitan Toronto, the gross national product per capita (in constant dollars), and the number of business establishments with 100 or more employees, though increasing at a slower rate, all doubled during the same period. Such doublings would lead us to anticipate a geometric increase in the number of elite positions at about 2.3 per annum during this period, if we assume that elite positions increased in proportion to general population, wealth, and corporate enterprise.

But the elite population – the potential dynasties – were reproducing at a much slower pace. Elite members had produced an average of only 2.5 children per father, about 1/6 less than persons in the same occupations at the same time, and many fewer than men in blue-collar or agricultural work. (This rate would imply an elite Gross Reproduction Rate of under 1.2 daughters per mother.)

To estimate the rate of natural increase of a population, we need to measure its mortality as well as its fertility level. Calculations based on published life tables and model life tables (United Nations, 1967) indicate that the elite's sons had a better-than-average chance of survival. Elite men lived on average about 5 years longer than the typical Ontario man.

At this mortality level, and with a Gross Reproduction Rate of about 1.2, the Toronto elite could not have grown through natural increase at a rate faster than $\frac{1}{2}$% (or .005) per annum (United Nations 1967: 117). Accordingly, any growth in elite positions above .005 per annum would allow for the infusion of new blood.

Let us, then, suppose that around 1925 the elite population was growing at .005 per annum and elite positions were increasing at .023 per annum. Further, assume compound growth of each at these rates from 1925 on. Then, by 30 years, or one generation later, at most only 58.7% of elite positions could be held by children of elite parents. Conversely, the access of children of nonelite parents to the elite would be given by

$$\text{Access}_t = \frac{(1 + dx)^t}{(1 + dy)^t}$$

where x_o = number of persons in the elite at t_o; y_o = number of elite positions at t_o (and $x_o = y_o$); dx = annual rate of change in the elite population; dy = annual rate of change in elite positions; and t = number of years since t_o. Substituting the estimated values into the equation yields an access value of 41.3%.

Porter (1965) found essentially this amount of inflow when examining his 1951 data on elites and Clement (1975: 216) found the same in his 1972 data. Almost half of all the elite positions were filled by persons originating outside the elite or upper class, because there were too few upper-class children to inherit all of the elite positions available without "doubling up" on positions. No more than 50–60% of elite positions could possibly have been filled by elite children. Note that the estimating procedure assumes that *all* upper class children are willing to fill elite positions. Had elite children refused this opportunity, additional elite positions would have been freed up.

If there is a decline in the growth of elite positions or a "doubling up" by position holders, a higher proportion of elite positions will be filled by the elite's children than earlier. Clement (1975: 218) has suggested as much in his study of the corporate elite by comparing the class origins of elite persons born after 1920 with those born before it.

But during the period from 1876 to 1976, excellent demographic opportunities for mobility opened up to persons in the middle class and below. The factors leading to this operated throughout the late nineteenth century: Low elite fertility and high rates of economic growth combined to inundate descendants of the Family Compact, rather than displace them. New men who entered the elite at this time came to control later recruitment. Indeed, they made the rules of the game.

Internal processes affecting elite continuity

Stable upper classes consist of dense, highly connected, close-knit networks. Members of the upper class tend to know one another. Upper-class networks are also *multiples*: Persons within the network are tied together by kinship, friendship, neighboring, and many other kinds of relationships simultaneously (Wellman, Carrington, and Hall, Chapter 6). This multiplexity provides a stronger bond between members of the network, ensuring long-term, emotionally significant relationships. This is an important basis for class solidarity, a basis for a community perhaps as strong as one that might exist among isolated preliterate people or immigrants to a foreign land. Even without class conflict – which tends to strengthen the internal cohesion of the upper class – loyalty and conformity are likely to be strong in this community.

Dynastic rule – rule by powerful families – is not common today. However, even democratic societies have their ruling families, power elites, hereditary upper classes, or establishments. Dynastic rule has not passed away so much as it has changed its form. Therefore, it becomes important for us to consider why some families in a country's hereditary elite or upper class today keep their wealth and power longer than others. What factors shape the history of dynasties?

In some sense, answering this question is no different from explaining why some royal families persist longer than others in a traditional dynastic system. Upper or ruling classes are made up of cooperating, stable dynastic families. Entry into elite positions in dynastic societies depends on kinship particularism: Upper-class children are preferred over others in the competition for elite positions. Thus, if dynasties fail to form or elite families fail to keep their prominence over many generations, it is at least partly because the upper class has lost some of its control over elite positions. Control over recruitment into the elite is, therefore, quite important.

Circulating succession

The external processes I have just discussed are important influences on the formation and persistence of dynasties. But three kinds of internal processes also influence the ability of dynasties to persist.

The first is circulating succession. Goody (1966) claims that, historically, the highly determinate "next-in-line" methods of succession that characterize modern European monarchies are rare. In the more common, less determinate, systems of succession, potential successors are more likely to fight with one another and, therefore, the state must use some means (e.g., election, combat, or appointment) to select new rulers. Depending on the means used, interregna between periods of relative stability may be long and troubled.

An alternative to this is a system of (fraternal or horizontal) succession, in which brothers can inherit rule from other brothers. By allowing brothers to assume the throne, a dynasty can draw upon a wider range of kin. Father–son relationships come under less strain. But the fraternal system results in older officeholders, hence shorter reigns and a higher rate of turnover, and the number of eligibles increases more or less geometrically with each generation.

On the one hand, this produces a corporate dynasty with many people committed to maintaining it. On the other, satisfying everyone becomes progressively more difficult with each generation.

In the extreme, corporate dynasties produce circulating succession. According to Goody (1966: 157), "circulating succession is a system whereby offices pass between two or more units of organization," each of which has a dynastic component. In effect, it produces a polydynastic system. The units of organization involved, Goody says, "may be dynastic segments, political parties, or even nation states" (Goody, 1966: 157).

Modern ruling classes, upper classes, or establishments are polydynastic systems of circulating succession. Within each, family property and power are accumulated and passed on to next of kin. This tends to concentrate power (Goody, 1966: 160). Upper classes function to distribute this power among families included within them. Intermarriage, then, maintains a balance between the concentration and dispersion of wealth and power that yields a corporate upper class. Thus, the class, not families, becomes the relevant unit of analysis for studying the exercise of power.

The advantages to forming a ruling class in a system of circulating succession are obvious: Rotation allows many more people to gain a direct interest in maintaining the unity of the state. This, as Goody points out, is particularly valuable when the state rules over many competing ethnic groups, spread over a large, sparsely populated area, as, for instance, in Canada.

Rotation also reduces or redirects tension outside the family. Conflicts over succession to office will not generally arise between father and son, or between brothers, but rather between persons who are more distant from one another: between neighbors or, better still, between acquaintances or even strangers.

Although the continued functioning of this upper-class rotation system is in the long-run interest of its members, it requires a willingness to forego immediate advantages. Participants must minimize deviance and conflict. Those holding positions may try to press their temporary advantage by recruiting their own successors from among protégés or family members. However, they generally avoid this course of action for several reasons. First, retaliation is possible, and even the powerful wish to avoid exciting the envy or anger of their peers. Second, the idea of rotation may be an accepted part of the elite political culture. Third, and most important, ties among dynastic families may promote or institutionalize trust. Private schools, clubs, and communities teach the self-discipline and collective self-awareness – the upper-class consciousness – which make circulating succession a continued possibility.

Preserving the upper class as a whole necessarily enhances the persistence of any particular dynasty. In a system of rotating power, no individual family can feel secure without the support of the others, since pressure from below will generally threaten to upset both the class and the dynasty. Thus, class loyalty melds into educated self-interest in the elite, as elsewhere.

Family support

Family support is critical in helping children to achieve and maintain elite status. Although fathers may play a critical role in promoting sons, others are often involved and these people are frequently the son's elite kinsmen.

For example, in studying the descendants of the Family Compact (Tepperman, 1972) I examined only the male line or patrilineages, for the obvious and expedient reason that such lines preserve the family name of the prominent progenitor, while the matrilineages do not. Thus, all references to the histories of elite families are only references to the male lines, and when every male line in the family has disappeared, I shall say that the family has disappeared. (However, I accept E. A. Wrigley's comment [personal communication] that "the behavior of families which had daughters but no sons would also be of great interest since many societies have informal equivalents of the formal adoption of a male successor, often cemented by the marriage of a daughter.")

Eighty initial elites gave issue to 580 male descendants at one or more generations removed. From these, 450 chains were generated, containing the characteristics of the initial progenitor, his son, and so on until the last son in the chain was reached. Less than one chain in seven extended five generations or more, and most chains terminated in various ways by the fourth generation: (a) through a failure of the last son in the chain to live to adulthood, to marry, or to reproduce; (b) through the failure, if reproducing, to father sons; or (c) as a result of our inability to discover information about the last son's descendants, if any did exist.

With each succeeding generation, a chain is less likely to contain prominent men. By the fifth generation, fewer than 10% of the existing descendants are prominent. Probably even this percentage is too high, for we are more likely to have found information about chains that maintained their prominence than those that did not. There may be many more nonprominent fifth-generation descendants in existence than we know of, and the ratio of prominent fifth-generation men may be much lower than 10%.

In his nineteenth-century classic *Hereditary Genius*, Sir Francis Galton (1962: 378) had asked, "If we know nothing else about a person than that he is a father, brother, son, grandson, or other relation of an illustrious man, what is the chance that he is or will be eminent?" Galton's answer was that the probability of eminence of such a person is inversely correlated with the number of links in a chain connecting that person and the illustrious kinsman. The smallest chain has only one link and is the relationship between a father

Table 15.1. *Measures of association between the prominence of ego and the prominence of ego's son, grandson, and great-grandson, by ego's generation*

Ego's generation	Measure of association with prominence of		
	Ego's son	Ego's grandson	Ego's great-grandson
1	0.380	0.109	0.076
2	0.363	0.235	0.109
3	0.218	0.206	n.a.
4	0.300	n.a.	n.a.

Note: The measure of association used is Cramer's *V*; n.a. indicates "not available."

and son; next are chains of two links, as between men and their grandsons or uncles, or men and their brothers (i.e., the chain passer through a common father); then chains of three links, as between men and their great-grandsons or nephews; and so on.

According to the data, Galton was right. Table 15.1 shows that the prominence of "ego" is consistently related to the prominence of ego's son in each of four generations. By contrast, association with the prominence of ego's grandson is weaker; and the association between ego's prominence and his great-grandson's prominence is weaker still.

The effect of prominent kinsmen on ego's status is complicated, as Table 15.2 suggests. If egos have many prominent uncles, their likelihood of inheriting father's status are not much affected one way or another. If they have many prominent cousins, the likelihood of their inheriting father's status is unaffected in two generations, and diminished to insignificance in another two.

However, if egos have *no* prominent uncles or cousins, their chance of inheriting father's status is (with one exception) much diminished, so that the association between father's prominence and ego's prominence disappears. This suggests that prominent kinsmen are most noticeable in their absence: If such kinsmen are present, the transmission of prominence from father to son is unaffected either positively or negatively. But an absence of such kinsmen makes transmission of prominence from father to son problematic.

Kinsmen are especially valuable when aspirants to elite status lack an elite father: Uncles and cousins can promote the entry of kinsmen into the elite even when father cannot. On the other hand, without elite kinsmen, an elite father can give his child relatively little help. The recruitment of a child into

Table 15.2. *Measures of association between the prominence of ego and the prominence of ego's father controlling for number of prominent supporting kin, by ego's generation*

| Ego's generation | None | Control variables | | | |
		Many prominent uncles	Many prominent cousins	No prominent uncles	No prominent cousins
2	0.380	0.348	0.429	0.293	0.485
3	0.363	0.317	0.346	0.000	−0.131
4	0.218	0.232	0.119	−0.073	−0.343
5	0.300	0.349	0.000	−0.000	−0.109

Note: The measure of association used is Cramer's V.

the elite appears to be beyond the control of a prominent father alone; that father depends on family members, perhaps even friends, to help secure his child's position. Therefore, a high degree of intergenerational elite inheritance implies a wide network of ties or mutual obligations among members of the elite, for these ties provide the help on which elite inheritance is obviously based.

The death of an upper classman is doubly consequential for his family: It both eliminates one prominent family member *and* one kinsman supporting other members of the family. Being doubly consequential, the loss of each prominent family member accelerates the family's drop from prominence. In one sense, then, an upper class is a system of intertwined kindred giving one another support. Added to class loyalty based on rotation is the loyalty due to kin ties and sentiments. Family support among extended kin is like a rope: Each strand is slender and weak, but when the strands are intertwined, the whole is stronger than the sum of these individual fibers. Historically, intertwining through cousin marriage and cooperative business enterprises have often supported family dynasties. Once some strands of a kindred are cut by death or untwined by exogamy, the remaining strands come under greater strain. The entire family is like a fraying rope.

Thus, individual fortunes are bound up in family fortunes, and family fortunes are bound up in class fortunes. Family status persists through collective rather than individual processes.

The apparent centralization of an upper class through marriage is at odds with Granovetter's (1973) "strength-of-weak-ties" argument. His thesis holds that egos often do better to stand at the center of *weakly* tied networks than *strongly* tied ones. "Weak ties," he argues (1973; 1379), "often denounced as generative of alienation, are here seen as indispensable to individual's opportunities and to their integration into communities; strong ties, breeding local cohesion, lead to overall fragmentation." As Rapoport (1957) showed, weakly tied networks open rapidly outward, and strongly tied networks do not. Thus, the outward diffusion of information from egos or the funneling to egos of information from a wide variety of sources is maximized by loosely bounded, weakly tied networks containing many members. This contradiction suggests that middle-class people attain and maintain status in ways different from upper-class people.

In the short run, endogamy and other forms of ascription may maintain a dynasty by giving it an advantage over others in a highly uncertain environment in which cohesion, internal control, and loyalty are at a premium. But this stability is purchased at the price of flexibility, which may carry costs in the long run. Strong ties are a luxury only the rich can afford, and then only at great cost. When the national or international balance of power changes quite suddenly, the most heavily committed (i.e., endogamous) dynasties are the most shaken. Closed, exclusive marriage systems, producing strongly tied networks, probably do not ensure dynastic well-being *in the long run* as well as weakly tied ones.

Differentiation of functions

Just as the structures of collective mobility have changed over time, so have the structures within which competition occurs. There is evidence that, in the past 100 years, elite activity has become more functionally specialized. Business elites have tended to withdraw from civic activity – especially overt political activity – and have concentrated almost entirely on business. Legal elites, always more diverse in their activities than business elites, have also reduced their political activity and have entered business.

Smith and I have analyzed these and related changes (Smith and Tepperman, 1974). To compare two kinds of Canadian elites at two points in time, we arbitrarily defined "elites" as men and women recognized for their authority, prominence, wealth, or influence in contemporary Canadian society by the editors of four biographical dictionaries of important people. From each of these dictionaries, we randomly sampled 50 people described as lawyers – that is, primarily active in the legal–judicial sphere – and 50 people described as principally businessmen, merchants, or industrialists. This provided a total sample of 200 persons: 100 from each century, and 100 from each sector of the occupational structure.

We found that these elites, whether in business or law, have become more alike in characteristics and experiences. Because organization, per se, has exerted more control over processes of entry and socialization into the elite, it is now possible to speak of a typical elite career. However the activities of legal and business elites have become more sharply differentiated from one

Table 15.3. *Elite persons who have held specified positions, by time of elite incumbency and situs (percent)*

Position held	Business		Law	
	19th century	20th century	19th century	20th century
Political appointment	48.0	10.0	44.0	16.0
Elected representative	60.0	8.0	60.0	10.0
Judicial position	16.0	4.0	46.0	20.0
$N =$	50	50	50	50

Note: All of the differences in this table are based on statistically significant cross-tabulations, such that $p \leqslant .05$.

another. If a line separated business and law in the nineteenth century, it was easily crossed. Today, careers in business are more distinct and segregated from careers in law, although lawyers may still choose to enter a business career. Not only have business and law become more mutually exclusive in the twentieth century, they are much more separate from public service and political and literary activity than they once were. A business or legal career today does not require the extra-professional activity it once did. Professional socialization may even discourage such outside activity.

In these senses, business and legal elites today seem to personify trends typical of socioeconomic development: bureaucratization, role segregation, and professionalization.

The twentieth-century exodus of business and legal elites from political life has been part of a general decrease in elite visibility. Elite lawyers have largely given up holding judicial positions. Few businessmen in the contemporary elite have held either elected or appointed political office (see Table 15.3). This contrasts strongly with nineteenth-century elite businessmen, almost half of whom served in an appointed office, and many more of whom held an elected office.

Today almost all elite businessmen sit on at least one board of directors and many sit on five or more such boards. This increase is somewhat less marked among elite lawyers, but is still noticeable. If corporate authority is wielded by groups today rather than by individuals, it is fitting that elite members should spend their leisure time in group activities where they may make connections and discuss corporate policy. Participation in voluntary and fraternal organizations has increased remarkably among both business and legal elites, although this increase has been most notable among businessmen.

In keeping with the "managerial revolution" (Burnham, 1945), the proportion of elite members who own or control the firms they manage has

Table 15.4. *Number of corporate directorships and businesses owned or controlled, by time of elite incumbency and situs (percent)*

	Business		Law	
	19th century	20th century	19th century	20th century
Number of corporate directorships				
None	56.0	4.0	78.0	56.0
One, two	20.0	40.0	20.0	28.0
Three, four	16.0	36.0	0.0	4.0
Five or more	8.0	20.0	2.0	12.0
$N =$	50	50	50	50
Number of businesses owned or controlled				
None	24.0	72.0	88.0	100.0
One, two	60.0	28.0	8.0	0.0
Three or more	16.0	0.0	4.0	0.0
$N =$	50	50	50	50

declined (see Table 15.4). Many members of the present business elite do not own or control any business firm. This was not true in the nineteenth century. The change among elite lawyers has been similar but less marked, as lawyers were never as involved as businessmen in business ownership and management.

Stratification of business firms indicates a trend toward the concentration of economic power in larger and larger holdings. As Levine (1972b), Clement (1975), Richardson (1982), and others have suggested, banks and other financial firms may act as foci for large conglomerates. Accordingly, business elites have increasingly tended to be connected with these corporate financial giants. Involvement in trading companies has decreased. Elite lawyers, however, are involved in approximately the same number of such firms as they were earlier.

There seem to be more roads to wealth in the twentieth century than in the nineteenth century. Law has seemingly become as good a road to wealth as the ownership of a large business firm, and holding a large number of corporate directorships – more characteristic of elite businessmen than lawyers or business owners – is another effective way to wealth. Public service in an elected office or judicial appointment is apparently not the best way to become wealthy today.

Of many changes in the past century, the increased importance of directorships for gaining elite rewards is most consistent and marked. Directorships are not only direct means of acquiring wealth and authority, they also increase the attainment of wealth and authority by helping one gain mercantile influence. Thus, the holding of many directorships seems to exert an indirect influence on wealth and authority by discouraging relatively nonremunerative nonprofessional activities of a political or judicial nature. Those holding directorships are also less involved with public service. Since the ability of directorships to confer great rewards has increased in the past century, the willingness of legal and business elites to participate in public service activities has accordingly diminished.

Finally, the role of director has changed with the separation of management and ownership. In the twentieth-century elite, self-employed status no longer directly influences one's amount of wealth or authority, and it appears slightly negatively related to the number of directorships held. Thus the ownership of one's own services and other means of production has become less advantageous for attaining wealth and power in the twentieth century. Not only has self-employment lost its direct effect on the attainment of elite resources, it has also lost its indirect effect via the attainment of directorships.

This important and pervasive change in the structure of the elite – the increased importance of, and changed routes to the directorship – recalls the opening concerns of this discussion: namely, that the stratification system today is a collection of internally stratified "islands" and the main actors are collectivities. Directorships are elite statuses in particular islands. As a largely inheritable status – given the inheritability of corporate shares and the connection between large share-holding and directorship status – directorships allow dynastic continuity in a world that typically denigrates kinship and other allegedly nonrational, nonefficient dynastic ties. It is a status protected in law and, given rules of limited liability, an efficient way of protecting family wealth.

Thus dynasties today depend not on landholding or officeholding, but on directorship holding and the political infighting that may go with that form of class organization. The rotation system is largely that of families and family members through private and public corporate boardrooms.

The structural basis of mobility

Social mobility is not the random, nor even the meritocratic selection of individuals for higher rewards. It is primarily the movement of collectivities relative to one another. Historically and even today, a principal collectivity influencing status inheritance and mobility is the family. A family that maintains a high status for many generations, a dynasty, is the building block of an upper class and thus the main source of recruits for a society's elite positions.

Thus, the persistence of dynasties, and conversely their failure to persist, offer insights into both the dynamics of class stability and the laws governing collective social mobility. In this respect, family dynasties are prototypical of all collective mobility, but also a special case – as long as the kinship inheritance of property continues – contributing to the processes of social stratification.

These dynasties persist for reasons other than their intrinsic merit. They organize in ways functional to collective survival and to adaptive relations with their external environment. Internal organization that contributes to collective survival chiefly involves a reduction of within-class conflict, orderly family succession, and kinship assistance and a symbiotic differentiation of elite functions. Given this combination of characteristics, dynasties seem unlikely to fail.

Yet, fail they do, if we allow a long enough time. "Clogs to clogs in five generations" says the peasant proverb. These dynasties do not often fail out of internal weakness. The reason appears most often to be an inadequate accommodation to the changing external environment.

Thus, the Family Compact disappeared because it failed to adapt to new commercial and political exigencies. A later Canadian elite failed to secure its exclusive hold – it is too soon to know whether they have failed as much as the Family Compact in creating powerful dynasties – because it could not fill all of the new elite positions (chiefly directorships) with their own children, although they may have filled them with nonkin protégés.

As Berkowitz (1980: 26) has written, "for structuralists, units of analysis themselves must be taken as problematic because of the complex interrelationships among the processes which systemic models are designed to represent. In a very fundamental way, as a result, structural models reject the notion of the 'independence' of effects upon which purely statistical models rest." This chapter has shown that dynasties and the upper classes they make up are systems that have boundary-maintaining properties and survival problems, as other systems do. A precise demonstration of cause-and-effect contributions to persistence is not yet possible. To go beyond the merely descriptive and conjectural, such a demonstration might be carried out by computer simulation under various hypothesized conditions (Delany, Chapter 16). Laws about systems are best tested by creating and examining hypothetical systems. However, this will not be possible except in very limited ways (Tepperman, 1976a; Tepperman and Tepperman, 1971) until preliminary research of the kind described here has been considerably extended.

NOTES

1. Some of the literature that reads this way includes (in the United States), Mills (1956), Baltzell (1958), Domhoff (1971), and (in Canada) Porter (1965), Clement (1975), Newman (1977). For an excellent critique of this conception of ruling classes, see Berkowitz (1975).
2. Pareto (1966: 256–60) characterized elite circulation in terms of an alternation of "lions and foxes": as Machiavelli knew well, different times demand different talents and virtues in a ruler. Implicitly, sometimes cleverness is needed for survival in power, and sometimes sheer perseverance.
3. The problem hinted at in Chamberlain (1972).
4. Responsible government means that the executive is responsible to, and removable by, the legislature through a vote of no confidence.

LITERATURE CITED

Acheson, T. W. "The Social Origins of the Canadian Industrial Elite, 1880–1885." In D. S. Macmillan (ed.), *Canadian Business History: Selected Studies, 1497–1971.* Toronto: McClelland and Stewart, 1972.

Baltzell, E. Digby. *Philadelphia Gentleman: The Making of a National Upper Class.* New York: Free Press, 1958.

Berkowitz, S. D. "The Dynamics of Elite Structure: A Critique of C. Wright Mills' 'Power Elite' Model." Ph.D. diss., Brandeis University, 1975.

"Structural and Non-structural Models of Elites: A Critique." *Canadian Journal of Sociology* 5 (1980): 13–30.

Blau, Peter M., and Otis Dudley Duncan. *The American Occupational Structure.* New York: Wiley, 1967.

Breiger, Ronald L. "The Social Class Structure of Occupational Mobility." *American Journal of Sociology* 87 (1981): 578–611.

Breton, Albert, and Raymond Breton. *Why Disunity? An Analysis of Linguistic and Regional Cleavage in Canada.* Montreal: Institute for Research on Public Policy, 1980.

Burnham, James. *The Managerial Revolution.* Harmondsworth, England: Penguin, 1945.

Chamberlain, Neil W. *Beyond Malthus: Population and Power.* Englewood Cliffs, N. J.: Prentice-Hall, 1972.

Clement, Wallace. *The Canadian Corporate Elite: An Analysis of Economic Power.* Toronto: McClelland and Stewart, 1975.

Domhoff, G. William. *The Higher Circles: The Governing Class in America.* New York: Vintage Books, 1971.

Durham, Lord. *Report on the Affairs of British North America,* ed. Gerald M. Craig. Toronto: McClelland and Stewart, 1963.

Edwards, Richard. *Contested Terrain: The Transformation of the Workplace in the Twentieth Century.* New York: Basic Books, 1979.

Featherman, David L., and Robert M. Hauser. *Opportunity and Change.* New York: Academic Press, 1978.

Feller, William. *An Introduction to Probability Theory and Its Applications. I.* New York: Wiley, 1968.

Galton, Sir Francis. *Hereditary Genius: An Inquiry into Its Laws and Consequences.* Cleveland: World, 1962.

Goody, Jack (ed.). *Succesion to High Office.* Cambridge Papers in Social Anthropology 4. Cambridge: Cambridge University Press, 1966.

Granovetter, Mark. "The Strength of Weak Ties." *American Journal of Sociology* 78 (1973): 1360–80.

    Getting a Job: A Study of Contacts and Careers. Cambridge, Mass.: Harvard University Press, 1974.

Johnson, Leo. "The Development of Class in Canada in the Twentieth Century." In Gary Teeple (ed.), *Capitalism and the National Question in Canada.* Toronto: University of Toronto Press, 1972.

Larson, Magali Sarfatti. *The Rise of Professionalism: A Sociological Analysis.* Berkeley: University of California Press, 1977.

Levine, Joel. "A Two-parameter Model of Interaction in Father–Son Status Mobility." *Behavioral Science* 17 (1972a): 455–65.

    "The Sphere of Influence." *American Sociological Review* 37 (1972b): 14–27.

Lipset, Seymour Martin, and Reinhard Bendix. *Social Mobility in Industrial Society.* Berkeley: University of California Press, 1967.

Mills, C. Wright. *The Power Elite.* New York: Oxford University Press, 1956.

Newman, Peter C. *The Canadian Establishment, I.* Toronto: Seal Books, 1977.

Pareto, Vilfredo. *Sociological Writings.* Selected by S. E. Finer. New York: Frederick A. Praeger, 1966.

Podhoretz, Norman. *Making It.* New York: Bantam Books, 1969.

Porter, John. *The Vertical Mosaic.* Toronto: University of Toronto Press, 1965.

Rapoport, Anatol. "Contribution to the Theory of Random and Biased Nets." *Bulletin of Mathematical Biology* 19 (1957): 257–77.

Reitz, Jeffrey G. *The Survival of Ethnic Groups.* Toronto: McGraw Hill Ryerson, 1980.

Reitz, Jeffrey G., Liviana Calzavara, and Donna Dasko. "Ethnic Inequality and Segregation in Jobs." University of Toronto, Center for Urban and Community Studies Research Paper 123. Toronto, 1981.

Richardson, R. J. "Perspectives on the Relationship between Financial and Non-financial Corporations: A Critical Review." University of Toronto, Structural Analysis Programme Working Paper 34. Toronto, 1982.

Saunders, R. E. "What Was the Family Compact?" *Ontario History* 49 (1957): 173–8.

Smith, David, and Lorne Tepperman. "Changes in the Canadian Business and Legal Elites, 1870–1970." *Canadian Journal of Sociology and Anthropology* 11 (1974): 97–109.

Tepperman, Lorne. "The Natural Disruption of Dynasties." *Canadian Review of Sociology and Anthropology* 9 (1972): 111–33.

    "A Simulation of Social Mobility in Industrial Societies." *Canadian Review of Sociology and Anthropology* 13 (1976a): 26–42.

    "Effects of the Demographic Transition upon Access to the Toronto Elite." *Canadian Review of Sociology and Anthropology* 14 (1976b): 285–93.

    "Status Inconsistency in the Toronto Elite of the 1920's." In James E. Curtis and William Scott (eds.), *Social Stratification: Canada.* Scarborough, Ont.: Prentice-Hall of Canada, 1979.

Tepperman, Lorne, and Barry Tepperman. "Dynasty Formation in Eight Imaginary Societies." *Canadian Review of Sociology and Anthropology* 8 (1971): 121–41.

Thernstrom, Stephan. *Poverty and Progress: Social Mobility in a Nineteenth Century City.* New York: Atheneum, 1969.

United Nations, Department of Economic and Social Affairs. *Manual IV: Methods of Estimating Basic Demographic Measures from Incomplete Data.* New York, 1967.

Warner, W. Lloyd, Marcia Meeker, and Kenneth Eells. *America: The Evaluation of Status.* New York: Harper Torchbooks, 1960.

Wiley, Norbert F. "The Ethnic Mobility Trap and Stratification Theory." *Social Problems* 15 (1967): 147–59.

16

Social networks and efficient resource allocation: computer models of job vacancy allocation through contacts

John Delany

In modeling the efficient allocation of scarce resources, researchers using traditional market and formal organization approaches have generally skirted the role played by informal social structure in the allocation process. This tendency to ignore the influence of communications among social contacts is partly due to the difficulty of formally positing specific resource transfers and efficiency measures in a social setting. It is also partly due to the difficulty of modeling the simultaneous nature of the allocation process among a large number of interdependent actors.

My objective here is to suggest one line of inquiry into the effect network social structure may have on the efficient allocation of insider information and scarce economic resources. I suggest that some of the obstacles to examining the relationship between social structure and allocation may be overcome by envisioning certain kinds of socially mediated resource transactions as *donative transfers* (Hansmann, 1980; Galaskiewicz, 1981). Furthermore, I demonstrate how abstract computer models of network allocation dynamics can be used to treat network interdependencies in a resource transfer process among a moderately large number of actors. By formalizing specific kinds of donative transfers in a multiperiod stochastic network simulation, it is possible to derive formal theoretical statements about the allocative efficiency of well-defined social networks.

The chapter is divided into five main sections, the first of which is a brief overview of the broad collection of empirical findings and theoretical developments that motivate the present inquiry. The second section outlines the rationale for developing stochastic computer models of network resource allocation processes (in lieu of mathematical models) and then discusses the general modeling framework. Results and theoretical implications are presented in the fourth section, with the aid of a number of examples of network allocation performance. In the Conclusion I offer some general comments on the potential of an abstract network simulation approach for modeling more complex network resource transfers. Attention is directed toward the problem of unemployment within the firm and to the problems of relaying information in stratified and segregated networks where there are clear biases in the allocation dynamics. Other ideas are presented for the theoretical analysis of interorganizational relationships, particularly as they pertain to the recruitment and donation of philanthropic capital among networks of nonprofit organizations.

Empirical and theoretical background

Despite the theoretical void one confronts upon inquiring about the efficiency properties of social structure, we may start piecing together theoretical insights from a plethora of empirical studies. A number of investigations have dealt, in one way or another, with the relationship between network structure and the flow of resources. As a kind of topical outline one might consider: the study of the diffusion of medical innovation (Coleman, Katz, and Menzel, 1957), the recruitment of individuals to social movements and religious sects (Stark and Bainbridge, 1980; Snow, Zurcher, and Ekland-Olson, 1980), matching individuals to job vacancies (Rees and Schultz, 1970; Granovetter, 1974), career mobility in a corporation (Kanter, 1977; Kanter and Stein, 1979), the interorganizational structure of resource flows in a community (Galaskiewicz and Marsden, 1978; Galaskiewicz, 1979) and in a world system (Snyder and Kick, 1979), patterns of interorganizational coordination (Van de Ven, Walker, and Liston, 1979), interorganizational resource flows in education (Clark, 1965), the myriad studies of interlocking directorates (e.g., Pennings, 1980; Burt, 1980), the generation of new business opportunities (*New York Times*, 1977), and more recently the flow of philanthropic capital (Galaskiewicz, 1981).

Within this menagerie of findings, the empirical seed for developing theoretical insights about the allocation properties of social networks is the work of Granovetter (1973, 1974). The crucial theoretical follow-up to Granovetter is Boorman's (1975) model of optimal contact, network formation. In what is proving to be a catalytic piece of sociological research, Granovetter made the discovery that individuals in a white-collar labor market frequently located their positions of employment through distant social acquaintances – their weak ties. In the present discussion, the salience of Granovetter's findings rests with the pivotal role played by idiosyncratic social ties for matching the demand for a scarce resource with its supply. In a "Granovetterian" world, weak ties are valued for relaying insider or impacted information, that is, information not circulating through public channels, but known to a small number of individuals.

Capitalizing on Granovetter's empirical result, Boorman proceeded to develop a static optimizing model of individual behavior for the formation of contact networks. Quite distinctly, Boorman added a twist to Granovetter's ex post result by posing the problem of job finding before job change ever actually occurs, so that network formation is viewed as rational strategy-building behavior by individuals. The central analytic issue focuses on how individuals should trade off their strong ties and weak ties to maximize their chances of receiving a job tip at some point in the future, when they might be out of work and need the information. Boorman showed that an "all-weak-ties" strategy is both optimal and stable for a given set of model parameters with per period expectations of unemployment ranging as high as .10 (Boorman, 1975: 232).

As a follow-up to Boorman's work, Delany (1978, 1980) developed a dynamic computer simulation version of the static optimizing model. The principal objective here was to establish a dynamic extension of Boorman's central weak-tie result by relaxing certain restrictive assumptions about individual decision-making and network topology. With a network simulation called JOBSEARCH, Delany demonstrated that Boorman's numerical analysis of optimal network strategies was remarkably robust for dynamic and decentralized network decision-making environments. Significantly, the optimality of devoting one's full-time budget to the maintenance of an all-weak-tie network, for the future receipt of a job tip, was demonstrated for per period expectations of unemployment as high as .19. This optimality result was displayed for both the static and dynamic models (see Delany, 1980a: chap. 3). Also significant was the abstract computer modeling method, established with JOBSEARCH, that would yield the foundation for exploring issues of network allocation efficiency.

At its inception, the JOBSEARCH simulation was analyzed primarily for the multiperiod perspective it yielded on contact strategy decision problems in large (100 individuals) social networks and the extent to which equilibrium in a dynamic network reflected equilibrium in the static analysis. A secondary interest also soon emerged concerning the relationship between individuals' contact-strategy decisions and aggregate network structure. (By analyzing the JOBSEARCH equilibrium contact networks with CONCOR, I observed a statistically significant tendency for individuals to maintain weak ties with contacts in network positions structurally different from their own.)

Focusing on the problem of job search before job termination occurs is a critical stopping point for both the static model and the dynamic simulation. Although issues of optimal and equilibrium network strategies and the kinds of structure one finds in association with contact selection decisions are inherently interesting, one is still left wanting to know how the network might perform when job finding becomes a necessity, and network members must rely on the contacts they have made to help them find a new employment slot.

Thus, the research started by Granovetter, and then pursued first by Boorman and next by Delany, developed questions about the efficiency of network resource allocation. Specifically, I am interested in extending the job-finding problem to the actual location of a new job by persons who are out of work. The primary source of new job information in this study is the contacts of the unemployed. The efficiency of a contact network is gauged primarily in terms of how quickly, on average, unemployed individuals return to work after job loss. Related perspectives are also established with respect to the influence of network structure on the average size of the unemployed pool and on the proportion of job vacancies filled.

The modeling framework

Consider now the two central questions in this inquiry: How may one envision certain kinds of resource transfers mediated by social structure as donative transfers? and How may one establish a stochastic computer simulation methodology with which to study the allocation properties of a network social structure?

Donative transfers

By relating issues of allocative efficiency to informal social structure, one raises a class of questions that are in many ways similar to certain questions economists have asked about price systems. Namely, we are interested in determining which properties of a social structure influence the delivery of decision-making information to far-flung (but interdependent) actors, so that excess demand for a given resource might be minimized. Similarly, an economist is interested in the properties of a price system for equilibrating supply and demand among a large number of economic agents.

Although social exchange theory has made some progress in explaining transactions intervened by social structure, in general little is known about how patterns of social structure, per se, affect the efficiency of resource allocations, especially when many individuals are considered simultaneously (however, see Marsden, 1981). Instead, social exchange theory has tended to concentrate on how social structure arises from exchange transactions (e.g., Blau, 1964; Emerson, 1976). As mentioned at the outset, a long-standing problem in exchange theory has been how to define formally the resources of social exchange and the nature of the transfers presumed to occur. When attempting to explain group social structure or its evolution, the social exchange theorist has also tended to discuss the transfers of many different resources simultaneously. Yet, without a consensus on resource definition, it is difficult to unravel efficiency and related optimality issues in the context of social exchange theory. This problem becomes acute when the modeler also has difficulty establishing an explicit set of barter conditions for the exchange of a specific resource, or cannot index transactions of numerous resources in terms of some numeraire good, or cannot rely on bureaucratic fiat as the criterion for resource transfer.

In establishing our particular theoretical perspective on allocative efficiency, we can bypass a number of the problems of social exchange theory by modeling the transfer of a single resource, the job tip, and by defining the *donative transfer criterion*. Specifically, in the models to follow, an actor relays information on a job vacancy only on the condition that at least one of the actor's contacts is out of work and can use the information *and* that the actor does not need it himself or herself (i.e., is employed). As exemplified in the offering of a job vacancy tip, the transfers are presumed to take very little time and it is not assumed that they incur an immediate reciprocal obligation (in the sense of Gouldner, 1960). (For one aspect of reciprocal obligation, see Delany, 1980a: chap. 6.)

Stochastic computer simulation

Progress has been achieved in this research by constructing a family of stochastic simulations that mimic various aspects of locating a job through contacts. In this discussion, we concentrate on the integral member of this family and comment in passing on one other related model.[1] Within this nested modeling methodology, I develop a perspective on allocative efficiency by systematically varying the assumptions about network structure and the decision rules for information transfer. The simulations are then executed under the various assumptions, and the statistical output of the different executions is subsequently analyzed.

The rationale for relying on abstract simulations to study network allocation properties arises from the necessity of dealing with nonlinear stochastic processes. The very basic interconnectedness of network life results in a nonlinear process of job matching that makes both the formulation and analysis of mathematical expressions extremely difficult. A dynamic simulation, however, affords the network modeler a way to preserve the formal assumptions of a theoretical model while sidestepping cumbersome mathematical expressions. Instead, one analyzes a set of statistics from a Monte Carlo simulation of network allocation performance. (The potential of this approach appears even stronger for more complex network transfer processes, as might occur in discrimination or promotion process, as noted later in the chapter.)

The statistics to be examined are indicators of network performance in the job-match process and are used to establish the perspectives on network efficiency. They measure, for example, the average size of the unemployed pool for the history of a simulation run or the proportion of job vacancies filled over the simulation time periods.

Note that since computer memory can indeed handle a large number of formal assumptions and decision rules, the investigator is forced to be absolutely specific about every single detail of network stucture and network dynamics. There is no notion of unexplained variance to employ as an escape-hatch for misspecified model constructions. Moreover, by virtue of the computer's ability to display each and every network event, the investigator can see exactly how modeling assumptions interact to produce observed network performance and statistical outcomes. In this sense, the simulation models are transparent to the initial assumptions.

The JOBMATCH model

The principal simulation producing the network efficiency benchmarks is called JOBMATCH (Delany, 1980a, 1980b). The strategy for theory building basically involves varying the network contact density over repeated JOBMATCH executions and examining the effect of these differential densities on the return-to-work times of the jobless actors, the average number of jobless, and the proportion of filled vacancies over the course of a simulation run. In other words, the efficiency statements are ascertained by comparing the statistics from JOBMATCH executions with different network densities.

The primary purpose of this chapter is to concentrate on the description and analysis of JOBMATCH, in order to establish a single benchmark for network efficiency. Mention is made, however, of the JOBRELAY simulation (see Figures 16.1 through 16.4 in the next section). This second model represents simultaneous variation in network density and the rules for information transfer between contacts (described more fully below; see Delany 1980a, 1980b for details).

JOBMATCH assumptions

JOBMATCH is a multiperiod simulation that relies on simple network imagery and conceptual design. There is only a single type of tie and it is not differentiated by strength of relationship (no distinctions between strong ties and weak ties). Each actor's individual contact network remains fixed over the entire execution of a simulation. The creation of job loss and job vacancy occurs at the beginning of each time period as exogenous events – so that some actors are thrown out of work and others (possibly some of those already out of work) are endowed with the control of a job slot to be filled.

Jobless individuals may find new employment by one of two ways. They may hear directly of job vacancies (in the start-of-period job creation) or they may be given information about job openings by contacts. The heart of the simulation consists of a straightforward job-tip allocation rule by which individuals who control job vacancies fill them with their unemployed contacts. The model can be summarized by seven basic assumptions:

1. *Discrete time periods.* All processes leading to unemployment and reemployment take place in discrete time, over a number of time periods specified by the investigator. At the start of each time period, two "shocks" are administered to network members. First, a number of individuals lose their jobs and become listed as unemployed. Second, another, possibly overlapping, set of individuals is listed as having heard directly of a job vacancy. (Each set of actors is selected by a set of Bernoulli trials.)

2. *One job, one controller.* In any given time period, each individual may act as a controller of at most one job opening, and each job opening is controlled by only one individual. It is assumed that hearing directly of a job tip is equivalent to acting as a controller of that vacancy.

3. *Single-period vacancy lifetimes.* Job vacancies last for only a single period, so that a fresh list of job controllers is created at the start of each time period.

4. *Indefinite duration of unemployment.* Once classified as unemployed, individuals remain out of work until a new job is found or until the simulation terminates.

5. *Ahistorical job loss.* Each actor may be repeatedly thrown out of work during the course of a single JOBMATCH execution; that is, if an unemployed actor locates a new job in period t, he or she may lose that job in period $(t + 1)$.

6. *Equal number of contacts.* Each actor is assigned the same fixed number of contacts; that is, all personal networks are of equal size. (Observe that this is a simple way to vary network density.)

7. *Random allocation of job tips.* If a given employed actor controls a job vacancy and has one or more unemployed contacts, the job is allocated randomly to one such contact. If the job controller is out of work, then he or she uses the tip.

JOBMATCH parameters

At the start of each JOBMATCH execution, the investigator is required to enter the values for six parameters that effectively bound the network performance problem; these are also the only inputs the user needs to make. Values are specified for

POP the size of the network population
NP the number of time periods to be simulated

UPR an individual's probability of becoming unemployed at the begin-
ning of each time period, if he or she is not already out of work
JPR an individual's probability of hearing directly of a job vacancy that
he or she may allocate to himself or herself or to another individual
OUT1 the number of individuals unemployed at the *start* of time period 1.
(The use of this parameter avoids having to start JOBMATCH from an
artificial full-employment position.)
B the number of contacts given to each person (a uniform distribution)

In the JOBMATCH executions summarized below, these six parameters were set
as follows:

$$POP = 300 \quad NP = 200 \quad UPR = .05$$
$$JPR = .04 \quad OUT1 = 168$$
$$B = 0,1,2,3,4,5,8,10,15,299$$

POP. The population size was dictated primarily by the storage limitations of
the IBM 5100 minicomputer used to develop and execute JOBMATCH (64
thousand bytes of memory) and the unavailability of a larger machine that
would run APL, the simulation language. Although 300 is certainly implausible for the size of an economy, this may well be a realistic size for discussing
certain internal labor market phenomena, such as nonpromotability problems
in a corporation or revitalization of stale matches of jobs and personnel.

NP. For the chosen parameter values, it was observed in trial executions that
approximately 40 time periods were needed for JOBMATCH to settle down to
its equilibrium performance level (also true for JOBRELAY). With NP = 200,
this leaves 160 "slack" periods to ensure that key simulation statistics (e.g.,
average level of unemployment or proportion of vacancies filled) are
oscillating in equilibrium regions.

JPR and UPR. The two parameters JPR and UPR were set small so that the
social system would be seen as changing with only moderate speed, for
example, on the average, 12 job controllers appear at the start of each period
and only 15 people lose their jobs. UPR was set slightly higher than JPR to
suggest a system in which there would be some pressure to rely on network
information.

OUT1. The number of individuals defined as beginning the first period out of
work (OUT1 = 168) was decided by approximating the equilibrium fraction
of unemployed individuals in a world without contact communication
(B = 0). When B = 0, no contact communication is possible and unemployed
individuals hear of jobs only directly. Thus, all relevant job-match statistics,

including the number of unemployed at equilibrium (OUT1), can be derived from a simple two-state (employed, unemployed) Markov model (see Delany, 1980a: 127, b: 131–2). The Markov numerical analysis was also checked with the NONET simulation that incorporates all of the JOBMATCH assumptions, save for permitting contact communication.

B Values. This investigation focuses on gauging the effects of increasing network density. Therefore a complete set of B values was explored for the low end of the B range. Since B = 10 and B = 15 closely approximate B = 299 ([POP − 1], see Figures 16.1 through 16.4), it was not necessary to explore more intermediate values. As just pointed out, network performance for the case B = 0 can be modeled by using a short-cut procedure, since a contact network does not actually have to be constructed. Similarly, the case of B = 299 can also be investigated without actually establishing a contact network. Since complete network connectivity amounts to perfect circulation of all job tips, it is impossible for a vacancy and an unemployed actor to exist simultaneously at the end of a time period. Therefore, network allocation performance can be modeled by simple numerical comparisons of the number of job openings and the number of unemployed in each time period. The FULLNET simulation handles this special case.

JOBMATCH computer operations. After the investigator enters the parameter values, the contact network is established in the computer by randomly selecting B other actors as contacts for each network member (no individual uses himself or herself for a contact; ties are not assumed to be symmetric). Also, before the start of the first time period, OUT1 individuals are selected at random and listed as unemployed.

Once into the first time period, a set of individuals, selected randomly from those still employed, is listed as just having lost their jobs and they join the previously disengaged OUT1 actors already looking for work. Another set of individuals, selected at random, is then named as being in control of job vacancies.

Now the matching process begins. Any unemployed individual who heard directly of a job takes it and is considered to have found work. Next, jobless actors who did not directly receive job information call on their personal contacts for help. If a contact with a job tip faces more than one request for the information, he or she allocates the job to one of his or her unemployed ties selected at random, and this individual returns to work. The first period ends when all matches that can be made through the network have in fact been made. All individuals still in search of work at this point enter period two on the unemployed list; all job controllers who failed to fill their job slots lose control of them, although they may be named controllers of new jobs in period two.

The processes of job loss, vacancy creation, and job matching continue for the remaining (NP − 1) periods specified by the JOBMATCH user. Throughout the full set of periods, event histories are kept of all job losses, vacancies established, job matches accomplished, types of matches made (either directly or through the network), and how long unemployed individuals took to find new jobs. From these tabulations, the user receives a highly refined profile of job loss and network vacancy allocation for all NP periods of JOBMATCH. We now select aspects of that profile.

Donative job information transfers and network efficiency

The central premise of this chapter is that smoothly functioning social networks may constitute a class of highly effective nonmarket and non-bureaucratic mechanisms for allocating insider information and scarce economic resources, interpreted here as job-vacancy information. So that our preliminary explorations into this claim may be conveniently summarized, the discussion of simulation results centers around four figures, each of which depicts a different measure of network efficiency.

The figures display one set of results for JOBMATCH and two sets of results for JOBRELAY. The main effect captured by JOBRELAY allows for chaining of job-tip transfers. In JOBRELAY, once an actor remains out of work for one period, he or she may ask one or two immediate contacts to help him or her find work in subsequent time intervals. Thus, an unemployed individual may receive a job tip from the contact of a contact in this simulation, as well as receive one directly or from an immediate contact. The results for asking one contact and two contacts for help are reported in the graphs as JOBRELAY(1) and JOBRELAY(2). Even though we display two sets of JOBRELAY results, the following discussion is based essentially on observations of JOBMATCH. Visual inspection of the figures shows that, as a general outcome, JOBRELAY only mildly improves JOBMATCH performance in each case.

For evaluation purposes, these graphs all display a measure of efficiency on the *y*-axis, versus network connectivity (B, the number of contacts per actor) on the *x*-axis. Note too that each data point represents the average of a number of simulation executions.

The duration of unemployed job search

Figure 16.1 shows the average number of periods absorbed as unemployed following job loss. When contact communication is not allowed (B = 0), it takes an unemployed individual 25 time periods, on average, to locate new employment. (Recall this may be ascertained by direct investigation of a two-

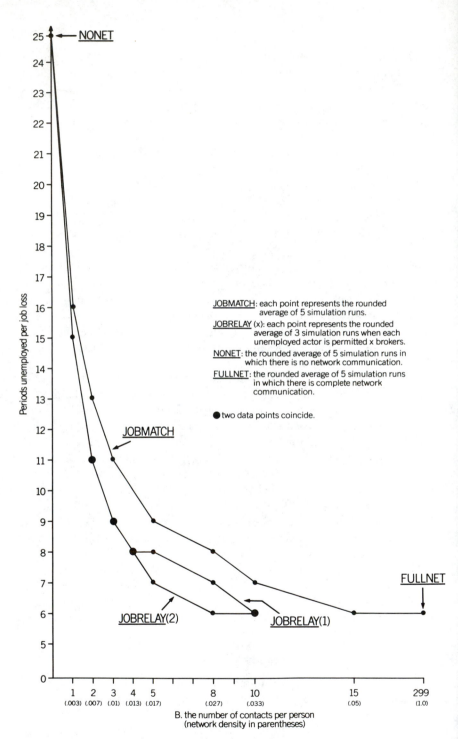

Figure 16.1. The average duration of job search unemployment following job loss, displayed as a function of B.

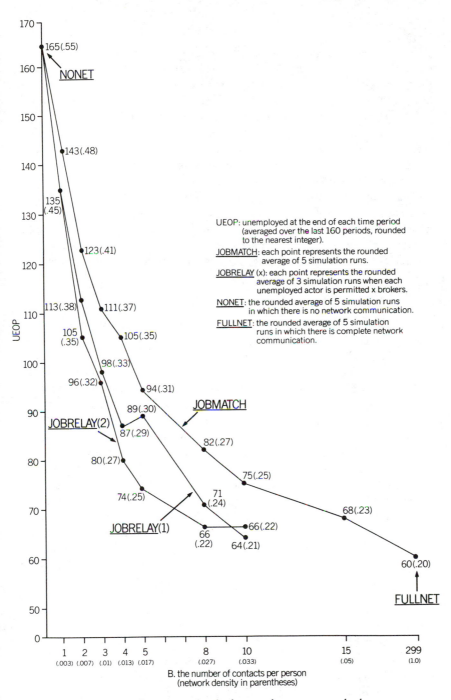

Figure 16.2. The average level of unemployment over the last 160 time periods. (Entries in parentheses show the unemployment rate corresponding to each level.)

state Markov model and by the NONET simulation.) Yet, with just one contact per person (B = 1), JOBMATCH indicates that the average search time for a new job drops by 9 time periods. As B is increased to 2, then to 3, job search duration continues to decline significantly. At B = 3, where network density is .1%, average waiting time has been reduced by more than 50%.

Beyond 3 contacts per person, the network begins to exhibit decreasing returns to contact investment. In passing from 5 to 8, 8 to 10, 10 to 15 contacts per person, mean waiting times decrease by one time period with each B increment. At 15 contacts per person (a network density of just 5%), the efficiency of the network for minimizing job search time is not noticeably different from a fully connected network. (Recall that results for complete network connectivity, B = 299, are obtained with the FULLNET simulation.) This informational equivalence between a very low density network and a complete-density network is perhaps the most striking result of the analysis.

Aggregate levels of unemployment

Obviously related to the length of job search is the average level of unemployment, displayed in Figure 16.2. In addition to the average number of unemployed over the last 160 time periods, there is a parenthesized proportion showing the employment rate that corresponds to each level.

As one would expect, Figure 16.2 tells a similar story to Figure 16.1. Beginning again with a simulation of no contact communication, one sees that permitting a single contact per actor reduces the unemployment level from 165 to 143. Significant welfare gains are made up through three contacts per person, where the number of jobless is down to 111. Above B = 3, the unemployment level drops from 5 to 12 individuals with each B increase, until at 15 contacts per person, 68 individuals are out of work on average.[2]

Before shifting our perspective to the demand (employer's) side of the job-matching process, one may comment that the unemployment rates observed in Figure 16.2 correspond to what would be disastrous rates in real societies. Obviously, a lower UPR and higher JPR would rectify this. However, for demonstration purposes, the present values enable one to visualize clearly the contrasts in system performance. (Again, however these rates may fit with selected reinterpretations of the model.)

The proportion of vacancies filled

Another efficiency perspective is offered in Figure 16.3. In order to portray how well the networks perform from the viewpoint of the job controllers, the proportion of vacancies filled is displayed as a function of B.

All the qualitative features noted in Figures 16.1 and 16.2 extend to the present perspective. Moreover, because the measures of performance are

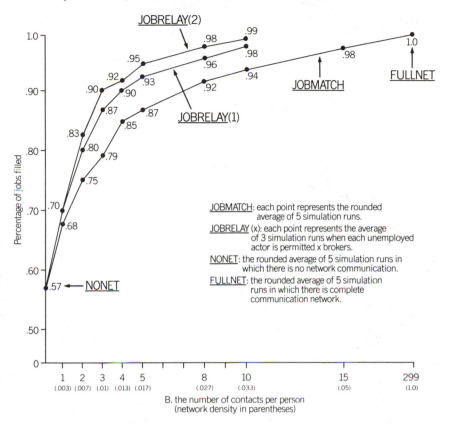

Figure 16.3. The percentage of vacancies filled, displayed as a function of *B*.

bounded by unity, these monotonic curves are all very close to each other with tightly clustered asymptotes once B ⩾ 10; that is, almost no job information goes to waste above B = 10. Hence, networks appear to be a remarkably efficient means of funneling individuals into job vacancies at the source of labor demand.

Network brokering

Finally, we summarize the load of job transactions borne by the network system. Figure 16.4 displays the percentage of all job matches made through the contact network. Although the curves appear similar to those already observed, note the absolute levels of the percentages. In both JOBMATCH and JOBRELAY, when the contact network density surpasses 1% (B = 3), the network is brokering between 58% and 73% of the job matches. (Because the

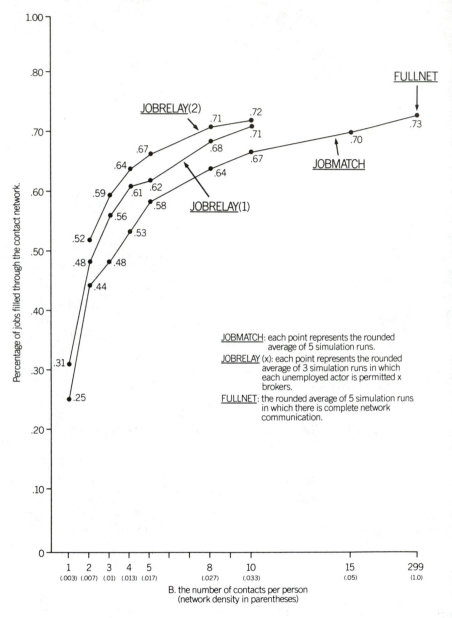

Figure 16.4. The percentage of job matches made through the contact network, displayed as a function of *B*.

FULLNET case amounts to general publication of all new vacancies, networks really reach their greatest role for B = 10 and B = 15.)

Summary

The overall impression from these figures is strong and clear. Even very sparse networks may sustain matchings of unemployed individuals to job openings at high levels of absolute efficiency. Furthermore, these gains from network communications are achieved rapidly and then diminish as the information capacity of the network is reached. It does not appear, however, that efficiency is significantly improved by the chaining of job-vacancy information. Rather, large increases in efficiency result from chains of length one, and the chains of length two in JOBRELAY only mildly improve on the JOBMATCH results. Put in terms of the tie maintenance activity required to sustain interpersonal networks, these findings suggest quite significant allocation returns, even when all individuals might put remarkably little effort into their personal networks, as they presumably do with weak ties.

Conclusion

Our central objective in this chapter has been to illustrate, in a hypothetical way, the performance of fixed social networks for the allocation of insider information about a scarce perishable resource. Strategically simple models have yielded impressive preliminary evidence indicating that sparsely connected social networks may in fact perform quite well, differing little in their efficiency from fully connected contact networks. Note that these structures may also be integral components for coordinating activities in both the marketplace (White, Chapter 9) and the firm (Kanter, 1977).

As the toehold here is made firmer in future research, it is hoped that the present results will branch out into a more complete family of nested theoretical statements. Underlying this hope is the largely untapped potential for expanding both the particular simulations and the general computer modeling methodology in a number of analytical and substantive research directions.

Expanding the benchmark result

Studies of the relationship between relational social structure and allocative efficiency are uncommon in sociology: Therefore, the central purpose here has been to communicate a single baseline result, generated from JOBMATCH, and one corollary amplification, generated from JOBRELAY. However, a significant amount of numerical analysis remains to be done so that the benchmark results obtained here can be broadened and a solid analytical foundation established for the continued study of allocative efficiency and network structure.

Obviously, fuller distributions of simulation output are needed for the parameter values with which these investigations began. Extensive results also need to be obtained for other combinations of parameter values. As mentioned above, work is under way to assess network performance for larger populations. Different parameter environments will also be explored through systematic variations in the values of UPR and JPR, held constant for this report.

What is perhaps more significant, the method of establishing network density implemented here (defining uniform contact distributions) ignores the differential access that actors have to network information in more realistic situations. Thus, experiments are in progress to establish contact budgets using, for example, Poisson and normal distributions. Another contrary-to-fact restriction of JOBMATCH and JOBRELAY, receiving high priority for modification, is the assumption of a random network topology. Plans are being made to permit network cliques, neighborhoods, or blocks like the ones observed in a variety of empirical network studies (Roethlisberger and Dickson, 1939; Newcomb, 1961; Sampson, 1968; White, Boorman, and Breiger, 1976; Breiger, 1976; Laumann and Pappi, 1976). Other approaches to the description of network social structure have focused on dyadic or triadic distributions (Holland and Leinhardt, 1975; Wasserman 1978; Galaskiewicz and Wasserman, 1981). Conceivably, network connectedness could be made to reflect varying distributions of these microstructures.

Network allocations in a corporation network

There are many possibilities to consider in developing the basic JOBMATCH model. However, the longer-run promise of this approach to theory development and further discussion of it might be better appreciated if we look at a different network context – that of a corporation or other formal organization.

An internal labor market analog to unemployment can be established by considering the repercussions of nonpromotability (Roseman, 1977) and the various modes of job disengagement that result from blocked opportunity, such as depressed aspirations, low commitment, withdrawal from job responsibility, increased social behavior, and attention to peer group relations (Kanter, 1977: chapt. 6). One can view destructive or stale job–personnel matches, or other forms of job dissatisfaction, as together constituting a mode of organizational failures that has the potential to detract significantly from organizational productivity. These failures can be seen, in effect, as various manifestations of "internal underemployment."

A fluidly operating company contact network may appreciably enhance the flow of information concerning personnel–position mismatches, employee dissatisfaction, and opportunities for more productive and desirable job–employee realignments. If organizational performance can be upgraded, at a reasonable cost, by relocating disenchanted individuals to other corporate positions, information passed through corporate contact networks may be seen as an aid to more efficient job transfers and job rotation – thereby buffering the organization against those productivity losses. (Presumably, job transfers designed to groom individuals for greater corporate responsibilities in the future might also be made more intelligently with the help of network information.)

If we superimposed this new interpretation on JOBMATCH, the parameters UPR and JPR would be reinterpreted, respectively, as an individual's probability of becoming dissatisfied with his or her job, while JPR would be seen as an individual's probability of hearing directly of another job slot in the company to which he or she could move. The basic network efficiency results obtained from JOBMATCH now become the comparison standard for proceeding to explore the impact of various job-matching requirements, network structures, and allocation biases with regard to the efficiency of personal matches.[3]

As a preliminary step in elaborating this hypothetical interpretation of JOBMATCH, one can relax the assumptions of completely identical employment positions and a homogeneous network population to outline an elementary personnel assignment problem. Now, instead of all actors appearing with identical productivity attributes (as in JOBMATCH), one establishes network subpopulations. All individuals belonging to a given subgroup are characterized by the same performance ability, productivity attribute, or other market signal (Spence, 1974). The employment slots in the company are also partitioned, but by their respective task requirements, or equivalently, by the kinds of abilities that they require from the job incumbents. Now the role of the contact network is to channel individuals who are mismatched to their present jobs into other positions that achieve a better fit with their individual performance strengths.

In this setting, the measure of network efficiency would focus primarily on the number of individuals, on average, who are mismatched to their jobs. Optimal productivity conditions for a given network structure would obtain when the proportion of mismatches (dissatisfied individuals) is at a minimum. Consider as a simple example, just two job categories, of, say, type x and type o. If the network members have an individual attribute that fits either an x or an o job classification, then the presumed productivity losses are minimized when the largest proportion of x ability individuals sit in jobs with x task demands, and the situation is similar for individuals with o-type ability. Although this is quite a simple matching problem, there are many ways to modify the models and make the assignment process more realistic. Individuals obviously have more than a single binary-valued talent, the vast majority of organizations are characterized by departments (network neighborhoods) and chain-of-command communication structures, sometimes job controllers cannot always distinguish true productivity signals (Spence's problem), frequently responsibility to fill a job rests with more than one individual (a collective decision), and, as discussed next, not everyone has equal access to job information.

Discrimination in network allocation dynamics

The creation of network subpopulations and the differentiation of individuals by selected market signals (Spence, 1974) also holds out the possibility of establishing a social network perspective on informal processes of discrimination and biased resource allocation. Both subjective and structural allocation distortions might be handled with modifications to the basic JOBMATCH simulation logic. In order to simulate structural conditions of unequal access to information, the disadvantaged network group could be given a lower value of JPR and a higher value UPR than the other group is given (if we continue to assume just two subpopulations). Another method of simulating structural discrimination in an informal social structure would be to permit the victims of discrimination fewer network contacts (either as a single model modification or in combination with differential JPR and UPR probabilities) than the other individuals are permitted. To approximate more subjective forms of discrimination, job controllers might be permitted to use a priority rule for the distribution of job information when there are competing claims for it, the advantaged group members always receiving the lower priority (this relaxes assumption 7 above).

All three of these potential modeling directions yield the possibility of exploring both group and system-wide welfare implications of discriminatory information transfers. Once some type of network equilibrium is reached in these systems (assuming one exists), it would also then be possible to experiment with various reverse discrimination policies in the network model to explore for the conditions that might return the disadvantaged group (or groups) to information-access parity.

Interorganizational resource allocation models

Another direction in which to expand our theoretical insights on network allocation processes would be to relax the rules about single-unit allocations of job tips to job controllers (assumption 2, above) and the single-unit demands for job vacancy information from unemployed individuals and simultaneously to redefine the network members as organizations. This leads one to consider a variety of models for analyzing the allocation of the philanthropic capital in interorganizational networks.[4]

Once again, one might define two network subpopulations, a group of corporate organizational donors and a group of nonprofit organizational donees. Each corporate donor would be assumed to possess an initial endowment for distribution, and each donee may be assumed to require a minimum donated income for continued operation. Network activity in the simulation would consist of requests for donations by nonprofits and the subsequent allocations of capital by corporate donors. The purpose of the simulation would be to search for organizational strategies that lead to efficient distribution of donated resources, as evaluated, for example, by the number of surviving nonprofits at the end of a simulation run and by the distributions of excess supply and excess demands of resources. A basic extension of this model would define prestige rankings among donors and donees that restrict their network communications.

Another possibility is to allow for congestion effects at various corporate actors that might block a donee's request; that is, the donors would already face too many grant requests, so that the latest donees would have to look elsewhere, an idea quite close to the contact dynamics in Boorman's (1975) model of network formation.[5] Another refinement of this simulation would permit the construction of a communication network for organizational donors, a nonoverlapping structure from both the network joining donors and donees and the network among the donees. The objective here would be to model the passing of tips on worthy grant applicants, the network acting as a certification mechanism to help break ties among competing organizational requests for funds. This idea may offer one way to approach the dilemmas of multiple signaling equilibria posed by Spence (1974).

NOTES

1. See Delany (1980a) for detailed elaborations of all models.
2. Differences between JOBMATCH and FULLNET observed here but not in Figure 16.1 result from rounding errors.
3. Under such a reinterpretation of JOBMATCH, a population of 300 may not be so implausible as an approximation to the size of middle- to upper-level management ranks. In addition, the unemployment rates displayed in Figure 16.2 may now appear unrealistically optimistic when reinterpreted as the percentage of less than fully satisfied workers. See Quinn and Staines (1977: Table 13.1, 210–11). Approximately 53% of the sample report were less than fully satisfied with their jobs and 60% would prefer a different one. Obviously, these percentages can be approached in the models by appropriate parameter adjustments.

4. I am indebted to Joseph Galaskiewicz for ongoing conversations on this topic.
5. This idea for modeling the dynamics of organizational stratification has been suggested by Joseph Glaskiewicz.

LITERATURE CITED

Blau, Peter. *Exchange and Power in Social Life.* New York: Wiley, 1964.

Boorman, Scott A. "A Combinatorial Optimization Model for Transmission of Job Information through Contact Networks." *The Bell Journal of Economics* 6 (1975): 216–49.

Brieger, Ronald. "Career Attributes and Network Structure: A Blockmodel Study of a Bio-medical Research Specialty." *American Sociological Review* 41 (1976): 117–35.

Burt, Ronald S. "Cooptative Corporate Actor Networks: A Reconsideration of Interlocking Directorates Involving American Manufacturing." *Administrative Science Quarterly* 25 (1980): 557–82.

Clark, Burton. "Interorganizational Patterns in Education." *Administrative Science Quarterly* 10 (1965): 224–37.

Coleman, James, Elihu Katz, and Herbert Menzel. "The Diffusion of Innovation among Physicians." *Sociometry* 20 (1957): 253–270.

Delany, John L. "Network Dynamics for the Weak-tie Problem: A Simulation Study." *Harvard–Yale Preprints in Mathematical Sociology* 10 (1978).
"Aspects of Donative Resource Transfers and the Efficiency of Social Networks." Ph.D. diss., Yale University, 1980a.
"The Efficiency of Sparse Personal Contact Networks for Donative Transfer of Resources: The Case of Job Vacancy Information." University of Minnesota, Industrial Relations Center Working Paper 80–03. Minneapolis, 1980b.

Emerson, R. M. "Social Exchange Theory." *Annual Review of Sociology,* 2 (1976): 335–62.

Glaskiewicz, Joseph. *Exchange Networks and Community Politics.* Beverly Hills, Calif.: Sage, 1979.
"Networks of Resource Allocation: Corporate Contributions to Nonprofit Organizations." Paper presented to the Albany Conference on Contributions of Network Analysis of Structural Sociology, State University of New York, Albany, April 1981.

Galaskiewicz, J., and Peter Marsden. "Interorganizational Resource Networks: Formal Patterns of Overlap." *Social Science Research* 7 (1978): 89–107.

Galaskiewicz, J., and Stanley Wasserman. "A Dynamic Study of Change in a Regional Corporate Network." *American Sociological Review* 46 (1981): 475–84.

Gouldner, Alvin W. "The Norm of Reciprocity: A Preliminary Statement." *American Sociological Review* 25 (1960): 161–78.

Granovetter, Mark S. "The Strength of Weak Ties." *American Journal of Sociology* 78 (1973): 1360–80.
Getting a Job: A Study of Contacts and Careers. Cambridge: Harvard University Press, 1974.

Hansmann, H. B. "The Role of Nonprofit Enterprise." *The Yale Law Journal* 89 (1980): 835–901.

Holland, Paul, and Samuel Leinhardt. "Local Structure in Social Networks." In D. R. Heise (ed.), *Sociological Methodology 1976*. San Francisco: Jossey-Bass, 1975.

Kanter, Rosabeth M. *Men and Women of the Corporation*. New York: Basic Books, 1977.

Kanter, R. M., and B. A. Stein (eds.). *Life in Organizations: Workplaces as People Experience Them*. New York: Basic Books, 1979.

Laumann, Edward O., and Franz-Urban Pappi. *Networks of Collective Action: A Perspective on Community Influence Systems*. New York: Academic Press, 1976.

Lee, Nancy Howell. *The Search for an Abortionist*. Chicago: University of Chicago Press, 1969.

Marsden, Peter "Restricted Access in Networks and Models of Power." Paper presented to the Albany Conference on Contributions of Network Analysis to Sturctural Sociology, State University of New York, Albany, April 1981.

Newcomb, Theodore. *The Acquaintance Process*. New York: Holt, Rinehart and Winston, 1961.

New York Times. "How CPA's Sell Themselves." September 25, 1977.

Pennings, Johannes. *Interlocking Directorates*. San Francisco: Jossey-Bass, 1980.

Quinn, R. P., and G. L. Staines. *The 1977 Quality of Employment Survey*. Ann Arbor: University of Michigan, Survey Research Center, Institute for Social Research, 1979.

Rees, A., and G. P. Schultz. *Workers and Wages in an Urban Labor Market*. Chicago: University of Chicago Press, 1970.

Roethlisberger, F. J., and W. J. Dickson. *Management and the Worker*. Cambridge, Mass.: Harvard University Press, 1939.

Roseman, E. *Confronting Nonpromotability: How to Manage a Stalled Career*. New York: AMACOM, 1977.

Sampson, S. F. "*A Novitiate in a Period of Change*." Ph.D. diss., Cornell University, 1968.

Snow, D. A., L. A. Zurcher, and S. Ekland-Olson. "Social Networks and Social Movements: A Microstructural Approach to Differential Recruitment." *American Sociological Review* 45 (1980): 787–801.

Snyder, David, and Edward Kick. "Structural Position in a World System and Economic Growth, 1955–1970: A Multiple-Network Analysis of Transnational Interactions." *American Journal of Sociology* 84 (1979): 1096–126.

Spence, A. M. *Market Signaling: Informational Transfer in Hiring and Related Screening Processes*. Cambridge, Mass.: Harvard University Press, 1974.

Stark, R., and W. S. Bainbridge. "Networks of Faith: Interpersonal Bonds and Recruitment to Cults and Sects." *American Journal of Sociology* 85 (1980): 1376–95.

Van de Ven, A. H., G. Walker, and J. Liston. "Coordination Patterns within an Interorganizational Network." *Journal of Human Relations* 32 (1979): 19–36.

Wasserman, Stanley. "Models for Binary Directed Graphs and Their Applications." *Advances in Applied Probabilities* 10 (1978): 803–18.

White, Harrison, Scott Boorman, and Ronald Breiger. "Social Structure from Multiple Networks. I. Blockmodels of Roles and Positions." *American Journal of Sociology*, 81 (1976): 730–80.

17

Occupational mobility: a structural model

Joel H. Levine and John Spadaro

When any employed person contemplates the job market, he or she is well aware that there is a structure to that market. It is very unlikely that someone now employed as a laborer will find employment as a professional next year. It is much more likely that a laborer will move into a supervisory position. Specialized skills, status differentials, geographical specialties and, presumably, many other attributes combine to create an occupational structure in which some patterns of mobility are far more likely than others.

In this chapter we develop a model of mobility proposed earlier by one of us (Levine, 1972) and apply it to a new end: We show how the model can serve as an exploratory device to map the occupational structure, and we demonstrate how a specifically structural view of occupational mobility resolves one of the outstanding problems in the study of mobility, namely, the modeling of longitudinal mobility as proposed by Blumen, Kogen, and McCarthy (1955) and Prais (1955).

Structural interpretation of mobility

The phrase "structural mobility" has been used to describe mobility induced by changes in the availability of jobs. If, for example, employment in agriculture has decreased while employment in white-collar occupations has increased, then a certain amount of structural mobility has been forced upon the population. Beyond the effect of simple availability or nonavailability of jobs, the job market also has a deeper structure. It has, to use Spilerman's (1972) term, "texture," provided by careers and institutions. Job skills, educational credentials, expertise, regional industrial specialties, and many other attributes combine to make an occupational structure in which some patterns of mobility are far more likely than others. It is a "macrosocial characterization of a whole society" (Pullum, 1975; Hope, 1976). This more

We wish to acknowledge our great debt to S. D. Berkowitz and Barry Wellman for their encouragement with this work. The work was supported under the generous research support policies of the Dartmouth College Library's data acquisition program and of Dartmouth College Time Sharing.

fully structural concept of mobility can be better understood by comparing a model of mobility to a medical X ray using trace compounds. If, for example, a physician has introduced a barium compound into someone's digestive system, then the X ray is a photograph of the shadow of the barium. Of course, the barium, per se, is of no interest to the physician, but the shadow is, because it traces the otherwise invisible structure through which the compound is moving. For our purposes, men and women moving from one job to another are like the barium: Their movement provides a trace of the occupational structure that guides and restricts their mobility. Mobility tables are the shadow by which the otherwise invisible structure can be seen.

In order to "see" the structure implied by these data we use a model. The parameters of the model describe the structure, and the predictions of the model allow us to compare the accuracy of two or more alternative descriptions.

The model

The model requires several components, one of which is a "law of motion": Sorokin's (1927) discussion and, indeed, popular descriptions of mobility refer to upward, downward, or lateral mobility. For heuristic purposes, we define social space literally and require a law of motion (or at least an approximating equation) by which frequencies of movement express the structure of this space. Such an equation, equation 17.1, was proposed by one of us (Levine, 1967, 1972, 1978) for use with intergenerational mobility. The equation generates the predicted frequency of moves from occupation i to occupation j as a function of two size effects and of the distance between i and j.

$$\hat{F}_{ij} = \frac{R_i C_j}{e^{P_2(d_{ij})}}. \qquad (17.1)$$

To some extent, this equation resembles a physical gravitation model. R_i is a size factor like mass, which, when it is small (or large), implies that occupation-of-origin i sends few (or many) persons to all destinations including itself. C_j is a second masslike size factor effecting recruitment from all origins into destination j. Completing the resemblance to gravitation, movements are inversely proportional to an exponential function of the distance between i and j, $\exp(d_{ij} + P_2 d_{ij}^2)$, where the distance d_{ij} is measured by a "corner distance" metric:

$$d_{ij} = \sum_{k=1}^{\#\text{dimen.}} |x_{ik} - x_{jk}| \qquad (17.2)$$

The second component of the model is the specification of reasonably appropriate categories. The partition of all jobs into categories must establish a set of reasonably homogeneous categories (Breiger, 1981). We believe, with Breiger, that the determination of homogeneous categories requires as careful attention as the more mathematical components of mobility models because the categories contain implicit hypotheses regarding the nature of mobility. Poor categories – that is, job categories whose definition does not correspond to the career-relevant attributes of the jobs – will limit the model's ability to fit the data. Thus, when Blumen et al. (1955) began their study of longitudinal mobility by using industrial categories (the categories that were available from social security data), they accepted a handicap that would almost certainly limit the ultimate fit of their model. The category "Service, Amusement, and Professions," for example, equated everyone from custodians emptying the wastebaskets to accountants filling them up, as long as all of them were employed within the same industry. For this work, we begin with a 17-category classification system combining criteria of occupation, industry, and "class" (salaried vs. self-employed), following Blau and Duncan (1967). Starting with this standard set of categories, we map the occupational structure and then show examples in which a redefinition of categories – that is, a revised hypothesis as to career-relevant attributes of the jobs – effects an improvement in the model. This fine tuning of the model, by redefining categories, provides a method for testing hypotheses about the social structure of jobs.

A third component of the model, one that is more of a practical than a theoretical necessity, is the goodness-of-fit criterion and the estimation procedure for the parameters. We assess goodness-of-fit between data and model by means of two chi-square–like measures and, more usefully, by direct examination of residuals. (These chi-square measures are given no probabilistic interpretation.) One measure is the ordinary chi-square statistic, equation 17.3, where the expected frequencies, $\hat{F}_{ij}$, are the values predicted by equation 17.1. Parameters of the model are estimated as those that minimize chi-square (estimated by steepest descent on χ^2).[1]

$$\chi^2 = \sum_{\text{all cells}} \frac{(F_{ij} - \hat{F}_{ij})^2}{\hat{F}_{ij}} \tag{17.3}$$

The second measure, χ_z, is a standardization of the χ^2, standardized according to the number of degrees of freedom, v, where v is the usual expected value of χ^2 and $(2v)^{1/2}$ is the usual standard deviation of χ^2. Taken only as a heuristic device without probabilistic interpretation, this provides a standardized measure that makes it possible to compare results obtained under assumptions that alter the number of degrees of freedom used by the model (for example, 3 dimensions versus 2 for the structure, or 17 categories versus 8 for the occupations).

$$\chi_z = \frac{\chi^2 - \nu}{(2\nu)^{1/2}} \tag{17.4}$$

First results

Our principal data are from the National Longitudinal Survey (NLS) (Parnes, 1975). However, as Hope (1976) notes, the touchstone for models of mobility has become the Glass and Hall data for intergenerational mobility (Glass and Hall, 1954). Thus, we begin with these data in order to compare our goodness-of-fit to the goodness-of-fit of various models summarized by Duncan (1979). Table 17.1 shows the data using Miller's 8 category transcription (Miller, 1960) and the fit. The goodness-of-fit is "acceptable" with $\chi^2 = 35.94$ for 34 degrees of freedom.

The fit is better than that of preceding models: It is both closer to the data and more ambitious in the scope of what it attempts to fit (Table 17.1). Note that earlier models have had such difficulty with the data on the principal diagonal that they have tended to abandon these data entirely, confining their attention to the off-diagonal cells. In the best of the models reported by Duncan (1979), $\chi^2 = 43.4$ (using off-diagonal cells) which is 21% more error than that obtained by the structural model (using both on-diagonal and off-diagonal cells; the number of degrees of freedom is the same in both cases).[2] χ_z^2 drops from 1.61 to 0.32. The structural model requires no separate hypotheses to explain the frequency of nonmobile (on-diagonal) individuals. It describes the movement as structural movement (following equation 17.1) among statuses located as estimated in Table 17.2.[3]

Having touched base by applying the model to this standard set of data, we proceed to Table 17.3, which shows data and application of the model to our first table from the NLS. These data are for 45- to 54-year-old males categorized according to "Current or Last Job" in 1967 (retrospective question) and in 1969.

Starting with the 17-category classification used by Blau and Duncan (1967), we can explore the "X ray" of the occupational structure. First, note that the map (first two dimensions graphed in Figure 17.1) is methodologically distinct from the "smallest space maps" (Blau and Duncan, 1967: 70, 74) of similar data: These maps, unlike the smallest space maps, are directly testable. These are the coordinates, which, when substituted into equation 17.1, generate the expected values. Thus, for example, the graph of χ_z against the number of dimensions used to describe the structure, Figure 17.2, indicates that it is a four-dimensional structure. χ^2 and χ_z are poor if the model is restricted to one dimension. Both measures improve as the number of

Table 17.1. *Glass and Hall intergenerational mobility data: counts, fitted counts, and parameters*

Category[a]	I	II	III	IV	Va	Vb	VI	VII
I Prof.	50	19	26	8	7	11	6	2
	48.	25.	23.	12.	6.	13.	3.	2.
II Manag.	16	40	34	18	11	20	8	3
	17.	35.	29.	19.	13.	23.	12.	4.
III Inspec.	12	35	65	66	35	88	23	21
	16.	32.	74.	60.	29.	90.	28.	18.
IV Inspec.	11	20	58	110	40	183	64	32
	9.	22.	63.	108.	49.	171.	59.	41.
Va Routine	2	8	12	23	25	46	28	12
	2.	8.	17.	27.	18.	49.	25.	12.
Vb Skilled	12	28	102	162	90	554	230	177
	10.	27.	93.	168.	88.	565.	236.	169.
VI Semiskill	0	6	19	40	21	158	143	71
	2.	8.	19.	37.	29.	149.	142.	75.
VII Unskill	0	3	14	32	15	126	91	106
	1.	3.	14.	30.	16.	128.	90.	106.

Chi-square = 35.9431

	Coordinates		Row multipliers	Column multipliers
I	0.849	−0.014	8.519	5.668
II	0.473	0.072	5.923	5.979
III	0.210	−0.033	8.984	8.283
IV	−0.037	−0.074	11.088	9.703
Va	−0.071	0.055	3.382	5.405
Vb	−0.294	−0.046	25.239	22.378
VI	−0.476	0.081	10.065	14.129
VII	−0.654	−0.042	9.481	11.133

Coefficients of the polynomial function of distance:

Power	Coefficient
1	1.0000
2	1.0911

[a]*Labels in full*:
  I   Professional and high administrative.
  II   Managerial and executive.
  III   Inspectional, supervisory, and other nonmanual (high grade).
  IV   Inspectional, supervisory, and other nonmanual (lower grade).
  Va   Routine grades of nonmanual.
  Vb   Skilled manual.
  VI   Semiskilled manual.
  VII   Unskilled manual.

Table 17.2. *Test statistics for six models*

Model	Degrees of freedom	G^2 (likelihood ratio)[a]	χ^2	χ_z
1. Independence	49	954.5		
2. Row effects	42	130.1		
3. Quasi-independence, diagonal excluded	41	446.8		
4. Uniform association, diagonal excluded	40	58.6	55.5^b	2.45^b
5. Row effects, diagonal excluded	34	45.9	43.4^b	1.61^b
6. *Structural model*				
Two dimensions, diagonal included	34	—[c]	35.9	0.32

Note: G^2 and χ^2 are both approximately chi-square distributed and, therefore, approximately comparable to each other.
[a]From Duncan (1979).
[b]Computed from fitted counts published by Duncan (1979).
[c]Not applicable.

dimensions is increased to four. But although χ^2 improves in five dimensions (it cannot get worse), χ_z increases, indicating that the cost (i.e., the improvement in fit compared to the additional number of coordinates required for five dimensions) is too high. Mobility in the "body" we are x-raying seems to be moving in 4-space; the mobility itself (rather than any a priori scaling of the categories) seems to imply this.

The first two dimensions of the map display a hierarchical situs arrangement: On the first dimension, occupations are organized in a hierarchy of status from "Farm Labor" through "Professionals"; with the exception of "Sales – other," a persistent exception noted in other studies as well (Blau and Duncan, 1967: 74). Identifiable industrial groups are clustered in two dimensions, noting "Farm" (including "Farm" and "Farm Labor"), "Manufacturing" (including "Labor," "Operatives," and "Crafts") and "Other" (including "Labor," "Operatives," and to a lesser extent "Crafts"). Where the categories allow the distinction to be made (at the left and right ends), salaried workers are sharply differentiated from the self-employed, and this distinction seems roughly consistent with the differentiation between "Manufacturing" and "Construction" in the center of the map. It may be hypothesized that the mobility from which these dimensions are inferred suggests that class and status are the differentiating dimensions of the structure.

The interpretation of the whole map, using the third and fourth dimensions as well as the first and second, is something we choose to treat lightly at this point. The differentiation among categories in these dimensions is small compared with the first two dimensions (standard deviations of the

Table 17.3. *National Longitudinal Survey 1967–1969, mobility data (males, age 45–54): counts, fitted counts, and parameters*

	Prof	Prof	MOP	MOP	Cler	Sale	Sale	Craf	Craf	Craf	Oper	Oper	Serv	Labor	Labor	Farm	Farm
Prof.(SE)	37	6	3	1	0	0	0	0	0	0	0	0	0	0	0	0	0
	36.	3.	1.	3.	1.	1.	1.	1.	1.	2.	2.	1.	1.	1.	1.	1.	0.
Prof.(Sal)	1	244	0	31	8	1	0	5	1	5	2	1	1	1	1	1	0
	1.	247.	2.	24.	9.	2.	4.	5.	1.	4.	3.	2.	2.	1.	1.	1.	1.
MOP(SE)	1	1	112	18	2	6	10	2	9	6	9	1	3	2	1	1	2
	1.	4.	123.	16.	12.	6.	9.	3.	5.	8.	6.	1.	4.	1.	6.	1.	1.
MOP(Sal)	1	17	12	237	16	9	13	6	2	10	4	5	2	0	0	0	0
	1.	24.	9.	243.	13.	7.	10.	5.	3.	10.	3.	4.	3.	1.	2.	1.	1.
Clerical	0	12	0	10	150	1	3	2	0	7	10	4	1	3	4	1	0
	0.	9.	7.	14.	144.	2.	2.	8.	3.	7.	7.	5.	4.	3.	2.	1.	1.
Sales, retail	0	0	3	6	1	40	1	1	0	1	0	1	1	0	0	0	0
	0.	1.	2.	5.	1.	39.	2.	1.	0.	1.	1.	1.	2.	0.	0.	0.	0.
Sales, other	0	1	4	9	2	4	68	0	1	0	4	1	1	0	0	1	0
	0.	4.	5.	10.	2.	4.	68.	1.	1.	2.	1.	1.	1.	0.	1.	1.	0.
Craft, Mfg.	0	9	4	7	5	0	0	229	8	11	28	6	8	3	1	0	0
	0.	6.	2.	6.	10.	1.	1.	232.	5.	14.	32.	5.	5.	4.	2.	1.	1.
Craft, Con.	1	3	4	2	3	0	1	6	165	11	2	9	3	1	8	4	1
	1.	2.	3.	4.	3.	1.	1.	5.	162.	16.	2.	10.	3.	1.	8.	3.	2.
Craft, other	0	4	7	11	9	1	2	13	9	233	3	11	4	3	11	0	1
	0.	4.	5.	10.	7.	1.	2.	12.	14.	235.	5.	14.	8.	2.	7.	1.	1.
Oper, Mfg.	0	2	4	1	6	1	1	34	3	3	328	11	9	18	9	2	1
	0.	4.	2.	3.	8.	1.	1.	31.	2.	5.	328.	10.	12.	18.	8.	2.	1.
Oper, other	0	5	5	6	6	2	2	1	9	20	13	240	6	3	24	0	4
	0.	2.	5.	5.	6.	1.	1.	6.	12.	19.	13.	233.	9.	5.	28.	3.	3.
Service	0	2	4	6	8	3	0	5	0	11	11	5	257	3	10	0	1
	0.	2.	3.	4.	5.	3.	1.	5.	3.	9.	13.	8.	255.	7.	9.	2.	1.
Labor, Mfg.	0	1	1	0	3	0	0	4	0	4	24	1	8	57	5	0	0
	1.	1.	1.	1.	3.	0.	1.	4.	1.	3.	21.	4.	7.	57.	6.	1.	1.

Labor, other	[illegible]	[illegible]	[illegible]	[illegible]	[illegible]	[illegible]	[illegible]	[illegible]	[illegible]	[illegible]	[illegible]	[illegible]	[illegible]	[illegible]	[illegible]	[illegible]	[illegible]
	0.	2.	6.	3.	3.	1.	1.	3.	11.	10.	10.	31.	11.	7.	160.	5.	5.
Farmers	0	2	2	1	1	1	1	4	3	2	1	4	4	2	5	230	10
	1.	4.	2.	2.	2.	1.	1.	2.	5.	2.	3.	4.	3.	2.	7.	231.	7.
Farm labor	0	0	0	0	1	0	0	3	2	1	0	5	2	2	11	2	86
	0.	2.	1.	1.	1.	1.	1.	1.	3.	2.	2.	4.	2.	2.	7.	7.	86.

Chi-square = 251.242 Chi-t = 3.08

	Coordinates				Row multipliers	Column multipliers
Prof. (SE)	2.940	3.456	−1.158	−0.166	9.902	3.626
Prof. (Sal)	2.900	−2.027	−1.157	−0.262	13.762	17.912
MOP (SF)	1.424	0.455	0.367	0.052	12.801	9.616
MOP (Sal)	2.263	−0.625	−0.715	0.026	13.781	17.611
Clerical	0.847	−1.329	−0.140	−0.262	10.833	13.331
Sales retail	2.363	−0.248	2.236	0.026	4.611	8.549
Sales other	3.803	−0.145	0.314	0.020	7.447	9.189
Craft, Mfg.	−0.504	−2.756	−0.724	0.052	14.607	15.887
Craft, con.	−0.503	2.001	−0.724	0.053	11.882	13.656
Craft, other	−0.344	−0.153	−1.276	0.256	13.765	17.059
Oper, Mfg.	−1.557	−2.566	0.313	−0.117	17.061	19.199
Oper, other	−1.554	0.292	−0.461	−0.418	16.002	14.562
Service	−1.132	−0.773	1.598	0.256	15.812	16.147
Labor, Mfg.	−2.389	−1.588	0.254	0.201	7.559	7.554
Labor, other	−1.696	0.886	0.213	0.256	13.855	11.536
Farmers	−2.918	3.693	0.481	0.052	19.319	11.951
Farm labor	−4.044	1.425	0.579	−0.024	11.725	7.339

Coefficients of the polynomial function of distance:

Power	Coefficient
1	1.0000
2	−0.0491

Labels in full: Professionals (self-employed); Professionals (salaried); Proprietors, commerce; Managers, operators, proprietors – other; Clerical; Sales, retail; Sales, other; Crafts, manufacturing; Crafts, construction; Crafts, other; Operatives, manufacturing; Operatives, other; Service; Labor, manufacturing; Labor, other; Farmers; Farm labor.

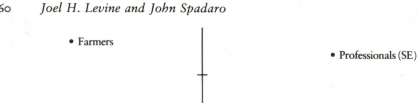

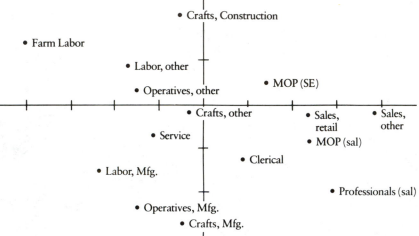

Figure 17.1. Structural map: Initial 17-category classification, first two coordinates.

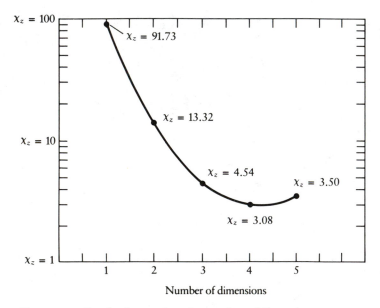

Figure 17.2. Graph of χ_z against the number of dimensions.

coordinates on each dimension are $s_1 = 2.3$, $s_2 = 1.8$, $s_3 = 0.96$, $s_4 = 0.19$). These dimensions are likely to change as the model is improved by redefining and, presumably, sharpening the definitions of the occupations.

Redefining the occupational structure

Examination of the residuals shows a relatively heavy concentration of error associated with the category "MOP-SE" ("Managers, Officials, and Proprietors – Self-Employed"). If one accepts as a working hypothesis that the equation of the model is correct, then the explanation for these errors must be that the boundaries of this category do not conform to the attributes of the underlying reality.

By analyzing the residuals and attempting to redefine categories, we can use the model as an exploratory device for mapping and testing hypotheses about social structure. We have hypothesized that the class distinction ("MOPs Salaried" versus "MOPs Self-Employed") is not the most important distinction and searched for a better alternative. Among the alternatives we tried was an industrial distinction between industries with a more complex division of labor and those with less complex divisions. This reduced χ_z from 3.08 to 1.7 (χ^2 from 251 to 224 with the same number of degrees of freedom). Still, the residuals were concentrated in one of the two (new) categories of MOPs. Close analysis of the residuals and repeated hunch testing (if not hypothesis testing) chipped away at the error until finally a sharp improvement was obtained when we defined a new category, "Proprietors – Commerce" comprised of self-employed middlemen engaged in wholesale and retail trade.[4] When these were distinguished from other MOPs, the residuals dropped throughout the table (not only in the rows and columns of the directly affected categories). χ_z dropped to 0.92 (χ^2 to 209).

With this new distinction among MOPs (Table 17.4), all of the categories move slightly, and the whole map (Figure 17.3) is brought a step closer to a focused image of the structure. The data indicate that the distinction between the salaried and the self-employed managers and proprietors is less important than the distinction between these self-employed middlemen and other managers and proprietors. The new category boundary gives us relatively homogeneous categories; the old one does not. The new category boundary is supported by its ability to cut the χ^2 by 20% (with no change in degrees of freedom) and by the decrease in χ_z from 3.08 to 0.92. These categories should now be subjected to detailed examination, and, indeed, there is room for alternative hypotheses. In this chapter we propose simply that the structural model provides a format in which to formulate and compare such hypotheses.

Table 17.4. National Longitudinal Survey, 1967–1969, mobility data (males, 45–54), revised categories: counts, fitted counts, and parameters

	Prof	Prof	Prop	MOP	Cler	Sale	Sale	Craf	Craf	Craf	Oper	Oper	Serv	Labor	Labor	Farm	Farm
Prof. (SE)	37	6	0	4	0	0	0	0	0	0	0	0	0	0	0	0	0
	37.	3.	1.	3.	1.	0.	1.	1.	2.	1.	1.	1.	1.	0.	1.	1.	0.
Prof. (Sal)	1	244	0	31	8	1	0	5	1	5	2	1	1	1	1	0	0
	1.	246.	1.	24.	9.	2.	4.	6.	1.	4.	3.	2.	1.	1.	1.	0.	0.
Proprietor	0	0	64	14	1	6	3	0	1	1	0	3	3	0	4	4	2
	0.	2.	65.	13.	3.	7.	4.	1.	3.	4.	1.	2.	3.	1.	1.	1.	1.
MOP, other	2	18	10	291	17	9	20	8	10	15	5	11	2	2	1	1	0
	1.	27.	8.	303.	15.	8.	16.	9.	6.	16.	5.	7.	4.	1.	2.	1.	1.
Clerical	0	12	0	10	150	1	3	2	0	7	10	4	1	3	4	1	0
	0.	9.	2.	13.	148.	2.	3.	6.	3.	7.	7.	5.	4.	2.	2.	1.	1.
Sales, retail	0	0	3	6	1	40	1	1	0	1	0	1	1	0	0	0	0
	0.	1.	3.	5.	1.	39.	2.	1.	0.	1.	1.	1.	2.	0.	0.	0.	0.
Sales, other	0	1	0	13	2	4	68	0	1	0	4	1	1	0	0	1	0
	0.	4.	2.	15.	3.	3.	67.	1.	1.	2.	1.	1.	1.	0.	1.	0.	0.
Craft, Mfg.	0	9	1	10	5	0	1	229	8	11	28	6	8	3	1	0	0
	0.	6.	1.	9.	7.	1.	1.	228.	6.	13.	31.	7.	6.	4.	3.	1.	1.
Craft, con.	1	3	1	5	3	0	1	6	165	11	2	5	3	1	8	4	1
	1.	2.	2.	6.	3.	1.	1.	5.	160.	15.	3.	10.	2.	1.	8.	3.	2.
Craft, other	0	4	4	14	9	1	2	13	9	233	3	11	4	3	11	0	1
	0.	4.	2.	14.	7.	1.	2.	11.	13.	233.	4.	12.	7.	3.	9.	1.	1.
Oper, Mfg.	0	2	1	4	6	1	1	34	3	3	328	11	9	18	9	2	1
	0.	3.	1.	5.	8.	1.	1.	31.	3.	4.	326.	12.	10.	19.	7.	2.	2.
Oper, other	0	5	2	9	6	2	2	1	9	20	13	240	6	3	24	0	4
	0.	3.	2.	9.	7.	1.	1.	9.	13.	17.	15.	237.	7.	4.	24.	3.	3.
Service	0	2	1	9	8	0	0	5	0	11	11	5	257	3	10	0	1
	0.	2.	2.	5.	6.	1.	1.	6.	3.	10.	11.	6.	256.	8.	11.	2.	2.

Labor, Mfg.	0.	1	0	1	3	0	0	0	4	0	4	8	1	24	8	57	5	0	0
	0.	1.	0.	2.	2.	0.	1.	1.	5.	1.	4.	7.	10.	21.	7.	56.	6.	1.	1.
Labor, other	0.	1	0	4	3	0	1	0	2	13	16	7	16	28	16	10	157	1	1
	0.	2.	1.	3.	3.	1.	2.	1.	4.	10.	13.	10.	13.	25.	13.	8.	162.	4.	5.
Farmers	0	2	2	1	1	0	0	0	3	3	2	1	4	4	2	2	5	230	10
	1.	2.	2.	2.	2.	0.	1.	1.	1.	6.	2.	4.	4.	5.	2.	2.	7.	231.	7.
Farm labor	0	0	0	0	1	0	0	0	3	2	1	0	1	0	2	2	11	2	86
	0.	1.	1.	1.	1.	1.	1.	1.	1.	3.	2.	3.	2.	4.	3.	2.	7.	7.	86.

Chi-square = 209.093   Chi-t = .923

	Coordinates				Row multipliers	Column multipliers
Prof. (SE)	2.484	3.009	−0.850	−1.163	9.181	3.995
Prof. (Sal)	2.186	−1.646	−0.868	−1.163	13.853	17.779
Proprietor	1.707	0.647	0.069	0.860	9.433	6.884
MOP – other	1.738	−0.660	0.080	−0.676	16.134	18.774
Clerical	0.417	−0.995	−0.924	−0.008	10.755	13.738
Sales, retail	1.946	−0.428	−0.138	2.156	4.626	8.524
Sales, other	3.393	−0.584	−0.083	0.075	7.365	9.140
Craft, Mfg.	−0.520	−2.241	0.137	−0.833	14.126	16.168
Craft, Con.	−0.239	1.751	0.137	−0.656	11.705	13.688
Craft, other	0.059	−0.067	0.770	−0.957	13.560	17.151
Oper, Mfg.	−1.711	−2.113	−0.098	0.075	16.840	19.333
Oper, other	−1.480	0.232	−0.399	−0.676	16.005	14.813
Service	−1.029	−0.780	0.710	1.337	16.224	15.799
Labor, Mfg.	−2.210	−1.458	0.770	−0.008	7.356	7.629
Labor, other	−1.480	0.781	0.710	−0.008	13.733	11.807
Farmers	−1.944	3.339	0.069	0.860	20.605	11.194
Farm labor	−3.317	1.214	0.069	0.786	12.062	7.168

Coefficients of the polynomial function of distance:

Power	Coefficient
1	1.0000
2	−0.0456

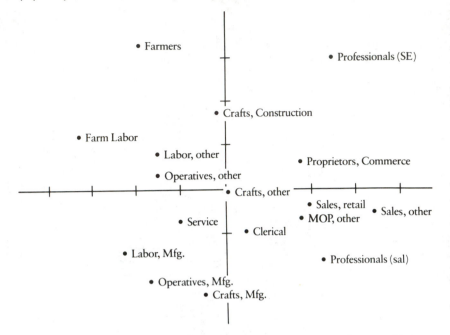

Figure 17.3. Structural map: Revised 17-category classification, first two coordinates.

Longitudinal mobility

Using this revised, but by no means completed image of the structure, we explore the use of the structural model for one other purpose: to begin resolving one of the outstanding tasks of mobility analysis, the modeling of longitudinal mobility. The problem of analyzing longitudinal mobility, as posed 25 years ago by Blumen et el. (1955), is to describe the relation within a sequence of mobility tables. The work of Prais (1955), McGinnis (1968), McFarland (1970), Mayer (1972), and Singer and Spilerman (1978) has been richly suggestive, but the actual results have been unsatisfactory. The simpler models failed to fit the data, while the more complex models were difficult to test: The number of parameters required became unreasonably large in comparison to the amount of data one could reasonably expect to have available. In simple terms, the problem with these models is that they do not work.

Without yet proposing a longitudinal model, consider the analysis of three separate tables for 1967–69 (Table 17.5), 1967–71 (Table 17.6), and 1967–73 (Table 17.7). If, as hypothesized, the coordinates describe the structure through which these men move, then the solutions would have to be almost the same (barring any major social upheaval between 1969 and 1973). Such is the case. The correlations between the four dimensions found above and the four dimensions found in the 1957–71 table, for example, are all greater than or equal to .99 ($r_{11} = .998$, $r_{22} = .998$, $r_{33} = .997$, $r_{44} = .990$). The difference lies in the standard deviations. A posteriori, this provides the necessary clue to the relations between short-term and long-term mobility.

Consider, for example, hypothetical extremes of very short-term and very long-term mobility. Aside from the data we actually have, a table representing extreme short-term mobility would be one in which essentially no mobility had taken place. Such a very short-term table based on U.S. data would resemble the long-term mobility data from some other, more immobile society in which caste-like statuses were socially far apart. If the model were applied to these hypothetical data, the analysis would yield large between-category distances.

Consider the second hypothetical case, that of extremely long-term mobility. A table representing extreme long-term mobility would be one in which origin and destination of workers had become nearly independent (being dominated by the accumulation of intervening events). Applying the model to these data would yield scaled-down short distances. For extreme short distances, the distance term, in effect, drops out of equation 17.1, and equation 17.1 approaches the standard null model for tables of independent variables, $F_{ij} = R_i C_j$.

The interesting cases, the ones for which we have actual data, lie between these two hypothetical cases. Where, as in these data, the macro social structure can be presumed to be approximately invariant, separate tables can be related by simply re-scaling the distances, using a large scale factor for short-term mobility and a small scale factor for long-term mobility. Thus, we generalize equation 17.1 to a longitudinal model by introducing a time-dependent scale factor s_t, equation 17.5.

$$\hat{F}_{ijt} = \frac{R_{it} C_{jt}}{e^{P(s_t d_{ij})}} \tag{17.5}$$

What is the relation between long-term and short-term mobility? Within this frame of reference, the key relation lies in the estimate of s_t with other effects absorbed by the R_{it}'s and C_{jt}'s.[5] We applied the generalized model to the data for the periods 1967–9, 1967–73, and 1967–73. The results are quite consistent with the hypothesis. For this series of tables, the χ_z is essentially unchanged from the result with a single table.

As we see from the residuals, the key point of comparison between this and earlier models is the effectiveness of this structural model with respect to the data represented along the principal diagonals of Tables 17.5, 17.6, and 17.7 (Table 17.8; see also Singer and Spilerman, 1978). For Blumen et al.'s (1955) models and for the Markov-based work that followed, the fit to the principal-

Table 17.5. *Revised categories: longitudinal model, 1967–1969, counts and fitted counts*

	Prof	Prof	Prop	MOP	Cler	Sale	Sale	Craf	Craf	Craf	Oper	Oper	Serv	Labor	Labor	Farm	Farm
Prof. (SE)	37	6	0	4	0	0	0	0	0	0	0	0	0	0	0	0	0
	36.	4.	1.	2.	1.	1.	1.	1.	2.	1.	1.	1.	1.	0.	1.	1.	0.
Prof. (Sal)	1	244	0	31	8	1	0	5	1	5	2	1	1	1	1	1	0
	2.	250.	1.	21.	9.	2.	4.	5.	2.	4.	3.	3.	2.	1.	1.	1.	1.
Proprietor	0	0	64	14	1	6	3	0	1	1	0	3	3	0	0	4	2
	0.	2.	65.	13.	3.	7.	3.	1.	3.	3.	1.	2.	3.	1.	3.	1.	1.
MOP – other	2	18	10	291	17	9	20	8	10	15	5	11	2	2	1	1	0
	1.	22.	8.	310.	12.	7.	15.	8.	7.	16.	5.	8.	5.	2.	3.	1.	1.
Clerical	0	12	0	10	150	1	3	2	0	7	10	4	1	3	4	1	0
	0.	9.	1.	11.	154.	2.	2.	5.	3.	7.	6.	6.	5.	2.	2.	1.	1.
Sales, retail	0	0	3	6	1	40	1	1	0	1	0	1	1	0	0	0	0
	0.	1.	3.	4.	1.	41.	1.	1.	1.	1.	1.	1.	1.	0.	0.	0.	0.
Sales, other	0	1	0	13	2	4	68	0	1	0	4	1	1	0	0	1	0
	0.	4.	2.	14.	3.	2.	70.	1.	1.	2.	1.	1.	1.	1.	1.	0.	0.
Crafts, Mfg.	0	9	1	10	5	0	1	229	8	11	28	6	8	3	1	0	1
	0.	5.	1.	8.	6.	1.	1.	238.	5.	11.	29.	7.	6.	4.	3.	1.	1.

	1	2	3	4	5	6	7	8	9	10	11	12	13	14	15	16	17
Crafts, const.	1 / 1.	3 / 2.	1 / 2.	5 / 7.	3 / 3.	0 / 1.	1 / 1.	6 / 4.	165 / 162.	11 / 14.	2 / 2.	5 / 8.	3 / 3.	1 / 1.	8 / 8.	4 / 3.	1 / 2.
Crafts, other	0 / 0.	4 / 4.	4 / 2.	14 / 15.	9 / 7.	1 / 1.	2 / 2.	13 / 10.	9 / 13.	233 / 237.	3 / 4.	11 / 13.	4 / 7.	3 / 2.	11 / 9.	0 / 1.	1 / 1.
Oper., Mfg.	0 / 0.	2 / 3.	1 / 1.	4 / 5.	6 / 7.	1 / 1.	1 / 1.	34 / 28.	3 / 3.	3 / 4.	328 / 332.	11 / 11.	9 / 9.	18 / 19.	9 / 7.	2 / 2.	1 / 2.
Oper., other	0 / 0.	5 / 3.	2 / 2.	9 / 10.	6 / 8.	2 / 1.	2 / 1.	1 / 8.	9 / 10.	20 / 18.	13 / 14.	240 / 239.	6 / 8.	3 / 4.	24 / 20.	0 / 3.	4 / 3.
Service	0 / 0.	2 / 2.	1 / 2.	9 / 6.	8 / 6.	3 / 3.	0 / 2.	5 / 6.	0 / 3.	11 / 8.	11 / 11.	5 / 7.	257 / 253.	3 / 7.	10 / 11.	0 / 2.	1 / 2.
Labor Mfg.	0 / 0.	1 / 1.	0 / 0.	1 / 2.	3 / 2.	0 / 0.	0 / 1.	4 / 4.	0 / 1.	4 / 3.	24 / 21.	1 / 3.	8 / 7.	57 / 59.	5 / 6.	0 / 1.	0 / 1.
Labor, other	0 / 0.	0 / 2.	1 / 2.	4 / 4.	3 / 4.	0 / 1.	0 / 1.	2 / 4.	13 / 10.	16 / 13.	7 / 9.	28 / 22.	16 / 13.	10 / 7.	157 / 168.	1 / 4.	1 / 4.
Farmers	0 / 1.	2 / 2.	2 / 2.	1 / 2.	1 / 2.	1 / 1.	1 / 1.	4 / 2.	3 / 6.	2 / 2.	1 / 4.	4 / 5.	4 / 4.	2 / 1.	5 / 6.	230 / 229.	10 / 7.
Farm labor	0 / 0.	0 / 1.	0 / 1.	0 / 2.	1 / 1.	0 / 1.	0 / 1.	3 / 1.	2 / 3.	1 / 2.	0 / 3.	5 / 4.	2 / 3.	2 / 2.	11 / 6.	2 / 6.	86 / 87.

Table 17.6. *Revised categories: longitudinal model, 1967–1971, counts and fitted counts*

	Prof	Prof	Prop	MOP	Cler	Sale	Sale	Craf	Craf	Craf	Oper	Oper	Serv	Labo	Labo	Farm	Farm
Prof. (SE)	33	7	0	3	0	1	0	0	0	1	0	0	0	0	0	0	0
	34.	4.	1.	3.	1.	0.	1.	1.	2.	1.	1.	1.	1.	0.	1.	1.	0.
Prof. (Sal)	3	208	2	28	8	1	1	5	0	7	3	2	3	1	1	3	0
	2.	218.	2.	25.	9.	2.	4.	5.	2.	5.	2.	3.	2.	1.	1.	1.	1.
Proprietor	0	1	62	19	0	7	2	0	2	1	1	1	2	1	0	2	2
	1.	3.	59.	15.	3.	6.	3.	1.	4.	4.	1.	2.	4.	0.	3.	1.	1.
MOP – other	1	20	8	280	13	10	20	9	11	20	4	8	7	1	3	0	1
	1.	23.	9.	298.	12.	6.	15.	9.	7.	17.	4.	9.	6.	1.	3.	1.	1.
Clerical	0	13	1	14	130	1	3	7	1	6	8	5	1	1	8	0	0
	1.	10.	2.	14.	135.	2.	3.	6.	3.	8.	6.	7.	7.	2.	3.	1.	1.
Sales, retail	1	0	2	5	0	34	2	0	0	0	0	4	2	1	0	0	0
	0.	2.	4.	7.	2.	38.	2.	1.	1.	1.	1.	1.	2.	0.	1.	0.	0.
Sales, other	1	2	2	15	2	2	65	1	1	1	3	1	0	0	0	1	0
	0.	5.	2.	17.	3.	2.	62.	1.	1.	2.	1.	1.	2.	0.	1.	0.	0.
Crafts, Mfg.	0	7	1	14	4	1	0	231	8	12	29	7	9	3	4	0	0
	0.	7.	1.	12.	7.	1.	2.	228.	6.	14.	29.	10.	8.	4.	4.	1.	1.

Crafts, const.	0	2	1	16	1	0	1	5	140	16	1	5	4	0	12	6	2
	1.	2.	3.	9.	4.	1.	1.	5.	146.	17.	3.	11.	4.	1.	10.	3.	2.
Crafts, other	0	5	5	20	7	2	0	10	17	221	2	18	7	1	11	0	1
	1.	5.	3.	20.	8.	1.	2.	11.	15.	224.	4.	17.	9.	2.	11.	1.	1.
Oper., Mfg.	0	3	1	8	8	0	0	38	3	11	313	19	12	20	9	2	4
	1.	4.	1.	8.	10.	1.	2.	37.	3.	6.	314.	18.	15.	20.	11.	3.	3.
Oper., other	0	4	3	12	13	1	1	3	6	23	11	243	9	1	21	2	4
	1.	4.	2.	12.	9.	1.	2.	9.	11.	20.	13.	238.	10.	3.	24.	3.	4.
Service	0	7	1	12	8	2	0	5	3	7	8	9	244	2	12	0	1
	0.	2.	3.	7.	7.	3.	2.	7.	3.	10.	10.	9.	246.	6.	13.	3.	3.
Labor, Mfg.	0	1	0	2	4	0	0	7	0	2	25	2	8	46	10	2	0
	0.	1.	1.	3.	3.	0.	1.	5.	1.	4.	22.	5.	10.	49.	8.	1.	2.
Labor, other	0	3	2	3	5	0	1	1	17	12	8	28	23	7	157	1	5
	0.	2.	3.	5.	4.	1.	1.	4.	11.	15.	9.	27.	16.	6.	166.	5.	6.
Farmers	0	1	1	2	4	0	0	3	5	1	1	9	8	4	5	215	10
	1.	2.	2.	3.	2.	1.	1.	2.	7.	3.	4.	7.	6.	1.	8.	218.	10.
Farm labor	0	0	0	0	3	0	0	0	1	0	3	2	3	2	12	5	93
	0.	1.	2.	2.	1.	1.	1.	1.	3.	2.	3.	6.	4.	2.	8.	7.	91.

Table 17.7. *Revised categories: longitudinal model, 1967–1973, counts and fitted counts*

	Prof	Prof	Prop	MOP	Cler	Sale	Sale	Craf	Craf	Craf	Oper	Oper	Serv	Labor	Labor	Farm	Farm
Prof. (SE)	28	10	0	2	0	1	0	1	0	0	0	0	0	0	0	0	0
	31.	5.	1.	3.	1.	1.	1.	1.	2.	1.	1.	1.	1.	1.	1.	0.	0.
Prof. (Sal)	4	210	2	30	11	0	2	6	0	3	0	2	2	1	1	4	0
	3.	209.	2.	29.	13.	3.	6.	6.	2.	5.	3.	4.	3.	1.	1.	1.	1.
Proprietor	0	1	57	11	0	6	2	2	3	3	0	2	3	1	0	3	2
	1.	3.	51.	14.	3.	6.	4.	1.	4.	3.	1.	3.	4.	0.	3.	1.	1.
MOP – other	4	26	11	251	14	11	25	8	12	21	3	12	11	1	3	1	1
	1.	26.	12.	269.	16.	8.	20.	10.	9.	18.	6.	12.	8.	2.	4.	1.	1.
Clerical	0	10	1	15	127	1	2	5	0	8	9	6	1	3	4	0	0
	1.	10.	2.	14.	121.	2.	4.	6.	4.	7.	7.	8.	8.	2.	4.	1.	1.
Sales, retail	0	0	1	7	2	32	3	0	0	0	1	2	3	0	0	0	0
	0.	2.	4.	6.	2.	33.	2.	1.	1.	1.	1.	1.	3.	1.	1.	0.	0.
Sales, other	0	1	3	14	2	4	61	0	2	2	3	1	0	0	0	0	0
	0.	5.	3.	16.	3.	3.	58.	1.	1.	2.	1.	2.	2.	1.	1.	0.	0.
Crafts, Mfg.	0	5	1	14	6	1	1	207	7	10	31	4	12	3	6	0	0
	0.	7.	1.	13.	9.	1.	2.	196.	6.	14.	32.	12.	10.	4.	5.	1.	1.

Crafts, const.	0	1	2	20	1	0	2	4	129	8	3	11	5	1	9	5	1
	1.	2.	3.	10.	5.	1.	2.	6.	231.	16.	3.	12.	5.	1.	11.	4.	3.
Crafts, other	0	5	5	18	6	3	3	8	19	188	5	28	9	0	15	1	1
	1.	6.	4.	22.	10.	2.	3.	14.	18.	186.	5.	21.	13.	3.	14.	2.	2.
Oper., Mfg.	0	3	1	10	11	1	1	38	4	9	273	20	16	19	12	2	5
	0.	4.	2.	8.	12.	2.	3.	36.	4.	5.	277.	20.	18.	20.	12.	3.	4.
Oper., other	0	1	2	13	12	1	1	4	8	21	17	213	14	1	26	3	3
	1.	4.	2.	13.	10.	2.	2.	10.	12.	18.	15.	208.	13.	4.	25.	4.	5.
Service	0	4	1	12	11	2	0	2	3	6	10	9	227	6	8	0	2
	0.	2.	3.	7.	8.	3.	2.	7.	4.	9.	11.	10.	223.	6.	14.	3.	3.
Labor, Mfg.	0	1	0	1	3	1	0	8	1	0	22	2	13	38	8	1	0
	0.	1.	1.	3.	3.	1.	1.	5.	1.	3.	21.	5.	11.	39.	8.	1.	2.
Labor, other	0	2	2	2	5	0	1	0	12	13	9	27	17	8	143	2	8
	0.	3.	3.	5.	5.	1.	2.	4.	12.	13.	10.	27.	19.	6.	138.	5.	6.
Farmers	0	1	4	2	3	0	2	1	11	2	4	8	8	2	5	197	12
	1.	2.	3.	3.	3.	1.	1.	2.	8.	3.	5.	8.	7.	2.	10.	200.	11.
Farm labor	0	0	0	0	2	0	0	1	3	0	6	1	3	3	10	6	79
	0.	1.	2.	2.	2.	1.	1.	1.	4.	2.	4.	6.	5.	2.	8.	7.	77.

Table 17.8. *Parameters: longitudinal model, 1967–9, 1967–71, 1967–73*

	Row multipliers			Column multipliers			Coordinates			
Profession (self-employed)	8.672	7.145	7.101	4.138	4.698	4.318	2.450	3.003	−1.221	0.994
Profession (salaried)	14.366	12.780	13.786	17.407	17.053	15.152	2.212	−1.445	−1.221	0.994
Proprietors, commerce	9.367	8.302	7.055	6.888	7.110	7.204	1.715	0.746	0.962	−0.083
Managers, operators, proprietors – other	16.472	14.350	15.047	18.833	20.776	17.846	1.649	−0.667	−0.643	−0.090
Clerical	11.021	10.476	9.510	13.962	12.902	12.766	0.252	−0.965	0.026	1.122
Sales, retail	4.655	5.344	4.297	8.850	7.164	7.569	1.993	−0.397	2.209	0.194
Sales, other	7.470	7.031	6.277	9.323	8.794	9.308	3.580	−0.629	0.034	−0.066
Crafts, manufacturing	14.666	15.124	14.517	16.255	15.099	13.477	−0.546	−2.458	−0.963	−0.228
Crafts, construction	11.737	11.597	11.032	13.835	12.562	11.833	−0.154	1.847	−0.643	−0.236
Crafts, other	13.758	13.336	14.135	17.239	16.786	13.147	0.080	0.003	−1.059	−0.878
Operatives, manufacturing	17.076	19.994	18.305	19.441	15.690	15.157	−1.788	−2.301	0.034	0.013
Operatives, other	16.019	14.808	13.964	14.940	16.049	14.904	−1.462	0.091	−0.689	0.383
Service	16.068	14.671	12.767	15.773	16.739	17.428	−1.019	−0.794	1.309	−0.699
Labor, manufacturing	7.580	8.221	7.014	7.782	5.904	5.505	−2.312	−1.521	0.068	−0.817
Labor, other	13.975	13.306	11.790	12.012	12.479	11.667	−1.462	0.814	0.019	−0.748
Farmers	20.359	20.780	19.289	11.228	10.493	10.348	−1.880	3.393	0.962	0.103
Farm labor	11.929	11.159	9.704	7.263	8.127	7.959	−3.307	1.278	0.814	0.041

Chi-square (χ^2)   Chi-z (χ_z)
732.226   .8339

Coefficients of the polynomial function of distance:

Power	Coefficient
1 = 1	1
2	−0.0483

Table scale factors
$s(1) = 1$
$s(2) = 0.902938$
$s(3) = 0.812644$

diagonal data was poor, so poor as to provide the impetus for Blumen et al.'s Mover/Stayer models and for much of the recent work. The structural model, with no Mover/Stayer hypothesis, fits the data, thereby obviating the need for these more complex hypotheses. It is more parsimonious for these data,[5] and its key parameters provide a relatively interpretable structural map that is amenable to improvement by relatively straight-forward research procedures.

Discussion

Rather than present the structural model in the context of the established, primarily Markovian, models we have chosen to present the model in its own terms, as a model of social structure and of movement through that structure. Nevertheless, it is reasonable to ask how it compares with these models: Clearly, in order to obtain this fit (particularly on the diagonals), we must have relaxed the Markovian assumptions. What has been altered is the assumption that a person's future occupation is, in principle, predictable from a complete description of that person's present state. Equation 17.1 and 17.5 introduce a balance between "supply" and "demand" where the Markov-based models are one-sided. In lay terms, it doesn't matter how well qualified you are for a job if there are no jobs to be had. The job market is one in which the employer as well as the employee, the recruiter as well as the candidate, must both be satisfied.

The structural model incorporates a variety of hypotheses, some of them explicit in the equations, some of them implicit in the definition of the categories. As in the medical X ray, the movements of individuals trace the structure. Modifying the definition of categories, and then testing the result, sharpens our understanding of the social structure: Is it important to differentiate between salaried and self-employed members of the same occupation? If so, then following the homogeneity principle, introducing this refinement among the categories will increase the homogeneity of mobility, and it will increase the accuracy with which mobility can be predicted. The distances inferred to exist between the salaried and the self-employed will show the importance of this dimension relative to other dimensions. Is it important to distinguish jobs according to the numbers of subordinates? If it is, then introducing this refinement will increase homogeneity of mobility and the accuracy with which mobility – in time series as well as in single tables – can be predicted. Do women and blacks and the young face a substantially different job structure? The structures through which they move can be traced from their movements. The structural model is designed to compare hypotheses about the structure of occupations and to trace the structure within which occupational mobility takes place.

NOTES

1. The ordinary chi-square is chosen over the likelihood ratio, G (Goodman, 1972; Bishop Fienberg, and Holland, (1975), frequently used for log-linear models (see Duncan, 1979, and Breiger, 1981) because of computational advantages: The ordinary chi-square is far more readily adapted to steepest descent estimation. (G is more difficult to adapt to steepest descent because the optimization must be constrained to the boundary condition $\Sigma F_{ij} = \Sigma F_{ij}$ without which the likelihood ratio is invalid.)

2. Duncan (1979) uses the likelihood ratio chi-square. This ordinary chi-square was computed from the fitted frequencies published by Duncan. Both measures are roughly comparable to the chi-square distribution and thus are roughly comparable to each other. Thus, the 21% difference in magnitudes is almost certainly a true difference, if not exactly equal to 21%.

3. The Glass and Hall data are analyzed more fully in Levine (1972).

4. Two-digit occupation codes 60 and 69 based on three-digit (U.S. Census) occupation codes 606–629 and 636–696.

5. The structural model uses 166 parameters (leaving 701 degrees of freedom) where a Markovian model would require 272 transition probabilities plus 17 initial row sums plus an unspecified number of stayer parameters (depending on the specific modification of the Markov model). Moreover, the advantage of the structural model would increase if the number of categories were to exceed 17: The number of structural parameters increases only linearly with the number of categories, whereas the number of transition probabilities increases more rapidly, increasing with the square of the number of categories.

LITERATURE CITED

Bishop, Y. M., Stephen Fienberg, and Paul Holland. *Discrete Multivariate Analysis: Theory and Practice.* Cambridge, Mass.: MIT Press, 1975.

Blau, Peter, and Otis Dudley Duncan. *The American Occupational Structure.* New York: Wiley, 1967.

Blumen, I., M. Kogen, and P. McCarthy. *The Industrial Mobility of Labor as a Probability Process.* Cornell Studies in Industrial and Labor Relations, Vol. 6. Ithaca, N. Y.: Cornell University Press, 1955.

Breiger, Ronald. "The Social Class Structure of Occupational Mobility." *American Journal of Sociology* 87 (1981): 578–611.

Duncan, Otis Dudley. "How Destination Depends on Origin in the Occupational Mobility Table." *American Journal of Sociology* 84 (1979): 793–803.

Glass, D. V., and J. Hall. "Social Mobility in Britain: A Study of Inter-Generational Changes in Status." In D. Glass (ed.), *Social Mobility in Britain.* Glencoe, Ill.: Free Press, 1954.

Goodman, Leo. "A Model for the Analysis of Surveys." *American Journal of Sociology* 77 (1972): 1050.

Hope, Keith. "Review of Pullum (1975)." *American Journal of Sociology* 82 (1976): 8–12.

Levine, Joel. *Measurement in the Study of Intergenerational Status Mobility*. Ph.D. diss. Harvard University, 1967.

"A Two-parameter Model of Interaction in Father–son Status Mobility." *Behavioral Science* 18 (1972): 455–65.

"Comparing Models of Mobility." *American Sociological Review* 43 (1978): 118–21.

McFarland, David. "Intragenerational Social Mobility as a Markov Process." *American Sociological Review* 35 (1970): 463–76.

McGinnis, Robert. "A Stochastic Model of Social Mobility." *American Sociological Review* 33 (1968): 712–22.

Mayer, Thomas. "Continuous Time Models of Intragenerational Mobility." In Joseph Berger, Morris Zelditch, and Bo Anderson (eds.), *Sociological Theories in Progress Volume II*. Boston: Houghton Mifflin, 1972.

Miller, S. "Comparative Social Mobility." *Current Sociology* 9 (1960): 1–89.

Parnes, Herbert, S. et al. *National Longitudinal Survey: 1966–73*. Ohio State University, Center for Human Resource Research. Columbus, 1975.

Prais, S. F. "Measuring Social Mobility." *Journal of the Royal Statistical Society A* 118 (1955): 56–66.

Pullum, T. *Measuring Occupational Inheritance*. New York: Elsevier, 1975.

Singer, Burton, and Seymour Spilerman. "Clustering on the Main Diagonal in Mobility Tables." In Karl Schuessler (ed.), *Sociological Methodology 1979*. San Francisco: Jossey-Bass, 1978.

Sorokin, Pitirim. "Social Mobility." *Social Mobility*. Harper and Bros., 1927.

Spilerman, Seymour. "Extensions of the Mover Stayer Model." *American Journal of Sociology* 78 (1972): 599–626.

18

Afterword: Toward a formal structural sociology

S. D. Berkowitz

What is structural sociology?

Sociology as an academic discipline developed out of systematic attempts to understand the massive transformations in Western society beginning in the eighteenth and nineteenth centuries. Although these changes – industrialization, urbanization, and secularization – directly altered individuals' lives and consciousness, their most profound result was a revolutionary rearrangement in the relationships between persons, groups, and the larger social order. Thus, early sociologists naturally came to focus on what they took to be explicitly *social* phenomena – classes and elites, bureaucratic organization, marriage and kinship systems, crime and suicide rates, religious movements, patterns of urban settlement – and on the complex ways in which changes in one sphere of activity brought about changes in others (Marx, n.d.; Durkheim, 1964a; Simmel, 1950).

In this limiting sense, sociology has always been concerned with the study of social structure. Given the complex relationships within even very simple societies, researchers have long recognized that dimensions of social organization cannot be fully understood in isolation from one another. Consequently, they have historically been interested in how the behavior of individuals, groups, or organizations is shaped by the positions they occupy or the roles they play within larger structures. But, until recently, empirically oriented sociologists had no concrete set of observables that closely corresponded to their notions of structure. As a result, instead of trying to examine social structures directly, they became adept at observing and measuring *structural outcomes* – in distributions of wealth or income, in intergenerational mobility, in career patterns, or whatever.

Social structure

Before the 1960s, the term "social structure" was commonly understood to refer to a loosely defined set of factors that constrained individuals' actions. When office workers had reacted in rigid ways to changes in their work environments, for instance, sociologists had based their explanations of this behavior on the inherent inflexibility of *bureaucratic structure*. When peasants had borrowed from village moneylenders rather than "modern credit facilities" provided by government programs, other researchers had found the culprit in peasants' residual attachments to traditional *economic structures*. In effect, the notion of structure was being used as a convenient way of tying together otherwise unrelated effects. Rigorous attempts to uncover explicit processes and mechanisms concretely linking these diverse social phenomena were rare, since, in large measure, the appropriate foundation for doing so did not exist.

As we noted in the first two chapters of this book, two important developments in the modeling of social phenomena played a large role in changing all of this. First, a group of primarily European social scientists systematically advanced approaches to their disciplines in which the notion of structure was a central or organizing concept. Roman Jakobson and Morris Halle, Claude Lévi-Strauss, and Jean Piaget had put forward perspectives on language, kinship systems, and child development that formally recognized the systematic, interdependent, and self-regulating dimensions of these phenomena (Jakobson and Halle, 1956; Jakobson, 1962; Lévi-Strauss, 1969; Piaget, 1971). While lacking the methodological elaboration that would be seen as characteristically structural analytic by the end of the decade, it is clear that this early work contained the germ of a new, holistic mode of social inquiry (Berkowitz, 1982).[1]

Second, by the mid-1960s most of the members of a small but influential mathematical specialty group had agreed that graphic devices, called *networks*,[2] could be rigorously used to map patterns of relationships between the parts of complex social structures.[3] This recognition had been sparked by the successful use of random and biased graphs in modeling the dynamics of friendship group formation (Rapoport and Horvath, 1961; Fararo and Sunshine, 1964), by the subsequent adoption of a "network metaphor" by a group of British social anthropologists (Mitchell, 1969; also see Wellman, Chapter 2), and by the adaptation of graphic theoretic techniques to represent the overall form or morphology of social structures (Harary, Norman, and Cartwright, 1965). Although some important scientific concepts do not refer to objects in the real world – and thus take on meaning only in the context of others that do – *constructs* of this kind (e.g., "marginal propensity to consume," "instantaneous velocity") need to be supported by closely defined formal models. Conceptualizing and operationalizing properties of social structures in terms of networks of effects had, for the first time, made it possible to think about modeling social structure in this way.

By the mid-1970s it was clear that these early theoretical and methodological advances had provided the foundation for a new research paradigm: *structural analysis*. Kuhn argues that sciences usually pass through a series of stages before they come to be dominated by a particular set of theories, methods, and bodies of fact that then function as the standard for practitioners within a particular field (Kuhn, 1970). When this paradigmatic or "normal" stage in the development of a science is reached, the scientific community formed around this standard becomes relatively closed to fundamentally new ideas. Only when anomalies – inconsistencies or failed experiments – within the paradigm become overwhelming, is it possible for a new and more inclusive paradigm to replace it. Although the social sciences have usually not been paradigmatic in the same sense as the physical or natural sciences, I have argued elsewhere that the emergence of structural analysis constitutes just such a radical break with conventional social scientific frameworks (Berkowitz, 1982).

At first, even those researchers who were later to play a leading role in the development of structural analysis were not fully aware that they were engaged in something radically new or different. Each of the established social sciences had, after all, evolved some notion of structure, and new methodological tools – such as factor analysis – had come along in the past without fundamentally changing the ways in which social science was being done. There was almost nothing on the surface to indicate that anything unusual was going on. Early structural analysts, in fact, had borrowed heavily from the conceptual language and techniques of various branches of conventional social science – in particular, small group research, game theory, general systems theory, epidemiology, interorganizational studies, and sociometry. Hence, there were no easy clues that could be used to distinguish between structural and nonstructural work.

Ironically, it was probably the sheer complexity of their two principal *methodological* tools – algebraic modeling and multidimensional scaling – that finally forced structural analysts to begin articulating the *theoretical* underpinnings of the framework they were developing. Since earlier forms of structuralism could not be easily translated into a set of explicit methodological rules, they had had relatively little impact on the actual conduct of empirical research. By contrast, North American structuralists had been preoccupied with *tool building*: constructing and testing new techniques for modeling the relations among elements within structures. Since most social scientists had been trained in methods that assumed that the elementary parts of a system were, for practical purposes, independent (e.g., statistical models), this work struck them as abstruse or exotic – certainly nothing that might be directly relevant to their own research practice. Hence, it was only when these structuralist tools had been honed through application to real data and commonly accepted research problems that conventional social scientists had begun to recognize that structural modeling was not simply a new way of doing the same thing, but embodied fundamentally different assumptions about how one goes about interpreting social reality. It was, in some sense, through articulating these differences – and drawing parallels to work taking place in Europe – that North American structural analysts first became fully aware of themselves as a distinct scientific community.

Structural analysis: an emerging paradigm and its implications

Over the course of its history, sociology has nurtured a wide variety of analytic styles. Although, at first glance, these "frameworks" or "traditions" appear quite different, most reflect very similar ideas about the goals of social inquiry, the appropriateness of particular methods, and the relative importance of specific research problems or issues. Thus, although the first impression of contemporary sociology often is of a welter of contradictory and conflicting ideas, models, and trends, beneath the surface there is a broad pool of agreement with respect to fundamental issues. In this sense, most approaches to doing sociology are best thought of as *interpretive schools* rather than paradigms.

The root of this apparent consensus among contemporary interpretive schools lies in the fact that they fundamentally accept the nominalist idea that somehow we can derive, a priori, a series of *categories* of actors, forms of *action*, and *roles* that can be shown intuitively to correspond to groups, events, and relationships in the real world. For most sociologists, for instance, there is nothing inherently problematic about the notion of "social class": classes are real, almost palpable. If we find a lower-than-expected association between some phenomenon – say, voting behavior – and class, then we must have made some error in operationalization or measuring our variables. If we discover that models based on social class, no matter how defined, are only weakly predictive – and this is frequently true – then some intervening factor must be at work. We must not, they assume, have adequately controlled for race, or region, or age, or whatever. Our sample must be improperly drawn, our data fouled, or our statistical techniques inappropriate. Categories, they imply, are sacrosanct and, consequently, as Howell noted (Chapter 3), conventional sociologists spend most of their time attempting to predict from one set of weak relationships among variables to another.

Structuralism in general – and structural analysis in particular – proposes a very different way of looking at things. Instead of assuming that classes or other categories of actors are real in themselves, structural analysts begin by recognizing that there are underlying *relationships* among the elementary parts of a social system that constrain their interactions with one another and shape the patterns of behavior in which they engage. Individuals, groups, and organizations, it maintains, are bound up with one another, simultaneously, in a number of quite different ways. Models of social structures must be designed in such a way that they reflect this, but, at the same time, allow analysts to resolve sometimes reinforcing and sometimes divergent *dimensions* of interaction into coherent and consistent patterns.

Categories and networks

In attempting to understand how this can be done, structural sociologists have tended to emphasize the *morphology* of the set of relationships that define a particular social structure. The central tenet of the structural analytic approach is that the form of a set of relationships will broadly determine or condition the effective boundaries between sets of actors, the range of action they will deem appropriate under various circumstances, and the regular or recurrent types of exchanges or other behavior in which they are most likely to engage (Cook, 1982). Thus, for structural analysts, classes do not simply exist: categories of actors are meaningful only to the extent that they reflect – or, as Blau (1981) says, "emerge from" – observed patterns of interaction. If individuals or groups are mutually *embedded* in a set of relations – that is, if they are tied together by participation in a common social form such as marriage or if they engage in recurrent contacts with one another such as the exchange of goods – we have reason to assign them to a particular category and expect them to behave in a specified way. Where no patterns of this kind are observed, we are not justified in doing so.

Scientific models are reductions, in both scale and detail, of the observable world. In creating them, model builders must therefore select those aspects of reality they want to represent in a given case and those which, for these purposes, they choose to ignore. Structural analysts recognize that we can arbitrarily create an almost unlimited number of categories to which we can assign individuals, groups, or organizations. Having made such assignments, we can then define attributes that will be shared to a greater or lesser degree by the members of these categories. By treating attributes as variables, we can then attempt to predict their orderly distribution across these sets. But if the classificatory schema we use do not reflect some robust property of the environment we are trying to model – that is, if categories are not more than random collections of elements or if their boundaries are improperly drawn – the results of any statistical tests we apply to relationships between these variables will be weak or inconclusive. By analyzing the morphology of systems, structural analysts are saying, we can uncover the forces that mobilize individual and collective actors and, hence, make our selection of categories more meaningful.

Thus, structural analysts argue, social classes cannot simply be aggregated together on the basis of some relatively arbitrary criterion such as income or occupation. They must consist of sets of individuals or groups sharing particular relationships (e.g., kinship ties, common institutional connections) over time. These relationships or exchanges – bounded ties or emanations – form patterns that can then be analyzed to determine structurally equivalent or structurally similar actors (Berkowitz and Heil, 1980; Berkowitz, 1982).

The specific types of ties that will allow us to specify patterns of class membership thus become, in each case, a matter for theoretical and empirical investigation. In given places during specific epochs, family connections – and the concrete access they provide to land or patronage – may be the most important dimension structuring class membership (Bodemann, Chapter 8). During others, a combination of mercantile ties, kinship links, and ethnic group bonds may be critical (Berkowitz, 1975). Although the concrete dimensions that analysts employ in uncovering patterns of class membership may vary in each instance, the notion that a class consists of a particular set of positions within a structure remains constant.

Structural analysts employ this same analytic strategy – what is called *clustering* – when they want to identify a number of different kinds of individual and collective actors. But a larger problem remains: If we stipulate categories on the basis of the *positions* their members occupy within a global system, we must also be concerned with how localized groups and structures come together to constitute a larger whole. Given, for instance, that we are able to cluster families occupying like positions within a village, can we then find a way of linking these clusters together into an overarching class structure?

This is the problem of "embedding the particular in the general" (Berkowitz, 1982). In addition to its gross morphology, every social structure has local or particular properties. Because they deal with presumably independent units, conventional model builders usually ignore this issue or treat local variation only as a source of measurement error. This can be misleading. Assume, for instance, that we are interested in the differential employment patterns of male and female rural–urban migrants in a rapidly industrializing society. We suspect that these are strongly influenced by the division of labor within households. Further assume that some part of the study population is organized into multidomicile, extended family households whereas the rest consists of nuclear families living in separate dwellings. A sample is drawn based, in the usual North American fashion, on the "number of related persons living under one roof." Respondents are selected from each unit and are interviewed about their employment histories. Unless a conventional researcher has some exogenous reason for being sensitive to the fact that *some* domiciles are linked together into larger structures, or unless some predetermined categorical distinction happens to coincide with this difference in household form, the tendency would be to lump all respondents together and to ignore these local variations. If work histories and reports about household labor were then analyzed, results would be likely to be inconclusive, not because of measurement error in the usual sense but because we were measuring different things.

Several important conceptual and methodological differences, then, underlie this apparently simple disjuncture in the ways in which structural and conventional sociologists define categories of actors. Having decided to focus on the relations among units rather than attributes, structural sociologists are forced to think *sociologistically*, that is, to draw inferences about the behavior of elements (*parts*) from aspects of the overall structure of systems (*wholes*). Most sociologists – indeed, most social scientists – reason *psychologistically*: They assume that systems (wholes) are nothing more than the sum of the attributes of their elements (parts). This type of reasoning is often simpler: By drawing inferences about wholes from parts they are able to isolate events from the complexities of the contexts in which they occur. Structural sociologists have no such luxury: Sociologistic reasoning implies constraint and, hence, mutually determinative relations among elements at each of several levels within a structure. Systemic effects are thus an explicit part of the "real world" that structural sociologists attempt to model.

Once one accepts this basic idea, a plethora of new research questions opens up. If social structures consist of sets of elements related to one another by patterned relations, then we would expect alterations in the behavior of some subset of these elements to generate discernible impacts throughout the system so defined. In the simplest example, one element – let us call it A – might have an effect on B, which, in turn, might have a similar effect on C. Under these circumstances, structural sociologists would be tempted to infer *transitivity* and conclude that A has exerted an indirect, second-order effect on C.

A series of indirect effects of this kind has important consequences for the overall structure of a system of relations. Take the example of friendship ties: If A is a friend to B, and B is a friend to C, then, by transitivity, A is involved in some sort of friendship with C – "friends' friends are friends." If we allow for N-order effects, we would expect to discover an overarching structure of friendship in this population that consisted of large clusters of individuals loosely linked together into long chains. This friendship structure would not, of course, function like a tight-knit group: We would not expect people who were, say, four-distant to behave like intimates. But structural sociologists have found that at some high orders of remove these kinds of weakly defined friendship networks can be used to obtain information, locate resources, and focus search processes (Granovetter, 1973, 1974; Lin and Dayton, 1976). When looked at in terms of kinship and strong friendship ties, structural analysts have discovered that these same indirect effects are the stuff out of which modern communities are built (Wellman, 1979; Wellman, Carrington, and Hall, Chapter 6).

A more complex example of the consequences of the propagation of effects within a social system would entail something like the impact of local structural change on the relations between large subgroups within a population. Consider the case of two highly endogamous and close-knit ethnic communities. Posit the creation of only a single mutually recognized marriage tie between them. Children from this marriage would not be wholly subsumed within either group, but would constitute some type of bridge. Both groups, moreover, would lose a certain amount of internal coherence as a result of the existence of this bridge: Over time, we would expect it to act as an avenue for cultural contact and, hence, for the interpenetration of group attitudes, customs, and cultural forms.

Levels and units

In larger scope, sociologistic definitions of group structure and recognition of the role played by transitive effects in establishing morphology lead us to the *problem of levels* and the *question of units of analysis*. In his famous monograph, *Rules of Sociological Method*, Durkheim defined a set of objects of study that are *external* to individuals' consciousness and at the same time act to *constrain* their behavior. He referred to these as "social facts" and maintained that they could be distinguished from individual facts by their origins in *collective action* – either undertaken by the society as a whole or by one of several possible "intermediate groups" (Durkheim, 1964b: 1–13).

Durkheim thought of social and individual facts as quite distinct. But if indirect effects are taken into account, his formulation of the "levels problem" needs to be modified. Durkheim recognized that intermediate groups can overlap or even subsume one another (e.g., "physicians" and "professionals") and thus that social effects can originate in groups of varying scope and complexity. But he did not systematically follow through on the implications of this: He did not see that if what he called "social facts" could be generated at each of several distinct layers of group organization, then some social effects must override or dominate others. This is why in discussing sociologistic and psychologistic reasoning we spoke of *directions* of inference (whole–part, part–whole) rather than "social" and "nonsocial" facts. Given this, how we go about establishing in which layer of systemic organization particular effects originate becomes problematic. If there are several such layers, which is likely to generate specific social facts?

Observe, for instance, an industrial process such as printing, which is undergoing rapid technological change. At the level of the industry as a whole, various parts of the process – typesetting, proofreading galleys, setting up pages, and so on – are being shifted about between enterprises as each new technological advance alters the relative cost of performing a particular task inside the boundaries of a firm or purchasing it outside. Markets are forming and falling apart. At the level of firms, departments or divisions are being reorganized so as to maximize benefits or minimize transfer costs, or both. And at the level of the shop, work groups and, hence, the relationships between workers, are being re-formed and reorganized. The effects of large-scale changes at the industry level, such as selling plants or introducing new equipment, are being broadcast downward: Departmental or divisional organization and the composition of work groups are being altered in response to them. Norms or standards of efficiency, measures of output, and accounting procedures are being changed and workers' views of one another and of the nature of their occupations and careers are being transformed as well. At the same time, lower-level social facts such as workers' attitudes are being felt in the form of demands on unions to control the rate at which new equipment is introduced into the workplace, new work and wage schedules are being created, and existing technology and jobs are being phased out. Bargaining and strike action by unions to achieve these ends places constraints on management's responses to changes in technology and organization. All of these interactions, moreover, are taking place in a context where craft production and small shops have been the historic norm, and this is becoming less common.

Social change of this kind, going on as it does within several system layers at the same time, is difficult to capture. Effects generated across levels are the most difficult to grasp. Without sharp analytic tools and a well-defined framework for assessing effects, structural sociologists argue, complex systemic effects such as these are likely to be lost.

Recent extensions of the problem of levels have centered on even subtler issues. Given a knowledge of the kinds of events that can the generated throughout a complex structure, how can we determine the appropriate *units of analysis* for capturing these events? Put another way, if groups can overlap both within and between levels, and if events can be propagated across them, how do we decide which of several possible definitions of the *boundaries* between sets of elements is the correct one for exploring a given phenomenon (Berkowitz, 1982; Laumann and Marsden, 1982)?

For instance, assume that we are interested in the organization of effective decision-making units within an economy.[4] We know from observation that there are hundreds of thousands of legal entities called firms that produce or sell goods and services, both to one another and to consumers. However, we also know that many of these firms are not independent, but are divisions within, or wholly owned subsidiaries of, larger units and are thus not free to make their own production or pricing decisions. Some of these decisions are taken at the level of what industrial organization economists call "enterprises" (sets of firms operating under common control), and some, de facto, are arrived at in the most general terms at the level of "groups" (sets of well-articulated enterprises, usually connected with core financial institutions). Since treating independent firms and ones that are part of multifirm enterprises as equivalent would be misleading if we were interested in something like management style or profitability, it is necessary to devise some consistent way of establishing the boundaries between enterprises. Similarly, since different groups may evolve distinct criteria for assessing enterprise performance, we must find some appropriate way of mapping enterprises into groups.

Structural sociologists have answered these and closely related questions in a variety of ways, but have utilized fundamentally similar approaches and techniques in doing so. Firms can be mapped into enterprises, for example, on the basis of ownership of common stock or shared directorships, or both (Berkowitz, Carrington, Kotowitz, and Waverman, 1978/79). Groups can be discriminated by virtue of their indirect connections with one another (Levine, 1972), relative centrality (Mintz and Schwartz, 1981), or by the fact that they form connected components of a graph. In each case, structural sociologists have (a) developed measures of relatedness that reflect the dimensions of the decision-making process at issue and (b) established criteria of robustness and reliability in an attempt to validate particular boundaries between subsets. In a number of cases, the arrays generated by these procedures have been juxtaposed to behavioral data and assessments have been made of the fit between boundary definitions and outcomes.

Structure and location

At the point where they have had a satisfactory map of the broad morphology of the relations representing a specific structural dimension and have had well-defined boundaries between units of analysis and among levels of interaction, structural analysts have then turned their attention to a class of problems centering around the relative roles played by specific individuals, groups, or organizations in channeling flows of information throughout a social structure. Some types of social effects, such as bilateral exchanges of goods or transactions that take place within a highly specific market, are confined to one locale or neighborhood. Others propagate throughout a system and shape or alter the behavior of every element within it to some degree. Structural sociologists recognize that, because of their locations within this system, some elements will be better able to control this flow of effects than others and, accordingly, have devised ways of identifying them.

The term *centrality* refers to the most important locational properties of elements that structural analysts have been able to discover to date. Centrality is the relative central location of given units within a structure. Versions of the concept were originally applied to emergent leadership positions within small groups: Early researchers designed a variety of experiments in which patterns of communication were restructured in such a way that different individuals would occupy "hubs" or the ends of "spokes" under different laboratory conditions (Freeman, 1979). More powerful and general ways of using the idea followed.

In its earliest reconceptualizations, centrality was interpreted in terms of *path-distances*: given a network in which every node is linked to every other at some remove (i.e., a *connected graph*), there exists a *path* (sequence of ties) of some length between every pair. If we compute the path-distances from all others to some target node, we have one kind of centrality measure: *reachability*.

Reachability comes close to capturing what we intuitively mean when we say someone is "at the center of things." Individual or collective actors who are difficult to reach tend to take a long time to find out what is going on. If, for instance, we modeled the flows of information among members of a scientific specialty group, we would expect scientists who were distant from others to be behind the times, working on problems others considered less critical, and, at least sometimes, not being recognized for their work because others had published similar findings before them.

The simplest elaboration of this concept is the notion of *degree*. Where two nodes are directly reachable from one another – that is, where they are only one path-distance apart – we refer to them as adjacent. The number of other nodes adjacent to a given node is its degree. When an element is close to others in this sense, it has a high potential capacity to influence them. Thus, for instance, whereas banks in the United States frequently own controlling blocks of shares in industrial corporations, their counterparts in Canada do not. Despite this, Canadian banks play an extremely central role in their economy because of the extraordinary number of first-order directorship ties they have to industrials.[5]

Structural sociologists concerned with the relative strategic importance of individual or collective actors have developed another notion of centrality that is based on the shortest paths (or geodesics) between pairs of nodes. All points falling on the shortest path – or on equally short paths – joining two nodes can be said to fall between them. By calculating the *betweenness* of given nodes, that is, how many paths they fall within, we can estimate the extent to which they are able to disrupt or distort system-wide communications (Freeman, 1979).

Extensions of these basic measures take into account things such as the centrality attributable to adjacency, that is, the extent to which an element's influence on communications is enhanced by the centrality of its neighbors

(Bonacich, 1972; Mintz and Schwartz, 1981), the isolatability or "inverse centrality" of nodes (Freeman, 1978/79), and a range of similar conditions.

The system level

Some measures of nodal properties, such as reachability or degree, can be transposed to the system level. We can talk, for instance, about the *compactness*, or average reachability of nodes within a network. Structuralists have devised a number of other measures of this kind (Hage and Harary, 1983). However, probably the conceptually and methodologically most important work undertaken so far on the integration of elements within a larger structure has followed an entirely different tack: *algebraic modeling.* Consider a network model of one specific structural dimension – say, job contacts in a population (Delany, Chapter 16). Define all such contacts as a relation of type J. Second-order contacts can then be represented by JJ or J^2, third-order ones by JJJ, or J^3, and so on. Add to this a second relation of type C, representing citations. Assume that we are interested in the extent to which individuals' embeddedness in their job-contact networks and scientific specialty groups coincide. By calculating all possible *composition* operations defined on these two graphs simultaneously, we can, in effect, algebraically compound these different types of relations. By reducing this algebra to a simpler form, we can then uncover sets of structurally equivalent and structurally similar actors, that is, nodes playing the same or similar roles – for example, liaison persons, job and information brokers – given the confluence of *both* dimensions of this joint structure (Lorrain and White, 1971).

More recent algebraic approaches include what is called *blockmodeling.* The weakness of algebraic techniques that depend on strict compounding is that they presume that all structurally relevant ties are actually made. This is an extremely strong assumption. In our previous example, for instance, it would require that all persons currently in the job market and actively publishing also appear in the citation data. Given lags in publication time, different work schedules in subfields, and so on, this would be extremely unlikely. Moreover, since the techniques involved require that ties be positively made, lost or missing data could lead us to very misleading conclusions.

The alternative proposed by blockmodelers is (a) to focus on the holes in a structure – to group elements together on the basis of their nonconnectedness to others, and (b) to use a more permissive standard of what it means to be unconnected:

A blockmodel is a structural abstraction of a data network.
In a blockmodel single "model nodes," called *blocs*, are used to

> represent *sets* of nodes in a *data network*. Ties between data
> nodes are represented by c graphs or matrices, on the same
> p nodes, then the model consists of an *image*, with c types of
> ties on b blocs $(b < p)$. (Berkowitz, 1982:133)

Blockmodels are deemed to be adequate if there is some mapping of the
p nodes into the b blocs such that the ties in the *image graph* will fit with those
in the data graph. Thus, given a fit that is less than perfect, we can provide
greater flexibility in the modeling process (Carrington, Heil, and Berkowitz,
1979/80).

Algebraic techniques are extremely general and have, consequently,
allowed structural analysts to test out a wide variety of hypotheses about
relationships among parts of structures. Blockmodeling in particular,
structural analysts have found, is sufficiently powerful to accommodate a fair
amount of local variation within a well-defined global pattern (Breiger, 1979;
Breiger and Pattison, 1978; White, Boorman, and Breiger, 1976). It has
therefore proved to be a very useful tool in circumstances where levels of
interaction within a system are problematic (Snyder and Kick, 1979).

Although locational measures such as centrality can be used to examine
some dimensions of social structure and algebraic modeling is useful in
exploring others, there is a class of systemic effects for which these tools, and
the conceptualizations upon which they are based, are simply inappropriate.
Consider the structural bases of phenomena such as individual or collective
intergenerational mobility, marriage patterns, or job markets (Levine and
Spadaro, Chapter 17; Tepperman, Chapter 15; Delany, Chapter 16). The
events that produce these phenomena – emanations or the making or
breaking of bonded ties – occur at relatively low rates over time. At a
maximum, intergenerational mobility can happen once, marriage or divorces
perhaps a dozen times, and the activation of job-contact networks perhaps
two or three times this during an average individual's lifetime. In a well-
bounded population, such as a small village or an elite group, it is possible to
encompass all the dimensions of these phenomena and to study them using
locational measures or algebraic techniques. But in any larger structure, the
ties in one's model would be too sparse: Measures such as relative degree
would yield such similar results as to be uninterpretable and blockmodels
would tend to be vacuous. Moreover, in each instance, individual tie
formation occurs within a shifting context: Intergenerational mobility takes
place over periods where economic and occupational change is likely to
occur, marriage choices are altered by demographic trends, and job contacts
are affected by a wide variety of factors.

Consider these phenomena sociologistically: Each involves an overarching
structure that is changing in response to powerful social effects that are only
detectable over long time periods. Although actions taken by individuals,

groups, or organizations can have an impact on these effects, they cannot do so quickly or easily: There are long feedback times associated with individual actions. Thus, individual or collective actors are trapped into making judgments and formulating choices on the basis of the options they perceive at the time.

Since a number of quite different structural effects are likely to come into play over long time periods, it is difficult to think about them deterministically. Some, but not all, of these effects can be anticipated, but their relative impact on structural parameters is hard to assess. Thus, failing some highly detailed knowledge of the processes and mechanisms at work, our best approach is to try to draw inferences about why actors behave as they do within the limits imposed at higher levels.

Structural analysts have used two kinds of tools for doing this: *multidimensional scaling* and *microsimulation*. Multidimensional scaling rests on an extension of the notion of social distances. Conceive of a matrix in which the rows and columns are elements and the cell entries are the number of contacts between them. It would be possible, but difficult, to find a graph that would satisfy all of these distances simultaneously. Given a network of N nodes, we can generate a perfect or exact representation of these distances in $N - 1$ dimensions. But given even a modest number of nodes, the resulting image would be well beyond one with which we could reasonably expect human beings to cope. Thus, in order to make sense out of what we have, it is necessary to compress these distances in such a way that they will "yield a more-or-less accurate three-dimensional picture ... [by utilizing] techniques generalized from those used in finding distances in normal or Euclidean spaces" (Berkowitz, 1982: 84). This compression is done by reducing the number of dimensions in the solution and only introducing those minimal distortions in interpoint distances necessary to bring this about. The representations that result from this procedure then constitute a general map to which individual or collective distances can be compared.

For instance, consider the case in which rows represent mothers' reported ethnic group memberships and columns show those of fathers. Off-diagonal entries indicate interethnic marriages. Use the number of these entries as a measure of interconnection. Plot highly connected ethnic groups closer together and weakly connected ones further apart. The resulting, say, three-dimensional mapping would constitute a resolution of all these intergroup marriage distances simultaneously. Compare the distances between any two pairs of ethnic groups and one has a roughly metric ("quasi-metric") notion of their relative position within the interethnic marriage market.

Microsimulations can be employed where more of the basic mechanisms underlying structural shifts are known. Since two of the best examples of these approaches have been given in the chapters by Howell (Chapter 3) and Delany (Chapter 16), only a broad outline of the techniques involved seems appropriate here. Briefly, researchers using simulations first establish the units whose activities they wish to model. This can be done either analytically or through boundary-establishing techniques of the kind referred to earlier. Relevant processes are then defined and embodied in a set of procedures. These should reflect conditions or events to which units will be subject. For instance, since Howell is dealing with kinship, in her case these conditions have to do with births, deaths, marriages, and so on. These processes are then constrained by intrinsic parameters where these are known. For Howell, this would include things like biological limits on women's fertility. Assumptions are introduced about the size and composition of the population of interacting units, and outcomes are produced over some specified time period. Results of these simulations are then compared to known parameters for a population or to ones that can be shown for a series of heuristic cases. Analytic results are derived from these comparisons, and new aspects of processes uncovered through these procedures are incorporated into the model.

The long-term purpose of structural modeling is, of course, to allow analysts to begin describing how the behavior of elements within a system is constrained by morphology and social processes so as to yield consistent and recurrent patterns. At the point where this can be done, it becomes practical for structural sociologists to formalize their understanding of the factors that produce these patterns in the form of a set of process equations. Despite some promising beginnings along these lines – such as Burt's work on market constraints and directorate ties (Burt, 1983) or White's reconstruction of the mechanisms involved in market formation (Chapter 9) – structuralists have, as yet, no clear general way of approaching the problem of behavior under constraint. This, however, is clearly the direction in which structural sociology is headed.

For most sociologists, of course, questions about the integration of parts and wholes and the underlying shifts that generate changes in structure are simply not issues. Variables are operationalized in terms of some set of observables and levels, and units or structural constraints are left to take care of themselves. This means that, from a structural analytic perspective, much of the work going on in contemporary empirical sociology is ill-defined. Although most sociologists pay lip service to the notion that social structure constrains individual action, the idea is simply not relevant to them under most circumstances. Most studies of group interaction or attitudes are abstracted from the contexts in which they occur. Since they are not rooted in concrete observables and since they seem to largely depend on researchers' preconceptions, conventional notions of community are largely ephemeral. Markets are largely left to economists. Social change is a catchall term for a range of observed differences in attitudes. behaviors, expectations, and national economies or polities. Intellectual life and social mobility are usually perceived psychologistically. In short, conventional sociology is, in large measure, unwilling to take on the hard questions.

Structure and substance

The most frequently voiced criticism of structural analysis is that it consists of "methods without theory." This criticism is rooted in the fact that, for many conventional sociologists, theorizing it is something theorists do, not a part of actual research practice. Apart from obligatory references to the appropriate sociological saints, most make few attempts to join limited theories – consisting of empirical generalizations or focused hypotheses – to general bodies of theory. True, in the area of deviance, for instance, one talks about conflict theories of crime or labeling theory, or the like. But the things referred to in this way are not theories in the ordinary sense of a set of law-like statements about the real world. They are more nearly statements of belief or orientation. Indeed, sociology does not have a well-formed and consistent philosophy of science – either on paper or in practice.

Methods are thought of in the same way: Both their development and application are seen as the proper province of a special class of experts called "methodologists." Most ordinary empirically oriented sociologists not only do not fashion their own tools, but they are not even aware in most cases of the deeper assumptions underlying them. Methods are simply there – on the shelf or in the computer package. Moreover, since graduate courses in theory or methods are segregated from one another, these sorts of attitudes toward research and practice are perpetuated over time.

So when conventional sociologists say that structural sociology consists of "methods without theory," they presume a particular view of research that structural analysts do not share. In the conventional worldview, one can either be sophisticated in the way one uses ideas – and, hence, theorize – or become mired in the prosaic business of actually gathering and analyzing data, at which point, if one uses some apparently complicated computer-driven method, one is labeled a methodologist. Implicit in this is the mistaken notion that there really are two kinds of sociology: rigorous sociology and interesting sociology. By implication, there is little ground upon which the practitioners of the former and latter can meet.

Structural analysts begin with a different perspective on the relationship between theorizing and research practice. Theory construction, they assert, is intimately bound up with the creation of appropriate methodological tools. Consider the case of algebraic modeling. Before Lorrain and White (1971) found a practical way of determining structurally equivalent actors within large and complex structures, organizational analysts were limited to dealing with the concept in the abstract: There was no way that structural equivalence could be examined concretely except in very regular, simple, and therefore theoretically and substantively uninteresting cases. By creating a method for rigorously examining *actual* organizational structures too complex to be understood through simple inspection, they made it possible for us to (a) identify anomalies or inconsistencies in the application of the term, (b) find instances where the concept-in-use needed to be modified to be consistent, and (c) discover extensions of it (e.g., structural similarity) that could be substantively explored in their own right. With the development of blockmodeling, this process could be carried further owing to its greater flexibility as a tool for uncovering categories of like actors (White et al., 1976). Formal modeling techniques then allowed for the extension of the concept and its generalization to a range of related ideas (White, Chapter 9). At each stage in the process, methodological advances fed back into theorizing so as to clarify the context within which theory was being developed.

The approach to theory-building, of course, is much closer to that normally associated with natural science than the one that has been traditional in sociology. Physicists or astronomers, or whatever, are accustomed to the idea that specific new devices will extend the range of their theorizing to encompass new or previously intractable phenomena – and they expect that this will occur when new tools are constructed. Social scientists in general, and sociologists in particular, do not anticipate these kinds of forced extensions of their theories because their models are seldom so closely specified that this will occur. Hence, they tend to think of theory in the most general terms and data analysis in the most particular. By joining the act of theorizing to the activity of tool building, structural analysts have gone a long way toward embodying the general in the particular and, hence, placing social sceince methods on the same footing as they are in other areas of scientific inquiry. This is essential to constructing tightly articulated hypotheses and, thus, laying out the outlines of a paradigm.

A final word

Despite some impressive beginnings, then, formal structural analyses of sociological phenomena are still in their infancy. Thus, the range of problems structural sociologists have dealt with to date has been, in some ways, quite restricted. We have as yet, for instance, only the first convincing structural analyses of legislative behavior, ethnic organization, or a variety of other political phenomena. This is significant because a number of the issues involved in these areas are ideally suited for treatment in a structural analytic fashion, and conventional approaches have more or less reached the limits of what they can do without resolving important anomalies. No structural sociologist has, to my knowledge, looked at schisms in fundamentalist churches (see Stark and Bainbridge, 1980), at the evolution of legal systems, or at a host of other substantive problems to which structuralist conceptualizations and methods seem particularly well adapted. Sampson's (1968) data on monasteries has been analyzed and re-analyzed a number of times, Heinz and Laumann (1982) have studied the organization of legal specialists, but this work, although important, has not begun to exhaust the possibilities for work on what has been referred to as institutional domains in social order.

Given its relatively brief history as a paradigm, structural analysis has been able to deal with an impressively wide variety of substantive problems. We have tried to convey a sense of this here. Despite this broad scope, however, the chapters included in this collection could not reflect all the kinds of work that might properly appear under the heading of structural sociology. Some of this is well covered elsewhere (Leinhardt, 1977; Holland and Leinhardt, 1979; Burt, 1982; Burt and Minor, 1983), and some cannot be easily put across in a relatively nontechnical treatment. Moreover, given the rate at which new work in the area is being done, we have probably reached the point where no single volume could do this. One of the coeditors of this book (Wellman) has spent a considerable amount of time editing an informal journal (*Connection*) that has kept track of what is going on. This task is becoming increasingly difficult. Perhaps scientific revolutions, like revolutions in other aspects of human affairs, are, to borrow Meisel's term, "accelerations in history," and, during the current phase in the development of structural analysis, trying to "keep up" would be like Charlie Chaplin's attempt to oil and adjust the machines in *Modern Times* – do-able, but futile.

Although much good structural analytic work is still at the stage of paper-and-pencil verbal models, it is clear from the history of work in the area that real advances have been made only when the process of joining theoretical model building and tool construction have been in full operation. In this sense, the completion of the scientific revolution that is implicit in structural analysis must await further formalizations that will allow for explicit juxtapositions of empirical findings to well-defined formal models. Without this, ironically, the structural analytic work under way at the present time would run the risk of being characterized not as a collection of methods in search of a theory, but as a collection of findings in search of a paradigm.

NOTES

1. For a detailed discussion of the implications of holism in practice, see Wellman's overview (Chapter 2).
2. The term is used here in its sociological sense to refer to a graph consisting of nodes or points and a set of relations or edges defined on them. Mathematicians prefer to reserve the term "network" for a class of directed graphs with valences associated with edges.

3. See Harary, Norman, and Cartwright (1965) and Berkowitz (1982) for a detailed treatment of the mathematical and sociological implications of these graphs.
4. See Berkowitz, Chapter 10, for an extended discussion of some of the issues raised here.
5. Degree can be standardized for the size of a network by computing a given node's relative degree, i.e., its degree as a proportion of all potential first-order contacts.

LITERATURE CITED

Berkowitz, S. D. *The Dynamics of Elite Structure: A Critique of C. Wright Mills' "Power Elite" Model.* Ph.D. diss., Brandeis University, 1975.
  An Introduction to Structural Analysis: The Network Approach to Social Research. Toronto: Butterworths, 1982.
Berkowitz, S. D., Peter J. Carrington, Yehuda Kotowitz, and Leonard Waverman. "The Determination of Enterprise Groupings through Combined Ownership and Directorship Ties." *Social Networks* 1 (1978–9): 391–413.
Berkowitz, S. D., and Greg H. Heil. "Dualities in Methods of Social Network Research." University of Toronto, Structural Analysis Programme Working Paper 18 (rev.). Toronto, 1980.
Blau, Peter, "Introduction: Diverse Views of Social Structure and Their Common Denominator." In Peter M. Blau and Robert K. Merton (eds.), *Continuities in Structural Inquiry.* London and Beverly Hills, Calif.: Sage, 1981.
Bonacich, Phillip. "Technique for Analyzing Overlapping Memberships." In Herbert L. Costner (ed.), *Sociological Methodology, 1972.* San Francisco: Jossey-Bass, 1972.
Breiger, Ronald L. "Toward an Operational Theory of Community Elite Structure." *Quality and Quantity* 13 (1979): 21–47.
Breiger, Ronald L., and Philippa E. Pattison. "The Joint Role Structure of Two Communities' Elites." *Sociological Methods and Research* 7 (1978): 213–26.
Burt, Ronald S. *Toward a Structural Theory of Action: Network Models of Social Structure, Perception, and Action.* New York: Academic Press, 1982.
  Corporate Profits and Cooptation: Networks of Market Constraints and Directorate Ties in the American Economy. New York: Academic Press, 1983.
Burt, Ronald S., and M. J. Minor (eds.). *Applied Network Analysis.* Beverly Hills, Calif.: Sage, 1983.
Carrington, Peter J., Greg H. Heil, and S. D. Berkowitz. "A Goodness-of-Fit Index for Blockmodels." *Social Networks* 2 (1979–80): 219–34.
Cook, Karen S. "Network Structures from an Exchange Perspective." In Peter Marsden and Nan Lin (eds.), *Social Structure and Network Analysis.* Beverly Hills: Sage, 1982.
Durkheim, Émile. *The Division of Labor in Society.* New York: Free Press, 1964a.
  Rules of Sociological Method. New York: Free Press, 1964b.
Fararo, Thomas J., and Morris H. Sunshine. *A Study of a Biased Friendship Net.* Syracuse: Syracuse University Press, 1964.
Freeman, Linton. "Centrality in Social Networks: Conceptual Clarification." *Social Networks* 1 (1979): 215–39.

Granovetter, Mark. "The Strength of Weak Ties." *American Journal of Sociology* 78 (1973): 1360–80.

Getting A Job. Cambridge, Mass.: Harvard University Press, 1974.

Hage, Per, and Frank Harary. *Structural Models in Anthropology*. Cambridge: Cambridge University Press, 1983.

Harary, Frank, Robert Z. Norman, and Dorwin Cartwright. *Structural Models: An Introduction to the Theory of Directed Graphs*. New York: Wiley 1965.

Heinz, John, and Edward Lauman. *Chicago Lawyers*. New York and Chicago: Russell Sage Foundation and American Bar Association, 1982.

Holland, Paul, and Samuel Leinhardt (eds.). *Perspectives on Social Networks*. New York: Academic Press, 1979.

Jakobson, Roman. *Selected Writings*. The Hague: Mouton, 1962.

Jakobson, Roman, and Morris Halle. *Fundamentals of Language*. The Hague: Mouton, 1956.

Kuhn, Thomas. *The Structure of Scientific Revolutions*. Chicago: University of Chicago Press, 1970.

Laumann, Edward O., and Peter V. Marsden. "Microstructural Analysis in Interorganizational Systems." *Social Networks* 4 (1982): 329–48.

Leinhardt, Samuel (ed.). *Social Networks: A Developing Paradigm*. New York: Academic Press, 1977.

Levine, Joel H. "The Sphere of Influence." *American Sociological Review* 37 (1972): 14–27.

Lévi-Strauss, Claude. *The Elementary Structures of Kinship*. Boston: Beacon Press, 1969.

Lin, Nan, and Paul W. Dayton. "The Urban Communication Network and Social Stratification: A Small World Experiment." Paper presented at the annual meetings of the International Communication Association, Portland, Oregon, 1976.

Lorrain, François, and Harrison C. White. "The Structural Equivalence of Individuals in Social Networks." *Journal of Mathematical Sociology* 1 (1971): 49–80.

Marx, Karl. *Capital*. Moscow: Progress Publishers, n.d.

Mintz, Beth, and Michael Schwartz. "Interlocking Directorates and Interest Group Formation." *American Sociological Review* 46 (1981): 851–69.

The Power Structure of American Business. Chicago: University of Chicago Press, 1985.

Mitchell, J. Clyde. *Social Networks in Urban Situations: Analyses of Personal Relationships in Central African Towns*. Manchester: Manchester University Press, 1969.

Piaget, Jean. *Structuralism*. London: Routledge and Kegan Paul, 1971.

Rapoport, Anatol, and William J. Horvath. "A Study of a Large Sociogram." *Behavioral Science* 6 (1961): 279–91.

Sampson, S. F. "A Novitiate in a Period of Change." Ph.D. diss, Cornell University, 1968.

Simmel, Georg. "The Metropolis and Mental Life." In Kurt H. Wolff, *The Sociology of Georg Simmel*. Glencoe, Ill.: Free Press, 1950.

Snyder, David, and Edward L. Kick. "Structural Position in the World System and

Economic Growth, 1955–70: A Multiple Network Analysis of Transnational Transactions." *American Journal of Sociology* 84 (1979): 1096–126.

Stark, R., and W. S. Bainbridge. "Networks of Faith: Interpersonal Bonds and Recruitment to Cults and Sects." *American Journal of Sociology* 85 (1980): 1376–95.

Wellman, Barry. "The Community Question: The Intimate Networks of East Yorkers." *American Journal of Sociology* 84 (1979): 1201–31.

White, Harrison C., Scott A. Boorman, and Ronald L. Breiger. "Social Structure from Multiple Networks I: Blockmodels of Roles and Positions." *American Journal of Sociology* 81 (1976): 730–80.

Notes on contributors

S. D. BERKOWITZ teaches sociology at the University of Vermont. He is the coauthor and editor of *Canada's Third Option* (1978), the author and editor of *Models and Myths in Canadian Sociology* (1984), and the author of *An Introduction to Structural Analysis* (1982). He is currently conducting research on market structure and new tools for analyzing intercorporate connections.

Y. MICHAL BODEMANN is Associate Professor of Sociology, University of Toronto. He has conducted fieldwork for many years in Sardinia (Italy) and has recently taught at the Free University, West Berlin. His major interests include Southern Italian society, ethnicity, and theoretical issues within Marxism. His recent publications deal with the role of Jews in pre- and postwar Germany, Marx's conception of class, and problems of fieldwork.

RONALD L. BREIGER is Professor of Sociology at Cornell University and a Faculty Associate of the Cornell Institute for Social and Economic Research. His current work is in the areas of social stratification, the evolution of role structures, and the development of network theory and models for the aggregation of social categories.

ROBERT J. BRYM is Professor of Sociology, University of Toronto. His recent books include *Soviet Jewish Immigration and Soviet Nationality Policy* (with Victor Zaslavsky, 1983) and *The Structure of the Canadian Capitalist Class* (1985). He is currently researching class voting, editing (with T. B. Bottomore) *The Capitalist Class: An International Study*, and writing (with B. Fox) *Sociology in English Canada*.

PETER J. CARRINGTON teaches sociology at the University of Waterloo and consults on research methods and applications. His current work includes a study of the functioning of the Canadian juvenile court system and a study of Canadian intercorporate links and their relationship with corporate profits.

JOHN DELANY holds a B.A. from Brown University and a Ph.D. in sociology from Yale. He is currently an account supervisor for Fallon McElligott, a Minneapolis advertising agency. Prior to that he was Assistant Professor of Sociology and Industrial Relations at the University of Minnesota.

BONNIE H. ERICKSON, Professor of Sociology at the University of Toronto, is conducting a study, with T. A. Nosanchuk, of a duplicate bridge network in Ottawa-Hull. She is the author (with Nosanchuk) of *Understanding Data* and of a variety of articles on topics in structural analysis. Recent publications include "The Allocation of Esteem and Disesteem," *American Sociological Review* (1984) and "How High Is

Up? Calibrating Social Comparison in the Real World," *Journal of Personality and Social Psychology* (1985). She is currently examining the size and status composition of personal networks, the effects of personal network variables and dyad characteristics on access to help, and individual and network factors in age and gender stereotyping.

HARRIET FRIEDMANN is Associate Professor of Sociology at the University of Toronto. Her principal publications are in the political economy of agriculture, especially family labor in relation to capitalist and precapitalist economies, and in international political economy. Recent publications include "The Political Economy of Food," *American Journal of Sociology* (1982), "Patriarchal Commodity Production," *Social Analysis* (1986), and "The Family Farm and International Food Regimes," in Teodor Shanin, ed., *Peasants and Peasant Societies.*

ALAN HALL is a doctoral student in sociology at the University of Toronto. His major interests are in the structural constraints of social class on mental illness and the political-economic origins of psychiatric policy and practice. His dissertation centers on the relationship between changes in the labor process and class–mental health patterns in advanced capitalism.

LESLIE HOWARD is Associate Professor of Sociology at Whittier College. His work has focused on interdependence and dependency in interpersonal networks as these are constrained by larger political and productive structures and processes. Another part of his work has dealt with organizational constraints on interprofessional politics in psychiatric settings. He is currently working on the intersection of organizational theory and social reaction theory.

NANCY HOWELL is author of *The Search for an Abortionist* (1969) and *The Demography of the Dobe !Kung* (1979). She was educated at Harvard in the Social Relations Department, where they forgot to tell her about the boundaries in the field. Hence, she reads, writes, and teaches in the areas of biology, demography, anthropology, and sociology. She is Professor of Sociology at the University of Toronto.

JOEL H. LEVINE is Professor of Mathematical Social Science at Dartmouth College. He is the author of articles on social mobility, corporate interlocks, and structural methods, including "A Two Parameter Model of Interaction in Father–Son Mobility," *Behavioral Science* (1972); "The Sphere of Influence," *American Sociological Review* (1972); and "Joint-Space Analysis of 'Pick Any' Data: Analysis of Choices from an Unconstrained Set of Alternatives," *Psychometrika* (1979). He is also the author of *Levine's Atlas of Corporate Interlocks* (1985).

H. GILMAN MCCANN studied at Allegheny College and Princeton University, where he received a Ph.D. in 1974. He has taught at the University of California (Santa Cruz), Princeton, the University of New Mexico, and has been at the University of Vermont since 1974. His research specialty is the sociology of science, and he is the author of *Chemistry Transformed: The Paradigmatic Shift from Phlogiston to Oxygen* (1978) and the coauthor, with Eugene Johnsen, of "Acyclic Triplets and Social Structure in Complete Signed Digraphs," *Social Networks* (1982). His current research interest is scientific communication networks and their changes over time.

JOHN SPADARO is a software consultant specializing in accounting and data processing. He maintains an active involvement in research on structural methods and stratification. He is a graduate of Dartmouth College and lives in Kingston, Rhode Island.

LORNE TEPPERMAN is Professor of Sociology at the University of Toronto. His publications include *Social Mobility in Canada* (1975), *Crime Control* (1977), and (with David Bell) *The Roots of Disunity* (1979), *The Social World* (with R. J. Richardson, 1986) and *Understanding Canadian Society* (with James Scott, 1988). The book manuscripts are nearing completion, one on the life cycle and another on the computerization of social services (with John Gandy).

CHARLES TILLY directs the Center for Studies of Social Change at the New School for Social Research. His work deals with collective action and large-scale social change, especially in France and Britain since 1600. Among his recent books are *As Sociology Meets History* (1981), *Class Conflict and Collective Action* (1981) (coedited with Louise Tilley), *Big Structures, Large Processes, Huge Comparisons* (1984), and *The Contentious French* (1986).

BARRY WELLMAN is Professor at the Centre for Urban and Community Studies and the Department of Sociology, University of Toronto. His principal interest is the analysis of the effects of such large-scale phenomena as industrialization and capitalism on the structure and content of urban social networks. He has recently completed a series of papers on the network bases of social support and on the impact of domestic and paid work on men's and women's personal communities. He founded the International Network for Social Network Analysis in 1976 and continues as its Coordinator and as Editor of its informal journal, *Connections*.

DOUGLAS R. WHITE is Professor of Social Sciences at the University of California, Irvine. With colleagues at Irvine, he developed the autocorrelation approach to causal inference that has formed the basis for the cross-regional replication of a labor-intensification model of variation in the sexual division of agricultural labor. He is currently working (with Karl Reitz) on formalizations of connectivity and density-based homomorphisms for the blocking and scaling of actors and relations in social networks. He is currently preparing (with Anthony Coxon) a volume on methods and applications of entailment analysis – containing work on the entailment algorithm, social behavior in kinship networks, and the implicational structure of other cognitive and behavioral domains.

HARRISON C. WHITE is Professor of Sociology at the University of Arizona. He is the author of *Chains of Opportunity* (1970), and of a series of papers on blockmodels in the 1970s and market models in the 1980s. At present he is collaborating with members of the faculty of the Harvard Business School on dual-interface models of executive control through decentralization into profit centers.

Author index

Subject index